American Foreign Policy

ARCTIC OCEAN

GREENLAND
(DENMARK)

RUSSIA

CANADA

NORTH
PACIFIC
OCEAN

UNITED STATES

NORTH
ATLANTIC
OCEAN

MEXICO

THE BAHAMAS
CUBA
JAMAICA   HAITI   DOM. REP.
BELIZE
GUATEMALA   HONDURAS
EL SALVADOR   NICARAGUA
COSTA RICA
PANAMA   COLOMBIA
VENEZUELA   GUYANA
SURINAME
FRENCH GUIANA
ECUADOR

PERU   BRAZIL

BOLIVIA

PARAGUAY

SOUTH
PACIFIC
OCEAN

NEW
ZEALAND

CHILE   URUGUAY

ARGENTINA

0   1000   2000 mi
0   1000   2000 km

American Foreign Policy

A FRAMEWORK FOR ANALYSIS

William O. Chittick
University of Georgia

with Lee Ann Pingel

A Division of Congressional Quarterly Inc.
Washington, D.C.

CQ Press
1255 22nd Street, N.W., Suite 400
Washington, D.C. 20037

Phone: 202-729-1900; toll-free, 1-866-427-7737 (1-866-4CQ-PRESS)

Web: www.cqpress.com

Photo Credits: Arko Datta/Reuters/Landov, 1; Library of Congress, 41, 82; David Brauchli/Reuters/Landov, 116; Jack Smith/EPA/Landov, 163; Amrel Emric/AP/Wide World Photos, 200; Aly Song/Reuters/Landov, 239; Ahmad Masood/Reuters/Landov, 281; Pablo Martinex Monsivais/AP/Wide World Photos, 310; Landov, 344; Eric Draper/AP/Wide World Photos, 378; Dennis Brack/Landov, 414; Amy E. Conn/AP/Wide World Photos, 447; Tannen Maury/Landov, 483; Jonathan Ernst/Reuters/Landov, 519

Cover design: Michael Grove, MG Design
Interior design: Octavio Design
Maps: International Mapping
Composition: Auburn Associates, Inc.

⊗ The paper used in this publication exceeds the requirements of the American National Standard for Information Sciences—Permanence of Paper for Printed Library Materials, ANSI Z39.48-1992.

Printed and bound in the United States of America

10   09   08   07   06   1   2   3   4   5

Library of Congress Cataloging-in-Publication Data

Chittick, William O.
    American foreign policy : a framework for analysis / William O.
Chittick with Lee Ann Pingel.
        p. cm.
    Includes bibliographical references and index.
    ISBN 1-933116-62-5 (alk. paper)
    1. United States—Foreign relations.   2. United States—Foreign
relations—1989–   —Case studies.   3. United States—Foreign
relations—Philosophy.   I. Pingel, Lee Ann. II. Title.
    E183.7.C475 2006
    327.73—dc22

                                                          2005037911

In memory of my son, Will,
and in honor of my daughter, Laura, and my son, Nathaniel

Brief Contents

Contents

Boxes, Tables, Figures, and Maps

Boxes

Tables

Figures

Maps

Preface

In a now classic study, researchers William G. Chase and Herbert A. Simon ran a series of chess experiments that demonstrated the importance of structure to the learning process. The experiments involved players with three different levels of skill: a master chess player, experienced Class A players, and novice players. They were all shown twenty-four chess pieces arranged randomly on a chessboard for five seconds on a monitor. They were then asked to reconstruct from memory the positions of each of the pieces. Interestingly, the master player was no better at this task than the Class A or novice players.

In the second stage of the experiment, the same players were shown a board on which the arrangement of chess pieces was taken from actual games in the middle of play. Again the players were asked to reconstruct the positions of the chess pieces after a five-second look. This time the master player performed much better than the Class A players who, in turn, performed much better than the novice players. How do you suppose the experimenters accounted for this outcome? They concluded that in the second stage the positions of the chess pieces stuck more with the master and even the Class A players than with the novices because the experts were better able to perceive the structure—the series of strategic moves by other players. The experimenters noted that all the participants in the experiment could "perceive structure in such positions and encode them in chunks." But because the master player had a superior knowledge of chess strategy, he had a better framework for making sense of the arrangements of pieces and could therefore reconstruct them more accurately. The Class A players also grasped playing strategy, but their lesser skill meant that their framework for identifying meaningful arrangements was less complete and therefore of less value in helping them reconstruct the board.

What have chess experts got to do with the study of American foreign policy? In an age of instant, continuous, global communications, opinions about American foreign policy abound. Although some individuals have more experience and greater expertise than others, all of us are bombarded by misleading and partisan information on foreign policy. Those who are exposed to online bloggers and radio and television call-in shows and other unfiltered media may be even more vulnerable than others. The proliferation of such opinions is not in itself a terrible thing—it at least appears to be democratizing—but the sheer volume of unedited information does create a special obligation for those who write foreign policy texts to structure information about foreign policy in a way that helps students separate the wheat from the chaff. Students don't necessarily need more information about foreign policy as much as they need to know how to prune and critically analyze the information to which they are already exposed. What truly separates the average bright student from an experienced foreign policy analyst, such as Condoleezza Rice, is that Rice can encode new information into a framework that she has developed over time and has learned to use effectively. Students, on the other hand, usually lack such a framework and therefore can make use of only slightly more information than they would be able to employ if they perceived the information as a random series of facts. But with a framework for analysis, even a novice student can make sense of political choices on various foreign policy issues and comment on them with confidence. Yet this is no small task, for it requires students to accept a disciplined language for describing foreign policies and a sophisticated framework for foreign policy analysis.

That's precisely what this text has to offer: a framework, based on a realistic understanding of foreign policy formulation and analysis that gives students a better structure for analysis. The origins of the framework can be traced back to Ole R. Holsti and James N. Rosenau's landmark public opinion study, wherein they identified three types of elite opinions on the Vietnam War. While replicating their study, I realized that what they perceived to be three *types* of individuals were actually one type of individual on three separate *dimensions* of opinion: security, economy, and community. I later discovered that these dimensions could be derived from the three basic motivations—power, achievement, and social affiliation—that some psychologists use to describe behavior. Because everyone has distinct opinions on each of these dimensions, one cannot assume that these types are mutually exclusive.

Because the foreign policy opinions of the elite and the general public in the United States are based on these motivations, why shouldn't foreign policy analysts employ these same three motivational dimensions to describe and explain foreign policy? The most obvious advantage of such a framework is that most individuals already use bits and pieces of it, albeit intuitively. The trick, then, is to come up with a formal way for students of foreign policy to recognize the three dimensions, to differentiate carefully among them, and to offer students a procedure that will enable them to integrate these same three dimensions into a meaningful whole. That, in a nutshell, is the basis for this text.

Throughout the book, I use a straightforward method to identify the choices that states and world leaders make on these three dimensions of foreign policy, offering many clear examples that demonstrate the range of preferences held by various individuals. Beginning in chapter 1, I use a matrix table that is very much like the "chunk" of the chessboard discussed above to display the "structure" of foreign policy. This matrix table enables students to stay informed about all three dimensions at the same time. Of course, students do not have to be master chess players to keep track of the dimensionality of foreign policies using my method. But the more familiar they are with the framework, the easier it will be for them to retain all the essential information about particular foreign policies; to link foreign policy inputs, outputs, and outcomes; and to compare various foreign policies.

The book's organization and its pedagogical features also support the framework. Because the framework is inclusive—that is, it incorporates the security, economic, and community dimensions as well as actor motivations—it is both more comprehensive and more flexible than the approach taken by many other texts in which the focus is primarily security concerns. The framework is equally suitable for analyzing both historical and contemporary cases of foreign policy as well as the inputs (sources), outputs (decisions and actions), and outcomes (consequences) of foreign policy. As a result, the text is organized into three self-contained parts—history, contemporary issues, and processes—that can be read or taught in any sequence. There is a short introduction to each part so that instructors can use the parts in any way they please.

For the sake of consistency, the same pedagogical features are employed in all parts of the book. For example, the matrix tables described above are used throughout the text. In parts 1 and 2 they are used to describe foreign policy outputs; in part 3 they are used to describe foreign policy inputs. Although the text focuses mainly on government or nongovernment actors, most chapters feature a "Profile in Action," a brief biography of a person who exemplifies how individuals can make a difference in foreign policy. In order to highlight the core terms of the field and help students review, key concepts are put in boldface when they first appear in the book as well as listed at the end of each chapter. The text also includes maps, tables, and other figures to supplement the narrative. Moreover, there is a short list of suggested readings for further study at the end of each chapter.

An Instructor's Resources CD-ROM is available free to adopters; it provides a host of materials to help with class preparation. Resources include a testbank featuring a series of exams, with midterms and final exams that are of the short essay variety; a more detailed discussion of how the framework can be used in the classroom; a series of class-tested exercises, handouts, and games that can be used in the classroom or assigned as homework; a set of PowerPoint lecture slides for each chapter; and all figures, boxes, and tables in .jpg and .ppt format for use in lectures. These ancillaries are organized by both chapter and part so that instructors can easily use them regardless of how they have organized their course.

Acknowledgments

I am indebted to many people for their help with this project. I have had the opportunity to work closely with three experienced diplomats: former secretary of state Dean Rusk, who was my colleague at the University of Georgia for twenty years, beginning in 1970; former U.S. ambassador to Paraguay and Nicaragua Lawrence A. Pezzullo, with whom I shared an office suite when he was an ambassador in residence at UGA from 1981 to 1982; and former U.S. ambassador to Hungary and West Germany Martin J. Hillenbrand, with whom I shared an office suite from 1982 to 2004. I also want to thank the many government officials, reporters, and NGO leaders I have interviewed over the years. In addition I want to thank those students, staff, and colleagues in the Departments of Political Science and International Affairs in the School of Public and International Affairs at the University of Georgia and elsewhere in the country for giving me ideas on specific chapters. I am especially indebted to Rick Travis, the graduate research assistant who was most involved in the data analysis; Lee Ann Pingel, a graduate student with whom I began this project; Keith R. Billingsley, my co-researcher for many years at UGA; and Martin J. Sampson, who actually used my framework in a course he taught on American foreign policy at the University of Minnesota.

I initially signed a contract to publish this book with Chatham House publishers, where I worked with Mellisa Martin, Donna Kimbler, Maggie Barberie, and Sabra B. Ledent. In October 2003, CQ Press acquired the Chatham House list. Because my eldest son, Will, died during this transition, I am especially indebted to director of College publishing Brenda Carter and chief acquisitions editor Charisse Kiino for facilitating a new review of the manuscript at that time. As I look back over this lengthy process, three people stand out: development editors Sabra B. Ledent for Chatham House and Elise Frasier of CQ Press and project editor Anna D. Socrates of CQ Press. These three individuals were marvelous in the professional care, restraint, and encouragement they gave me in developing the manuscript for publication. Thanks also go to Anne Stewart for her photo research and to the following reviewers: Linda Adams, Baylor University; J. Joseph Hewitt, University of Missouri; Ole R. Holsti, Duke University; the late Joseph Lepgold, Georgetown University; Roy Licklider, Rutgers University; James A. Mitchell, California State University–Northridge; Benjamin Page, Northwestern University; and Stacy Vandeveer, University of New Hampshire.

CHAPTER 1

An Inclusive Framework for Foreign Policy Analysis

WITH LEE ANN PINGEL

The framework for analysis employed in this text emphasizes three essential elements in any foreign policy endeavor: community, security, and prosperity. All three elements are represented in this picture. The Iraqi woman on the left, Lubna Said Janad, is a member of the city council of Ad Dajayi, a town near Tikrit, about 110 miles north of Baghdad. She is receiving instructions about the provincial elections to be held in the fall of 2003. These elections were one of the first steps in building a new community in Iraq. U.S. Captain Kerrie Pate of the Fourth Engineer Battalion is explaining how for security reasons a thirty-four member governing council is to be chosen from a list of 120 Iraqis handpicked by the U.S. army. The Iraqi woman brings a plate of fruit, which represents a certain level of prosperity.

IN THE MONTHS LEADING UP to the U.S.-led war in Iraq in 2003, the Bush administration launched a concerted effort to justify its invasion policy to the American people, U.S. allies, and the global community of nations. The argument for going to war was grounded on two central premises, both of which highlighted the administration's security concerns. First, the administration claimed that evidence demonstrated that Saddam Hussein planned to develop more weapons of mass destruction (WMDs), in direct violation of the UN-imposed post–Gulf War requirements. Second, they claimed clear ties linked Saddam Hussein to al Qaeda. Both circumstances, it argued, made Iraq a breeding ground for future attacks against the United States and justified the invasion.[1] Indeed, Secretary of State Colin Powell appeared before the UN Security Council in February of 2003, using those twin claims as the centerpiece of his argument for going to war.

Critics of the Bush administration's policy objected, noting that UN weapons inspectors had not found any evidence of WMD production since sanctions were introduced in 1991, and that evidence purportedly linking Hussein to al Qaeda was tenuous at best. As hindsight now indicates, those critics appear to have been correct. But do these miscalculations of the level of threats to the United States necessarily mean that the Bush administration made a bad or erroneous foreign policy decision to go to war with Iraq? Does this mean that its critics were entirely correct in their criticisms?

The answers to these questions depend in part on the extent to which one takes economic and community values as well as security values into account. Arguably, the U.S. invasion of Iraq could further other legitimate foreign policy goals—economic stability and improving relations with and among the community of states in the Middle East. The Bush administration recognized that Iraq controlled a significant portion of the world's oil reserve and, at least from the perspective of the United States, a successful regime change in Iraq could have a salutary effect on relationships throughout the entire Middle East region. But these economic and community benefits were deduced from and ancillary to the certainty of military success. They were not assessed independently.

Were administrative critics guilty of the same error of over-simplification? They, too, argued against the invasion on the grounds that a unilateral invasion would violate important international norms, an argument based primarily on community values. Did they also not take into account possible economic and security interests? The answer ultimately depends on the outcome of an independent assessment of security and economic values. If the security threat had been genuine and if there had been no other way of dealing with the security problem, then it might have been appropriate to invade Iraq. But this was not the case.

Of course, this is not the first case in history in which questionable judgment had frustrated American foreign policy. The military policy of

American Indian removal in the first half of the nineteenth century did not consider the community issue of relationships between Native Americans and other Americans during this and later stages. And the military decision to prop up the noncommunist government of South Vietnam in the 1950s and 1960s did not sufficiently consider the legitimate right of the Vietnamese people to choose their own form of government.

This text offers a foil for such oversimplifications, arguing that policy makers as well as students of foreign policy must carefully consider **economic values** and **community values** as well as **security values** before making foreign policy decisions. These three sets of values must be considered both independently and collectively.

What would it look like in practice for policy makers to consider these three values in tandem? In the case of Iraq, from the security perspective, they would have to weigh the advantage of ousting Saddam Hussein's corrupt regime (with its desire to have nuclear weapons and its support for suicide bombers against Israel) against the disadvantage of the immediate prospect of military and civilian casualties on all sides as well as the long-term consequences of such an invasion. The long-term security consequences would include future support for the American military both inside and outside the country and resistance movements inside Iraq itself and by other peoples and groups outside Iraq who generally oppose the U.S. presence in the Middle East.

From an economic perspective, policy makers would also weigh the prospect of securing better access to Iraq's rich oil reserves against the danger that these oil fields would be destroyed during the war. They must also consider the prospect that Western attempts to secure Middle East oil could backfire, and that the American presence in Iraq might actually increase oil prices and threaten American access to the much larger oil reserves throughout the Middle East, including those in former Soviet republics.

Finally, from the standpoint of community values, policy makers would measure the prospect of initiating democratic reform throughout the Middle East against the danger that a war that could be seen as violating traditional international norms and might weaken international institutions, undermine the relationship between the United States and its Western allies, and even create a more fundamental breach between the Arab world and the West.

This chapter will lay the groundwork for exploring American foreign policy through an analytical framework that considers each of these three core values—community, security, and economics—without oversimplifying foreign policy problems. The chapter will first define foreign policy in terms of actors *in situ* and then identify the major approaches used by scholars and practitioners to account for foreign policy behavior.

The Definition and Nature of Foreign Policy

Foreign policy, like any other policy, is a set of behaviors used to obtain a desired result—that is, a policy maker selects a particular method to achieve a particular objective in a particular situation. A policy can be characterized in terms of either its methods (e.g., using force or relying on negotiations) or its objectives (e.g., complete domination or accommodation). Such a characterization is especially necessary when a policy maker takes an action without reference to an objective or when an objective is attributed to a policy maker who has not yet acted. For instance, a policy maker might withdraw from a conference without stating the reason for doing so, or a policy maker might feign peaceful intentions but make no effort to realize them. Both the objective to be achieved and the actions undertaken to achieve that objective contribute to the understanding of a policy. But unless there is an obvious link between the action and the objective, it is difficult to understand the logic of the policy.

Like other kinds of policy, foreign policy focuses on the behavior of an actor—that is, it is actor-oriented. **Foreign policy** differs from other kinds of policy in that the referent actor is usually, though not always, a **state**, and the situation within which the action takes place is the **international system.** A state refers to the population associated with a defined territory under the control of a sovereign government. A state is considered **sovereign** if it has absolute and independent control over the population in this territory and is so recognized by the governments of other states in the international system. Both the United States and the United Kingdom are states in this sense. The international system refers to all the material and nonmaterial forces that affect an actor—in this case the state. These forces, which often transcend state borders, may be military, economic, technological, and cultural in nature.

Who Acts in Foreign Affairs?

The use of one term, state, to refer to the actor and another term, nation—which forms the root of the word "international"— to refer, not to the actor, but to the situation in which the actions of states take place requires additional explanation. The state is considered the primary actor in foreign policy studies because its government claims to represent all the people residing in a given territory. But the people within a given state often identify themselves primarily as members of a group called a **nation.** A nation is a group of individuals who believe they share a common heritage and a common future. Thus, a nation, as opposed to a state, reflects a genuine, albeit subjective, sense of unity. For example, the government of the United Kingdom claims to represent all the people living in the British Isles, but the Scots, Welsh, or Northern Irish may each perceive their community and what contributes to its security and prosperity quite differently.

In most cases there are several if not many different nations within a state. For example, there are ethnic, racial, political, cultural, and even geographic nations in the United States, such as Irish Americans, African Americans, libertarian Americans, and Southern Americans. There are also trans-state nations such as the diaspora Chinese and the Zionist movement. Even al Qaeda could be considered a nontraditional nation. Because all these nations can draw the primary loyalty of people over and above the state in which they happen to reside, they are a powerful force in international relations and foreign policy.

Both state and nation are abstract concepts. These corporate actors are actually represented by concrete individuals. In each case there is "an 'internal decision structure' that institutionalizes and authorizes [this kind of] collective action" although this mechanism is usually more formally established in the case of the state than the nation.[2] Because the leaders of nations (those not formally recognized as states) as well as international and interstate bodies are not sovereign actors, they will be referred to as **nonstate actors** in this textbook. For instance, the quartet that developed the road map for the 2003 negotiations between Israel and the Palestinians in the Middle East consisted of two state actors, the United States and Russia, and two nonstate actors, the United Nations and the European Union.

The definition of foreign policy must then be broad enough to encompass the intersection of state and nonstate actors and their environments in order to incorporate both states and nonstates in foreign policy analysis. Foreign policy includes the internal sources and consequences of an actor's external affairs as well as the external sources and consequences of an actor's internal affairs. An earthquake in Turkey becomes a matter of U.S. foreign policy only if either the government or people of the United States respond to this event in some way, thus an external event can have internal consequences for a state. Bills passed or not passed by the U.S. Congress only become matters of American foreign policy if they affect at least one other state; thus the internal events of a state can have external consequences. Similarly, events in Chile only become a foreign policy problem for the AFL-CIO if these external events affect that organization's own unions in some way. A labor dispute involving the AFL-CIO in the United States only becomes a foreign policy issue for the AFL-CIO if it has a bearing on labor relations of interest to that organization in another state. This book's main focus is on U.S. foreign policy because the U.S. government is the primary actor.

State Actors.   A number of organizations and individuals within the U.S. government purport to represent the people of the United States as a whole. They include the president, members of Congress, the secretaries of state, defense, and other departments, as well as a growing list of other officials and their subordinates. Although Americans like to think that these individuals and institutions speak with one voice in foreign affairs, that is seldom true.

One difficulty these individuals face in representing the United States is that although the U.S. territorial borders have hardly changed in over 150 years, the makeup of its population is constantly changing—not only generational changes, but geographic and demographic changes and changes in voting behavior. Immigration, which varies both in size and in composition over time, is another source of change. Such changes serve as a reminder that the relationship between a population and the state is not necessarily static or harmonious. The composition of nations is constantly changing.

Nonstate Actors.   Because individuals form groups that are more exclusive and/or more inclusive than the population of a state, there is a plethora of nonstate actors. Some of these nonstate actors may even be U.S. government actors, but they are not part of the U.S. internal decision-making structure for foreign policy. Just as the original colonies had foreign relations before the federal government was even established, today most state governments and many large cities regularly engage in international trade and investment through their foreign offices. Unlike the individual foreign policy actors in the federal government, these people and institutions do not speak authoritatively for the United States as a whole, but they do speak authoritatively for the state and local governments they represent.

In addition, tens of thousands of U.S. **nongovernmental organizations** (NGOs) are found across America, many of them foreign policy actors. For instance, American NGOs like the AFL-CIO and the Mennonite Central Committee have the international staff and resources needed to influence events abroad. American business NGOs, like Citicorp, are usually classified separately as **transnational national corporations** (TNCs).

Moreover, there are thousands of **international governmental organizations** (IGOs) at the regional and global level, e.g., the North Atlantic Treaty Organization, the United Nations, the World Bank. Although IGOs have states as members, they are considered nonstate actors because they lack the sovereign powers claimed by ordinary states. Then there are tens of thousands of **international nongovernmental organizations** (INGOs), such as the International Red Cross, the International Peace Academy, and the Global Citizens Association. INGOs are usually composed of NGOs and/or individuals from various nation-states. Once again, business **multinational corporations** (MNCs) are usually classified separately from other INGOs.

But societal participation in international affairs is not limited to formal organizations, whether at the national or international level. Informal groups such as African Americans and the loosely allied groups and individuals constituting the environmental movement in the United States or abroad as well as global networks of individuals and organizations using the Internet can have an important effect on U.S foreign relations.

Although individuals generally can augment their influence by working through formal organizations, anyone can play an important role in foreign policy if he or she is sufficiently motivated. Box 1.1 describes how Amy Curtis, a Kentucky housewife, became an important actor in U.S.-Russian

---

BOX 1.1

Profile in Action: Amy Curtis

Amy Curtis, a housewife from Madisonville, Kentucky, was so moved by the economic hardships of the Russian people after the collapse of the Soviet Union in 1991 that she asked the State Department to identify one Russian family for her to help. Neither the U.S. State Department nor Gorbachev's office was able to assist her, so she contacted a Russian correspondent in New York.

He helped Amy by contacting local radio stations in Russia. One of the women who heard Amy's offer of help was Ludmila Starchenkova, a single parent with two children in Chulyaninsk, an industrial region on the border of Siberia. Before long Amy had received about 200 letters from people in Russia, including one from Ludmila. Amy, overwhelmed by the response, got a local newspaper editor to help her contact other Americans who might help her respond appropriately to these letters.

At one point Amy reported that about 1,600 American families had been linked with the same number of Russian families, and there were still 4,000 Russian families waiting for help. By that time Amy's private aid operation had moved from her bedroom to her dining room. Eventually the State Department offered to help Amy with shipping expenses, and she found a young man in Chulyaninsk, Yuri Zaitsev, to help her make deliveries in Russia.

Five months after Ludmila first wrote Amy, she received a phone call from Yuri. A box from America had arrived in her name from a Nancy Brazil of Columbus, Indiana. The 50-pound box was stuffed with useful items, and Nancy and Ludmila began corresponding with one another. Eventually Ludmila even got a sewing machine! Later, Amy got a State Department grant to help her establish a self-sustaining operation in Russia. Who says individuals can't have foreign policies?

Source: Story adapted from broadcast by Anne Garrels, *All Things Considered*, National Public Radio, May 4, 1993.

relations when she decided that she could make a difference to one Russian family.

The U.S. government recognizes that nonstate actors are sufficiently important for foreign policy institutions throughout the U.S. government to keep in touch with them. For example, the State Department's Office of Intergovernmental Relations maintains contact with the foreign trade offices of state and local governments. Congress, the White House, and federal departments and agencies with a stake in foreign policy also have offices that correspond with, send speakers to, and otherwise keep in touch with U.S. nongovernmental organizations both at home and abroad. The U.S. government also works closely with many international and transnational organizations.

Although these various foreign policy actors maintain contact with one another, they remain largely autonomous because each represents different interests and values and because each therefore defines its internal and external environment somewhat differently. For all these actors, the state is a common reference point, but it is not always the main referent.

Where Does the Action Take Place?

The international system has often been described in terms of material forces such as human nature, natural resources, geography, forces of production, and forces of destruction.[3] It can also be described in terms of intangibles, such as ideas or beliefs. However it is described, most scholars and practitioners of foreign policy accept the idea that the international system is anarchic—that there are no inherent rules that govern states' behavior—because there is no central authority at the international level. Despite this common assumption, scholars have many different interpretations of how the system actually does work. Some believe that the existence of many independent states places a premium on security. Others believe that the anarchic international system leads states to pursue what is most advantageous for them economically. Still others believe the international anarchy will eventually lead states to accept common norms of communal existence.

Each of these interpretations is linked to one of the three core approaches to international relations and connected to one of the three core values identified previously. According to Alexander Wendt, realists and neorealists characterize the international system as a state of war among states even if war is not actually taking place; thus they value security interests most highly. Liberals and neoliberals characterize the international system as competitive because states are perceived as economic rivals rather than enemies; and idealists, or in contemporary parlance, constructivists, characterize the international system in terms of cooperation and community because they perceive states as potential friends.[4]

The Realist Approach. Most realists describe the international system in terms of the distribution of power among states and claim that because there is no central authority in the international system, states constantly fear that other states will use their power against them. Thus the fear of war compels each state to primarily emphasize the use of force as a method of providing for its security. But the realist approach can also be described in terms of ideas and beliefs by assuming that Self (one actor) and Other (other actors in the system) accept two rules: first, that Other "does not recognize the right of the Self to exist as an autonomous being," and, second, that Other "will not willingly limit its violence toward the Self." [5] Thus whether this system is based on an assumed nature of man or on shared norms among system participants the result is the same—a system in which there is a "war of all against all" without limit.

This view of the international system is usually associated with the dominant approach to the study of international politics—**realism** and **neorealism.** Realism is concerned exclusively with the state, which is assumed to function as a unitary, rational decision maker. In the absence of a central authority, these decision makers are motivated by fear and are primarily interested in power and security. Although realists such as Hans J. Morgenthau and John J. Mearsheimer discuss international politics in terms of "a struggle for power," they do not always assume that this appetite for power is insatiable.[6] And although neorealists such as Kenneth N. Waltz assume that states are fearful, they do not always assume that they behave in an offensive manner.[7] Both realists and neorealists emphasize configurations of power.

The Liberal Approach. Most liberals describe the international system in terms of competition. They claim that states have similar as well as different interests and that competition within a set of general constraints is desirable. Liberals envisaged a system in which states first accepted each other's right to exist, and, second, they agreed to limit conflict among themselves. Within this system, conflict among states is still possible, even likely. However, states pursue self-interests that do not entail the destruction of others but actually depend on the participation of others in joint endeavors. Institutions developed to limit conflict also create an environment conducive to joint endeavors (e.g., international organizations established to promote collective security).

The liberal approach to the study of international politics has its roots in the thought of Jeremy Bentham and other utilitarians as well as in the free market liberalism of economic theorists such as Adam Smith. **Liberalism** stresses the importance of individuals and institutions within the state. Liberals believe that people are largely motivated by the desire to better themselves: the profit motive. For example, most liberals believe that states participating in a free market can actually serve both their individual interests and the common good. Neoliberals, such as Robert O. Keohane and Joseph S. Nye, emphasize the role that international institutions, such as the European Union, play in the international system.[8] **Neoliberalism** stresses "the cultural-institutional context for state action."[9] Both liberals and neoliberals emphasize a link between capitalism and democracy.

The Idealist Approach.   **Idealism** tends to view the international system in terms of the shaping power of ideas and emphasizes the potential for change. Idealists envisage a system in which states become friends and allies. Such a system would be based on two norms: first, "disputes will be settled without war or the threat of war" (the rule of nonviolence), and, second, states "will fight as a team if the security of any one is threatened by a third party (the rule of mutual aid)."[10] Similarly, the idealist system is reflected in the efforts of contemporary states to pursue collective security arrangements and total disarmament. Such a system depends on the growth of international law and the rejection of the use of force as an acceptable way to deal with conflicts.

This third view of the international system developed more recently and has become associated with **sociological institutionalism** and **constructivism**, because these schools of thought stress the impact of ideas and norms on the behavior of decision makers as well as on the ways in which these decision makers define their own needs. Sociological institutionalists show how global culture can "shape and define the preferences of actors in ways not related to internal conditions, characteristics or functional needs."[11] Constructivists such as Wendt emphasize the importance of shared norms, such as global opinion or culture, which have developed through social interaction. Constructivists further argue that "actors cannot know what their interests are until they know what they are representing—'who they are.'"[12] Both sociological institutionalists and constructivists emphasize shared ideas and cultures.

Each basic approach—realism, liberalism, and idealism—posits a different international system that could have been described either in terms of material realities or shared ideas. In this case the descriptions of the systems focused on shared ideas, rather than material realities. But there is one commonality these approaches share: they all assume that foreign policy actors will behave purposively. That is, all the approaches assume that individuals and states will take particular actions to achieve particular objectives—in short, they behave rationally.

Rational Explanations of Foreign Policy: Rationalists and Political Psychologists

Rationality refers to the logical relationship between ends and means. The ends of foreign policy are the goals and objectives sought by foreign policy actors; means are the methods and actions employed by foreign policy actors to obtain these ends. Both ends and means involve motivation. **Motives** are the needs and desires that arouse actors to pursue foreign policy ends. Motives are also what prompt foreign policy actors to take actions in order to fulfill those ends. For instance, most states want peace, but some of these states desire more armament and others less armament as a means of preserving peace.

Because motives are central to both the ends and the means of foreign policy, they pose a problem for many foreign policy analysts. After all, scientific inquiry requires that causes be separate from effects. If the same motives are behind both ends and means, there is no way to independently verify propositions based solely on those motives. Thus, in order to offer scientific explanations of foreign policy, theorists must use something other than motivation to explain behavior. Social scientists have developed two general solutions to this problem: rationalist explanations and psychological explanations.[13] Rationalists find causal explanations for behavior arising out of the physical environment of the foreign policy actor, while those favoring psychological explanations find causation arising out of the individual's perceptions of the situation.

How do Rationalists Explain Foreign Policy?

Rationalists—neo-classical economists, behaviorists, and rational choice theorists—explain behavior with reference to observable, material factors in the environment.[14] They emphasize the physical environment, that is, the "situation as it actually exists and affects the achievements and capabilities" of an actor.[15] They believe that this physical environment creates incentives that account for the behavior of foreign policy actors. In short, rationalists posit a direct relationship between the environment of an actor and the actor's behavior.

In order to avoid the charge that they are actually taking motives into account in examining both ends and means (and are thus unscientific), rationalists assume that the process whereby incentives are converted into actions in the human mind is rational. In short, they bypass the human mind and motivation by substituting how individuals *should* make foreign policy decisions for how they will actually do so. Rationalists assume that individuals will do what they should do under particular circumstances, and rationalists usually rely on deductive logic, statistics, and probabilities to determine what a foreign policy actor would be likely to do.

Rationalists further assume that the preferences of actors are both consistent and stable. For example, when there are two alternatives, A and B, the actor either prefers A over B, or B over A, or finds each equally desirable—and will maintain that same preference over time. Second, they assume that the actor can identify all the available options, and determine the likely consequences of choosing each option in terms of their own values and interests. Finally, they assume that the actor will choose the option with the highest expected utility, or that which affords the greatest return in terms of their values and interests. This is sometimes called the **optimizing model** because it represents perfect rationality.

The optimizing model may require more of decision makers than they are capable of delivering, however. Therefore, some scholars have developed a second version of the rational decision-making model, the **satisficing model.** This model, which is also referred to as "bounded rationality," means choosing a course of action without taking into account all of the possible responses. It recognizes limits to the computational abilities of decision makers. First, it does not require an exhaustive ordering of preferences so much as a determination of the minimum objectives in a situation. Second, it does not attempt to identify all possible options. Indeed, it usually involves successive limited comparisons between only two options, one being the present policy. Third, it does not seek the best policy but rather the first policy that will satisfy minimum requirements. And fourth, it does not predict policy at all—only the process by which the decision is made. The satisficing model is considered rational because the process is believed to be sufficiently coherent to lead to a satisfactory outcome.

The Cuban Missile Crisis of 1962 is often used by scholars to illustrate a rational decision-making process. In October 1962 the United States discovered that the Soviet Union had secretly placed nuclear missiles in Cuba. After discussing the issue, President John F. Kennedy and his top advisors set as their objective the removal of the missiles without precipitating a general war. They seriously considered as many as six options: do nothing; exert diplomatic pressure; approach Cuban leader Fidel Castro secretly; or launch either an invasion, air strike, or blockade. The last two options—the air strike and the blockade—ultimately received the most attention, and they eventually settled on the blockade, because it seemed to have the best chance of success without increasing the danger of an all-out war.[16]

How do Political Psychologists Explain Foreign Policy?

The second rational explanation is based on psychology. Political psychologists also look at the relationship between the environment and behavior, but they believe that the incentives emphasized by rationalists are actually a product of the human mind. Thus they emphasize the psychological environment that refers to an "individual's perceived image of a situation, an image that may or may not correspond to reality."[17] Since political psychologists maintain that the perceived images of the environment trigger incentives, they focus on other aspects of the mind to establish a causal link between ends and means.

Political psychologists emphasize the relationship between motives and both cognition and affect. Cognition is the process whereby people come to know things; it includes "perceiving, thinking, and remembering."[18] Affect refers to emotional states of the mind. Because cognition and affect are separate from motivation, they also provide a basis for causal explanations of behavior; thus political psychologists are able to satisfy the requirements of scientific inquiry. Since cognition and affect are not directly observable, however, political psychologists generally employ inductive, empirical methods, such as experimentation and case studies to infer cognition and affect.

By emphasizing cognition and affect, political psychologists focus on how decisions *are* actually made. They look for a correspondence between evidence of perceptions, beliefs, states of mind, and feelings on the one hand and observable behavior on the other. They employ the logic of appropriateness to explain behavior: behavior is rational to the extent that it corresponds *appropriately* to the beliefs and feelings of the actor.

Because political psychologists emphasize the actual process of decision making, they do not assume that the process of decision making is coherent. For them it is sufficient if there is a correspondence between what individuals believe or feel and how they behave. For example, political psychologists have shown that individuals are more likely to be aggressive if they have a right-wing authoritarian personality, which is associated with obedience, conformity, aggression and—most famously—prejudice toward groups that are "different." [19]

Although many political psychologists, like rationalists, avoid motivation in order to make their studies seem more scientific, others have incorporated motivation in their analyses. The latter have generally identified three basic human motives: **power, achievement,** and **social affiliation.**[20] Power, broadly defined, is the desire for control over one's environment; achievement is the desire to accomplish personal goals, such as material well-being; and social affiliation is the desire to associate with and be respected by others. Foreign policy analysts employ the three motives of power, achievement, and social affiliation in the formulation of approaches and values, but they often use somewhat different language. For example, in the *History of the Peloponnesian War* the ancient Greek historian Thucydides based his analysis of the Athenian empire on the motives of fear, profit, and honor, or, as Thucydides defined it, reputation. Fear and the quest for power could be viewed as forming one motivational complex. The pursuit of profit, if the term is interpreted broadly enough, can be explained by the need for achievement. Finally, the quest for honor, or reputation, is intimately connected with the human need for social affiliation.

These three basic motives not only define foreign policy ends but also the most appropriate means of achieving those foreign policy ends because motivation plays a key role at every stage of the foreign policy-making process: defining objectives, analyzing various courses of action, deciding which course of action to take, and evaluating the success of that action.[21]

Both the rationalist and psychological methods of explaining behavior are rational because they link motives as commitments to actions. However, the logic connecting ends and means differs, depending on the character of the ends. Thus prosperity requires that means optimize ends; security only requires that means satisfy ends; and community only requires that the means correspond to the ends; Thus the three different kinds of rationality are related to the three basic motivations and the three primary approaches to the study of international relations and foreign policy discussed earlier.

The Logic of the Three Basic Approaches to Foreign Policy

Each approach—realism, liberalism, and idealism—uses a different form of logic. That is, each approach assumes a different kind of connection between means and ends. Realists seeking to increase security are satisficers. They emphasize the logic of effectiveness because they want their minimum needs met. The logic of effectiveness places an emphasis on relative differences between the outcomes achieved by actors. For example, an American realist would not be too concerned about the fact that a lesser ally gained more from a military exchange than the United States did so long as this exchange did not threaten the relative power of the United States over that state.

Liberals seeking to maximize economic benefit are optimizers. They emphasize the logic of efficiency because they believe actors want to maximize their gains and minimize their losses. The logic of efficiency places a premium on absolute differences in outcomes between actors. For example, an American liberal would only conclude an economic exchange with another country if the United States would gain more from that exchange than it would without it.

Idealists seeking to define the basic values underlying community emphasize the logic of acceptability because they believe that actors want to act in accordance with the norms of the community with whom they identify the most. The logic of acceptability places an emphasis on the correspondence between objectives and behavior. For example, an idealist would only accept UN enforcement if it was approved by the Security Council according to the UN Charter.

Table 1.1 shows how each approach employs a different logic because it focuses on a different set of values. Realists emphasize the logic of effectiveness because they are preoccupied with security. Liberals prefer the logic of efficiency because they are most interested in prosperity or economic values. And idealists use the logic of acceptability because they are most concerned with the values of community.

Although it is convenient to separate these values and the approaches based on them for analytic purposes, it is essential to remember that all three dimensions come into play when analyzing a foreign policy issue.

Table 1.1. Essential Elements of the Three Foreign Policy Approaches

Approaches	Principal Actors	Views States as	Operates according to logic of	Motive	Value Orientation
Realism/Neorealism	States	Combative; states are enemies	Satisficing, emphasizing the logic of effectiveness	Power	Security
Liberalism/Neoliberalism	States and corporations	Competitive; states are rivals	Optimizing, emphasizing the logic of efficiency	Profit or achievement	Economic/ prosperity
Idealism/Constructivism Sociological Institutionalism	Individuals in government and society	Cooperative; states are potential friends	Acceptability, emphasizing the logic of correspondence between objectives and behaviors	Social affiliation	Community political

The question is, should these three approaches and the values they represent be treated separately or collectively?

The Case for Treating These Approaches Separately

Because these three basic approaches feature different forms of logic, adherents of these approaches tend to assume the approach with which they are most familiar provides a better explanation of foreign policy than other approaches. On the one hand, realists and neorealists believe that security values are the most important goals of foreign policy, and they tend to use the logic of effectiveness to explain and predict most foreign policy behavior. For example, in his *Theory of International Relations* the neorealist Waltz contends that because the United States is more capable than other states (it has what he calls "relative advantage"), it will be willing to pay higher prices for economic goods, undertake more costly military campaigns, and pay higher political costs to maintain institutions it favors so long as these actions maintain U.S. superiority over other states.[22]

On the other hand, liberals and neoliberals believe that economic prosperity is the most important value, and they use the logic of efficiency to explain and predict most behavior. For example, Barbara Koremenos, Charles Lipson, and Duncan Snidal contend that rational choice analysis can explain the development of institutions better than either realism or constructivism because state actors use international institutions to maximize their benefits and minimize their losses.[23]

Although constructivism is a more recent approach, its advocates are also beginning to show that constructed ideas regarding community are as useful, if not more useful, in explaining foreign policy choices than either realist concerns regarding power and security or liberal concerns regarding economic interests. For example, Craig Parsons shows that ideas about community played a key role in establishing the European Union (EU), and Amitov Acharya indicates that ideas about sovereignty played a key role in the local interpretation of common rules by members of the Association of Southeast Asian Nations (ASEAN).[24]

In the absence of a theory of value preferences that could definitively explain which values are most important and which logic should be given priority, advocates of different approaches usually claim that their toolbox is the most useful. But by treating these values as essentially competitive, they overlook the fact that these values are integral parts of the human psyche, and that all three values are involved in every foreign policy.

The Case for Treating These Approaches Collectively

The truth is these three sets of values are distinct parts of a larger whole. It is not possible to determine what best serves the security or prosperity of a foreign policy actor without first defining who that actor is in terms of the community values that actor represents. For example, until one realizes that the United States is part of a world that values basic human rights, one cannot devise an appropriate strategy either for its extended security or its wider prosperity. Likewise, one cannot make a community secure without having the capacity for prosperity. And one cannot become prosperous without having a minimum level of security. For example, in the years following the invasion of Iraq, the United States got itself in a bind because the Iraqi interim government could not solve the security problem until average Iraqis had adequate electricity, water, and jobs and because Iraqis blamed the United States for their economic woes. And the interim government on its own could not provide improved electricity, water, and jobs without first getting U.S. help in providing Iraqi citizens with minimum security.

For these reasons this text assumes that all three basic sets of values and the logics associated with them are integral to any given foreign policy. In this sense foreign policy is not the result of just one or even two of these factors, it is the product of all three. A good foreign policy is one that fulfills community, security, and prosperity needs. Anything less is, as suggested earlier, a gross over-simplification of foreign policy. The recognition of this tripartite structure is the basis for the new framework for foreign policy analysis employed in this text.

A New Framework for Analysis

The new framework for foreign policy analysis is based on three assumptions. The first assumption underlying this analytic framework is that the three basic human motives—power, achievement, and social affiliation—organize what individuals know about foreign policy, and *should* also shape how they make their decisions. These basic motivations are expressed in the three sets of values—security, prosperity, and community, respectively. Throughout the remainder of this text these values have been reordered—putting community before security and prosperity—because the values associated with community define the actor whose security is to be protected and whose prosperity is to be enhanced.

All three sets of values are expressed in terms of both ends and means, and each employs a different form of logic. Thus the motive of social affiliation is associated with the ends and means of community and invokes the logic of acceptability. Put another way, all actors want to be accepted within a community, but they may differ as to what community is most acceptable to them and what actions they feel will be most acceptable to that community. Similarly, the motive of power is associated with the ends and means of security and utilizes the logic of effectiveness. Thus all actors want security, but they may differ as to what kind of security is possible and what actions are most effective in achieving that kind of security. Finally, the motive of achievement is associated with the ends and means of prosperity and employs the logic of efficiency. All actors want prosperity, but they may differ as to what kind of prosperity is feasible and what actions may be most efficient in achieving that level of prosperity.

The second assumption underlying this analytic framework is that the differences among individuals in their beliefs about what community ends and means are most acceptable, what security ends and means are most effective, and what prosperity ends and means are most efficient exist along three separate continua, each going from one extreme position to the other. For instance, if an actor defines security in terms of complete domination, that actor will favor the use of force; whereas if an actor defines security in terms of accommodation, that actor will oppose the use of force. These two diametrically opposed positions would appear as the extremes on each end of the continuum. These three continua are referred to here as "dimensions."

The final assumption underlying this analytical framework is that all three dimensions are necessary to describe, explain, and evaluate any foreign policy because all three dimensions are integral parts of the human psyche. Each of these assumptions will be addressed separately.

The Structure of Foreign Policy Values

If psychologists are correct in identifying these three basic human motivations, then it follows that human beings will categorize the words and ideas used to describe the values and logic associated with these values into three separate categories. That is, words and ideas associated with community and the logic of acceptability would be put in one category; words and ideas associated with security and the logic of effectiveness would be put in another category; and words and ideas associated with prosperity and the logic of efficiency would be put in still another category. We can actually test this proposition using opinion data from the Chicago Council on Foreign Relations (CCFR).

Beginning in 1974, the CCFR conducted general public surveys of American opinion on U.S. foreign policy every four years. [25] The CCFR also conducted a special computer public survey in 2004. The most frequently used goal questions were:

How important a foreign policy goal should [each of the following] be?

- Defending our allies' security
- Protecting the jobs of American workers
- Combating world hunger
- Protecting weaker nations against aggression
- Promoting and defending human rights in other countries
- Protecting the interests of American business abroad
- Helping to improve the standard of living of less developed nations
- Strengthening the United Nations, and
- Helping to bring a democratic form of government to other nations

In each of these surveys respondents were asked whether they thought each goal was "very important," "somewhat important," "not important at all" or given the option to answer "don't know." None of the surveys include exactly the same set of questions—on each occasion one or more questions were added, others dropped—but nevertheless, some key questions have been employed throughout the existence of the surveys, and many of the questions that were dropped resemble those that were later added. Unfortunately, the 1990 and 2002 surveys cannot be used for this test of whether responses to foreign policy questions can be sorted into these three value categories because all respondents were not asked to answer all the goal questions in those years. However, the surveys of 1974, 1978, 1982, 1986, 1994, and 1998, as well as the 2004 computer survey, can be used for this test.[26] It is also important to realize that other pollsters and scholars have replicated these goal questions, so even though this test is restricted to the six CCFR quadrennial surveys and the 2004 survey, judgments about the fit of questions that have not been used frequently in these surveys are based on experience with other similar surveys. Based on what we know from political psychologists, we can expect that the attitudes of respondents toward these questions will reflect their value preferences with respect to community, security, and prosperity.

Though each survey asks a total of between 13 and 18 questions, we can hypothesize that respondents answer the questions in each as if they were actually answering only three *underlying* questions because the words and ideas incorporated into these questions will invoke values associated with the three motivational categories. Thus it seems to us that questions that suggest one's identification with the values of community will be answered one way; questions that conjure up values of security, another way; and questions that invoke values of prosperity, yet another way.

This expectation should not lead us to think that all individuals surveyed will feel the same way about the values in each set. For instance, those who identify more with the global community will say that community goals are "very important" whether the question deals with the environment, human rights, or the standard of living in less developed nations. And those who do not identify primarily with the global community are more likely to report that each of these goals is "somewhat important," "not important at all," or "don't know."

As expected, when the answers to the foreign policy goal questions in these seven surveys are factor analyzed, they reveal three underlying factors that correspond to each of the three sets of values.[27] Box 1.2 groups the questions that were answered in a consistent way in these seven surveys into three parts. Each part represents a separate factor or set of values: Part I corresponds to community values, Part II to security values, and Part III to economic values. The questions within each part are ordered by the

BOX 1.2

CCFR Survey Results

Part I, Question: "I am going to read a list of possible foreign policy goals that the United States might have. For each one please say whether you think that it *should* be a very important foreign policy goal of the United States, a somewhat important foreign policy goal, or not an important goal at all, or you don't know. How important a foreign policy goal *should* [the following] be?"

Community Values:

1. Combating world hunger	7 of 7[a]
2. Helping to improve the standard of living of less developed nations	7 of 7
3. Strengthening the United Nations	7 of 7
4. Promoting and defending human rights in other countries	5 of 5
5. Improving the global environment	3 of 3

Part II [Same question as above]:

Security Values:

1. Maintaining superior military power worldwide	3 of 3
2. Preventing the spread of nuclear weapons	3 of 3

degree to which each question fits into the particular value category. The first number represents the number of times the question fits into the particular value category; the second number represents the number of times the question was asked.

Community Values. The five items in Part I of Box 1.2 appear to express community values because those who agree that these goals are "very important" seem to accept the need to treat people in other countries as equals and to regard them as members of the same global community. According to the individuals who responded affirmatively to the high importance of these goals, it would be an essential foreign policy aim to build up these people and the organizations, such as the United Nations, designed to further their interests. These goal questions generally have a longer shared history than those in other categories.

Security Values. The questions in Part II of Box 1.2 are believed to express security values because those who agree that these particular goals

3. Defending our allies' security — 6 of 6
4. Helping to bring a democratic form of government to other nations — 6 of 7
5. Protecting weaker nations against aggression — 5 of 7
6. Combating international terrorism — 1 of 2

Part III [Same question as above]:

Prosperity Values:

1. Stopping the flow of illegal drugs into the United States — 3 of 3
2. Controlling and reducing illegal immigration — 3 of 3
3. Protecting the jobs of American workers — 6 of 7
4. Protecting the interests of American business abroad — 5 of 6
5. Securing adequate supplies of energy — 3 of 7
6. Reducing our trade deficit with foreign countries — 1 of 3
7. Promoting market economies abroad — 0 of 1

a. The first number represents the number of times the item defined the expected factor at the .30 level or higher out of the number of times (the second number) the item was included in the seven surveys.

are "very important" seem to perceive threats to their security. Some of the questions long used in this category, such as "containing communism," have been abandoned, and others have been added or reworded as the nature of international threats has changed. The one question that might at first not seem to fit as well in this category is the one about "helping to bring a democratic form of government to other nations." In this context it is important to remember that the goal of bringing democracy to non-democratic states is frequently (and increasingly) used by U.S. leaders to justify military action. One question that might have fit this category better is the one about "combating international terrorism." When this question was first asked in 1998, respondents seemed to give it more of an economic interpretation.

Prosperity Values. Most of the seven questions in Part III of Box 1.2 deal with economics and are believed to express prosperity values. But two of the questions—one on drugs and another on immigration—deal with basic social issues. The presence of both social and economic issues in this category suggests that the well-being or prosperity of the actor should be broadly defined.

The grouping of the questions in each of the three parts of Box 1.2 raises similar value choices, but it is important to remember that different individuals make different choices with respect to these values. Now it is time to examine the differences between individuals within each of these value categories. Each of the three dimensions of the value categories will be depicted as a continuum with extreme positions on each end.

Dimensions of Foreign Policy

In interpreting these results we need to consider the full range of questions that might have been asked. The fact that some respondents may not have found that any of the goals mentioned in a category were "very important" does not mean that they believe all possible goals in this category were unimportant. It may simply mean that they were not asked about goals that they thought were "very important." Sketching out the full range of goals in each of these categories, therefore, requires speculation about what questions should have been asked that weren't.

Primary Dimension for Community Values. All of the questions asked about community values appear to favor an inclusive community. It is assumed that those who answered "somewhat important," "not important at all," or "don't know" to these questions may have had a more exclusive community in mind. After all, it is quite common in the United States for individuals to identify more with the United States, or even with groups more exclusive or inclusive than the United States, than they do with the world as a whole.

For example, the leaders of the Cuban American National Foundation (CANF), representing Cuban exiles in South Florida, view the foreign policy of the United States differently than other Americans. They define U.S. interests mainly in terms of values that accentuate the differences between Castro's Cuba and the United States, and their view of the Castro regime is different from that of most other American citizens. These differences became especially apparent in early 2000 during the dispute over Elián González, the six-year-old Cuban refugee whose Cuban relatives in South Florida wanted him to stay in the United States despite the efforts of his father to return him to Cuba.

It is also possible for U.S. citizens to identify with communities that are larger than the United States but still smaller than the global community. For example, Latinos in the United States might identify with Brazilians, Colombians, and Cubans (other "Americans") and express concern about any U.S. foreign policies that might adversely affect these Latin American countries.

In fact, most individuals identify with multiple communities—their family, town, profession, country, and various other groups. When these loyalties to various communities conflict, however, individuals, including those in policy-making positions, tend to make decisions that reflect the primacy of one community over the other. Therefore, the main concern here is with the community to which an individual foreign policy actor feels most strongly committed when making foreign policy choices.

Ultimately that choice involves a preference for the values that individuals associate with community. If the actor stresses the unifying values and goals of equality, universality, and generality, then that actor will identify with a more inclusive community. Such a view is often referred to as **cosmopolitan.** If the actor emphasizes the individualistic values and goals of liberty, freedom and independence, then that actor will identify with a more exclusive community. Such a view is often referred to as **communitarian.** Figure 1.1 shows how the primary dimension in the community domain, when defined in terms of values and goals, ranges from unification, at one extreme, to independence, at the other extreme.

It is important to describe each of the three dimensions, but especially the community dimension, in terms of methods as well as goals because the activation of goals involves means as well as ends. On the one hand, foreign policy actors who most value a unified community tend to act on a **multilateral** basis, attempting to coordinate their actions with the other parties involved or even to avoid acting altogether without support from their allies. For example, U.S. decision makers have traditionally consulted their counterparts in North Atlantic Treaty Organization (NATO) countries on matters of mutual interest. On the other hand, U.S. decision makers may place the highest value on the independence of the United States of America and act in a unilateral manner, not consulting officials in any other state. For example, when the United States put forth the Monroe Doctrine in 1823, it consulted neither the British who had originally suggested the policy, the European states whose foreign policies it was meant to corral, nor the Latin American countries who might benefit from it.

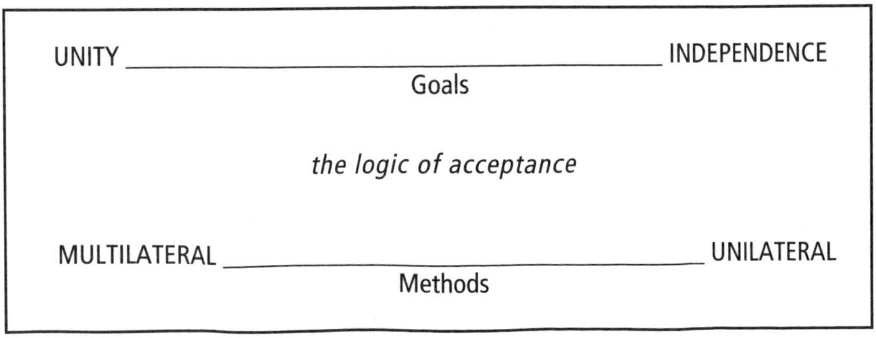

UNITY _____ INDEPENDENCE
                              Goals

                    the logic of acceptance

MULTILATERAL _____ UNILATERAL
                              Methods

Figure 1.1. Primary Dimension for Community Values

For a policy to be truly multilateral, three conditions must be satisfied. First, the policy must be based on a general principle rather than on an *ad hoc* decision. This usually means that at least three states are involved, although one or two states can act according to a multilateral principle if they have developed that principle in concert with other states beforehand. Second, multilateral agreements are indivisible in the sense that they cannot be reduced to a series of bilateral measures. For instance, the United States often negotiates with its NATO allies on a one-on-one basis before NATO as a whole ratifies an American initiative. And third, multilateral policies are characterized by **diffuse reciprocity**, which means that the parties do not expect their actions to balance one another all the time.[28] A **unilateral** policy is more easily recognized, because it is produced by a state that determines for itself what it wants to do. A bilateral policy, one developed in consultations between two states, is more difficult to deal with, because one country can shape the position of the other. In this text bilateral policies are usually also classified as unilateral policies because the United States is so much stronger than other countries that it almost always shapes the position of the other player at the table.

Differences in preferred methods rather than preferred goals are used to label the dimensions in this book because foreign policy must be implemented in order to affect outcomes. Thus the primary methods dimension for community values is multilateral–unilateral. However, this emphasis on methods rather than goals does not mean that motives are any less involved in guiding foreign policy because motives take different forms at various stages of the foreign policy-making process.

The distinction between multilateral and unilateral is not always easy to make. In contemporary diplomacy, so many different actors are engaged in such a variety of forums, dealing with the same issue, that it is often difficult to know whether a given set of negotiations is multilateral or bilateral. For example, it appears that the March 1999 NATO decision to employ air strikes against Serbia was multilateral, because all NATO member countries were involved in approving the decision at some level. But it is also possible that the NATO decision really grew out of a series of bilateral arrangements between the United States and other member countries. At the all-European level and certainly at the global level, however, the decision was not multilateral, because the United States surely would have sought the support of both the Contact Group and the UN Security Council if it could have obtained the support of these institutions.[29] But Russia, which is a member of both the Contact Group and the Security Council, and China, which is a member of the Security Council, opposed NATO air strikes.

Primary Dimension for Security Values. The questions grouped together in Part II of Box 1.2 seem to share a concern with security. The respondents who believed these foreign policy goals were "very important" seemed to perceive an objective, external, security threat. But what about those who felt that these threats were only "somewhat important," "not important at all," or answered "don't know? It seems to us that these other respondents may also be motivated by security concerns, but the CCFR surveys may not have included the issues with which these individuals were most concerned.

Although many individuals seem to interpret the cold war and the September 11, 2001 attacks as objective threats from an external source, others seem to envisage threats coming from quite different sources. For example, the individuals involved in the bombing of the Alfred P. Murrah Federal Building in Oklahoma City in April 1996 appeared to have had ties to some of the many militia groups in the United States. The ideology and rhetoric of members of some militia groups demonstrate that a few Americans may perceive their own government as the main threat to their community, and the fact that the Oklahoma City bombing involved Americans attacking Americans demonstrates that attacks can come from within the community.

Challenges to a community's values can also be interpreted as security threats. For example, the cold war was very much driven by an arms race between the United States and the Soviet Union, but much of the hostility and anxiety stemmed from the clash of values. In fact, certain Americans felt so threatened in the 1950s that, led by Republican senator Joseph McCarthy, the country went to extraordinary and often unjustifiable lengths to expel "communists" from two repositories of American cultural values: the educational system and the entertainment industry.[30]

The goal dimension underlying security values is based on the actor's perception of different levels and kinds of threats. If a state (actor) perceives a high level of threat, it usually wants to put itself in a position of control that would provide something approaching absolute security. If a state perceives a lower level of threat, it may be satisfied with the relative security that comes from a more balanced situation. Figure 1.2 illustrates how foreign policy actors pursue goals in the security category that vary from domination to accommodation.

An actor's choice of security goals affects its preferences for methods. If a foreign policy actor such as a state feels that to be secure it must dominate others, it will be more prepared to use or threaten force to reach its goal. **Coercion** implies one state's willingness to compel another state to do something against its will. It could involve the threat or use of military force, but economic or environmental measures are possible as well. If a state believes that true security depends on mutual consent, then it will favor **noncoercive** methods. Such methods might entail negotiation (when all actors involved participate in reaching a satisfactory outcome) or persuasion (when one actor tries to convince another by suggesting the

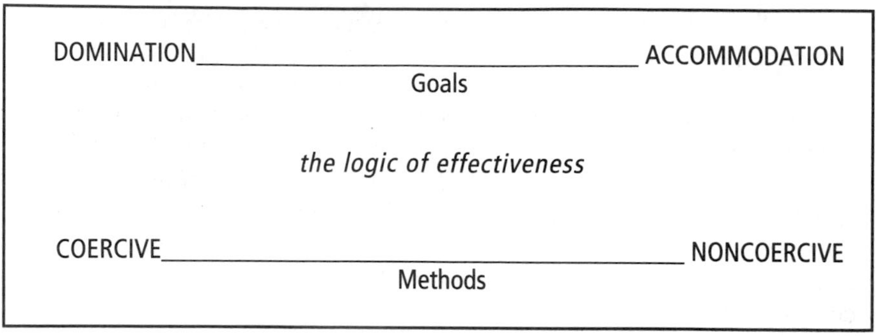

DOMINATION_____ ACCOMMODATION
                            Goals

                  the logic of effectiveness

COERCIVE_____ NONCOERCIVE
                           Methods

Figure 1.2. Primary Dimension for Security Values

benefits that might materialize if its advice is followed). The primary differences in security measures among actors for security are thus shown along the coercive–noncoercive dimension depicted in Figure 1.2.

One of the most unusual forms of coercion was exercised by the Muslim women of Srebrenica in Bosnia when Gen. Philippe Morillon, the French commander of the UN protection force (UNPROFOR), visited their besieged city in March 1993. For weeks the surrounding Serb forces had been shelling the city and it was about to fall. General Morillon hoped to negotiate with the Serbs both a cease-fire and a corridor for humanitarian aid convoys into the city. But the citizens of Srebrenica were convinced that if he left the city, even to negotiate on their behalf, the Serbs would resume the shelling. According to one account, "Morillon was surrounded by a sea of women and children. Some women lay in front of his vehicle. He could not move." [31] A week later, the Srebrenica war council allowed General Morillon to leave the city in the hope that he could get the Bosnian Serbs to agree to a demilitarization of the city. At first General Morillon thought he had reached an agreement on demilitarization with the Bosnian Serbs, but when the forces aligned against the city continued to attack, he turned his attention to the negotiation of the exodus of some of the women and children. The initial decision of the people of Srebrenica to prevent General Morillon from leaving the city was coercive; the later decision to let him go was made under duress.

Primary Dimension for Prosperity Values. The questions in Part III of Box 1.2 seem to express a common concern with the economic and social welfare of the United States. The respondents who answered "very important" to these questions appeared to be most concerned about the domestic costs that international relations may impose on the American society. But those who responded only "somewhat important, "not important at all," or "don't know" to these questions may be just as interested in the economic and social well-being of the United States as other

Americans. Indeed, these respondents might have answered quite differently if the CCFR had asked questions about the benefits associated with the free flow of money, goods, and services abroad.

Foreign policy actors often define the state's interests in terms of broad goals such as growth and development. Under the influence of globalization, a state's interests often take the form of very tangible goods and services. But pride in one's culture and religion is also an important aspect of foreign policy. Prosperity includes the strength and vitality of a state's culture as much as its economic strength and vitality. For example, the competition between Arab states and the West involves religious and cultural differences as well as economic disparities.

The primary dimension for prosperity values is based on a state's level of confidence in relation to others. Generally speaking, the greater the state's confidence in its own culture and economy, the more open its foreign policy. A confident state perceives itself, if not superior, at least secure with respect to others and welcomes open relationships with other states, because it expects to benefit from them. With little to fear from the international environment, confident states will attempt to *maximize their benefits*. By contrast, the less confident a state is, the more pessimistic it is about enhancing its prosperity by opening itself to outside influences. Such states expect to be taken advantage of and tend to avoid relationships in an effort to *minimize the costs* of their participation in the international system. Thus the underlying value in the prosperity category is well-being: either trying to get more, or just trying to preserve what one has. Figure 1.3 illustrates the extremes of the prosperity goal dimension as maximizing benefits and minimizing costs.

An actor's prosperity goals influence the methods it prefers for achieving them. Foreign policy actors that seek wealth and maximum benefits will be **proactive**. Such actors generally believe that their purposes are best served by participating actively in the international exchange of goods, people, and ideas. Actors concerned mainly with

MAXIMIZING BENEFITS	Goals	MINIMIZING COSTS
	the logic of efficiency	
PROACTIVE	Methods	REACTIVE

Figure 1.3. Primary Dimension for Prosperity Values

meeting basic needs and minimizing the costs of participating in the international system will be **reactive**. They will be cautious and even defensive when it comes to international exchanges. Thus the primary methods dimension for prosperity values is proactive at one end and reactive at the other.

Disagreements as to how active a state actor should be can pit one governmental department against another. Such a disagreement clearly arose in the case of the former Yugoslavia, particularly in relation to Bosnia. In 1995, when the U.S. government was preparing for the Dayton, Ohio negotiations among the Balkan rivals, U.S. military and civilian leaders differed over the mission to be pursued by the international implementation force (IFOR) that eventually would enter Bosnia. The military, with the support of both the Joint Chiefs of Staff and the NATO countries, wanted to keep the mission of these forces as narrow as possible so that IFOR would not get involved beyond its capabilities. The civilians in the State Department and the National Security Council wanted a broader mandate for IFOR so that, among other things, the forces would arrest indicted war criminals and help civilians in Bosnia reclaim their homes. Richard Holbrooke, the head negotiator, believed that "the narrower the military mission, the longer [IFOR] would have to stay," because without the help of the military, things would not get better very quickly. The eventual compromise recognized that the military would "have authority but not the obligation, to undertake the additional tasks." [32] In this case, the narrower mission represents a reactive policy; the broader mission, a proactive one.

All three dimensions—community, security, and prosperity—are incorporated into Table 1.2, which shows how these dimensions are related to the three basic approaches discussed earlier. The fact that three distinct factors emerge from this analysis does not mean that individual items in one section of Box 1.2, which contained the questions for the CCFR surveys, do not correlate with individual items in another section. Indeed, the need of individuals to satisfy all three sets of values sometimes leads them to substitute one set of values for another or to interpret the values differently at different times. For instance, the question on "combating international terrorism" was interpreted quite differently in the 1998 survey and the 2004 survey. This kind of confusion has been evident since the end of the cold war, particularly after the September 11, 2001 attacks.[33] Such interpretive shifts underscore the need for an explicit procedure for combining the three dimensions.

Integrating the Three Dimensions of Foreign Policy

As indicated earlier, there are no generally accepted rules for integrating the three dimensions of foreign policy. Scholars and analysts acknowledge the existence of these different motives, values, methods, and logics; but in the absence of a general theory of value preferences, students of foreign

Table 1.2. Essential Elements of the Three Foreign Policy Approaches, Including Primary Dimensions

Approaches	Principal Actors	Views States as	Motive	Operates according to logic of	Value Orientation	Value continuum "Dimension"
Realism/Neorealism	States	Combative; states are enemies	Power	Satisficing, emphasizing the logic of effectiveness	Security	Coercive–noncoercive
Liberalism/Neoliberalism	States and corporations	Competitive; states are rivals	Profit or achievement	Optimizing, emphasizing the logic of efficiency	Economic/prosperity	Proactive–reactive
Idealism/Constructivism Sociological Institutionalism	Individuals in government and society	Cooperative; states are potential friends	Social affiliation	Acceptability, emphasizing the logic of correspondence between objectives and behaviors	Community political	Multilateral–unilateral

policy often ignore one or more sets of values. Moreover, the absence of such rules encourages foreign policy analysts to misconstrue one or more of these dimensions for another. For example, there is no clear distinction in general public discourse between multilateral and international (proactive) behavior on the one hand or unilateral and isolationist (reactive) behavior on the other hand, although these terms apply to two different dimensions of behaviors, which are pursued for two different types of goals.

As a consequence, it should come as no surprise that politicians often misconstrue dimensions in order to serve their own purposes. The fact that polar positions on some dimensions, i.e. multilateral, coercive, and proactive, are often viewed more favorably today than others, i.e., unilateral, noncoercive, and reactive, makes it inviting for politicians to substitute one dimension for another in order to have a desired political effect. For example, when the Bush administration was being criticized by its opponents for pursuing a unilateral foreign policy in Iraq, it tried to convince the public that its policy was multilateral by stressing the number of states involved in its coalition. However, a "coalition of the willing" is more appropriate to and characteristic of a proactive foreign policy in pursuit of efficiency or economic well-being than it is to a multilateral policy in pursuit of acceptability or community-building. The number of U.N. members does not constitute collective action by the United Nations when key members of the Security Council such as France and Russia have not approved the action.

In other circumstances political parties and individuals have mischaracterized multilateral foreign policies as pacifist (noncoercive) or isolationist (reactive) ones in order to characterize those policies in a negative way. For example, in the early 1990s, Bill Clinton's foreign policy in Bosnia could be classified as multilateral, coercive, and proactive because he wanted to undertake joint air strikes against Serbian forces in Bosnia. When his European allies were unwilling to take joint action, however, Clinton decided not to act unilaterally. Clinton's critics characterized his foreign policy as pacifist and isolationist rather than multilateral because it was politically desirable for them to do so. Yet the difference between his preferred foreign policy and the foreign policies that his opponents supposedly favored was on the multilateral–unilateral dimension, not the coercive–noncoercive or proactive–reactive dimension.

Whether conscious or unconscious, the problem of mistaking one dimension for another is common, because all three dimensions are part of every foreign policy. This makes it incumbent upon us to distinguish carefully between all three dimensions regardless of whether we initially define that foreign policy as a community, security, or prosperity issue. After all, the tendency to confuse dimensions may lead analysts to prioritize the wrong dimension because the essential criterion for choice may not always be the one associated with the values defining the issue. For example, the Cuban Missile Crisis of 1962 is generally classified as a security problem. But the choice between a blockade (quarantine) and an air strike was not made solely on the basis of their relative effectiveness—the criterion for choice for security values. The choice of the blockade rather than an air strike was made primarily on the basis of the criterion of acceptance—the criterion for choice for community values. After all, Kennedy ultimately wanted to take an action that would be acceptable to the Soviet Union, thus avoiding World War III.

In order to avoid such errors there must be a systematic way of combining the three dimensions. The analytic framework adopted in this book contributes to this end by requiring careful consideration of all three dimensions of foreign policy regardless of the values initially assigned to a foreign policy event or issue. This rule may make the study of foreign policy somewhat more complicated, but the student will be well rewarded by an increased understanding and more complex picture of foreign affairs. In order to avoid narrow, linear thinking in foreign policy analysis, it is essential to place any given foreign policy in a three-dimensional space. In this context each dimension of foreign policy choice is represented by a separate line. These lines should be drawn at right angles (perpendicular) to one another to show that they are causally independent as shown in Figure 1.4.

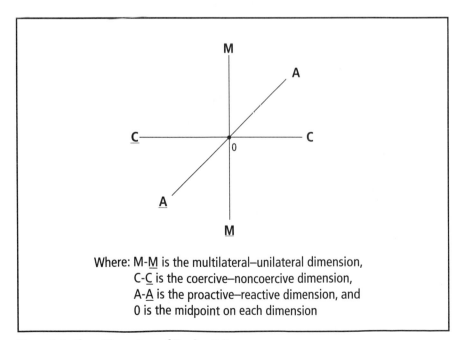

Where: M-M is the multilateral–unilateral dimension,
C-C is the coercive–noncoercive dimension,
A-A is the proactive–reactive dimension, and
0 is the midpoint on each dimension

Figure 1.4. Three Dimensions of Foreign Policy
The dimensions should be read clockwise rather than from left to right.

In Figure 1.4, the vertical line **M–M** represents the multilateral–unilateral dimension; horizontal line **C–C**, the coercive–noncoercive dimension, and diagonal line **A–A**, the proactive–reactive dimension. Because foreign policy is conceived as the result of independent choices on these three dimensions, foreign policy can seldom be represented as a point on any of these lines. A given foreign policy is best described as the common point of intersection based on the choice of a foreign policy actor on each of these three dimensions (lines). This common point of intersection represents an integrated foreign policy and symbolizes a foreign policy that satisfies all three basic human goals. The location of this common point can be determined by means of triangulation.[34]

Given the limitations of representing on a two dimensional page the location of a common point in three dimensions and because of measurement problems, this book also offers a more general way of identifying foreign policies in three-dimensional space. All three dimensions are dichotomized, and each foreign policy is described in terms of its position on three dimensions, beginning with the **M–M** dimension, then the **C–C** dimension, and finally the **A–A** dimension. For example, **MCA** represents a foreign policy that is multilateral, coercive, and proactive, whereas **MCA** represents a foreign policy that is unilateral, noncoercive, and reactive. There are six other possible types reflecting unique combinations of dichotomous positions on these three dimensions. Figure 1.5 illustrates all of these possibilities.

In this text the **MCA** notation is used to refer both to the precise location of a particular foreign policy and the location of a general type of foreign policy, depending on the context. Of course, the locations of these foreign policies will change as positions on these three dimensions change over time. These locations can also be used to compare the foreign policies of different actors at various times.

Organization of the Book

The text is divided into three parts. Part I focuses on the history of U.S. foreign policy; Part II, on contemporary U.S. foreign policy; and Part III, on U.S. foreign policy decision making.

Part I is divided into three chapters. All these chapters deal with all three sets of values, but each historical period highlights a different value. Chapter 2 deals with the formative period between 1607 and 1865 in which the primary values at stake are community values—that is, independence versus unity. Were there to be thirteen independent states or a single, centralized state? That question was first broached by the adoption of the U.S. Constitution in 1789, but as a practical matter it was not finally settled until the end of the Civil War in 1865.

Chapter 3 covers the transition period between 1866 and 1941 in which the primary agenda involved values of prosperity—that is, whether

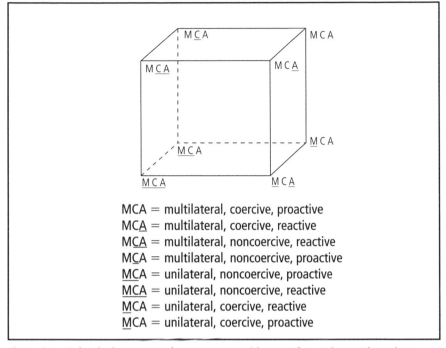

MCA = multilateral, coercive, proactive
MCA = multilateral, coercive, reactive
MCA = multilateral, noncoercive, reactive
MCA = multilateral, noncoercive, proactive
MCA = unilateral, noncoercive, proactive
MCA = unilateral, noncoercive, reactive
MCA = unilateral, coercive, reactive
MCA = unilateral, coercive, proactive

Figure 1.5. Eight Ideal Types Based on Extreme Positions on Three Primary Dimensions.

the country should be proactive or reactive. During this period, the chief issue was the degree of American involvement in the wider world, and that choice was not resolved until the United States recognized how American "isolationism" in the 1920s and 1930s had contributed to the onset of the Second World War.

Finally, Chapter 4 looks at the period between 1942 and the present, one in which security values held the nation's attention—that is, dominance versus accommodation. The inability of the allied states to work together during and after World War II as well as the advent of new weapons of mass destruction largely accounted for the attention given to security. Although the end of the cold war in 1990–1991 seemed to presage the end of the dominance of security considerations in foreign policy, the September 11, 2001 attacks quickly refocused global attention on security matters.

Part II analyzes contemporary U.S. foreign policy by casting U.S. foreign policy preferences as independent variables, and by using foreign policy dimensions to explain foreign policy behavior and outcomes. Addressing each of the different values of foreign policy, the three chapters in this part reveal how U.S. foreign policy preferences in all three dimensions are translated into foreign policy actions and how the interactions among states may affect the outcomes of such behavior.

Chapter 5 shows how preferences on community values have been formulated in the contemporary period and then examines foreign policy options on several issues of special concern, including immigration, asylum, and human rights, as well as prospective foreign policies designed to cope with humanitarian intervention and environmental justice. Chapter 6 illustrates how different perceptions affect foreign policy preferences with respect to security, and how these preferences in turn affect foreign policy behavior. The chapter deals specifically with U.S. concern for international terrorism, the disposition of nuclear weapons, and the threats posed by developing countries. Finally, Chapter 7 addresses prosperity values and examines the role of the United States in the international economy through such issues as international trade and investment, economic development, and economic sanctions.

Part III looks at the process of U.S. foreign policy making through the framework of the three foreign policy dimensions. The six chapters in this Part examine various approaches to the study of how foreign policy is made. These chapters show the kinds of influences (causes) that account for foreign policy decisions (effects), and decisions are revealed as the outcome of commitments to realizing certain objectives.

Concerned with the relationship between government and nongovernment actors in the policy-making process, Chapter 8 shows how different actors are key players in various approaches to the explanation of foreign policy decisions. Chapter 9 then explains how institutions, especially Congress, are used to influence individuals and organizations engaged in foreign policy making.

Chapter 10, which focuses on the U.S. foreign policy bureaucracy, deals primarily with organizational behavior theories. Although these theories are evident at all levels of the bureaucracy, they usually are associated with middle- and lower-level officials in the government. Presidents are the subject of Chapter 11—their personalities and their relationships with their top advisers.

In addressing the impact of society as a whole on U.S. foreign policy, Chapter 12 explores majoritarian theories of foreign policy making, emphasizing the difference between elections, public opinion, and political culture. It attempts to answer the question of how political leaders are able to develop a consensus in support of their foreign policies.

Chapter 13 focuses on pluralist theories of foreign policy, looking mainly at the effect of organized groups on foreign policy outputs and outcomes. Elitist theories of foreign policy making are covered in Chapter 14. Although evidence of elite dominance as opposed to elite influence is weak, this chapter explores the notion that certain elites may control foreign policy decisions by examining their role in policy planning and in the mass media.

Chapter 15, the concluding chapter, addresses the issues of democracy and foreign policy raised both in this introductory chapter and throughout the text.

Key Concepts

achievement   13

coercion   25

communitarian   23

community values   3

constructivism   10

cosmopolitan   23

diffuse reciprocity   24

economic values   3

foreign policy   4

idealism   10

international governmental
    organizations   6

international nongovernmental
    organizations   6

international system   4

liberalism   9

motives   11

multilateral   23

multinational corporations   6

nation   4

neoliberalism   10

neorealism   9

noncoercive   25

nongovernmental organizations   6

nonstate actors   5

optimizing model   12

power   13

proactive   27

rationality   10

reactive   28

realism   9

satisficing model   12

security values   3

social affiliation   13

sociological institutionalism   10

sovereign   4

state   4

transnational national
    corporations   6

unilateral   24

Suggested Readings

1. Chittick, William O., Keith R. Billingsley, and Rick Travis. "A Three Dimensional Model of American Foreign Policy Beliefs." *International Studies Quarterly* 39 (1995): 313–331.

2. Chittick, William O., and Annette Freyberg-Inan. "The Impact of Basic Motivation on Foreign Policy Opinions Concerning the Use of Force." In *Public Opinion and the International Use of Force,* edited by Philip Everts and Pierangelo Isernia, 31–56. London: Routledge, 2001.

3. Friedman, Thomas L. *The World Is Flat: A Brief History of the Twenty-First Century.* New York: Farrar, Straus and Giroux, 2005.

4. Gaddis, John Lewis. *Surprise, Security and the American Experience.* Cambridge, Mass.: Harvard University Press, 2004.

5. Jewett, Robert and John Shelton Lawrence. *Captain America and the Crusade Against Evil.* Grand Rapids: W.B. Eerdemans, 2003.

6. Packer, George. *The Assassins' Gate: America In Iraq.* New York: Farrar, Straus, and Giroux.

PART I

The History of American Foreign Policy

FOREIGN POLICY IS CONSTANTLY CHANGING, not only because the circumstances in which the action takes place change, but also because there are subtle changes in the value choices made by key actors. Although these changes pique one's interest in future policy, that doesn't mean that one can afford to ignore past foreign policy choices. Indeed, understanding the choices actors have made in similar circumstances in the past are crucial to understanding future foreign policy directions. As a consequence, Part I focuses on the historical development of American foreign policy. This history has been divided into three broad periods: (1) the formative period between 1607 and 1865; (2) the transition period from 1866 to 1941; and (3) the most recent period from 1942 to the present.

In order to describe and explain foreign policies in each of these periods one needs to consider each of the three values—community, security, and prosperity—on all three dimensions because all three values are involved in foreign policy decisions. At the same time, one of these three dimensions seems to best characterize the foreign policies in each of these periods. The primary issue from 1776 to 1865 seems to have been independence versus unity. Once the thirteen colonies declared their independence from England, the initial question was whether they could function as united colonies. By 1789 the question had evolved to become whether the new federal government could exercise sovereign powers or whether those powers remained with the several states. That question was not settled until the end of the Civil War in 1865.

The principal issue between 1866 and 1941 seems to have been superiority versus inferiority. This period is often described as isolationist, but that is not really appropriate. The United States has generally been proactive. The real question during this period was not whether to expand, but where and for what purpose. Initially the question of expansion was whether to occupy the Great Plains that were already inhabited by various Indian tribes. Then it was whether to incorporate territories in the Caribbean, Latin America, and the Pacific. Finally, it was whether to become involved in European wars. The attack on Pearl Harbor seems to have settled that question.

The primary issue between the Second World War and the early twenty-first century seems to have been domination versus accommodation. Although the United States was the dominant power throughout this period, it generally sought to accommodate old enemies—Germany and Japan—but it found it difficult to meet the demands of an erstwhile friend—the Soviet Union. As the cold war between these two superpowers ensued, other threats to world order were either amplified or ignored, such as the spread of nuclear weapons, wars of national liberation, the global environment, world poverty, and disease. Although the cold war with the Soviet Union ended in about 1991, U.S. security remained a paramount issue because these other threats had not only grown but were linked by the overriding threat of international terrorism.

Although one dimension has been placed above others in each of these chapters, the question of which dimension should receive priority is always contested. From the beginning Americans have taken great pride in developing a unique democracy under one of the oldest, living constitutions in the world. But the values of security (effectiveness) and prosperity (efficiency) have always competed with democracy, that is to say, community, or acceptance. This issue has usually taken the form of asking whether democracy is compatible with foreign policy, meaning the requirements of efficiency and effectiveness in foreign policy. This perennial question will be revisited throughout the text.

Foreign policy has been defined in terms of a state's relationships with other states. Democracy is defined as a system of governance that emphasizes the equal participation of the members of society on a continuing basis.[1] Actual equal participation was not realized in the United States until well into the twentieth century. Women did not receive the right to vote until 1919, and most African Americans were unable to vote until the civil rights movement in the 1960s tore down the last barriers to full suffrage. Most people in the United States now have the right to vote, although many citizens believe that moneyed interest groups continue to deny them true equal participation in government. Yet despite problems in the system, Americans continue to participate in an increasingly complex system of governance and to push for openness in public affairs.

The United States was hardly a full-fledged democracy in the nineteenth century. Yet when French nobleman, writer, and politician Alexis de Tocqueville visited the United States in the early 1830s, he set out to write the first comprehensive foreign appraisal of the American experiment with democracy.[2] Although Tocqueville asked the readers of his work, *Democracy in America,* to "suspend judgment" on the ability of the young U.S. government to conduct foreign policy until time had produced more evidence, he himself argued that "democratic governments appear decidedly inferior" to aristocracies in this respect. Yet the American democracy has survived many foreign and domestic crises and is proud that it continues to govern itself under one of the oldest written constitutions in the world.

In assessing Tocqueville's criticism of democracy's ability to conduct foreign policy, it is important to realize that his criticism had a lot to do with his ideas about how foreign policy should be conducted, not just with his ideas about the nature of a democracy. Essentially, Tocqueville felt that the American constitution established a weak executive branch that would be ineffective in foreign affairs. According to Tocqueville, democracy favors the growth of the state's internal resources; it extends material well-being and develops public spirit; and it strengthens respect for law in the various classes of society—none of which has more than an indirect influence on the standing of one state in respect to another. More so than an aristocracy, a democracy finds it difficult to coordinate the details of a great undertaking, to fix on some plan and to carry it through with determination in spite of obstacles, and to combine secrecy with waiting patiently for the result: all factors usually associated with security issues.[3]

The requirements of foreign policy also have changed somewhat since Tocqueville visited America. In the early nineteenth century, diplomacy was mainly conducted on a bilateral basis (between two countries at a time). Europe was the center of diplomacy. Most foreign policy of consequence emerged from just a few European capitals, and few procedures had been established for conducting multilateral diplomacy. By contrast, today bilateral diplomacy takes place in the context of multilateral diplomacy, and hundreds of international organizations function in the international system. The number of independent states has multiplied, and the number of nonstate actors engaged in international affairs—among them nongovernmental organizations (NGOs), transnational corporations, and international networks—has grown much faster than the number of state actors.

These dramatic changes in both democracy and foreign policy raise a new set of questions. If Tocqueville is correct and democracy only indirectly affects foreign policy, what accounts for the many successes the United States has experienced in foreign affairs? Those successes are all the more puzzling because the United States often fails to behave in the manner Tocqueville recommended: with unity of action, steadfastness of purpose, and secrecy in its dealings with other nations. Could it be that democracy *does* positively influence foreign policy? If so, how? On the one hand, perhaps a division of opinion on what policies the United States should pursue can actually serve U.S. objectives: the ability to change one's mind and reverse course could be a strategic advantage. Perhaps openness supports American interests abroad. On the other hand, what if unity, patience, and keeping secrets really are critical to a successful foreign policy? Can the United States behave that way if necessary?

Tocqueville's assumption that the only requirements of foreign policy that really matter are those related to executive security functions such as coordination, planning, implementation, and secrecy, in effect dismisses any legislative or judicial functions that might be better performed in a democracy. The assertion that democracy is incompatible with foreign policy is just one more example of the oversimplification of foreign policy. This text will show that democracy (acceptability) can sometimes contribute to effectiveness and efficiency, thus proving Tocqueville wrong. This issue will be raised throughout the text and then revisited in the final chapter.

CHAPTER 2

The Nation's Formative Period: 1607–1865

WITH LEE ANN PINGEL

om 1776 to 1865 the primary issue for the people of e United States was independence versus unity. The eclaration of Independence presented the unity of the lonies, as well as proimed their independence om Great Britain. The signg of the Emancipation Procmation on January 1, 1863 affirmed the unity of states, well as granted freedom to e slave population in the onfederacy. President Abraim Lincoln and his secretary state, William H. Seward, own here, worked closely to eserve the Union. Although ey were naturally concerned at foreign governments ight recognize the Confedacy, their main effort in prerving the Union was to craft olicies for the border states at would make it easier for ncoln, a Union Party candiate, to be reelected in the orth, and for the warring outh to rejoin the Union, after e cessation of hostilities.

PRESIDENT LINCOLN AND SECRETARY SEWARD SIGNING

THE PROCLAMATION OF FREEDOM

JANUARY 1ST 1863.

A MERICA HAS PLAYED A UNIQUE role in the history of the modern era. The thirteen American colonies were the first British colonies to revolt against Crown rule, and their uprising inspired rebels in the French Revolution in 1789 and in Latin America's wars of independence from 1808 to 1833. In many ways, the American Revolution also marked a turning point between the Age of Absolutism, which began in Europe in the sixteenth century and reached its apex in the eighteenth century, and the Age of **Enlightenment**, which began in the eighteenth century and extended into the nineteenth and twentieth centuries.

This chapter describes the significance of this turning point, as well as the relationship between the American colonies and Britain before the Revolutionary War and the foreign policies of the new American government from the Declaration of Independence through the Civil War. Although the road from independence to unity involved all three dimensions of foreign policy, this period of American history was mainly about defining community. But because many of the events and ideas that shaped American foreign policy during this period originated in Europe, the chapter begins with an overview of the relevant events on that continent.

Europe's Transition from Absolutism to Enlightenment

The most prevalent form of government in medieval European political history was the feudal system, which took shape in the ninth century with the collapse of the Holy Roman Empire and continued in most of Western Europe until the fifteenth century. During the early feudal period most people lived as serfs in rural villages in which they were required to make regular payments in service and kind to the local landed nobility. The local village emphasized self-sufficiency. In the middle feudal period, towns, which were essentially communes, began to develop. By the late feudal period, some towns developed much faster than others, and they developed craft guilds in which artisans became increasingly dependent on the merchants who employed them. Throughout the feudal period, public authority rested in private hands, mostly those of the local nobility.[1] The nobility was, however, subject to two sources of higher authority: the Catholic Church and the regional king. Still, neither the church nor the kings had much success in achieving power over the local lords until a different kind of king emerged—the "new monarch" of the modern state system.[2] With the arrival of these kings, the Age of Absolutism was born.

The Age of Absolutism

Any understanding of the evolution of the modern state system rests on knowing how the feudal kings gradually wrested power from the local nobility, on the one hand, and the Catholic Church, on the other. See Figure 2.1 for a timeline for key events in American and European history.

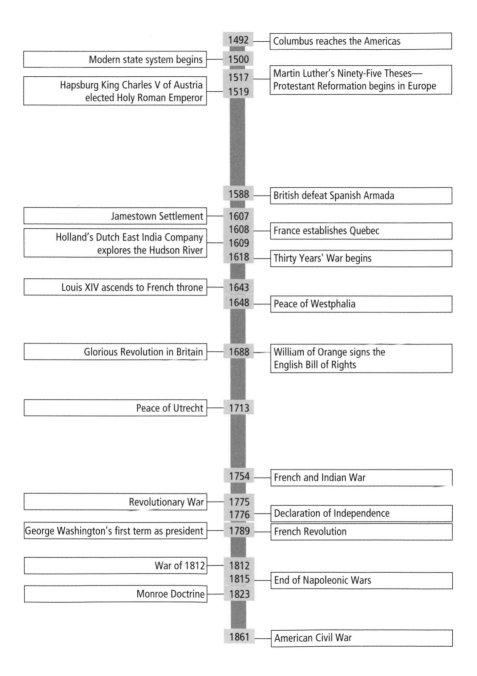

Figure 2.1. Key Events in American and European History 1492–1861.

The regional kings gradually reasserted their claims of homage from the local nobility as these nobles, in turn, required more assistance from the kings. As commerce expanded, the nobility began to accept monetary payments from the peasant classes in lieu of the time required to perform personal services, such as agricultural labor, and it was easier for the kings to assert their claims over the nobles because they too could require monetary payments. The merchant class in towns also financed the regional kings who protected their local monopolies. In the early modern period, kings found it easier to raise revenues by selling monopoly and guild privileges than by collecting taxes.

The kings gained their freedom from the Catholic Church in a more abrupt fashion, precipitated by the Protestant Reformation. Beginning as early as the Crusades in the middle feudal period, Catholicism got away from its original practices and permitted practices like the sale of indulgences, for which there was no scriptural authority. By the sixteenth century the lax and corrupt practices of Catholic churches had bred discontent among theologians and religious scholars, so that when a previously obscure monk named Martin Luther openly criticized those practices in 1517, a violent rift ensued between believers that rocked the continent for most of the next 150 years. In the upheavals that followed, both Catholics and Lutherans sought the protection of secular monarchs although in most cases the monarch made the decision about religion—sometimes out of sincere religious conviction and sometimes by making a political calculation of which side in the religious wars was more advantageous to back. Thus the development of commerce, followed by the unrest of the Reformation and the Catholic Counter-Reformation, combined to elevate the new monarchs to positions of absolute authority.

The last of the religious upheavals of the sixteenth and seventeenth centuries, the Thirty Years' War, ended with the Peace of Westphalia in 1648. That date is usually accepted as the point at which the institutions, such as a centralized bureaucracy and a standing army, associated with the modern state system gained prominence. These institutions were built on the principle that the king's will was law.[3] This principle was extended to more and more areas by the new monarchs, who claimed absolute authority over all the residents of their territory. Monarchical authority was based in turn on a new concept, **sovereignty,** which claimed that the people had surrendered to the monarch nearly all of their personal powers and freedoms in exchange for his protection, thus the power of the sovereign was both absolute and indivisible.

To exercise sovereign power, each of the new monarchs centralized his control over large expanses of territory by gathering in the reins of legal and financial administration and by building up his military forces. Although the kings of England, Holland, Spain, and Austria all strengthened the power of the state during the sixteenth and seventeenth centuries, the rise of the modern state is most identified with France, under the seventy-two-year rule of Louis XIV from 1643 to 1715.

The growth of state power had important implications for the relations between states. If each state through its monarch possessed absolute sovereignty, who was to regulate the relations among them and how? The assertion of absolutism within the state (internal sovereignty) naturally led to a search for the power that each state could wield over other states (external sovereignty). In the absence of any higher authority, the conclusion was that these states were equal to one another. Each state, then, could act as it wanted in relation to other states, subject only to the reactions of these other states and whatever constraints were mutually agreed on by all the states.

Because at first there were relatively few rules to constrain states' exercise of external sovereignty, states were free to pursue their ambitions at the expense of other states. Almost from the beginning, however, the system saw the emergence of a **hegemon**—one state powerful enough to impose its sovereignty on the others. At the beginning of the sixteenth century, shortly after the discovery of America in 1492, the central rivalry in Europe was between France and the combined power of Spain and Austria under the Hapsburg dynasty. In 1519 King Charles V of Austria (also known as King Charles I of Spain) was elected Holy Roman Emperor. With both the military power of a strong monarchy and the moral power of the Catholic Church invested in one man, it appeared for a brief period in the 1520s that Charles and his kinsmen, who controlled Spain, the Netherlands, and parts of Germany as well as Austria, were in a position to impose a "universal monarchy" throughout Europe. The ambitions of the Austro-Spanish Hapsburgs were eventually blocked, however, by a coalition headed by the kings of France in a series of conflicts that became known as the Thirty Years' War, and the Hapsburg threat came to an end in 1648 with the signing of the Peace of Westphalia.

Each time the position of dominance in Europe shifted (from the Hapsburgs in the sixteenth century to France under Louis XIV in the middle of the seventeenth century, and then to England in the late eighteenth century), various coalitions formed to prevent the dominant state from taking over the rest. These joint efforts to check the power of dominant states illustrate the concept of **balance of power.** Political practitioners used the concepts of balance and equilibrium to make sense of the constant feuding and fighting among the European states.

Out of the uncertainties of international relations grew the "classic age of diplomacy" in the eighteenth century. According to historian Felix Gilbert, at this point "the aim of diplomacy was to evaluate correctly the interplay of opposing forces and interests and to create a constellation favorable to conquest and expansion."[4] This traditional diplomacy, or **power politics,** featured secrecy, deception, and aggressive action, and was justified in terms of **reason of state**—the idea that the first duty of the state is to preserve itself. In effect, classic diplomacy elevated foreign affairs over domestic issues, in that the security of the state from outside aggression was held to the highest value.

The economic policy of the day, **mercantilism**, granted monopoly trading privileges to merchants both at the local and national level. These monopoly grants were an important source of revenue for states, such as England and France. Because mercantilists confused money with wealth, they preferred exports to imports, a reversal of the economic policies of the feudal period. Of course, imports from their own colonies were treated as different from imports from other states, so mercantilist states organized trading companies, such as the British East India Company, to maximize the returns from their colonies. Not only were economies in the service of the states, but diplomacy was also a profession devoted to the necessities of states, which, because of the absolute rule of the monarchs, owed nothing to the people residing in the states.

Yet the foreign policies of states were not always dictated by external exigencies. Toward the end of the seventeenth century, a series of events in England had an enormous impact in Europe. In 1685 British king James II, a Catholic, made it clear that he intended to reinstate Catholicism as the state religion in England. Protestant leaders, fearing for their safety should their religion fall out of favor, secretly approached William of Orange, a Dutch Protestant who headed the Dutch army, was married to James's Protestant daughter Mary, and was third in line of succession to the English throne, and asked him to help them depose James II. In response, William led a large army to England, setting off a largely bloodless revolution in which James II fled to France and William took the British throne. In the process, however, William, believing that it only defined existing law, unwittingly signed the English Bill of Rights, a document that would undo absolutism in England and eventually transform the British monarchy into a constitutional monarchy.

This turn of events had two important consequences that earned it the label the "Glorious Revolution." First, the Dutch and British forces, now combined, posed a credible threat to France, the current European hegemon. Second, the English Bill of Rights, which strengthened Parliament's power as against the Crown's, became the foundation for a movement that threatened the very soul of the absolutist system. Some political philosophers of the day, most prominent among them John Locke, took several steps beyond the English Bill of Rights. These philosophers had been developing and writing about the concept of **natural rights**—rights that men possessed simply because they were living human beings.[5] "The philosophies"—as natural rights and related ideas were known—looked beyond the power of absolute monarchs for the "hidden forces" that actually determined events. A new age was dawning.

The Age of Enlightenment

John Locke's *First Treatise of Government* challenged the hereditary and divine right of kings to rule. His *Second Treatise of Government* provided a convincing justification for revolution by the people if the government did not protect their natural rights to life, liberty, and property. Locke used the same rational thinking that natural scientists used to explain the physical world to provide a natural law explanation for the social and political world. He argued that all men had been free to enjoy their own life, liberty, and property before they contracted with government for security. If government did not protect these fundamental rights, men had every right to overturn their government.

Locke, who is well known for establishing the idea of **limited government**—government constrained by a constitution—advocated a series of measures that would help to ensure that governments would be more representative of the people they served. His advocacy of civil—or natural—rights, separation of powers, and other limitations on the powers of government quickly caught the imaginations of oppressed people throughout Europe. Thus, even as the new absolutist monarchs were affirming their authority in a hierarchical society and consolidating a centralized state, novel ideas were already beginning to challenge their legitimacy.[6]

Although these ideas were known throughout Europe, they had the most immediate effect on England itself, because the power of the English king was already balanced by a parliament through the English Bill of Rights. Although the debates in the British Parliament were closed, important speeches were often printed in broadsides and discussed in public. Members of the British public, then, were more aware than ordinary people in other countries of their government's foreign policy problems and options, such as whether England needed to play an active role in struggles to maintain the balance of power in continental Europe.

Meanwhile, Enlightenment thinkers, especially the French *philosophes*, argued that the old diplomacy that emphasized the balance of power was ineffective at peacemaking or peacekeeping, and peacetime activities such as trading.[7] They wanted to abandon power politics that emphasized differences among states in favor of economic policies that would further the common interests of individuals. In other words, they wanted the people to take over the political life of the country and establish a new diplomacy that would be the opposite of the old diplomacy. Under such a system, there would be no difference between the norms that rule the relations among people and the norms that rule the relations among states. Because they did not make a clear distinction between politics and economics, they thought commercial agreements could replace formal treaties, and the relationships between states could rest in the hands of people trading with each other, not governments.[8]

The ideas associated with the Age of Absolutism and the Age of Enlightenment fit neatly into the framework of dimensions presented in Chapter 1. As Table 2.1 shows, the **old diplomacy** espoused foreign policies that were unilateral, coercive, and reactive (or M$\underline{CA}$); the **new diplomacy** advocated foreign policies that were multilateral, noncoercive, and proactive (or $\underline{M}$C$\underline{A}$). (The matrix format of Table 2.1 will be employed throughout the text to illustrate the dimensions of foreign policy situations.) Both sets of ideas had a profound effect on the development of the British colonies in North America.

The Colonial Period in America: 1607–1776

During the sixteenth century, Spain and Portugal dominated exploration of the New World. But after the defeat of the Spanish Armada in 1588, the British, Dutch, and French began to encroach on Spanish territory and hegemony in North America and established settlements of their own further north. England founded Jamestown in 1607; France established Quebec in 1608; and the Dutch East India Company made the first inroads into the New York area in 1609, when Englishman Henry Hudson, exploring for Holland, sailed up what is now known as the Hudson River. By 1664, however, the English had shut the Dutch out of the Hudson River valley, and by 1689 Spain's position in North America had weakened considerably, and Spanish territorial boundaries were pushed further and further to the South and West throughout the seventeenth and eighteenth centuries.[9]

Eventually the British and the French became the main rivals for North America. The British settled on the eastern coast of North America; the French explored and developed the middle of the continent, using the St. Lawrence and Mississippi Rivers to reach deep into the interior of the continent. The colonial competition between the British and the French did

Table 2.1. Dimensions of Foreign Policy: Old and New Diplomacy

| | Multilateral | | Unilateral | |
	Coercive	Noncoercive	Noncoercive	Coercive
Proactive		New diplomacy		
Reactive				Old diplomacy

The old diplomacy is M$\underline{CA}$—unilateral because each state exercises its external sovereignty, coercive because absolute rulers are prepared to use force, and reactive because these rulers employed mercantilist policies to maximize internal wealth.

The new diplomacy is M$\underline{C}$A—multilateral because it emphasizes the common interests of people and states, noncoercive because it emphasizes diplomacy, and proactive because it advocates free trade between states.

not reach a crisis until the middle of the eighteenth century. When that clash occurred, however, it had important repercussions for the relationship between the British colonies and their mother country.

Years Leading Up to the French and Indian War: 1607–1754

The settlers of the British colonies in North America were motivated by all three of the basic motivations described in Chapter 1: power, achievement, and social affiliation. Although this chapter is concerned primarily with social affiliation or the community dimension, it is important to take all three motivations into account. For that reason, the prosperity and security dimensions are also discussed in this section.

Prosperity Values.   Although the promise of monetary gains was one of the factors that led settlers to embark on the dangerous voyage to the New World, no royal funds were used to develop the British colonies. Indeed, at first there was no British imperial policy; the colonies were largely a "private endeavor" funded by joint stock companies such as the British East India Company, which were granted royal charters to establish settlements in the New World. In the absence of more specific provisions or written charters, most colonies relied upon common law procedures. Under common law, legislative supremacy rested with the British Parliament, and statutes passed by that body could alter common law. At first the possible conflict between laws passed by the British Parliament and colonial assemblies did not become an issue because Parliament did not concern itself that much with colonial affairs. But as Parliament gradually replaced the crown as the primary British actor in colonial affairs, conflict arose because British merchants, who now looked to Parliament rather than the crown for assistance, began to seek special privileges from that body, and colonial policy makers began to question the constitutional bases on which the colonies were founded.[10]

By the 1660s the British and the French governments were using various trade regulations to bind their respective settlements in North America to them. For example, Britain, by means of Navigation Acts, required all colonial imports from continental Europe to be routed through Britain. Likewise, various exports from the colonies, such as tobacco, had to be shipped to Britain for reexport to other countries.[11] These mercantilist policies favored the mother countries at the expense of the colonies.

The British, however, found it more difficult than the French to enforce these kinds of regulations, because the British government had not imposed rigorous mercantilist controls from the beginning. The British colonies had been engaged mainly in self-sustaining agriculture, and only about 15–20 percent of colonial produce went overseas. Yet even though the absolute amount of international trade was small, colonial merchants and planters were sensitive to these new controls because they had already developed their own markets in the West Indies and southern Europe, and by the end of the seventeenth century, the independent colonial trade was fairly well established. The colonies were expected to provide food and other raw materials to England, and they depended heavily on that country for manufactured goods. To afford to import these goods, they simply had to develop export crops and engage in international trade. In view of America's abundant natural resources and scarce labor, the only solution seemed to be to export resource-based commodities and import labor-intensive ones. This trade involved not only England but also other markets in Europe, North Africa, the Caribbean, and South America.

In such a situation, an individual colony's mix of self-sustaining and export-oriented agriculture largely determined how it would develop. Because of variations among the colonies in climate, quality of land, and availability of good ports, they developed quite differently. The middle colonies, with their especially rich land, developed first. Tobacco became an important crop in Virginia and Maryland, but later the southern colonies began to produce both tobacco and rice. As large cash crop agriculture became more predominant in the South, the slave trade grew briskly as well, to compensate for the labor shortage, with the number of slaves rising from almost 15,000 in 1680 to more than 500,000 by the outbreak of the Revolutionary War. New England, by contrast, overcame its poorer agricultural climate and rocky soil by capitalizing on its harbors and becoming a major trading and shipping center.

The British encouraged immigration into the colonies, first from England and later from the rest of Europe, because it augmented trade and increased national strength. By the mid-eighteenth century, the British colonies in America were thriving. The population growth rate of the colonies was twice that of Europe, doubling every twenty-five years. Philadelphia was not only the largest city in North America but also the second largest in the British Empire. The port cities of Boston, New York, and Charleston also were becoming important commercial centers. The growth of population and cities in North America put the colonists in a better position to challenge the mother country.

Community Values. In addition to the economic incentives, many people came to the New World to build a more perfect social order. Because many of the settlers were religious dissidents, they developed a variety of tightly knit local communities of true believers who were not necessarily any more tolerant of religious dissenters once they were the dominant religion. The communities differed both from those of England and from each other. For example, the American colonists developed a very different sense of local autonomy than that practiced in England itself. According to historians Harold T. Parker and Marvin L. Brown Jr., "English lawyers generally likened a colony to a municipal corporation: an inferior and subordinate body. . . . The colonists saw themselves in a different light. Their lower houses were miniature Houses of Commons." [12] Moreover, the loyalty of the colonists to Britain diminished over time. This was especially true in later years when immigrants were more likely to come from the continent than from England itself.

Although the charters that defined the relationship between the colonies and the mother country were somewhat different, they all relied on British common law. But local circumstances led them to develop legislation that was different in important ways from the corresponding laws in England. The colonists placed special emphasis on representation in their lower houses or assemblies. And Americans developed a much stronger sense of *equal* representation than the British, for whom

> the privilege of sending two representatives to the House of Commons had been accorded to each county and to certain specified boroughs, but there had never been any thought of creating electoral districts of equal population. However, when each colony first delimited its districts for the election of the lower house of the colonial assembly, it tended systematically to outline regular electoral districts roughly equal in population. Then, when the western districts in each colony filled with people and they protested that they were under-represented, they based their protest on a principle of equal representation that was not accepted in England, or anywhere else in eighteenth-century Europe.[13]

A governor appointed by the Crown presided over each of the colonies' assemblies. These governors represented Britain's primary source of power over the colonies, but they gradually lost control of their wards because of the diverging interests of the colonies and their mother country. Eventually, each of the colonies also established agents in England to represent their interests before Parliament and the Crown. At first, most of these colonial agents were Englishmen. As the lower houses became more powerful in the colonies, however, these agents tended to be loyal to the assemblies rather than the governors. In later years, colonists such as Benjamin Franklin of Pennsylvania and Arthur Lee of Virginia became colonial agents in London.

Security Values.   It was not until the latter part of the seventeenth century that the British began to pay special attention to security threats to the colonies. Britain had believed that the superiority of the British fleet was sufficient to deter serious challenges to their colonies from other states and that colonial militia units were perfectly able to deal with the threat posed by Native Americans. The colonists had learned that killing the game on which the Native Americans depended for food would force the tribes inland away from established settlements. Although Native Americans were skillful individual fighters, the tribes found it difficult to unite and fight a sustained war against the colonists. For their part, the colonists found they were able to meet their primary security needs simply by arming all able-bodied males. Largely as a result of this experience with militias, the colonists developed concepts of self-government that did not primarily emphasize maintaining standing armies.

After the "Glorious Revolution" in 1688, however, strategic and military considerations became more important to Britain, and it began to commit military and naval forces to the defense of its American colonies.[14] In 1754 Benjamin Franklin's newspaper carried a report by an obscure officer of the Virginia Militia, named George Washington, which described a skirmish between a small group of Virginia volunteers under his command and a much larger force of French and Indians near Fort Duquesne (Pittsburgh) on the Ohio River. Franklin quickly grasped the danger that the French and Indians posed to the western frontiers of the colonies, and in an accompanying cartoon depicted the colonies as a snake broken into eight parts, with the caption "JOIN, OR DIE."

Shortly thereafter, the British Board of Trade asked the governors of seven colonies to hold an intercolonial conference in Albany, New York. At this conference Franklin proposed a "Plan of Union," suggesting that the colonies might even establish two new colonies in the West and charge them with providing for the common defense. Although the Plan of Union received the approval of the conferees, it was rejected by both the colonies themselves and Britain. Neither Britain nor the colonies were prepared to relinquish any control over colonial affairs. As for the French threat, Britain decided to commit the military resources needed to defeat France.[15] Map 2.1 shows how the British eventually came to dominate North America as a result of the French and Indian War.

From the French and Indian War to 1776

The French and Indian War, which began in 1754, soon spread to other British colonies in the West and East Indies. Two years later, in 1756, the colonial war precipitated a war on the European continent between Britain and France. The conflict, later known as the Seven Years' War, soon involved nearly every country in Europe. When the Seven Years' War ended in 1763, France surrendered to England all its claims to Canada and to the region from the Appalachian Mountains west to the Mississippi River. When British forces took Havana, Cuba, from its Spanish colonists, Spain agreed to cede its Florida territory to Britain in order to retain control of Cuba.

One consequence of this war was that Britain, France, and the other European powers became more aware of North America's importance in the overall balance of power in Europe. Because the British had greatly increased their holdings in North America, they needed to give some thought to how they might govern and defend those territories in the future. Realizing that the French could become involved in North America

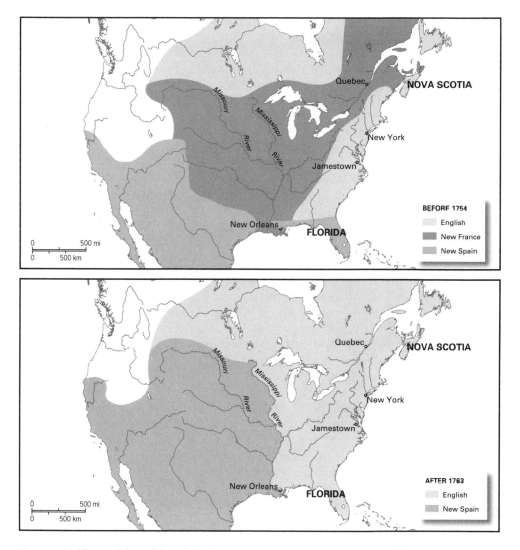

Map 2.1 British, Spanish, and French Settlement in North America, 1754 versus 1763
Prior to the French and Indian War, the English occupied the eastern coast of North America; the French,
the interior; and the Spanish, Florida and the Southwest. After the war the English claimed everything
east and north of the Mississippi River.

again at a later point, Britain decided to increase its military and administrative presence in the New World and worked quickly to exert more control over its American colonies. The most important change was that the
British stationed six thousand British troops in North America (to defend
the colonies against possible attacks by the Indians and Spain) and expected that the colonists would contribute annually to the troops' upkeep.

To prevent future Indian wars, the British king himself also forbade whites to settle west of the Appalachian Mountains and designated the interior of British North America as an Indian reservation.

These measures widened the gulf of misunderstanding that separated the two societies at this point in time. The more the British became persuaded that their own security and well-being depended on retaining the colonies, the more hastily they attempted to exert control over their North American outpost. But the more the British tried to exercise control over the colonies, the more the colonies perceived a threat to their autonomy. Indeed, the British were not the only ones to come out of the war with a greater awareness of the importance of the colonies; American colonists also had gained a sense of self-importance. Moreover, the colonists had begun to think of the British Empire as more of a federal system, and they were not prepared to accept the omnipotence of the British Parliament. From their perspective, it was only fair that they, a colony of English subjects, be taxed only by an assembly of their own elected representatives.

The British decision to station troops in the colonies was not nearly as troublesome to the Americans as the way the British were going to pay for it. The British had practically doubled the size of their national debt during the recent war, and the British, as well as the Dutch, were already paying the highest taxes in Europe. So it is not surprising that Britain wanted the Americans to help pay for their own defense.

The British decision to restrict settlement west of the Appalachian Mountains came as a severe blow to land speculators and others in America who had hoped to benefit from the opening of new lands in that region. The Proclamation Line of 1763, which demarcated the boundary of white settlements, was perceived by Americans not only as an unnecessary limitation on their economic prospects but also as a threat to their security, because they equated the settlement of western lands with the security of their land holdings on the eastern coast.

The British also instituted other acts that the colonists resented. The first was the Currency Act of 1764, which forbade colonies other than those in New England from issuing any paper currencies that would be contrary to British interests. The Sugar Act of 1764 effectively limited colonial trade with the West Indies and other parts of Europe. The Sugar Act was followed by the Stamp Act of 1765, which was a direct tax on the colonies to pay for the British troops stationed there. Public protest of the Stamp Act was particularly strong, and the colonists' resentment toward the British deepened.

The turbulence generated by the Stamp Act was reflected in the shifts in attitude of the American colonial agents in England. At first, Benjamin Franklin, one of the London-based colonial agents, actually nominated one of his personal associates in Philadelphia to be a stamp tax collector. Once Franklin correctly perceived the scope and depth of the protests at home, however, he led the effort in London to have the act repealed.

Although the British government eventually repealed the Stamp Act, the colonists maintained their opposition to taxation without their consent. The British government continued to make concessions to the colonies through 1773, but when the British cabinet offered to sell surplus tea to America for less than the colonists were paying for smuggled tea to avoid the Townshend tax, the Americans thought it was a sly way of getting them to accept the British tax. The colonists' resulting act of defiance, known as the Boston Tea Party on December 16, 1773, provoked Britain into issuing the punitive 1774 Coercive Acts, which closed the port of Boston and stripped the colonists of nearly all of their rights to self-governance. These punitive measures were intolerable to the American colonists, who then agreed to convene a congress to address the crisis. In 1774 the first Continental Congress prohibited all trade with Great Britain. When the second Continental Congress met in 1775, it created a Secret Committee of Correspondence to identify potential allies abroad.

The Wars of Independence: 1776–1815

Although present-day Americans usually assume that the colonies won their independence at the close of the Revolutionary War, a good case can be made that true independence was not achieved until the Americans and the British settled most of the issues between them and established normal trading relationships, which did not happen until after the War of 1812, referred to herein as the Second War of Independence.

This section, which is divided into three periods—the Confederal Period, the Federalist Period, and the Republican Period—employs the framework developed in the first chapter. Before the Declaration of Independence, the colonies did not qualify as states, and so they had no basis for conducting their own foreign policies. In the fall of 1775 France sent a secret agent, the dramatist Pierre-Augustin de Beaumarchais, to the American colonies to encourage their insurrection. But it was not until March 1776 that the Second Continental Congress sent its first emissary, Silas Deane, to France.

The Confederal Period: 1776–1788

To invest meaning in the Declaration of Independence, the Americans had to deal with two problems simultaneously. First, they had to learn to work together. Second, they had to win the war with Britain. Although they worked on the two tasks concurrently, the second task took precedence over the first. This section describes the former colonists' efforts to win the war before they attempted to achieve a perfect government.

Winning the War.   Writing in Philadelphia where the Continental Congress was meeting, Thomas Paine, a relative newcomer to America, published in 1776 a widely read pamphlet entitled *Common Sense*. In it he urged Americans to abandon any hope of freedom under the English throne, to declare their independence, and to establish good trade relations with France and Spain. After all, the elimination of trade with Britain did not pose a very serious problem because Americans were largely self-sufficient. In April 1776 the Continental Congress followed Paine's recommendations and ordered that American ports be open to the ships of all nations except those of Britain.

Once Congress signed the Declaration of Independence in July, work began on securing trade treaties with the other countries of Europe, because the government realized the former colonies needed outside help to win the war. Diplomacy was essential to acquiring uniforms, munitions, and other supplies. Although the Americans were reluctant to seek help from the French, with whom they had just fought a war, they realized that France was the only country that had both the capability and the motivation—revenge against Britain—to help them. In September 1776 the Congress also sent Arthur Lee and Benjamin Franklin to France to join Silas Deane. The inexperienced Deane and Lee could be considered "militia diplomats," but Franklin was already an experienced diplomat, as well as one of the nation's most prestigious citizens. Box 2.1 discusses Franklin's diplomatic career. France finally signed a formal Treaty of Alliance and a commercial treaty with the Americans in 1778.

Despite this coup with the French treaty, America's "militia diplomats" were only partly successful. In 1779 Congress renewed its efforts to ally with other European states. It assigned its emissaries in France somewhat different tasks: Franklin was to work primarily with the French government; John Jay was given special responsibilities in relation to Spain; and John Adams was expected to work directly with Britain. Adams made little headway with Britain, but he was successful in signing a treaty of commerce with the Netherlands. On the whole, then, Congress and its emissaries experienced little success in obtaining financial resources elsewhere, and the individual colonies and Congress were forced to issue paper money, which fueled inflation.

After six years of bloodshed and hardship, the former colonists finally defeated the British army at Yorktown in 1781, but a formal peace agreement was not signed until September 1783. The Americans could not have won their independence without the help of France and, to a lesser extent, Spain and Holland.[16] Even then, the victory would not have been possible had Britain's forces not been spread so thinly across its worldwide empire.

The Treaty of Paris, which ended the war with Britain, did not resolve all of the foreign policy issues between the two countries. The Americans still faced major problems such as trade discrimination by Britain and its refusal to relinquish frontier posts, as well as Spain's restrictions on American use of the Mississippi River. Some of these issues would not be settled until after the Second War of Independence. The fact that so few countries recognized the new government only added to its ongoing dilemmas.[17] The founders finally addressed some of these fundamental problems at the Constitutional Convention of 1787.

Perfecting the Government. In addition to winning the war, the Continental Congress—which was a government, not simply a legislature—took other actions that proved to have far-reaching consequences for the development of the United States. One of the most significant measures was the Northwest Ordinance of 1787, which divided land between the Ohio and Mississippi Rivers (known as the Northwest Territory) into territories that could become states when their population reached sixty thousand. This ordinance was critically important not only because it opened up the western land for settlement but also because it defined the rules under which new states could join the thirteen original states on equal terms. As America grew over the next sixty some years, the conditions under which new states would be added became a crucial issue.

At the same time, Congress encountered several difficulties that hampered the development of the nation's foreign policy. One difficulty was the lack of effective executive leadership. Although America's "militia diplomats" had been successful in getting help from France and to a lesser extent from Spain and the Netherlands during the recent war, they were no more successful after the war than they had been during the conflict in obtaining either diplomatic recognition from or commercial agreements with other European states.[18] Congress's difficulties in developing a coherent foreign policy led leading political thinkers to call for a stronger, more centralized government that could play a more dominant role in international relations.

Another difficulty facing the new government was in developing coherent domestic policies, namely that Congress did not have the power under the Articles of Confederation either to tax the former colonies or to regulate commerce among them. Lacking the power to regulate interstate commerce, Congress found it difficult to facilitate trade with other countries, such as France, because each of the thirteen states had its own system of tariffs and duties. The terms of trade with Britain also became problematic, because although the British had been quite generous in allowing the former colonies to resume trade with England under the Treaty of Paris, the Americans lost their commercial privileges within the British Empire. The inability to tax or receive revenue created other difficulties for Congress. Although most states were eventually able to pay off their war debts, Congress itself could not do so without the power to tax or receive revenues.[19] And although the Treaty of Paris called for compensation for the properties left behind by British loyalists, Congress could not compel state courts to order restitution.

These and other problems under the Articles of Confederation led the states to call for a convention that would consider ways of enabling the

BOX 2.1

Profile in Action: Benjamin Franklin

No one grappled more persistently with the issue of independence versus union during the latter half of the eighteenth century than Benjamin Franklin. From 1754 until his death in 1790, Franklin, both as a politician and publisher at home and as a diplomat abroad, worked actively to promote a union of Britain's thirteen American colonies. At first, he believed that this harmony of interest could include both the colonies and Britain. But when he realized that King George III was unwilling to allow the colonies to act individually or jointly, he pushed hard for independence.

As described in the text, Franklin's initial "Plan of Union" was rejected in 1754, and so the individual colonies had to protect their own western frontiers. Franklin himself served briefly as a general in the Pennsylvania militia. Then, in 1757, the Pennsylvania assembly sent Franklin to Britain where he successfully negotiated a new understanding about the right of Pennsylvania to tax millions of acres belonging to the Penn family as proprietors in the original Charter. Franklin returned to Philadelphia in 1762.

When the British attempted to increase their control over the American colonies after the French and Indian War, Franklin was sent back to Britain to seek redress. This time he represented New Jersey and Georgia in addition to Pennsylvania. As the primary spokesperson for the American colonies in London, and one able to benefit from his fame as a scientist and a printer, Franklin led the fight against the Stamp Act in 1765. Massachusetts asked him to represent that colony as well in response to British oppression after the Boston Tea Party in 1773. Franklin remained in Britain for nine years.

On his return to his home in Philadelphia in early 1775, Franklin was appointed a member of the Continental Congress, but he was disheartened be-

central government to deal with problems. The convention, which met in Philadelphia in May 1787, decided in the end to draft a new constitution for the fledgling republic rather than revamp the Articles of Confederation. Alexander Hamilton, who was a proponent of the old diplomacy, argued in *The Federalist Papers,* a series of essays written in support of state ratification of the Constitution, that the United States needed a stronger executive. James Madison, another contributor to *The Federalist Papers* and a key player in the Constitutional Convention, also wanted a stronger central government, but he advocated putting internal checks in place to prevent it from stealing too much power away from the former colonies. The debate on the new constitution demonstrates that the values of com-

cause the Pennsylvania delegation was under the control of an old rival, John Dickerson, who still thought George III would provide relief to the colonies. Despite his feeling of isolation while serving in Congress, Franklin drafted a Declaration of Independence and Articles of Confederation, which in his mind were part of the same document. Most members of the convention were unprepared to consider such strong actions, however, and so his work was only accepted as a talking paper. (Jefferson's draft of the Declaration of Independence was not accepted until 1776 and the Articles of Confederation in 1781.)

Although Franklin was heavily involved in the work of the Continental Congress, he was sent to France in 1777 to arrange treaties of defense and commerce with that country. Franklin succeeded in getting the French treaties approved in 1778, but he stayed on in France until 1785.

While in Europe, Franklin was not just trying to achieve independence of the united colonies from Britain, but also seeking to achieve the kind of rapprochement with the mother country that would allow the two nations to work in harmony in the future. Franklin ultimately failed to secure this broader peace both because Britain was unwilling to make the required concessions and because France, Spain, and Holland were unprepared to accept a strong and unified America.

Franklin returned to the United States in 1785 just in time to participate in the Constitutional Convention. Despite his age, he became heavily involved in the fight for ratification. Although Franklin is correctly associated with American independence from Britain, he was even more committed to unity—both the unity of the thirteen original colonies and the unity of American and British interests. As a result of his experience in London and later in Paris, he came to realize that independence was an essential step toward a genuine unity with Britain. In this sense, Franklin's personal foreign policy is best described as MCA: multilateral, noncoercive, and proactive.

munity, security, and prosperity were involved in American foreign policy discussions from the beginning. The dilemmas of American foreign policy during this period could all be expressed in terms of the conflict between the old diplomacy and the new diplomacy along the value dimensions.

Dilemmas of Foreign Policy.   The choice between unilateralism and multilateralism was a choice between the old diplomacy's emphasis on divergent state interests and the new diplomacy's preference for the unity of mankind. At the international level the founders were intent on satisfying the special needs of the new country, but they were also cognizant that they had won the war only by acting in concert with other states.

Although the founders may not have realized it fully at the time, the dilemma of unilateralism versus multilateralism was a familiar and underlying element of the domestic debate over federalism. On the one hand, the original colonies—now states—had different priorities and viewed the federal government as an instrument to meet these varying interests. On the other hand, they had common objectives that could not be fully realized unless they put aside their differences and recognized that the central government best represented their common aspirations for the future.

Traditional governments were based on two precepts of internal sovereignty: absolute power and indivisible power. The new republic challenged both of these fundamental principles, because it limited the powers of government by means of a written constitution and because it divided the remaining power between one federal and several state governments. In rejecting these precepts of the old diplomacy, the founders also expected to challenge the European practice of external sovereignty. The Americans believed that foreign policy was the outgrowth of a country's domestic politics, and they expected their relations with other countries to reflect democratic principles.

The choice between coercion and noncoercion was a choice between the old diplomacy's emphasis on military force and the new diplomacy's preference for negotiations. Although recognizing the need for some sort of armed force, the founders preferred nonmilitaristic means and believed that the primary instrument of the new diplomacy would be free trade. They were reluctant to create a large standing army under the command of the central government, even though they realized the difficulty of building an adequate military force through voluntary enlistments. Many feared that a strong federal army might some day be used against the states and a strong military was inimical to democratic government.

The choice between a proactive foreign policy and a reactive foreign policy was a choice between the new diplomacy's emphasis on free trade and the old diplomacy's commitment to mercantilism. The founders were also profoundly aware that, earlier republics in Greece and Rome had failed. They realized that in their efforts to establish a functioning republic, they were engaged in "a great experiment." Although their geographic isolation gave them the opportunity to develop their republic without undue influence from abroad, most Americans thought that their country might have a positive influence on the wider world. Many of the founders believed that God had specially blessed their new country as a modern "promised land" of freedom and possibility. As a result, they were highly conscious that they worked not just in their own interest or even in the interest of the country, but in the interest of God. They were acutely aware of what the new United States represented in the eyes of many people around the world, and so often felt compelled to offer advice and assistance abroad. Because foreign policy was the most direct way in which America's voice was heard, the members of the first national government deliberated long and hard on the proper course to take in international relations.

The Federalist Period: 1789–1800

Under the first two American presidents, George Washington and John Adams, the government endeavored to set a clear course for the country in foreign affairs. For the most part, the founders had assumed that the foreign policy of the new republic would simply be an extension of the principles of its domestic politics. They believed that the U.S. republic would be a peace-loving society that based its relations with other countries on the principles of open diplomacy and free trade. Although they realized that Americans would face many threats and opportunities from abroad, they foresaw no inherent divisions among Americans over the conduct of foreign policy. If divisions sprang up among Americans, the founders expected the divisions to arise in the arena of domestic politics.

Domestic and foreign policy divisions appeared in George Washington's first cabinet, not too long after Washington appointed Thomas Jefferson as his secretary of state and Alexander Hamilton as his secretary of the Treasury. These two men soon came to represent opposite sides of opinion on an issue that plagued the country for the next quarter-century—how to handle American relations with France and England. The enmity between those countries made it difficult for the United States to be neutral; each country sought to gain advantage over the other by developing the closest ties to American resources.

When the French Revolution broke out in earnest in the last decade of the eighteenth century, the United States was still in the midst of fine-tuning its brand-new domestic government. But with the overthrow of the French royal house and France's later declarations of war on several European powers—the so-called Napoleonic Wars—President Washington and his cabinet faced a serious foreign policy crisis.[20]

Relations with France.   The treaties of alliance and commerce drawn up in 1778 between the United States and France under Louis XVI made dealing with the new republican government in France more complicated for the Washington administration. Jefferson and Hamilton debated vehemently over whether these treaties were still valid and more generally over how to proceed with U.S.-French relations. The difference in their views stemmed less from their philosophical disagreement over the nature of the French Revolution than from their opposing interpretations of U.S. obligations under the 1778 treaties.

Jefferson was a strong proponent of the ideals of democracy, preferring a weak federal government to a strong one, and an agricultural economy to one of commerce and manufacturing. Named minister to France in 1785, Jefferson found his five years there to be "among the happiest of his life," and he returned to the United States a faithful ally of France. His belief in reform for the French government allowed him to support the republicans against the monarchy and to draw a strong parallel between the French and American Revolutions. He also distrusted the British Empire and desired to implement an economic plan he had designed to break Britain's monopoly of the American market.

Hamilton was in many respects the exact philosophical and political opposite of Jefferson. He supported a strong central government and the development of commerce and manufacturing. Hamilton mistrusted the French Jacobins, fearing that their example of extremist popular revolution may "have unhinged the orderly principles of the People of this country [America]" and that "a further assimilation of our principles with those of France may prove to be the threshold of disorganization and anarchy." [21] Instead, he sided with Britain, primarily because the success of his own economic system depended on revenues earned from trade with Britain. And rather than place the American and French Revolutions in the same league, Hamilton regarded the French war as overly bloody and "sullied by crimes and extravagancies." [22]

President Washington had publicly advocated a policy of neutrality in the French–English conflict but regarded the alliance with France under the 1778 treaties as worrisome. This alliance stipulated that, first, the United States might be required to help defend French holdings in America, such as the French West Indies, and, second, French ships could purchase supplies in American ports, but France's enemies could not do so. Should the United States honor the alliance with France and risk having to fight as France's ally—a potentially devastating development for the young republic—or should it break the alliance with France and risk provoking France into declaring war on the United States as well? Washington convened his cabinet to discuss this question. Not surprisingly, Jefferson and Hamilton came out on opposite sides of the debate, with Jefferson advising that the United States honor its alliance with France and Hamilton advising that it be abandoned. Each developed a report analyzing and explaining his position to the president.

Hamilton possessed a pessimistic certainty that the United States would find itself in danger if it were to honor the treaties. His report carefully constructed a variety of hypothetical situations that could result in American involvement in the war, such as a British attack on the French West Indies. Furthermore, Hamilton asked, what would become of U.S.-French relations if the Jacobin rebellion failed? After all, it had been the French *king* who had sent aid to the United States during the American Revolution. Such a good turn did not deserve to be repaid with hostility and betrayal.

Jefferson argued that America was honor-bound to recognize the treaties, because the preeminent writers on the natural law governing international relations stated that treaties could be nullified only if honoring them meant the "absolute *ruin* or *destruction* of the state. . . not merely . . . being disadvantageous, or dangerous." [23] The rest of Jefferson's report patiently refuted any threat of imminent danger to the United States from either France or any French enemy as a result of honoring the treaties, and showed that Hamilton's fears were based on hypothetical possibilities that were quite unlikely to come to pass.

In the end, Washington accepted Jefferson's view and did not abrogate the alliance. The events that followed did indeed prove Jefferson's analysis of the situation to be true. It is likely that Jefferson's deeper understanding of France based on his service there enabled him to predict French behavior more accurately than Hamilton. However, this was one of the few instances in which Washington followed Jefferson's advice; he tended overall to more closely share Hamilton's views and support his policies. Jefferson's frustration with this situation rose to such a level that he resigned his post in late 1793 to create an opposition movement against Washington's administration and Hamilton's followers. In the new Republican Party, Jefferson shared the helm with the much younger but ideologically compatible James Madison.[24] Perhaps as a result of Jefferson's desertion of the administration, he was not able to prevent the eventual souring of relations between the United States and France.

The Jay Treaty.   As the war in Europe intensified, both the British and the French "impressed" or kidnapped American sailors and placed other restraints on American trade. Outraged, Americans contended that "free ships make free goods"and that a neutral flag should protect a ship's crew and cargo against attack. At Hamilton's suggestion, Washington sent John Jay, who had been secretary of foreign affairs under the Articles of Confederation, to England to resolve some of America's disputes with that country. Jay did manage to draw up a treaty with England, but it accomplished almost none of things sought by President Washington, and most significantly, it did not prevent British warships from stealing goods and sailors off American trading ships. Even so, Hamilton favored the Jay Treaty as a first step toward rapprochement with Britain since the Revolution, and it was ratified with Washington's help.

The signing of the Jay Treaty came as a severe blow to France—with whom the United States still had a formal alliance—and therefore to Jefferson and the Republicans. In their eyes, the United States not only was failing to live up to its 1778 treaty obligations, but also was actually aiding the British under the guise of an official policy of neutrality. As Jefferson had predicted, France was sorely offended and abrogated the 1778 alliance with the United States. From 1797 to 1800, then, France and the

United States were engaged in an undeclared war that would persist into the presidential tenure of Washington's Federalist successor, John Adams.

The schism that developed between the Republicans and the Federalists—as the followers of Hamilton were known—over U.S. foreign policy toward France and Britain was totally unexpected. The difficulties this animosity caused in day-to-day governing highlighted the danger that could result when one party, or faction, gained undue influence over policy making. Madison, in particular, had been adamant in warning against factionalism, and his ideas had been well circulated publicly in *The Federalist Papers*. However, the founders had expected to see this sort of trouble arise in issues of domestic governance and not in the area of foreign policy. Contrary to their initial expectation that the democratic process would smooth the process of implementing foreign policy, the difficulty encountered in developing foreign policy could potentially disrupt the democratic process.

Yet foreign policy of the new republic was not always divisive. An incident during Adams's presidency fostered American unity rather than diversity on foreign policy issues. In 1798 three American emissaries sent to negotiate an end to the hostilities with France were told by three French agents, "X," "Y," and "Z," that they would not be received unless the United States offered a large loan and paid a bribe. When President Adams informed Congress of this turn of events, it declared the treaties with France void. Americans were greatly offended, and, as historian Thomas A. Bailey later described, "the masses of the republic were no longer pro-French or pro-British—but pro-American." [25]

Dimensions of Foreign Policy. America's relations with France and Britain during this period reflect their leaders stances on all three dimensions of foreign policy. The Federalists pursued decidedly unilateral policies, in keeping with the practice of the old diplomacy. They did not formally consult other states on what joint policies they might pursue in relation to the struggle then going on among European powers. Washington's call for "no entangling alliances" in his Farewell Address advised Americans to focus on the unique interests of their own country and thus to forge their own national identity independent of overbearing historical and political ties to other nations.

America's security was obviously threatened by the wars on the European continent, with a real possibility that the young United States could be drawn into the conflict. Presidents Washington and Adams both responded to the threat by pursuing strictly noncoercive measures. When the British confiscated goods from American ships and impressed their seamen, Washington limited his government's actions to the realm of negotiation. Certainly this strategy stemmed in part from America's military weakness vis-à-vis Britain, but Washington could have chosen to retaliate by forging closer ties with France and generally assisting that country's campaigns against England. Later, when U.S. relations with France soured, Adams ensured that the "war" remained undeclared. Although Congress voted to increase military preparedness and authorized U.S. ships to retaliate if attacked, neither the United States nor France allowed offensive hostilities or the seizure of private goods.

America's security dilemma heavily affected its commerce and economic prospects. President Washington tried to steer a middle path between a proactive and a reactive policy. On the one hand, he fervently believed that his primary task was to develop and maintain the integrity of America's new institutions of government. On the other hand, he knew that U.S. prosperity relied on international trade and acceptance. Washington perceived a great risk in becoming too embroiled in European politics and strove to assert the seafaring rights of neutral countries. The Federalists generally pursued a unilateral, noncoercive, proactive foreign policy, shown as <u>MC</u>A in Table 2.2.

The Republican Period: 1801–1815

The Republicans gained power in 1801, when Thomas Jefferson reentered the government as the third president of the United States. Early in his administration, Jefferson learned that France might be willing to sell the Louisiana Territory west of the Mississippi River. In 1803 Jefferson won congressional approval of the Louisiana Purchase. Very popular among Americans and a source of confidence for the new republic, the purchase provided full navigation rights along the Mississippi River and a large expanse of western territory, as shown on Map 2.2.

During Jefferson's first administration, relations with France improved for a time, and the increase in foreign trade stimulated economic growth in the United States. Although Jefferson had wanted to provide France

Table 2.2. Dimensions of Foreign Policy: The Federalists

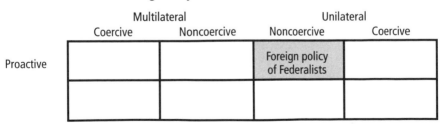

| | Multilateral | | Unilateral | |
	Coercive	Noncoercive	Noncoercive	Coercive
Proactive			Foreign policy of Federalists	

The two Federalist presidents, George Washington and John Adams, generally pursued a neutral foreign policy. Their policies were <u>MC</u>A—unilateral because they were careful to exercise the sovereign prerogatives of a new state, noncoercive because they tried to avoid military involvement in European wars, and proactive because they tried to build commercial relationships with other countries.

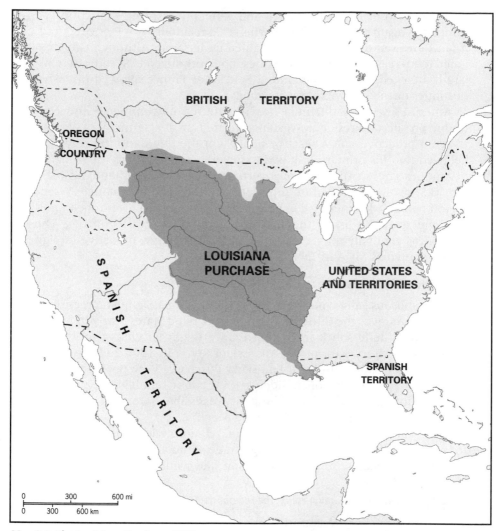

Map 2.2 The Louisiana Purchase, 1803
The Louisiana Purchase of 1803 almost doubled the size of the United States. The United States was bounded by Spanish territory in Florida and the Southwest, English territory to the North, and the Oregon country in the Northwest.

with limited aid a decade before, he no longer felt the United States had a particular stake in a French victory on the European continent, and he continued Washington's and Adams's policy of neutrality. Like his predecessors, he was against any entangling alliances that might lead to war.

Jefferson also had strong nonmilitaristic leanings and opposed defense expenditures, especially the cost of building expensive frigates. He did send the marines against the Barbary pirates, but only after the pirates had declared war on the United States. Generally, he sought peace through negotiations.

As the Napoleonic Wars continued, however, both Britain and France continued to impress American seamen and confiscate cargo from American ships, which brought about a shift in Jefferson's policies. He decided that the only way to force both Britain and France to respect U.S. neutrality was to break off all trade with those countries. In 1807 he pushed an Embargo Act through Congress that closed American ports to French and English ships and prevented American ships from leaving for foreign ports. The embargo had more of an effect on American prosperity than European, however, and quickly sent American trade into a depression. New Englanders, who depended on shipping for their livelihood, were especially unhappy.

In 1809 James Madison, who succeeded Jefferson as president, replaced the Embargo Act with the watered-down Non-Intercourse Act, which allowed Americans to trade with other neutral countries. Even so, Madison knew that these efforts at economic coercion were failing and that the United States would be forced into war. Although France eventually lifted some of its restrictions on American trade and although Great Britain was about to make similar concessions, these actions occurred too late to prevent the Second War of Independence with Britain, also called the War of 1812.

Dimensions of Foreign Policy.   Jefferson and Madison pursued foreign policies that were very different from those of the Federalists. Jefferson and the Republicans continued the Federalist policy of unilateralism. Willing to stand up to harmful incursions into their commercial activities by undoubtedly stronger governments, the Republicans pursued an independent foreign policy tailored to further what they saw as the unique features of the world's only free society. However, Jefferson was much more likely than the Federalists to justify his actions in terms of multilateral principles.

Although Jefferson was known for his nonmilitaristic predispositions, his economic embargo, which he thought of as peaceful coercion, did eventually lead to war with Britain. In the end, Jefferson was prepared to employ coercive measures to bring about the desired changes in the external environment. Thus, unlike the noncoercive Federalists, Jefferson reluctantly practiced coercion.

In many ways Jefferson was more proactive than the Federalists. He not only wanted to extend America's trade relations with other countries but also prepared to overlook the absence of any constitutional authority to add new territory to make the Louisiana Purchase. Similarly, his economic embargo was designed not just to eliminate Britain's hold over U.S.

commerce, but also to establish in international law a precedent for the political and economic rights of neutral countries to pursue their policies unmolested by warring parties.

Jefferson's foreign policies are more difficult to classify than Washington's or Adams's policies because his rhetoric often obscured his actions. For example, Jefferson's embargo was coercive, but nonmilitary; justified in multilateral, not unilateral, terms; and served proactive aims although it involved closing down American ports in the short term. If one takes both objectives and action into account, Jefferson's embargo policy was MCA—unilateral, coercive, and proactive, as is shown in Table 2.3.

Growth and Segmentation: 1815–1865

The War of 1812 was popular among northern war hawks who wanted to acquire Canadian territory and among southern war hawks who wanted to take Florida. During the war, Americans made three unsuccessful attempts to take Canada, but they had moderate success in Florida. In the meantime, Britain occupied and burned the new capital city of Washington, D.C., and generally prevailed over U.S. forces. But the war in Europe was taxing British resources so severely that Britain was forced to end the conflict on terms that were very favorable to the United States. For the first time since the Declaration of Independence, Americans had the commercial treaty with Britain they had been seeking. This peace agreement introduced a period of economic growth and expansion, but that very progress precipitated an internal crisis.

In the first thirty years after the end of the War of 1812, the United States steadily increased development of its lands east of the Mississippi River. Then in three short years, from 1845 to 1848, growth and development west of the Mississippi exploded, with the country increasing its occupied territory by more than 50 percent, to about 3 million square

Table 2.3. Dimensions of Foreign Policy: Jefferson's Trade Embargo

	Multilateral		Unilateral	
	Coercive	Noncoercive	Noncoercive	Coercive
Proactive				Jefferson's trade embargo policy
Reactive				

Jefferson's trade embargo against the belligerents in the Napoleonic Wars, was MCA—unilateral because it was shaped exclusively by the U.S. government, coercive because it was designed to assert the rights of non-belligerents (and eventually it caused the War of 1812), and proactive because he closed American ports in the short term in order to extend the rights of neutrals to free trade in the long term.

miles, with the settlement of the Louisiana Purchase territory. This sudden, vast expansion brought the issue of factionalism once again to the fore of political debate, because it was uncertain whether a republican government was feasible over a large territory and because of the extension of slavery. Madison had argued earlier in *Federalist* no. 10 that the republican use of elected representatives made it possible for a republic to grow very large, because every citizen did not have to vote on every government decision. However, the larger the population, the greater was the possibility of serious and debilitating factions developing. The sections that follow examine the consequences of this domestic growth for American foreign policy, looking first at the period of steady economic growth and limited territorial expansion between 1815 and 1849 and then at the period of rapid territorial expansion accompanied by political division between 1850 and 1865.

Growth and Expansion: 1815–1849

The citizens of the United States rapidly settled unoccupied areas east of the Mississippi River in the first half of the nineteenth century. As the nation moved west, its values and interests also changed in all three dimensions of foreign policy.

Prosperity Values.   One of the unintended consequences of Jefferson's economic embargo was that capital and labor were forced into manufacturing, especially in the Northeast, thereby stimulating American industrial expansion. Domestic investment increased both the rate of national economic growth and the degree of internal regional specialization. The growth of the domestic market reduced the importance of international trade, which made up less than 10 percent of the country's gross national product (GNP) by 1850. International trade played an important role in the nation's commerce, but it was not as vital to the country's growth as it had been earlier in the century.

Simultaneous increases in three factors of production—land, population, and capital— fueled the growth of the domestic market. For example, the area north of the Ohio River and east of the Mississippi was transformed from frontier farming to settlement farming, as the frontier moved west of the Mississippi. This period also saw a population growth rate of 3 percent per year, one of the highest rates of sustained population growth ever recorded.

In addition, the distribution of the population changed. First, the flow of people to the West was so strong that by 1865 a majority of the population lived to the west of the thirteen original states. Second, there was movement from rural to urban centers. Indeed, in 1815 only 7 percent of the population lived in urban areas, defined as cities with populations of 2,500 or more, and eight of ten jobs were in agriculture. By 1865, 20 percent of the population was residing in urban areas, and farming accounted for more than half of total employment.[26]

Of the three factors of production, the rate of change in the supply of capital was particularly pronounced. Much of this capital was invested in better transportation systems, such as canals and steamboats, which played a key role in the improvements in agriculture and business after 1815 and lessened the isolation of the West. Railroad construction began in the early 1830s, but America remained dependent on steamboats plying the natural waterways for moving both goods and people.

The strength of the domestic market encouraged different regions to specialize in producing the goods that made the best use of their natural resources. The South specialized in cotton and other staple crops, the Northwest in grains and meat, and the Northeast in manufacturing. As a result, the Northeast began to outstrip the other regions in wealth and development. Much of its success stemmed from cheap transport—canals, and later railroads—which enabled the North to take advantage of its own intrasectional market and then to pull the South and West into further and fuller dependency on its manufactured goods. Indeed, "the West and South assumed an almost colonial relationship with the North, not unlike that of the earlier colonies with England." [27]

Although most of this growth occurred east of the Mississippi, it required large amounts of foreign capital and immigration from abroad, and it whet the appetite of Americans for new resources from areas west of the Mississippi and other parts of the world.

Security Values.   Meanwhile, the United States was steadily securing its borders east of the Mississippi River. The first area to be incorporated was Florida. Even before 1812 the United States had occupied much of the territory of West Florida, but it was not until after the Second War of Independence that the United States moved against East Florida, which still belonged to Spain. In 1817 President James Monroe asked Gen. Andrew Jackson to protect American settlers from attacks by Seminole Indians in Spanish East Florida, thus providing a pretext for occupation of the area by Jackson's troops. In 1819 Spain, weakened by its involvement in the Napoleonic Wars, ceded East Florida to the United States and gave up its claims to Oregon and the Pacific coast in exchange for U.S. recognition of Spanish claims to Texas.

Spain's readiness to surrender its North American claims is largely explained by the deterioration of its position both in Europe and in its South American colonies. By 1815 the Spanish American colonies were in full revolt. Fueled by the revolutionary rhetoric of Napoleon's army, similar revolts also were occurring in European Spain, to such an extent that only the joint effort of the "Holy Alliance" of Russia, the Austrian Empire, and Prussia was able to restore the Spanish monarchy to its throne. American fears that the Holy Alliance might try to restore Spanish rule in South America as well prompted President Monroe to issue the Monroe Doctrine of 1823. Monroe announced the doctrine, which outlined American hegemony in the Western hemisphere, in his seventh annual message to Congress. It informed European governments, especially Britain and Russia, that the northwest coast of the North American continent was no longer open to colonization; it warned the allies of Spain and Portugal in Europe to stay out of the Southern Hemisphere; and it promised that the United States would not get involved in Europe's internal affairs.[28] This doctrine did not have any immediate effect—because it was Britain, not the United States, that was in a position to enforce it—but it did lay the foundation for American foreign policy in Latin America for next the 150 years.

When feasible, the United States used diplomatic means to settle border disputes and questions. Earlier Monroe had also fixed the border with Great Britain's Canadian possessions in the North from the Lake of the Woods to the Rockies. The Convention of 1818 also settled a dispute with Canadian fisheries.

During the 1820s and 1830s the United States also acquired land by removing Native Americans from regions desired by white settlers. In fact, the government brutally forced five great Indian nations—the Choctaw, Creek, Chickasaw, Seminole, and Cherokee nations—from the South into unwanted lands west of the Mississippi. The U.S. government also fought the Sauk and Fox tribes, but most of the northern tribes chose to withdraw to west of the Mississippi River rather than continue to fight a losing battle.

Community Values. As Tocqueville predicted, growth and expansion during this period put enormous pressure on the country's political institutions. The South had become increasingly dependent on its ever-increasing slave population, which produced its cash crops of rice and, more important, cotton, but the growing industrial areas of the North were increasingly opposed to slavery. So when importation of slaves into the United States ended in 1808, the internal slave trade within the South and even from border states in the North to the South increased. The Missouri Compromise of 1820 largely settled the slavery issue between these two communities by allowing slavery in Louisiana territories south of latitude 36 degrees 30 minutes— the southern border of Missouri—but not above that line. This satisfied the South for the time being because most slave holders did not really want to move west anyway.

The slavery issue did not really rise again until the mid-1840s because the emergence of national parties largely blurred sectional differences. The change in party structure can be traced back to the election of 1824. The 1824 presidential contest saw the emergence of a key political figure of this period—Andrew Jackson, a military hero and political aspirant. All five candidates for the office of president were Republicans, including Jackson. Although Jackson won a plurality of both the popular and Electoral College votes, John Quincy Adams won the presidency through indirect election in the House. Outraged at this inequitable practice and unable to attain a position of prominence in the Republican Party, an embittered Jackson left to form the Democratic Party and thereby provide a political base for his presidential campaign in 1828. Over the next several years the Republican Party would dwindle away, losing its members to the Democratic Party and the Whig Party, which had replaced the old Federalist Party and advocated free trade and internal improvements

A severe critic of President John Quincy Adams and his supporters, Jackson built his 1828 campaign on two main planks: a return to President Washington's principle of "no entangling alliances"—particularly with regard to the newly independent states of the former Spanish America—and faster expansion of U.S. settlement into Texas, which then belonged to Mexico. As early as 1821 the Mexican government had allowed Americans to acquire tracts of land in Texas as long as the settlers agreed to become Mexican citizens and join the Catholic Church. Later, however, Mexican authorities regretted that decision and tried to reverse their earlier policy. When Jackson became president in 1828, he was eager to annex territories west of the Mississippi River, including the Texas lands settled by white settlers, whose numbers reached about 30,000 by 1835.

Throughout this period the relationship between the United States and Mexico was extremely sensitive. Skirmishes were common between native Mexicans and the immigrants from the United States, leading eventually to an all-out Texan revolt against Mexican authority in 1836. The famous siege and defeat of the rebel Texans at the Alamo rallied the settlers and outraged many in the United States who thought of the Texans as Americans, despite their Mexican citizenship. With aid from the United States, the Texans quickly defeated the Mexican forces, and Texas declared itself an independent country in 1836.

Texas then requested admission into the Union, but this step ignited controversy between southern states, where the institution of slavery was widespread, and northern states, where there was a growing movement to abolish slavery. Southerners welcomed the addition of Texas, because it would greatly expand slave territory, while Northerners favoring the abolition of slavery vehemently opposed annexation. Jackson sensed that the issue could easily split the Democratic Party, which it could ill-afford if it wished to see its policies implemented. The Whig Party was generally against landed expansion, though it favored modernization, economic expansion, and internal improvements in territories already held, and the Democrats would need a united vote to defeat a Whig presidential candidate. Therefore, Jackson decided to reject Texas's application, thereby forestalling dissension in the Democratic ranks.

When the United States denied their request for statehood, Texans cunningly approached England and France for trade agreements and other economic assistance. This move played on lingering American fears of European interference in U.S. territory. After all, America was surrounded by a strong English presence in Canada and the Caribbean, a still very hostile Mexico to the south and west, and an expansion-minded Russia in the Pacific Northwest and Alaska. With tensions so recently resolved between various European countries and their former New World colonies, and among the European countries themselves, it was not unreasonable that the United States would be a little nervous.

Americans' craze for new land and westward expansion lay not only in fear of European encroachment, but also in their belief that the United States, as a nation blessed by God, was destined for unchecked growth. This sentiment received its most succinct expression in the words of New York newspaperman John L. O'Sullivan, a Democrat, who wrote in mid-1845 that it is "the fulfillment of our manifest destiny to overspread the continent allotted by Providence for the free development of our yearly multiplying millions." [29] Now popularly known as America's "manifest destiny," this drive for land and political influence—even outright governance—over other lands would eventually include ambitions in Asia, the Pacific, Central America, and the Caribbean.[30] Indeed, O'Sullivan warned in 1848, when the territories of California and the rest of Texas were obtained from Mexico, that "a State must always be on the increase or the decrease." As time passed, this "law of movement" knew no bounds and gave the young country the gumption to assert itself in dealings with older and stronger countries.[31] Map 2.3 illustrates the territorial expansion that grew out of Americans' assumption that if their country was not expanding, it was not succeeding.

England, however, was still a significant factor in U.S. foreign policy, especially because both countries were still sharing the Oregon Territory. The boundary of American holdings continued to be in dispute. Britain claimed that U.S. lands extended only as far north as the Columbia River (near the northern border of present-day Oregon). The Americans rejected this claim, because they would be left without the seaport they needed to conduct trade with Asia. The United States countered with a demand for control over land as far north as the 54th parallel. As the governments argued, the feverish rhetoric of war rose on both sides of the Atlantic. Neither country truly wanted to fight, however, so they agreed to divide the territory along the 49th parallel, which remains the modern boundary between the state of Washington and Canada.

Oregon's entry into the Union allowed Congress to finally go ahead with the annexation of Texas, because Oregon, as a free state, would balance Texas's entry as a slave state. The addition of Texas quickly led to other problems, however. The southern border of Texas had not been settled

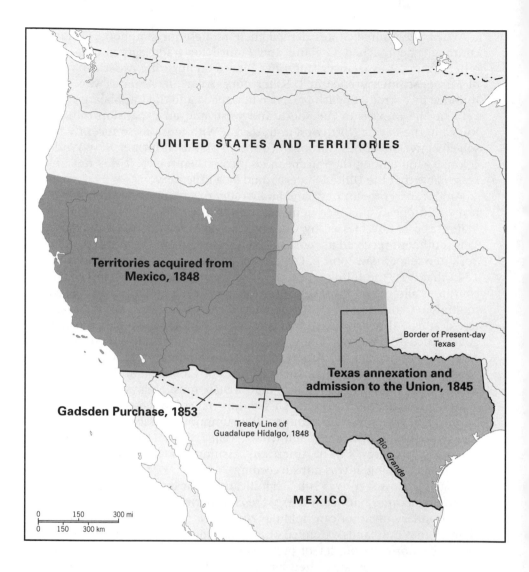

Map 2.3 U.S. Territorial Acquisitions from Mexico, 1848–1853
When the United States annexed Texas in 1845, it claimed all territory north and east of the Rio Grande. The western boundary of Texas was moved about 200 miles to the east of the Rio Grande when the United States acquired the Mexican Cession territories in 1848.

after the revolt against Mexico. The United States claimed land as far south as the Rio Grande, but Mexico insisted that the U.S. holdings ended at the Rio Nueces. When Mexico broke off diplomatic relations with Washington, President James K. Polk sent an army to the disputed territory, but was reluctant to act on the offensive. Conveniently for Polk's ambitions, American casualties were reported the very next day. Polk had a pretext to begin a war that eventually would lead Mexico to cede all of its claims, not only to the Rio Grande but also to its lands in California.[32]

At the time the Mexican government referred to all the lands west of Texas and the Louisiana Purchase as "California." But the Mexicans living in California did not consider the area east of the Sierra Nevada to be part of California, and so the area between California and Texas is referred to here as Mexican Cession territory. This territory is especially relevant to the definition of community values in this period because efforts to deal with it helped rekindle the sectional controversy between the North and the South.

When the prospect of Mexican Cession was first considered in Congress, Northern Democrats tried to pass the Wilmot Proviso, which would prohibit slavery in Cession territories. Southern Democrats opposed the proviso, and a few Northern Democrats, who were interested in finding a suitable compromise, proposed *popular sovereignty* where the settlers themselves would decide the slavery issue. Instead President Polk recommended that the Missouri Compromise line be extended to the Pacific Coast, despite the fact that Mexico had earlier outlawed slavery in California, including other Cession territories. Although most Southern leaders were not interested in the extension of slavery per se, they increasingly perceived the proposed prohibition on slavery as an affront to their rights.

Dimensions of Foreign Policy.   American foreign policy between 1816 and 1849 can best be described in terms of the foreign policies of John Quincy Adams and Andrew Jackson. Adams had been a member of the American delegation to the peace conference in Ghent in 1814, Monroe's secretary of state from 1817 to 1825, and president from 1825 to 1829. Jackson was president from 1829 to 1837, and two of his associates, Martin Van Buren (1837–1841) and James Polk (1845–1849), succeeded him as president.

The long-term goals of both individuals were very similar. Table 2.4 illustrates how they both pursued foreign policies that were unilateral, coercive, and proactive, or MCA. However, Adams was the more cautious of the two because he recognized that a too rapid expansion could both impel Spain and Britain to intervene and exacerbate internal divisions within the United States. Jackson was aware of the potential for disunity between the North and the South, but he pushed for expansion nevertheless. Thus when it came to tactical considerations, Adams sought U.S. dominance first through diplomacy whereas Jackson favored immediate forceful action.[33]

Identity Crisis: 1850–1865

Growth and expansion, especially in the North, encouraged the development of third parties because sectional divisions prevented national

Table 2.4. Dimensions of Foreign Policy: John Quincy Adams and Andrew Jackson

| | Multilateral | | Unilateral | |
	Coercive	Noncoercive	Noncoercive	Coercive
Proactive				Foreign policies of John Quincy Adams and Andrew Jackson
Reactive				

The foreign policies of John Quincy Adams and Andrew Jackson were <u>MCA</u>. They were unilateral because their policies were based exclusively on U.S. interests, coercive because they were prepared to use force, and proactive because they actively sought the economic benefits of territorial expansion. They differed mainly in the degree to which they were prepared to use force as the preferred instrument of policy.

Democrats and Whigs from taking advantage of new causes. For example, the Free Soil Party emerged in the mid-1840s among those who opposed the Democratic idea of popular sovereignty; the Know Nothing Party arose in the mid-1850s as an anti-Catholic, anti-foreign party; and the Republican Party sprung up in the mid-1850s when it became clear to northern Whigs and even some northern Democrats that they could not effectively oppose slavery within either of the two national parties.

When Zachary Taylor of the Whig Party became president in March of 1849, he tried to get the Cession territories to apply for statehood before Congress reconvened in December, bypassing the need for Congress to determine the character of their territorial governments. In this way the Whigs could get the credit for defining these territories and at the same time damage both the Free Soil Party and the Democratic Party in the North. But New Mexico put off its application for statehood, and the Mormons in Utah tried unsuccessfully to become part of California. As a consequence, Congress was compelled to deal with the issue when it returned.

The issue was addressed in what became known as the Compromise of 1850. Congress labored through July of 1850 to fashion an omnibus bill, but it could not do so. The main point of contention was the boundary between New Mexico and Texas. The main break came when President Fillmore, who replaced Taylor earlier that month after Taylor died in office, received word that Texas was planning to send an armed force to Santa Fe to secure its western border. Fillmore decided to reinforce the federal troops already in Santa Fe, and the Senate quickly approved the present border, which is 150 to 200 miles east of the Rio Grande. Within a week the Senate accepted California as a free state and New Mexico as a territory organized on the basis of popular sovereignty. Later, the territory of

Utah was also organized on the basis of popular sovereignty. By the middle of September the House had passed similar measures, and both houses passed a Fugitive Slave Act for Washington, D.C. This compromise was supposed to settle the slavery issue.

However, the compromise did not last very long. The admission of California as a free state theoretically gave the North an advantage over the South in the Senate as well as the House. Because the arid states of the southwest were not suited to the labor-intensive cash crop agriculture of the southeast, and thus did not give southern Democrats much hope of reversing this imbalance, they looked for other possibilities for the extension of slavery. One such opportunity came out of the pressure in the North for a transcontinental railroad and settlement in Kansas and Nebraska. Accordingly, southern Democrats urged William O. Douglas, who was then chairman of the Senate Committee on Territories, to open Kansas and Nebraska for settlement on the same basis as New Mexico and Utah, that is, popular sovereignty.

Southern Democrats and southern Whigs eventually helped northern Democrats (who were evenly divided on the issue) pass this legislation in the form of the Kansas-Nebraska Act of 1854. The act overturned the Missouri Compromise of 1820, which had limited slavery in the Louisiana territory to the area south of a line extending west from the southern boundary of Missouri. By 1856 northern displeasure with the Compromise helped the Republican Party gain ground at the expense of the Know-Nothings, Free Soilers, northern Democrats, and northern Whigs. The reactions of anti-slave northerners to the 1857 *Dred Scott* decision by a Supreme Court dominated by southerners further aided Republicans and dealt a final deathblow to the national Whig party.[34]

With the demise of the two-party system and its adhesive effect on the Union, political affiliations gave way to sectional divides. The southern states had been outstripped by the northern states in land, immigration, wealth, and congressional representation. Individuals and groups in the South made some last desperate efforts to add new slave territories in Central America, Cuba, and Mexico.[35] With the election in 1860 of the Republican president Abraham Lincoln, the South believed that it had finally lost control of its destiny. With repeated efforts to acquire new land for slaves having failed, many southerners felt they had no alternative other than secession from the Union.

Lincoln's Foreign Policy. Lincoln was dismayed at the prospect of civil war but saw that there was little hope of avoiding it. William H. Seward, Lincoln's secretary of state, proposed a desperate, ludicrous scheme of provoking a war with a European power, most likely England, on the pretense that European trade with the Caribbean hindered U.S. plans for southward expansion.[36] Seward, a prominent figure in the politics of his day, hoped that such a war would serve to rally the states around a common cause and thereby forestall civil war. Many people, including Seward himself, considered Seward an abler statesman than Lincoln, who had to struggle to overcome his image as a rail-splitting bumpkin from the Midwest. Lincoln disregarded Seward's preposterous plan and concentrated on preparing for the imminent civil war.

Both the North and the South were aware that outside powers could affect the course of the war. Lincoln actually tried to avoid a formal state of belligerency, but when the South hired privateers to interfere with northern trade, he had no choice but to blockade southern ports. Early in the war foreign sympathies seemed evenly matched. Russia, which placed a high strategic value on the use of northern seaports, favored the Union. France, which was dependent on southern cotton, favored the Confederacy and even established a friendly regime in Mexico.[37] Americans on both sides saw very clearly that Britain would play a key role. Loss of its support would be a harsh blow to either group. But Britain, for various reasons, including the strong antislavery sentiment among vocal liberals, declared itself neutral in the conflict. Its huge textile industry imported 80 percent of its cotton from the South, but it had an ample supply of cotton for several years. Besides, it also depended on grain grown primarily in the Union.

In many ways the most relevant foreign policy problem for President Lincoln was how to bring the South back into the Union. This problem was all the more perplexing because, unlike his Democratic opponents, he represented a purely sectional party. Northern and southern Democrats could conceivably mend their differences, but Lincoln, as the leader of a Republican Party whose radical elements were an anathema to the South, had no political basis for reaching out to the South prior to, during, or after the war. The three dimensions of foreign policy are helpful in understanding how Lincoln tried to overcome this difficulty.

Dimensions of Foreign Policy.   During the Civil War Lincoln's personal foreign policy is best understood in terms of his efforts to bring the states of the Confederacy back into the Union. Toward this end Lincoln, working primarily with Seward, pursued a foreign policy that was diametrically opposed to the one preferred by his fellow Republicans in Congress. Congressional Republicans, protective of their comfortable position of dominance over a Democratic Party divided into pro-North and pro-South wings, favored stripping pro-South Democrats of political privileges and using military might to smash the South into submission as punishment for its promulgation of secession and slavery.

Meanwhile, Lincoln occupied a weaker political position than his party members on Capitol Hill. Whereas most members of Congress represented strongly Republican districts, Lincoln faced much stiffer competition for votes at the national level. To win reelection in 1864 Lincoln knew he would have to broaden his support in the North to include not just anti-slavery northerners, but also more moderate voters in the West and border states, such as Missouri, Tennessee, and Maryland, who favored both the Union *and* slavery. Therefore, not wanting to create permanent enemies of these voters, Lincoln preferred luring southerners back into the Union by diplomatic and political means over harsh military ones. He thus aimed most of his political actions and appointments at reconstituting the Republican Party into a new Union Party that would be anti-Democratic, while espousing a more moderate stance on emancipation and extension of political power to former Confederates.

Over and above his political ambitions, however, Lincoln worked for the establishment of the Union Party, because he considered it to be key to reunification of the country. He had always been a firm believer that a republican government was one of, by, and for the people. For example, in a July 1861 message to Congress President Lincoln pointed out that war would eventually reveal "that ballots are the rightful, and peaceful, successors of bullets; and that when ballots have been fairly, and constitutionally, decided, there can be no successful appeal back to bullets." [38]

Disenfranchising the South would therefore be anathema to restoring a healthy republic. This goal also explains the conditions set out in Lincoln's Preliminary Emancipation Proclamation of September 22, 1862, which stipulated that Confederate and other slave states that returned voluntarily to the Union by January 1, 1863, when the proclamation went into effect, would be exempt from abolition. Lincoln, then, clearly viewed emancipation as a step toward quickly restoring the Union and not as a measure taken to punish Southerners.

Therefore, if Lincoln's foreign policy is defined narrowly in terms of the relations between the Union and the Confederacy, his foreign policy was opposite that of the early Republicans and Democrats. He pursued a multilateral, noncoercive, and proactive, or MCA, foreign policy, not unlike the foreign policies recommended by the Enlightenment *philosophes*. His policy was multilateral in that it aimed to establish a more inclusive community by looking to bring the South back into the Union after the cessation of hostilities. It was noncoercive in that it primarily emphasized diplomatic and political strategies rather than military actions, despite having to fight the Civil War. Finally, Lincoln's policy was proactive in that he actively tried to gain the confidence of Southern sympathizers in the border states as well as disaffected Southerners in Union-occupied areas in the South. Table 2.5 illustrates how President Lincoln, then, pursued an MCA foreign policy.

Conclusion

When the young nation's political leaders gathered to draft a new constitution in 1787, they were familiar with the dilemmas of foreign policy

Table 2.5. Dimensions of Foreign Policy: Abraham Lincoln's Foreign Policy of Union

| | Multilateral | | Unilateral | |
	Coercive	Noncoercive	Noncoercive	Coercive
Proactive		Lincoln's policy of union		
Reactive				

Lincoln's foreign policy toward the Confederacy during the war years was MCA—multilateral because Lincoln sought eventual unification with the Confederacy, noncoercive because he and his secretary of state wanted to bring the South back into the Union largely through political means rather than by imposing a punitive military occupation on the defeated South, and proactive because he actively tried to gain the confidence of Southern sympathizers in border states as well as disaffected Southerners in Union-occupied areas in the South.

represented by the dimensions defined here as multilateral–unilateral, coercive–noncoercive, and proactive–reactive. Each of these dilemmas had been a facet of the debate between the old diplomacy, represented by power politics in Europe, and the new diplomacy advocated by the Enlightenment *philosophes*. Advocates of the old diplomacy were in favor of policies that were unilateral, coercive, and reactive (MCA). Advocates of the new diplomacy favored those that were multilateral, noncoercive, and proactive (MCA).

Most of the founders were attracted to the new diplomacy and initially tried to implement those principles and practices. Somewhat ironically, the analysis described here shows that the Federalists probably came closer than Republicans to practicing the new diplomacy. Although both the Federalists and Republicans clearly favored proactive, unilateral policies, the Federalists were noncoercive; whereas the Republicans and later Democrats were coercive.

If there is one persistent element in early American foreign policy, it is unilateralism. In one sense, however, American statesmen did gain experience with multilateralism, and that was in the realm of internal politics. Except for the period just before the Civil War, American leaders tried to fulfill the promise of republican government by getting individual states to act together in both domestic and foreign affairs. That effort failed during the 1840s and 1850s, only to be restored by force of arms during the Civil War.

Key Concepts

balance of power   45
Enlightenment   42
hegemon   45
limited government   47
mercantilism   46
natural rights   46

new diplomacy   48
old diplomacy   48
sovereignty   44
power politics   45
reason of state   46

Suggested Readings

1. Fleming, Thomas J. *Alexander Hamilton, Aaron Burr, and the Future of America.* New York: Basic Books, 1999.

2. Fischer, David H. *Washington's Crossing.* New York: Oxford University Press, 2004.

3. Holt, Michael F. *The Fate of Their Country.* New York: Hill and Wang, 2004.

4. Isaacson, Walter. *Benjamin Franklin: An American Life.* New York: Simon and Schuster, 2003.

5. McCullough, David G. *John Adams.* New York: Simon and Schuster, 2001.

CHAPTER 3

The Transition Period: 1866–1941

WITH LEE ANN PINGEL

From 1866 to 1941, the primary issue for the people of the United States was prosperity, that is, whether the country would play a role in the wider world commensurate with its growing industrial strength or whether it would allow other states to direct the course of world events. The opening of the Panama Canal on August 15, 1914, just a few days after the beginning of the First World War, symbolized America's importance as an industrial power. As a consequence of the canal and other innovations, international trade became more important for the United States, especially the Northeast, the region which most strongly favored American involvement in both the First and Second World War.

T HE UNITED STATES AND GERMANY set the pace for industrialization during the last third of the nineteenth century. Moreover, the
United States maintained its economic lead throughout the first third of
the twentieth century, but the United States did not generally play a commensurate role in international political affairs. Because of this differential
between the country's economic and political powers, its foreign policy
from 1866 to 1941 is frequently misunderstood. Often it has been described as **isolationist,** yet U.S. foreign policy has never been decisively
and wholly reactive, and this period is no exception. In the period between the Civil War and the Spanish-American War differences between
the president and Congress inhibited territorial expansion; and in the period between the First and Second World War the preference for private
initiatives and public reactivity led to the appearance of inactivity. But although America's territorial expansion was sometimes delayed and occasionally arrested during this period, its economic and cultural drive for
absolute advantage was relentless.

After the Civil War the U.S. government was intent on extending its
influence into the Pacific, the Caribbean, and South America. But it was
not the only developing country to covet new territories in these and
other areas. Germany and Italy emerged as new, unified states in Europe
at about this time, and as latecomers to colonialism, they were interested
in acquiring new territories. In the Caribbean and South America, the
United States had to compete with Germany as well as other traditional
European countries; and in East Asia, the United States had to compete
with Germany and Japan as well as traditional European colonial powers
for influence.

U.S. imperialism was different from that of other states for several reasons. For one thing the U.S. Constitution created barriers to colonialism
that these other states did not face. After all, the idea that government
rests on the consent of the governed is a fundamental principle underlying the U.S. Constitution. Did the U.S. Constitution even allow for the
incorporation of colonies or non-self-governing territories? For another
thing, some of the regions the United States wanted to conquer and settle
were already part of its territory. What really was the status of the Great
Plains Indian tribes under the Constitution?

In addition, the United States also had to consider the power relationships between itself and its rival colonizers. Industrialization, urbanization,
population growth, and technology had transformed all these societies as
well as the international system in which they operated. The United
States was constantly on guard against the machinations of other imperial powers, especially Britain and Germany, and to a lesser extent Russia
and Japan. How could the United States guarantee that it would have access to new markets and could proliferate its beliefs abroad? Should the
United States become engaged in European wars? Thus developments in

Europe heavily influenced the foreign policy of the United States in this period.[1]

The European System after the Napoleonic Wars

From the end of the Napoleonic Wars in 1815 to the beginning of the First World War in 1914, Europe enjoyed a century of relative peace. This peace could be attributed initially to the "balance of power" established by Metternich and other peacemakers at the Congress of Vienna in 1815 and subsequently to the adroit diplomacy of Bismarck of Germany up to about 1890. The Napoleonic Wars also ushered in domestic changes that affected relations among the **Great Powers** of Europe during the next century. The most prominent of these were the forces of **liberalism** and **nationalism**.[2] Equally important was the rapid rise of **industrialization** in Europe during this period. With improvements in manufacturing, transportation, and communications technologies, it was possible to expand the size of both states and empires. All these changes created in turn the unstable balances of power that led to the two world wars of the twentieth century.

Liberalism and Nationalism

The French Revolution shook the very foundations of the absolutist system, and as a result, Europeans began to advocate the liberal values of individual rights, limited government, private property, and economic freedom that were also embodied in the American Constitution. As the inhabitants of European states asserted their own rights, they inevitably challenged the absolute powers claimed by the monarchs of Europe. Groups that perceived themselves as sharing common attributes—such as territory, history, culture, and language—developed a sense of national unity. Although this national identification eventually strengthened the nation-state, it initially undermined the authority of those who claimed the sovereign right to rule these countries single-handedly. Rising nationalism also led to instability in large, multinational empires such as the Austrian Empire and the Ottoman Empire.

Weary of war and confronted by restive populations and revolutionary forces within their borders, the monarchs who ruled the Great Powers of Europe had every reason to cooperate with each other so that international events would not exacerbate their domestic problems. In 1815, at a peace conference known as the Congress of Vienna, the victors in the Napoleonic Wars (Britain, Russia, the Austrian Empire, and Prussia) established through the Treaty of Vienna a system to guarantee the stability of Europe. The treaty called for, among other things, independence for Belgium and Holland, the permanent neutrality of Switzerland, and the restoration of a Polish state between Russia and Prussia. The four victorious powers also agreed to restore France to the position of a Great Power within a few years.

To maintain this stability, the monarchs agreed to meet periodically and settle any disputes arising among them at a series of conferences that became known as the Concert of Europe. Other factors that contributed to European stability were the Holy Alliance among Russia, the Austrian Empire, and Prussia, all of which feared the liberal forces arising within their societies, and Great Britain's interest in preserving its far-flung empire, which was vulnerable to invasion by a strong and ambitious European power. In theory, Britain was always prepared to help reestablish the balance on the continent if necessary.

The first challenges to this stability came in the early 1820s with uprisings against conservative rulers in Spain, Portugal, and Naples and Piedmont (small states in Italy). The Holy Alliance authorized Austria and France to suppress the revolutions in Naples and Spain, respectively. As noted in Chapter 2, Britain and the United States were concerned that the Holy Alliance would attempt to restore Spain's empire in the Americas. But in one of the first signs of discord within the Concert of Europe, Britain blocked the efforts of the monarchs in Europe to help Spain reclaim its former colonies in the Americas. Indeed, Britain took advantage of Spain's plight by becoming the most important trading partner of most of these South American countries.

Another series of popular revolts in Belgium, Germany, Italy, and Poland was prompted in 1830 by a liberal uprising in France in opposition to the attempts of Charles X to reestablish the old order in that country. These revolts were soon suppressed, but in 1848 a series of liberal revolts again erupted in France, Prussia, the Austrian Empire—especially Hungary—and Greece, as liberals attempted to take control of their respective governments. Although these revolts failed, they compelled the monarchs to meet many of the liberals' demands for representative or parliamentary institutions. By mid-century, the Great Powers were having difficulties balancing the domestic and international forces pushing for change. The social and economic changes brought by industrialization only added to their woes.

Industrialization

Although the beginnings of industrialization can be traced back to the 1700s, nineteenth-century improvements in iron making and the steam engine and other labor-saving devices increased the pace at which machines replaced manual labor. Factory production rapidly replaced cottage industry, and eventually the increased competition among factories spurred the development of larger and larger firms. The accompanying advances in transportation and communications changed the European landscape. Meanwhile, an increase in population and a shift of population from rural to urban areas accompanied the growth in production.

These developments profoundly affected relations among the Great Powers as trade both within and between states grew dramatically. Moreover, colonies became valued sources of raw materials and resources to feed the new factories and valuable markets for the manufactured goods. Great Britain, with the largest number of colonies, found itself in the most advantageous trade position. France, Russia, the Austrian Empire, Belgium, Holland, and other states also sought secure trade arrangements with colonies.

Industrialization and improvements in transportation and communications affected various states in different ways. For example, the development of railroads allowed continental powers such as Germany and Russia to move military forces from one border to another more readily. This capability threatened Britain, whose empire depended on its command of the world oceans, which in turn was based on its control of a limited number of key waterways such as the English Channel, the Straits of Gibraltar, the Bosphorus Strait, and later, the Suez Canal. Now the newly mobile land powers could bypass some of Britain's naval choke points.

In mid-century the anxiety created by these changes reached a breaking point when Russia pressed the weakening Ottoman Empire for special rights over Christian sites in Palestine on behalf of Orthodox Christian believers. The dispute over which state had the right to protect the sites in Turkish-controlled Palestine provoked a conflict with France, which claimed the right, under an obscure treaty, to protect the access of Catholics to these sites. When the sultan of Turkey objected to the Tsar's second demand to intervene in Ottoman Turkey to protect Orthodox believers, Russia occupied Turkish principalities on the Danube River. In response, Turkey declared war on Russia in 1854, and Britain and France came to Turkey's aid. Britain was particularly concerned that Russia might defeat Turkey and block Britain's Mediterranean sea routes to India, Britain's most valuable colony.

In 1855 Britain and France won what became known as the Crimean War. In the 1856 peace treaty the Black Sea was declared neutral, the Great Powers pledged to respect the integrity of the Ottoman Empire, and the Turkish sultan agreed to deal justly with the Christian population in his empire. The war marked the final breakdown of the Concert of Europe. The period that followed was marked by changes in both the size and identity of states and in the relations between them.

Redistribution of Power in Europe

Having lost the war, the Russian tsars found it more difficult to cope with liberal challenges to imperial rule, and so in 1861 Tsar Alexander II emancipated the serfs.[3] The war also exposed Russia's difficulties with the Austrian Empire. Russia had expected the support of the Austrian Empire in the Crimean conflict, but the latter, fearing Russian expansion in the Balkans, had remained neutral. In the meantime, the Austrian Empire was facing its own domestic problems. Franz Josef, an ethnic Austrian who had become emperor in 1848, was facing challenges from his disaffected

Hungarian subjects and was therefore forced to grant a degree of self-government to the outer regions.

The weakening of Russia and the Austrian Empire provided an opportunity for first Italy and then Germany to emerge as unified states. The nationalist struggles of Italy and Germany compelled Franz Josef to placate his restive Hungarian minority by dividing his empire into two parts—Austria and Hungary—in 1867, with the result that he became emperor of Austria and king of Hungary. After further continental unrest solidified the union of the German states, Germany emerged as the strongest state on the continent. Because of the diplomatic skills of its chancellor, Otto von Bismarck, Germany was, for the most part, able to remain at peace with the other European states by maintaining better relations with France, Austria-Hungary, Italy, and Russia than any of them had with each other. After about 1890, however, Germany found it more difficult to maintain this delicately balanced alliance system. For one thing, the competition between Russia and Austria-Hungary over the Balkans became more serious. For another, Germany realized that if it were going to compete with Britain for world power, it would have to expand its influence on a global level. That realization complicated its already difficult relations with France. And finally, the new Kaiser, Wilhelm II, seemed disinclined to follow the advice of Chancellor Bismarck and lacked Bismarck's diplomatic finesse.

Redistribution of Power at the Global Level

Although the Concert of Europe had been fairly effective in maintaining the peace on the continent prior to the Crimean War, it had not tried to control the competition among its members elsewhere. France and Britain competed for colonies in Africa and Asia, and Belgium, Spain, Portugal, and the Netherlands held on to territories they had claimed earlier. South and Central America had been excluded largely from the competition because the British dominated trade with most of these countries and were prepared to use their navy to prevent other European countries from meddling in these areas. Moreover, the United States had announced in the Monroe Doctrine that it would not tolerate European expansion into the Western Hemisphere.

Because Germany and Italy had unified later than the other European colonial powers, they had not established colonies in Africa and Asia and so felt deprived. In the end, both countries were allowed to take over some of the less-attractive areas that remained—for the Germans, Southwest Africa or Namibia, the Cameroons, and East Africa; for the Italians, Libya. From 1870 until World War I, Germany, in particular, was anxious to establish bases and trading areas throughout the world.

Russia also was actively seeking to expand its holdings during this period, but the areas it incorporated into its territory were contiguous regions. Thus Russian imperialism, like American imperialism, was not quite as visible. By the end of the 1880s Russia essentially reached the borders of Afghanistan and Persia, where it posed a serious threat to British India. Russia also had extended its territory into the Far East, where it competed with Japan and, to a lesser extent, Germany for control of northern China.

Although Britain was perceived as the world's leading military and economic power from 1870 to 1913, its percentage share of world manufacturing production declined vis-à-vis both the United States and Germany, even though Britain's economy actually grew during this period. This loss of manufacturing supremacy had significant repercussions for Britain's status as the world's leading power. Militarily, Britain did not really perceive its decline until it became engaged in the Boer War against the Dutch and German settlers in South Africa from 1899 to 1902. To win this war against a poorly equipped, but highly determined, opponent, Britain had to drastically reduce its forces throughout the empire. The Boer War highlighted Britain's military and strategic weaknesses in managing a worldwide empire and caused it to wonder what would happen if a major opponent, such as Russia, challenged it for control of its prize possession, India.

The key to British strength was its command of the world's seas, but during the 1870s and 1880s first France and then Italy, Germany, Russia, and the United States began to build modern navies. By 1902 Britain realized that it no longer could claim to control the oceans of the world. With the prospect of the interoceanic Panama canal in the Western Hemisphere, the British could not compete successfully with the United States in those waters, and with the emergence of a Japanese navy, Britain would have to reach some accommodation with Japan in the Pacific.

Even in Europe, Britain's "two-power standard"—its claim of superiority over the next two most powerful navies—was in jeopardy. Britain could claim to be more powerful than its two most likely opponents, France and Russia, only because of its friendly relations with Italy, the third-ranked naval power after Britain and France. More seriously, the British realized that Germany held the balance of naval power in Europe and was the main threat to British control of the English Channel, the North Sea, and the Mediterranean.

France, even more so than Britain, feared a powerful and increasingly bellicose Germany. Because Germany was clearly the strongest state on the European continent, France began to search for additional guarantees for its security. It first looked to Britain for that support, but the British were not willing to provide any guarantees. Consequently, France had to ally itself with Russia in the hope that Germany would be deterred by the prospect of the two-front continental war that by now appeared inevitable. The British eventually realized that they had a stake in protecting

France because France and its ally, Russia, could help contain Germany. As the British accommodated American interests in the Western Hemisphere, the friction between the United States and Germany increased. For example, Germany became the most intransigent opponent of both international arbitration procedures and of controlled disarmament at the Second Hague Conference in 1907, both measures that the United States supported.

In 1914 these increasingly rigid alignments brought Britain, France, Russia, and Italy into array against Germany and Austria-Hungary in the continent-wide conflict of World War I. The United States finally joined the Allied countries in the spring of 1917, and even though Russia quit the war in late 1917, an overextended Germany sued the remaining Allies for peace in late 1918.

World War I is particularly interesting when examined from the standpoint of relations among the Great Powers. Randall Schweller contends that the only states that should be considered first-tier Great Powers—or poles—as opposed to lesser Great Powers are those that have 50 percent or more of the power capacity of the most powerful state.[4] Applying these rules to the data in Table 3.1 reveals that the United States was the only first-tier Great Power at the time. This observation is important because it suggests that the United States could have prevented World War I if it had been prepared to play an active role in European affairs. But it chose not to do so.

The United States and Japan were the only states that emerged from World War I stronger than they had been before the war. According to Schweller's rules for defining Great Powers—a comparative assessment of

Table 3.1. Power Capacity of the World's Most Powerful States, 1870–1913[a]

Period	United States	Germany	United Kingdom
1870	0.73	0.42	1.00
1881–1885	1.00	0.49	0.93
1896–1900	1.00	0.55	0.65
1906–1910	1.00	0.45	0.42
1913	1.00	0.44	0.39

a. The poles—that is, those countries that have 50 percent or more of the power capacity of the most powerful state—are shaded.

Source: Power capacity is based on percentage share of the world's manufacturing, as reported in Aaron L. Friedberg, The Weary Titan: Britain and the Experience of Relative Decline, 1895–1905 (Princeton: Princeton University Press, 1988).

relative economic strength—the United States remained the only pole until the early 1930s. At that point the balance of power in the world changed very quickly as Table 3.2 illustrates. First, Stalin's rapid industrialization program propelled the Soviet Union into Great Power status. Then by 1935 Germany became a Great Power as a result of remilitarizing the Rhineland and undertaking an ambitious armaments program under Adolf Hitler's leadership.

By 1938, Schweller argues, the unipolar system had been transformed into a very unstable **tripolar system** because two of the three poles, Germany and the Soviet Union, were revisionist states—that is, they wanted to change the balance of power.[5] If the two states had joined together against the United States, they might have won, contends Schweller. But he also recognizes that the two revisionist states would not have been able to agree on a division of the spoils in Europe, and so inevitably they would end up fighting each other. What foreign policy should the United States have pursued? On the one hand, it was not entirely unreasonable for the United States to stay aloof, hoping that the two revisionist states would fight. On the other hand, the United States might have prevented both world wars if it could have played the role of balancer on the European continent. A look at the domestic conditions that influenced the development of American foreign policy from 1866 to 1941 will go far toward explaining why the United States refrained from proactive involvement in Europe during that period.

Table 3.2. Power Capacity of the World's Most Powerful States, 1933–1940[a]

Year	United States	Soviet Union	Germany	United Kingdom
1933	1.00	0.84	0.31	0.31
1934	1.00	0.81	0.48	0.33
1935	0.99	1.00	0.54	0.39
1936	1.00	0.87	0.59	0.39
1937	1.00	0.89	0.62	0.40
1938	1.00	1.00	0.80	0.42
1939	1.00	0.85	0.99	0.52
1940	1.00	0.74	0.84	0.45

a. The poles—that is, those countries that have 50 percent or more of the power capacity of the most powerful state—are shaded.

Source: Power capacity is based on calculations by Randall L. Schweller, *Deadly Imbalances: Tripolarity and Hitler's Strategy of World Conquest* (New York: Columbia University Press, 1998), Table 1.2.

The American System after the Civil War

Although the United States quietly overtook Britain to become the world's most productive country in the decades immediately after the Civil War, it did not assume a comparable position of leadership until well into the next century. Indeed, throughout this period of tremendous growth no country in Europe even considered sending a representative of ambassadorial rank to Washington, D.C. The explanation for the disparity between American wealth and the exercise of American influence in the world is examined in the rest of this chapter. The discussion is divided into four periods in which there was: (1) intervention within, 1866–1889; (2) intervention without, 1890–1920; (3) intervention postponed, 1921–1932; and intervention delayed, 1933–1941.

Intervention Within: 1866–1889

During this period many leaders in the North were, like those in the South just before the Civil War, seeking to expand the country. After all, the primary obstacle to expansion before the war had been the issue of the extension of slavery, and the war had settled that issue. Yet by the time President Grover Cleveland, the first Democrat to be elected president after the Civil War, began his second term of office in 1893, the United States had added territorially only Alaska in 1867, the Midway Islands in 1867, and basing rights in Samoa in 1878. A specific look in this section at all three aspects of foreign policy—prosperity, security, and community,—will explain this outcome.

Prosperity Values. At the time that Italy and Germany were emerging as unified states in Europe, the United States was engaged in national reconstruction after its Civil War. And while the productive capacity of the Great Powers of Europe was growing at the impressive rate of 2–3 percent a year, America's industry was growing at an annual average rate of 5 percent. Almost every sector of the American economy contributed to this remarkable rise.

With the benefit of the Homestead Act of 1862, farmers quickly settled the new frontier between the Mississippi River and the Rocky Mountains. A "combination of strong demand, high prices, and labor shortages convinced many farmers that the time had come to make the change from hand power and hand tools to horse power and the new horse-drawn machines, such as McCormick's reaper. The result was the first American agricultural revolution." Although the sharp increases in production during this period eventually leveled off, demand continued to grow, resulting in the general equilibrium between supply and demand and slowly rising prices that produced the "golden age of agriculture" between 1898 and 1919.[6]

The growth in the U.S. manufacturing sector was even greater. By 1885 the United States had surpassed Britain's share of the world's manufacturing output, and by 1899 manufacturing's contribution to the U.S. gross domestic product (GDP) had increased by a factor of six, to $6.3 billion. By 1900 total capital invested in U.S. manufacturing was at $8.2 billion and increased to $20.8 billion in the next decade and a half. By 1900 the U.S. economy already consumed more energy than the other industrialized nations combined, with the exception of England.[7]

This unprecedented long-term industrial growth changed the structure of the American economy. In 1860, 58 percent of employed workers worked on farms; in 1880 about 50 percent worked in industry and 50 percent in farming; and in 1900 farm workers constituted only 38 percent of the total workforce.[8]

Meanwhile, the population was growing rapidly, assisted by immigration. Large jumps in the growth rate between 1869 and 1873 and again between 1912 and 1916 more than doubled the population, from 41 million to 100 million. The nationality of the immigrants also changed. Most immigrants to the United States came from northern and western Europe, until the 1880s, when immigration from southern and eastern Europe began to increase dramatically, so that by 1900 over 80 percent of the immigrants to the United States came from southern and eastern Europe.[9] Most of these new immigrants obtained manufacturing and mining jobs in the northeastern and midwestern United States.

Industrialization in the decades after the Civil War not only attracted waves of new immigrants who challenged Americans' sense of identity, but also affected the way Americans did business with one another, as the new capitalists sought ways to enhance their competitive position. Because during this period industrial production rose even faster than demand, it was characterized by boom and bust cycles—periods of growth and expansion followed by downward swings in employment and prices. To deal with this highly competitive situation, business entrepreneurs expanded their operations westward to avoid government controls, reduce competition, and take advantage of economies of scale by combining, merging and acquiring operations.

This horizontal formation of trusts and monopolies, the **spread effect,** is associated with some of the most famous names in American industry: Andrew Carnegie, Edward H. Harriman, John D. Rockefeller, J. P. Morgan, George Westinghouse, and George Pullman. As one example of the trust and monopoly formation of these "robber barons," during this period, Rockefeller, president of Standard Oil Company, brought about 90 percent of the refining capacity of the kerosene industry under one management.

During this period railroads replaced waterways as the primary means of transportation. By 1914 the United States had more than 250,000 miles of railroad lines, including a transcontinental railroad, thereby exceeding the rail capacity of all other industrialized countries taken together.[10] Such improvements in transportation and the invention of the telegraph and the telephone in communications paved the way for the development of a truly national economy by allowing the nation's regions to come together. Regional integration took two forms: the Great Lakes region was absorbed into a manufacturing-commercial core that produced new building materials such as concrete, steel, and glass, and the Pacific area became part of the country's new resource base that featured oil, electricity, and coal.

Foreign trade accounted for only a small portion of the national income during this period, but developing trade with international markets was very important to the United States because the United States was producing far more than it could consume. Although about 85 percent of American foreign trade during this period was with Europe, America's infant industries could not compete effectively in the established markets of Europe without the tariff protection they enjoyed at home. The Republican Party, which dominated the government throughout most of this period, happily obliged by implementing the higher tariffs that industries in the Northeast preferred. Meanwhile, the United States sought to develop new markets in Latin America, the Pacific Islands, and the Far East.

Security Values.   In the period immediately after the Civil War, America generally encountered more opportunities for expansion abroad than threats from abroad, though the United States perceived threats on its borders from European nations. At the end of the Civil War the North had some 600,000 men in uniform. Conceivably, the United States could have used this force to deal with some of the perceived threats on its borders. For example, most Americans felt that Britain had favored the South in the Civil War, and there was some sentiment for incorporating all or part of Britain's Canadian territory into the Union at that time. During the same period France had established Maximilian as the ruler in Mexico, and Spain had temporarily retaken Santo Domingo in the Caribbean. Nevertheless, these perceived threats soon disappeared, and the United States quickly reduced the size of its military forces.

The War Department chose instead to deploy the much smaller army of about 25,000 men that remained after demobilization almost exclusively against the Native Americans who roamed the Great Plains between the Mississippi River and the Rocky Mountains. Because the Constitution treats these Indian nations as independent entities within the territory of the United States, they are considered here in the context of American foreign policy.

The five Indian nations of the South—Cherokee, Chickasaw, Choctaw, Creek, and Seminole—had been moved in the 1830s and 1840s to the area now known as Oklahoma. When the Civil War began, the Confederacy sent representatives to the southern tribes to seek their support. At first, some of the Indian leaders were reticent, but a combination of

Southern promises and Northern neglect prompted many of the Indian nations to favor the Confederacy. John Ross, the primary chief of the Cherokee nation, held out the longest, preferring to remain neutral and fulfill his obligations under the treaty with the United States, as is described in Box 3.1. Eventually, though, both factions of the Cherokees allied themselves with the Confederacy.

BOX 3.1

Profile in Action: John Ross

When President Andrew Jackson became president in 1829, he decided that the five great Indian nations in the South should be moved to what is now the state of Oklahoma. The policy of removal divided the Cherokees. The main faction under Principal Chief John Ross opposed removal on the grounds that it violated their treaty rights; another faction under Chief Stand Waite accepted removal. Ross's position was supported by the U.S. Supreme Court in *Worcester v. Georgia* (1832), but Jackson would not enforce it.

Although John Ross was only one-eighth Cherokee, he grew up among the full-blooded Cherokees and was accepted by them. By 1838, when Ross finally led his people on the Trail of Tears to Oklahoma, he had already become an experienced negotiator. In the 1840s and 1850s he concentrated primarily on obtaining suitable compensation for the members of his tribe who had been forced to move west.

At the beginning of the Civil War, Confederate agents tried to convince the five Indian nations in Oklahoma to ally themselves with the Confederacy. The Waite faction favored the proposed alliance, but Ross preferred to keep the existing treaty with the U.S. government, avoid the war, and continue negotiating with the Union for better compensation for the Cherokee nation.

It was not until Northern troops essentially abandoned the Indians in the West that Ross accepted the new alliance with the Confederacy. Later, in a meeting with President Abraham Lincoln, Ross argued that the North had no one to blame but itself for the actions taken by the Cherokees and that he had been forced to sign the treaty with the Confederacy. Lincoln remained unconvinced.

Ross can be classified as a multilateral, noncoercive, and reactive (MCA) foreign policy maker. His multilateralism stemmed from his belief that the Cherokee nation had an obligation to abide by its international agreements. He was noncoercive because he wanted to maintain only a domestic police force within the Cherokee nation. And he was anti-involvement because he wanted to focus exclusively on the internal affairs of the Cherokee nation and not become entangled in the war between the North and the South.

In early military campaigns in the West between the North and the South, both sides enlisted some Indians as cavalry, and the Indian troops fought bravely and well, especially for the Confederacy; but when the North won the war in the West, the South largely abandoned the Indian nations. At that point, the North took the position that these nations had abrogated their original treaties with the U.S. government, and so new treaties would have to be promulgated. The government used this justification to extend the policy of concentration begun before the war; and after the Civil War it reduced by half the territory given to Native Americans.

The story in the northern Great Plains was similar, although it took over two decades for the policy of concentration to take full effect there. In the 1850s the northern Indians were cleared out of the Minnesota River Valley to make room for settlers. But when the food and supplies they were promised in exchange for moving were not forthcoming, some Indians murdered a small group of settlers in 1862. The government then decided to push the Indians farther west and establish posts at strategic locations to ensure they remained far removed from white settlements.

As white settlers moved west in search of free land and as American industry sought to establish railroad rights-of-way through Indian territory after the Civil War, they came into inevitable conflict with the relocated Indian tribes, and the U.S. Army was increasingly called upon to deal with the Indians who naturally defended their territory. Sometimes the army did try to stop the settlers, but when the settlers would not halt their movement, the army gave priority to protecting the settlers from the Indians.

In the early 1870s about 400,000 homesteaders lived on the prairies between Kansas and the northern border of the United States, and about 239,000 Indians lived in the entire West. Not all of the northern Indians fought with the settlers, but those who did—mainly the Teton Sioux, the northern Cheyennes, and the northern Arapahos—fought determinedly. Because of the vast areas of land involved and because the Indians were nomads, it was very difficult for the army to pin down the Indians and apply its superior firepower. Finally, the U.S. generals determined that the best time to attack the Indians was during the winter, when they stayed in one place and could not easily regroup and counterattack. As a result of this strategy, by the late 1870s almost all American Indians had been reduced to disarmed bands living on government reservations.

While the U.S. Army was fully engaged on the Great Plains, the U.S. Navy was allowed to atrophy, although it continued to maintain some presence in various parts of the world. No new ships were built until the 1880s when U.S. naval policy changed and became more expansion-minded.

Community Values.   In the nation's earliest days, Americans' confidence in their unique institutions was associated to some extent with the availability of free land. As Americans proceeded to fill up the Great Plains in the postbellum period, it became apparent that the American frontier was disappearing. In 1878 John Wesley Powell, the director of the U.S. Geographical and Geological Survey of the Rocky Mountain Region, reported that most of the remaining unsettled land could not be cultivated. The census report of 1890 confirmed that the American frontier was disappearing, which prompted the historian Frederick Jackson Turner to formulate his famous **frontier thesis,** which stated that the development of the democratic institutions that largely define America were tied to this frontier, and with the closing of the frontier those institutions were, therefore, in jeopardy.

Although the belief that foreign expansion might be needed to replace the lost frontier did not become popular until the 1890s, **"frontier anxiety"** did manifest itself in the attitudes of Americans toward immigrants in the 1870s and 1880s. In the West the settlers directed the cry of "America for Americans" at alien landholders, particularly those from southern and eastern Europe. The attitudes of white Anglo-Saxon Protestants in the Northeast, whose cities drew most of the new immigrants, were similar to those of the settlers in the West. On the whole, however, the attitude of Americans toward recent immigrants was determined by the newcomers' willingness to become assimilated linguistically and culturally into American society.

This emphasis on **Americanization** also became the new policy toward American Indians, once the policy of concentration had forced them onto reservations by the end of the 1870s. The new policy—not to be mistaken for Jefferson's policy of assimilating Native Americans and their assets in the Louisiana Territory and the Pacific Northwest—rested mainly on the notions of land reform and a government-sponsored educational program for Indian children. The first measure was designed to convince the Indians to accept the concept of private property; the second was intended to separate Indian children from their parents by sending them to distant boarding schools where they could learn how to function in American society. Americans' desire to maintain their identity as a unique group of people was a national phenomenon, but the cost was high: hundreds of immigrant and Native American groups lost their unique linguistic and cultural identity.

Dimensions of Foreign Policy.   It is particularly difficult to classify American foreign policy in the period immediately following the Civil War because there is such a sharp division between Congress and the executive branch of the government over the extent and nature of executive power. Lincoln had exercised unprecedented executive power, such as authorizing the suspension of the writ of habeas corpus, as president during the Civil War. In the immediate post-war period Congress sought to reassert its prerogatives. For example, Congress not only tried to impeach Lincoln's successor, the unpopular Andrew Johnson, but the Senate repeatedly refused to consent to expansionist treaties signed by his popular successor, President Ulysses S. Grant. Congressional negativism was reinforced by several factors, including a huge federal debt accumulated during the Civil War, a small executive branch largely controlled by congressional patronage, and a series of corruption scandals, some of which involved members of Grant's own administration.

Intense bickering between Congress and the executive during the period seemed to verify the Tocqueville thesis that democracies could not achieve the kind of unity of action required in foreign affairs. Indeed, the weakness of the American government was so apparent at the time that a future president, Woodrow Wilson, proposed in an 1885 publication, *Congressional Government*, that the United States adopt the British system in which executive powers were controlled by a cabinet chosen by and accountable to Parliament.

Nonetheless, if one focuses more on executive intent than congressional action—or inaction—it is possible to locate American foreign policy in the period along the three dimensions as is shown in Table 3.3. Generally speaking, the expansionistic U. S. foreign policy remained largely unilateral, although the United States did participate in some European treaties and sponsor a Pan American conference. American expansionistic foreign policy was also coercive at least insofar as the Indian nations on the Great Plains were concerned. Though ostensibly undertaken to secure the frontier, many of the military engagements in the Indian wars are

Table 3.3. Dimensions of Foreign Policy: The Postbellum Period

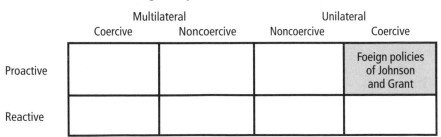

| | Multilateral | | Unilateral | |
	Coercive	Noncoercive	Noncoercive	Coercive
Proactive				Foeign policies of Johnson and Grant
Reactive				

The major difference between the antebellum period described in Chapter 2 and the postbellum period described in this chapter is that the domestic obstacles to external expansion had changed. Prior to the Civil War the problem was the political division over slavery; after the Civil War the problem was largely the division between the president and Congress over whose prerogative it was to initiate expansion. Both Presidents Andrew Johnson and Ulysses S. Grant favored an <u>M</u>CA policy of expansion. The policy was unilateral because they saw little need to consult with other countries, coercive because they were prepared to use force if necessary, and proactive because they actively sought external markets, even though these markets weren't open to American goods. Congress, however, refused to accept their initiatives.

properly characterized as massacres. And U.S. foreign policy was basically proactive because it absorbed the economic assets of Indians living on the plains, and it promoted new markets for American goods abroad.

Intervention Without: 1890–1920

By 1890 many of the developments that had weakened the federal government and inhibited American territorial expansion in the decades immediately after the Civil War, such as the struggle between Congress and the executive and the national debt from the Civil War, were no longer factors. Moreover, the factors driving industrialization and territorial expansion gained further impetus as the horizontal integration of firms—"the spread effect"—was followed by vertical integration as firms sought control of both their sources of raw materials and manufacturing and marketing functions further up the line. This vertical growth of large corporations, coupled with the horizontal growth—the **size effect**—spawned a reform movement that sought to strengthen the federal government's ability to regulate these corporations and monopolies through new laws, such as the 1890 Sherman Antitrust Act, and new agencies, such as the establishment of the Interstate Commerce Commission in 1887. The progressive reform movement, together with the civil service reform that was spreading throughout the federal bureaucracy, weakened party patronage and Congress (which controlled patronage through its appropriations power) and resulted, by the end of the nineteenth century, in a presidency and bureaucracy much more capable of exercising leadership in both domestic and foreign affairs.

In the meantime, many of the factors that favored overseas and extra-territorial **expansionism** in the earlier period became even more significant in the 1890s. The most important of these factors was Frederick Jackson Turner's famous pronouncement in 1893 that the American frontier had disappeared. New and noncontiguous territories would now have to be annexed. American business also looked abroad for new markets and investment opportunities, and the competition for influence and territory in the Caribbean, the Pacific, and East Asia heated up, particularly because of competition with Germany's expansionistic and imperialistic aims.

Just as in Europe, the leading intellectual figures of the day fueled the perception of these opportunities and threats through an ideology of expansionism based on bellicose nationalism, as well as the consciousness of newly acquired industrial wealth and feelings of racial superiority. Josiah Strong, a Protestant minister, popularized the idea of external expansion as the "final competition of races." Social Darwinists such as William Graham Sumner believed "that the fittest, most highly developed races would naturally conquer the weaker ones." Indiana senator Albert J. Beveridge argued that it was "America's divine mission to civilize inferior races." Intellectual Brooks Adams contended that "if Americans could now develop and increase their commercial activities overseas—west of the Pacific continental boundary—then their country would become the center of world trade and commerce."[11] The "yellow" journalists in the popular press, such as Joseph Pulitzer's *New York World* and William Randolph Hearst's *New York Journal American*, sensationalized these sentiments for mass audiences.

And so, just as in the three-year span from 1845 to 1848 during which the United States rapidly annexed Texas, the Oregon Territory, and the California Territory, it now extended its reach to Hawaii, Cuba, Puerto Rico, Guam, Wake Island, the Philippines, and Samoa—all in 1898.

Latin America, the Pacific, and East Asia. President William McKinley, who served from 1897 to 1901 and who actually opposed colonization, had been elected largely with the expectation that he would build up the domestic economy. Nevertheless, as president, he quickly became immersed in foreign affairs.

The event that precipitated American imperialism at the turn of the century was the 1896 revolution in Cuba. Americans were appalled by the harsh measures Spain purportedly employed to quell the rebellion in its Caribbean colony, by the April 1898 sinking of the battleship *Maine* in Havana's harbor, and by the possibility of lost investments in Cuba. The yellow press especially played up the Spanish atrocities and the *Maine* incident. McKinley worked steadily during his first year in office to resolve the issue peacefully. He offered U.S. mediation, and he tried to convince the Spanish to give the Cubans more autonomy in the hope that such a step would solve the problem. When he realized that Spain could not resolve the situation, he asked Congress for a declaration of war against Spain, and on April 25, 1898, it obliged.

By seeking war with Spain, President McKinley unleashed a chain of events that neither he nor most others anticipated. Acting in accordance with a contingency plan developed by the U.S. Navy, Adm. George Dewey defeated a small Spanish fleet in Manila Bay in the Philippines. But because the army and navy had no contingency plans for an invasion of Cuba, some time was required to assemble the American ground forces needed to defeat Spain. The war ended in December 1898 with the signing of the Treaty of Paris, and the United States found itself propelled into the arena of world politics as a major player. Although the United States acquired both Cuba and the Philippines in the Treaty of Paris, McKinley was not eager to incorporate either of those territories, and no decision on how the United States might dispose of them had been made when the treaty came before the Senate for ratification.

The Senate debate on the treaty over the issue of expansion was one of the great debates of American foreign policy. Some Republican supporters of the treaty, such as Henry Cabot Lodge of Massachusetts, argued that "the Treaty merely cedes the Philippines to us. It commits us to no course of action."[12] Others, such as Republican senator George Hoar, also of Massachusetts, opposed the treaty on the grounds that "the American conquest of the Philippines violated the principle that government rests on the consent of the governed."[13] But McKinley succeeded in separating ratification of the treaty from any decision on colonization, and it was finally approved with only one vote to spare.

Meanwhile, shortly before the Senate passed the Treaty of Paris, the United States annexed the Hawaiian Islands, an acquisition that it had been considering for some time. But annexation became a reality only after the Japanese expressed interest in the islands.

The American drive for expansion was more economic and ideological than territorial. For example, some American businessmen and missionaries aggressively pursued opportunities in China, despite the fact that American access to China was jeopardized by the competition between Japan, Russia, and Germany for exclusive **spheres of influence**. John Hay, who was secretary of state under both McKinley and his successor, Theodore Roosevelt, sent notes to each of the powers operating in China, asking them "to allow equal commercial opportunity within the spheres" of influence, thus sparing the United States the expense and headache of trying to acquire or administer actual colonies and spheres of influence.

But Hay's notes advocating an **Open Door policy** in China were just one form of American interventionism or imperialism. In 1900, when Chinese nationalists, with the encouragement of the Chinese government, objected to the continuing efforts of foreign powers to interfere in Chinese affairs and attacked foreigners near Peking, the United States joined in the European-led rescue force sent to suppress the uprising, known as the Boxer Rebellion. U.S. trade with China was never very extensive during this period though, and by 1910 Americans had turned their attention to Latin America and Europe.

Much of the effort to extend American influence abroad from 1890 to 1920 was focused on the countries in the Caribbean and bordering the Gulf of Mexico. The United States had been interested for some time in an inter-oceanic canal, but construction had been stymied by the Clayton-Bulwer agreement with Britain, which required joint control of any such canal. Once Britain decided to accommodate American interests in the Western Hemisphere, the United States was free to act on its own; and in 1904 President Theodore Roosevelt moved quickly to build the canal at the Isthmus of Panama. The canal finally opened in 1914.

While the Panama Canal was being built, European governments were lending large amounts of money to countries in the Western Hemisphere and then claiming the right to intervene when instability or revolution in these countries caused them to default on their loans. President Roosevelt moved to forestall these dangers by adding a corollary to the Monroe Doctrine, which said that the United States could intervene in order to recover such investments.[14] In some ways the Roosevelt Corollary turned the Monroe Doctrine on its head. Whereas the United States had originally tried to support revolutionary movements in Latin American countries by keeping European states from intervening in the hemisphere, it was now, in effect, advocating American intervention to prevent such revolutions.

Roosevelt was prepared to use force to discourage European meddling in hemispheric affairs. His successor, William Howard Taft, preferred **dollar diplomacy,** whereby increased private American investment in the Western Hemisphere would woo Central American and Caribbean nations and force the Europeans out of the region. When Woodrow Wilson replaced Taft in 1913, he rejected both Roosevelt's "big stick" and Taft's "dollar diplomacy," because he recognized that both policies supported undemocratic forces in Latin America. Wilson believed that democratic government was essential to world peace, and he saw the need for democratic revolutions and national self-determination in that region.

The opportunity for President Wilson to implement his policy in Latin America arose early in his administration. The Mexican Revolution began in 1911, before he came to office. But in February 1913 a counterrevolution emerged, supported by various Western powers, as well as the American ambassador. President Wilson fired the ambassador and refused to recognize the new Huerta regime. He quickly learned from his special envoy to the revolutionaries in Mexico that a democratic revolution did not go far enough; there also must be economic revolution. Thus Wilson decided to use American military force, when necessary, to sustain the radical revolution in Mexico. Wilson felt responsible for maintaining a level playing field so that the Mexicans themselves could determine their form of government, yet another example of Wilson's policy of national self-determination.

Dimensions of Foreign Policy.   Overall, although their specific objectives were quite different, Table 3.4 shows how Presidents William McKinley, Teddy Roosevelt, and even Woodrow Wilson pursued foreign policies in Latin America that were unilateral, coercive, and proactive, or MCA.

Europe.   When World War I broke out in Europe in August 1914, President Wilson declared a policy of **neutrality** and tried to keep the United States out of the fighting. He also presented a four-point program for peace based on ideas that were popular in intellectual circles at the time:

1. No nation shall ever again be permitted to acquire an inch of land by conquest.

2. There must be a recognition of the reality of equal rights between small nations and great.

Table 3.4. Dimensions of Foreign Policy: U.S. Relations with Latin America during the Progressive Era

| | Multilateral | | Unilateral | |
	Coercive	Noncoercive	Noncoercive	Coercive
Proactive				Foreign policies of McKinley, Theodore Roosevelt, and Wilson
Reactive				

Although their specific objectives were quite different, Presidents William McKinley, Theodore Roosevelt, and even Woodrow Wilson pursued MCA foreign policies in Latin America. These policies were unilateral because they did not consult other countries, coercive because they were prepared to use force if necessary, and proactive because they rigorously pursued these policies abroad.

3. Munitions of war must hereafter be manufactured entirely by the nations and not by private enterprise.

4. There must be an association of nations, all bound together for the protection of the integrity of each, so that any one nation breaking from this bond will bring upon herself war; that is to say, punishment, automatically.[15]

These four points were later incorporated into the Fourteen Points bulletin that he later presented to the world following World War I. For example, Point Four anticipated the central idea behind the League of Nations, collective security, which was important throughout the period covered in the remainder of this chapter.

Wilson's multilateral idea was not as sharp a break with the past as it first appeared. The ideas of arbitration and conciliation as a way of settling disputes among nations had been suggested previously. The Hague Peace Conferences of 1899 and 1907 had produced the Permanent Court of Arbitration as well as a set of rules for fighting wars. Theodore Roosevelt had proposed some kind of league of nations when he formally accepted the Nobel Peace Prize in 1910. And President Taft, and especially Secretary of State William Jennings Bryan under Wilson, concluded some twenty bilateral treaties providing for conciliation periods, mostly with Latin American countries. (**Arbitration** is the process in which disputing parties are induced to accept terms of settlement defined by a neutral third party, whereas **conciliation** is the process in which the disputing parties meet and come to agreement on their own.) Wilson later believed that if the

European powers had made these kinds of treaties on a multilateral basis, World War I might have been prevented.

Shortly after the war began, President Wilson and his advisor, Col. Edward House, began to work on a Pan-American Pact, which could serve as the blueprint for a new collective security plan for peace. The model could first be employed in the Western Hemisphere and then extended to other countries once the war was over. However, Chile had reservations about the pact, and so Wilson did not make the pact public until early 1916. As part of his announcement, he explained that the Monroe Doctrine had been a unilateral declaration by the United States, but "now countries of the Americas were uniting to guarantee to each other, absolutely, political independence and territorial integrity."[16]

In preparation for the election of 1916 Wilson made a conscious effort to "harmonize domestic and foreign policy." He built a new coalition of Democrats and Progressives who favored domestic reform legislation and an international peace program. The Progressive Party arose during the late nineteenth century to deal with the problems created by rapid industrialization and urbanization in America. They wanted to strengthen government at all levels in order to fight the abuses of corporate power, protect natural resources, and promote social services. The Progressive Party also favored a variety of peace-making proposals. Among other things Wilson emphasized the multilateral character of the Pan-American Pact, arguing that his peace program would only come into effect "when nation shall agree with nation that the rights of humanity are greater than the rights of sovereignty." However, the single most divisive issue in the 1916 election was military preparedness. Theodore Roosevelt, the Republican candidate, urged the country to prepare for war in order to bolster the Allied states against Germany, but Wilson opposed a large standing army.[17]

Wilson won a narrow victory in 1916 and soon thereafter made his "Peace without Victory" speech, which led to an open debate in the country over war aims. Wilson hoped that the United States could remain neutral in the war, so that he could become the key arbitrator in the peace negotiations that would follow. However, a renewal of German submarine attacks on neutral shipping, including that of the United States, to the Allied nations and the British release of the infamous Zimmerman telegram containing details about a possible alliance between Germany and Mexico led Congress to declare war on Germany on April 2, 1917.[18]

America's entry into the war came just three weeks after the Russian tsar, Nicholas II, abdicated his throne. The two events contributed to a sense of greater unity among the Allied countries, who now saw themselves as democratic nations fighting Germany and old absolutist empires. But that unity was quickly shattered in November 1917 when the Bolsheviks, under the leadership of communist revolutionary Vladimir Ilyich Lenin, overthrew the provisional government in Russia, and the eastern front began to collapse. Within days the new communist government in Russia called for a cease-fire in order to arrange a peace conference the next month. Russia invited its Western allies to join with it in seeking peace on the basis of no "annexations and contributions with the right of all nations to self-determination."[19]

Russia's proposal to return conquered territories to the status quo antebellum was consistent with Wilson's four-point program for peace and with Wilson's commitment to national **self-determination.** Although Germany was eager to end the war in the east so it could concentrate on its western front, it was not prepared to accept a status quo antebellum in the east because it expected to gain significant territory at Russia's expense. After all, German forces were in a superior position in the east, and many of the nations dominated by Russia under the tsars were already seeking independence from Russia, including Poland, the Ukraine, Lithuania, Latvia, Estonia, and Finland in the north as well as the Transcaucasus region in the south. For its part, Russia believed its peace proposal would be more attractive to Germany if the Western allies joined Russia at the peace table. After all, Germany was prepared to give up northern France, Belgium, and parts of Serbia if the Allies did not claim any other territory or indemnity payments from Germany on the western front. When the West did not accept negotiations with Germany on the basis of the terms suggested by Russia, Germany and Russia reached a separate agreement, the Treaty of Brest-Litovsk, in March 1918.

Russia's allies scrambled to deal both with the collapse of their eastern front and with their differences over war aims. The British published a "Memorandum on War Aims" in late December. President Wilson and Colonel House put together the American war aims in the Fourteen Points bulletin issued on January 5, 1918 (see Box 3.2). Wilson was committed to the idea of national self-determination,[20] but he was not unsympathetic to the plight of Russia on the eastern front, and he recognized that Russia's position on the western front was closer to his own than that of either Britain or France because he also did not agree with British and French demands for compensation and indemnities from Germany.

After its entry into the war in 1917, the United States required over a year to mobilize its military forces and make an impact on the western front. On September 27, 1918, a week after the first significant action by American forces in Europe, Wilson outlined five practical guidelines for a settlement, based on the Fourteen Points, in a speech before some 6,000 people at the Metropolitan Opera House in New York City, including national self-determination and the rejection of indemnity payments by the defeated nations. He challenged the other Allied states to state openly whether they agreed with his war aims. Shortly thereafter, Germany asked for negotiations on the basis of Wilson's Fourteen Points, especially after Wilson's address of September 27, 1918.

As Germany edged toward acceptance of an armistice on Wilson's terms, former president Theodore Roosevelt renounced the Fourteen Points in their entirety. Even former president William Howard Taft, who headed the League to Enforce Peace, denounced Wilson's armistice plan. On November 5, 1918, the very day that Colonel House secured Allied approval for the Fourteen Points, President Wilson lost his Democratic Progressive majorities in both houses of Congress in the midterm elections. Had the armistice been released earlier and had voters realized that it was, for all practical purposes, an unconditional surrender for Germany, it is possible that the elections might well have turned out differently. Shortly after the election Wilson appointed a five-member American Commission to Negotiate Peace and included on it only one Republican, a career diplomat.

In December 1918 Wilson and the commission left for Europe. The most important document Wilson took to the peace conference was a draft treaty for a League of Nations. The League's covenant put forth the idea of collective security and required all nations to unite against an aggressor. Enormous crowds in Paris, Rome, and London triumphantly greeted Wilson's arrival in Europe. The tremendous outpouring of public support enabled Wilson, despite his recent congressional defeat, to restore his leadership in the peace process when the Paris Peace Conference opened on January 18, 1919. On the basis of this European popular support, Wilson was able to obtain most of the treaty provisions he wanted for the League of Nations before returning to the United States in late February 1919.

One of the problems Wilson confronted at home was the fact that some of his socialist supporters prior to America's entrance into the war, such as Max Eastman and John Reed, had been arrested under the Espionage Act of 1917. Although liberals and socialists had repeatedly pleaded with Wilson to repeal the act and release the prisoners now that the armistice had been accepted, he did not do so. The result was that the progressive coalition he had built for the 1916 presidential election was in a shambles, leaving Wilson without the support he needed for his proposed League of Nations. Just prior to Wilson's return to Europe, Sen. Henry Cabot Lodge, the Republican chairman of the Foreign Relations Committee, prepared a resolution opposing U.S. acceptance of the covenant of the League of Nations. Thirty-seven Senate Republicans then signed the resolution, more than the one-third votes plus one necessary to defeat in the Senate the covenant of the League of Nations, which was considered a treaty requiring Senate ratification.

Thus Wilson's domestic critics sent him back to Europe with the knowledge that he would be forced to make many of the changes regarding territorial divisions, indemnity payments and assignment of war guilt to Germany wanted by the representatives of the other Allied states. Indeed, even before Wilson returned to the negotiations at Versailles in late March, Colonel House had agreed to give France permanent control of the German Rhineland and to separate the League from the treaty itself.

BOX 3.2

Woodrow Wilson's Fourteen Points

I. Open covenants of peace, openly arrived at, after which there shall be no private international understandings of any kind but diplomacy shall proceed always frankly and in the public view.

II. Absolute freedom of navigation upon the seas, outside territorial waters, alike in peace and in war, except as the seas may be closed in whole or in part by international action for the enforcement of international covenants.

III. The removal, so far as possible, of all economic barriers and the establishment of an equality of trade conditions among all the nations consenting to the peace and associating themselves for its maintenance.

IV. Adequate guarantees given and taken that national armaments will be reduced to the lowest point consistent with domestic safety.

V. A free, open-minded, and absolutely impartial adjustment of all colonial claims, based upon a strict observance of the principle that in determining all such questions of sovereignty the interests of the populations concerned must have equal weight with the equitable claims of the government whose title is to be determined.

VI. The evacuation of all Russian territory and such a settlement of all questions affecting Russia as will secure the best and freest cooperation of the other nations of the world in obtaining for her an unhampered and unembarrassed opportunity for the independent determination of her own political development and national policy and assure her of a sincere welcome into the society of free nations under institutions of her own choosing; and, more than a welcome, assistance also of every kind that she may need and may herself desire. The treatment accorded Russia by her sister nations in the months to come will be the acid test of their good will, of their comprehension of her needs as distinguished from their own interests, and of their intelligent and unselfish sympathy.

VII. Belgium, the whole world will agree, must be evacuated and restored, without any attempt to limit the sovereignty which she enjoys in common with all other free nations. No other single act will serve as this will serve to restore

All in all, Wilson found it difficult just to keep faith with his own principles, especially the provision that there would be no annexation or indemnities.

The Senate Committee on Foreign Relations began its hearings on the Treaty of Versailles on July 2, 1919. In September President Wilson began a train tour of the western and midwestern states in order to build public sup-

confidence among the nations in the laws which they have themselves set and determined for the government of their relations with one another. Without this healing act the whole structure and validity of international law is forever impaired.

VIII. All French territory should be freed and the invaded portions restored, and the wrong done to France by Prussia in 1871 in the matter of Alsace-Lorraine, which has unsettled the peace of the world for nearly fifty years, should be righted, in order that peace may once more be made secure in the interest of all.

IX. A readjustment of the frontiers of Italy should be effected along clearly recognizable lines of nationality.

X. The peoples of Austria-Hungary, whose place among the nations we wish to see safeguarded and assured, should be accorded the freest opportunity to autonomous development.

XI. Rumania, Serbia, and Montenegro should be evacuated; occupied territories restored; Serbia accorded free and secure access to the sea; and the relations of the several Balkan states to one another determined by friendly counsel along historically established lines of allegiance and nationality; and international guarantees of the political and economic independence and territorial integrity of the several Balkan states should be entered into.

XII. The Turkish portion of the present Ottoman Empire should be assured a secure sovereignty, but the other nationalities which are now under Turkish rule should be assured an undoubted security of life and an absolutely unmolested opportunity of autonomous development, and the Dardanelles should be permanently opened as a free passage to the ships and commerce of all nations under international guarantees.

XIII. An independent Polish state should be erected which should include the territories inhabited by indisputably Polish populations, which should be assured a free and secure access to the sea, and whose political and economic independence and territorial integrity should be guaranteed by international covenant.

XIV. A general association of nations must be formed under specific covenants for the purpose of affording mutual guarantees of political independence and territorial integrity to great and small states alike.

Source: www.yale.edu/lawweb/avalon/wilson14.htm

port for the treaty. But on September 26 he became ill in Pueblo, Colorado, and was forced to return to Washington, where he suffered a massive stroke on October 2, which left him incapacitated. On November 19 the Senate defeated the Treaty of Versailles by a vote of 55 in favor, 39 opposed. On March 8, 1920, another vote failed, this time by 49–35—seven votes short of a two-thirds majority.[21]

Dimensions of Foreign Policy.   Although there were many different elements in Wilson's plans for peace, his Fourteen Points qualify him as a
MCA foreign policy maker—that is, his postwar policies were multilateral,
noncoercive, and proactive, as Table 3.5 shows.

Intervention Postponed: 1921–1932

During World War I—the height of the Progressive era—the national government had been strengthened to the point that it was able to procure
one-fourth of the national output and mold the economy to meet war
needs. It was not surprising, then, that at the end of the war many Americans felt the government was playing too large a role in society. In order
to counter this feeling, liberals and socialists implored Wilson to undertake the domestic reforms—such as recognizing collective bargaining, establishing a national minimum wage, and setting up a program of health
insurance—that were the counterpart of his progressive internationalism,
but he did not do so. As a consequence, Americans became disillusioned
with the war effort especially once the country failed to join the League of
Nations. And so although the United States came out of World War I in
better shape than any other major power, Americans did not have a positive view of the country's World War I experience. The result was that the
United States spent the next twenty years abdicating any responsibility as
one of the world's Great Powers.

Private Initiatives: In 1920 Republican Warren G. Harding was elected
president after an election campaign dominated in part by the question of

Table 3.5. Dimensions of Foreign Policy: Wilson's Post–war Collective Security Policy

	Multilateral		Unilateral	
	Coercive	Noncoercive	Noncoercive	Coercive
Proactive		Foreign policy of Wilson		
Reactive				

Woodrow Wilson's Fourteen Points peace plan qualifies him as a MCA-type foreign policy
maker—that is, his policy evolved to a multilateral, noncoercive, and proactive policy. But his personal style of diplomacy was very unilateral in that he seemed to prefer to dictate the multilateral
principles that others should follow. Though Wilson had shown willingness to use force in the past,
his foreign policy evolved into a noncoercive stance, based on his assumption that public opinion,
coupled with disarmament, conciliation, and other noncoercive measures, would forestall future
conflicts under the League of Nations before any enforcement measures would have to be taken.
Wilson's personal proactive pursuit of this policy, both in attending the peace conference abroad
and undertaking the long cross-country train tour in the United States, ruined his health.

U.S. participation in the League of Nations. One of the most important figures in the new Harding administration was Herbert C. Hoover, his secretary of commerce. Hoover had developed an enviable national reputation both as an engineer and as head of American postwar relief efforts overseas. He joined the Harding administration with the understanding that he would play an important role in foreign affairs, and he continued that role in the Calvin Coolidge administration before he himself became president in 1929.

Hoover had definite ideas about what the U.S. role in international affairs should be. Although he was an **internationalist**, that is someone who believes that one's country should play an active role in international affairs, and had supported the League of Nations in 1919, Hoover wanted to reduce the role of the government in international affairs—a reactive position—and to enhance the role of private enterprise by removing foreign affairs from government politicians influenced by an emotional public and placing them with experts who could settle them according to established principles of business. For example, Hoover believed that competition forced business leaders to make rational decisions, so he often urged them to join together in trade associations in order to develop and share vital information about the cost of production and distribution and about available markets. Thus in the 1920s American banks and corporations expanded their overseas activities with the encouragement of the government. Hoover discovered, however, that private corporations usually made investments for short-term gains and not for the purpose of building infrastructure or long-range relationships. As a result, the investments abroad did not make lasting improvements to foreign economies, especially those of the new nations in Eastern Europe.

Hoover miscalculated with domestic economic policy as well as international policy. Domestically, the government could not control private investment. Although the Great Depression did not arrive until 1929, elements of society and regions of the country were already in financial distress as early as 1920. One of the first troubling indications was the collapse of American agricultural prices in 1920: the average price of a bushel of wheat fell from $2.16 in 1919 to $1.03 in 1921. The drop in grain prices affected the overall economy and precipitated the Great Depression.

Internationally, Hoover was convinced that Germany and other European debtors could still continue to pay their obligations to the United States despite high U.S. tariffs. Hoover believed that the United States could essentially subsidize foreign purchases of American products by lending and investing private capital abroad. But American investors gradually reduced their activities abroad—in part because of the attractiveness of the domestic market in the late 1920s. Then when the American stock market collapsed in 1929, they stopped lending and investing overseas altogether. Although Hoover, as president, eventually declared a moratorium on German reparations and other foreign debts owed to the United States, his actions came too late to save the European economies, especially those of the new Eastern European nations. A worldwide depression ensued in the early 1930s, which weakened America and its erstwhile allies at the same time that both Stalin's Russia and Hitler's Germany were becoming more powerful.

Dimensions of Hoover's Foreign Policy.   Hoover believed that moral persuasion, not physical force, was the real instrument for peace; he generally opposed the coercive aspects of government. Perhaps the crowning achievement of the Hoover period was his noncoercive policy of nonintervention in Latin America; he abrogated Theodore Roosevelt's corollary to the Monroe Doctrine. Hoover also believed that the government had an important role in disarmament and conciliation. He and his colleagues were especially pleased when the Washington Disarmament Conference negotiated a battleship ratio of 10:10:6 for the U.S., British, and Japanese navies, respectively.

Hoover wanted to regulate international behavior by establishing multilateral principles. For example, he was very supportive of declaratory policies such as the Kellogg-Briand Pact, which pledged governments to reject war as an instrument of foreign policy. He also supported the Stimson Doctrine in which the United States refused to recognize Japan's takeover of Manchuria in the hope that other countries might follow suit.

Although Hoover is known for his international relief work, international conciliation, and cooperative action, he was seldom prepared to bind countries to follow the prescribed course of action. He supported high protective tariffs. He wanted to leave countries free to determine for themselves whether or not they would accept their international obligations. Overall, Hoover pursued a foreign policy that was multilateral, noncoercive, and reactive or MCA as shown in Table 3.6.

Intervention Delayed: 1933–1941

Although Franklin D. Roosevelt preferred a foreign policy very different from Hoover's, he did not at first push his international agenda, giving priority to his domestic efforts to deal with the Great Depression. Even when the rise of fascism and militarism abroad threatened international stability Roosevelt was constrained by domestic political considerations from pursuing his preferred proactive foreign policy. The problem was that he, like Wilson, lacked the two-thirds vote required to pass important treaties in the Senate. Thus although a majority of the American public appeared to support proactive foreign policies, it rejected the multilateral commitments required by most treaties. Roosevelt might have challenged the public on this multilateral–unilateral dimension, but he preferred to hold back so as not to jeopardize his domestic programs.

Table 3.6. Dimensions of Foreign Policy: Herbert Hoover and Franklin D. Roosevelt

| | Multilateral | | Unilateral | |
	Coercive	Noncoercive	Noncoercive	Coercive
Proactive	Foreign policy of Franklin D. Roosevelt			
Reactive		Foreign policy of Herbert Hoover		

Despite Herbert Hoover's success at getting many of his foreign policies adopted, especially in the years before he became president, he could not prevent the United States and the world from sliding into the Great Depression. Hoover is best understood as pursuing an MCA foreign policy. The policy was multilateral because Hoover placed so much emphasis on moral principle, noncoercive because it rejected force as an instrument of national foreign policy, and reactive because he endorsed reactive policies whether it was the protectionist tariff, the reduced role of government, or his insistence on voluntary action. The fact that his successor, Franklin D. Roosevelt, pursued a multilateral, coercive, and proactive, or MCA, foreign policy in the same period is one of the great reversals of American history.

The Period of Neutrality: Although American foreign policy during 1933–1941 is often labeled isolationist, in fact, no politician or national political party ever advanced the idea that the United States should isolate itself from the rest of the world. Rather, the term isolationism refers to a set of beliefs that can be identified along all three of the foreign policy dimensions used here— multilateral–unilateral, proactive–reactive, and coercive–noncoercive. According to the historian Wayne Cole, the set of beliefs labeled as isolationism "was a caricature of the policies the United States actually had pursued, and that caricature, that distortion, was designed to make those earlier policies appear worse than they actually were so that it might be easier to turn the United States in new directions in world affairs."[22]

In the 1930s the Republicans in Congress sought to avoid making any permanent commitment to other nations—in keeping with George Washington's advice to avoid entanglements—and such a policy is best understood as unilateral. In accordance with the unilateralist leanings of the Congressional Republicans, the United States not only refused to participate in the League of Nations but also stayed out of the Permanent Court of International Justice. Roosevelt, however, was a multilateralist, and he gradually turned the country in that direction.

Because unilateralism was the most important element of this isolationist sentiment, Roosevelt tried to use the Monroe Doctrine—the centerpiece of unilateralism in American foreign policy—as the foundation for building a more multilateral policy. In 1936 Roosevelt attended the Inter-American Conference for the Maintenance of Peace at Buenos Aires, where he argued that all countries of the Western Hemisphere should join together to maintain the peace and security of the region, turning the Monroe Doctrine from a unilateral U.S. policy into a multilateral regional one. Like Wilson before him, he hoped that multilateralism in the Western Hemisphere might be extended worldwide at a later point.

Another component of isolationism was its reactive strain. In the 1930s the country's economic circumstances were so dire that many Americans felt that domestic affairs had to be given priority. This was particularly true of rural America. Although agricultural interests realized that they were dependent on overseas markets, they were very suspicious of the efforts of urban interests to involve the country in projects in which they did not perceive an immediate personal stake. For example, they opposed a naval buildup because they did not want to subsidize the northeastern manufacturers who made and fitted the ships or to have these ships sent overseas in order to defend the interests of northeastern financiers.

Finally, a closely related aspect of isolationism was its security concerns. In 1931 the Japanese had occupied most of Manchuria. The United States had tried to block Japan through the Stimson Doctrine's refusal to recognize the legitimacy of Japan's takeover, but that had not been effective. Hitler's rearmament policy in Germany was equally alarming to the isolationists, and though they did not want to use force abroad, they were prepared to use coercive measures in defense of the homeland. Although Roosevelt signed the Neutrality Acts passed by Congress in the mid-1930s, he was willing to use coercive measures abroad as well as in defense of the homeland. His objectives were very different from those who wanted the legislation to keep the United States out of war in Europe or the Far East, however; in that Roosevelt wanted legislation that gave him the discretion necessary to pursue whatever policy he thought was in the national interest at the time.

By 1936 international tensions, and thus the prospects for war, had increased significantly. Throughout the late 1930s Roosevelt began to prepare the public for intervention, but a large segment of Americans continued to oppose a foreign war—that is, they favored military defense but opposed sending American forces overseas.

World War II in Europe began in 1939 when Germany attacked Poland. The United States was divided into two groups: those favoring and those opposing intervention. Yet as during World War I, it became increasingly difficult for the United States to maintain a position of neutrality. The isolationists thought that the steps Roosevelt described as "aid short of war" were actually just "short steps to war." When Roosevelt announced the destroyers-for-bases, or Lend-Lease, deal between the United States and Great Britain on September 3, 1940, many isolationists joined the newly created America First Committee, which set forth the following principles favoring defense at home but opposing any deviation from strict neutrality:

1. The United State must build an impregnable defense for America.

2. No foreign power, nor group of powers, can successfully attack a prepared America.

3. American democracy can be preserved only by keeping out of the European War.

4. "Aid short of War" weakens national defense at home and threatens to involve America in war abroad.[23]

The America First Committee and two opposition committees—the Committee to Defend America by Aiding the Allies and the Fight for Freedom Committee— battled between September 1940 and December 1941. But when the Japanese attacked Pearl Harbor on December 7, 1941, the America First Committee lost the argument at once, as the majority of the country now supported going to war with Japan.

Dimensions of Isolationist Foreign Policy.   Although they never had majority support outside of Congress, the isolationists of the 1930s made an indelible impression on the history of American foreign policy because of the way in which Roosevelt discredited them. Their <u>MCA</u> policies were unilateral because they disapproved of collective actions, coercive because they were prepared to use force to defend the United States, and reactive because they were prepared to restrict American commerce abroad in order to avoid getting involved in a European war. Under Franklin Roosevelt, however, American foreign policy, particularly at the close of the period, was clearly MCA: multilateral, coercive, and proactive, as shown in Table 3.7.

Conclusion

It seems unreasonable to characterize this period of American foreign policy after the Civil War and before the Second World War as isolationist when a clear majority of the population favored a proactive foreign policy. Yet for one reason or another, the United States vacillated not so much about whether to become actively involved, but rather about who would take the lead and what role the United States would play in the imminent conflict.

After the Civil War, the U.S. government intervened actively to incorporate Indian territories in the Great Plains, but with a few exceptions it could not reach agreement on acquiring territories outside the United States. Postbellum presidents proposed treaties of acquisition, but with the exception of Alaska and the Midway Islands, the Senate refused to accept these presidential initiatives. By the 1890s that issue of how active the

Table 3.7. Dimensions of Foreign Policy: Prewar Policies of Franklin D. Roosevelt and the America First Committee

| | Multilateral | | Unilateral | |
	Coercive	Noncoercive	Noncoercive	Coercive
Proactive	Foreign policy of Franklin D. Rooselvet			
Reactive				Foreign policy of the America First Committee

Although they never had the support of a majority of the American public, the isolationists of the 1930s made an indelible impression on the history of American foreign policy because of the way in which Roosevelt discredited them. Their MCA policies were unilateral because they disapproved of collective actions, coercive because they were prepared to defend the United States, and reactive because they were prepared to suffer economic constraints rather than become involved in a world war. Under Franklin D. Roosevelt American foreign policy, however, particularly at the close of the period, was clearly MCA: multilateral, coercive, and proactive.

president should be in foreign affairs had largely been resolved in favor of the president, and the United States did incorporate a number of new territories in the Pacific and the Caribbean into the United States in 1898. But even when it did so, the country was still deeply divided over the constitutionality of incorporating non-self-governing territories into the Union.

The outbreak of World War II in Europe presented a third set of problems. Once again, a majority seemed to believe that the United States had a stake in these conflicts, but they could not agree on the terms of engagement. Of those Americans supporting military intervention, some wanted to assist France and the other Western Allies; others to overcome the threat to their independence posed by militaristic and dictatorial states; and others, especially in World War I, wanted to stay out of the war in Europe but play a more decisive role in establishing a new system of collective security that could prevent similar outbreaks in the future. Of course, there were others, especially before World War II, who wanted to remain neutral that developing this country's own national defense. Only the last group was really isolationist. The Japanese attack on Pearl Harbor decisively overrode these divisions by demonstrating the need for immediate intervention.

Key Concepts

Americanization 96	expansionism 98
arbitration 102	frontier anxiety 96
conciliation 102	frontier thesis 96
dollar diplomacy 101	Great Powers 84

industrialization   84
internationalist   109
isolationist   83
liberalism   84
nationalism   84
neutrality   101

Open Door policy   100
self-determination   104
size effect   98
spheres of influence   100
spread effect   92
tripolar system   90

Suggested Readings

1. Friedberg, Aaron L. *The Weary Titan: Britain and the Experience of Relative Decline, 1895–1905*. Princeton: Princeton University Press, 1988.

2. Cole, Wayne S. *Roosevelt and the Isolationists: 1932–1945*. Lincoln: University of Nebraska Press, 1983.

3. Dog, Mary Crow. *Lakota Woman*. New York: Harper Perennial, 1991.

4. Knock, Thomas J. *To End All Wars: Woodrow Wilson and the Quest for a New World Order*. New York: Oxford University Press, 1992.

5. Schweller, Randall L. *Deadly Imbalances: Tripolarity and Hitler's Strategy of World Conquest*. New York: Columbia University Press, 1998.

6. Zakaria, Fareed. *From Wealth to Power: The Unusual Origins of America's World Role*. Princeton: Princeton University Press, 1998.

CHAPTER 4

The Hegemonic Period: 1942–Present

WITH LEE ANN PINGEL

From 1942 to the present, the primary issue for the people of the United States was security. And, from the end of World War II until the collapse of the Soviet empire, the dominant security issue was the cold war between the United States and the Soviet Union. That era abruptly ended on November 9, 1989, with the fall of the Berlin Wall. In this picture, a demonstrator pounds away at the wall while East Berlin border guards look on from above the Brandenburg Gate. Once the Soviet Union had collapsed, the primary security issue became nuclear weapons. But the September 11, 2001 attacks on the twin towers of the World Trade Center in New York and the Pentagon in Washington, D.C. with jet airplanes hijacked by al Qaeda operatives redefined the security issue as terrorism.

W HEN THE UNITED STATES entered World War II in December 1941, American foreign policy entered a new era that would last at least sixty years. The United States was the dominant state throughout this period, best defined by the foreign policy dimension of security. U.S. security was initially challenged by revisionist states—first Germany and Japan and then the Soviet Union. By the time that the threat from the Soviet Union finally dissipated in 1991, the United States confronted a series of threats that affected states throughout the world: the proliferation of nuclear weapons, world poverty and disease, global environmental damage, and destabilizing wars of liberation. Although some of these threats arose from rogue states, the greatest danger seemed to arise from nonstate sources—international terrorist groups.

Virtually all of these challenges can be traced to the Second World War because the strategies developed by the United States and its allies during the course of that war determined the leadership role that the United States would subsequently play on the world scene. Thus in order to understand how these issues developed and why the United States took the positions which it did toward them, it is important to know how the United States fought the Second World War.

Defeating Germany and Japan, 1942–1945

The Second World War resulted in the destruction of the industrial centers of Europe and East Asia, the conquest of many colonies in non-industrialized areas, the breakdown of international institutions, and the emergence of new technologies for war. These events, which defined the most important postwar issues, such as the need to rebuild Europe, the demand by the former colonies for independence, the call for a new peace organization, and the search for ways to control nuclear weapons, were determined as much, or more, by the decisions of generals than they were by the choices of diplomats. So in order to understand American foreign policy after the war, it is necessary to know how the war was won.

How the War Was Won

To understand issues that arose from the aftermath and conduct of the war, one needs to go back to its beginning. The Axis powers, especially Germany and Japan, attacked quickly and changed the character of warfare, and thus the international system.

The Axis Advance.   After overrunning Poland in September 1939 in a lightning operation known as "blitzkrieg," Germany moved on to overcome France and the Low Countries of Belgium, Luxembourg, and the Netherlands. The British were able to evacuate most of their army from France at Dunkirk in a May 1940 naval operation and save their air power to defend their homeland from the attempted German air invasion.[1] The

Battle of Britain commenced in July 1940, but when Adolf Hitler realized that it would be more difficult than expected to defeat the island nation, he told his generals to prepare for the invasion of the Soviet Union. Before Hitler could carry out his attack against the Soviet Union, however, Benito Mussolini, his Italian ally, attacked British forces in Egypt in September 1940 and a British ally, Greece, in October. Hitler had not approved these actions in advance and was furious that Mussolini's tactics had delayed his plan to invade the Soviet Union—in both instances, Hitler had to send in German forces to prevent the defeat of the Italians and had to delay the invasion of the Soviet Union until the summer of 1941.

Although Soviet leader Joseph Stalin expected that his country would eventually have to go to war with Germany, despite the existence of the secret Nazi-Soviet Pact of 1939, he was surprised when the Germans attacked in June 1941, and the Red Army was ill-prepared for war. Based on the initial success of the German surprise attack, Hitler expected to occupy the Soviet capital of Moscow within three months. However, tactical errors, such as commencing the invasion too late in the year, left him short of his goal. In the meantime, Germany's other ally, Japan, also upset Hitler's plans by launching the surprise attack on the U.S. naval base at Pearl Harbor on December 7, 1941. This brought the powerful United States into the war against Germany before Hitler had properly defeated the Soviet Union.

Yet despite these setbacks, by the middle of 1942 Germany controlled a swath of Europe stretching from the outskirts of Moscow and Stalingrad in the east to the Pyrenees in the west, as Map 4.1 shows. In Asia, by the end of 1942 Japan occupied much of East and Southeast Asia and the Pacific Islands, as Map 4.2 shows. Meanwhile, the United States prepared to go to war by putting its economy on a war footing and fully mobilizing its military capabilities.

The Allies' Victorious Response.   Although Stalin appreciated the supplies that the Americans provided his forces, he desperately needed the United States and Britain to open a western front in order to divide German forces. However, President Franklin D. Roosevelt and British prime minister Winston Churchill chose to delay the invasion of France until they had more landing craft and instead invaded French North Africa in November 1942. The Allies followed their success in North Africa with the invasion of Sicily in July 1943. At this point Mussolini called a meeting of his rubber-stamp parliament, which, to his surprise, promptly deposed him. The new government, headed by Marshal Pietro Badoglio, sued the Allies for peace. Alarmed that Italy would go over to the Allies, Hitler intervened, rescued Mussolini, and installed him as head of a puppet regime in Northern Italy. The German forces successfully delayed the U.S.-British plans to capture Italy for almost two years.[2]

In the meantime, Stalin became increasingly frustrated by the failure of the United States and Britain to invade France and open a western front. In 1943 Churchill and Roosevelt considered other intermediate actions such as a modest invasion of the Balkans or southern France before undertaking the main invasion. A date for the invasion of Normandy was finally set at the Tehran Conference held in late 1943.

In June 1944 the long-awaited invasion of Normandy occurred. Once Allied forces had established a western front in France, Stalin began his final offensive against Germany in the east in August 1944. Finally, Germany was caught in an Allied vise. At first it looked as though the Allied victory would come before the end of the year. But a German counterattack, the Battle of the Bulge, delayed the British and American advance in the west until the spring of 1945. When some Allied forces were ready to make the final push toward Berlin, Gen. Dwight D. Eisenhower, the supreme Allied commander, decided to hold up their advance until the Soviets had taken Berlin and could occupy their assigned sector of East Germany.

Although America was giving priority to the war in Europe, it also began a methodical two-pronged invasion of Japanese-held areas in the Pacific. One effort focused on recapturing the Philippines; the other focused on an island-hopping strategy in the Central Pacific. The first American victory in the Pacific was in the Battle of Midway in June 1942 (see Map 4.2.) By the time the war in Europe ended in May 1945, the United States had retaken the Philippines and most of the island nations occupied by the Japanese. Despite the extensive U.S. bombing of Japanese cities, in the summer of 1945, the United States assumed it would need six months or more to transfer U.S. forces from Europe to the Pacific for a final invasion of Japan. President Harry S. Truman's decision to resort to atomic warfare against the Japanese cities of Hiroshima and Nagasaki in August 1945, however, brought the war in the Pacific to an earlier than anticipated end.

How the War Defined Post–war Issues

Throughout the war, Churchill, Roosevelt, and Stalin, the representatives of the three major Allied powers, met to discuss military strategy and address the peace to follow. These meetings of the Big Three—held in Moscow and Tehran in 1943 and Yalta and Potsdam in 1945—were important because they defined the issues that the United States in particular would have to deal with once the war ended: (1) rebuilding Germany and Japan; (2) working out new relationships with its wartime allies, mainly the Soviet Union; (3) meeting the demands of colonial states for political independence; (4) addressing the rising demands of these same states for economic development; (5) establishing a new international organization for peace; and (6) controlling the new weapons of mass destruction.[3]

Map 4.1. Nazi Germany and German-controlled Territories, 1942
By late 1942 Germany, with the help of Italy and Vichy France, controlled much of Europe and North Africa. Portugal, Spain, Sweden, Switzerland, and the Vatican were self-interested noncombatants. Turkey did not declare war on Germany and Japan until February 23, 1945.

Planning the Future of Europe and East Asia. As the Allies began to free various countries from German occupation during the latter years of the war, they had to decide how to deal with their enemies in the post–war period. The United States and Britain actually set the precedent in Europe that one had to participate in the liberation of a country in order to share in its administration when they rejected Stalin's bid at a foreign ministers'

Map 4.2. Axis Japan and Japanese-controlled Territories, 1942
By late 1942 Japanese forces controlled Korea, the eastern portion of China (including Manchuria), Southeast Asia, the western Pacific Islands (including the western Aleutian Islands), and threatened India.

meeting in Moscow in October 1943 to participate in the occupation of Italy. Stalin was no less determined to control the governments of those countries freed exclusively by Soviet forces. In Tehran in December 1943, Churchill and Roosevelt tentatively agreed to allow the Soviets to take the lead in establishing new governments in Eastern Europe. At the Yalta Conference, Roosevelt and Churchill accepted Soviet prominence in

Poland and the other Eastern European countries being liberated by the Red Army, but thought they had provided for broad participation by all interested parties in free elections. Vague drafting of the agreements, however, allowed Stalin to bypass the requirement for free elections and establish his own regimes in many of these countries. Roosevelt even considered the need for Allied occupation of Vichy France, but in July 1944 he reluctantly accepted General Charles de Gaulle's provisional government-in-exile, the French Committee of National Liberation, as the official government of France.[4]

All of the Allied leaders initially took a harsh stance toward Germany itself. Indeed, Roosevelt had refused to accept the distinction between the reprehensible regime in Germany and the German people as a whole. In practice, then, Roosevelt called for the destruction of all vestiges of the Nazi government in Germany before establishing a new government. His statement also implied that some form of Allied supervision would be required to make this new system of government work.

The question of how post–war Germany would be governed and administered related to the question of how well the Allies would continue to collaborate with each other. Because the United States and Britain had been allies since the beginning of the century and because Churchill and Roosevelt had signed the Atlantic Charter that defined Allied war aims without consulting Stalin, he was very suspicious of the two Western leaders. The Soviet Union had also been exceedingly frustrated by Western delays in opening a second front in France. Over the course of the war in Europe, Western suspicions of Stalin also grew when it became apparent that he planned to maintain significant forces in the countries "liberated" by the Red Army.

In the Pacific, the United States worried that the Soviets would not assist in the invasion of Japan because the Soviet Union had signed a non-aggression pact with Japan before the war. However, after the United States used the atomic bomb, Soviet help did not prove necessary, and the United States alone occupied Japan.

Meanwhile, the more immediate question was how to rebuild Europe and Asia. By the end of the war most of the industrial areas of Europe and Asia, especially those in Germany and Japan, had been destroyed. At first Roosevelt and Churchill agreed with Stalin that Germany would have to pay reparations for its aggression, but by the Yalta Conference in July 1945 the Anglo-American position on reparations had changed. Now the challenge was how to rebuild the industrial economies of Europe. Although the Soviets proceeded to move whole factories from Germany and its associated states back to the Soviet Union to replace factories that had been destroyed by the Germans, the United States and Britain were beginning to realize that the skills and resources of the German people would be needed to help the rest of Europe recover. The same issue arose in Asia and the Pacific, but there it was less controversial because the United States alone was in control of Japan.

Dealing with the Colonial Areas.   The rapid collapse of British, French, and other colonial areas to the advance of Axis armies in Africa and especially in Asia and the Pacific had inspired independence movements in the colonies. Roosevelt had recognized even before America's entry into the war that one of the main problems in the post–war period would be how to meet the rising expectations of the colonies for political independence and prosperity. Indeed, he had insisted that the right of self-government be one of the general principles of the 1941 Atlantic Charter between the United States and Britain.

Roosevelt pressed Churchill about the colonial question throughout the war, but Britain, France, and other European countries wanted to retain their special interests and responsibilities in Africa, Asia, and the Middle East. The Western colonial powers felt that they needed the human and material resources of these areas to help them recover economically. They also recognized that these countries, once independent, would want to develop themselves economically. Because of their disagreements, the Allies took little action on these issues at the time.

Maintaining the Peace.   The Allies were also very aware that they had to address the question of how to maintain the peace after the war. Roosevelt was the first to use the term "United Nations" to describe the countries fighting the Axis powers. The first official use of the term emerged on January 1, 1942, when 26 countries, including the United States and Britain, signed the Declaration by the United Nations. The signatories pledged to support the Allied effort and not to make peace separately with the enemy. Roosevelt formally proposed the establishment of the United Nations at the Tehran Conference in 1943. The broad structure of the present United Nations organization—comprising both a Security Council and a General Assembly —was approved in 1944 by the foreign ministers of China, Britain, the United States, and the Soviet Union at a conference at Dumbarton Oaks in Washington, D.C. Roosevelt envisaged a Security Council in which the four permanent member countries—China was included to balance the Soviet Union in East Asia—would be primarily responsible for preserving the peace after the war. When Roosevelt first proposed the plan for the United Nations publicly, he referred to these four powers as the "Four Policemen." Roosevelt had proposed that each Security Council member have veto power in the Security Council; Stalin agreed, but he wanted the veto to cover procedural as well as substantive matters. It was only at the Yalta Conference in February 1945 that Stalin agreed to limit the veto power to substantive issues.[5]

Although Roosevelt died two months later while vacationing in Warm Springs, Georgia, the delegates of 50 countries met in San Francisco from

April to June 1945 to draft a charter establishing the United Nations organization. The UN Charter generally retained the basic character of the Dumbarton Oaks agreements, but there were some changes. For example, human rights became part of the charter, the Economic and Social Council was given a wider role, a draft statute of the International Court of Justice was included, and the Trusteeship Council was made one of the six principal organizations of the United Nations.

While the San Francisco conference was taking place, Roosevelt's challenges became the responsibility of his vice president, Harry Truman. Unfortunately, Truman had not been part of Roosevelt's foreign policy decision-making circle. Although many in government rallied around the new president, he was inexperienced in foreign affairs and so required some time to prepare at the same time that many important decisions and actions had to be taken.

In July the Allied leaders met in Potsdam, Germany, for the last of their big war conferences. While there, Truman learned that a successful test of an atomic weapon had been conducted in the United States. Although the Truman administration was now confident that it could end the war in Japan without Soviet help, it realized that it could not actually exclude Soviet participation. Truman ordered the use of atomic bombs against Japan in early August. By the end of August American forces were landing in Japan, but Allied leaders were now facing yet another challenge posed by the war—how to control new weapons of mass destruction. (The control of nuclear weapons will be discussed more extensively in the next section.) Table 4.1 shows the contrast between Roosevelt's and Truman's foreign policies.

Restoring Industrial Centers: 1946–1952

Once the war was over President Truman had to turn his attention to domestic affairs. Having survived first the Great Depression and then a world war, the American people expected the president to bring home the troops and to shift the domestic economy to a peacetime footing. At the end of World War II the United States and the Soviet Union had roughly twelve million men in uniform. By the end of 1947 the United States had reduced its forces to 1.4 million, the Soviet Union to 4 million. Truman delegated most of the responsibility for dealing with specific international issues to experts in whom he had confidence—that is, generals such as Gen. Douglas MacArthur in Japan, Gen. Lucius Clay in Germany, Gen. John Hodge in Korea, and Gen. George Marshall in China.[6]

The primary problem at the end of the war was how to fill the enormous vacuum created by the demise of Germany in Europe and Japan in Asia. Yet as the United States and the Soviet Union rushed to fill this vacuum, neither could dismiss entirely its suspicions of the other. Hesitancy on the part of either Great Power could leave it in an inferior position, and so each moved ahead. Truman's dilemma was how to confine

Table 4.1. Dimensions of Foreign Policy: Final Years of the War

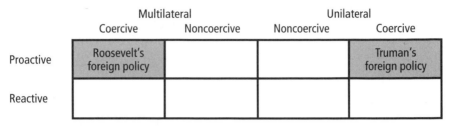

	Multilateral		Unilateral	
	Coercive	Noncoercive	Noncoercive	Coercive
Proactive	Roosevelt's foreign policy			Truman's foreign policy
Reactive				

Roosevelt's foreign policy during the war years was MCA. It was multilateral because despite his suspicions of Soviet intentions, Roosevelt realized that real progress on so many of the issues being discussed depended on Stalin's cooperation, coercive because he realized that military power was going to be an essential instrument in the post–war period, and proactive because he recognized that the United States would have to play a leading role in post–war reconstruction.

Truman's foreign policy at the end of the war was _M_CA. It was _more_ unilateral than Roosevelt's policy because Truman lacked Roosevelt's experience and confidence in working with Churchill and Stalin throughout the war, coercive because Truman felt that sole possession of atomic weapons gave the United States a decisive advantage in post–war planning, and proactive because he, like his predecessor, felt that the United States had worldwide responsibilities.

Soviet ambitions in Eastern Europe while also maintaining a cooperative relationship with the Soviets. That task was complicated by the fact that by 1949 the Soviet Union had 175 divisions in Europe compared with just 14 divisions for the Western allies. But the Truman administration was willing to challenge the Soviet Union both because it believed that the overall economic capacity of the United States was so much greater than that of the Soviet Union and because it alone had atomic weapons. Together, these two factors allowed the Truman administration to assert American interests whenever it came into conflict with Soviet actions, although it continued to acknowledge the need for Allied unity (multilateralism).

Because the United States was fully engaged in both the European and the Pacific wars, it devised a global strategy for dealing with the post–war situation. But it did not expect to defend every corner of the globe. Rather, it believed it could maintain various strong points from which its strategic air force could deliver unacceptable damage to the enemy.[7] Soon after the war defense officials had identified hundreds of potential bases and airfields around the world that the United States could use in bringing its strategic forces to bear on various problem regions. Although George Kennan believed there "were only five centers of industrial and military power . . . important to us"—the United States, Great Britain, Germany and Central Europe, the Soviet Union, and Japan—it was important to be alert to dangers in other areas, such as the Middle East.[8]

Because the Big Three had already drawn the lines between East and West in Europe and because the United States was the sole occupying power in Japan, it was in southeastern Europe and the Middle East that the United States first responded to Soviet maneuvers. Britain and the Soviet Union had each stationed military forces in Iran during the war with the understanding that they would withdraw them six months after the end of the war. When it appeared that the Soviets might not withdraw their troops on schedule, the United States and Britain threatened to take action. At about the same time, the Soviets began to demand special rights of passage through Turkey. The United States responded by sending a naval task force into the eastern Mediterranean. Then in the summer of 1946 the Greek communists renewed their war against a Greek republican government supported by Britain. In Greece, as in Turkey and other key locations in the Middle East, the United States expected Britain to provide military assistance if America supplied economic assistance. The United States thought that once its Western allies had fully recovered from the recent war, they would be able to police some of these regions, much as the United States had policed the Western Hemisphere in the early twentieth century.

The United States recognized, however, that it might ultimately have to intervene in some of these areas with its strategic weapons. For that reason it was very guarded when the issue of submitting atomic weapons to international control arose. Strong public support for international control forced Truman to appoint the Acheson-Lilienthal Committee to investigate the issue.[9] Nevertheless, the American military was counting on the recently developed atomic weapons for the nation's defense, and Truman himself was not willing to share industrial applications of the new technology until adequate safeguards were established. With these concerns in mind, Truman appointed senior statesman Bernard Baruch to negotiate an appropriate atomic weapons agreement with the Soviet Union. Baruch cleverly revised the plan so that it would win the support of the American public and at the same time invite Soviet opposition. This move was calculated to make the United States look like a responsible, upstanding party while it actually avoided submitting its nuclear technology to international control and abiding by the rules it had itself proposed.[10]

By the winter of 1946 the leaders on both sides felt the need to interpret recent international events in terms of a long-range strategy. In his address to the Communist Party in February, Stalin reaffirmed Lenin's thesis that war among capitalist countries and between capitalist and communist countries was inevitable. Two weeks later Churchill delivered his "iron curtain" speech in Fulton, Missouri, one of the first uses of the phrase.[11] At about the same time George Kennan, counselor to the American embassy in the Soviet Union, sent his long telegram from Moscow to Washington in which he defined the essential aspects of what was to become the U.S. policy of containment. Kennan argued that Soviet power must be contained at critical strongpoints, because it was relentlessly propelled by a unique combination of absolute power and communist ideology.

Events in Europe in the Immediate Post–war Period

Despite the hostile rhetoric, Soviet and American actions were not as polarized during the immediate post–war period as they would be later. The Soviet Union allowed noncommunist parties to play a role in the governments of Eastern Europe, just as the Western powers allowed communist parties to participate in the politics of Western states. As long as the actions of each side were confined to the areas of influence defined by the wartime agreements, foreign policy actors believed that there would be little danger of an intentional war.

It was at this point that the British government, severely pressed by economic problems, informed the American government that it did not have the resources to support the Greek government in its struggle against the communist guerrillas. The British admission coincided with Truman's difficulties in convincing the Republican-controlled Congress to support economic assistance for Europe. In his effort to build public and congressional support for military and economic aid to Greece and Turkey, Truman emphasized the danger of communism more generally. Then in June 1947 Secretary of State George Marshall announced a plan for the economic recovery of Europe, which, although open to all countries, also alluded to the dangers of communism.

These two policies, the Truman Doctrine and the Marshall Plan, are often identified with the beginning of the cold war. Table 4.2 illustrates the essential difference between the two plans. The Truman Doctrine involved military assistance and provided for direct American intervention in host countries. The Marshall Plan involved only economic assistance

Table 4.2. Dimensions of Foreign Policy: the Truman Doctrine and the Marshall Plan

	Multilateral		Unilateral	
	Coercive	Noncoercive	Noncoercive	Coercive
Proactive		Marshall Plan		Truman Doctrine
Reactive				

The Truman Doctrine was M̲CA. It was unilateral because it was developed and implemented by the United States, coercive because it was designed to provide military assistance, and proactive because the United States sent military advisers and assistance overseas. In contrast, the Marshall Plan was MC̲A. It was multilateral because all the countries involved had to develop a common economic plan, noncoercive because the United States only provided economic assistance, and proactive because economic assistance was sent overseas.

and encouraged the participating governments to develop their own coordinated plans for economic recovery, which the United States would
then try to finance. The Soviet Union and some other Eastern European
countries initially showed an interest in the Marshall Plan, but they pulled
out when the Soviets realized that the Americans were insisting on access
to the national budgets of participating countries as well as on a requirement that recipients buy American goods for the most part.

The situation in Europe finally reached a crisis point in 1948, when, first,
communists took over the democratic government of Czechoslovakia in
late February and, then, in June, the Soviets blocked land access to Berlin,
which though divided into western and eastern sectors was deep inside East
Germany, as an indirect means of preventing the Western powers from so-
lidifying their hold on West Germany. The Western allies successfully resisted this effort by airlifting supplies to the over two million people of West
Berlin for almost an entire year. Stabilizing Germany as the heart of central
Europe was clearly the center of America's strongpoint defense.

Because the Soviets feared the rise of an industrialized Germany tied to
the West, they proposed a neutral government for a united Germany, but
the West did not take this and subsequent proposals very seriously because
Stalin was never willing to guarantee free all-German elections.[12] As a result, the West used the productive capacity of the western zones of Germany to pull the rest of Western Europe out of its economic malaise. The
French initially were also very suspicious of a revived German state on their
border but eventually accepted the idea, and even eventually proposed establishment of a European Coal and Steel Community and a European Defense Community that included West Germany. Although the United States
had thought at first that the Europeans could maintain the balance of
power on the European continent once they had gotten back on their feet,
it now realized that it would have to maintain a presence there. In 1949,
then, the United States and its European allies created the North Atlantic
Treaty Organization (NATO) to serve as an integrated defense alliance.

Events in East Asia in the Immediate Post–war Period

The task of reindustrializing Asia was somewhat easier because the United
States alone controlled Japan, although the economic and political situation in China was quite unsettled. During the war, the Japanese had controlled most of the coastal areas of China as well as the industrial areas of
Manchuria; the Nationalist Chinese under Chiang Kai-shek had become
established in southern China; and the Communist Chinese under Mao
Zedong occupied the remote northwestern portions of China. At the end
of the war, the Soviets occupied parts of industrial Manchuria and the
Americans occupied some areas along the coast.

In 1946 Truman sent Secretary of State Marshall to China to end the
nineteen-year-long war between the Nationalists and the Communists.

Even Stalin seemed to be working toward this end by pressuring Mao to join a coalition government in China. But Marshall was unable to bring an end to the civil war, and he concluded that it was not in America's interest to invest additional resources in a corrupt and unpopular Nationalist government.

The United States fully expected the Chinese communists to take over much of the populous areas in the industrial north, but it thought that Chiang's Nationalists could hold on to much of the South. The Americans also expected the Chinese communists to turn toward the Soviet Union, but they also were convinced that the Soviets had little to offer. Thus when the Chinese communists swept to victory over all mainland China in 1949, the Truman administration took it in stride, convinced that in time America could use its superior resources to drive a wedge between the Soviet Union and China. Remnants of the Nationalist Chinese army and government escaped to the island of Formosa (later known as Taiwan) where they established themselves.

The loss of China came as a shock, however, to many Americans, and the Republicans in Congress used this apparent defeat to embarrass the Truman administration. They asked how the administration could expect the American people to provide economic support to combat communism in Europe when it was so cavalier about losing China to communist followers of Mao Zedong. Because China experts in the State Department had predicted and accepted this result, the Republicans blamed them for bringing it about. Thus began the **McCarthy era,** in which Sen. Joseph R. McCarthy of Wisconsin began a five-year witch hunt for communist sympathizers throughout American institutions, including those concerned with foreign affairs.

The situation in Korea was different. Kim Il Sung, then living in the Soviet Union, accompanied the Soviets when they occupied North Korea in 1945. The Americans supported the anticommunist Syngman Rhee in South Korea, where he won free elections in 1948. The Americans suggested a division of the country, with the thirty-eighth parallel dividing North and South Korea, and the Soviets and the United States withdrew their forces from the Korean peninsula in 1948 and 1949, respectively.

Elsewhere in Asia, the former colonial powers of Europe were trying to reestablish their colonies. Although the United States had felt that orderly decolonization was the key to co-opting the nationalist movements that had sprung up throughout the colonized world, and although Britain agreed to relinquish control over its former colonies, France held on to as many of its territories as it could. For example, the French ousted a communist government under Ho Chi Minh in the north of Vietnam and established a government responsible to France under emperor Bao Dai.

The international landscape changed in July 1949, when the Soviets successfully tested their first atomic bomb and an alarmed Truman asked the National Security Council to comprehensively reevaluate American foreign policy. By this time the idea of a strongpoint defense had yielded to the notion of a defense that would be more comprehensive and more aggressive. In the spring of 1950 the State Department's director of policy planning, Paul Nitze, under the direction of Secretary of State Dean Acheson, prepared a general political strategy for the cold war that took the form of a National Security Council paper (NSC-68). The paper gave first priority to co-opting the industrialized areas of Europe and East Asia. Maintaining access to the raw materials and markets of the developing countries received second priority. It gave virtually no priority to rolling back Soviet control in Eastern Europe and China. The main purpose of the paper was to justify additional economic aid and military expenditures, especially in Europe, because America did not possess forces commensurate with its responsibilities around the world.

The Korean Conflict.   In June 1950 North Korea attacked South Korea and pushed South Korean troops into a perimeter around the port of Busan. Apparently Stalin had permitted the attack, assuming that the United States would not respond. However, the United States sent forces already stationed in Japan to Korea almost immediately, assuming that the attack was the first step in a coordinated strategy planned in Moscow.

Intent on developing a multilateral approach to security issues, the United States promptly took the issue to the United Nations. The Soviet representative just happened to be absent from the Security Council at that time, protesting the UN's failure to seat the Communist government of China. The Nationalist representative of China, who happened to be chairing the council that month, ruled that the Soviet absence should not be considered a veto and the council passed a resolution calling for a UN police action against North Korea. Although the Soviet delegate hurried back to New York, the damage had been done, and sixteen nations eventually sent military forces to assist South Korea.

In September 1950 General MacArthur, designated by Truman as the commander of UN forces, landed UN forces behind enemy lines at Inchon, the port for Seoul, and quickly forced the North Koreans to retreat across the thirty-eighth parallel. At this point the course of the Korean War became driven largely by misperceptions on all sides. Given its broader view of the conflict, the United States was not too surprised when the Vietnamese army, the Vietminh, launched an offensive against the French in North Vietnam at about the same time. Realizing that the Chinese might also take advantage of the situation, the United States sent its ships into the Formosa Straits as a precautionary measure to separate the Communists on the mainland from the Nationalists on Taiwan. In all likelihood the Chinese communists perceived U.S. action as a pro-Nationalist maneuver. Accordingly, the Chinese communist foreign minister Zhou Enlai warned the Americans through India that China would consider any attack north of the thirty-eighth parallel in Korea as a threat to China. The United States did not receive the warning, however, and MacArthur crossed the thirty-eighth parallel and pursued the North Koreans almost to the Yalu River on their border with China. At that point the Chinese communists entered the conflict and sent American forces reeling back toward the thirty-eighth parallel.

As American forces were being pushed southward, the Truman administration took another hard look at the conflict. General MacArthur wanted to widen the war by attacking Chinese bases in Manchuria. But President Truman and his advisers did not want to extend the conflict because they expected Moscow to follow the attack in Korea with attacks in other areas. Their response was to heed NSC-68 and build up America's military capacity in order to meet what they perceived to be a global challenge. Because MacArthur was prone to make statements and take actions without consulting Washington first, Truman removed him from his command. Then, once again, the president faced the wrath of congressional Republicans who believed they were witnessing one more failure of U.S.-Asia policy. The administration also constrained MacArthur's replacement, General Matthew Ridgeway, in an attempt to contain the conflict. Finally, the United States and China agreed to a cease-fire in June 1951.

Ramifications of the Korean Conflict.   The Korean conflict played a pivotal role in the cold war. President Truman used the conflict as a vehicle for implementing the military buildup called for in NSC-68. Indeed, Truman had proposed a budget of only $13.5 billion prior to the opening volley of the Korean conflict in 1950, but in early 1951 the president submitted a $50 billion defense budget, recommending an increase in troop size to 3.5 million and in number of divisions from 14 to 50. Moreover, in June 1950 the United States had fewer than 300 atomic weapons; by late 1950 it had 500 atomic bombs and some 264 aircraft capable of carrying nuclear weapons. Although America's defense budget tripled from 1950 to 1951, clearly this buildup was to address global challenges as only about one-fourth of the $54 billion available in 1951 was used in Korea.

Another consequence of the Korean War was the change in American policy toward Japan. The United States speeded up its plans for a peace treaty with Japan, which would allow Japan to shift from the status of occupied country to independent ally of the United States. The time was particularly opportune because Japan's leaders had finally shown their willingness to accept the permanent stationing of American forces on Japanese soil. By September 1951 the United States and forty-eight other states, excluding the Soviet Union and China, had signed a peace treaty with Japan.

The United States also decided to support the Chinese Nationalist government on Taiwan, because America could not afford to lose Taiwan and the other offshore islands to the Chinese communists. Southeast Asia was considered particularly important for the economic future of Japan, and the United States and its allies, including Japan, were greatly concerned about the security of that region.

The Korean War and the expansion of the United States' security concerns also had repercussions in southeastern Europe. Turkey, which had not originally been invited to join NATO, became increasingly concerned about guarantees for its security in this period, and both Turkey and Greece joined NATO as full partners in 1952.

Overall, the greatest achievement during this period of American foreign policy was the industrial restoration of the former enemy states of Germany and Japan. This decision to make permanent military and political commitments to both Europe and Japan underscores the Truman administration's movement toward a more MCA type foreign policy after the Korean War: coercive, proactive, and—to a greater degree than ever before—multilateral, as Table 4.3 shows.

Republicans attacked the Truman administration's more globally oriented anticommunist policy. One group of Republican conservatives opposed the proactive character of that policy; another group of Republican liberals believed that the foreign policy of the United States was not proactive enough. This intraparty debate was partially settled when Dwight D. Eisenhower, the liberal candidate, defeated the conservative candidate, Robert Taft, in the race for the Republican Party nomination in 1952. When Eisenhower then became president, the question was just how proactive the liberal Republicans would prove to be.

Table 4.3. Dimensions of Foreign Policy: U.S. Strongpoint Defense prior to the Korean War

| | Multilateral | | Unilateral | |
	Coercive	Noncoercive	Noncoercive	Coercive
Proactive				Strong effort to aid Europe
Reactive				Weak effort to aid China

President Harry Truman's foreign policy was generally MCA. Although U.S. foreign policy under Truman evolved to become more multilateral, it was in an absolute sense unilateral because the United States was able to control its allies, coercive because it placed great emphasis on the use of force, and proactive because it developed a global strategy that featured economic as well as cultural instruments. The strongpoint defense is illustrated by the difference in degree between U.S. foreign policy in Europe and Asia. The United States was much more proactive in Europe than in China, because of the higher priority accorded to Europe.

Securing Colonial Areas: 1953–1968

In 1953 both the United States and the Soviet Union experienced pivotal changes in leadership. Eisenhower became the first Republican president in the United States in twenty years. Two months later Stalin, in power since the mid-1920s, died. The changes in leadership opened up the possibility that the priorities established in NSC-68 might be changed. Indeed, Eisenhower's new secretary of state, John Foster Dulles, was prone to talk about the need to "roll back" the iron curtain that the Soviets had erected between East and West. But if there was a change in priorities, it related to determining where the administration should place its emphasis —on the industrial centers of Europe and Japan or on the newly emerging countries in Asia and Africa. Although the established industrial centers remained America's first priority, the developing countries played an increasingly important role in the confrontation between East and West. This section looks specifically at how all three dimensions of American foreign policy—prosperity, community, and security—evolved in this period, especially in developing areas.

Prosperity Values

The growth and development of the economies and cultures of states in this period cannot be separated from security alignments because most cross-border exchanges were among members of the same defensive alliances. As the economies of Western Europe improved, more and more attention was devoted to their military defense. NATO provided a structure of commitments, but it did not ensure the existence of adequate forces or provide for their effectiveness. With American pressure the French had proposed an integrated force in the form of a European Defense Community to include France, Italy, Belgium, the Netherlands, Luxembourg, and West Germany. But in 1954 the French Assembly failed to ratify the EDC. The failure of the EDC proposal drew the United States even more fully into the defense of Europe. After taking stock, the United States and Britain led an effort to create a European Defense Union in 1955, which paved the way for West Germany to join NATO. Six days later the Soviets responded by creating a counterpart to NATO, the Warsaw Pact, a formal military alliance among seven East European satellites and the Soviet Union.

Early on the Eisenhower administration attempted to tighten the noose around the Soviet Union. The fact that so many European colonies were seeking independence from their mother countries complicated the administration's efforts. As early as 1947, Britain had been forced to grant independence to the population of the Indian subcontinent. In 1948 Britain also ended its mandate in Palestine and signed an agreement with Egypt in 1954 to withdraw its forces from the Suez Canal. At the same

time, France was having great difficulty sustaining its position in North
Vietnam. France was also heavily engaged in guerrilla wars in North
Africa; it was eventually forced to grant both Morocco and Tunisia independence in 1956 and Algeria in 1962. Most African countries gained
their independence in the 1960s.

Despite these complications, the West proceeded to organize regional
defense agreements in Asia and the Middle East. In 1954 the United
States, Britain, France, Australia, New Zealand, Pakistan, Thailand, and
the Philippines formed the Southeast Asia Treaty Organization (SEATO).
This treaty also protected South Vietnam, Cambodia, and Laos under a
protocol attached to the treaty. After the Korean War broke out in 1950,
the United States, France, and Britain had asked Egypt to assist them in
developing a Middle East Defense Organization (MEDO). Egypt, however,
was not interested, and the British eventually had to shift their base of
operations from the Suez to Iraq. In 1955 Turkey proposed a Middle East
Treaty Organization (METO), or the Baghdad Pact, which included
Turkey, Iraq, Iran, Pakistan, and Britain. However, the 1959 revolution in
Iraq brought an anti-Western Republican government into power, and so
the Baghdad Pact was reorganized, without Iraq, into the Central Treaty
Organization (CENTO) in 1959.

From the perspective of the United States and its European allies, these
regional organizations were defensive alliances, **balancing** against threats
posed by the Soviet Union and other communist states. However, from
the perspective of the non-European members of these alliances, **bandwagoning** was involved because they perceived the United States and its
allies as the stronger party. They joined with the expectation of receiving
significant economic assistance, especially in the form of defense support.

As the alliances between countries of the communist world and the "Free
World," as Eisenhower called it, became tighter, those countries that remained outside the two armed camps began to feel left out. The first international conference of newly independent African and Asian states was
held in Bandung, Indonesia, in 1955. Many of these nations were part of
what was generally called the **nonaligned movement,** but just what non-
alignment meant differed from one leader to the next. According to Indian
prime minister Jawaharlal Nehru, the "third world" was more of a "third
force" that would try to exercise some moral power over the competition
between the superpowers.[13] For Egyptian prime minister Gamal Abdel
Nasser, the nonaligned movement was a means of playing one side against
the other in order to acquire maximum benefits for developing countries.

Because of its greater economic strength, the West offered economic assistance programs to these countries, whereas the East was more likely to
offer military assistance. As the struggle for political independence and economic development grew more intense within these countries, the competition among them for resources from the West and/or the East also became

more profound. Some of these states, such as Pakistan, chose to become part of the bipolar alliance system; others, such as India, chose to remain non-aligned. But virtually all of these states became involved in balancing and bandwagoning in order to prosper and survive. For example, Pakistan signed a Mutual Defense Agreement with the United States in 1954. The United States wanted Pakistan as an ally in order to provide *local* balance against the Soviet Union in an area in which the United States needed military bases. Pakistan may have been led to believe that the agreement with the United States would help it balance against its stronger neighbor, India. From the perspective of Pakistan, the agreement with the United States probably represented bandwagoning because Pakistan stood to gain large amounts of economic assistance. Table 4.4 shows how both Pakistan and India became involved in balancing and bandwagoning during 1953–1968.

Interestingly, the Indian president, Nehru, visited the Soviet Union for the first time shortly thereafter, in December 1955. Although India was non-aligned during the cold war, it must have felt that it wouldn't hurt to improve relations with the world's other great power. India's need for outside support increased as a result of the Sino-Indian War in 1962. As a consequence, India eventually signed a Treaty of Peace, Friendship and Understanding with the Soviet Union in 1971. India probably saw this treaty with the Soviet Union both as a means of balancing against China and bandwagoning with the Soviet Union.

Community Values

But what is really remarkable about the 1953–1968 period is the unprecedented extent to which the United States consulted its allies over foreign policy. To some extent such consultations came naturally because the United States had not been as actively engaged in some of these areas as Britain or France, and so it often needed their expertise. And it was only natural that the United States wanted to share some of the costs associated with decolonization with the former colonial masters. Yet from a historical perspective it was most uncommon to see the United States employ mutual defense arrangements as much as it did during this period.

Many of these regional pacts, such as CENTO, were formal agreements among states that had little in common, and it was not always clear how committed these states were to joint action. In this sense NATO was different because it seemed to come closer than most associations to representing a community with a common interest in security matters as well as economic ones. It was always more difficult for the NATO community to define its common interest when NATO operated outside its own territory, however, a circumstance that the Suez crisis best illustrates.

Multilateralism and the Suez Crisis.   By the summer of 1956 the Anglo-French influence in the Arab world had largely dissipated. The Egyptians

Table 4.4. Dimensions of Foreign Policy: Balancing and Bandwagoning

| | Multilateral | | Unilateral | |
	Coercive	Noncoercive	Noncoercive	Coercive
Proactive			Pakistan band-wagoning with the United States against the Soviet Union in 1954 and India bandwagoning with the Soviet Union against China in 1971	Pakistan balancing against India in 1954 and India balancing against China in 1971
Reactive				

The alliance between the United States and Pakistan in 1954 is a good example of balancing be-cause the United States pushed to have Pakistan as an ally because it wanted local help in bal-ancing against the Soviet Union by organizing friendly states to the south of the Soviet Union and because Pakistan wanted to gain U.S. support in balancing against the regional power of India. This MCA policy is unilateral because each made its decision without consulting the most relevant third party, India, coercive because it was a military alliance, and proactive because it en-tailed economic and social as well as political and military commitments. India also signed the Treaty of Friendship with the Soviet Union in 1971 in order to balance against China.

  Both Pakistan and India were probably bandwagoning in their relationship with the United States and the Soviet Union, respectively, because they were both more concerned with regional enemies than they were with great power aggression. Pakistan received large amounts of mili-tary and defense support from the United States as a result of the 1954 pact, and India received economic assistance from the United States throughout the 1950s and 1960s. India also received some economic and much military aid from the Soviet Union during this period. These MCA poli-cies are unilateral because neither felt obligated to consult the other in arranging for this aid, noncoercive because they were not primarily concerned with an attack by a great power, and proactive because they gained economic and other benefits.

had nationalized the Suez Canal, now the key route for oil tankers rather than Britain's passageway to India, and Britain, France, and Israel all felt threatened by Nasser's new regime in Egypt. In the fall of 1956 Israel at-tacked Egypt, and Britain and France intervened on the pretense of pro-tecting the canal. The situation left the United States in a quandary. It was allied with Britain and France in NATO and committed to the defense of Israel. Yet it also was obligated under Article 51 of the UN Charter to join other states in opposing aggression. The United States, then, was caught in a conflict between its defensive alliance commitments under NATO and its collective security obligations under the charter.

In this instance, the United States supported the UN Charter, and it was partly motivated to do so because of the failure of Britain and France to consult with it under the multilateral provisions of NATO.[14] Britain and France assumed that the United States would support them in maintaining free passage through the Suez Canal. But the United States was so upset by the failure of its closest allies to adhere to the requirement for multilateral consultations that it abandoned its allies and took action against them under the provisions of the charter. The United States was able to use economic sanctions against its regional allies, and, with the help of UN forces, it compelled Britain, France, and Israel to withdraw.

What makes this incident particularly interesting is that at the same time the Soviet Union was faced with independent actions by one of its European satellites, Hungary, as is shown in Table 4.5. After Nikita Khrushchev, the new Soviet premier, criticized Stalin's exercise of power earlier in the year, some of the Eastern European countries began to take advantage of this apparently more liberal climate to establish some independence from Moscow. The Kremlin had successfully negotiated with Poland earlier in the year in order to prevent any embarrassing deviations from Moscow's policies. However, Hungary had gone so far that Khrushchev felt compelled to send in Soviet as well as Warsaw Pact troops to quell the rebellion.

The coincidence of these two events is interesting for two reasons. First, America's preoccupation with the unilateralism of its principal allies at

Table 4.5. Dimensions of Foreign Policy: U.S. Policy in the Suez Crisis and Hungary

	Multilateral		Unilateral	
	Coercive	Noncoercive	Noncoercive	Coercive
Proactive	U.S. action against Britain, France, and Israel			
Reactive			U.S. inaction in relation to the Soviet invasion of Hungary	

U.S. policy toward its allies in the Suez Crisis is best understood as MCA. It was multilateral because the United States honored its obligations under Article 51 of the UN Charter, coercive because the United States was instrumental in developing a UN peacekeeping mission in Egypt, and proactive because the United States expended its time and resources abroad.

U.S. policy in the Hungarian crisis was MCA. It was unilateral in that the United States planned no coordinated response with other countries, noncoercive in that the United States did not threaten to intervene once the Soviets and Warsaw Pact countries had acted, and reactive because no action was taken.

Suez prevented it from developing a response to Soviet actions in Hungary. Notwithstanding the Eisenhower administration's rhetoric that the United States should help Eastern Europeans break away from the Soviet Union, when the first real opportunity presented itself, the United States took no action whatsoever. Second, the coincidence revealed that unilateralism was the norm in the Warsaw Pact, whereas the United States perceived a multilateral norm operating in the NATO alliance. But the Suez incident was not the only occasion on which the United States had to deal with the independent, unilateral actions of its allies.

French Unilateralism. In 1957 Charles de Gaulle was called back to power in France to deal with the crisis in Algeria. De Gaulle's strong nationalist sentiments served him well when it came to extracting France from that difficult situation, but his unparalleled determination to uphold the honor and prestige of France led him to develop an independent nuclear force and eventually to drop out of NATO military commitments. Although NATO was able to move its headquarters and other military bases out of France, the French action underscored the propensity of individual NATO members to pursue independent courses of action despite their dependence on each other for collective security. Indeed, de Gaulle's unilateralism was based on his recognition that the United States had no choice but to defend France regardless of its aberrant behavior.

Although the Soviet Union tried to keep a tight rein on its associated states, it too encountered serious difficulties. In addition to its problems with Poland and Hungary, the Soviet Union faced insurmountable problems with China. The Chinese were particularly upset about the close relationship between the Soviet Union and China's regional rival, India. A dispute rose as well over the long Chinese-Russian border. More generally, from the very beginning of the cold war these two communist giants pursued independent policies, and as the cold war progressed, they found it difficult to work together, despite their ideological similarities.

Security Values

At the end of 1952 the United States successfully tested a hydrogen weapon, only to be followed just nine months later by the Soviet Union's tests. As a result, the year 1953 marked the point at which the possibility of a nuclear confrontation between the two superpowers began to cast a dark shadow over American foreign policy.

When the Republicans took office in 1953 they were determined both to bolster the defense against communism and to reduce the federal budget. To deliver on both promises President Eisenhower placed a limit on defense expenditures. The result was what the Eisenhower administration called the "new look" in defense policy—that is, an emphasis on strategic deterrence forces over the more expensive conventional forces used at the time of the Korean War. Because the United States still had a tremendous advantage over the Soviet Union in the number of weapons of mass destruction and the means of delivering them, it was in a position to threaten **massive retaliation**—that is, the United States could deter communist aggression in peripheral areas by threatening to respond in a disproportionate manner.

The Eisenhower administration also developed or refined new instruments for meeting the Soviet threat. The use of clandestine operations became a favorite way for the administration to deal with threats that were not amenable to other military strategies. As early as 1953 the Central Intelligence Agency (CIA) toppled the prime minister of Iran, Mohammed Mossadegh, simply by inciting street mobs against him. With this simple but effective maneuver the United States replaced a suspected communist sympathizer with an ally, Shah Mohammed Reza Pahlavi. A year later another suspected communist leader, Jacobo Arbenz Guzmán of Guatemala, was duped into leaving office when the CIA led him to believe that his country was under attack by elements supported by the United States.

So long as the Soviet Union did not challenge American interests around the world, massive retaliation seemed credible. Indeed, for a time at least it appeared as though the Soviets had become less rigid and doctrinaire after the death of Stalin. The United States assumed that Moscow was orchestrating the following actions by the Soviet Union's communist allies. First, the Chinese and the Americans were able to arrive at a prisoner exchange agreement in Korea in 1953. Then, under the negotiated settlement reached a year later in Vietnam, the French pulled out of North Vietnam. The boundary between East and West also was clarified in Europe as Soviet and Western forces withdrew from Austria under the stipulation that the country would remain neutral. Finally, in 1956 the Soviet Union, Britain, and France held a summit meeting in Geneva to discuss mutual problems.

By 1956, though, Khrushchev had emerged as the Soviet leader, and he, like Stalin, felt that the Soviet Union should have as much influence as the United States in world affairs. Earlier in the year, in addressing the Twentieth Congress of the Communist Party in Moscow, Khrushchev had indicated that the Soviet Union had made sufficient progress in both economic development and the acquisition of nuclear weapons to allow it to control its own destiny. Moreover, Khrushchev saw new opportunities for the Soviet Union to use its nuclear status to force favorable agreements and to support **wars of national liberation** throughout the developing world. The Soviet Union's more aggressive posture soon became evident in its security policies.

In October 1957 the Soviet Union successfully launched its first satellite, *Sputnik*. This development suggested that the Soviets might soon be able to launch nuclear weapons against targets in the United States. Indeed, the Soviets could potentially skip over the intercontinental bomber stage of delivery (where the United States had an advantage) and go directly to the intercontinental missile stage of delivery (where the Soviet Union had the advantage, at least temporarily). Because intercontinental ballistic missiles (ICBMs) could hit their targets within a matter of 20 to 30 minutes, whereas intercontinental bombers required four to six hours, the United States was faced with the prospect of a **missile gap**. Although the credibility of massive retaliation had been questioned earlier, it was clear that the United States could no longer unilaterally threaten such retaliation when it now seemed so vulnerable itself.

The Berlin Crisis.   One of the first measures that Nikita Khrushchev took to demand more respect for the Soviet Union centered on Berlin. In November 1958 Khrushchev announced that because Britain, France, and the United States had all violated provisos of the Potsdam agreement related to Berlin, he was prepared to hand over to the German Democratic Republic, the East German government, sovereign authority over the Allies' access to Berlin.[15] Because Berlin was nestled deep in East German territory, the United States became engaged in a series of diplomatic efforts to forestall such action and to negotiate continued access to the city.

The Berlin issue was still unsettled when President John F. Kennedy met with Khrushchev in Vienna in June 1961. At that time Khrushchev reiterated his determination to settle the issue before the end of the year. Then, in August 1961, the East Germans built a wall around West Berlin to stem the increasing flow of refugees from East Germany into the Western sector. The West continued to insist on formal access to East Berlin, but it did not attempt to tear down the wall.

In the meantime, the successful 1959 revolution in Cuba—just ninety miles off American shores—had become a tremendous concern to the United States because Fidel Castro, the leader of the nationalist and communist revolutionary movement, opposed U.S. influence in Cuba and soon turned to the Soviet Union for support. For the first time the Soviets had a foothold in the Western Hemisphere. By the end of the Eisenhower administration events occurring elsewhere appeared to indicate that relations with the Soviet Union had deteriorated. In the spring of 1960 a U-2 reconnaissance flight shot down over Soviet territory led to the cancellation of the Paris summit between Eisenhower and Khrushchev. That summer the Soviet-supported regime in the former Belgian Congo collapsed, and Khrushchev not only threatened to stop paying for UN peacekeeping in that country but also insisted that the Soviet Union would not support the United Nations unless it accepted a *troika* in the secretary-general's office.[16] The Russians also began to make trouble in Laos.

Thus President Kennedy took office in 1961 amid especially tense relations between the two superpowers. At first, Kennedy had mixed success. He was effective in Laos when his threats to send troops into that area induced the Soviets and their allies to back down. But when he tried to overturn the Castro regime in Cuba—using a plan similar to the covert operation successfully used in Guatemala in 1954—he failed miserably. The U.S-sponsored invasion at the Bay of Pigs in Cuba in April 1961 was an embarrassment not only because it failed, but also because the United States initially lied about its involvement.

To meet the threats posed by the missile gap with the Soviet Union and the Soviet-supported wars of national liberation, Kennedy and Secretary of Defense Robert McNamara introduced important changes in strategic doctrine and force composition. Among other things, to deter a possible Soviet nuclear missile attack the United States placed a thousand Minuteman missiles in underground silos. These ICBMs were designed to meet the challenge of any new Soviet missiles with the idea that if the United States could ensure the destruction of 25–30 percent of the population and 65–70 percent of the industrial capacity of the Soviet Union, then the Soviets would be effectively deterred from starting a conflict in the first place. The policy was given the label of **mutual assured destruction** (MAD). This new policy was soon tested in the Cuban Missile Crisis in 1962.

The Cuban Missile Crisis.   In the fall of 1962 Nikita Khrushchev appeared incensed that the United States had placed intermediate-range nuclear missiles in Turkey on the border of the Soviet Union, whereas the Soviet Union had no comparable missiles close to the U.S. border. Seeking to correct this imbalance, Khrushchev secretly sent intermediate-range nuclear missiles to Cuba in 1962.

Although unofficial reports of missiles in Cuba were numerous, they were denied by Soviet diplomats and could not be independently confirmed by U.S. government sources at first. Once the United States had photographic proof that such missiles were being assembled in Cuba, President Kennedy secretly called together his chief advisers to decide on a course of action.

Secretary of Defense McNamara initially suggested that Kennedy ignore the problem because the location of the missiles did not change the overall balance of strategic power, but President Kennedy did not feel he could do so. Two courses of action were seriously considered: an air strike against nuclear sites in Cuba and a blockade of Cuba. After considerable debate, the president decided in favor of the blockade or quarantine of Soviet ships headed to Cuba. Although this action did not affect the missiles per se as an air strike would have, it did force a confrontation that could have easily escalated into a nuclear war. Eventually, the Kremlin called back its ships and ordered the deactivation of the Cuban missile sites. As Secretary of State Dean Rusk described it, "We're eyeball to eyeball, and I think the other fellow just blinked."[17] What was not known at the time was that the United States secretly agreed to remove its missiles from Turkey as part of the bargain. From the outside, then, the agreement looked more lopsided than it actually was. But from within the Kremlin, Khrushchev's position was undermined by the agreement because in exaggerating Soviet nuclear strength he had been forced to back down. Many scholars and policy analysts regard this episode as the most serious crisis of the cold war.[18]

In 1963 the United States and the Soviet Union agreed to install a direct communications hot line between the White House and the Kremlin and a limited nuclear test ban treaty. But, for the United States, the danger of an all-out nuclear confrontation between the two superpowers was not necessarily the most pressing issue. Washington also needed to develop a strategy for coping with more limited threats to its security around the world.

Vietnam. At about the same time the Kennedy administration was developing its MAD nuclear strategy, it also was developing a strategy for **graduated deterrence,** a NATO strategy based on a capacity to meet the enemy at every possible level of aggression. This strategy then evolved into the more general strategy of **flexible response.** In a direct reversal of Eisenhower's belt-tightening strategy, the administration built up the nation's conventional forces, adding special forces that could deal with a wide range of contingencies, so threatening nuclear war would not be the only available strategic option.

The capabilities of graduated deterrence and flexible response were soon called into action. By 1964 there were reports that regular North Vietnamese forces were infiltrating South Vietnam, where the United States had established a puppet government after the overthrow of the unpopular Diem government. Even though Kennedy had already sent a large number of U.S. military advisers to South Vietnam, the situation there continued to deteriorate. Although Lyndon B. Johnson, who succeeded to the presidency in 1963 after Kennedy was assassinated, promised in the campaign of 1964 to stay out of the war in Indochina, an August 1964 incident in which North Vietnamese allegedly attacked American ships off North Vietnam led Johnson to seek the authority to enter the conflict if necessary. Congress responded with the Gulf of Tonkin Resolution.[19]

In early 1965, after some American advisers lost their lives in attacks in the central highlands of South Vietnam, President Johnson ordered air strikes against North Vietnam based on the authority granted him by the Gulf of Tonkin Resolution. By spring American ground forces were being prepared to enter the war. The marines went in first to protect strategic airfields; army units were then deployed to occupy strategic locations in the highlands. Congressional opposition to the war emerged almost immediately, and the nightly news exposed the American people to different plans for strategic engagement. By 1966 almost 500,000 U.S. forces were in South Vietnam. Based on questionable data, the United States claimed to be winning what was essentially a war of attrition, as Box 4.1 shows, but the end was not in sight.

The Vietnam War was difficult to fight. Although the United States had hoped to face regular North Vietnamese forces in the field, the war itself was largely a guerrilla insurgency, and so it was often difficult, if not impossible, to separate the military combatants from ordinary civilians. American ground forces had to send out patrols to find the enemy, and once U.S. troops located enemy forces, they often had to call in artillery and air strikes on their own positions. Indeed, the distinction between friend and foe was so obscure on the battlefield that the United States was frequently accused of "destroying villages in order to save them." In 1969 and 1970 all Americans had to confront war crimes committed by American troops, with the highly publicized investigation of a massacre at the village of My Lai, where an American lieutenant, who was later court martialed, ordered his troops to kill large groups of women, children, and the elderly.

The beginning of the end occurred in January 1968, on the Chinese New Year, with the launching of the Tet offensive by the Viet Cong (the Vietnamese Liberation Front). The offensive consisted of simultaneous attacks against some forty cities and strongholds. Although these attacks were eventually repelled at great loss to the Viet Cong, the attacks themselves demonstrated the Viet Cong's capacity and determination to carry on the war that belied the Johnson administration's expectations. Once the Tet offensive was over, and amid growing antiwar sentiment domestically and abroad, President Johnson announced that he would not run for reelection and would give his primary attention to ending the war. His vice president, Hubert H. Humphrey, became the Democratic candidate for president, but he was at a distinct disadvantage in relation to the Republican nominee, Richard M. Nixon, because he "could not attack his own administration nor did he dare defend the issue before the electorate." [20] For an illustration of the contrast between the antiwar protesters' and the Johnson administration's attitudes toward the Vietnam War, see Table 4.6.

Balancing Commitments and Capabilities: 1969–1984

The Vietnam War played a pivotal role in the history of U.S. foreign policy during the cold war because it demonstrated that the United States could not continue to assume the same role it had assumed in the world during the previous decades without increasing its economic and military capa-

BOX 4.1

Profile in Action: Sam Adams

Sam Adams was a young analyst in the Central Intelligence Agency during the Vietnam War, working as an order of battle specialist, that is, he was studying the composition of enemy forces. Adams was specifically asked to study the state of enemy morale, and he began by examining data on Viet Cong defections. The data appeared to show that the Viet Cong were not only suffering numerous defections and a large number of casualties, but they were also having trouble recruiting new soldiers. He estimated that they were losing at least 50,000 troops every year out of an estimated 270,000. At first Washington welcomed this good news. However, when Adams traveled to Vietnam to corroborate his findings with people in the field, he found no evidence that the Viet Cong forces were either short-handed or demoralized.

Adams finally figured out the discrepancy between what his figures indicated should be happening and what people in the field said was taking place: the U.S. government's official tally grossly underestimated the total number of Viet Cong forces, as Table 4.6 shows. If Adams's calculations based on the new data were correct, the total number of Viet Cong forces was 470,000, not 270,000. The importance of this finding was monumental, because all the U.S. calculations, including the number of U.S. forces needed, were based on the ratio between U.S. and VC forces. The United States already had about 350,000 soldiers in Vietnam, and everyone was talking about "force ratios." Some experts maintained that in a guerrilla war the U.S. side needed to outnumber the enemy by a ratio of about ten to one; others said five to one; the most optimistic said three to one. If Adams's figures, based on the new data, were correct, the force ratio actually favored the Viet Cong. When Adams tried to find out the source of the U.S. government's numbers, he concluded that

bilities. Up to this point the United States had experienced such rapid economic growth at home that it could play a leading role overseas without disrupting its own domestic economy and society. Now, however, it had to make a choice: either reduce its commitments abroad or increase its domestic capabilities by putting the economy on a war-time footing as was done during the Second World War.

During the period covered in this section, Presidents Richard Nixon and Jimmy Carter, for all their differences in personal style, pursued a very similar foreign policy strategy: they both attempted to balance costs by reducing U.S. commitments abroad. In his first term President Ronald

they were probably supplied by the South Vietnamese, who had every reason to tailor these figures to suit their own particular needs.

Viet Cong Order of Battle

Communist regulars	About	110,573 (figure varied monthly)
Guerrilla-militia	Exactly	103,573
Service troops	Exactly	18,553
Political cadres	Exactly	39,175
Total forces	Approximately	271,301

Adams continued to study the Viet Cong order of battle. Eventually he was invited to an order of battle conference in Hawaii, where he confronted U.S. Army personnel studying this issue. The army disputed his findings at the conference, but one official told him privately that they had instructions to keep the total order of battle figure at less than 300,000—the Defense Department was responsible for fighting the war and so they would decide how many enemy they were fighting.

The order of battle statistics that Adams worked with in the CIA were not some obscure figures that were only available to a few government experts; they were regularly presented to the American public. A table similar to Table 4.6 appeared on national television at least once a week. In a war of attrition—where victory depends on which side suffers the highest casualties—order of battle statistics are particularly important; it's how you "keep score." Apparently, the United States started using the South Vietnamese–supplied data early in the war and never confirmed the figures. By the time it became obvious that the order of battle statistics were in error, it was too late to change them without undermining the whole war effort.

Source: Based on the article by Sam Adams, "Vietnam Cover-up: Playing War with Numbers," *Harper's* (May 1975).

Reagan attempted to deal with the same problem by increasing defense expenditures.

Ending the Vietnam War

Nixon's first task was to extricate the United States from the Vietnam War. His plan was similar to the one Eisenhower had offered some sixteen years earlier for Korea. Nixon planned to use the threat of strategic bombing to force the North Vietnamese to negotiate. The problem was that Nixon had to carry out much of this bombing covertly because he also had promised the American people that he would withdraw American

Table 4.6. Dimensions of Foreign Policy: U.S. Debate over Vietnam Policy in 1968

	Multilateral		Unilateral	
	Coercive	Noncoercive	Noncoercive	Coercive
Proactive				Johnson's Vietnam policy
Reactive		Vietnam Protesters		

Johnson's Vietnam policy was M<u>C</u>A—unilateral because it was undertaken without the support of key allies to say nothing of other concerned states, coercive because it was based on the use of force, and proactive because it involved extensive overseas commitments.

Most Vietnam protesters were M<u>C</u>A—multilateral because they explicitly argued that the United States should only act when there was a broad international as well as domestic consensus, non-coercive because they felt that the Vietnam War showed that force was not an answer, and reactive because they felt the United States should not be engaged in the internal affairs of another state.

ground forces from Vietnam and replace them with South Vietnamese forces, in a process called **Vietnamization.**

Nixon's policy, however, was an abysmal failure. The North Vietnamese would not negotiate in good faith because they saw American troops withdrawing. The United States could not sufficiently pressure the North Vietnamese by bombing because there were not enough suitable targets in North Vietnam, and even if there had been, the North Vietnamese were prepared to suffer the consequences in order to gain national independence. The South Vietnamese were not willing to support the negotiations either because they could not afford to replace U.S. forces. As a result, Secretary of State Henry Kissinger eventually signed a peace treaty that allowed North Vietnamese forces to remain in South Vietnam. Soon after the last American forces had left, the North Vietnamese army swept away the South Vietnamese government. Meanwhile, the United States lost not only South Vietnam but also Laos and Cambodia to communist revolution.

Although the results in Indochina were not the ones hoped for, Nixon's policy in South Vietnam was part of a larger effort to restructure American foreign policy based on new assumptions. In this sense Nixon's Vietnam policy was a microcosm of U.S. foreign policy as a whole during the 1970s. The Nixon Doctrine attempted to reduce American commitments in developing countries, but Nixon's main effort was to pursue a policy of relaxing tensions, or **détente**, with the Soviet Union and open relations with China.

Nixon and Détente

After its perceived embarrassment in the Cuban Missile Crisis, the Soviet Union devoted more and more of its resources to catching up with the

United States in strategic nuclear armaments. By 1969 it had generally succeeded. Indeed, on the day of Nixon's inauguration the Soviet Union proposed bilateral negotiations to limit both nuclear delivery vehicles and defensive systems. A week later Nixon accepted this proposal and acknowledged that the Soviet Union had reached virtual parity with the United States in strategic nuclear forces. In 1972 the United States and Russia negotiated a ceiling on the number of intercontinental ballistic missiles (ICBMs) that each side could deploy over the next five years as well as limitations on the number of launchers and sites for antiballistic missile systems (ABMs).

At about the same time, Washington acknowledged that it could no longer guarantee the value of the American dollar. In 1971 Nixon announced that the dollar would no longer be convertible into gold and that the United States would impose a 10 percent surcharge on imports.

The factors that produced these adjustments in American foreign policy also lured some of America's European allies into considering new policy initiatives. For example, French president de Gaulle attempted to create a more independent center of power in Europe under French leadership. Once de Gaulle's effort failed, Willy Brandt, the new foreign minister of West Germany, sought to normalize his country's relations with the communist bloc. Whereas de Gaulle had taken a hard line against the Soviet Union, Brandt was eager to develop friendly relations with Germany's eastern neighbors.

At the same time that the United States was confronting these independent policy initiatives from its NATO allies in Europe, the Soviet Union was facing problems of its own. Although the Soviets were pleased with their progress on the nuclear front, they were having trouble with China and some of their other allies. For example, in the summer of 1968 they sent troops into Czechoslovakia to overturn a communist government under Alexander Dubček that allowed domestic dissent. Then in 1969 serious border clashes broke out between Russia and China. The time had come on both sides of the iron curtain to reassess capabilities and commitments.

Germany took the lead in the West. Ever since the Cuban Missile Crisis there had been an interest on both sides of the cold war in signing a nuclear nonproliferation treaty. The main stumbling bloc was the effect it might have on regional defense agreements, such as NATO. Germany helped break the impasse by signing such a treaty in November 1969 and then a nonaggression pact with the Soviet Union in 1970. By 1971 the four occupying powers had agreed not to act unilaterally on the Berlin issue; by 1972 the German Democratic Republic (East Germany) had signed a treaty with the Federal Republic, normalizing relations between the two Germanies; and by 1974 the two Germanies joined the United Nations. Although Nixon and Brandt were forced from office by scandals in 1973, President Gerald R. Ford, who succeeded to the presidency when Nixon resigned, was able to pursue détente to the point where thirty-five nations, including the Soviet Union, the United States, and Canada, signed the Final Act of the Conference on Security and Cooperation in Europe (also known as the Helsinki Accords) in August 1975. In this final act the participating countries recognized the existing political boundaries of Europe and provided for improved economic and cultural relations between them. From this politically binding agreement arose the Organization for Security and Cooperation in Europe (OSCE). In the years that followed, Western investment in East Germany and other Eastern European countries, including the Soviet Union, increased rapidly and limited travel and cultural exchanges were allowed between East and West.

During this same period the United States moved forward in East Asia. In 1969 the Nixon administration relaxed certain trade and travel restrictions on China in the hope that America would develop a new relationship with that country. In 1971 the Chinese government invited the American table tennis team that was competing in Japan to come to China. Events then moved quickly: Nixon revoked the U.S. embargo against China in June, and by July his national security adviser, Henry Kissinger, was meeting secretly with Zhou Enlai and Mao Zedong. In February 1972 Nixon himself visited China and forged a new relationship with that country.

While détente generally characterized the relations between the United States and the Soviet Union, on the one hand, and the United States and China, on the other, America's relations with many developing countries became more difficult. To some extent these new tensions resulted from gradual decolonization and emergence of many newly independent states with a voice in the UN General Assembly. But it also was triggered by the Arab oil embargo of 1973. Although developing countries were not the target of the embargo, they were the ones least able to cope with the rising oil prices. By the mid-1970s these developing countries had formed the Group of 77 (now 132) and began to vote as a bloc in the United Nations.

In the North-South confrontation that ensued in the UN, the developing countries of the South (many in South America and Africa) sought to gain economic concessions from the developed countries of the North (largely those of Western Europe, North America, and Japan). This alignment offered new opportunities for the Soviet Union in the developing world, and Leonid Brezhnev, the Soviet leader, was quick to take advantage of the situation. For example, the Soviets concluded a treaty of friendship with the African country of Somalia. When Ethiopian dictator Haile Selassie fell from power, the Soviets were able to exert their influence in that country. The Soviets then established communist governments in the former Portuguese colonies of Angola and Mozambique. In response, the United States poured its resources into these and other African states with the result that détente began to break down over conflicts in Africa and the Middle East.

In the meantime, relations in Latin America also began to fall apart for the United States. With Cuba almost entirely dependent on the Soviet Union, the United States became increasingly concerned that the Soviets would use Cuba as a base for exporting communism into other countries in the hemisphere. The United States' concern about the leftist regime in Guatemala led the Organization of American States (OAS), the regional collective security organization in Latin America, to impose sanctions on Cuba in July 1964. Then, beginning with its intervention in the Dominican Republic in 1965, the United States increasingly turned its economic development programs in the hemisphere into counterinsurgency efforts. Perhaps the most notable episode during this period was the U.S.-orchestrated overthrow of the freely elected communist leader of Chile, Salvador Allende, which resulted in his assassination. As Latin Americans became more and more suspicious of U.S. foreign policy, they began to steer their trade increasingly toward Japan and Europe.

Carter and Human Rights

When Jimmy Carter became president in 1977, he too sought to reduce American commitments abroad. According to David Skidmore, Carter's initial strategy was to (1) restrain overall defense spending and shift priorities from strategic and developing country intervention forces to NATO forces; (2) withdraw U.S. troops from South Korea; (3) reduce U.S. arms sales and military aid abroad; (4) restrict CIA covert actions; and (5) avoid military entanglements in peripheral regions and concentrate on key areas.[21]

However, Carter's methods for selling his policy to the American public were very different from Nixon's. Carter believed that Nixon and his secretary of state, Henry Kissinger, had gotten into trouble because their secretive and sometimes militant tactics were often incompatible with their détente strategy. Carter's foreign policy also was pragmatic, but he tried to wrap it in moral character. He wanted to place less emphasis on the coercive–noncoercive security dimension than his predecessors and more emphasis on the multilateral–unilateral community dimension. Carter also hoped to build positive support for his foreign policy by replacing America's reactive containment policy with a proactive human rights policy, as well as policies designed to protect the global environment and improve the lives of peoples in the developing world. One of the most dramatic foreign policy achievements of the Carter administration was the Panama Canal treaty, which gradually returned control of the Panama Canal to the government of Panama.

Although many of Carter's foreign policies were quite successful, the American public generally did not see it that way. They did not really understand the linkage between Carter's pragmatic efforts to limit U.S. commitments abroad and the normative aspects and ethical rhetoric of his foreign policy. From the standpoint of the public, Carter's criticisms of foreign leaders on human rights grounds were counterproductive—though the criticisms may have been deserved—because some of the leaders he criticized were from countries that staunchly supported the United States, such as Iran, South Korea, Argentina, the Philippines, and Nicaragua. What was not so clear to the public was that many of these dictators were going to fall anyway. But it took some time before the democratic forces unleashed by America's more humane policy in these and other countries could manage to replace these authoritarian leaders. Indeed, new democratic governments did not begin to emerge in Central and South America, Africa, and Asia for almost a decade. In the meantime, events abroad seemed to confirm the problems cited by Carter's critics at home.

Reasserting American Preponderance: 1979–1984

Shortly after the U.S. midterm congressional elections in 1978, the shah of Iran, who was probably America's staunchest ally in the Middle East other than Israel, saw major street demonstrations break out in his country. At first the United States assumed that the shah would survive these troubles as he had in the past, but in January 1979 the shah was forced to resign. He was replaced by a Shiite religious leader, the Ayatollah Ruhollah Khomeini. Khomeini encouraged the anti-American feelings of his supporters to the point that in November 1979 militant students entered the U.S. embassy in Tehran and took fifty-two embassy workers hostage. For the remainder of Carter's term adverse publicity on the hostage situation reminded Americans daily of the limits of American power overseas. The crisis also suggested to many that Carter's human rights policy may have undermined the power of many authoritarian governments friendly to the United States and might result in governments hostile to the United States coming into power. After all, similar pressure was being put on other friendly governments such as those of South Korea, Nicaragua, and the Philippines.

Then in December 1979 the Soviet Union invaded Afghanistan to save the leftist government of that country. Because the United States was already feeling pressure from communist activities in Africa and Central America, President Carter responded by turning more toward coercive actions, such as increasing the 1981 defense budget by 5 percent, placing an embargo on wheat shipments to the Soviet Union, boycotting the 1980 Summer Olympic Games in Moscow, and delaying consideration of the SALT II (Strategic Arms Limitation Talks) treaty, which was already bogged down in the U.S. Senate.

Another series of events that turned the Carter administration more toward coercion were changes in the balance and structure of the nuclear forces of the United States and the Soviet Union. Although Carter and Brezhnev had signed the SALT II treaty in June 1979, both countries were changing the character of their weapons systems. The Soviet Union not only had gained an advantage over the United States in the size and number of its land-based nuclear missiles but also had introduced a new long-range bomber, the "Backfire," and had begun to place MIRVs (multiple independent reentry vehicles) on their missiles in order to challenge areas in which the United States had an advantage in strategic nuclear weapons.[22] To compensate for these "losses," Carter had in turn authorized a new mobile missile, the MX, and ordered an array of cruise missiles, Trident submarines, and the B-1 bomber. American support for an arms agreement finally evaporated, however, when the Soviets decided to replace their old SS-4 and SS-5 intermediate-range nuclear missiles in Europe with more advanced SS-20s.

Both the Soviet Union and the United States agreed to put the ratification of SALT II on hold, and the United States decided to place new missiles in Europe. Although the European governments had approved this move, many Europeans were opposed to hosting these more powerful missiles on their territory. In response, the United States adopted a two-track policy in which it attempted to negotiate with the Soviet Union a reduction in intermediate-range missiles in Europe, while at the same time preparing to place new Nike missiles in Europe if the Soviet Union refused to negotiate.

Additional problems arose in Latin America. When the Sandinista rebels in Nicaragua were about to depose strongman Anastasio Somoza, President Carter decided to pursue a different policy than that used against Castro and other communists in Latin America in which the United States opposed these governments as soon as the United States suspected that their leaders were communists. Instead, the Carter administration chose to work with the Sandinistas. Carter believed the United States could compete successfully with communist countries for influence with these new regimes because it had so much more to offer them in terms of resources. This policy was very well received by Latin Americans, but it was difficult to implement because it frequently caught the rhetorical crossfire of Republicans in Congress and the Sandinista leaders in Nicaragua.

Despite all these policy innovations in the direction of community values, Carter attempted to run for reelection in 1980 as a militarist. But his inability to release the hostages in Iran and the continuing difficulties in Afghanistan and elsewhere put him on the defensive in relation to his Republican opponent, Ronald Reagan, who won the election handily. Reagan's reputation for pursuing peace through military strength was so well known that the guerrilla forces fighting in El Salvador actually began a military offensive between Reagan's election in November and his inauguration the following January in order to make headway before Reagan assumed the presidency and could act against them. Carter responded promptly to the crisis by sending military aid to the Salvadorans, who successfully blunted what turned out to be a premature offensive.

Reagan and the Evil Empire

Once in office President Reagan pursued an MCA foreign policy: unilateral, coercive, and proactive, as is shown in Table 4.7, and it contrasts with the foreign policies of Carter and Nixon, in Reagan's willingness to employ coercion. Reagan's foreign policy was built on a greatly strengthened American military. He immediately called for an expenditure of $1.6 trillion over a period of five years to gain a military advantage over the Soviet Union.

Reagan, like Carter, objected to the reactive character of the containment policy. But the resemblance ends there because the Reagan Doctrine was designed to use additional military strength, not human rights, to help noncommunist groups fight Soviet-supported governments worldwide. For example, Reagan formed and financed a separate Contra force to fight the Sandinistas in Nicaragua. He armed anticommunist forces in

Table 4.7. Dimensions of Foreign Policy: U.S. Efforts to Balance Commitments and Capabilities

	Multilateral		Unilateral	
	Coercive	Noncoercive	Noncoercive	Coercive
Proactive			Carter's emphasis on human rights	Reagan's increase in defense expenditures
Reactive			Nixon's emphasis on détente	

President Nixon attempted to lessen U.S. commitments abroad by improving relations with former enemy states. This MCA policy was unilateral because it was primarily a U.S. initiative especially in regard to China, noncoercive because it was supported by a series of arms control agreements, and reactive because it emphasized a lower level of involvement on both sides.

President Carter attempted to lessen the U.S. military burden by strengthening the positive aspects of American policy. This MCA policy was unilateral because the definition of human rights being utilized was American, and not universal, noncoercive because it sought to bypass the need for military forces, and proactive because the United States was prepared to use these human rights criteria as a basis for rewarding or punishing the states involved.

President Reagan's effort to increase U.S. military capabilities is clearly an MCA policy. It is unilateral because it was something the U.S. did regardless of the policies of other states, coercive because it emphasized the credibility of the American threat, and proactive because it was intended to have an impact abroad.

Angola and supplied Stinger missiles to the mujaheddin fighting the Soviets in Afghanistan. When his support for the forcible overthrow of the Sandinistas in Nicaragua aroused opposition in Congress, Reagan used covert means to get what he wanted, as illustrated by the Iran-Contra deal.[23]

Still, the most distinguishing characteristic of Reagan's foreign policy was its unilateralism. Since the formation of the Group of 77, the United States had found itself outvoted in the United Nations and associated organizations. Unlike his predecessors, Reagan was prepared to take independent actions on a whole array of issues from the environment to the use of force. As for aid packages, he generally preferred bilateral over multilateral ones so that the United States could maintain more control. In the United Nations, he withdrew from some UN councils and encouraged Congress to delay payment of U.S. annual dues in an effort to force the United Nations to reform itself in ways preferred by the United States.

Once Reagan established his armaments program, he became more interested in disarmament. In 1983, the same year that he referred to the Soviet Union as the "evil empire," he proposed his Strategic Defense Initiative (SDI). SDI was an effort to build weapons that were capable of protecting people not just by deterring nuclear strikes by others but also by avoiding the destructive effects of nuclear weapons even if they were used. For Reagan, SDI was not designed as a bargaining tool; it reflected the president's genuine interest in moving beyond mutual deterrence as a stand-in for real peace. These efforts at developing the SDI system continued under Presidents George H. W. Bush, Bill Clinton, and George W. Bush.

From an Improbable Victory to Preemptive War

Ironically Reagan, the man most responsible for this intensification of the cold war, also played a key role in getting the United States out of the cold war altogether. Over the course of the next twelve years (1985–1997) Presidents Reagan, George H. W. Bush, and Bill Clinton oversaw one of the most remarkable peaceful transformations in history. Although the Americans cautiously accepted the improvement in relations, the real impetus for disarmament in the fortieth year of the post–war period originated in the Soviet Union.

Reagan and Gorbachev

When Mikhail Gorbachev came to power in 1985, he was determined to improve the Soviet economy, which had suffered during the Brezhnev years. Gorbachev sensed that the resources the Soviet Union needed to bolster its domestic economy had to be siphoned off from its increasingly burdensome military sector. The country could afford to reduce its military expenditures, he believed, because the United States would also eventually reduce its military efforts if the Soviet Union appeared less threatening to the West.

Apparently, Gorbachev gleaned many of his ideas from the Western books he read in the Politburo library,[24] which reported that liberal critics of Reagan's defense policy were arguing that if the United States would reduce its armaments, the Soviet Union would do likewise. That policy made sense to Gorbachev, so he proceeded to develop an MCA foreign policy: multilateral, noncoercive, and reactive. The direction of Gorbachev's new Soviet foreign policy provided the opening needed for genuine progress on disarmament. See Table 4.8.

By December 1987 Gorbachev and Reagan had signed a separate Intermediate Nuclear Force Treaty, which provided for the removal of all intermediate-range nuclear missiles from Europe. In early 1988 Gorbachev took another giant step by announcing a unilateral reduction of Soviet troops in Europe and renouncing the use or threat of force to advance Soviet interests in Eastern Europe. Later that same year Gorbachev announced that all Soviet troops would be withdrawn from Afghanistan in ten months. By 1990 Gorbachev and the new American president, George H. W. Bush, had signed the Conventional Armed Forces in Europe (CFE) Treaty, which provided for the reduction of Soviet conventional forces in Europe. Also, the first Strategic Arms Reduction Treaty (START I), which was originally negotiated in 1982 under Reagan, was eventually signed by Bush in July 1991. START I provided for a 30 percent reduction in strategic nuclear forces. Thus these years witnessed a major demilitarization both in Europe and at the strategic nuclear level.

George H. W. Bush and the New World Order

The end of the cold war began in 1989, as first Czechoslovakia and then Hungary overturned their communist governments, and the Soviet Union announced that it would take no action. The most noteworthy single event was the fall of the Berlin Wall on November 9, 1989. Shortly thereafter, one Eastern European government after another tumbled, but the collapse did not end there. In early 1990 Estonia declared its independence from the Soviet Union, followed by Lithuania. The Soviet Union did send in troops to protect Lithuania's large Russian population, but eventually it agreed to withdraw them. Gorbachev found himself caught in a situation in which one peripheral nationality group after another broke away from the Russocentric Soviet Union. By December 25, 1991, the Soviet Union had formally dissolved, to be replaced by the Commonwealth of Independent States.

Gorbachev's policies have been criticized, particularly in the Soviet Union, because they led to the demise of that country. But if *perestroika*—the "restructuring" of the Soviet bureaucratic and economic system—had succeeded in reviving the economy before *glasnost*—the policy of greater "openness" of the political system—had been introduced, the economy of the country might not have collapsed as it did. It is also important to recognize that the MCA foreign policy that failed to preserve the Soviet Union actually strengthened the United States. The difference in outcomes for the two states results from the contrast in their strategic positions in the world. Because the strength of the Soviet Union depended almost entirely on its military power, the Soviet government could not surrender military capability without relinquishing its power both within the Soviet bloc and within the Soviet Union itself. However, the United States was not dependent solely on these strategic weapons for its status in the world and could match many of the Soviet steps in strategic nuclear disarmament without undermining its position.

Moreover, the willingness of Reagan and Bush to pursue nuclear disarmament with the Soviet Union did not preclude them from using conventional military force. U.S. foreign policy remained coercive and proactive even as the Soviet Union began pulling out of its strongholds in the nonindustrialized countries. The coercive, proactive character of American foreign policy is evident throughout the period. For example, the Russian decision to withdraw from Afghanistan was partly the result of Reagan's decision to provide the Soviets' opponents in that conflict with a significant number of Stinger missiles. Reagan also conducted an air strike against Mu'ammar Qadhafi of Libya in 1987. If American policy was any less militarist or interventionist in this period, it is only because the Soviet Union had pulled out of so many contested areas. The coercive, proactive character of American policy under George H. W. Bush was manifest in the U.S. military response to Iraq's invasion of Kuwait in 1990 and in Bush's decision to order military action in Panama.

Both Reagan and Bush also remained unilateralist in their approach to American foreign policy. Both presidents undertook unilateral policies in support of democracy and capitalism abroad. Their financial support for the United Nations was conditional. Even though Bush used the Security Council of the United Nations as the vehicle for legitimizing the coalition he organized against Iraq in the Gulf War, it was quite clear that the United States was prepared to act unilaterally if the United Nations did not do so.

Because Bush was president during the time the cold war ended and the post–cold war period began, many of the issues that President Clinton dealt with during his eight years in office were tied to the actions or inactions of the Bush administration. Although Bush was primarily interested in foreign affairs, he never effectively defined the **new world order,** perhaps because he was comfortable with the cold war and essentially interested in bringing stability in an era of change. For his part, President Clinton was also slow to define a new direction for U.S. foreign policy

Table 4.8. Dimensions of Foreign Policy: U.S. and Soviet Policies at the End of the Cold War

| | Multilateral | | Unilateral | |
	Coercive	Noncoercive	Noncoercive	Coercive
Proactive				Ronald Reagan's and George H. W. Bush's conventional force policy
Reactive	Reagan's[a] SDI policy	Gorbachev's foreign policy		

Gorbachev's foreign policy in the late 1980s became increasingly MCA. It was multilateral because he wanted as much as possible to work jointly with his principal opponent, the United States, and even through the United Nations, noncoercive because he was eager to reduce the emphasis on the military, and reactive because he hoped that the United States would disengage from the cold war as the Soviet Union disengaged.

Reagan's Strategic Defense Initiative (SDI) was MCA. It was multilateral in that he saw it not just as a national defense but a defense available to all countries, coercive because it depended on the use of force, and reactive because he foresaw that each country could decide for itself to use it.

Reagan and George H. W. Bush maintained U.S. conventional force capabilities and generally pursued an MCA policy insofar as these capabilities were concerned. The conventional arms policy was unilateral because the United States alone decided when these forces would be used, coercive because military forces were employed, and proactive because they were aggressively employed abroad.

[a]Reagan's notion was that this capability would be shared at least with the Soviet Union.

Source: BBC Interview cited by Mark W. Davis in "Reagan's Real Reason for SDI," *Policy Review* (Oct. 2000).

both because he was not as interested as Bush in foreign affairs and because he could never really decide what to do.

The major exception to this scenario of lesser involvement was U.S. foreign policy toward Eastern Europe where the Bush administration immediately supported German unification. The United States succeeded in convincing the Soviets to accept German economic assistance in exchange for accepting a united Germany. This development set the stage for progress toward establishing the European Union as well as for President Clinton's policies toward Eastern Europe such as Partnership for Peace and NATO expansion.

Enlargement and Engagement under Clinton

President Clinton characterized his foreign policy in terms of **engagement** and **enlargement**. Engagement is best exemplified by the policy of actively promoting American exports abroad. Clinton enhanced the role of the Department of Commerce so that it could reach the ten big emerging markets—China (including Hong Kong and Taiwan), India, Indonesia, South Korea, Mexico, Brazil, Argentina, Poland, Turkey, and South Africa. He also called for expanded trade with Russia and Eastern Europe. But the Clinton administration was not initially prepared to deal with the international financial problems that accompanied this rapid expansion of trade and investment. As a result, a series of financial breakdowns emerged in Mexico, Thailand, South Korea, Indonesia, and other countries in Southeast Asia, as well as in Brazil and eventually Russia.

Clinton's concept of enlargement built on the efforts of his predecessors—Carter, Reagan and Bush—to promote human rights and democracy in Eastern Europe and other areas of the world. At first it appeared that the end of the cold war had paved the way for the settlement of many of the world's ongoing conflicts. Within a few years significant progress was made with the help of the United Nations in dealing with internal conflicts in South Africa, Nicaragua, Guatemala, El Salvador, Cambodia, Northern Ireland, and even Israel.

Clinton was endeavoring to promote **democratic peace**—that is, to develop a community of states—namely, market economies and democratic governments that would not go to war with one another because they shared governments and economies conducive to cooperative relations, as exemplified in the EU. The efforts to promote human rights and democracy were often a secondary consideration in countries such as China and Russia, however. There, priority was given to immediate economic and security concerns. Nevertheless, these community values were still an element of U.S. foreign policy in those countries.

From Multilateralism to Unilateralism

But engagement and enlargement did not fully describe Clinton's security policy. The end of the cold war spawned new conflicts that challenged both the United Nations and the major powers. Some of these conflicts involved medium-range powers that either felt threatened by the new order or were prepared to take advantage of it. George H. W. Bush's administration had identified five rogue states—Iran, Iraq, Libya, North Korea, and Cuba. Their existence justified a more cautious approach to disarmament and concern about downsizing the military.

Other new conflicts revolved around small powers or breakaway republics within larger powers in which regional organizations or the United Nations had become involved because of the gross atrocities being committed by one side or both. The Clinton administration inherited many of these problems—Bosnia, Haiti, and Somalia—from its predecessor, but in each case these problems seemed to require **peacemaking** as opposed to **peacekeeping** forces. Peacemaking forces must have the ability to compel one or more sides in a conflict to do something contrary to their will. Although Clinton initially flirted with the idea of working through the United Nations to deal with these situations, he eventually decided to work mainly through NATO by employing air strikes in Kosovo.

Lacking confidence in the UN's peacemaking capabilities, Clinton decided to turn organizations that had originally been designed to provide collective defense within NATO into a "coalition of the willing" that could be used outside NATO. Table 4.9 illustrates the foreign policy dimensions of the unilateral peacemaking policy with NATO forces that Clinton first employed in Kosovo in 1999.

During the last years of the Clinton administration and the first years of the George W. Bush administration it seemed as though the world was increasingly divided into two parts. One part—represented by an expanding EU and NATO—was experiencing the political stability and economic progress associated with the democratic peace. The other part—represented by less developed countries and especially rogue states—was imperiled by poverty, disease, and political instability.

George W. Bush and Preemptive War

When George W. Bush became president, he threatened to extend a coercive and unilateral preemptive policy to the rogue states he identified as "the axis of evil," namely Iran, Iraq, and North Korea. What really gave this policy of preemption impetus, however, was the al Qaeda attack of

Table 4.9. Dimensions of Foreign Policy: Bill Clinton and George W. Bush

	Multilateral		Unilateral	
	Coercive	Noncoercive	Noncoercive	Coercive
Proactive	Clinton's policy with respect to Bosnia in 1993			Bill Clinton's policy in Kosovo and George W. Bush's policy in Iraq
Reactive				

Bill Clinton's foreign policy with respect to Bosnia was MCA—multilateral in the sense that the United States consulted broadly with the United Nations and NATO in regard to what action should be taken in Bosnia, coercive in that the Clinton administration was prepared to use force if others agreed, and proactive because the United States was willing to become involved even though these attacks could involve casualties on all sides.

Clinton's foreign policy with respect to Kosovo and George W. Bush's foreign policy are MCA—unilateral because the United States is willing to act regardless of the opinions of other key states, coercive in that they envisage the use of force, and proactive because they planned preemptive strikes to keep dangerous situations under control.

September 11, 2001, on New York's World Trade Center and the Pentagon in Washington, D.C. The fact that al Qaeda was a nonstate actor and used U.S. commercial planes against American targets undermined people's faith in the traditional concepts of just—or defensive—war and deterrence. How could the government of the United States limit itself to self-defense when it faced such an elusive enemy?

At this point George W. Bush rallied a united nation against the al Qaeda network that was clandestinely headquartered in Afghanistan by invading that country. In its effort to destroy al Qaeda and its leader, Osama bin Laden, the United States successfully invaded Afghanistan. But when bin Laden's capture became problematic, President Bush decided to tie the war against terrorism to Iraq, one of the states belonging to the previously identified "axis of evil." In his 2002 National Security Strategy paper Bush argued that the threat of international terrorism justified pre-emptive war whenever it was determined that there was a significant terrorist threat.[25] The difference between the MCA foreign policy in Afghanistan and the MCA foreign policy in Iraq is shown in Table 4.10.

The invasion of Iraq took place in the spring of 2003. The Bush administration justified the invasion on the grounds that Saddam Hussein, the leader of Iraq, would eventually supply weapons of mass destruction (WMD) to international terrorists. Although neither WMD nor formal ties between Iraq and al Qaeda were discovered once Saddam Hussein's government was overthrown, the United States has become engaged in an

Table 4.10. Dimensions of Foreign Policy: U.S. Policy in Iraq and Afghanistan

| | Multilateral | | Unilateral | |
	Coercive	Noncoercive	Noncoercive	Coercive
Proactive	Policy of George W. Bush in Afghanistan in 2001			Policy of George W. Bush in Iraq in 2003
Reactive				

George W. Bush's policy in Afghanistan in 2001 was MCA—multilateral because it had the support of the UN Security Council, coercive because it involved the use of force, and proactive because it carried the U.S. response to the September 11, 2001 attacks to suspected al Qaeda bases in Afghanistan. George W. Bush's invasion of Iraq in 2003 was MCA—unilateral because it proceeded without the active support of China, France, Russia, and other key states in the UN Security Council, coercive because it employed the whole panoply of military power, and proactive both because it had devastating effects in Iraq and because it created negative public reactions abroad.

ambitious war for seemingly limitless and vaguely defined ends—peace, democracy, and freedom—in Iraq.

Conclusion

The United States entered the Second World War determined to defeat Germany and Japan with the hope that it could depend on its allies to maintain the peace once it had been won. After the war the United States largely succeeded in building friendly relationships with its former enemies, but it was not able to accommodate the demands of its Soviet ally. A cold war between these two superpowers largely prevented the United States from addressing many of the global issues raised by the Second World War—with regard to decolonization, economic development of the former colonies, development of an effective United Nations with peacekeeping abilities.

When the cold war ended, the United States moved once again to accommodate its main rival—now Russia—and even made friends with most of the states formerly associated with the Soviet Union. But the issues of development and peace that had been largely deferred during the cold war remained and even sired new security issues. Thus despite its dominant position of power in the world for over a century and a quarter, the United States now faces a range of community, security, and prosperity issues. These issues will be discussed in more detail in Part II.

Key Concepts

balancing   134
bandwagoning   134
democratic peace   157
détente   146
engagement   156
enlargement   156
flexible response   142
graduated deterrence   142
massive retaliation   139

McCarthy era   129
missile gap   140
mutual assured destruction   141
new world order   155
nonaligned movement   134
peacekeeping   157
peacemaking   157
Vietnamization   146
wars of national liberation   139

Suggested Readings

1. Allison, Graham and Philip, Zelikow. *Essence of Decision: Explaining the Cuban Missile Crisis.* New York: Addison Wesley Longman, 1999.

2. Fordham, Benjamin O. *Building the Cold War Consensus: The Political Economy of U.S. National Security Policy, 1949–1951.* Ann Arbor: University of Michigan Press, 1998.

3. Gaddis, John Lewis. *Strategies of Containment: A Critical Appraisal of American Security Policy during the Cold War.* rev. and exp. ed. New York: Oxford University Press, 2005.

PART II

Contemporary Foreign Policy

CHAPTERS 5 THROUGH 7 focus on different dimensions of foreign policy, that is, community, security, and prosperity. These dimensions represent the goals or values associated with three basic motivations: social affiliation, power, and achievement, respectively. The framework assumes that there are differences among individuals with respect to the values on each of these dimensions. For example, some people prefer equality; others, liberty on the community dimension. Some prefer domination; others, mutual consent on the security dimension. And some prefer to maximize benefits; others, to minimize costs on the prosperity dimension. Although all foreign policy choices reflect these three motivations, it is helpful to appraise the policies on each dimension separately. Thus Chapter 5 deals with the community dimension; Chapter 6, the security dimension; and Chapter 7, the prosperity dimension.

All three chapters are organized similarly. They begin by asking the question: what are the foreign policy preferences of actors on this dimension? Because foreign policy actors have multiple goals, it is difficult to predict what they will do without knowing both what their specific objectives are on each dimension and how they order their preferences for these objectives. Because foreign policy involves other actors, the initial dispositions of an actor for various goals become specific objectives only once the actor takes into account the likely responses of other actors. For example, President George W. Bush's initial goal in August 2002 was to oust Saddam Hussein as the president of Iraq, but whether that ultimately became his foreign policy objective depended, at least in part, on his expectations for what people in Iraq would do and what other members of the UN Security Council would do. Thus in the first section of Chapters 5 through 7, the predispositions and perceptions of actors are discussed before any attempt is made to identify and order objectives.

But having a clear set of objectives is not sufficient to define a foreign policy; it is also necessary to identify the methods used to achieve those objectives. By developing at least one option in each cell of the 2 × 2 × 2 tables employed in Chapters 2 through 4, the text provides a menu from which to choose suitable methods. Each prospective method for implementing a preferred policy involves choices among alternative courses of action on each of the three dimensions. For example, if the aim of a policy is to promote human rights, it is important to know who should act (the state or the international community), what instrument should be used (coercion or persuasion), and how vigorous the action should be (proactive or reactive). Thus the second section of Chapters 5 through 7 develops alternative courses of action or options.

Finally, a judgment needs to be made as to which method is likely to be the most appropriate or best for achieving a given set of objectives. The three criteria suggested by the three dimensions—acceptability on the community dimension, effectiveness on the security dimension, and efficiency on the prosperity dimension—are useful in making this determination. Chapter 5 raises all three criteria in relation to two community policy issues: humanitarian intervention and environmental justice; Chapter 6, the disposition of nuclear weapons and stability in the developing world; and Chapter 7, prosperity-related policy in the form of economic development and economic sanctions.

Although the organization of each of these chapters is similar, the methods of analysis vary not only because each focuses on a different dimension and set of values but also because different approaches can be employed in analyzing dispositions, perceptions, objectives, and options. In order to avoid needless repetition and present a broader range of methods, different techniques are employed in these chapters. Thus the careful reader should ask himself or herself whether the approach employed in one chapter is equally applicable in another.

CHAPTER 5

Community Policies: Humanitarian Intervention and Environmental Justice

One way in which Americans differ from one another is how they define the community in which they live. Some are communitarians because they draw a sharp distinction between citizens and aliens. Others are cosmopolitans because they emphasize the similarities between foreigners and themselves. When it comes to issues such as immigration, communitarians usually want to stop illegal immigration at all costs; cosmopolitans are more sympathetic to those who want to enter the United States, regardless of their status. The picture above depicts the press of legal entrants—both American and Mexican—waiting to cross into the United States from Tijuana, Mexico. Communitarians would see this as just the tip of the iceberg because an estimated 800,000 illegal immigrants enter the country every year; cosmopolitans would view this scene with somewhat more equanimity, recognizing that immigration, both legal and illegal, is primarily the result of huge economic disparities that exist between countries.

THE STATE IS THE PRIMARY actor in American foreign policy, but what the state represents depends on the values, norms, and identities of the people who act on behalf of the state at any given time. Usually the people who matter the most are those who hold official positions in the government, but the leaders of nongovernment organizations, and even private individuals acting alone—such as Amy Curtis—or collectively, also play an important role in making foreign policy. To the extent that these individuals share common values, expectations, and beliefs about appropriate behavior, they give the foreign policy of a state a sense of stability and continuity. But individuals often hold different values, norms, and identities. When this occurs, particularly during transitions in government, these differences create an expectation of change and perhaps a sense of instability.

This chapter is concerned with the impact of ideas about community on American foreign policy. People often assume that states represent a unified people who share a common culture, but virtually all states encompass multiple cultures, and the people within those societies have a wide variety of beliefs. Because such a variety of people make up any state, those who hold key leadership positions may have very different ideas from each other and from some or all of the people they claim to represent about the identity of the state and about the norms that should govern its behavior. For example, some individuals may identify the state with a particular religion, class, or ethnic group; others may identify the state as a protector of human rights, a global policeman, or an advanced economy; and those in key leadership positions may both disagree with one another or identify with one viewpoint over another. These different identities and the norms implicit within them influence the foreign policy behavior of states.

Because ideas shape the self-identification of states and their understandings about how they ought to behave, different conceptions of community will invariably affect the objectives states pursue and the methods they prefer. Once the foreign policy analyst identifies these policy preferences and methods, the analyst can assess a number of key community foreign policies. Although this chapter emphasizes the logic of acceptability, such policies must also satisfy the criteria of effectiveness and efficiency.

Identifying Foreign Policy Objectives

The objectives of foreign policy are not always easy to identify. The foreign policy analyst must discover which of the many goals desired by the foreign policy actor are actually the objectives for which that actor is willing to make sacrifices. Thus the analyst must filter the basic needs and desires—or dispositions—of the actor through the actor's perceptions of a foreign policy situation. Then the analyst is able to define the actor's objectives and order the actor's preferences for those objectives.

The Dispositions of Foreign Policy Actors

In the Chapter 1 description, community values ranged from freedom, liberty, and independence on the one hand to equality, generality, and universality on the other. Once all these values were reduced to the polar values of independence and unity, they could be arrayed along a single dimension. Independence was the frequent rallying point of those favoring more exclusive communities, whereas unity was the most cherished value of those favoring more inclusive communities. Now in order to elaborate the kinds of community values that motivate foreign policy actors, these values will be described as **visions**. A vision refers here to the gut feeling or hunches people have about how things are accomplished in the real world. A vision reflects a general disposition or inclination rather than a preference in a specific situation.[1]

The Communitarian Vision.   One vision—held by **communitarians**— is based on the idea that more exclusive values are derived from the shared history, geography, culture, and laws of a community. Communitarians believe that an "individual finds meaning in life by virtue of his or her membership in a political community."[2] That community may be large or small, but it does not encompass the entire global community. For this reason, communitarians usually make a fairly sharp distinction between the citizens of a nation-state and aliens. President George W. Bush and former New York mayor Rudolph Giuliani are good examples of communitarians.

Communitarians assume that the boundaries of the community of the nation and the state are coterminous, and as a result, communitarians usually emphasize the sovereign authority of the state to protect the freedom and independence of its citizens. From the communitarian perspective, the state's duty is to defend and promote the values of the community—that is, the national interest.

The communitarian vision of community creates a diverse international system in which "ethical and moral standards differ in different places and times."[3] The world of communitarians is divided into a large number of separate nations or civilizations, each of whom may believe that only it understands the world as it really is. For example, those figures whom Israel labels as terrorists would be regarded as freedom fighters by many Palestinians.

The Cosmopolitan Vision.   The other vision—one held by **cosmopolitans**—is based on the idea that individuals have a shared moral personality in a sense that states do not. The term, cosmopolitan, as used here derives from the ancient Greek understanding of the term. In ancient Greece most people identified mainly with their *polis* or city-state; people who identified with the *cosmos* were cosmopolitans. Cosmopolitans

believe that all individuals have the same rights and obligations regardless
of the particular community in which they happen to reside. Former president Jimmy Carter, the late Martin Luther King Jr., and even former president Bill Clinton are examples of cosmopolitans. Unlike communitarians,
cosmopolitans do not make a sharp distinction between citizens and aliens,
because they believe all people have the same basic human rights regardless of citizenship or where they happen to be at a particular time.

Moreover, cosmopolitans do not attach deep moral significance to differences in class, ethnicity, gender, race, and citizenship status; rather,
they emphasize the values of equality, generality, and universality.[4] They
envisage a world in which all individuals should have similar rights and
obligations and share common interests. Cosmopolitans give more cre-
dence to global interests than to national interests, or at least define national interests in terms of global interests. For guidance on an issue,
cosmopolitans may look to the some sixty conventions and covenants
signed and ratified by the member countries of the United Nations, such
as the Universal Declaration of Human Rights, the International Covenant
for Political and Civil Rights, and the International Covenant for Economic and Social Rights.

Two Visions of the Law.   Traditional international law incorporates elements of both the communitarian and the cosmopolitan vision. It favors
communitarians by recognizing the sovereignty of individual states and
by embracing the principle of noninterference in the affairs of other states.
Thus within various states communitarian norms are likely to prevail,
particularly in domestic affairs. However, the very idea that all states are
equal and should respect the sovereign authority of other states implies
that there are generally agreed upon norms at the international level that
confer responsibilities as well as rights on states. To the extent that these
rights and responsibilities are based on the inherent worth of the people
who compose the state, they are based on cosmopolitan norms.

Communitarians and cosmopolitans may accept many of the same
norms or values, but communitarians give primacy to the norms developed within their own communities, accepting more general norms that
regulate their behavior toward other communities only when they have
consented to those norms. Cosmopolitans give priority to universal standards or norms, accommodating some differences between various communities. Although a communitarian and a cosmopolitan could agree that
the same rule should apply at various levels of society, it does make a difference whether one asserts that communitarian or cosmopolitan rules
are primary. Liberal communitarians are more likely than conservative
communitarians to incorporate the norms employed by other communities, and conservative communitarians are less likely than their counterparts to do so.

Not all of the rules governing state behavior at the international level have the same standing. A distinction is usually made between practices, norms, and laws. Practices are rules that states and individuals generally follow in large part because they have predictable physical consequences. For example, it is a wise practice to oppose aggressors because if a state does not do so it may encourage further aggression. Norms encompass ethical rules that define what ought to be done. Norms often contain principles of justice and equity, which individuals and states employ to deal fairly and honestly with one another in domestic and international societies throughout the world. For example, people in most societies extend hospitality to foreigners, although the character of that hospitality is likely to vary significantly from one country to another. Laws incorporate written or codified principles such as those embodied within the treaties and conventions that states have formally adopted, such as the Charter of the United Nations.

Both communitarians and cosmopolitans have to identify the rules that are applicable to them. In some ways cosmopolitans may have a more difficult task, because they must justify rules that can serve as universal standards for behavior. But communitarians face two difficulties. First, communitarian standards are also difficult to discern because many of the differences that exist in the world at large are also reflected in local communities. Second, communitarians must define the boundaries of the community because communitarian values may change depending on who is considered part of the community. For example, the John Birch Society defines America much differently than the American Civil Liberties Union.

There are two ways of thinking about the boundaries created by communitarian foreign policies. One way emphasizes actual physical boundaries; the other, the manner in which a state's foreign policy decisions create winners and losers regardless of residence or citizenship. For decisions emphasizing boundaries, the division is always between citizens and aliens regardless of the decision. But for decisions that create winners and losers regardless of citizenship, the division is between those who favor a decision and those who oppose it. The former are likely to view themselves as winners, and the latter to view themselves as losers.

However one defines community, there will always be some people who do not regard themselves as part of it. This is the reason for a foreign policy. In order to determine the objectives of that foreign policy one needs to consider one's perception of this situation, including one's perception of the values of other actors.

Different Perceptions

This section will consider some of the most important events since the end of the cold war and how different perceptions of these events and varying priorities assigned to them led Americans and others to create very different visions of the kind of world in which they were living. These varied conceptions steered many Americans toward one of three very different scenarios: the rise of a **democratic community,** the descent into a more profound **anarchistic community,** and the emergence of a **global community.**

A Democratic Community.   Many liberal communitarians viewed the disappearance of communist governments in the late 1980s and early 1990s in most Central and Eastern European countries and the emergence of new, market-oriented democracies in their place as the most striking change in the character of the global community at the end of the cold war. Because new democracies had already emerged in Latin America, Asia, and even Africa in the 1980s, the prospect for the emergence of a community of democratic states throughout most of Europe seemed to be good—indeed almost too good to be true.

Yet a late eighteenth-century German philosopher, Immanuel Kant, had predicted that a community of **republics**—governments in which people choose representatives who in turn make political choices for them—would eventually emerge. Kant even foresaw the possibility that some republics might extend the methods they used to govern themselves internally to their relations with each other and form a democratic league. He also hoped that one day this democratic league might influence other states to join in this democratic peace. Thus when Americans saw that Europeans who had formerly lived under communist rule were now embracing the ideals of both democracy and capitalism, these Americans perceived the opportunity to extend their democratic community across the whole of Europe and possibly beyond.

Progress came quickly as West Germany, the leading developed state in Europe, incorporated the former communist East Germany into a united Germany. Germany then deepened its commitment to the European Union (EU) first by ratifying the Maastricht Treaty in 1992 and then by working for a common European currency. Most other Western European states followed suit. The United States supported these efforts and took the initiative in creating the Partnership for Peace program between the NATO countries and the countries of Central and Eastern Europe. The Partnership for Peace aimed to develop NATO's political and economic potential for building new relationships with the fledgling market democracies of Eastern Europe.

The United States also took the lead in convincing the newly independent states of Ukraine, Belarus, and Kazakhstan to return the nuclear weapons they had inherited from the former Soviet Union to Russia, thus removing one of the primary obstacles to the democratic peace in Europe. In addition, the United States sought to build broader economic communities around key democratic states by adopting the North America Free

Trade Agreement (NAFTA) and by promoting the Asia-Pacific Economic Cooperation (APEC) forum. By 1995 the United States, with the help of most other countries in the United Nations, had moved a step closer to a democratic peace by renewing indefinitely the Nuclear Nonproliferation Treaty.

But the prospects for a democratic peace were not just reflected in the emergence of new democracies and evidence of cooperation among the older democracies and the new states. The possibilities of a democratic peace were reflected in the willingness of individual states to submit the most difficult issues to decision by elections or by negotiations. For example, in early 1992 white South Africans approved the reform plan proposed by President F. W. de Klerk for bringing blacks and other minorities into the governing process in South Africa—a decision that swept aside the entrenched policy of apartheid (the strict separation of blacks and whites) in that country. In the elections that followed in 1994 under the careful eye of UN observers, Nelson Mandela, the long-imprisoned leader of the African National Congress, replaced de Klerk as president. Elsewhere in Africa, the United Nations facilitated negotiations between socialist regimes in Angola and Mozambique and their opponents.

A negotiated peace even seemed possible in the Middle East. Israel had administered the West Bank and the Gaza Strip since the 1967 Six-Day War between Israel and its Arab neighbors, and the prospects for a homeland for Palestinians had seemed improbable during the cold war because the United States supported Israel and the Soviet Union supported the Palestinians. However, the inability of the Arabs to count on communist support after the collapse of the Soviet Union and America's ability to get Israel to refrain from military action during the 1991 Persian Gulf War set the stage for Arab and Israeli leaders to meet in Madrid in 1992 to begin the negotiation process. By 1993 Israel and the Palestinian Liberation Organization had signed an agreement to allow some Palestinian self-government in Gaza and limited areas on the West Bank.

Elsewhere, Russia, China, and the United States supported a UN program for negotiations and free elections in Cambodia in 1993. The UN assisted as well in negotiated solutions in Central American nations, such as Nicaragua, El Salvador, and Guatemala, where communist rhetoric had often justified internal wars. This spirit of compromise even reached Northern Ireland where the conflict between British Protestants and Irish Catholics had smoldered for centuries.

By the end of the first two years of the George W. Bush administration many American cosmopolitans could take heart from the expansion of NATO and the EU, but some of the progress toward democratic union had already come unraveled, especially in the Middle East. Liberal communitarians believed that America had proven itself to be "the city on the hill" by extending the democratic community from Eastern Europe to the

United States to Japan and possibly beyond. However, conservative communitarians, such as the Librarian of Congress James H. Billington, warned that there was a "real risk Russia will produce an authoritarian regime and that the establishment of such a regime or movement toward it could result in a giant version of the violent disintegration of Yugoslavia." [5]

An Anarchistic Community. While liberal communitarians were relishing the prospects of a democratic community, conservative communitarians in the American Security Council and other conservative organizations were perceiving a very different kind of post–cold war world, as exemplified in Billington's warning. The prospects for a democratic community, especially in Europe, had been built at least in part on the desire of people for independence and improved standards of living. But when these same motivations led various ethnic groups to seek self-determination from some of the newly independent states of Central and Eastern Europe, the prospects for a democratic peace were quickly shattered for conservative communitarians, to be replaced by the specter of internal war and abject poverty.

As early as 1991, war broke out in Yugoslavia, resulting in the emergence of several new states, one of which, Bosnia, became embroiled in a particularly bloody civil war. Internal wars also broke out in just under half of the former Soviet republics, including Armenia, Azerbaijan, Moldova, Tajikistan, Georgia, and Russia itself. In Bosnia, the bloodshed lasted over four years. Then several years later a civil war also flared up in Kosovo, a province of Serbia (what remained of the former Yugoslavia). In 1999 NATO employed air strikes to deal with the conflict between Serbs and Albanians in Kosovo. Although as of 2005 Bosnia and Kosovo were still under UN administration and NATO protection, the ethnic and economic conflicts that fed these internal wars were hardly settled. Likewise, tensions continued in some of the republics of the former Soviet Union.

Perhaps no conflict exemplifies the dangers of the post–cold war period better than the 1991 Persian Gulf War. Saddam Hussein, the leader of Iraq, invaded the neighboring state of Kuwait in the name of the impoverished masses of the Middle East. Although the United States mobilized a coalition of mostly democratic states under the UN banner to drive Hussein out of Kuwait, Saddam Hussein quickly reestablished his position within Iraq.

Meanwhile, the United Nations was eager to demonstrate its capacity for maintaining the peace now that Russia and the West were cooperating in the Security Council. But Russia opposed any UN peacekeeping operations in any former Soviet territory, preferring instead to have the regionally based Commonwealth of Independent States do so. Nevertheless, in February 1992 UN Secretary General Boutros Boutros-Ghali presented "An Agenda for Peace" in which he called on the United Nations to undertake **nation-building** and peace enforcement activities as well as its traditional peacekeeping ones. As a result, the United Nations became involved in almost as many peacekeeping situations in a period of about three years as it had in the previous forty years.

The United Nations first became involved in Yugoslavia in late 1991. It sought to maintain peace by placing peacekeeping forces in two of the Yugoslavian republics that were seeking independence—Croatia and Bosnia. The situation was particularly dangerous in Bosnia, where there were more Muslims than either Serbs or Croats. There, in the midst of a civil war, the UN undertook a broad range of activities such as humanitarian aid and refugee assistance, peacekeeping, human rights monitoring and protection, peacemaking, and peace enforcement. Although UN forces managed to hold things together until the Dayton accords, UN forces constantly had to choose between saving themselves and protecting people in UN-sponsored "safe havens." More often than not, they chose to save themselves.

Unfortunately, the crises in the East African nations of Somalia and Rwanda in the early 1990s demonstrated that many of the countries that had achieved political independence during the cold war years had not developed viable governments. By the end of 1992 the government of Somalia had collapsed and its people were facing starvation. In response, both the United States and the United Nations sent forces into the country to restore order and assist citizens and refugees. When U.S. and UN forces began to disarm the forces under the local warlords, eighteen U.S. Army Rangers were killed, and the United States eventually pulled its forces out of Somalia. The United Nations was unable to replace them and had to change its mission to work with the warlords.

A little over a year later, the United Nations was asked to protect the Hutus in Rwanda from raids by Tutsi rebels in Uganda. Almost immediately, however, that small UN force also had to contend with widespread retaliatory attacks on the Tutsi in Rwanda by the ruling Hutus. Unable to convince either the great powers or other African states to support more decisive action during the height of the Rwandan genocide, the Security Council first pulled its small contingent out of Rwanda altogether and then allowed a small French force to undertake a brief rescue mission. Eventually the Tutsi army defeated the Hutus, who fled to neighboring countries. The UN was never able to protect the Hutu refugees either from the armed killers in their midst or the Tutsi outside the refugee camps, and eventually a great many Hutus were killed when Tutsi-led forces chased the refugees out of the camps in Zaire.

In both the Balkans and East Africa, UN forces failed to achieve many of the goals assigned to them. In commenting on the Rwandan crisis, the new secretary general of the United Nations, Kofi Annan, noted that there was more than enough blame to go around. Many American cosmopolitans and some liberal communitarians were prepared to intervene in these crises with humanitarian aid, but conservative communitarians generally thought that the United States and the UN had already overextended themselves trying to bring about changes that could not be controlled by outsiders. They argued that the United States should only become involved if its interests were directly affected. Liberal communitarians and cosmopolitans warned that in an interdependent world it is often difficult to separate one's own interests from those of the wider world.

Under the George W. Bush administration the collapse of Israeli-Palestinian negotiations, the renewal of the war in Chechnya, Russia, continuing wars in Africa, the increase in terrorism, and the chaos in Iraq demonstrated that anarchy remained a viable perspective on the world. Yet the United Nations had rebounded from some of its earlier tribulations and continued to play an essential role throughout the world, especially in Afghanistan, Africa, the Balkans, and Iraq. But periodic wars were not the major problem; many people felt that the basic problem was structural and endemic to the very organization of the global community.

The Global Community.   Since the 1960s the leaders of many developing countries had been striving to elevate economic development rights to the same level as political and civil rights. They argued that international justice required that everyone be given a chance to enjoy the good life. Now that the cold war was over, developed countries were obligated to turn their attention to the problems of poverty throughout the developing world. Most cosmopolitans, such as members of the World Federalist Movement, would support this perspective.

The impetus for dealing with economic disparity throughout the world also came from the growing awareness that modern industrial practices threatened the global environment. If something was not done to control the destruction of the world's habitat, developed countries could not hope to maintain their standards of living and developing countries could not hope to catch up through industrialization. The greatest fear, at least among developed countries, was that greenhouse gas emissions would result in **global warming**, which would have catastrophic effects on economies throughout the world. Because no one country or even group of countries could effectively address this problem on their own, a major collective effort through the United Nations was needed.

The best opportunity to address global environmental and economic issues arose in June 1992 with the convocation of the Earth Summit in Rio de Janeiro, Brazil. The International Conference on Environment and Development's acceptance of a healthy environment and sustainable economic development as fundamental human rights was expressed as the first principle of its declaration: "Human beings are at the centre of concern for sustainable development. They are entitled to a healthy and productive life in harmony with nature." [6]

By the end of the conference, which was attended by 120 heads of state, including the leaders of the G-7 group of industrialized countries, 150 countries had signed three important documents: the Climate Convention, Biodiversity Convention, and Agenda 21. What is less commonly realized is that the developing countries implicitly agreed that they would accept some responsibility for environmental issues such as global warming, deforestation, and the loss of biodiversity if the developed countries would increase economic and other forms of assistance to them.[7]

In the decade after the Earth Summit, however, the amount of economic and other types of assistance from developed countries to developing ones actually decreased. The $65 billion in aid from all sources in 1992 dropped to less than $54 billion in 2000. This decrease in assistance occurred despite the growing disparity between the world's richest and poorest countries. For example, the richest 20 percent of the world's population was reportedly 30 times better off than the poorest 20 percent in 1960, and 75 times wealthier in 1996.[8]

When developed countries failed to provide additional assistance, the developing countries did not feel obligated to curtail their plans for industrialization. And in 1997 when developing countries boycotted the Kyoto Protocol on climate change, which called for all countries to reduce greenhouse emissions to 1990 levels by 2010, developed countries failed to take any concrete actions to meet this target. The prospect for successful action by developed states dropped significantly in 2001, when President George W. Bush renounced the Kyoto Protocol, although other developed countries renewed their commitments to show concern.

In the United States, various groups perceived the emergence of global issues requiring joint action by all countries quite differently. Cosmopolitans accepted the seriousness of these global problems and prepared to do their part. Liberal communitarians were willing to help but also anxious to preserve U.S. interests, and they were not prepared to solve the world's problems at America's expense. Conservative communitarians felt the United States was already paying more than its fair share of UN expenditures; they were unwilling to do more than what was absolutely required.

Communitarians and cosmopolitans place different levels of acceptability on each of the three scenarios: democracy, anarchy, and globalism. However, because all three motivations are relevant, acceptability is not the only consideration in each scenario; people also need to weigh the effectiveness as well as the cost and benefits of efforts to realize outcomes. For example, cosmopolitans may find anarchy unacceptable, but they cannot ignore either the need to respond to such dangers or the cost of failing to do so. Thus they may place a higher priority on dealing with this scenario than they give to one they find more appealing.

Consequently, the objectives arising out of each scenario will represent some combination of an actor's own dispositions as well as that actor's perceptions both of the events themselves and of other actors' likely objectives. The next section shows the order of preferences Presidents Bill Clinton and George W. Bush developed in response to these post–cold war scenarios.

Value Preferences

Although this chapter is primarily concerned with community values, that is with actions foreign policy actors view as acceptable, actions people view as being effective and efficient also affect such judgments. Like primary colors, the three basic dimensions can assume a grayish hue when they are mixed. Thus the foreign policy objectives of actors take on hues of gray that make it difficult to order the foreign policy preferences of actors. This section shows that although it may not be easy to prioritize these objectives, with practice, students of foreign policy can learn to do so.

Clinton's Preferences.   Clinton did not comprehensively describe his foreign policy direction until a September 1993 speech to the UN General Assembly. Clinton repeated themes that other members of the administration had previously tested, including his national security adviser, Anthony Lake, who proclaimed that America's primary objectives were to "strengthen the world's established market democracies," promote the "new market democracies" in Europe and elsewhere, oppose the anarchy that threatened these new market democracies, and promote human rights elsewhere in the world on a selective basis.[9] If the first two objectives are combined, then the goals of American foreign policy would reflect the three post–cold war scenarios of democracy, anarchy, and globalism described in the previous section.

Clinton's first goal was to promote and extend the democratic community. In his inaugural address, Clinton argued that America's "greatest strength" was the power of its ideas—"our hopes, our hearts, our hands are with those on every continent who are building democracy and freedom."[10] During his first year in office, Clinton went further than any of his immediate predecessors in saying that "enlarging the community of market democracies" was the primary objective of his foreign policy.[11] Clinton did not acknowledge that this community value might conflict with the values of American security and prosperity. Indeed, he argued that "nothing will strengthen our own security more in the long run" than "defending and expanding the community of democratic nations."[12] Because these democracies were also the most developed countries in the world and the countries with which the United States had the strongest trade and investment ties, such a goal would also serve U.S. prosperity interests.

Because both cosmopolitans and liberal communitarians could heartily endorse this democratic community, it was especially attractive to U.S. political leaders. Even those conservative communitarians who pointed to the difficulties facing these newly democratic governments in becoming mature market democracies often saw no choice other than to give these countries the opportunity to succeed.

Clinton's second goal was to prevent aggression by **rogue states** or wars of self-determination from disrupting efforts to build this democratic community. Particularly in relation to the so-called rogue states, the United States made it clear that it was prepared to employ force on either a unilateral or a multilateral basis to defend this democratic community.[13] The goal of preserving the political independence and territorial integrity of existing states may not be well recognized as a goal of American foreign policy. Yet the United States has consistently preferred larger political units, arguing that they are more viable from both an economic and security standpoint. For example, the United States had tried to keep the former Yugoslavia from disintegrating, and once Bosnia gained its independence, the United States made every effort to prevent its dismemberment. The United States also preferred autonomy to outright independence when the Kosovars sought self-determination and independence from Serbia.

America's commitment to the third goal of promoting human rights—broadly defined to include economic development and environmental protection—was less firmly established, despite pronouncements that these rights were as important as political and civil rights. Clinton was willing to sign treaties such as the Biodiversity Treaty that his predecessor would not sign, but was unwilling or unable to convince the Senate to consent to the treaties. The United States acknowledged that the rights to a healthy environment and sustainable economic development are inalienable, universal, and indivisible from the political and civil rights so long touted by Americans,[14] but did not follow up this declaration of principle with specific actions and programs.

George W. Bush's Preferences.   The September 11, 2001 attacks on New York and Washington, D.C. shaped Bush's foreign policy. Although President Bush had defined aspects of his foreign policy earlier, a formal statement of his "national security policy" was not transmitted to Congress until September 20, 2002, a year after the attacks.[15] In the introduction to that document Bush makes it clear that "the first and fundamental commitment" of the federal government was to defend the United States against its enemies. Bush had earlier labeled these enemies as "the axis of evil," including Iraq, Iran, and North Korea, as well as international terrorist organizations.[16]

His second priority of "protecting America's freedoms" was closely related to the first. Although Bush called upon the United States to "champion the rights of human dignity," he clearly defined human dignity in terms of a "distinctly American internationalism." Bush reiterated

America's commitment "to lasting institutions like the United Nations, the World Trade Organization, the Organization of American States, and NATO," but the most newsworthy aspect of the whole document was his determination not to "hesitate to act alone, if necessary, to exercise our right of self-defense by acting preemptively against terrorists, to prevent them from doing harm against our people."

Bush's concern for security and his insistence on the unilateral right to take preemptive action overshadowed his third general objective "to extend the benefits of freedom across the globe." By this phrase he did not mean equality so much as the opportunity to enjoy economic freedom. Bush promised to "deliver greater development assistance through the New Millennium Challenge Account to nations that govern justly, invest in their people, and encourage economic freedom." However, the wars in Afghanistan and Iraq made it increasingly difficult to fulfill these commitments.

Though in these policy statements both Presidents Clinton and Bush remained true to their visions—that is, cosmopolitan and communitarian, respectively—their perception of contemporary events shaped their specific objectives and order of preferences. Clinton's statement emphasized prosperity first, security second, and community third. Bush's rhetoric pronounced security first, community second, and prosperity third. Table 5.1 shows how differently Presidents Clinton and Bush prioritized these three dimensions.

These differences in preference are important because they illustrate how disparate two foreign policies might be even if they happened to end up being on the same side of all three bifurcated dimensions. For example, Presidents Clinton and Bush might both pursue a unilateral, coercive, and proactive policy, but those policies would look very different depending on the priority they gave each of the objectives on these three dimensions.

This problem is further complicated by the fact that foreign policies are not self-implementing measures; foreign policy actors must develop specific methods of achieving these objectives. As a consequence, one always has to pay attention to how these foreign policies have been implemented in foreign policy situations. The foreign policy analyst must constantly compare the expressed objective with the concrete methods employed to reach that objective. Both must be considered in determining which foreign policy option was chosen.

Identifying Foreign Policy Options

Before describing this action menu , however, it is important to review the distinctions between the types of foreign policies described on each of the three dimensions. Unilateralists are communitarians because they want to preserve and promote their own value system. They prefer bilateral relationships with other countries so they can maximize their own values and interests. Multilateralists are cosmopolitans because they want to build a

Table 5.1. The Order of Value Preferences: Bill Clinton and George W. Bush.

Order of Preference for Foreign Policy Objectives	Clinton's preferences	Bush's preferences
First preference	"Engagement and enlargement" (Prosperity values)	"War on terrorism" (Security values)
Second preference	Control rogue states (Security values)	Protect "American freedom" (Community values)
Third preference	Strengthen global environment and human rights (Community values)	Help those who are prepared to help themselves (Prosperity values)

For Clinton "engagement and enlargement" was the most important foreign policy objective because although it primarily enhanced American prosperity, it contributed to all three aspects of foreign policy because the advanced economies were democracies and were the basis for projecting American security worldwide, controlling rogue states was the second most important because it provided security for the realization of the first objective, and strengthening the global environment and human rights, the community value dimension, was least important because it was viewed as unachievable in the short-term.

For Bush the war on terrorism was the most important foreign policy objective because the security threat appeared imminent, American freedom was the second most important because, rhetorically at least, this was what was ultimately at stake, and helping those who were prepared to help themselves was the least important because we first had to save ourselves.

consensus among as many states as possible. Multilateralism involves cooperative agreements that are (1) based on general principles; (2) indivisible in the sense that they cannot be reduced to a series of bilateral measures; and (3) characterized by diffuse reciprocity, which means that the parties do not expect their actions to balance one another all the time.[17]

The security dimension involves the use of force whether actual or implied. Generally speaking, government actions are coercive because the coercive power of the government is behind these actions even if that is not the government's intent. Most nongovernment actions are noncoercive because most nongovernmental organizations are not authorized to use force. However, government actions might be considered noncoercive if there is no hint of force. And nongovernment actions might be considered coercive if they have the ability to punish a vulnerable party. Because the community and security dimensions are considered independent of one another, there is no fixed relationship between communitarians, cosmopolitans, and the use of force.

The prosperity dimension is concerned with efforts to enhance one's well-being. Proactive foreign policies are aimed at strengthening benefits;

reactive foreign policies place a premium on reducing costs. There is no necessary relationship between communitarianism, cosmopolitanism, coercion, noncoercion, and prosperity. A proactive foreign policy may or may not involve coercive actions; a reactive policy may or may not involve noncoercive actions. Cosmopolitans and communitarians may employ a wide range of actions to pursue either security or prosperity goals.

If one bifurcates each of the three dimensions, one gets eight different combinations of actions. To clarify further the eight types of foreign policy actions (methods) employed to achieve community values, this section takes a closer look at one issue that has a communitarian bias—immigration and refugee policy—and one issue that has a cosmopolitan bias—human rights—and highlights the differences between communitarian and cosmopolitan actions in each case. These various combinations will be illustrated in the next four tables.

Immigration and Refugee Policy

Before the development of nationalism in the nineteenth century, the governments of states did not pay much attention to the migration of people from one state to another, because the monarch's control over subjects was based on that monarch's protection of people within the monarch's domain, rather than on the subject's nationality. After the French Revolution, however, these subjects became citizens with rights, thus governments began to regulate immigration and nationalization more carefully.[18] In theory, governments had complete control over immigration, although once they had allowed aliens into their country, governments were required under international law to treat them decently.

People choose to immigrate for many reasons, but one group of immigrants has special rights—the **refugees** who seek a safe haven from their country of origin "because of persecution or a well-founded fear of persecution on account of race, religion, nationality, membership in a particular social group, or political opinion."[19] But international law does not place a corresponding duty on states to provide **asylum**—that is, to take in refugees—and so governments must decide for themselves whether to allow refugees to enter their country.

In 1950 the United Nations attempted to deal with this problem by creating the position of UN High Commissioner for Refugees (UNHCR). Although the occupant of this position was responsible for ensuring the rights of refugees, the 1951 Convention Relating to the Status of Refugees protected the right of refugees to leave their country of origin but did not actually require states to grant asylum to refugees. As a consequence, the UNHCR can only provide these refugees with legal protection until some state offers them asylum.

A **displaced person**, as opposed to a refugee, is someone who has been driven out of his home as a result of a natural disaster or a human conflict but who is still living in his original state. In 2004 there were an estimated 11.9 million refugees worldwide, 7.35 million of whom had been warehoused for 10 years or more. At the same time there were 23.6 million displaced persons worldwide, 5.28 million of whom are newly displaced.[20] Many of these displaced persons depend upon private voluntary organizations for essential services.

Immigration Policy.   The U.S. Immigration Act of 1965 established annual immigrant quotas and generally gave preference to those seeking visas for reasons of family unification over those seeking visas for employment opportunities or those with refugee status. Where U.S. immigration officials are giving preference to uniting families or obtaining skilled workers, they may be thought of as pursuing unilateral, coercive, and proactive immigration policies, or MCA. Table 5.2 illustrates this type of immigration policy as well as the other three types of communitarian immigration policies: the efforts of the government to stop illegal immigration, the efforts of nongovernmental, private groups to promote immigration, and the efforts of nongovernmental, private groups to stop illegal immigration.

Because many more people want to immigrate into the United States each year than the quota system allows, the main effort of the U.S. Citizenship and Immigration Services is to prevent illegal immigration into the United States. In an effort to get control of its southern border, the Immigration Reform and Control Act of 1986 even conferred legal status on the three million undocumented aliens living in the United States and sought to reduce further illegal immigration. But the flow of illegal immigrants into the United States has not been reversed. Recently President Bush has proposed a guest worker program that would allow Mexicans to work in the United States for a period of three years. These workers would not be allowed to apply for permanent guest worker status or legal immigration. It is not known whether this program would have any effect on the flow of illegal immigrants into the country.[21] In addition to armed border patrols the State Department has developed a Border Industrialization Program in Mexico that seeks to provide Mexicans with better job opportunities on their side of the border so that they will not attempt to cross into the United States illegally. And in the 1990s the State Department actually negotiated an agreement with Cuba in which the United States would admit 20,000 Cubans each year in return for Cuba's promise that it would prevent its citizens from fleeing for the U.S. mainland by boat.[22] All these efforts to stop illegal immigration may be classified as unilateral, coercive, and reactive immigration policies, or MCA.

Some American ethnic groups are active in promoting emigration. For example, the Cuban American National Foundation (CANF), which represents Cuban Americans who earlier fled Fidel Castro's Cuba, actively

Table 5.2. Dimensions of Foreign Policy: U.S. Immigration Policies of the Last Half Century

| | Multilateral | | Unilateral | |
	Coercive	Noncoercive	Noncoercive	Coercive
Proactive			Efforts by some American cities to assist legal immigrants in getting settled in the U.S.	Efforts by State Department to unite families and obtain skilled workers
Reactive			Efforts by anti-immigration groups to create obstacles for illegal immigrants	Efforts by Department of Homeland Security to limit illegal immigration

The U.S. Citizenship and Immigration Services' efforts to unite families and obtain skilled workers are MCA—unilateral in that this policy is an official government policy, coercive in that the United States is prepared to back these decisions with force if necessary, and proactive because they facilitate immigration.

The Department of Homeland Security's efforts to prevent illegal immigration are MCA—unilateral because these officials are acting under U.S. law, coercive because they are prepared to use force if necessary, and reactive because they restrict immigration.

The efforts of U.S. NGOs to assist legal immigrants are MCA—unilateral because whatever the motive of these groups, it serves national interests as defined by the U.S. government, noncoercive because the immigrants come at their own volition, and proactive because these groups encourage such immigration among the target populations.

The efforts of private organizations to make it difficult for illegal immigrants to stay in the United States are MCA—unilateral because these organizations are asserting a national definition of rights over a universal definition of rights, noncoercive because these groups use persuasive means, and reactive because they hope to reduce illegal immigration into the country.

encourages other Cubans to emigrate as a means of weakening the Castro regime. Similarly, the American Israel Public Affairs Committee (AIPAC) actively promoted the emigration of Russian Jews before the fall of the Soviet Union. Many communities throughout the United States have large immigration populations and ethnic neighborhoods. They often facilitate immigration. For example, the mayor of St. Paul, Minnesota, went to Cambodia in 2004 in order to welcome and offer assistance to some 5,000 Cambodians who were scheduled to join the large Cambodian community in that city.[23] The communitarian immigration policies of these groups are unilateral, noncoercive, and proactive, or MCA.

In addition, there are a number of private anti-immigration groups, such as the Immigration Reform Caucus, the Council of Conservative Citizens, and the American Border Patrol, that use security issues to place restrictions on immigration. One example of their efforts is the passage of the Real ID Act of 2005 that will require new drivers who want a license to have a valid identification card. These groups favor a unilateral, non-coercive, reactive, or <u>MCA</u>, immigration policy.

Refugee Policy.   The 1951 Convention relating to the Rights of Refugees expects individual countries to provide asylum to refugees, and the United Nations does not generally use its coercive power to compel countries to accept refugees. The exception occurred in Iraq in 1991. In the 1980s and early 1990s, the UNHCR was finding it increasingly difficult to locate asylum for the growing number of refugees, to say nothing of the displaced persons whom it was not legally authorized to help. When Saddam Hussein turned on the Kurdish people living in northern Iraq at the close of the Persian Gulf War and when the government of Turkey refused to allow these same Kurds to enter its country, however, the UN Security Council passed Resolution 688, which authorized the international community to take all the actions necessary, including military intervention, to rescue refugees trapped on the border. This was the point at which the United States and Britain created "no-fly zones" in northern and southern Iraq and brought Kurdish refugees fleeing Saddam into this country. These cosmopolitan or liberal communitarian actions under the Security Council Res. 688 were multilateral, coercive, and proactive, or MCA. Table 5.3 shows the dimensions of U.S. enforcement of Res. 688 and the next three examples of refugee policy: efforts by the U.S. government to deny asylum to refugees, efforts by some U.S. NGOs and INGOs to provide asylum to refugees, and efforts by some U.S. NGOs to deny asylum to refugees.

However, the United States government has also been known to deny asylum to qualified refugees. This happened frequently in the 1980s and early 1990s because so many refugees were fleeing friendly, though repressive, governments such as El Salvador and Guatemala. In the early 1990s the U.S. government actually violated the terms of the 1951 convention and the rights of refugees leaving Cuba and Haiti by forcibly returning them to their respective countries without a hearing (a multilateral, coercive, and reactive, or MC<u>A</u>, refugee policy). But the government later provided "shipboard screening" in the region so that Haitians could find protection on a temporary basis.[24] By following the procedures set forth in the 1951 convention, the United States was once again conducting a cosmopolitan refugee policy that was at least partly a multilateral, coercive, and proactive, or MCA, refugee policy.

The UNHCR works mainly with states to provide legal protection to refugees; it depends on individual countries, such as the United States, to grant asylum to refugees and displaced persons. The UNHCR has entered into agreements with INGOs such as the International Rescue Committee

Table 5.3. Dimensions of Foreign Policy: U.S. International Refugee Policies

	Multilateral		Unilateral	
	Coercive	Noncoercive	Noncoercive	Coercive
Proactive	In 1991 UN Security Council asks countries to protect displaced Kurdish nationals in nothern Iraq	Assistance by U.S. NGOs, such as Jubilee Partners, and INGOs to find asylum in the United States for refugees and displaced persons		
Reactive	U.S. government decision to deny asylum to foreign nationals fleeing friendly governments such as El Salvador and Guatemala	American NGOs that favor legislation that will limit asylum to refugees and displaced persons		

Efforts to protect displaced persons in northern Iraq in 1991 were MCA—multilateral because they were authorized by the UN Security Council, coercive because countries were asked to use all necessary means including force, and proactive because it meant providing asylum to some Kurds in this country.

The refusal of the United States to extend asylum to refugees fleeing friendly governments is MCA—multilateral because the United States accepts its obligation to provide relief to qualified individuals under the 1951 convention, coercive because those who were refused as unqualified were held in stockades and returned to their country of origin against their will, and reactive because these actions restricted the granting of asylum to these individuals.

Efforts by U.S. NGOs, such as Jubilee Partners, as well as INGOs to provide refugees with asylum were MCA—multilateral because they acted on the basis of international law, noncoercive because the refugees wanted help, and proactive because they facilitated the award of asylum to these individuals.

Efforts by some American NGOs to limit asylum to refugees and displaced persons are MCA—multilateral because they are dealing with international human rights law, noncoercive because they are using persuasion to influence legislation, and reactive because they want to deny asylum to these individuals.

and CARE to provide humanitarian assistance to these groups while they are waiting for asylum. A number of American NGOs typically work with these INGOs and government agencies to settle refugee populations. The U.S. government has been particularly helpful in accepting refugees from communist countries or those with special needs, such as the "Lost Boys of Sudan." All these efforts are examples of cosmopolitan refugee policies that are multilateral, noncoercive, and proactive, or MCA. Box 5.1 profiles Don Mosley, one such activist.

It is more difficult to identify American NGOs who actively oppose granting asylum to refugees and displaced persons. However, groups such as Families for a Secure America were active in supporting the National Intelligence Reform Act of 2004 that makes it more difficult for those seeking asylum to find refuge in the United States and easier to return refugees and asylum seekers to countries with repressive regimes. Such policies would be multilateral, noncoercive, and reactive, or MCA.

Human Rights Policy

No foreign policy issue is dearer to cosmopolitans than human rights. Initially the United States played a crucial role in the acceptance of universal human rights at the global level. In 1945 the forty-two American non-governmental organizations attached to the American delegation to the San Francisco conference that launched the United Nations succeeded not only in getting the preamble of the UN Charter to state "We the Peoples of the United Nations" rather than the usual "We the High Contracting Parties" but also in getting human rights recognized as one of the four specific purposes of the United Nations and in achieving creation of a Commission on Human Rights. Former first lady Eleanor Roosevelt played a key role in the adoption of the Universal Declaration of Human Rights in 1948.

In the 1950s and 1960s the United States played a smaller role in promoting and defending human rights for at least two reasons. First, the country was not well positioned to assume the kind of leadership many wanted to take in human rights because of the discrimination against African Americans in the United States before the start of the Civil Rights movement. Second, the priority placed on security considerations largely crowded out human rights as an issue during the early cold war period. Thus it was not until the United States began to tackle its own problem of racial discrimination in the 1960s and put its heightened security concerns aside during the détente period of the 1970s that the United States explicitly began to incorporate human rights into its foreign policy.[25]

By the 1970s a division had emerged between those who considered state sovereignty a "non-negotiable principle" and those who believed that the international community had a responsibility to investigate human rights abuses wherever they occurred.[26] In addition, the United States had traditionally given preference to civil and political rights over economic, social, and cultural rights. This issue tended to divide countries on a North-South basis, because, according to Stephen Marks, the "have" states of the North tended to regard "the repressive behavior of state authorities as the major impediment to enjoyment of human rights" whereas the "have-not" states of the South tended to regard "poverty and social injustice not only as major impediments to full enjoyment of such rights but even as a violation of human rights and a priority for UN action."[27] Although American leaders agreed in principle, as signatories to

BOX 5.1

Profile in Action: Don Mosley

Don Mosley is the privileged son of a millionaire Texas businessman who was expected to take over the family business. But when his father took Don on a round-the-world trip after his high school graduation, what he saw in the refugee camps in Egypt and the Middle East changed his life. Although he completed his engineering degree, he went on to take courses in Anthropology, serve in the Peace Corps, and join Koinonia Partners, a Christian community in South Georgia where Millard Fuller was developing the Habitat for Humanity project.

In the spring of 1979 Don and his wife Carolyn became one of three couples that left Koinonia to establish a new Christian community in northeast Georgia called Jubilee Partners.[a] The group was first moved to address the refugee problem because of the stories coming out of Southeast Asia about the "boat people," refugees of the long-standing conflicts in that region arising out of the Vietnam war and its aftermath. But by the time the community was ready to receive refugees in 1981, it found itself aiding the flood of Cuban refugees in Florida. Later, it helped refugees from Cambodia. For each group of refugees, Jubilee Partners fed and housed thirty to forty men, women, and children while they waited for permanent sponsors in the United States. The partners also provided the refugees with English language training and cultural information.

By 1982 the Partners learned that most Guatemalans and El Salvadorans seeking asylum in the United States were being returned to the countries they had just fled. Jubilee also learned that the Canadian government had a refugee law similar to the U.S. law and was prepared to accept refugees that the United States had rejected. Jubilee therefore worked out a precarious arrangement

the Vienna Declaration of 1993, that the "right to development" is an inalienable, universal, and an integral part of human rights, the United States has a long history of rejecting that position in practice.[28]

Global Human Rights Policy.   The International Bill of Human Rights includes the Universal Declaration of Human Rights (1948), the International Covenant on Economic, Social and Cultural Rights (1966), the International Covenant on Civil and Political Rights (1966), and well over 100 conventions and protocols dealing with specific issues such as racial discrimination, discrimination against women, torture and other cruel, inhuman or degrading punishment, and the rights of the child. Unfortunately, unless the Security Council is willing to take action, the United Na-

with the U.S. and Canadian governments to send its representatives to the U.S. refugee detention centers in Texas to select refugees they knew would qualify for asylum in Canada. The refugees were then bused to Jubilee's site in Comer, Georgia, to await interviews with Canadian consulate officials located in Atlanta and to complete the necessary paperwork. In the final step, Jubilee Partners would bus the refugees to Canada where they received asylum.

Jubilee Partners continued to funnel Central American refugees from Texas to Canada until 1990 when negotiations between the United States, Canada, and Mexico over NAFTA mysteriously resulted in Mexico blocking the flow of refugees and Canada changing its refugee policy. Nevertheless, the Partners continue to help refugees. The most recent ones are from Afghanistan, Vietnam, Bosnia, and Africa. Over the years Jubilee Partners has helped over two thousand refugees settle either in the United States or Canada.

Although Don and other partners have devoted most of their attention to the refugee issue, they have also participated in a variety of humanitarian causes, including opposition to the death penalty, control of nuclear weapons, and Vietnam. These beliefs have occasionally cost him dearly. For example, although Don only receives a few dollars a week as a partner, his parents established a trust in his name, and this has brought him into conflict with the Internal Revenue Service because of his refusal to pay taxes during the Vietnam War on the annual interest earned by the trust. As a consequence, Don had to serve sixty days in prison in 1989.

a. Jubilee refers to the biblical idea that every fifty years people should celebrate their good fortune by acts of justice and mercy.

Source: See Don Mosley with Joyce Hollyday, *With Our Own Eyes: The Dramatic Story of a Christian Response to the Wounds of War, Racism, and Oppression* (Scottsdale, Penn.: Herald Press, 1996).

tions has only a limited capacity to enforce universal human rights. The Commission on Human Rights has developed three mechanisms for investigating human rights violations: (1) a "confidential procedure" for investigating abuses by states when it would be politically impossible to do so openly; (2) a more "public procedure" for investigating human rights complaints against particular countries; and (3) the appointment of special *rapporteurs* to investigate various types of violations. The commission operates with the consent of its fifty-three government members including the United States.

To strengthen the enforcement powers of the commission, the UN member countries created both a Centre for Human Rights and a High Commissioner for Human Rights in 1994. These institutions are examples of efforts to undertake cosmopolitan human rights actions that are multi-lateral, coercive, and proactive (or MCA) global human rights policies. Table 5.4 shows this example of cosmopolitan human rights policies and the next three examples of such cosmopolitan policies: the efforts of national governments to weaken universal human rights, efforts of NGOs

Table 5.4. Dimensions of Foreign Policy: International Human Rights Policies

	Multilateral		Unilateral	
	Coercive	Noncoercive	Noncoercive	Coercive
Proactive	Efforts by the Security Council and the Commission on Human Rights to enforce the International Bill of Human Rights	Efforts by INGOs, such as Amnesty International and the World Council of Churches, as well as U.S. NGOs to identify human rights victims and assist them		
Reactive	Partial or inconsistent enforcement of universal human rights conventions by U.S. government	Efforts by some American NGOs to deny universal economic, social, and cultural rights		

The covenants and protocols included under the International Bill of Human Rights are MCA—multilateral because they are meant to be universal, coercive because the Security Council and the International Criminal Court can, if necessary, enforce them, and proactive because they should be practiced at every level of society, in domestic as well as international situations.

The covenants and protocols that make up the International Bill of Human Rights are considered law-making treaties, because they are applicable to all states as long as most states ratify them. Thus when United States signs but does not ratify, they are still valid assuming that most countries ratify them. Therefore, the refusal to sign or ratify such documents may be considered MCA—multilateral because they are established international law, coercive because the Security Council or some other state may in fact enforce them, and reactive because from the U.S. point of view they are not applicable in the United States.

Efforts by INGOs, such as Amnesty International and the World Council of Churches, as well as U.S. NGOs to promote human rights laws abroad are MCA—multilateral because they are promulgating universal rights, noncoercive because they seek to persuade, and proactive because they are trying to maximize these rights all over the world.

Efforts by some U.S. NGOs to restrict universal economic, social, or cultural human rights are MCA—multilateral because these rights are universal whether these groups choose to recognize them or not, noncoercive because these groups seek to persuade, and reactive because these groups deny the existence of these rights.

and INGOs to establish human rights policies, and the efforts of some national NGOs to weaken universal human rights.

Unfortunately, some of the governments that have been the worst violators of universal human rights have sought membership on the Commission on Human Rights explicitly for the purpose of weakening that body. This is not true of the United States, although the United States has failed to ratify key international conventions including those on women's rights and worker's rights and is one of only a few countries in the world that has failed to ratify the Convention on the Right of the Child.[29] Moreover, when the United States does ratify such conventions, it often exempts itself from these obligations, particularly where international human rights law grants safeguards and remedies that are not available under U.S. law.

The U.S. government has also worked with other governments to keep the budget for the Centre for Human Rights very low. The U.S. government also saw to it that the Centre's headquarters would be located in Geneva, rather than in New York, where it would be difficult for the Centre to integrate human rights with other UN operations. Although President Clinton played a pivotal role in establishing a High Commissioner for Human Rights, he refused to sign the Convention on an International Criminal Court until his last days in office because the convention does not require Security Council control over the jurisdiction of the proposed court. In 2002 President Bush nullified that action because he feared that other countries might take advantage of these new laws to punish Americans for, among other things, engaging in preemptive wars.

Since the attacks of September 11, 2001, the United States has also refused to extend the protections of the Geneva Conventions to members of al Qaeda, as well as any others who they say are engaged in jihad. Efforts by the Bush administration to redefine torture and to carry over interrogation practices initially developed in Afghanistan and Guantanamo Bay into the insurgent population of Iraq have undermined the Geneva accords. All these actions by the United States and other countries have weakened the International Bill of Human Rights and may be classified as multilateral, coercive, and reactive, or MCA, human rights policies.

Because governments, the United States among them, purposively limited the ability of the Commission on Human Rights and other offices to be as effective as they might otherwise be in implementing human rights at the global level, some observers have requested that fact-finding and implementation of human rights policies be handled whenever possible "by independent outside experts." [30] Others have called for nongovernmental organizations such as the World Council of Churches, World Medical Congress, International Commission of Jurists, International League for Human Rights, and Amnesty International, which are independent of these governments, to identify human rights violations and help victims."[31] Proof of the value of these independent activities lies in the fact that states found to have violated such rights often try to remove human rights organizations from the list of those accredited to play a role in official proceedings.

Because of the efforts of governments to prevent local groups from pressing their governments on human rights abuses, the adoption groups of Amnesty International located around the world almost always deal with "prisoners of conscience" in societies other than their own. In this way local human rights groups in China and Kenya are monitoring and assisting victims in the United States, and groups in the United States are dealing with human rights problems in Hungary and Paraguay. Some local groups also try to implement universal human rights in the United States. For example, Amnesty International USA is active in fighting the discriminatory character of the death penalty as practiced in many locales in this country. Whether these INGOs and NGOs are operating at the global or local level, their cosmopolitan human rights actions are multilateral, noncoercive, and proactive, or MCA, global human rights policies.

Few American NGOs would oppose universal human rights by which they mean civil rights. But many communitarian groups, such as the Foundation for Economic Education, Libertarian Alliance, and Downsize DC, emphasize individual liberty and responsibility, private property, free markets, and constitutionally limited governments rather than support the full range of other economic, social, and cultural rights. The efforts of these NGOs can be classified as multilateral, noncoercive, and reactive, or MCA, universal human rights policies.

U.S. Human Rights Policy.   Americans take pride in the rights guaranteed to them in the U.S. Constitution. But the U.S. Bill of Rights is different from international human rights in the sense that Americans, unlike the United Nations, place much more emphasis on civil rights than economic, social, and political rights. This distinction is essential in understanding the character of the U.S. human rights policies that became so important to American foreign policy beginning in the 1970s. At that time Congress and the Carter administration made respect for human rights a factor in determining America's relations with foreign countries. Under Carter the United States was prepared for the first time to terminate military support, deny most-favored-nation trade status, and oppose financial assistance to countries that engaged in a consistent pattern of gross violations of internationally recognized human rights, that is civil rights. In the 1990s the State Department attempted to strengthen human rights practices in other countries by financing efforts by American professionals to support legal reform and train judges and law enforcement officials.

All these human rights policies were unilateral, coercive, and proactive, or MCA. Table 5.5 shows this example and the next three examples

Table 5.5. Dimensions of Foreign Policy: U.S. Human Rights Policies

| | Multilateral | | Unilateral | |
	Coercive	Noncoercive	Noncoercive	Coercive
Proactive			Efforts by U.S. NGOs and TNCs to promote nationalist interpretations of human rights around the world	Efforts by Congress and the Carter administration to promote U.S. civil rights as a regular instrument of their foreign policy
Reactive			Efforts by some US NGOs and TNCs to deny Americans some civil rights in the name of national security	Efforts by the Department of Homeland Security to enforce provisions of the Patriot Act of 2001 that may violate the civil rights of Americans

Efforts by U.S. government, such as those of the Carter administration, to promote the American conception of human rights abroad are MCA—unilateral because economic, social, and cultural rights were not included, coercive because the United States punished states when necessary, and proactive because these actions were designed to maximize the acceptance of civil rights abroad.

Efforts by the Department of Homeland Security to implement the Patriot Act of 2001 are MCA—unilateral because these officials are carrying out U.S. laws, coercive because, if necessary, these officials are authorized to use force, and reactive because many people believe that some of these measures violate the civil rights of many Americans.

Efforts by U.S. private groups, sometimes working with U.S. government departments or agencies, to promote U.S. preferred rights abroad are MCA—unilateral because they may not emphasize all universal rights, noncoercive because the effort is usually made to persuade other parties, and proactive because these organizations want to extend these rights.

Efforts by U.S. NGOs or transnational corporations (TNCs) to deny economic, social, and cultural rights to people are MCA—unilateral because they are employing a national interpretation of human rights, noncoercive because they seek to persuade, and reactive because they are trying to deny or restrict the rights of these individuals.

of U.S. liberal communitarian human rights policies: the efforts of the U.S. government to reconcile the respect for human rights with security requirements after the September 11, 2001 attacks, the efforts of U.S. NGOs to promote U.S. human rights policies, and the efforts of some private NGOs to whittle away at traditional U.S. human rights.

Prior to the September 11, 2001 attacks, most foreign visitors to the United States were able to enjoy many of these same rights; however, these rights have been curtailed by the Patriot Act of 2001. Now it is more difficult for most foreigners to get visas to enter the United States. The U.S. government has also developed surveillance techniques and confinement procedures under the Patriot Act that make it more difficult for Americans to practice what they assumed were freedoms enjoyed by all Americans. All these government efforts to prevent terrorism by screening individuals here and abroad are examples of communitarian human rights policies that are unilateral, coercive, and reactive, or MCA.

Many religious, professional, civic, and ethnic groups in American society also conduct human rights programs at home and abroad. For example, the American Civil Liberties Union (ACLU) has an international reputation for helping isolated citizens and aliens defend their rights in the United States. American labor organizations have also helped workers in other countries develop democratic unions. For example, the Polish trade union, Solidarity, received financial support from the AFL-CIO in its early years. When the government cooperates with these groups, its human rights policies can usually be considered noncoercive. These communitarian human rights policies are unilateral, noncoercive, and proactive, or MCA, human rights policies.

Finally, some private organizations, especially those that emphasize the importance of homeland security, such as the Center for Security Policy, have resisted challenges to the Patriot Act. Although these groups stop short of arguing for the denial of basic human rights, they contend that some civil rights may have to be compromised in order to provide better domestic security. These communitarian human rights policies are unilateral, noncoercive, and reactive, or MCA.

Choosing the Best Foreign Policy

Thus far this chapter has described the objectives or value preferences Americans may have for community policies (both communitarian and cosmopolitan) and the types of community actions they may choose to employ. The rest of the chapter will assess these actions in terms of those preferences. Because this text cannot deal with all of the contemporary issues worth investigating from this perspective, it will deal with just two of the most important issues: humanitarian intervention and environmental justice. Humanitarian intervention is a crucial issue because cosmopolitans must confront communitarians where it is most difficult for the communitarians to give ground—interfering in the business of other states. Environmental justice is equally critical because communitarians in both developed and developing states confront cosmopolitans on the issue of just how far the cosmopolitans should go in promoting global equality.

Interestingly, both of these issues deal with the nature of the universal global community and the role Americans should play in it. On this role, Americans are divided. All Americans would probably prefer that other states respect the human rights of their own people, yet what values are Americans willing to sacrifice, if any, to ensure that other states respect human rights? Similarly, all Americans would like to live in a world that is both environmentally healthy and just. But again, what values, if any, are they prepared to sacrifice to realize that kind of world? On these questions cosmopolitans not only disagree with communitarians, but individuals within each group are likely to disagree among themselves.

Humanitarian Intervention

To what degree should the United States intervene in the internal conflicts of other states in order to defend and promote universal human rights? **Intervention** in this context means separating the warring parties and enforcing the peace either on a unilateral or a multilateral basis.[32]

Because traditional international law is based largely on the principle of noninterference in the internal affairs of states, the norms guiding intervention in these affairs are not well developed. Although the norms governing conflicts between states do not apply directly to internal conflicts, a brief look at them may reveal what norms might be more appropriate for internal conflicts.

Collective defense or self-defense is the main justification for wars among states, and the primary emphasis is placed on the party that started the conflict. In internal wars, however, it is even more difficult to determine who fired the first shot. Because the purpose of humanitarian intervention in internal wars is to defend universal human rights, the burden of proof falls on those who intend to intervene—that is, they have to show that human rights would be better served from intervention than from its absence. Thus the intervening states would have to demonstrate that it is the purpose of one or both parties to an internal conflict to destroy fundamental human rights, or that the means employed by one or both parties is likely to do so to a remarkable extent. The civil war in Rwanda is a good example of a conflict where both sides were guilty of human rights violations.

Once the intervention is justified, what limitations, if any, should govern its conduct? If, as Robert W. Tucker says, the "essential condition for the observance of distinctively human rights in inter-state war is the continued observance among the belligerents of the rights of states," then it may be especially difficult to exercise meaningful restraints on the use of force in internal wars because at least one, if not both, participants in an internal war is a nonstate actor.[33] What rights and obligations do nonstate actors such as al Qaeda have in internal conflicts? It is also more difficult to distinguish between combatants and noncombatants in internal wars than in interstate wars. Nevertheless, because humanitarian intervention is designed to preserve human rights, it is even more incumbent upon those intervening to conduct themselves in a way that minimizes the destruction of human rights. Given these special difficulties, it is particularly important to define the values at stake in internal wars and consider the full range of actions that might be taken in relation to them.

Values at Stake.   All internal wars involve conflicts of values. One or more of the parties engaged in an internal conflict are promoting exclusive (communitarian) values that threaten the values of other parties. When efforts to maintain or extend these communitarian values deny basic human rights to others, the parties appeal to outsiders for assistance. Thus whatever the character of the value conflict between the internal parties, it becomes a conflict between the right of either an existing state or a group seeking to create a new state to enjoy its communitarian values and the allegations of another group that their basic human rights have been violated. In Kosovo, for example, the Serbs claimed the sovereign right of their government to preserve the independence of their state from internal insurrection. The Kosovars claimed the right of self-determination in a province in which 90 percent of the population is ethnic Albanian, not Serbian. Both the Serbs and the Kosovars claimed that the basic human rights of some of their people were being destroyed. But because it is not unusual for minorities to feel that their rights are being thwarted in multicultural states, humanitarian intervention becomes necessary only when these threats manifest themselves as genocide, ethnic cleansing, systematic and pervasive discrimination, or massive starvation.

Under these circumstances, it is not just the values but the lives of members of minorities and ethnic groups that are in imminent danger. Increasingly, such danger results from the flow of refugees into neighboring countries or the emergence of large numbers of displaced persons in their own country. Because these refugee and displaced populations may include remnants of those actively engaged in the conflict, it is particularly difficult to ensure the safety of the refugee camp inmates and the surrounding inhabitants, especially because of the danger of an internal conflict escalating into a wider conflict involving sympathizers in neighboring countries. For example, the Kosovo conflict contained the danger of involving Albania and Macedonia, followed by Greece, Bulgaria, Turkey, and possibly others.

Any state contemplating humanitarian intervention must review its value preferences in relation to the conflict quite frequently. Such preference orderings are crucial because they determine which of several possible actions will be chosen.

Main Options.   The kinds of actions that the United States might take when facing the possibility of intervening in another country for humanitarian purposes fall into three broad categories. First, the government could embrace the traditional doctrine of **noninterference** in the affairs of other states—an <u>MCA</u> action—for example, the U.S. government's position on the war in Chechnya, Russia. Of course, this does not prevent the government or private voluntary organizations from providing relief and other assistance to refugees or displaced persons in such societies. This option assumes that the U.S. government has no formal responsibility for the destruction of individual human rights in other countries. This position might also be justified on the theory that the outcomes of internal struggles ultimately depend on the correlation of forces within those societies and that outside parties can have only a marginal effect on such situations.

The second option is that the U.S. government should intervene in internal conflicts in other countries for humanitarian reasons only when it is in America's national interest to do so—an <u>MCA</u> action. For example, when weapons of mass destruction (WMD) and ties to al Qaeda were not found in Iraq in 2003, the U.S. government argued that it was justified in ousting Saddam Hussein from power because he violated the human rights of his own people. This option usually assumes that the U.S. government should promote and defend human rights only when the destruction of those rights impinges directly on the interests of the United States. Adherents to this position might argue that the United States has more of a stake in the defense of human rights in Europe than in Africa.

The third option is that the United States could intervene in internal conflicts whenever the UN Security Council or some other **international security organization** to which it belongs determines that international action is required to prevent the gross denial of fundamental human rights—an MCA policy. To implement this option the U.S. government would either support the development of a permanent international force or train a contingent of its own forces to serve in ad hoc international forces when required. Private American groups, particularly transnational organizations, also would be encouraged to participate—M<u>C</u>A and MCA actions. This option is based on the assumption that the international community can best promote and defend human rights if states and societies and organizations are committed to working together.

Assessing Options.   The first option best suits conservative communitarians who might argue that the independence of states best serves U.S. security and prosperity values in these situations over the long run. The option favors the dominant local powers and the values represented by existing states. It largely ignores the claims of minorities that their fundamental human rights are being violated, and, to the extent that other states and international organizations depend on the United States for rapid transport and other kinds of support, it may also deprive these states or organizations of the capacity to help those in need. A true cosmopolitan might argue that adopting this option would make the United States at least partly responsible for these abuses. This option may also discourage minorities in other countries from taking some risks in the short run, but it is unlikely to do so in the long run. As a consequence, an even more serious security situation may emerge in the future. Likewise, this option may avoid expenditures in the short run, but it may lead to conditions that will eventually require even more costly interventions in the future.

The second option is most attractive to liberal communitarians because it acknowledges that America's security and prosperity values sometimes require an extended view of community. It both ensures that the United States can intervene unilaterally when abuses of human rights are perceived as directly impinging on its national interests and permits the United States to avoid involvement when such abuses seem to be less relevant to its national interests. Under this option, American security interests are given more weight than human rights considerations. And it allows the United States to act unilaterally or multilaterally in any given situation, although the ad hoc character of America's commitment to international forces would adversely affect the overall capabilities of these forces. By limiting the number of such interventions the United States might keep its overall costs down, but its failure to intervene in other cases may result in more costly interventions in the future.

The third option is best for cosmopolitans who place universal human rights above considerations of national security and prosperity. Unlike the other two options, this option would strengthen cosmopolitan norms possibly at the expense of communitarian norms. And it would enable the United States to work with other countries to establish general guidelines and plans for when and how international forces would be employed for intervention. Assuming that these humanitarian interventions were effective, they might deter states and dominant parties in local situations from violating the basic human rights of the people under their control. But this option also could involve the United States in situations in which it has no apparent interest and lead to the establishment of an inexperienced and ineffective government. Moreover, the initial costs of undertaking these interventions might be quite high.

Environmental Justice

Since the signing of the Climate Convention in Rio de Janeiro in June 1992, the signatory countries have met eleven times—most recently in Montreal in November 2005—to establish stronger commitments to reduce greenhouse gases. These efforts faltered in 2001 when George W. Bush pulled the United States out of the Kyoto Protocol. According to Mihaly Simai, the stalemate arises because the "developed industrial countries generate about 80 percent of the total global pollution . . . and developing countries . . . do not want to sacrifice their development in order to manage the problems caused by the industrialized countries." [34]

The developed countries view the drive for industrialization in the developing countries as the real problem, because an estimated 45 percent of pollution in the near future will be attributable to these countries. The industrialized countries fear that if the developing countries do not commit themselves to sustainable development now, their large and growing populations will drive global pollution to even more dangerous levels. The developing countries point out that most of the pollution is attributable to the populations of developed countries, and that developing countries only create a fraction of the current pollution because their per capita consumption is so much lower. Nevertheless, the Kyoto Protocol became operational in Europe on February 16, 2005, when Russia finally accepted her commitments.[35]

Values at Stake.   Most Americans recognize that environmental pollution is a   serious issue even though their government and society as a whole have not yet decided what they will do about it.[36] Environmental pollution potentially affects community, security, and prosperity values. Historically, the prosperity of the United States has been tied to its productivity, which cannot continue unless people in both this country and abroad consume its products. Unfortunately, the production and consumption of these goods cause both the drain on resources and the pollution that threatens the environment. Ultimately, Americans will have to decide what kind of environment they want to live in.

At first, environmental problems were viewed largely from a local perspective. The United States was concerned about the quality of its own air and water and the availability of resources for American uses. But in the 1980s Americans became aware of the global threats—global warming and climate changes—posed by environmental issues. By now most Americans recognize that even if the United States did everything in its power to address some of these environmental issues, problems such as holes in the ozone layer, which cause global warming, would continue.

Thus environmental justice is a problem of prosperity and security both at the local or state level and at the global level. Above all, environmental justice is a community problem; national communities must cooperate at the global level if they are going to significantly correct the problem. However, the corrective actions required may severely affect the character of these communities. What changes in lifestyle should national communities undergo to ensure the quality of air and water resources at the level of the global community?

So far it appears that most Americans hold prosperity as their preferred value. Americans enjoy one of the highest standards of living in the world, and they are not willing to sacrifice that standard of living unless they are convinced that it is absolutely necessary. Ironically, the whole environmental movement in the United States has had to counter a conservative movement that views government regulation as anathema. Although this conservative antigovernment movement began in the 1970s and 1980s, it did not peak until 1994 with Newt Gingrich's Contract with America.

At the same time, many Americans are concerned about the threats to their environmental security. They have experienced enough aberrant weather and drought to pay attention to the predictions of global warming. Some Americans are already prepared to sacrifice their standard of living to solve these environmental problems. Indeed, beginning in the 1970s many Americans began to modify their homes, change their diets, and control their buying habits in ways that could contribute to a better environment. Some of these actions have been taken in response to government programs, but most of them have been taken voluntarily as individuals and groups have tried either to improve their local situation or to contribute to the solution of environmental justice problems in the wider world. Yet for now many Americans look mainly to their own government to provide relief rather than changing their lifestyle or reducing their prosperity. The dilemma is how the United States can continue to prosper without jeopardizing its security, yet at the same time contribute to environmental justice at the global level?

Main Options.   Three possible responses to this question are described in this section. First, there is the neoclassical economic response, better known as **corporate environmentalism**. Under this option, the United States would "incorporate the costs of environmental degradation into the internal costs of production." [37] Advocates of corporate environmentalism believe that developed countries can sustain growth by allowing the market to account for environmental costs. This option usually envisages a quota system in which countries and companies adhere to limits placed on the pollution they can produce unless they can find ways to purchase excess pollution allowances from others— basically a bounded MCA policy. Advocates of corporate environmentalism emphasize the role of countries and companies. Countries would have to agree on overall controls and establish limits on the amount of pollution allowed. Then companies would invest in science and technology to develop the most efficient ways of getting the most production out of the fewest resources with the least amount of pollution.[38] Corporate environmentalists believe technology would allow American consumers to have their cake (prosperity, security, and community) and eat it too (conservation of resources and minimal pollution).

The second option is based on **ecology and science** and calls for the United States to limit its quantitative growth while striving to enhance the quality of life of its people. This option requires using fewer resources and causes less pollution, but it suggests that Americans can cut production without sacrificing their quality of life. States would collectively set limits on the use of resources and pollution, but the most difficult task would be developing and enforcing changes in lifestyle appropriate to a system based on fewer material resources. Indeed, this expanded MCA option suggests that Americans can actually enhance their quality of life by making some adjustments in what they value—that is, by placing less emphasis on material things and more emphasis on leisure activities and relationships. This second option assumes that there are limits to growth and to technology.

The third option is referred to as **deep ecology**. Deep ecologists go even further than the advocates of science and ecology in advancing an eco-centric type of values. They advocate "subjectivity for nature." [39] Whereas the neoclassical economists would turn public lands over to private parties and enable the market to protect the environment, the deep ecologists would give rights to nature by advocating for both animate and inanimate objects. Although governments would supposedly limit both the use of resources and pollution, the deep ecologists would include the needs of nature that would have to be included in this transformed system, an extreme MCA policy. The deep ecologists assume that the only way to protect resources is to give them the same rights as people. [40]

Assessing Options.   The first option is the most attractive to conservative communitarians who want to maximize prosperity, particularly for developed countries, and who are less concerned about global environmental security and global community. Advocates of this option hope to preserve the communitarian values of many developed countries, particularly the United States. Because it envisages some limits on global pollution, this option offers some progress on global environmental security but not at the expense of prosperity. This option also provides developing countries with an opportunity to develop if they purchase environmentally sound technology from developed countries with the capital they earn by selling their pollution allowances, but it does not require that they do so or guarantee that they will improve their position vis-à-vis developed countries.

The ecology-science option would be more acceptable to liberal communitarians who would identify local security and local prosperity with the broader community. It calls for reductions in productivity and consumerism in the hope that changes to current standards of living can be made without sacrificing the quality of life. Indeed, advocates of this option argue that the quality of American life can continue to grow only if the use of finite resources and the problem of pollution are controlled. By decreasing their own resource requirements and pollution, the developed states can help nonindustrial states develop in ways that will not threaten environmental security; however, it is not clear how much progress these

nonindustrial countries can make without pressing the limits of both resources and pollution.

Cosmopolitans might support the third option, which defines global security and prosperity in terms of environmental justice. They call for a
transformation in current lifestyles and standards of living. Indeed, they
would change the very character of society to attain environmental security. They do not really address the quality of human life in developed and
developing countries except to note that many people in developing
countries already value natural resources. At least in this sense, deep ecologists would probably ensure a greater measure of justice for developing
societies.

Conclusion

Because people make foreign policy and foreign policies influence people,
this chapter has examined the ideas people have about the community dimension. People choose their foreign policy objectives as well as their
methods, and so their identities, values, and norms do make a difference.

This chapter assumes that the values represented by most people's foreign policy goals, like the hue of primary colors, are bright. However, once
these same individuals consider a specific situation, their mixed objectives
sometimes appear in shades of gray. This "graying" of foreign policy makes
it difficult, but by no means impossible, to establish a clear, well-ordered
set of foreign policy objectives

But knowing an actor's foreign policy objectives does not go far
enough. The foreign policy student also must know what methods might
be used to reach those objectives. Although some means readily present
themselves, others may have to be carefully developed. This chapter assumes that it is important to consider a wide range of methods. The next
chapter shows that the most appropriate or best foreign policies may involve a combination of such actions.

Finally, how these choices are made is important. The priorities of an
actor determine which criteria—acceptance, effectiveness, or efficiency—
are the most important for foreign policy. Of course, acceptability is the
key criterion in the community domain, but which foreign policy is most
acceptable often hinges on matters of effectiveness and efficiency. The
next chapter addresses questions of effectiveness, but efficiency and acceptability will also be relevant considerations.

Key Concepts

Suggested Readings

1. Anand, Ruchi. *International Environmental Justice: A North-South Dimension.* Burlington, Ver.: Ashgate, 2004.

2. Cambridge, Vibert C. *Immigration, Diversity, and Broadcasting in the United States, 1900–2001.* Athens, Ohio: Ohio University Press, 2005.

3. Dolan, Chris J. *In War We Trust: The Bush Doctrine and the Pursuit of Just War.* Burlington, Ver.: Ashgate, 2005.

4. Iweala, Uzondinma. *Beasts of No Nation.* London: HarperCollins, 2005.

5. Lawrence, John Shelton and Robert Jewett. *The Myth of the American Superhero.* Grand Rapids: W. B. Eerdmans, 2002.

CHAPTER 6

Security Policy: International Terrorism, Nuclear Weapons, and Instability in Developing Countries

WITH LEE ANN PINGEL

Americans also hold different views toward conflict. Some feel that the United States should adopt an offensive posture against putative foreign threats. Others feel that the United States needs to find ways to accommodate differences. Because the United States has the most powerful military forces in the world, it is the only country capable of projecting its power anyplace in the world, but many of the security issues that the United States faces today involve winning the hearts and minds of other people. This raises questions about what kind of forces the United States should have and how they should be employed. The contradiction between the two types of military involvement—peacekeeping and straight-up military intervention—is represented in the picture above in which U.S. soldiers, members of a NATO-led peacekeeping force in Bosnia, greet children on their way to school as the soldiers patrol through the village of Bulatovci, fifteen miles east of Tuzla.

WHEN PRESIDENT BILL CLINTON ASSUMED office in 1993, many observers assumed that U.S. security policies would change significantly as the country approached the millennium. That assumption was based less on the incoming president's ideas about foreign policy than on the changes in the international security situation. As the first post–cold war president, Clinton was expected to behave differently, because he would supposedly be free of the compulsions and constraints inherent in the dominant relationship between the United States and the Soviet Union during the cold war. Most observers hoped the United States could forge new relationships not only with Russia but also with other countries. Because security issues had dominated international relations during the cold war, the prospect for the pursuit of new foreign policies depended largely on the shape of future American security policy.[1]

Ordering Value Preferences

The framework employed in this text suggests that security policies are usually motivated by fear, and that the level of security to be sought depends on the extent to which a threat is perceived. The primary threat to the United States during the cold war was the Soviet Union. During the cold war, domination was the primary goal of American security policy, although beginning in the 1970s and certainly in the late 1980s accommodation also became an important security goal. Each of these security goals is associated with a distinct vision of how things work, as was the case with the community goals in the previous chapter.

Dispositions

Traditionally, two visions have influenced thinking about security goals. The first assumes that the international system is basically competitive. Proponents of this vision, known as realists, believe that providing security in a highly competitive situation depends on the ability of an actor to confront other actors. Because the term "realist" suggests that these individuals have a better grasp on reality, it is important to recognize that realists are no more capable of perceiving the objective environment than others. They are realists because they posit an anarchical world in which states must provide for their security by enhancing their power vis-à-vis other states.

The second vision assumes that the international system is essentially cooperative, a situation in which actors hope to accommodate whatever differences threaten their security. The most effective conflict resolution strategy is through mutually acceptable compromises—that is, seeking symmetry, not asymmetry or superiority.[2] Those who subscribe to this vision are often called idealists. In Chapter 1 idealism is presented as an approach associated with the community dimension because idealists envisage an ideal world in which human beings share values inclusively. In such a world, most conflicts can be resolved by accommodation. In the context of the security dimension, realists often use the term, idealist, to discredit those who believe that negotiations will work. And because idealists are commonly associated with ideas or, worse yet, ideologies, they are often accused of being unrealistic. It is important, then, to point out that idealists are no more or less capable of perceiving the objective environment than realists. They are idealists because they assume the existence of a global society in which states can ultimately work out their differences with other states. Yet in such a world, accommodation is the best security policy.

Proponents of these two visions have always been part of the human response to security issues. Under a wide range of circumstances, foreign policy actors have adhered to both visions, but not the same actors at the same time. Although psychologists believe that people's adherence to such visions are quite stable, that does not mean that people never change their vision. This does suggest that changes in vision are unusual, and that when they do occur they usually are quite gradual.

As in the last chapter, however, these visions are influenced by an actor's perception of contemporary events and the actor's assessment of other actors' positions in light of these events. The next section considers how events since 1990 have affected perceptions of threat, opportunity, and community relevant to the security dimension.

Perceptions

During the cold war most observers were concerned either that conflicts among advanced states (the North) or among developing states (the South) might escalate into an East–West conflict. In the post–cold war period, especially after the September 11, 2001 attacks, they were increasingly concerned about the escalation of North–South conflicts. In surveying these changes in perceptions it is essential to remember that people with the same vision—either realists or idealists—may perceive these events differently.

How Events Affect Perceptions of Threat.   The collapse of the Soviet Union transformed the perception of threats to an unprecedented degree. One author refers to this transformation as a "quiet cataclysm." [3] Beginning in 1990 with the Conventional Armed Forces in Europe (CFE) Treaty, the threat posed by conventional arms in Europe diminished considerably. Within a period of two years the ideological threat of communism also vanished as one Soviet-style government after another fell, including the communist government of the Soviet Union. Indeed, by 2003 most former Warsaw Pact states were either full-fledged members of NATO or were slated to become members. [4] Even Russia, which had been the security concern that initially gave rise to NATO, was now included in many NATO deliberations. [5]

The end of the cold war also lessened the threat of strategic nuclear forces. Under the first Strategic Arms Reduction Treaty (START I) of 1991, America and Russia reduced their nuclear forces by 30 to 40 percent as Box 6.1 details.[6] Both the United States and Russia had about 6,000 warheads at the end of 2002. In the Treaty of Moscow signed by Russian president Vladimir Putin and U.S. president George W. Bush on May 24, 2002, the two main nuclear powers agreed to further limit themselves to between 1,700 to 2,200 nuclear warheads by the year 2012.

As the threat of a major war between the United States and the former Soviet Union receded, the prospects for more cooperation between them increased, including joint efforts to bring about a more peaceful resolution of conflicts in countries once trapped in the confrontation between the two major powers. The ability of President George H. W. Bush to organize a large coalition of states against Iraq in the Persian Gulf War in 1991 is just one example of the enhanced possibilities for collective action as the cold war ended. In the early 1990s the United Nations engaged in thirteen new peacekeeping operations, more than it had seen in all forty-five years of its existence. UN involvement in Somalia, Bosnia, El Salvador, Guatemala, Angola, and Cambodia are just a few examples of greater cooperation.

The 1991 Persian Gulf War brought about more meaningful negotiations in the seemingly endless conflict between Israelis and Palestinians in the Middle East. The willingness of some Arab countries to work closely

---

BOX 6.1

START I Agreement

START I, a multilateral treaty among the United States, Russia, Ukraine, Kazakhstan, and Belarus, limits the United States and Russia to 1,600 strategic nuclear delivery vehicles each and places a ceiling on each country of 6,000 "accountable" warheads. It also requires Russia to limit the number of its heavy intercontinental ballistic missiles (ICBMs) in fixed silos to half the number possessed by the former Soviet Union. Finally, it requires Ukraine, Kazakhstan, and Belarus to rid themselves of all nuclear weapons that they have. The weapons reduction called for under START I was completed by December 2001, seven years after the treaty entered into force. START I accomplished a 30–40 percent reduction in the strategic nuclear arsenals deployed at the time of the treaty signing.

Source: Harold A. Feiveson, ed., *The Nuclear Turning Point: A Blueprint for Deep Cuts and De-alerting of Nuclear Weapons* (Washington, D.C.: Brookings Institution, 1999), 10.

with the United States and its allies during the war, as well as the willingness of Israel to refrain from military action even when the target of Iraqi missile attacks, provided a foundation for the 1993 Declaration of Principles on Interim Self-Government Arrangements (also known as the Oslo accords). Under these accords, Israel and the Palestinian Liberation Organization (PLO) made the first real progress toward some form of self-rule for Palestinians in the Gaza Strip and selected areas in the West Bank.

But the reduced threat of external war between traditional states soon gave way to new dangers, such as the threat of internal wars within states and the likelihood that a significant number of conventional and even nuclear weapons would end up with rogue states and terrorist groups whose use of these weapons could not be so easily deterred.[7] The danger of a limited nuclear war arising from rogue states and nonstate actors is different in degree from the danger of a cataclysmic war between the United States and the Soviet Union; however, rogue states and nonstate actors are more difficult than traditional states to deter because they present fewer targets of opportunity and because they often reject the traditional constraints agreed to by normal states.

Indeed, as the overwhelming threat of a catastrophic war between superpowers receded, the number and variety of other threats to security seemed to swell. Nuclear weapons were not the only weapons of mass destruction available to these new actors. In some ways, the danger of chemical and biological weapons became even more serious because these unconventional weapons were easier to make and, most important, easier to hide. Besides, military threats were not the only security threats; the threats of global warming, financial market collapses, communications breakdowns, mass hunger, and infectious diseases could destroy as many or more lives than most wars. The concept of security became so diffuse in the mid-1990s that the respondents' estimates of the importance of foreign policy goals associated with the security dimension in the questionnaire results discussed in Chapter 1 could not always be differentiated from the importance of goals associated with the community and prosperity dimensions.[8]

However, when George W. Bush became president in 2001, his administration tried to give the public a much clearer sense of what they thought were the real threats to the United States. They invariably eschewed environmentalism, nation-building, and negotiations in favor of crisis diplomacy. They redefined military threats by emphasizing just three states—Iraq, Iran, and North Korea—whose efforts to attain nuclear weapons constituted an "axis of evil" in the world.[9]

Although the al Qaeda attacks on the World Trade Center towers and the Pentagon on September 11, 2001 were not the work of the "axis of evil" previously defined by the administration, that event so shocked the citizens of the United States, and to a lesser extent the rest of the world, that it gave sustenance to the Bush administration's earlier threat perceptions. Although the nature of the surprise attack was unimaginable to many and came from an organization, al Qaeda, that was largely unknown to the general public, it gave shape to all of the amorphous, nontraditional threats in a way that no government public relations effort could have achieved. The Bush administration then used this heightened sense of insecurity to justify a new doctrine, the right of a great power to undertake a preemptive war should a rogue state or terrorist group threaten the world.

But even the shock of the September 11 attacks and the idea of an "axis of evil" could not wholly unify threat perception because Americans had very different views not only of what would be the most effective way to meet this threat but also what would be the most efficient and acceptable ways to do so.

How Events Affect Perceptions of Opportunity.   The collapse of Soviet power in 1991 placed the United States in a position of superiority. The performance of American conventional forces in the first Gulf War, coupled with the difficulties Russian conventional forces confronted in the breakaway republic of Chechnya, demonstrated beyond any doubt that the United States possessed the world's premier conventional force. Indeed, the United States was the only state that could deploy significant conventional forces all over the world. The outcomes of START I and START II also left the United States with an advantage in nuclear forces.

Russia's weakness left a vacuum in East-Central Europe that was occupied not only by states that were under the control of the former Soviet Union but also by some states that were Soviet republics. In the mid-1990s many security analysts saw this as an opportunity, but that did not mean that they agreed on what should be done.

Some security experts thought the United States should encourage Western Europe to incorporate as many Eastern European countries as they could into the European community. After all, most Eastern European countries, even Russia, now identified with the West and espoused market democracy. These countries were particularly interested in joining the European Union because of the economic benefits they hoped would result from EU membership.[10]

These analysts perceived the possibility of creating "One Europe," which had been the dream of Europeanists since Charlemagne at the end of the first millennium. According to this scenario, the United States would provide the stability required to build common economic and political institutions across all of Europe, including even Russia. Eventually the United States would withdraw, hoping that its initial support and encouragement would establish a permanent bond between America and

Europe, but Europe would ultimately determine its own identity and future.

These experts argued that Europe, like Japan, was perfectly capable of defending itself in the post–cold war period. They noted that in the past major powers, such as the British Empire, had too often overextended themselves by maintaining expensive military commitments overseas only to discover that these defense burdens severely hurt their domestic economies.[11] These experts hoped that the United States could finally reap the long-hoped-for "peace dividend" that was to result from the end of the cold war.

Indeed, some analysts even argued that an isolationist policy would strengthen American security, because as political scientist Richard Betts suggested, "American intervention in troubled areas is not so much a way to fend off such threats as it is what stirs them up." [12] Developing countries in particular are reluctant to have permanent American bases on their territory. For example, U.S. support for Israel and U.S. use of bases in moderate Arab states are a constant irritant to Arab and Islamic nations. The United States has already been forced to relinquish some of its most important bases abroad, such as Subic Bay in the Philippines.

Other security experts maintained that there would always be an East–West division in Europe because of the historic fear of the Soviet Union on the part of many East-Central European countries. They argued that the United States should incorporate as many East-Central European countries as possible into the Western alliance. With the help of NATO the Clinton administration launched the Partnership for Peace (PFP), a program that provided military assistance to these former communist states and increased their capacity to act in concert. Later the Clinton administration made it clear that PFP membership was the first step to becoming a full-fledged member of NATO.[13]

This bifurcation of Europe assumes that the United States would continue to play an active role in Europe. Although the U.S. contribution to the balance between the Western and East-Central European countries, on the one hand, and Russia and its allies, on the other, may decrease over time, it is unlikely that the U.S. role would disappear altogether. Because the United States and its Western European allies would have the advantage of additional East-Central European states on their side, they could keep Russia and its allies at bay without undertaking a new military buildup.

Another group of security experts perceived that the real security threats in the future would arise across the whole Eurasian continent.[14] If the United States was going to remain dominant, it could not afford to commit itself to any one state or group of states. From this perspective the United States would have to influence the correlation of forces in both Europe and Asia to prevent any one coalition from gaining control of the

Eurasian continent. In this strategy the United States would have to pursue a flexible policy; it could not afford to become permanently allied with any particular states.

Under this strategy the United States would build **coalitions of the willing** in Europe and elsewhere to deal with security issues outside Europe or at least outside NATO territory, for example, the U.S. efforts to get NATO members to undertake air strikes in 1999 against Serb forces in Kosovo. Subsequent efforts by President George W. Bush in Afghanistan and in Iraq to lead a coalition of the willing both in NATO and elsewhere to counter international terrorism and deal with rogue states suggested at least initially that the new or prospective NATO members in East-Central Europe might often be more interested in participating in these coalitions than some of the longer-standing NATO members.

The different perspectives on the opportunities arising out of the collapse of the Soviet bloc show how many different kinds of communities are involved in security issues. Now it is important to identify these communities and to show how beliefs about them affect the perception of what moral and legal constraints, if any, should influence the conduct of security policy.

How Events Affect Perceptions of Community.   During the cold war, analysts not only perceived a distinction between the West, mostly democratic countries, and the East, virtually all communist countries, but also between the developed countries and the Third World, consisting mainly of developing countries. Once the cold war ended and most Eastern-communist countries expressed an interest in becoming market democracies, observers were tempted to divide the world into two broad communities. One community incorporated countries that either were or soon aspired to become advanced, democratic countries; the other community consisted of developing countries that for various reasons could not be accepted into the first community.

The line between the two communities was roughly defined in terms of membership in the Organization for Economic Cooperation and Development (OECD), which included Australia, Canada, Iceland, Japan, Korea, Mexico, New Zealand, the United States, and Turkey as well as twenty-one European states. The line separating the two communities in Europe became a focal point for much post–cold war maneuvering among East-Central European countries, including Russia, to be accepted into the advanced-democratic category.

The United States not only distinguished between Western Europe and East-Central Europe, it distinguished between those former Warsaw Pact countries that were ready to be accepted into the Western community— Czechoslovakia, East Germany, Hungary, and Poland—and those who were not—Romania and Bulgaria.[15] One of the reasons for the breakdown of Yugoslavia was that the republics of Slovenia and Croatia were deemed ready for admission to the Western community, whereas Serbia, Bosnia, Montenegro, and Macedonia were not.

There was an even sharper distinction between these countries—all of whom might eventually be accepted as advanced-democratic countries— and all of the developing countries throughout Africa, Asia, and South America. Although some of these countries were more developed than others, for reasons of culture, geography, history, and religion, they were considered outside the pale. Now having distinguished between these two broad communities of states—advanced-democratic countries and developing countries—it is necessary to differentiate between U.S. leaders who perceive these distinctions as quite rigid and those who regard them as more diffuse.

The former are communitarians, and they sharply delineate the United States and other advanced democracies from the developing countries. They perceive the greatest threats to the United States and the advanced democracies as emanating from the developing world. More specifically, the danger allegedly comes from terrorist cells in these countries, particularly those located in the so-called rogue states. Because of the sharp distinctions communitarians have made between terrorists and others, or rogue states and others, they have demarcated these particular actors as existing outside the so-called civilized community. In effect, these actors have been classified as barbarians, and as such they are not parties to the usual norms and laws of the international community. This is the reason that the United States or a "coalition of the willing" led by the United States is justified in taking preemptive action against these elements, even if the rest of the international community does not agree.

The latter are cosmopolitans, who contend that even though the so-called terror cells and rogue states engage in unacceptable behavior, they, and their people, are members of the international community. Cosmopolitans perceive these people as having certain basic human rights, which they lose only if one carefully follows established procedures for depriving these persons of their rights, procedures comparable to the constitutional protections accorded accused persons in criminal court. In effect, these individuals, groups, and states must be dealt with within the rules of the international system. A preemptive strike against these individuals, states, or groups could only be justified if there was uncontestable evidence that they were about to violate the law, and even then it would be best if the UN Security Council coordinated the action against them because only the Security Council has the legal right to deal with "threats to the peace," which are deniable.

As this discussion suggests, foreign policy actors not only have a particular vision that predisposes them to favor dominance or accommodation but often perceive situations and assess the responses of other actors to those situations in ways that reinforce their visions. The next sections show how these visions and perceptions combine to form a more or less coherent set of foreign policy objectives.

Preferences

There are essentially two different theories about how state and nonstate actors form preferences. One theory assumes that the state is guided by a coherent set of value preferences as if a single individual dictated the foreign policy of a state. The other theory assumes that those who act on behalf of the state have multiple preferences, which means that foreign policies are determined through a political process. Because foreign policy is a continuous process, the focus should not be on the ranking of value preferences at a particular point in time, but rather the ranking of objectives over a period of time.

A Coherent System of Preferences.   Those who assume that American foreign policy actors have a coherent set of value preferences usually arrive at that conclusion in one of two ways. The first way is to contend that the objective environment, particularly the security dimension, is so salient that most if not all people would perceive it the same way. This means that even people with different visions come to the same conclusion about the requirements of a given situation. To the extent that an objective situation defines a security threat, then the people acting on behalf of the state will have no real choice as to how they respond. Realists would also assume that the security of the state is more important than any other value.

The second way to arrive at a coherent system of value preferences is by positing that a single individual acts on behalf of the state. Under the U.S. Constitution this person is the president of the United States. As commander in chief, the president has the opportunity to establish orderly preferences on security policy. Both Congress and the bureaucracy look to the president for leadership on such policies, especially during crisis situations. As presidential appointees, the principal officials in the executive branch of the government also seek to implement the policies of a democratically elected president, even if they do not always agree with those policies. If these officials cannot agree with the president's foreign policies, they are expected to resign from office.

Because both paths can actually work in concert, many observers believe it is reasonable to assume that the government's security policies are coherent—that is, they are consciously derived to maximize a consistent set of value preferences. However, this is often more true in theory than in practice. Presidents may have trouble convincing others that their assessments of various situations are correct, and events may later demonstrate that presidents' assumptions are faulty. For example, the Bush administration argued in 2003 that it was necessary to take military action against Iraq in order to prevent that country from using nuclear weapons (which it later turned out Iraq did not have), whereas it was not wise to take such action against North Korea (which later admitted to having such weapons.) Not everyone in the government, media, or general public agreed with the Bush administration's assessments or supported the administration's policies at the time.

Although the Bush administration's treatment of the two cases was distinct because of the differences it perceived in the character of the two regimes, the administration would not negotiate with both regimes until they had fulfilled their international obligations by disavowing nuclear weapons. As this occurrence illustrates, administrations will make fine distinctions between cases such as Iraq and North Korea, and base different policies on those distinctions. It is also easy to see how people inside as well as outside the administration might have very different views as to what ought to be done in each case. Because every administration would like to arrive at some degree of consensus on such issues, however, it is important to consider the situation that exists when individuals involved in the decision-making process hold varied or **multiple preferences**.

Preferences of Multiple Actors. What happens when decision making is shared among the members of large and small groups? Political scientist James DeNardo, who studied the preferences of undergraduate students with respect to various strategic nuclear arms situations in the early 1990s, provides an answer to this question.[16] DeNardo asked 169 students to order their value preferences in four concrete strategic choice situations, involving decisions as to whether the United States should have or not have a particular weapons system, depending on what decision they thought the Soviet Union would make. Because the well-established theoretical literature had already identified the optimal outcomes in these situations, DeNardo expected most students to settle on a few well-established preference orderings.

To his amazement, the students actually identified 60 different preferred outcomes. Indeed, relatively few students agreed on even the most popular of the preferred outcomes! At first DeNardo dismissed this surprising outcome on the grounds that the students just didn't know very much either about nuclear weapons or nuclear strategy. But when he subsequently administered the same exercise to nuclear experts at the Rand Corporation, a private think tank, he discovered that the experts were almost as divided as the students on what should be the preference ordering.

Because the security experts as well as the students displayed such a wide range of preferences on these security outcomes, even experts, with access to information about weapons technology and the best thinking about how these weapons can be used, may have difficulty reaching agreement. Even experts will have different visions of what is likely to promote security, as well as different perceptions of both actual situations and the preferences of other relevant actors.

DeNardo's finding has major implications for decision making in any group context. It suggests that whether the group is a very large one such as the national electorate, a medium-size one such as the Senate, or a very small one such as the National Security Council, the preferences of those involved are likely to vary greatly. This also means that if a president needs to go beyond his own preferences and build a wider consensus on strategic policies, he may well encounter significant differences in value preferences. Of course, the president can ignore these differences, but if he chooses not to—and there are many reasons why he may not want to ignore them—he must find some compromise that is acceptable to the group. (This issue will be explored further in Part III.)

Chapter 5 contrasts the general foreign policy preferences of Bill Clinton in 1993 and George W. Bush in 2002. Clinton gave first priority to the development of democratic-market economies, especially in Europe, second priority to protecting this security community from the anarchical tendencies rampant in the rest of the world, and only third priority to developing a just global society. By contrast Bush gave first priority to fighting international terrorism and the axis of evil, second priority to maintaining freedom of choice in the form of capitalism and consumerism, and only third priority to satisfying the economic demands of society at the moment.

There are many explanations for the differences in Clinton's and Bush's foreign policy preference orderings. They may be the result of changes in the post–cold war situation between 1993 and 2003. They may also reflect differences in the preferred visions and perceptions of the two individuals. Moreover, they may mirror differences in both the composition of decision groups and the decision processes employed by the two presidents in those groups. Whatever the source, the differences in the ranking of these objectives are essential to understanding the foreign policies of these two administrations and the likelihood that these foreign policies will change over time.

The priorities of each president, shown in Table 5.1, are based largely on official statements of foreign policy. Such statements are useful, but they are seldom sufficient in themselves to define a foreign policy. One also needs to consider the methods chosen to implement these foreign policies, the subject of the next section.

Identifying the Options

After the Soviet empire collapsed, the character of American diplomacy and the configuration of American military forces also had to change.

Exactly what changes would take place was not entirely clear. The first congressionally mandated Quadrennial Defense Review took place in 1997 and produced little substantive change, except for overall force reductions, but as a consequence of the September 11, 2001 attacks and problems associated with the post–war occupation of Iraq, the need for major restructuring of the military became increasingly clear.

Currently some military analysts are calling for two distinct force structures: one to fight big wars; the other to build states in the developing world. The more traditional conventional and nuclear forces would be used to deter violent conflict between states and to deal with rogue states. New methods would have to be developed to strengthen developing countries.[17] This section explores the options emerging for both these traditional and nontraditional methods.

Traditional Methods

The United States has the world's only deep-water navy, the largest airlift fleet, the capacity to strike anywhere in the world from U.S. airbases, and the ability to rapidly deploy supplies.[18] Military analysts recommend that this diverse set of special operations, strategic, transportation, and joint forces commands will have to be maintained at the level required to deal with the danger of interstate conflict anywhere in the world.

Traditional Coercive Methods.   Military strategists plan to use the bulk of the Defense Department, particularly the Navy and the Air Force, for dealing with threats from near-peer states, such as China or Russia, or rogue states. For example, when George W. Bush decided to back up his threat to oust Saddam Hussein if Iraq did not give up its nuclear weapons program, he sent an invasion force to the Persian Gulf area in 2002–2003. This was an MCA security policy—unilateral, coercive, and proactive—because many other members of the UN Security Council felt that UN inspectors could accomplish the same result without placing an invasion force on Iraq's doorstep. Table 6.1 will illustrate this and the next three examples of traditional, coercive methods of security-based foreign policy: the National Missile Defense system, a mutual No First Use defense policy, and collective security actions, such as the 2001 war against Afghanistan.

Although the United States relied mainly on its **forward defense** during the cold war, some security analysts, such as Eric Nordlinger, argued that in the post–cold war period the most appropriate security policy would be a **continental defense**.[19] A forward defense means defending oneself by bringing the fight or the means to fight to the enemy by stationing troops and supplies overseas, whereas a continental defense means keeping one's forces within one's borders. In the 1980s Ronald Reagan developed a Strategic Defense Initiative (SDI) as a form of continental defense. Although successive presidents considered the idea of

Table 6.1. Dimensions of Foreign Policy: Traditional Coercive Methods

| | Multilateral | | Unilateral | |
	Coercive	Noncoercive	Noncoercive	Coercive
Proactive	George W. Bush's war against al Qaeda and the Taliban in Afghanistan in 2001			George W. Bush's decision to send an invasion force to the Persian Gulf in 2002–2003
Reactive	Reagan's proposal for a mutual No First Use nuclear policy			George W. Bush's plan for a National Missile Defense system

George W. Bush's decision to send an invasion force to the Persian Gulf in 2002–2003 was MCA—unilateral because it was opposed by many members of the UN Security Council, coercive because it envisaged the use of force, and proactive because it expected substantial benefits from a quick victory.

The Bush administration's decision to abrogate the Anti-Ballistic Missile treaty and develop a National Missile Defense system finally came in 2002. This traditional, classic defense security policy is MCA—unilateral because the United States decided to undertake this policy despite the opposition of Russia, China, and others, coercive because it calls for a military defense, and reactive because it would supposedly only be employed in self-defense. (Some analysts would argue that a NMD system is actually an offensive rather than a defensive weapon because it may make it possible to employ U.S. offensive capabilities anywhere in the world.)

The fact that nuclear weapons have not been used since 1945 is a promising sign. But a mutual policy of No First Use among nuclear powers, such as that proposed by Ronald Reagan, would certainly allay fears that this tacit understanding could be overturned at any time. Mutual policies of No First Use would be MCA—multilateral because they would be based on the agreement of all parties concerned, coercive because they involved the use of nuclear weapons, and reactive because they contemplate using nuclear weapons only in self-defense.

George W. Bush's war in Afghanistan is MCA—multilateral because in the wake of the September 11, 2001 attack the UN Security Council unanimously supported Resolution 1378 on November 14, 2001 which authorized the attack, coercive because it involved military forces, and proactive because it sought to punish al Qaeda by destroying their home bases in Afghanistan.

building a missile defense system, that step was not taken in earnest until George W. Bush finally abrogated the 1972 Anti-Ballistic Missile (ABM) treaty, opening the way for more extensive testing of such a system in 2002.[20] If and when this National Missile Defense (NMD) system becomes operational, it is an example of an MCA security policy.

The tacit agreement among states not to initiate an atomic or nuclear attack unless they are themselves the object of such an attack represents a third type of traditional, coercive policy. As a consequence, no nuclear state has initiated the use of atomic or nuclear weapons since 1945. When former president Reagan introduced SDI, he also considered giving this capability to the Soviet Union so that both countries could defend themselves and neither country would have an incentive for using nuclear weapons against the other.[21] In theory if all countries agreed to have a mutual **No First Use** defense policy, there would be little danger of a nuclear exchange. However, such a policy might prevent a state, such as the United States, from effectively extending its deterrence to third parties, such as Japan. In 1993 Russia briefly announced a No First Use policy, although that declaration was rescinded when it became evident that Russia's ability to defend itself in the war with Chechnya with conventional arms alone was suspect. Although mutual No First Use is just a theory, it is a good example of a MCA security policy.

The 2001 war against al Qaeda and the Taliban regime in Afghanistan is considered a collective security action under Article 51 of the UN Charter because the UN Security Council authorized it in Resolution 1378 on November 14, 2001. Although the UN Security Council has occasionally issued general calls for help in international peacekeeping, it has more frequently developed ad hoc peacekeeping forces that were acceptable to the combatants. Sometimes the Security Council has asked a single state to accept most of the responsibility for carrying out its mandate. For example, the United Nations chose Australia to take the lead in implementing its security policy in East Timor in 1999 and France to do the same in the Ivory Coast in 2002–2003. Also, the disarmament agreements such as START I and START II between both superpowers and the Nuclear Nonproliferation Treaty, which was ratified by most countries in the world, are good examples of MCA security policies.

Traditional Noncoercive Methods. At the end of his second term in office Bill Clinton devoted much time trying to achieve a settlement of the Israeli-Palestinian conflict. Although these efforts eventually failed, the two sides came as close as they have come thus far to reaching an accord. Unfortunately, minorities on both sides preferred a continuance of the conflict to the compromises proposed by the United States. This U.S. mediation effort is a good example of an MCA security policy. Table 6.2 will illustrate this and the next three examples of traditional, noncoercive security foreign policies: Bush's policy of non-involvement in the Arab-Israeli conflict, civilian defense such as that involved in the fall of communism in Eastern Europe, and the UN's efforts to bring about peace by mutual consent in Cambodia.

As a result of this failure President George W. Bush decided to reassess the progress the immediate parties to the conflict in the Middle East could make. Left to their own devices the Israelis and the Palestinians became engaged in a bitter conflict that some observers have labeled the sixth

Table 6.2. Dimensions of Foreign Policy: Traditional Noncoercive Methods

	Multilateral		Unilateral	
	Coercive	Noncoercive	Noncoercive	Coercive
Proactive		Anticommunist movements in Eastern and Central Europe in 1989–1991	Bill Clinton's efforts to settle the Israeli-Palestinian conflict in 2000	
Reactive		Nuclear freeze movement in Western Europe in 1983	George W. Bush's decision not to become involved in Middle East negotiations in 2001	

Clinton's efforts to negotiate a settlement in the Middle East in 2000 was MCA—unilateral in that although many other parties were interested in the proceedings, he was acting largely on behalf of the United States, noncoercive because the peace process was based mostly on negotiations among the parties directly concerned and participation in the negotiation process was voluntary, and proactive because all the participants were prepared to accept costs in order to realize positive benefits.

George W. Bush's decision not to become involved in negotiating an Israeli-Palestinian settlement in 2001 was MCA—unilateral because it was done without the consent of all of the interested parties, noncoercive because this issue did not involve the use of force, and reactive because the Bush administration did not think the prospects of a settlement would outweigh the costs.

The nuclear freeze movement in Western Europe in 1983 was an MCA policy—multilateral because citizens throughout Western Europe rallied around the anti-nuclear principle, noncoercive because they used peaceful protests as their main method, and reactive because they were mainly concerned about the potential costs of the deployment of new intermediate nuclear weapons in Europe.

The anticommunist revolutions in Eastern and Central Europe at the end of the cold war were MCA—multilateral because they represented a more or less spontaneous decision on the part of the peoples of these countries as news of one revolution sparked a chain of revolutions in the region, noncoercive because they were basically peaceful efforts by the local populations to communicate a lack of confidence to their communist governments, and proactive because ordinary civilians were prepared to take personal risks in order to gain their freedom from communist regimes.

Arab-Israeli War. Whether the United States might have prevented this latest war by encouraging negotiations is an open question, but the decision to stay out of the conflict for a time is a good example of an MCA security policy. (Now that Israel has pulled out of the Gaza strip, the Bush administration may become more active in pursuing a settlement.)

Sometimes it is possible to bring about peaceful change without becoming actively involved. The anticommunist revolutions in the six

Eastern European countries in 1989–1990, former republics of the Soviet Union in 1990–1991, and eventually the Soviet Union itself in late 1991 are examples of peaceful change that happened with little outside involvement. Although Western examples and universal values were important in each of these revolutions, the fall of communism in Eastern Europe was largely a homegrown phenomenon. Because governments generally require the support and cooperation of the populations they rule, a population can sometimes bring the government down by refusing to provide the support the government needs. Although Martin Luther King Jr., the civil rights leader, is best known in the United States for using the strategy of civil disobedience to end formal racial inequality in America in the 1960s, a political scientist, Gene Sharp, has written more extensively about **civilian defense** in general, as Box 6.2 shows. Civilian-based defense aims to deter and defeat aggression by making a society ungovernable and by maintaining a capacity for self-rule. Although civilian defense is rarely considered as a national security policy, especially in the United States, it is one of the most intriguing types of security policy. The fall of communism in Eastern Europe is a good example of a MCA security policy.

In 1982 the Soviet Union decided to place new SS-20 intermediate missiles in Eastern Europe in order to counter the missiles the United States already had in Western Europe. In response the Reagan administration proposed placing new cruise and Pershing II missiles in Western Europe in order to assure NATO governments that the U.S. deterrence in Europe was still viable. By the fall of 1983 the nuclear freeze movement in Europe had become so vehement that the United States had to alter its foreign policy by offering a "two-track" proposal including a "zero" option that would cancel the plan to introduce the new missiles into Western Europe. This protest movement is a good example of an MCA security policy.

These traditional methods were designed to deal with interstate wars or states, but they are not suitable for dealing with international terrorism, post–war conflicts such as the United States' attempts at reconstruction in Iraq beginning in the spring of 2003, or intrastate conflicts such as the conflict in Kosovo or Rwanda. New, nontraditional methods will have to be developed to deal with these types of conflicts.

Nontraditional Methods

After the September 11, 2001 attacks the George W. Bush administration introduced new methods for dealing with rogue states and nonstate actors. According to the administration's critics, these new methods undermine existing national and international norms. For example, they challenge the strictures in international law regarding the violation of the territorial integrity of states. Some of these methods are discussed below.

Nontraditional Coercive Methods.   The United States now employs a variety of military methods that would have been unacceptable only a few years ago. For example, the Bush administration has refused to abide by the rules governing the treatment of prisoners under the Geneva Convention because it claims that those rules apply only to military personnel of states and al Qaeda is a nonstate actor. This decision was originally made with respect to prisoners captured in Afghanistan and later transferred to detainment camps at the U.S. Naval Base in Guantanamo Bay, Cuba, so that these prisoners would not have access to the protection of U.S. law. Later, these same practices were extended to Iraq. Prisoner abuses have been identified in all of these locales. The United States also reserves the right to violate another country's sovereignty in order to effectively engage alleged terrorists, such as when a U.S. Predator drone fired a Hellfire missile that killed six suspected al Qaeda terrorists in a vehicle speeding along a highway in Yemen. Although U.S. agents had been working with Yemeni authorities on combating terrorism in that country, there is no reason to believe that the United States would have refrained from acting if the Yemeni authorities were not available. Table 6.3 illustrates these two examples of MCA security policy and the next three examples of the new, nontraditional coercive policy: the reduction in the number of screening personnel at U.S. airports, the efforts of member states to reduce financing for terrorism, and the U.S. withdrawal of some of its officials from UN peace-keeping missions.

Of course, one of the first steps taken after the September 11, 2001 attacks was to beef up domestic security measures, especially at some 429 commercial airports in the United States. Prior to the attacks most Americans assumed that people could move and talk freely within the United States without being subjected to restraint or supervision. After the attacks, however, many Americans have been subjected to compulsory searches at airports, and Americans with Arab and Muslim backgrounds have been subjected to compulsory interviews and in some cases detention. A number of Arab and Muslim aliens who have lived in the United States for years have also been deported. In 2003 the Department of Homeland Security had to cut back as many as 6,000 federally hired and trained screening personnel at these airports in order to meet budget requirements. This scaling down of personnel is a good example of nontraditional coercive MCA security policy.

Because the al Qaeda network exists in many different countries, it is important to get these countries to undertake their own antiterrorism actions. Accordingly, Resolution 1373 passed by the UN Security Council on September 28, 2001, asks all member countries to prohibit money transfers to international terrorists through their banking systems. Although the resolution calls for all states to act, each state is allowed to determine what measures are most appropriate within its domestic jurisdiction. The

BOX 6.2

Profile in Action: Gene Sharp

Gene Sharp began his studies of peace and war as a student at Ohio State University in the late 1940s. He wrote his senior honors thesis on war in 1949 and his master's thesis on nonviolence in 1951. Almost twenty-five years later this expanded thesis became a classic three-volume work on nonviolent action.

Sharp completed his first book on Mahatma Gandhi in 1953, the same year that he was imprisoned in New York as a conscientious objector to the Korean War. Once he was paroled in 1955 he moved to Europe where he worked and studied at the University of Oslo and the Institute for Social Research that was located in that same city.

The book on Gandhi was first published in 1960 in India as *Gandhi Wields the Weapon of Moral Power,* with a foreword by Albert Einstein. By this time Gene Sharp had moved to England where he completed the first draft of his three-volume work on *The Politics of Nonviolent Action* at St. Catherine's College in 1963.

He returned to the United States in 1965 to complete his dissertation in political theory as a research fellow at Harvard University's Center for International Affairs. After he received a PhD from Oxford University in England in 1968, he accepted positions at the University of Massachusetts and Southeastern Massachusetts University.

Security Council has even established an Implementation Committee that periodically reports progress made by various states to the Security Council. These financial measures are examples of nontraditional coercive MCA security policies.

The United States has signed some 90 bilateral agreements with various countries that bar prosecution of U.S. officials under the International Criminal Court (ICC), which is located in The Hague, Holland. Because there has been such strong opposition abroad to the abuse of Iraqi prisoners in Iraq, the United States has now abandoned this effort to exempt itself. However, in June 2004 the United States did withdraw two small contingents from the UN peace-keeping missions in Ethiopia-Eritrea and Kosovo because these Americans were no longer exempt from international prosecution in the ICC for war crimes. This action is a good example of a MCA security policy.

Nontraditional Noncoercive Policies. American military forces have learned that there is no clear separation between fighting a war and

When the three-volume study on nonviolent action, with a foreword by Thomas Schelling, was finally published in 1973, it became the classic work on nonviolent action. In the preface to an earlier work on civilian defense, with an introduction by David Riesman, Sharp explains "that all power, of all groups and all governments, derives from sources in the society, and the availability of these is determined by the degree of cooperation and obedience offered by the people."

In the first volume Sharp deals with the nature and control of political power. In the second volume Sharp lists 198 methods of nonviolent action, including those that fit under (1) protest and persuasion, (2) social noncooperation, (3) economic noncooperation, such as boycotts and strikes, (4) political noncooperation, and (5) nonviolent intervention.

In the third volume Sharp deals with the dynamics of nonviolence, especially various ways of dealing with efforts to repress nonviolent action. He argues that there are three ways to achieve success: conversion, accommodation, and nonviolent coercion.

One of the advantages of nonviolent defense is that it is not threatening to other societies. Although Americans have not generally embraced nonviolent defense, it was successfully employed by Martin Luther King Jr. and the civil rights movement to achieve racial equality in this country. It has also been employed in many other countries over the centuries.

Sources: Gene Sharp, *The Politics of Nonviolent Action* (Boston: Porter Sargent, 1973); Gene Sharp, *Exploring Nonviolent Alternatives* (Boston: Porter Sargent, 1970), vii.

post–war state-building or nation-building. The United States tried to establish this division of labor in Afghanistan. Once the Taliban government and al Qaeda forces in Afghanistan were scattered and forced into hiding, commonly held international norms expected the United States and other countries to do as much as possible to rebuild that country. Since George W. Bush did not believe that U.S. troops should be used for nation-building, the 10,000 U.S. troops in Afghanistan were largely engaged in efforts to deal with remnants of al Qaeda and the Taliban, whereas NATO forces engaged in nation-building. During the occupation of Iraq, however, U.S. military forces could not offload nation-building on NATO because those countries opposed the war. Consequently, U.S. forces and private contractors had to engage in economic reconstruction and election protection activities at the same time that they were conducting security operations. These nation-building efforts in Iraq are good examples of the new MCA security policies. Table 6.4 illustrates this reconstruction effort and the next three examples of nontraditional, noncoercive security

Table 6.3. Dimensions of Foreign Policy: Nontraditional Coercive Methods

	Multilateral		Unilateral	
	Coercive	Noncoercive	Noncoercive	Coercive
Proactive	The cooperative efforts of many governments to reduce the flow of financial resources to terrorists under UN Resolution 1373 (2001)			Readiness of Bush administration to treat terrorists differently from prisoners of war and violate other countries' territoriality in the war on terror
Reactive	The withdrawal of U.S. military officers from UN peace-keeping missions in Ethiopia-Eritrea and Kosovo			The reduction in force of some 6,000 federal airport screening personnel by the Department of Homeland Security in 2003 to meet budget requirements

The readiness of the Bush administration to deny Geneva Convention protections to terrorist prisoners and to violate territorial norms in pursuit of terrorists was MCA—unilateral because the United States is asserting its own prerogatives, coercive because it involved using extreme violence against some prisoners, and proactive because the decision was made in the hope that it would maximize the amount of good information gleaned from these terrorists.

The decision by the Department of Homeland Security to reduce federal screening personnel at U.S. airports by some 6,000 in 2003 in order to meet budget requirements was MCA—unilateral because the decision was made by the U.S. government, coercive because these screeners had coercive powers, and reactive because the government was trying to lower the costs of homeland security.

The cooperative efforts of UN member states to stop the international financing of terrorists under U.N. Res. 1373 (2001) was MCA— multilateral because the efforts were pursuant to a Security Council resolution, coercive because member states were expected to use government action to force member banks and other institutions under their jurisdiction to comply, and proactive because the members expected to benefit by restricting terrorism.

The withdrawal of small contingents of U.S. military officers from UN peacekeeping missions to Ethiopia-Eritrea and Kosovo was MCA— unilateral because the United States made this decision, coercive because it involved military personnel on peace-keeping missions, and reactive because it reduced U.S. participation in these missions.

policy: the election and reconstruction efforts of the UN in Iraq, recruitment of citizens and neighborhood watch groups in the domestic war against terrorism, and local efforts to bolster human rights that might be violated in the war against terrorism.

Table 6.4. Dimensions of Foreign Policy: Nontraditional Noncoercive Methods

| | Multilateral | | Unilateral | |
	Coercive	Noncoercive	Noncoercive	Coercive
Proactive		Efforts by UN to coordinate and deliver other assistance to Iraq once the interim government was formed in June 2004	Nation-building efforts by U.S. military forces in post–war Iraq	
Reactive		Efforts by individual cities to refuse assistance to U.S. federal authorities who they believe may be violating the basic rights of their citizens	Attorney General Ashcroft's call for American citizens to report suspicious activities to the U.S. government	

Nation-building efforts of U.S. military forces in post–war Iraq are a good example of MCA security policy—unilateral because many important countries would not participate so long as the United States ran the interim government, noncoercive because these activities were seen as distinct from their security assignment, and proactive because the United States expected to benefit from these activities.

The efforts of the United Nations to encourage countries who had not participated in the multinational force to contribute to the reconstruction of Iraq is a good example of a MCA security policy—multilateral because the UN Security Council is authorized to act on behalf of the international community, noncoercive because the UN assumed no responsibility for security other than to review the mandate for a multinational force at the request of the government of Iraq every twelve months, and proactive because the UN hoped to contribute to the reconstruction of Iraq.

Attorney General Ashcroft's call for American citizens to report suspicious activities was MCA—unilateral because it was made solely in his capacity as a U.S. official, noncoercive in that only voluntary action was requested, and reactive because neighborhood watch is one of the more passive methods of preventing crime.

Efforts by some U.S. municipalities to prevent their officials from cooperating with federal enforcement officers when they believe that these actions violate the basic human rights and civil rights of local citizens is MCA—multilateral because they are guided by what they perceive to be universal human rights, noncoercive because it is an effort to persuade the U.S. government to desist, and reactive because these measures are suggested to reduce the costs of antiterrorist measures.

On June 30, 2004, an interim government under Ayad Allawi assumed sovereign authority in Iraq. In anticipation of that event the UN Security Council passed Resolution 1546, which endorsed the formation of the Iraqi interim government, endorsed the proposed timetable for Iraq's political transition to democratic government, and assumed responsibility to work in three areas: political process, reconstruction, and the rule of law. The UN did not assume any responsibility for the U.S. reconstruction effort, but rather "contribute[d] to the coordination and delivery of reconstruction, development and humanitarian assistance." [22] This is a good example of MCA security policy.

The fact that nonstate actors planned and committed the September 11 attacks from within the United States also led the U.S. government to seek the help of ordinary citizens in its war against terrorism. Attorney General John Ashcroft announced in March 2002 that he was recruiting neighborhood watch groups across the United States to help the government detect terrorists. For example, in October of 2002 a Georgia woman alleged that she heard a group of Arab-looking men talking about terrorist acts. She called the police, and the men involved were eventually stopped and interrogated in Florida. Because nothing suspicious was found either on the men or in their car, they were released. But the medical convention that they were planning to attend no longer welcomed them because of the adverse publicity. Although the federal officials could get helpful information in this way, this example shows that the information thus gained is not always helpful. This is an example of the new MCA security policies.

Of course, the government's extraordinary efforts to ferret out terrorists in American society were resisted by groups and individuals who felt that such actions undermined American freedoms as well as global human rights. Some local communities, such as Amherst, Massachusetts, have even passed resolutions prohibiting local officials from assisting the federal government in carrying out measures that may violate the civil rights or liberties of individuals suspected of terrorist activities. These local efforts to bolster human rights that might be trampled by the government's efforts to pursue possible terrorists in the United States are examples of MCA nontraditional, noncoercive security policies.

The identification of traditional and nontraditional types of security policies is important, but the single most difficult task is to determine which combination of actions, out of all the possibilities, ought to be examined in greater detail. Although the framework for analysis is particularly useful in elaborating the full range of actions (a **divergent process**), it also helps in extracting the most relevant options (a **convergent process**). This convergent process is illustrated in the next section.

Selecting the Most Relevant Option: International Terrorism

Although it is important to consider all possible actions, most decision makers want to identify what combination of actions are likely to work best in a given situation. For example, in order to identify two to three convergent strategies for solving the terrorist problem, policy makers would have to make some assumptions about the motivations of their opponents, as well as the circumstances that would likely affect the outcome of their actions. Because the leadership of al Qaeda is highly motivated to continue its actions, policy makers have little choice but to apprehend the organization's leaders and end their operations. However, the organization's activities have continued despite U.S. efforts to disrupt the leadership. Accordingly, the prospect of ending al Qaeda's activities depends on the extent to which the al Qaeda leadership is supported by its network, which includes thousands of people scattered across some sixty countries, as well as the extent to which this network in turn is supported by a much larger body of sympathizers around the world, especially in Arab and Islamic countries.

As a consequence, policy makers have developed their options by positing different assumptions about al Qaeda's ability both to maintain internal control over its terrorist network and to build outside support for its cause. Toward this end it may be useful to distinguish between different levels of support for al Qaeda leadership among members of the al Qaeda network and among Arabs and Muslims generally. For example, it might be useful to ask whether al Qaeda rank-and-file support for its leadership is thick (strong) or thin (weak). Similarly, it might be helpful to know whether sympathizer support for al Qaeda is thick or thin.

Hoping that support for the al Qaeda leadership was thin, both inside and outside its network, the United Nations' and the United States' first option was to convince the Taliban government in Afghanistan, which was harboring this leadership, to give them up.[23] When the Taliban refused to do so, the U.S. government, with the support of UN Security Council Resolution 1378, proceeded to topple the Taliban government and scattered al Qaeda forces within Afghanistan. The diplomatic effort to get the Taliban government to give up Osama bin Laden was an MCA security policy; although the United States took the lead, the concomitant military policy of forcing the Taliban and al Qaeda out of Afghanistan was an MCA security policy. Table 6.5 shows the first strategic option in the war on terrorism.

Although some of the al Qaeda leadership in Afghanistan was disrupted, it appeared that Osama bin Laden and other elements of the al Qaeda leadership survived, and it became necessary to assume that the support for the al Qaeda leadership among those inside its network was thick even though outside support for the leadership among the population of Arab and Islamic countries might be thin. Under this set of assumptions it might be enough to hunt down the rank-and-file members with the help of the governments of states associated with the United States throughout the world. This second option would require the United

Table 6.5. Dimensions of Foreign Policy: Strategy of Defeating al Qaeda Leadership

	Multilateral		Unilateral	
	Coercive	Noncoercive	Noncoercive	Coercive
Proactive	Option 1			
Reactive				

The U.S. strategy for apprehending and punishing the al Qaeda leadership was multilateral because there was widespread support within the UN for this policy, both noncoercive and coercive because the United States both offered to help the Taliban government of Afghanistan if it gave up Osama bin Laden and to punish the Taliban government if it did not do so, and proactive because both elements of the policy anticipated large benefits with minimum costs. (If the Taliban voluntarily gave up Osama bin Laden, the United States would gladly provide assistance to Afghanistan; if the Taliban did not surrender bin Laden, the cost of forcibly ousting the Taliban regime in Afghanistan was not considered that high.)

States to work in conjunction with governments all over the world to deal with al Qaeda cells in their countries (an MCA security policy). Because individual countries would have to make sacrifices in order to destroy the network, the cost would be high because the network might be deeply imbedded in some of these societies (an MCA security policy). Because such a policy is unlikely to be successful unless all countries were prepared to use force, these security policies would all be coercive. Table 6.6 sets out these options.

If sympathizer support for al Qaeda was thick, especially in Arab and Islamic countries, however, it would be necessary to pursue a third option that would involve many ordinary citizens both in the United States and abroad in the effort. Newspaper columnist Thomas Friedman argued that to get to the root of sympathizer support for al Qaeda it is essential to help developing countries democratize and modernize their own societies. This would not only require efforts to deal effectively with Arab American and American Muslim populations, but also to assist Arab and Islamic populations in other countries. Among other things it would require the U.S. government to distance itself from the authoritarian regimes that oppress Arab-Muslim populations and give al Qaeda the unhealthy context that makes its violent actions acceptable to some people. In order to work effectively with Arab American and American Muslim populations the U.S. government and private groups would have to conduct MCA and MCA security policies. In order to operate effectively abroad, the U.S. government and nongovernmental groups would have to conduct MCA and MCA security policies abroad. Table 6.7 sets out these options.

Table 6.6. Dimensions of Foreign Policy: Strategy of Destroying the al Qaeda Rank-and-file Network

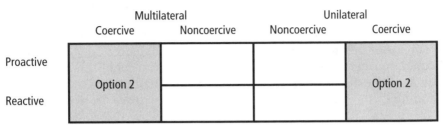

| | Multilateral | | Unilateral | |
	Coercive	Noncoercive	Noncoercive	Coercive
Proactive	Option 2			Option 2
Reactive				

TThe strategy for eliminating the al Qaeda network throughout the world was both unilateral and multilateral because although the United States took the brunt of the action, the strategy could not be implemented successfully without the support of many other countries, coercive because this strategy required the use of air, ground, and naval forces as well as police forces, and both proactive and reactive because both the benefits and the costs were recognized as being high.

Table 6.7. Dimensions of Foreign Policy: Strategy of Undermining al Qaeda's Support among Sympathizers

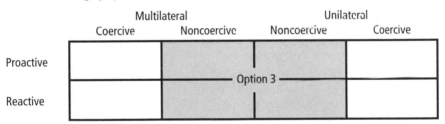

| | Multilateral | | Unilateral | |
	Coercive	Noncoercive	Noncoercive	Coercive
Proactive		Option 3		
Reactive				

The strategy of depriving the al Qaeda network of a support base among sympathizers both at home and abroad would work best if all the world's governments and peoples would cooperate, but the United States might have to offer special inducements where cooperation is not forthcoming, noncoercive because these people have to be persuaded that their lives are getting better and that violence has no place in their future, and both proactive and reactive because there would be benefits for all concerned, but the costs of such programs could be enormous especially if this strategy was not pursued from the beginning.

Choosing the Best or Most Appropriate Foreign Policy Option

So far this chapter has shown how the framework for analysis advances both the understanding of preference rankings, that is the prioritizing of objectives, and the development of strategic options, that is the determination of which methods will best reach these objectives. This final section is concerned with how preferences (objectives) can be used to assess strategic options (methods). But before one makes these assessments it is useful to think of these preferences in terms of criteria for judging various actions.

Applying the Three Criteria

Earlier objectives of foreign policy were defined in terms of dimensions. A separate criterion was associated with each primary dimension. Thus effectiveness was seen as the most appropriate criterion for assessing outcomes on the security dimension; acceptability, on the community dimension; and efficiency, on the prosperity dimension. Each of these criteria will be discussed separately before applying them to the objectives and methods associated with two foreign policy issues: nuclear weapons control and combating instability in developing countries.

Effectiveness Criterion.   States and political leaders are frequently tempted to employ military measures to reach their objectives. For one thing, coercive measures are often the most direct means of getting results; the use of force not only gets people's attention, but can produce immediate consequences. For example, from 1992 through much of 1995, Bosnian Serbs were unwilling to negotiate with Bosnian Croats and Bosnian Muslims. It was not until 1995 when the better-armed Croatian and Muslim forces began to push Bosnian Serbs out of areas they had held since the beginning of the war and NATO finally agreed to use its air power to force Bosnian Serbs from key positions around Sarajevo and other protected areas in Bosnia that the Bosnian Serbs agreed to negotiate. Within a matter of months, all three groups in Bosnia signed the Dayton accords that provided for a cease-fire, a NATO-led Implementation Force (I-FOR), and the partitioning of Bosnia under a decentralized system of government. None of these measures had been possible until the use of force on the ground and in the air.

However, military actions also have disadvantages in terms of their effectiveness. For one thing, the use of military force often causes collateral damage. The 1999 NATO air strikes in Kosovo may have forced former Serbian leader Slobodan Milosevic to end his operations in Kosovo, but the collateral damage in Serbia also stiffened his resistance to the terms of the agreement ending the war.[24] Moreover, the effectiveness of military measures often lasts only as long as the requisite coercion is applied. As soon as that force is withdrawn, the suppressed conflict is likely to reappear. For example, the various armies and air forces engaged in the war in Bosnia in 1995 may have forced the local parties to accept the Dayton accords, but the NATO-led Stabilization Force (S-FOR) eventually placed in Bosnia could not easily compel the Serbs, Croats, and Muslims in Bosnia to form a single community.

From the standpoint of effectiveness, noncoercive actions present advantages as well. For one thing, nonmilitary measures are usually based on mutual consent. Thus once these measures take effect, they can result in a permanent solution. If NATO and OSCE had been able to convince all three ethnic groups in Bosnia to establish multiethnic communities in accordance with the Dayton accords, then it might have been possible for all Bosnians to live peacefully within the borders of a single state once again. None of the three ethnic groups has yet lived up to their agreements in this regard, but they could eventually do so. If nothing else, noncoercive efforts to bring about change are less likely than military measures to elicit negative reactions, including the use of counterforce.

Mutual consent in not easily achieved, however. It may take years, even decades, before the parties will come to terms. In the meantime, it may not always be clear that the parties are working on such agreements in good faith.

Acceptability Criterion.   What are the advantages of multilateral actions? In 1990–1991, when George H. W. Bush organized a large coalition of states to oust Iraq from the territory of Kuwait, he did so with the legitimizing support of the UN Security Council, although he indicated that he was prepared to act unilaterally if necessary. To the extent that this was a multilateral action, however, it allowed the United States to use air bases, ports, and other facilities in Saudi Arabia, Turkey, and other neighboring countries. Allies such as Germany and Japan that did not provide troops were willing to share the financial burden. As a consequence, the United States was able to push Iraq out of Kuwait in less than one hundred hours.

Some of the disadvantages of employing multilateral measures are that the process of obtaining broad support for joint action is often very time-consuming; and it is always possible that other states will end up rejecting common action altogether. Moreover, even if other states agree to act in concert, the resulting security policy may be so watered down that it cannot be effective. For example, many people feel that U.S. forces should have pursued Saddam Hussein's army all the way to Baghdad to ensure that Iraq could not threaten its neighbors again. At least one reason they did not do so was that the UN Security Council and many of America's allies were not prepared to go beyond the agreed-upon objective of ousting Iraq from Kuwait.

This is just one of the reasons why states often prefer to act unilaterally. Unilateral actions are usually more easily initiated because other states do not have to sign on. In 1998, and again in 2002–2003, the United States was not able to achieve the same level of international support for a possible war against Iraq that it had during the Persian Gulf War. But it was able to launch the 2003 invasion according to its own timetable, and it was able to manage the post–war phase of the conflict on its own terms.

Unilateral action also carries disadvantages. By invading Iraq without the approval of the UN Security Council in 2003, the United States was deprived of the support of many of its most capable allies, such as France and Germany. The United States also found it difficult to get help from other states after the first stage of the conflict was over because other states felt no obligation to help. When the security situation and the reconstruction effort became more difficult than expected, the United States had to manage it alone for the most part.

Efficiency Criterion. Under the traditional international legal system states are supposed to respect the territorial integrity and domestic jurisdiction of other states. Occasionally, however, the relationship between two states is such that it is difficult to adhere to this principle. Proximity and mutuality may result in interference in each other's affairs. In such instances the costs and benefits of interdependence become manifest.

A reactive foreign policy is costly by definition. For example, when a military coup ousted Jean-Bertrand Aristide, the newly elected president of Haiti, in 1991, democratic and human rights groups in the United States called on the U.S. government to restore Aristide to power. The U.S. government chose not to restore Aristide to power because of the costs involved in intervention. Instead, it imposed economic sanctions on Haiti. (This policy is considered reactive here because it was designed to show U.S. displeasure with events in Haiti rather than to actually restore Aristide to power.) The economic sanctions hurt Haiti's ordinary citizens far more than its military leadership, and a flood of refugees sought political asylum in the United States, many in dangerous makeshift boats. George H. W. Bush then faced a dilemma. Because he did not want to appear to be lessening the pressure on Haiti's military government, he maintained the economic sanctions. Yet he was not prepared to accept the cost of the increasing number of refugees who were fleeing deteriorating conditions in Haiti that were caused, at least in part, by the economic sanctions. (If a policy is considered the "least bad" alternative, it is reactive.)

During the 1992 presidential campaign, Bill Clinton was critical of the Bush policy, arguing that the United States should take more effective action. Once Clinton became president, the Haitians naturally expected the new president to at least accept Haitian political refugees, and the number of refugees increased significantly. But Clinton proved no more prepared than Bush to accept additional costs. Like Bush, he was unwilling either to end the economic sanctions or to accept the Haitians as political refugees. As conditions worsened in Haiti, however, various groups in the United States, particularly the African American leadership, began to protest the president's policy. President Clinton finally decided in 1994 to send troops into Haiti if necessary to restore Aristide to power. At this point Clinton perceived that the domestic political benefits of a proactive policy were greater than the costs of his reactive policy.

Once the United States decided to intervene in Haiti, it sought the support of the Organization of American States (OAS) and the UN Security

Council. Apparently, the United States and the other countries then concluded that direct military intervention in Haiti was the only way to oust the junta. Fortunately, in September 1994 a three-person negotiating team headed by former president Jimmy Carter was able to negotiate an end to the junta's rule before the use of U.S. military force was necessary.[25] This proactive policy was more beneficial than expected, and the United States stationed about 20,000 troops in Haiti to protect Aristide and to train a new police force for Haiti. In March 1995 the American-led force left Haiti. When Aristide's successor was elected president, the American-led force was replaced by a 6,000-person UN mission, which included only 2,400 Americans.

But the situation in Haiti did not improve. Aristide returned to power in the 2000 election, but the international community felt that the election of some members of parliament was fraudulent. The United Nations and the United States periodically withheld economic assistance, hoping that Aristide would agree to new elections for the parliament. On April 30, 2004, the United States finally sent troops into Haiti for the purpose of escorting Aristide out of the country. The situation had reached the point where the George W. Bush administration decided to cut its losses in Haiti. This was a reactive security policy because it emphasized the costs of staying in Haiti.

So far this chapter has demonstrated how the framework can contribute to the enumeration and ordering of foreign policy objectives and the identification and linking of strategies for foreign policy action. The last section of this chapter shows how the ranking of objectives can be used to select the best or most appropriate course of action.

Although a wide range of security issues might have been selected for this purpose, two contemporary issues stand out. One is how the world will control and deal with nuclear weapons; the other is the problem of instability in the developing world. Both problems arose after the Second World War, and the end of the cold war significantly altered both. Indeed, in the post–cold war period these two issues, which were largely separate problems in the cold war, converged because of the danger of international terrorism. Although they are treated separately here, it is important to recognize that these and other security issues are linked in the expanded security awareness of the United States in the post–cold war period.

Nuclear Weapons Control

Although on September 11, 2001, the attackers employed a combination of simple devices, such as box cutters, and modern technology, such as civilian airplanes and cell phones, to attack symbols of American capitalism and militarism—the World Trade Center towers and the Pentagon—these attacks raised the possibility that even more significant damage could have been wrought with nuclear weapons or other types of WMD.

Because chemical and biological weapons are quite different in character from nuclear weapons and because they require distinct countermeasures, this section will focus exclusively on the danger of nuclear weapons.

Although the threat of a major nuclear exchange between the two superpowers diminished after the fall of the Soviet Union, it did not disappear altogether. One problem is that many of the former Soviet early warning stations were no longer under Russia's control. Another difficulty is that about 62 percent of Russia's remaining missiles have outlived their guaranteed service life and are no longer as reliable as they once were.[26] As a consequence, Russia is more likely to make a mistake in assessing the possibility of an attack, and might also feel more pressure to use its missiles in retaliation against a possible attack because Russia would not know how many of its surviving missiles would actually work.

This problem of nuclear control is exacerbated by the United States' decision to abrogate the ABM treaty in order to develop a national missile defense and refusal to ratify the Comprehensive Test Ban Treaty (CTBT). A U.S. missile defense system makes Russia nervous because it may render its retaliatory capability ineffectual. The refusal to ratify the CTBT leads Russia to think that the United States has not abandoned the effort to obtain a dominant nuclear capability. As a consequence, Russia may feel that its nuclear deterrent is insufficient, and that it needs to do more to protect itself.

But the most critical danger seems to be that as the two major powers reduce the number of active nuclear warheads, other states will become more, not less, interested in acquiring nuclear weapons. Despite the large number of states that have signed and ratified the Nuclear Nonproliferation Treaty, the prospects for proliferation may have actually increased in the post–cold war period both because second-tier nuclear states, such as China, are increasing their capability and because rogue states and terrorists may be able either to purchase or steal the technology and resources needed to build nuclear weapons. Each of these possibilities needs to be assessed separately.

Both India and Pakistan in South Asia have had the ability to produce nuclear weapons. As India's main regional rival, China, has increased its nuclear capability, India decided that it could no longer afford not to test its weapons capability. But once India had become a nuclear state, its regional rival, Pakistan, felt vulnerable. As a consequence, both India and Pakistan have developed and tested nuclear weapons despite the pressure not to do so from the United States and other signatories of the Nuclear Nonproliferation Treaty.

The problem of theft arises because it is not really possible at this juncture to permanently dispose of nuclear material. Both the United States and Russia are deactivating weapons, but Russia is less able than the

United States to safeguard nuclear materials. Thus the United States has actually purchased large amounts of this material from Russia for peaceful purposes. But Russia still has large amounts under its control and because of its economic woes, it cannot afford to safeguard these materials. As a result, weapon-grade Russian nuclear materials are reportedly lost or unaccounted for in Russia.

Because the science and know-how needed to make nuclear weapons is readily available in many countries, there is genuine concern that key technology, skills, and resources might be purchased or stolen by states or organizations who want even a small nuclear capability. Thus the real danger in nuclear control is that small quantities of nuclear weapons will be acquired by state or nonstate actors who are not constrained by the rules of the international system.

Values at Stake.   Because of the destructive power of even small nuclear weapons in the hands of unscrupulous actors, nuclear weapons pose a danger to large population centers. During the cold war strategists assumed that by threatening to destroy a significant percentage of an opponent's population—say 25 percent—one nuclear power could deter an attack by another. But now it is clear that if a rogue state or terrorist network could credibly threaten even a single population center with destruction, it could blackmail an entire society.

Because of the destructiveness of these weapons, the world has a major stake in the norm against first use of these weapons. The last time an atomic or nuclear weapon was used occurred when the United States employed two atomic weapons in Japan in 1945. Although most Americans believe that the United States would not actually use nuclear weapons in anger, the U.S. government has repeatedly threatened to use these weapons if it, or other key areas such as Berlin, were attacked. Moreover, the United States has been unwilling to explicitly adopt a No First Use nuclear policy. Because of these ominous signs, the world has an obvious stake in the tacit agreement among existing states not to actually use such weapons. The question is whether the global community can trust rogue states and terrorists to abide by the same kind of constraint.

Finally, the world has a stake in keeping the costs of security down. Because absolute security is unachievable, the real question is what price individual states are willing to pay for an additional increment of security. This cost consideration is further complicated by the fact that there are many other possible threats to national security, and a state cannot protect itself against every one of them. Because the financial resources of states are limited, even a state like the United States must decide which threats are worthy of additional expenditure.

The framework cannot determine which of the values associated with its three dimensions should be given more weight than others. That is a determination that each analyst must make. What the framework can do is suggest how the ranking of these value preferences or objectives can be used to evaluate various courses of action. The next section identifies three options for addressing the disposition of nuclear weapons.

Main Options. What are the three main options for nuclear strategists? The first option is deep cuts leading to **nuclear disarmament**. The United States and Russia have already talked about the possibility of implementing a START III by 2007, a START IV by 2014, and a START V by 2020. One group has argued that the United States and Russia should retain only two hundred nuclear weapons each, and that France and Britain together should have another two hundred nuclear weapons, and China another two hundred weapons.[27] By eliminating the most vulnerable weapons first and by ensuring the survivability of those that remain, arms negotiators could, assuming an adequate system of verification, achieve stability. This program of reduction would eliminate **launch-on-warning** and would rely instead on **de-alerting** and **deactivating** warheads so that smaller conventional forces and UN forces could deal with international conflicts.[28] This option assumes that residual forces would "be small enough to mark a clear break from past nuclear strategy and to provide a transition to possible elimination of nuclear weapons."[29]

The second option would be to maintain existing capabilities for **nuclear deterrence**—that is, keep in place existing land-, sea-, and air-based nuclear weapons systems. It also would involve theater, that is local or regional, missile defense capabilities. Under this status quo option, the United States would continue to work with other countries to prevent the spread of nuclear weapons as well as the accidental or unauthorized use of such weapons. To maintain existing capabilities, the United States would have to continue to invest in all current phases of its nuclear program. This option assumes that until the technology for nuclear defense is developed, old nuclear weapons can be replaced by newer ones, but these new nuclear weapons should not be capable of performing new functions.

The third option would be to develop a new national **missile defense system**. Such a system would be able to stop incoming strategic nuclear weapons. Although a partial defense could conceivably reduce the damage to the United States, such a defense would have to be fairly robust to discourage efforts to overcome it with more and smarter offensive weapons. This option assumes that if an effective defense were available at an acceptable level of cost and risk, any responsible decision maker would authorize it.[30] Of course, if this third option enhanced America's ability to project its power throughout the world, it would invite resistance from those who oppose an American empire.[31]

Assessing Options.   If one's primary objective is effectiveness, then one might favor building an NMD system because that might improve a state's dominance. Assuming that such a system were fully operational, it might either force other states to match the effort or acknowledge that they had lost their nuclear deterrence capability. Because the technology required for such dominance does not yet exist, the cost of such a policy would likely be very high. From a normative standpoint the policy of dominance would undermine the norm of No First Use because at least tacitly dominance would have no value unless others thought it might be used. Of course, President Putin has suggested that the United States might share this capability with Russia if and when it comes into existence just as Reagan had earlier offered to share his SDI system with Gorbachev. Were this to happen, a situation of **unified deterrence** based on mutual defense could come into play and might actually strengthen the norm against use.

If the primary objective were to maintain the advantages that the United States already has without incurring significant new costs, then continued reliance on nuclear deterrence would probably be the best or most appropriate nuclear policy. Although the cost of maintaining a deterrence capability would not be negligible, because both the warheads and the delivery systems would have to remain operational, that cost would be less than building new weapons systems. Also because these weapons represent offensive capabilities, their existence would undermine the norm against first use unless all states adopted such a deterrence policy. Such a policy might undermine the ability of states to extend deterrence to others.

If the primary objective were to strengthen international norms against the use of nuclear weapons, then the best or most appropriate nuclear strategy might be to disarm all nuclear states to the lowest level considered feasible. This reduction could only occur if all parties became convinced that nuclear weapons would serve no real purpose. One advantage of such an approach would be that the large and continuing cost of maintaining such weapons and developing new ones could be used for other purposes, such as enhancing economic development.

As the United States and Russia reduce the number of nuclear warheads and as the possibility that even one rogue state or terrorist group might acquire such weapon increases, the threat ratio between developed and developing countries diminishes. One rogue state or terrorist group may pose as much danger to the United States—particularly psychologically—as the United States poses to that rogue state or terrorist group both because it may be difficult to locate and isolate the offending parties and because world opinion would probably find a retaliatory nuclear attack as barbaric as the original attack. This equalization of threat underscores the importance of dealing with the second problem mentioned above, instability in the developing world.

Instability in Developing Countries

The process of globalization has made access to information, technology, capital, and transportation available to key individuals and groups throughout the world. Greater connectivity among the world's people is often associated with the values of peace and development. However, the benefits of greater connectivity are not evenly distributed. Although globalization has standardized the capabilities of some state and nonstate actors, it has paradoxically increased inequalities both within states and between states. As a consequence, a few fanatics can use some of these inequities to justify wreaking havoc and terror throughout the world.

Access to the Internet, modern transportation, science, and technology have made it is possible for an isolated individual with a grudge to operate on a world stage and command world attention. For example, Osama bin Laden could have access to the capabilities of advanced countries to attack them from a cave in Afghanistan. Kofi Annan, the secretary general of the United Nations, correctly pointed out that the world must learn to deal with what he called the **butterfly effect**—the fact that the world is so interconnected that even a small butterfly flapping its wings on one side of the world can have momentous consequences on the other side of the world.

Although there are many cultural, ethnic, governmental, geographical, racial, and religious differences between the developed and developing worlds, the main difference—as the labels imply—is economic. Developed countries are generally located in the northern hemisphere; developing counties are mostly in the southern hemisphere. Developed societies have better education, health, and standards of living; many people in developing societies suffer from illiteracy, ill health, and poverty. Although there may be many different reasons for this disparity, the inequality of economic means is staggering. The average per capita income in the developed world is 75 times greater than the average per capita income in the developing world. These inequalities, particularly within developing states and between developed and developing states, are a source of great instability and constitute a major security problem for the whole world.

Values at Stake.   The poverty and powerlessness in developing countries present a number of security threats to the United States and other developed countries. The most direct threat is that radical groups often based largely in developing countries might launch surprise attacks on key facilities or symbolic targets in advanced countries. The attack in the United States on September 11, 2001, the Japanese subway attack, the Madrid train attack, and the London subway bombings are constant reminders of this danger. Internal wars within developing countries or wars between developing countries could possibly spill over into the developed world because of the dependence of developed states on resources, such as oil, located in the developing world.

Disturbances within and among developing countries might possibly undermine values and constraints that have proven effective in preserving the peace of the world. The international legal system is largely based on customs and treaties developed first among advanced states. As nonstate actors or rogue states in the developing world challenge these norms, they not only shatter the international legal system but also undermine less formal international norms. There is a concern that continued violations of these laws and norms will lead to more and more humanitarian interventions in developing countries.

Finally, poverty in the developing world may create such pressure for immigration that the United States and other developed societies will be forced either to admit even more people into their borders or forced to expend capital and resources in an effort to develop those societies more fully. The costs of dealing with the lack of connectiveness in less developed areas of the world may be very high whether the United States and other developed nations take a proactive or passive approach to them.

Before one considers what priority ought to be given to objectives in each of these domains, it is important to examine the main options available to the United States. Three such options stand out.

Main Options.   One option would be for the United States to pursue **U.S. hegemony** in the world. This strategy is similar to the one proposed by former national security adviser Zbigniew Brzezinski on the Eurasian continent.[32] This strategy assumes that the United States could preemptively strike at those points in the developing world that threaten the peace of the international system as a whole.[33] The United States could employ its traditional war-fighting capabilities or new state-building services once these situations have been stabilized. The United States would not depend on particular allies in the developed world to get this job done, but instead would employ coalitions of the willing, such as those used in Afghanistan in 2001 and Iraq in 2003. This option assumes that the United States can create winning coalitions on an ad hoc basis.

The second option calls for the United States to work within the framework of the United Nations. The United States could work within the UN Security Council to deal with breaches of the peace originating in the developing world. This would require the United States and other key developed states to designate forces to serve on **UN peace-keeping missions**. It would also mean that the United States would follow the lead of the Security Council in determining where and when collective action under UN auspices is desirable. Moreover, this option would require the United States to work through the specialized organizations under the General Assembly and the United Nations Social and Economic Council to provide substantial assistance to developing countries. This option assumes that developed countries can act jointly to reduce the instabilities of the developing world.

The third option is for the United States to withdraw its forward defenses from the developing world and deal with these countries as ordinary states. By withdrawing U.S. military forces and acting like an **ordinary state** the United States would be less likely to antagonize these countries and give these countries less cause for blaming the United States for their problems. The United States would continue to provide assistance to these countries and work with them on a bilateral basis. This option assumes that developing countries have the will to overcome their lack of development if they are also treated like ordinary states.

Assessing Options.   If a foreign policy actor's primary objective was U.S. national security and the main emphasis was effectiveness, then it might be most appropriate for the United States to develop coalitions of the willing under its leadership to deal with the most dangerous security threats. Such a policy would probably mean that the United States would rely on different states each time. The cost of such a policy would be quite high because the United States would have to maintain a significant warfighting capability on its own, although it would supposedly only be necessary to intervene if U.S. national security was directly threatened. Because the United States would not depend on stable allies, it would be more difficult to get other countries to contribute to the state-building efforts required in these countries. As a practical matter, U.S. norms would replace other international norms as a guide to behavior. This policy might also cause other countries to view U.S. policy as arrogant.

If an actor's primary objective were to promote global accommodation, then it would make sense for the United States to join other developed countries in accepting responsibility within the UN to keep the peace. The fact that the United States would be working with the UN would strengthen the norms of the current system. The United States would also have to subscribe to group norms, assuring other countries that when military action is required, the United States could be counted on. This would require the United States to participate in principle even when its immediate national interests were not engaged. Under this option the United States would also share in the task of providing multilateral assistance to developing countries. Although the cost of this effort might be quite high, various states would share equitably in the expense.

If one's primary objective were to keep costs down, then the United States might look for ways to withdraw its military forces from forward bases around the world. In doing so the United States would perhaps receive less blame for what is going on in developing countries. The United

States and other developed countries would provide for their own homeland security. The United States could continue to provide assistance to developing countries when it was mutually advantageous. This option would emphasize respect for the political independence and territorial integrity of other countries.

Conclusion

Both the methods employed and the objectives pursued in security policy changed significantly after the September 11, 2001 attacks. Although these attacks focused the American people's attention on security matters more than before, they also broadened the concept of security. Security no longer was a military function, it also dealt with communications, the economy, the environment, and the health of a population. This expansion of the concept of security made it even more difficult to arrive at mutually acceptable solutions, much less dominate other states and groups.

These new concerns also raised the need for creating new norms. To what extent were the old rules that focused on states as the members of the international system appropriate for dealing with nonstate actors? Was there now a need to intervene in other states' affairs in order to prevent intrastate wars? Did the danger of terrorism or the existence of rogue states justify preemptive policies?

The mix of security threats also raised questions about the benefits and costs of addressing threats. At what level should these threats be addressed? What costs are acceptable? What benefits are achievable? The next chapter considers the economic ability of the United States to deal with these and other threats.

Key Concepts

butterfly effect 234	multiple preferences 210
civilian defense 216	ordinary state 236
coalitions of the willing 207	missile defense system 232
continental defense 212	No First Use 214
convergent process 222	nuclear deterrence 233
deactivating 232	nuclear disarmament 232
de-alerting 232	UN peace-keeping missions 235
divergent process 222	unified deterrance 233
forward defense 212	U.S. hegemony 235
launch-on-warning 232	

Suggested Readings

1. Barnett, Thomas P. M. *The Pentagon's New Map: War and Peace in the Twenty-First Century.* New York: G. P. Putman's Sons, 2004.

2. Brzezinski, Zbigniew. *The Grand Chessboard: American Primacy and Its Geostrategic Imperatives.* New York: Basic Books, 1997.

3. DeNardo, James. *The Amateur Strategist: Intuitive Deterrence Theories and the Politics of the Nuclear Arms Race.* Cambridge: Cambridge University Press, 1995.

4. Jewett, Robert and Lawrence, John Shelton. *Captain America and the Crusade Against Evil.* Grand Rapids: W. B. Eerdmans, 2003.

5. Nordlinger, Eric A. *Isolationism Reconfigured: American Foreign Policy for a New Century.* Princeton: Princeton University Press, 1995.

CHAPTER 7

Economic Policy: Investment, Trade, Development, and Sanctions

Another issue facing Americans is how to deal with economic competition from foreign countries. Millions of Americans have lost well-paying manufacturing or service jobs as a result of offshoring to China or outsourcing to India, respectively. Some observers believe that in the years to come, American workers will face even more competition from the better quality goods and services produced by an increasingly better-educated, more productive work force abroad. In this photo, Chinese workers sew clothes at a garments factory in Shanghai. Can the United States compete? What should the United States do?

THE DECLARATION OF INDEPENDENCE PROMOTES the values of "life, liberty, and the pursuit of happiness." "Life" represents security; "liberty" is the community goal most cherished by Americans; and the "pursuit of happiness" is the broadest possible interpretation of the goal of prosperity. From the 1870s to the present, the United States has consistently produced more goods and services than any other country, but U.S. international economic policies have been at times controversial. Throughout the period the country has been divided over both the objectives of foreign economic policy and the methods best suited for achieving those objectives.

Defining Value Preferences

In a capitalist society it may seem obvious that the primary objective of most actors in the prosperity sphere is to seek greater wealth. But this is not necessarily so. As in the case of other spheres, it is essential to differentiate between people's dispositions and perceptions before reaching conclusions about their preferences.

Dispositions

At the individual level people generally share one of two fundamental visions about the prosperity dimension: developing your greatest strengths or seeking to be well rounded. The first vision is one of strength; the second is one of acceptance.[1] At the societal level the goal of strength is usually represented as growth for growth's sake; the goal of acceptability is a combination of things that include modest growth tempered by full employment and a more equal distribution of wealth. In this section the two visions are labeled **growth** and **equitability.**

Growth.   Visions of strength, or growth, can be explained either at the micro- or macroeconomic level of analysis. Growth at the micro level of analysis emphasizes the perspective of the entrepreneur and the firm. Entrepreneurs prosper and firms grow by employing more inputs: land, labor, capital, and, especially today, better information and technology. By increasing these inputs, entrepreneurs increase outputs, which allows them in turn to enjoy a higher standard of living and to reinvest in productive resources. The most appropriate measure of prosperity is **productivity** per unit of labor. At the macro level, productivity is usually expressed as the annual percentage increase in a nation's gross domestic product (GDP). During the early cold war period GDP in the United States increased at the rate of about 3.5 percent a year; during the 1990s it generally hovered at about 2.3 percent a year.

Visions of strength, or growth, are therefore based on the notion of a **virtuous circle**. The circle of life is perceived as virtuous if one invests the additional resources received from working longer hours back into the work, so that one can work more efficiently, thus becoming increasingly productive. As productivity rises, income rises, allowing people to invest additional resources into the production of more goods and services, which in turn will lead to even greater productivity. This is the vision held by Scottish economist Adam Smith, who believed that if individual actors pursued their own selfish interests in a competitive market, they would all benefit in an absolute sense.

Other measures of prosperity, such as unemployment rates and income distribution, are recognized, but productivity is by far the most important because "a rising tide lifts all boats." As one proponent of growth explains, "Were the [U.S.] economy to grow 3.5% per year from 1996 to 2050 instead of 2.3%, GDP in 2050 would be $68 trillion instead of $36 trillion." [2] Given the magnitude of the gain, the advocates of growth might ask why one would want the economy to grow at a slower pace when it could surely grow at a faster one.

Advocates of growth acknowledge that all individuals, families, and even countries will not share equally in the general prosperity that accompanies growth, and they recognize that some jobs will be lost and some environmental and social concerns will surface. But they argue that "aggregate economic growth benefits most of the people most of the time; and it is usually associated with progress in other, social dimensions of development." [3] Indeed, Benjamin Friedman contends that economic growth is essential to "greater opportunity, tolerance of diversity, social mobility, commitment to fairness and dedication to democracy." [4] Moreover, advocates of growth contend that it is unwise to disrupt a virtuous circle, because efforts to regulate the process introduce both direct and indirect costs that will undermine the results.

Equitability. The second vision also can be described at the micro level, but the emphasis is on the **median income** of households rather than entrepreneurs or firms. Advocates of equitability argue that unless fairness is explicitly considered in economic planning, "the skills and talents of [many] people are ignored and stunted." [5] Thus they seek sustained growth, which is balanced with employment, income distribution, health, the environment, and productivity. The advocates of equitability want growth, but, especially in developed countries, they fear that the single-minded drive for efficiency and productivity may raise unemployment, and that differences among actors in efficiency and productivity will contribute to major inequalities in the distribution of income and other social and environmental problems. At the macro level they would rather sacrifice some gains in productivity in order to ensure steady employment, high median wages, low **inflation**, and **sustainable development** or growth in harmony with the environment.

In effect, the advocates of equitable growth fear a **vicious circle** in which attempts to maximize investment for the purpose of increasing productivity, such as providing tax breaks for the rich, may or may not decrease employment; but it usually reduces median family income, increasing inequalities in the distribution of wealth within and among societies. Indeed, this is precisely what economist Paul Krugman says is happening in the United States. Although GDP grew at the rate of 4.2 percent in 2004, "real median household income—the income of households in the middle of the income distribution, adjusted for inflation—fell for the fifth year in a row." [6]

Proponents of equitable growth rely more than the proponents of unregulated growth on the government to protect society from the ups and downs of the business cycle and to regulate the economy to prevent a vicious circle in which the pursuit of ever-greater wealth may actually lead to a recession. For example, the government may not want to reduce unemployment beyond, say, 5 percent, because, even though that would be desirable in itself, lower unemployment might cause inflationary wage and price increases. The advocates of equitability prefer more modest rates of growth to ensure more sustainable and equitable development.

As this discussion indicates, both visions rely on competitive markets to foster growth. But the proponents of growth and equitable growth take very different positions on fiscal policy—that is, on the role of government in taxation and spending. On the one hand, the advocates of unregulated growth generally want to keep government taxation and spending as low as possible. According to one economist, "If [government] spending declines along with taxes, the economy benefits from the switch of resources to private use and from the effects of permanently reduced tax distortions." [7] These measures are identified with **supply-side economics**, which emphasize the importance of tax cuts in encouraging economic growth. On the other hand, the advocates of **demand-side economics** believe that government fiscal measures, such as expenditures and taxation, are essential tools for preventing imbalances in the market and society. They usually want the government to provide a safety net for those who are unemployed; they favor some redistribution of income to ensure a level playing field; and they support government intervention to save the environment. These measures are identified with demand-side economic policies at both the national and global levels.

The advocates of growth and equitability also recognize the importance of money and prices in a market economy, but they hold different views on the role that government or a central bank should play in monetary affairs. The advocates of growth usually believe that society should rely primarily on the free market to determine prices and interest rates, as well as foreign exchange rates, although they usually prefer interest rates that favor investment. For example, the advocates of growth are less concerned than the advocates of equitable growth about the danger of inflation, arguing that industry cannot afford to raise prices because the competition of the global market is so rigorous that those who raise prices will simply lose sales. The advocates of equitability are more likely than the advocates of unregulated growth to want the government to regulate wages and prices and to fix foreign exchange rates because they want to avoid market instabilities. They also may want the government to control interest rates.

Most economists have accepted the principle of **comparative advantage**, which holds that free trade will benefit all parties because each can take advantage of its natural circumstances. However, recent research shows that there are inherent conflicts in international trade.[8] Because of the evidence that international trade hurts some parties more than others, advocates of growth and equitability are increasingly likely to take different positions on trade. Advocates of growth are likely to rely upon individual entrepreneurs and companies to decide what goods and services to produce and market; advocates of equitability are likely to turn to the government for help in determining national priorities, that is, **industrial policy**.

These alternative visions of prosperity are affected by visions of security and community. The fear of the Soviet Union and other communist states during the cold war distorted America's economic relationships with all countries as visions of growth and equitability were modified by visions of dominance and accommodation in the security domain. The perceived need to dominate the Soviet Union made the United States much less interested in investing and trading with that and other communist countries. Yet, at the same time, its desire to dominate the Soviet Union also led the United States to favor greater equitability among its allies. For example, America's desire to maintain security forces in Japan may have led it to accept growth-oriented Japanese economic policies at the expense of the U.S. economy.

At the same time, communitarian and cosmopolitan visions also affected America's economic visions. America's identification with Europe, one form of communitarianism, has made the United States more likely to adopt policies or make investments in areas populated by people with whom Americans have cultural, geographical, and historical ties than in areas populated by people who do not share those ties. Thus the cultural distance perceived between the United States on the one hand and some Middle Eastern and African countries on the other hand has made it much easier for the U.S. economy to grow at their expense or for investors to bypass these countries. At the same time, American cosmopolitanism is often credited for its generosity in the form of foreign assistance.

America's perceptions of the international economic situation, including its perceptions of the preferences of other relevant actors, color its economic actions. These perceptions have changed significantly over the last sixty years. In the 1950s and 1960s the United States pursued equitable growth abroad while pursuing growth at home. But by the 1980s the United States was forced to pursue a policy of growth both at home and abroad. After the fall of the Soviet Union, the United States followed a many-sided policy of growth and equitable growth.

Perceptions

At the close of World War II the world depended on the United States for both primary goods, especially food, and manufactured goods. Indeed, the United States accounted for about 50 percent of the World Gross Domestic Product (WDP), and manufactured goods accounted for roughly 30 percent of America's GDP. Today, the United States accounts for only about 22 percent of WDP, and only about 20 percent of that consists of manufactured goods.

American Preponderance.   From 1944 to 1969 the United States, large and rich in resources, was the preponderant economic power. With the return of its soldiers from the war and with skilled immigrants seeking to rebuild their lives, the country was assured of an ample supply of labor. Despite its war debt, the United States also had large gold reserves, a strong dollar, and a high rate of savings and investment. Moreover, all the traditional factors of production favored economic growth. As a result of its general superiority, the United States preferred an open international economic system and hoped that Britain and other economic powers would quickly regain their economic strength.

As early as 1944 the United States invited forty-three other countries to meet at Bretton Woods, New Hampshire, for the purpose of building a new international economic system. Together these countries established the International Monetary Fund (IMF), the International Bank for Reconstruction and Development (IBRD or World Bank), and the General Agreement on Tariffs and Trade (GATT). But none of these institutions was able to deal with the severe economic problems that existed in Europe and Asia immediately after the war, and so the United States became directly involved.

The first order of business was to restore the former industrial areas of Western Europe and Japan. Between 1948 and 1952 the United States provided $17 billion to Europe through what is commonly known as the Marshall Plan. The Committee for European Economic Cooperation, now called the Organization for Economic Cooperation and Development (OECD), coordinated these funds. As the European economies began to respond to this infusion of government capital, the amount of private foreign direct investment (FDI) going from the United States to Europe dramatically increased, beginning in the late 1950s. This investment was intended to give U.S. companies a unique advantage overseas so that they could participate more effectively in international trade. Because the money provided by the Marshall Plan went largely for the purchase of U.S. goods, it encouraged the growth of U.S. multinational corporations (MNCs) with subsidiaries in Western Europe. (This is one reason why Stalin didn't want Eastern European countries to participate in the Marshall Plan.)

U.S. government assistance to Japan took a different form and did not begin until after North Korea attacked South Korea in June 1950. The United States pumped some $31 billion into Japan in the form of defense support. Foreign direct investment was tightly controlled by the Japanese, but Japan did purchase some $5 billion in Western (mostly American) technology in the form of "licensing agreements" and sent numerous study groups to the United States.[9] By the end of the 1950s Western Europe and Japan had largely recovered economically, and as a result of six rounds of trade reductions between these countries and the United States under the auspices of GATT, ending with the Kennedy Round in 1967, international trade was increasing. But many countries continued to restrict capital flows because they wanted to prevent the United States from gaining control of foreign industries and to control their own monetary policies.[10]

In the meantime, developing countries requested help in the form of aid and trade. These states received modest help in the form of loans from the U.S. government and the World Bank, but they had hoped for an international trade organization that could give them preferential treatment. When the United States rejected that idea in the late 1940s, many of them pursued "import substitution" strategies in which they attempted to produce for themselves some of the goods they had been importing from developed countries. When neither aid from nor trade with the developed countries satisfied their need for industrialization, the developing countries formed the Group of 77 (which now includes over 130 countries) to press their demands for a "new international economic order" in the UN Committee for Technology and Development (UNCTAD).

Initially the American economy was so strong that it could afford to both sustain rapid domestic growth and extend capital abroad. But by 1960 the outflow of American dollars was beginning to affect the economy, and, for the first time, foreign dollar holdings exceeded U.S. gold reserves. The pressure on the dollar continued to rise during the 1960s, as private American companies began to buy a controlling interest in overseas firms and as multilateral banks began to operate in the United States and Europe. The result was a burgeoning Eurodollar market in Europe.[11] According to economist Joan Edelman Spero, "As long as other countries would absorb dollar outflows [without insisting on convertibility into gold], the United States did not have to take domestic measures to balance international accounts." [12]

But in the mid-1960s the Johnson administration intensified the dollar's problems by deciding to both expand domestic social programs and fight the Vietnam War without raising taxes. Thus the dollar was being undermined both at home and abroad. Europe and Japan wanted "a deflationary American policy, arguing that the dollar outflow and the expansion of the American economy were causing inflation abroad," but Richard Nixon wanted "to re-inflate" the American economy in 1970 to improve his party's position in the 1972 election. The Europeans and the Japanese complained about the American deficit, but they refused to do anything about their growing surpluses.[13] No one was prepared to assume responsibility for the management of the international monetary system.

Assimilation of Europe, Japan and New Industrial States. In August 1971 Nixon finally took unilateral action on the trade deficit by placing a 10 percent surcharge on imports into the United States and abandoning the fixed rate of exchange between gold and the American dollar. Although the United States eventually devalued the dollar several times, it was not enough to sustain fixed rates of currency exchange at the international level. Global inflation continued, and by 1973 a new era of floating exchange rates was in effect.

In 1973 the decline of the dollar plus another Arab-Israeli war led the Organization of Petroleum Exporting Countries (OPEC) to quadruple the price of oil, and Western oil companies passed the increased prices on to their consumers. The spiraling oil prices affected both developed and developing countries, but developing countries were especially hard hit because of their lack of capital. Because the oil-producing countries were unable to absorb most of their gains from the high prices, they invested heavily in private Western banks. These banks then made loans to non-oil-producing countries so they could afford to buy the energy they required. By this time, developing countries were receiving more money from private banks than they were from government aid.

Therefore when a second oil shock occurred in 1979 as a result of the fall of the shah of Iran, many developing countries were caught between both high oil bills and large debts that they could not repay. Some of these countries, such as Mexico, had invested heavily in future oil production in the hope that they too could make money on oil, but these investments soured when the bottom later fell out of the global oil market. As a result, Western banks with huge outstanding loans in developing countries were forced to extend additional loans to these countries to avoid writing off previous loans.

The oil shocks and the debt crises reflect some of the changes in capital flows after 1973 and especially in the 1980s. During this period, most countries removed restrictions on the movement of capital. Brokerage houses, securities firms, insurance companies, and pension funds rather than banks handled financial transactions increasingly.[14] Private assistance became more prominent than government assistance in developing countries. Large capital flows were used to finance government debts, and new financial instruments such as hedge funds and derivatives were developed to take some of the risk out of fluctuating currencies. According to Spero, the IMF "forced the debtor countries to shift the focus of their economic policy from development to financial stability and debt repayment." [15] This change in policy had profound effects on the developing countries.

Some developing countries were able to industrialize, partially in response to these international pressures. The newly industrialized countries (NICs) that emerged in the Far East—Hong Kong, Singapore, Taiwan, and South Korea—soon had company as some members of the Association of Southeast Asian Nations (ASEAN), such as Thailand, Malaysia, and Indonesia, also underwent industrialization. Thus one result of this transition period was the growing differentiation among developing countries—oil producers and non-oil producers, NIC and least developed, debtor and non-debtor, and so on.[16] The developing South thus began to find it increasingly difficult to maintain unity in its negotiations with the industrialized North.

In the meantime, America's economic relations with its main allies became even more competitive. When Ronald Reagan took office in 1981, he reduced taxes, increased defense spending, and pursued a tight monetary policy to fight inflation. One result was high interest rates, which attracted huge inflows of foreign capital into the United States, especially from Japan. In turn, most foreign countries raised their interest rates to prevent even more capital from flowing to the United States. Many of these countries suffered from a recession as well as capital outflows.[17] But Japan seemed to be an exception to the recession and continued to invest heavily in its own economy as well as the U.S. economy.

As the competition between Europe, Japan, and the United States intensified, all began to resort to one form or another of protectionism. One popular form of protectionism was voluntary export restraints (VERs) in which one country would agree to limit exports that were threatening industry and increasing unemployment in another country.[18] Industrial policies were another form of protectionism, in the form of tax preferences or subsidies to selected industries so they could be more competitive abroad. These **nontariff barriers** became increasingly common.

This period also marked the real beginning of trade between the developed countries of the West and the communist countries of the East. Although the United States had always conducted some trade with the Soviet Union, that trade had been severely restricted during the 1950s for fear that Western trade might contribute to communism's strength. Beginning with grain sales in the 1960s, however, American business successfully pursued some trade with the Soviet Union, China, and Eastern Europe. Western Europe and Japan became more active in East-West trade than the United States when the Reagan administration attempted to use trade as a stick rather than a carrot.

Competing with China, India, and Former Soviet States   The collapse of the Soviet Union in 1991 and the entry of China, India, and many former communist states into the global market potentially added almost three billion people to the global economy, virtually doubling its work force.[19] These new workers are not only willing to work at a fraction of the rate of workers in more advanced countries, but they are often willing and able to develop new skills. As a consequence, Thomas Friedman argues that "the world [economy] is [becoming] flat" because China and India as well as Europe and Japan will increasingly be able to compete on roughly equal terms with the United States.[20]

Changes in the flow of capital and information have been particularly striking. In 1971, 90 percent of all foreign exchange transactions were for trade and investment. Twenty-five years later, over 90 percent is attributable to speculation and less than 10 percent to trade and investment.[21] More than $1 trillion may move from one account to another in the new global economy in a single day; but most of this money is "virtual money"—that is, it is created primarily by currency trading and not by economic activity such as investment, production, consumption, or trade.[22] Speculation and virtual money can, however, affect both the fiscal and monetary policies around the world, such as the creation of asset bubbles like the tech stock bubble and the global housing bubble.

These new capital flows are made possible by the revolution in the flow of information. With the development of personal computers connected by cross-oceanic fiber-optic cables one can now easily use workflow software to browse Web sites anywhere in the world. This has resulted in near universal access to information via Google and Yahoo, and it has been greatly facilitated by the fact that many of the basic codes have been made available to all participants in the World Wide Web. These innovations in telecommunications have made it possible for Indians in Bangalore and elsewhere to handle routine service calls for customers in the United States, which is called **outsourcing**, and for American companies to move manufacturing plants to locations in China and elsewhere, which is called **offshoring**.

Offshoring is particularly feasible given the development of worldwide air, sea, and land transportation systems. Many national and multinational firms have developed complex **supply-chains**, which allow businesses to assemble resources from disparate locations on a just-in-time basis, and then distribute merchandise to scattered customers on a timely basis. For example, Wal-Mart uses its supply chains in combination with weather information to provide needed supplies such as water, generators, and plywood to areas being threatened by hurricanes. Other distributors such as Federal Express and United Parcel Service are engaged in **insourcing**, which means that they provide a range of services, such as repairs or financing, while they are distributing goods for large or small companies. The fact that Fed-Ex and others can now reach 5 billion people in 200 countries in at most 2 days has permanently changed the manufacturing process.[23]

All of these factors have affected international trade. Although the overall rate of increase in international trade has not exceeded long-term trends, important structural changes have occurred since 1990. Perhaps the most important single event was the completion of the Uruguay Round of trade negotiations in 1994. The Uruguay Round not only reduced traditional barriers to trade by about 40 percent on average but also promised to incorporate effective measures for free trade in services and adequate protection for intellectual property rights. In addition, the Uruguay Round produced a permanent World Trade Organization (WTO), empowered to establish the rules of the game for international trade and settle trade disputes.

As the dawn of this burgeoning new global market arose, developed countries began to protect themselves from the onslaught of competition. So, despite the prospect of a new WTO, developed countries began to protect themselves by developing regional trade agreements (RTAs). As a consequence, almost half of all international trade occurs among states on a regional basis, and intraregional trade is growing faster than interregional trade. Regional agreements can facilitate trade because they involve countries with similar concerns and cultures, but by creating preferential arrangements among members they can also discriminate against nonmembers. Indeed, most RTAs "are driven in large measure by geopolitical considerations."[24]

For example, it is generally recognized that the members of the European Community approved the Maastricht Treaty in 1992, which created the European Union (EU), as a means of improving their competitiveness with the United States and Japan. The United States responded in 1993 by extending the U.S.-Canadian free trade arrangement to include Mexico in NAFTA, at least in part to protect itself from the growing competition from the new EU. In 1993 the United States also took the lead in developing the Asia Pacific Economic Cooperation (APEC) forum among eighteen Asian Pacific countries largely in the hope of bringing this productive region into its orbit.[25] However, opposition by Venezuela, Argentina, Bolivia, and Brazil has stymied President Bush's efforts to promote the Free Trade Area of the Americas Act in 2005.

The emergence of the new global market had immediate consequences for Western Europe and Japan. West Germany, the leading European economy before the collapse of the communist bloc, was the most affected, because shortly after the fall of the government of East Germany, the government of West Germany moved toward reunification. To meet the large expenditures required and to prevent rampant inflation, Germany pursued a tight-money policy to maintain the value of the deutsche mark. Because of the importance of the German economy in Europe, other Western European governments such as France followed similar tight monetary policies. But unlike Germany, their economies experienced recessions because they did not face the same inflationary tendencies that Germany did. Eventually these recessionary pressures rebounded back on Germany itself. The result was high unemployment and large government deficits throughout Europe in the 1990s.

Japan's economic problems are quite different. The Japanese yen was so strong in the late 1980s that Japan was taking in more money than it could invest appropriately at home. So Japan invested an increasing amount of this surplus in the newly industrialized countries of East Asia and Southeast Asia. But American companies became more competitive in the early 1990s, and Clinton opened up trade and investment with China to an extent that was entirely unexpected by the Japanese. The emergence of China as a major trading country in the late 1990s had a profound effect on its neighbors; China began to compete successfully with some of the NICs as well as ASEAN countries. As China's economic prospects improved, those of many neighboring countries declined, and Japanese investments in East Asia and Southeast Asia began to sour. In short, the Japanese faced both a banking crisis at home and competition abroad. Consequently, Japan was not in a position to lift the NICs and ASEAN countries out of their financial crisis.[26] (It is important to realize that the 1997 Asian financial crisis is different from others in that it involved private, not public, debt.)

The emergence of the new global market in the 1990s also affects the United States. The main change in interregional trade at the global level involves China. (The entrance of India and Russia into the global market, except for computer skills and fuels, respectively, has been much slower, although India's trade with China and the EU is expanding rapidly.) In the 1990s China and other industrializing countries in Asia, Africa, and Latin America captured a larger share of the market in manufacturing goods because of cheaper labor costs. As a result, the world trade in manufactured goods is now almost evenly divided between developing and advanced countries. The gap between U.S. imports and exports, which was over $650 billion in 2004 and is largely the result of U.S. imports from Japan and China, could only be sustained because those countries continue to invest so heavily in U.S. debt.

Although some economists believe that industrial countries, such as the United States, may benefit the most from increased trade with less developed countries,[27] many Americans are less hopeful. Their main fear is that by trading with the developing countries of the South with their abundance of unskilled labor the United States will place its own workers at risk.[28] Of course, this trade with the South would not take place if consumers in the United States were not benefiting from it, but consumer satisfaction with lower prices and a greater variety of products does not placate those in the United States who are losing manufacturing, market share, and jobs. Many Americans also believe that the outsourcing of jobs occurs because plants in developing countries are not forced to maintain the same environmental and **social standards** as U.S. plants. (Social standards refer to items such as health benefits and worker safety standards.) They fear that capital and jobs will move to countries with lower standards, thereby triggering a race to the bottom, as one observer put it.[29]

To avoid such a race many in the United States have pushed for the inclusion of environmental and labor standards in the WTO rules. Either a higher standard would be applied to the goods and services of the developing countries or advanced countries would be allowed to levy a tariff against the implied subsidy represented by lower standards. Indeed, the United States has already repeatedly restricted imports by resorting to measures such as "anti-dumping and countervailing duty sanctions against Canadian softwood lumber and safeguard actions regarding steel and Chinese textiles."[30]

But the problem with interregional trade is not just a race to the bottom; it is also a race to the top. China, whose productivity has increased by about 17 percent per year, is also challenging the United States in terms of education, innovation, and quality. For example, the National Science Board reports that both Asia and Europe produced more bachelor's degrees in science and engineering in 2003 than the United States. "In engineering, specifically, universities in Asian countries now produce eight times as many bachelor's degrees as the United States."[31] The fear is that the United States and the rest of the industrial North will be "caught between low wages and high tech" in India, China, and East Asia.[32]

As individuals, companies, and countries scramble to deal with the leveling effect of "three billion new capitalists,"[33] American citizens will have to come to terms with their multiple identities. As shown in Chapter 1, everyone identifies with communities that are more exclusive and more inclusive than the nation-state. When individuals have to compete for jobs on a worldwide basis and when corporations truly become multinational entities, these individuals as well as the leaders of these companies and countries may find it increasingly difficult to determine whose costs and whose benefits really matter. This makes it especially important to understand how the perceptions, such as those discussed above, affect individuals' preference orderings.

Preferences

When Bill Clinton took office in 1993, the American economy was recovering from one of its low points. As Clinton noted in his first State of the Union address, Americans had experienced two decades of low productivity and stagnant wages; persistent unemployment and underemployment; years of huge government deficits and declining investment in the country's future; exploding health care costs and lack of coverage; legions of poor children, education and job training opportunities inadequate to the demands of a high-wage, high-growth economy.[34]

Clinton's Preferences.   Clinton declared the country's immediate priority was to create jobs. The Clinton plan sought to reverse the economic decline by jump-starting the economy in the short term and investing in people and jobs in the long term.[35] Although he clearly focused on domestic results, Clinton also recognized America's responsibilities to the wider world. The Clinton administration supported international trade and investment so long as it was both free and fair. (Many trade scholars, especially those who are growth-oriented, believe that free trade is inherently fair, but that position is being challenged by evidence that "countries can close off a market to foreign competition." [36]) And it used diplomacy abroad to fill the needs of and create opportunities for American industry and workers. The Clinton administration emphasized "competitiveness" in international markets.

Clinton later described his strategy of three main objectives: "First, to put the nation's economic house in order so our businesses can prosper and create new jobs; second, to expand trade in American products all around the globe; and third, to invest in our people so that they all have the tools they need to succeed in the Information Age." [37] Because all three of these objectives can be interpreted as promoting long-term growth, one might assume that growth or productivity was his primary objective. However, an examination of his discussion of these objectives reveals that the ultimate purpose of the first objective was not just growth but rather the creation of new jobs in circumstances where prices were relatively stable—that is, where inflation was under control. The second objective of expanding exports also was discussed in terms of the need to promote jobs through trade that was both free and fair. And the third objective of investing in people was clearly aimed at lowering the differences in income among individuals, and particularly families.

Thus Clinton promoted growth to foster employment and deal with the unequal distribution of incomes in American society. He later confirmed that equitable growth rather than growth per se was his primary objective when he boasted in 1996 that the United States had the lowest combined rate of unemployment and inflation in twenty-seven years.[38] As Clinton later explained, "[t]he lesson of America's history is that the good life is about more than individual liberty and material well-being; it's about cultivating community relationships and attending to public concerns." [39]

Bush's Preferences.   Not all Americans accepted the idea that employment and distribution of income should have priority over growth in productivity at the national level. The Republican Party promoted the need to get the U.S. government off the backs of American entrepreneurs, who, they argued, were the ones who actually invest in new growth. The Republicans claimed to also want full employment, but they believed it was self-defeating for government to intervene for this purpose, because the global market ultimately would determine this outcome. Moreover, fiscal conservatives saw little danger in inflation, because "the ability to move production all over the world and the entry of over one billion people into the global workforce will keep significant downward pressure on prices and wages." [40] They believed that the rising tide of economic growth in the aggregate "benefits most people most of the time and provides the means to achieve many of society's goals." [41]

President George W. Bush presented his economic priorities in a speech to the Economic Club of Chicago on January 7, 2003. He said

> Our first challenge is to allow Americans to keep more of their money so they can spend and save and invest—the millions of individual decisions that support the market, that support business, and help create jobs. . . . Our second challenge is to encourage greater investment by individuals and small business—the kind of investing that builds personal wealth and helps company expand [sic] and creates new jobs. . . . A third challenge facing our country is the need to help unemployed workers and prepare them for the new jobs of a growing economy.[42]

The Bush tax cuts clearly emphasized growth as the top priority, as they benefited the wealthier taxpayers and corporations.

The economic preferences of Presidents Bush and Clinton are different. But the preferences of economic policy makers are not self-executing; they have to be translated into specific strategies and actions. That is why preferences are at least partly deduced from the actions taken by policy makers. After all, "the world economy is a system—a complex web of feedback relationships—not a simple chain of one-way effects. In this global economic system, wages, prices, trade, and investment flows are outcomes, not givens." [43] In such a system economic policy makers are not at liberty to follow their own dispositions; they must work within the constraints they perceive to be operating within the international economic system as a whole. Thus in assessing the preferences of economic policy makers it is necessary to look for ways in which they attempt to nudge the system either in the direction of growth or equitability. If they prefer growth, then they are likely to be proactive. If they prefer equitability, they are likely to be reactive.

Identifying All Options

In the American capitalist system private entrepreneurs, companies, investors, and consumers are supposed to dominate the action; government is expected to play the role of a facilitator. It is the private sector, not the

government sector, that determines what goods and services are produced, what jobs are created, and what investments are made, although
the government does influence all of those choices. In a domestic
economy with a GDP of over $10.9 trillion, government accounts for only
about 14 percent of total GDP, which means that roughly 86 percent of
American goods and services are produced by the private sector. Thus
when Clinton bragged about the creation of ten million new jobs between
his inauguration in 1993 and 1996, he recognized that 93 percent of these
jobs had been created by the private sector.

So far the American economy has been treated here as though it is
strictly a domestic economy. But certain sectors are highly sensitive, if not
vulnerable, to international exchanges. For example, manufacturing and
agriculture account for only about 20 and 1 percent, respectively, of
America's GDP, but as much as 45 percent of these goods are involved in
international trade. Moreover, trade in manufactured goods, especially
exports, represents a very significant percentage of the new jobs being created in the American economy. For that reason, much attention is devoted to manufactured goods in international trade. By contrast, U.S.
trade in services makes up about 70 percent of America's GDP, but less
than 3 percent of the services trade is international. Yet international
trade in services is important because foreign trade in services is growing
and because the United States still sells more services overseas than it buys
from foreigners, as Figure 7.1 shows.

U.S. Economic Growth Policies

Eighty-seven percent of America's economy is based on domestic exchanges of money, goods, and services (including governmental services); international trade and investment account only for about 13
percent. The domestic economy is so large that even though Americans
save at a much lower rate than most Japanese or even most Europeans
(in June 2004 the U.S. savings rate was almost zero), private investment
in the United States ($2,246 billion in 2004) is often greater than that of
Japan, Germany, Britain, and France combined. The United States has a
very active venture capital market (the New York Stock Exchange and
NASDAQ National Market), and U.S. banks, companies, and individuals,
as well as foreigners, invest in a variety of American enterprises. Generally speaking, U.S. **foreign direct investment** (FDI) is greater than the
flow of foreign FDI into the United States because of the decline of the
value of the dollar in relation to the euro and the British pound. Since
the dotcom bust in 2000, foreigners have also lost some interest in the
U.S. stock market, that is, **portfolio investment**, in the United States.
These private growth investment activities are examples of MCA economic policies: unilateral, noncoercive, and proactive. Table 7.1 shows
the dimensions of these private investment growth policies and the

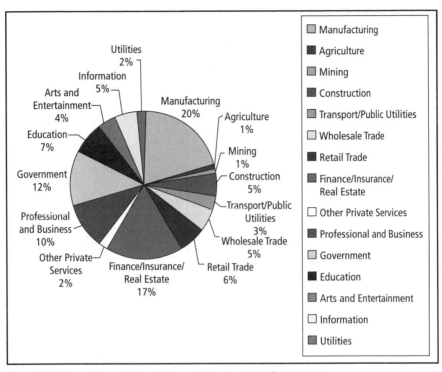

Figure 7.1. Percentage of Gross Domestic Product by Industry, 2003
Source: Data compiled by author from the Bureau of Economic Analysis.

next three examples of other economic growth policies: government investment policies, government efforts to promote trade, and private participation in free trade, including outsourcing, offshoring, and supply-chaining.

It is not possible to understand this level of private investment, especially in view of the low savings rate, without considering what the U.S. government does to encourage investment. George W. Bush's tax cuts for higher-income Americans were especially designed to encourage those with capital gains to use these tax savings for investment. As a consequence of these tax cuts, rising defense expenditures, and the growing costs of Social Security and Medicare, the U.S. debt soared to over $650 billion in 2004. The government could not sustain this level of government expenditure if it were not for the fact that foreign central banks are purchasing large quantities of relatively low yielding U.S. treasury bills. [44] Government economic policies geared to promote both foreign and domestic investments in U.S. growth are examples of MCA economic policy: unilateral because they are communitarian, coercive because the government influences the rates, and proactive because they are designed to stimulate U.S. growth. Of course, foreign governments such as China

Table 7.1. Dimensions of Foreign Policy: U.S. Economic Growth Policies

| | Multilateral | | Unilateral | |
	Coercive	Noncoercive	Noncoercive	Coercive
Proactive			*Investment:* Private U.S. venture capital markets, such as N.Y. Stock Exchange and NASDAQ National Market	*Investment:* U.S. government use of its tax powers to encourage domestic investment; government efforts to encourage foreigners to invest in U.S. Treasury bills
			Trade: Efforts by private U.S.companies to increase efficiency by offshoring, outsourcing and supply-chaining	*Trade:* U.S. government efforts to promote free trade through WTO and RTAs
Reactive				

Private U.S. participation in open investment markets and free trade are MCA—unilateral because they are self-interested, noncoercive because they are voluntary, and proactive because they are growth-oriented.

The U.S. government efforts to attract investment and promote trade are MCA—unilateral because they are self-interested, coercive because they involve the enforcement powers of the government, and proactive because they are growth-oriented.

and Japan would not invest in U.S. treasury bills if the U.S. government did not encourage Americans to spend their money on the cheaper imported goods and services available in the domestic market because of its free trade policies. The Office of the U.S. Trade Representative and U.S. participation in the WTO and various FTAs encourages these imports and consumerism generally.

In order to keep this imbalance of imports over exports from becoming even wider (it was $618 billion in 2004) the government also promotes exports. For example, during the Clinton administration the United States promoted exports by American companies by providing small and medium-size firms with the know-how needed to compete in overseas markets. It developed a national export strategy that targeted ten big emerging markets:

the Chinese Economic Area (including Hong Kong and Taiwan), Mexico, South Korea, Indonesia, Brazil, Argentina, India, South Africa, Turkey, and Poland. These pro-growth policies are MCA: unilateral, coercive in the sense that they involve enforceable decisions and that they authoritatively determine the character of public expenditures, and proactive.

As a result of these government policies, U.S. private companies and individuals are heavily engaged in offshoring, outsourcing, and supply-chaining. American consumers are benefiting from the cheaper goods that are available in the domestic market. Some jobs are also being created because of new opportunities for exporting American goods and services abroad. These private trade activities MCA: unilateral because they are self-interested, noncoercive because they are voluntary, and proactive because they are based on free trade principles.

However, these international trade flows have also caused a lot of turmoil in the domestic market. The jobs of many workers have been cut, and they must often develop new skills and/or take jobs in different locations that pay less than their former jobs. This is where equitable growth policies become especially important.

U.S. Equitable Growth Policies

In demand-side economics the government is expected to intervene in the economy to promote more equitable growth. Many foreign governments have aggressive industrial policies designed to ensure jobs and market share; however, laissez-faire economists in the United States have generally opposed such industrial policies. Clinton was probably more interested in government investment in the economy than most presidents.[45] He tried to increase government-sponsored civilian research and development in the United States through agencies like the National Science Foundation. He also developed educational and training programs for those who had lost their jobs so that they might find even better paying ones, although such programs are expensive and not always well funded.[46] Clinton's efforts to intervene in the market in order to make Americans more efficient are all examples of MCA investment policies—unilateral because they are communitarian, coercive because they represent government interventions in the market, and reactive because they are designed to introduce greater equitability. Table 7.2 shows the dimensions of government equitable growth policy as well as three other equitable growth policies: private investment policy, private trade policy, and government trade policy.

Because of increased competition, private American firms are changing the basic terms of employment. Rather than offering new workers security, American firms now offer pay and bonuses based on performance. The workers are expected to assume more responsibility for their own security. Some companies are attracting new workers by offering training programs that might make these workers more valuable because of their

Table 7.2. Dimensions of Foreign Policy: U.S. Equitable Growth Policies

| | Multilateral | | Unilateral | |
	Coercive	Noncoercive	Noncoercive	Coercive
Proactive				
Reactive			*Investment:* U.S. private efforts to provide additional training for their work force so that these workers will remain employable	*Investment:* U.S. government investments to save jobs or preserve market share; education and training programs for unemployed workers
			Trade: "Buy American" campaigns; U.S. consumer boycotts of foreign goods	*Trade:* U.S. government protections for intellectual property rights, the environment, and animal rights

U.S. government policies designed to ensure equitable growth are MCA—unilateral because they are communitarian, coercive because the government is using its enforcement power, and reactive because they are intended to save American jobs and market share.

Private efforts to protect workers and market share are equitable growth, or MCA, policies—unilateral because they are communitarian, noncoercive because they are voluntary, and reactive because they are designed to reduce the perceived costs of open exchanges.

versatility and, it is hoped, more employable throughout their careers. For example, International Business Machines (IBM) "spends $750 million a year on employee education, and $400 million of that is earmarked for training its workers in the skills that the company is betting it will need soon." [47] Such efforts are examples of MCA investment policies: unilateral because they are self-interested, noncoercive because they are voluntary, and reactive because they are designed to keep jobs and market share.

Of course, U.S. citizens also play a role in protecting jobs in this more competitive business environment. U.S. companies and their workers often urge citizens to buy American-made goods to save jobs. Private efforts to promote products "Made in the U.S.A." and even to boycott foreign goods are examples of MCA trade policies: unilateral, noncoercive, and reactive.

The U.S. government also intervenes in the market to protect American consumers and producers from foreign practices that it feels are unfair. For example, the U.S. government tries to get foreign governments, such as China, to respect intellectual property rights so that Americans can export more goods and services. The United States also blocks foreign goods that have been produced in ways that are harmful to wildlife. For example, the U.S. Marine Mammal Protection Act bans tuna caught by driftnets that kill dolphins. Such trade interventions are examples of MCA trade policies: unilateral, coercive and reactive.

Although national governments, private companies, and individuals play the lead role in international investment and trade, further liberalization of the global economy clearly requires collective solutions and international cooperation. A variety of international organizations contribute to this objective.

Multilateral Economic Growth Policies

The IMF and the World Bank provide financial help and development support to poor countries that are able and willing to open themselves to international market forces. Both institutions can enforce the international rules preferred by developed states because they have systems of weighted voting that favor financially strong states, such as the United States. By making assistance available to developing countries only if they accept certain terms of **conditionality**, such as stringent domestic budgets, these financial institutions can force even the poorest countries to give priority to paying their international debts and accepting other free market principles rather than attending to the immediate needs of their own people. The IMF and the World Bank have even tried to impose conditions on some more advanced states such as South Korea, Russia, and Brazil. These actions are all examples of MCA economic policies: multilateral, coercive (conditional aid), and proactive. Table 7.3 illustrates the dimensions of this and the next three examples of multilateral economic growth policies: efforts by INGOs to promote capital flows, INGO efforts to promote trade, and efforts of the WTO and RTAs to promote free trade.

Although the four Regional Multilateral Development Banks (Africa, Asia, Europe, and Inter-American) are also concerned with achieving economic growth and increased competitiveness in their regions, they may be more sympathetic to the problems faced by economically poor countries. To the extent that the loans made by these banks are based largely on economic criteria, they are engaged in MCA investment activities: multilateral, noncoercive, and proactive.

Because both countries and companies are suspicious of possible collusion among private actors at the international level, there are fewer forms of INGO coordination in the trade realm. Nevertheless, the UN Commission on International Trade Law (UNCITRAL) meets annually in New York to foster the harmonization and unification of trade law in international law. There is even an International Institute for the Unification of

Table 7.3. Dimensions of Foreign Policy: Multilateral Economic Growth Policies

| | Multilateral | | Unilateral | |
	Coercive	Noncoercive	Noncoercive	Coercive
Proactive	*Investment:* Conditional loans by the World Bank and the International Monetary Fund, which require developing countries to pursue growth strategies often against their will	*Investment:* Loans by regional banks, such as the Inter-American Bank for Development, which provide loans on the basis of likely financial returns;		
	Trade: Efforts by the enforcement panel of the WTO to overcome obstacles to free trade, such as the privileged position that the EU granted some countries with respect to bananas	*Trade:* Efforts by UNCITRAL, ISO, and UNIDROIT to facilitate trade by unifying the law and standardizing goods and services		
Reactive				

Conditional loans by the World Bank and WTO enforcement of free trade are MCA policies—multilateral because they are collective actions, coercive because the subject states have little recourse, and proactive because they are designed to promote growth.

Efforts by multilateral regional development banks to finance the most efficient projects and efforts by INGOs to unify the law and standardize products are MCA policies—multilateral because they are the result of collective decisions, noncoercive because they are voluntary, and proactive because they are intended to promote growth.

Private Law (UNIDROIT) that is trying to establish a uniform system of internal law around the world, and an International Organization for Standardization (ISO) that publishes international standards. These are examples of MCA trade policies: multilateral, noncoercive, and proactive.

Efforts to enforce free trade agreements are still in their infancy, but the WTO and various RTAs do have mechanisms for eliminating some barriers to trade. In the mid-1990s the Chiquita company petitioned the United States to formally complain to the WTO that by extending preferential treatment to some Commonwealth islands in the Caribbean the EU was unfairly preventing Chiquita from selling bananas grown mainly in South America to the EU.[48] This finding is an example of an MCA economic growth trade policy—multilateral, coercive, and proactive.

International organizations are also involved in promoting equitable growth policies. This is particularly important because inequalities among and within states are even more rampant at the international level.

Multilateral Equitable Growth Policies

A large number of IGOs, such as the UN Development Programme (UNDP), the UN Children's Fund (UNICEF), and the World Food Programme (WFP), provide **official development assistance** to developing countries; and an even larger number of INGOs, such as Oxfam International, the International Red Cross and Médecins Sans Frontières, provide private development assistance to these same countries. Some international organizations have also developed micro-loan programs that are designed to provide capital to the poorest people in developing countries. These programs were first established in Bangladesh in the mid-1970s, and they have been successfully emulated in urban and rural communities in both developing and developed states. Box 7.1 profiles Muhammad Yunus, an activist who headed one such program. These activities are all examples of MCA investment policies: multilateral, coercive, and reactive. Table 7.4 illustrates this and the next three examples of multilateral equitable growth policies: efforts by the World Bank and the IMF to help some of the least developed countries, efforts by settlement panels of the WTO to aid small vulnerable economies (SVE), and efforts by MNCs and TNCs to engage in socially responsible business practices.

Individual governments and private banks often write off debts in order to improve their credit ratings, but the World Bank and the IMF "contend that their bylaws prohibit them from granting debt relief or canceling debts.[49] As "preferred creditors" they put enormous pressure on developing countries to service their debts. In 1996 the World Bank and the IMF established an initiative to help the most Heavily Indebted Poor Countries (HIPC) reach sustainability. Unfortunately, this initiative has not been very successful. If these international financial institutions and the developed countries that sustain their policies would give up some of the leverage they have over these countries, this initiative would be an example of an MCA investment policy: multilateral, coercive, and reactive.

Because some countries' non-tariff barriers to trade are designed to help the poorest countries, the WTO is supposed to provide small vulnerable economies (SVE) with special differential treatment. In the Chiquita banana case mentioned above, the WTO ruling in favor of the United States will virtually destroy the economies of the Windward Islands of the Caribbean. It is not yet clear what form this special differential treatment

BOX 7.1

Profile in Action: Muhammad Yunus

In 1967 Muhammad Yunus received a Fulbright scholarship to study economic development at Vanderbilt University in the United States. While teaching in Murfreesboro, Tennessee, Yunus learned that a war had broken out in his native East Pakistan. He soon became involved in the push for U.S. diplomatic recognition of Bangladesh as a separate country, and in late 1971 he returned home to an independent Bangladesh.

Yunus became head of the Economics Department at Chittagong University in Bangladesh where he noticed that the fields adjacent to the university were not being used during a famine. Upon investigation he discovered that the poorest people in the local village were unable to take the most obvious steps to meet their basic needs because they lacked reasonable access to capital. (Regular banks would not make loans to the poor because they lacked collateral.) In short, the poor were being victimized by local money lenders who only provided very small, short-term loans at high rates of interest. As a consequence, the poor worked hard only to become more impoverished.

Yunus came up with the idea of lending money to the "hard-core" poor in the village so they could break this vicious cycle of poverty. He offered long-term micro-loans (as little as $27) to the poorest people in the village at 20 percent interest, rates that were better than those obtained from local money lenders. He developed a system to help these inexperienced loan recipients make good decisions and pay back their loans. In his system no one could get a micro-loan

will take.[50] This is an example of an MCA trade policy—multilateral, coercive, and reactive.

Finally, private individuals and companies often prefer to adhere to universal standards of behavior as a matter of choice. Some MNCs and TNCs have used the bargaining power they have over their supply chains to deal with problems such as child labor, extortion, hazardous materials, and pollutants. For example, IBM, Dell, and HP have developed a new Electronic Industry Code of Conduct to prevent these problems in companies in other countries.[51] The Global Sullivan Principles of Social Responsibility, named after the Reverend Leon H. Sullivan who proposed them for American companies operating in South Africa in the 1970s and 1980s, are another example of this kind of program. Such trade policies are multilateral, noncoercive and reactive, or MCA.

The framework employed in this text depicts foreign policy actions in terms of the same three dimensions used to describe preferences. This is

until he or she had become part of a group of five potential loan recipients. These "groups of five" then met weekly for the purpose of making and monitoring loans as well as collecting the two percent weekly payments on each one-year loan. The local project was so successful that Yunus was able to develop the Grameen (village) Bank at the national level.

Because women were severely restricted in Bengali society, Yunus made a special effort to include them. Now over 60 percent of those receiving micro-loans in Bangladesh are women. One of the most interesting things about these loans is that Yunus does not provide micro-loans to people for the purpose of receiving job training. He discovered that even the poorest people in a village could improve their lot without special training. What they lacked was capital, not knowledge, skills, or dependability to pay back loans. Indeed, he found that 98 percent of these poor recipients repaid their loans, a much higher percentage return than that obtained by regular banks. Of course, in a poor country such as Bangladesh people faced many natural and made-made disasters that could prevent them from repaying their loans. In these situations the Grameen Bank also provided disaster loans.

The typical borrower in Bangladesh receives a succession of micro-loans—each one larger than the previous one—as the financial capacity of the borrower improves. The micro-loan idea has been so successful that it has spread to scores of developed as well as developing countries. Millions of borrowers have collectively received billions of dollars under these plans.

Source: Muhammad Yunus, *Banker to the Poor: Micro-Lending and the Battle Against World Poverty* (New York: Public Affairs, 1999)

helpful because it keeps the value choices implicit in all foreign policies in mind. But it does not mean that one's actions are always aligned with one's preferences, and this is especially true when it comes to assessing the outcomes of foreign policies especially in economics. One hopes that one's actions are in tune with one's preferences; and that one's actions result in the expected outcomes. But outcomes also depend on the desires, expectations, preferences, behaviors, strategies, and capabilities of other foreign policy actors.

Choosing the Best Economic Policy

In order to establish a template for assessing the outcomes of foreign policy, it is useful to interpret the value of prosperity, that is the proactive–reactive dimension, in terms of the criterion of efficiency. Does a given foreign policy strategy or action promote growth or equitability? Since there is neither time nor space to illustrate the use of this criterion with

Table 7.4. Dimensions of Foreign Policy: Multilateral Equitable Growth Policies

| | Multilateral | | Unilateral | |
	Coercive	Noncoercive	Noncoercive	Coercive
Proactive				
Reactive	*Investment:* Efforts by the World Bank and IMF to reduce the debts of HIPCs *Trade:* Efforts by the WTO to provide special differential treatment to small vulnerable economies (SVE)	*Investment:* Official development assistance by IGOs and INGOs on the basis of need; micro-loans by the Grameen Bank and others *Trade:* Efforts by IBM, Dell, and HP to establish an Electronic Industry Code of Conduct; voluntary acceptance of the Sullivan principles by MNCs		

Efforts by IGOs, INGOs, MNCs, and TNCs to provide assistance to the poorest countries and the poorest people in those countries are MCA—multilateral because they are guided by cosmopolitan principles, noncoercive because they are voluntary, and reactive because they are designed to promote equitability.

Efforts by the WTO and the IMF to help countries that are heavily in debt or endangered are MCA—multilateral because they are based on joint agreements, coercive because they have some enforcement powers, and reactive because they have equitable ends.

respect to all of the actions described above, this section evaluates two specific kinds of economic policies according to the criterion of efficiency: development assistance and economic sanctions. Development assistance is usually thought of in terms of granting benefits; sanctions, in terms of imposing costs.

Economic Development

The American electorate is greatly confused as to the extent of the United States' generosity when it comes to foreign development assistance. Every couple of years the current president will announce a new initiative granting developing countries billions of dollars for multi-year development programs. No wonder the American people incorrectly believe that as much as 24 percent of the federal budget is devoted to foreign aid.[52] The fact is that the United States is the "largest international economic aid donor in dollar terms ($15,791 billion in 2004), but is the smallest contributor among the 21 major donor governments when calculated as a percent of gross national income (0.14 percent of GDP)." [53] To put this in perspective, the United States' contribution to foreign aid was 16 times as much in 1947 as it was in 2004 (in constant 2004 dollars).

At the same time Americans have been more generous with their private donations than the citizens of other donor countries. "Americans privately give at least $34 billion overseas—more than twice the United States' official foreign aid of $15 billion." [54] However, $18 billion of this $34 billion consists of personal remittances from people (mostly foreign nationals) to relatives in developing countries. These remittances probably have a negative effect on economic growth in these countries because the money goes mainly for private consumption.[55] This underscores the importance of official aid from the United States.

All foreign aid is not official development assistance (ODA). In order to separate ODA from the larger foreign aid program, Figure 7.2 breaks down the way in which U.S. foreign aid is categorized. Bilateral development assistance is the largest category. Multilateral aid is similar to development assistance, except it goes to international organizations such as UNICEF, UNDP, and the World Bank. Humanitarian aid, which goes to refugee relief, food aid programs, and support for democratic institutions, is also considered development assistance. Economic and political/secu-

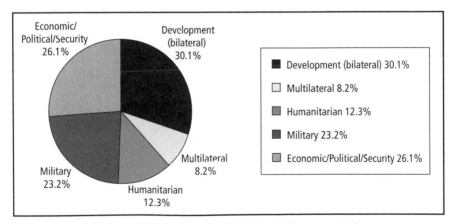

Figure 7.2. Composition of U.S. Aid Program, Excluding Aid to Iraq, 2004ᵃ
a. In fiscal year 2004 the Office of the President held nearly $23.7 billion for long-term reconstruction programs in Iraq compared with the $20.65 billion included in the traditional aid programs represented in this pie chart.

Source: Data compiled by author from the Bureau of Economic Analysis.

rity aid supports U.S. strategic goals abroad. The last category of aid is military. It is used to help friendly and allied states acquire military equipment and training. Only the first three categories involve ODA.

It is also important to note that in 2004 Congress and the president allocated about $80 billion for Iraq, $23 billion of which is for economic reconstruction in Iraq. The dollar amount for economic reconstruction alone in Iraq is more than all five categories of development assistance for the rest of the world. This money would generally be considered military aid and economic and political/security aid, but in this case it is controlled by the White House rather than by the Department of Defense and the Agency for International Development in the State Department, who normally control aid of these two types.

Most U.S. foreign aid is highly political. This becomes clear if one looks at the 15 top recipients for U.S. foreign aid for 1994 and 2004. Figure 7.3 shows that the bulk of U.S. foreign aid in 1994 went to Israel and Egypt as compensation for their participation in the Camp David accords and former Soviet States. Figure 7.4 shows that most aid in 2004 is going to Iraq.

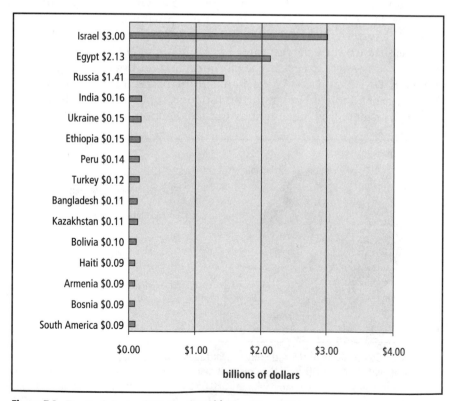

Figure 7.3. Top Recipients of U.S. Foreign Aid, Fiscal Year 1994
Source: Data compiled by author from Bureau of Economic Analysis.

In addition to Israel and Egypt, the other primary recipients are countries that are considered vital in the war against terrorism, such as Afghanistan, Jordan, and Pakistan, and the war against drugs, such as Columbia.

Although private investment and trade now overshadow official development assistance to developing countries, these instruments do not address some of the most pressing needs of these countries. They do not build infrastructure, feed the world's most destitute people, or deal with the most glaring inequalities both within and between states and societies. Thus the issue of ODA remains an important one.

Values at Stake. The need for development assistance arises from the existence of global inequalities that sustain poverty throughout the world. All of the aspects of the lives of the people living in this condition are affected: they have little money, few goods, or means for meeting life's requirements such as food, water, shelter, clothing, health, and education. If countries, groups, or individuals lack any of these key resources, they are likely to be deficient in the others as well. Thus poverty is ubiquitous, but even if one were to think of poverty solely in terms of hunger, the numbers associated with the extent of global hunger are staggering.

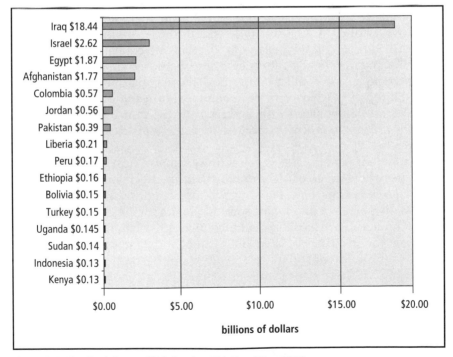

Figure 7.4. Top Recipients of U.S. Foreign Aid, Fiscal Year 2004
Source: Data compiled by author from Bureau of Economic Analysis

Approximately 1.2 billion people suffer from hunger (deficiency of calories and protein). Some 2 to 3.5 billion people have micronutrient deficiency (deficiency of vitamins and minerals). Yet, some 1.2 billion suffer from obesity (excess of fats and salt, often accompanied by deficiency of vitamins and minerals).[56]

Poverty, or the lack of prosperity, results largely because people are denied access to trade and resources. Not only is aid necessary, but trade is the key. Developing countries need development assistance and other forms of investment because they are given very limited access to the markets of advanced countries. The barriers to trade in advanced countries are especially high on agricultural goods and textiles: the goods that developing countries most want to sell. As a consequence, developing countries go into debt because there is not enough outside investment to meet their needs. Because of the high rate of interest charged on their debt (often about 20 percent), however, developing countries cannot hope to get ahead. For example, Nigeria owed all creditors about $19 billion in 1985; and although it paid them approximately $37 billion in principle and interest between 1985 and 2004, it still owed about $36 billion in December 2004.

This begins to explain why ODA—limited as it is—is so vital to developing countries. But ODA is not just something that affects the prosperity of developing countries; it is also essential to their security. After all, poverty is a threat to the lives of people in those countries. The danger from AIDS, tuberculosis, malaria, and other infectious diseases is very high in many developing countries. These countries are also more likely to experience group conflict. Most internal wars and other forms of militarized disputes take place in developing countries. Moreover, the incidence of international terrorism and crime, such as the international drug trade, is at least indirectly associated with the injustices associated with poverty.

In addition, poverty affects community values. Most developing societies offer only limited participation by their members in society. Women and children seldom have equal rights, including the right to an education. Many people in developing societies do not own the land they work. Labor conditions are harsher and much more unsafe in developing countries, and the incidence of child labor is much higher. The laws in developing countries do not guarantee the rights of freedom of association or expression. In short, poor countries do not afford people the same basic human rights that are available to most people in advanced countries. So, what can developing countries do about it?

Main Options.   This section considers three options for dealing with the problem of development at the global level. All of these options are MCA—multilateral because they involve cooperative action based on universal principles, noncoercive because they are voluntary, and reactive because they are designed to promote equitability. The first option does not envisage the most radical possible **redistribution** of economic resources; rather, it calls for developed countries to contribute about 0.7 percent of their GDP to a fund that would then total about $150 billion—not only enough to meet basic needs but also to invest in some development in every developing country except China, which is now in the best position to take advantage of world trade.[57] The most development assistance would go to those countries with the greatest need. This option is based on the **convergence theory of growth**, which posits, "poor countries grow faster than wealthier ones because they enjoy a higher rate of return to capital investment." [58]

The second option is to help those who are "most able to help themselves." The U.S. government is promoting this option in the form of the Millennium Challenge Account. The World Bank and the IMF also favor it. This growth option would funnel development aid to a select group of "low- or low-middle income countries that have shown a strong commitment to political, economic and social reforms." [59] The United States has already proposed spending billions of dollars for this purpose by 2006. If the United States and other countries in the United Nations follow through with their plans under the Millennium Challenge, this program could also provide in the neighborhood of $150 billion dollars for development assistance for selected developing countries.

The third option is to help only those "least able to help themselves." In effect, this option creates a safety net for people in the developing world who are living below the poverty line. It envisages a fund of about $60 billion that would be distributed to least developed states so that they, in turn, could deal with the most pressing needs without erasing the feeling of crisis in their societies. Perhaps some of these funds would take the form of micro-loans to those who are in the most desperate situations. This option assumes that advanced countries should emphasize refugee relief and food aid rather than development assistance.

Assessing Options.   The first option is desirable because it seeks sustained development in every developing country; it also is affordable. By giving the most aid to those countries with the most need, it takes into account the fact that, initially at least, conditions are different in various developing countries. But there is little evidence that those countries that do not have policies favorable to development will actually be able to use the funds effectively. As a result, much of this development assistance will be wasted when it could have contributed to development elsewhere. Moreover, this kind of development assistance could raise unreasonable expectations for improved living conditions, which could in turn create security problems both among developing countries and between developing and developed countries. If successful, this option also could exacerbate environmental problems as more countries are in a position to consume the world's resources.

The second option is designed to get the most out of the development dollar. It gives development assistance to select countries that have already demonstrated they can use such funds effectively. By focusing on the most promising countries, this option allows the United States to reduce its administrative costs. Such a policy also may inspire other developing countries to make the reforms needed to qualify for development assistance in the future. This option ignores, however, the least-developed countries and the problems they pose for the international system. It ignores the fact that much development assistance is a response to domestic politics, and it resembles the "conditionality" imposed on developing countries by the World Bank and the IMF, which most developing countries claim has adverse effects on development. But, most important, it ignores the right to development, which increasingly is being put forth as a universal human right, by ignoring the least developed countries.

The third option meets the minimal needs of most human beings and, in doing so, the minimal obligations of the developed world to the people of the developing world. It provides relief to developing countries whose populations face natural disasters such as drought, famine, and tsunamis. This option is the least expensive of the three, but in a larger sense it may be very costly because it does not promise any long-term solutions. Moreover, by allowing inequalities to continue to grow among countries, this option may create security problems down the road.

Economic Sanctions

Although economic sanctions are associated with the prosperity dimension, they are usually thought of as "economic measures directed to gain political goals." [60] When this occurs, these economic measures are reactive and have to be judged in terms of their political benefits. They can be employed for military gains as well, but that is usually known as economic warfare. Of course, they may also be used for purely economic reasons.

> Economic sanctions may take many forms: arms embargoes, cutbacks or halts in foreign assistance, limitations on exports and imports, frozen assets, hikes in tariffs, lower import quotas, revocation of most-favored-nation trade status, or prohibitions against credit, financing, and investment. Perhaps less obvious sanctions with economic repercussions are unfavorable votes in international organizations, such as the World Bank or IMF, withdrawal of diplomatic relations, visa denials, and cancelled air links. [61]

Although sanctions have been used throughout history, they have been employed especially frequently since World War II because they have more effect during periods of growing interdependence among states and because they are believed to be less likely than other forms of coercion to escalate into full-scale nuclear war. It is estimated that over half of all countries have either been threatened with or suffered from U.S. economic or trade sanctions.[62]

Countries are usually thought to be the targets of economic sanctions, but some recent applications have been directed at individual firms or groups within countries. For example, in August 2003 the administration froze the assets of six top leaders of the radical Palestinian group Hamas in the United States and levied sanctions against five charities that are linked to Hamas but operate largely outside the United States. And in April 2004 the U.S. Department of State imposed economic sanctions against five Chinese companies for exporting equipment and technology to Iran that might aid in the development and production of missiles and WMD.

Values at Stake.   Because economic sanctions are often used to protest the violation of community norms, values such as human rights and state sovereignty are often at issue at least on the surface. For example, when the United States froze all of the economic assets of both Kuwait and Iraq on August 2, 1990, the very day that Iraq invaded Kuwait, it justified that action in terms of aggression against a sovereign state rather than its concern for the potential loss of Middle Eastern oil. Four days later, the UN Security Council passed Resolution 661, which imposed comprehensive economic sanctions against Iraq. This action also was justified in terms of community values, not economic ones.

Economic sanctions may also involve security values. For example, in December 1981 the United States tried to impose economic sanctions on European firms profiting from the construction of a trans-Siberian pipeline. The sanctions were based on security considerations as well as on America's anger over the Soviets' involvement in the hard-line policy adopted by the Polish government against the trade union Solidarity earlier that year. Economic sanctions also may be the first step in a series of actions leading to conflict. For example, in 1990 the UN Security Council initially imposed economic sanctions to force Iraq out of Kuwait. Then at the close of the Persian Gulf War on April 3, 1991, the Security Council lifted the ban on food and some other supplies but set new standards for determining when the remaining sanctions would be lifted. The new standards called for Iraq to destroy WMD and establish a compensation fund for Kuwaiti victims of the Persian Gulf War. Two days later the Security Council condemned Iraq's repression of its own civilian population. The George W. Bush administration cited the alleged failure of these sanctions more than ten years later as the reason for its invasion of Iraq in 2003.

Whatever the stated purpose of economic sanctions, they are usually expected to have some affect on the prosperity of the target state or firm. However, it is possible that economic sanctions are as costly to the initiating state as they are to the target state. For example, U.S. farmers felt that cutting off the sale of U.S. wheat to Russia in the late 1970s and early 1980s, because of the 1979 Soviet invasion of Afghanistan, was more damaging to U.S. agriculture than to the Soviet Union. This suggests that economic sanctions are often a blunt instrument, and an effective protest against the violation or loss of community and security values may involve significant economic loss to the states imposing sanctions.

Main Options.   For sanctions, there are three broad alternatives. **Comprehensive sanctions,** the first alternative, normally entail a total embargo of all economic trade and freezing all financial assets, although some exceptions might be made for strictly humanitarian purposes. The UN Security Council employed this kind of sanction against Iraq in 1990. The Iraq sanctions were an MC<u>A</u> policy: multilateral, coercive, and reactive—because they were designed to punish Iraq for violating Kuwait's sovereignty. Comprehensive sanctions usually require enforcement by land, sea, and air to block all cross-border exchanges. They are based on the premise that the offending party will be forced to accept the terms of those enforcing the sanctions because most states are dependent on international trade and investment.

Comprehensive sanctions work best when they involve the participation of most states, but the United States has attempted to employ comprehensive sanctions unilaterally against states such as Iran, Libya, and Cuba. In order to strengthen these <u>MC</u>A comprehensive sanctions, Congress passed the Iran-Libya Sanctions Act in 1996. This act tried to enhance the effectiveness of U.S. unilateral sanctions against Iran and Libya by targeting foreign firms doing business with those countries. Similar legislation, the Helms-Burton Act, was passed in 1996 to strengthen U.S. unilateral sanctions against Cuba. But other countries have resisted efforts to extend the reach of unilateral sanctions. For example, the EU passed a law barring European companies from complying with such extraterritorial restrictions.

Partial or **selective sanctions**, the second option, are tailored to deal both with the severity of the violation and the identity of the perpetrators. For example, when the United States froze the assets of members of the military junta in Haiti in 1993, it was adding a selective sanction to the UN Security Council's embargo on all fuel and arms to that country. Sanctions may also be partial because the party or parties applying the sanctions do not expect full compliance. So when the United Nations passed the "oil-for-food" program in 1996, it in effect converted comprehensive sanctions against Iraq into selective sanctions. Moreover, if sanction legislation allows the president to grant waivers on specific sanctions, the U.S. government can use them more selectively.[63]

In **constructive engagement**, the third option, the offended state may use a wide variety of means, ranging from diplomacy to a show of force, to convince the offending state that it may eventually be the target of economic sanctions. This option is based on the premise that the threat of sanctions is more effective than sanctions themselves because it keeps the lines of communications open and gives the target state more opportunities to make amends. For example, the United States prefers to use the threat of sanctions in its relations with China because of the importance of the Chinese market. The threat of sanctions may also be more effective than actual sanctions against countries, such as North Korea, with whom the United States has very limited trade.

Assessing Options.   Comprehensive sanctions are most likely to be effective if they can be implemented quickly by most or all other states. Iraq was the target of comprehensive economic sanctions from 1990 until at least 1996. The United States froze most of Iraq's financial assets immediately after it attacked Kuwait and was able to block trade within a matter of weeks, if not days. Moreover, the United States had the support of most members of the United Nations, including the neighboring countries of Saudi Arabia, Turkey, Syria, and even Jordan. These sanctions were effective in forcing Saddam Hussein to dismantle his WMD program in the early 1990s.[64] Part of the effectiveness of the sanctions against Iraq was based on its high vulnerability: approximately 61 percent of Iraq's GDP was based on the sale of oil that accounted for 90 percent of its export earnings.

Unfortunately, the effects of comprehensive sanctions are most devastating to members of the general population. In the case of comprehensive sanctions against Iraq approximately one million out of a population of twenty million were seriously affected. The impact on the general population was reflected in the decline in Iraq's annual per capita income, which fell from about $335 in 1988 (using the free-market exchange rate) to about $44 in 1992.[65] (The United Nations defines a poverty-stricken state as one with a per capita income of less than $100).

Although the reduction in per capita income gives some sense of the devastation to the general population that the comprehensive sanctions involved, the human toll is most evident in the data on the younger generation. In a 1995 report on the nutritional situation in Iraq, the Food and Agriculture Organization found that, based on similar surveys conducted in 1991,

the percentage of children under five with *wasting* had quadrupled, to 12 percent, and *stunting* had more than doubled, to 28 percent.[66] (Wasting occurs when weight for height is two standard deviations below the median value; whereas stunting occurs when height for age is two standard deviations below the median value.)

When the UN Security Council learned of the full effects of the sanctions, there was strong pressure from humanitarian organizations to modify the sanctions in order to allow more food to get through to the general population. This is when the Security Council set up the "food-for-oil" program. Although Iraq suffered the most from comprehensive sanctions, it is important to recognize that trade is reciprocal; all parties normally receiving oil from Iraq would have been affected to some extent.

Unilateral efforts to apply comprehensive sanctions, even when undertaken by a super power, are less effective. The U.S. effort to use comprehensive sanctions to change the regimes in Cuba and Iran are good examples. But the Libyan case, which was ultimately successful, is more complex. The United States started out by designating Libya a state sponsor of terrorism in 1979. At first the United States banned the sale of military and dual-use products, prohibited bilateral U.S. assistance, and opposed loans or aid to Libya by international financial institutions. In 1986 the United States froze Libyan assets in the United States and ended bilateral trade with Libya. Then in 1992 the UN sanctioned Libya with a ban on all air links and ended arms sales: an action that was multilateral, coercive, and reactive, or MCA. In December 2003 Libya announced that it would abandon its WMD programs; earlier it had set up a $2.7 billion compensation fund for the families of victims of the Pan Am 103 (Lockerbie, Scotland) bombing. There may be many reasons why Libya chose to change its foreign policy; the most significant factor seems to have been the UN-imposed, multilateral economic sanctions, including the debilitating international air travel ban.[67]

Partial sanctions may be justified in part on the ground that the offending country would be particularly vulnerable to an embargo on one or two key resources such as food or oil. For example, when various nations contemplated instituting partial sanctions against South Africa in the 1970s and 1980s as a means of ending that country's policy of racial apartheid, they believed that South Africa was particularly vulnerable to a cutoff of oil supplies. But this idea was abandoned when it became apparent that partial sanctions would only force South Africa to develop synthetic fuels, which could actually strengthen, not weaken, South Africa in the long run. Moreover, partial sanctions may require levers of control that are not available in a society. For example, when President Carter tried to abruptly halt U.S. food exports to the Soviet Union in 1980, the United States was unable to cut off the aid that was already in the pipeline, and later American farmers resented the private market losses in the United States caused by the embargo.[68]

Partial economic sanctions have generally been most effective when applied to foreign firms dependent on U.S. markets or U.S. suppliers. In the 1980s economic sanctions against South African computer and telecommunications firms were particularly effective since they were areas in which the United States had a dominant market position. Even when such sanctions are not effective, however, they may be employed because they provide an acceptable way of demonstrating one's contempt for the guilty party. With that in mind, individual cities, universities, and companies adopted sanctions to punish South Africa for its apartheid policy even though they knew that they did not have the capability, either individually or collectively, to change that policy. Yet by the end of 1989, in a display of moral determination, some 200 of the estimated 350 U.S. firms operating in South Africa had withdrawn, even though most had been doing a lucrative business in the host country. [69]

Given the costs and uncertainties that accompany the use of sanctions, it is not surprising that many people believe that the threat of employing sanctions is more effective in bringing about the preferred changes than the sanctions themselves. This is the policy that Ronald Reagan pursued in relation to South Africa in the early 1980s and that George H. W. Bush and Bill Clinton tried to apply to China in the 1990s. For China, the success of threats seemed to depend largely on calculations of self-interest and will. The United States failed to get the Chinese to improve their human rights record in order to get most favored nation status; but the Chinese succeeded in getting the United States to separate trade from human rights by threatening to deny American firms access to Chinese markets. However, the United States did succeed in getting the Chinese to clamp down on the piracy of foreign videos by threatening a "100 percent putative tariff on $1 billion worth of Chinese goods in the spring of 1995, and $2–3 billion of Chinese goods in the spring of 1996." [70]

Conclusion

Because the United States is the wealthiest country in the world, it has a greater capacity than other countries to influence the international economic system. But the American people are probably less conscious of international investment and trade than other nationals because the United States is less dependent than other states on foreign trade and investment. Yet it depends more on international trade and investment than many people within the country believe it should, both because it runs such a high current deficit and because it uses so much outside energy.

As international war becomes more costly, the United States has paid more attention to foreign economic policies both as a way of disciplining other states and as a way of assisting them. But international economic instruments such as trade and aid are often two-edged-swords; they can have both negative and positive affects on the state employing them.

Key Concepts

Suggested Readings

1. Friedman, Thomas L. *The World is Flat: A Brief History of the Twenty-first Century.* New York: Farrar, Straus, and Giroux, 2005.

2. Gomory, Ralph E. and William Baumol. *Global Trade and Conflicting National Interests.* Cambridge, Mass.: MIT Press, 2000.

3. Prestowitz, Clyde. *Three Billion New Capitalists: The Great Shift of Wealth and Power to the East.* New York: Basic Books, 2005.

4. Yunus, Mohammad. *Banker to the Poor: Micro-Lending and the Battle Against World Poverty.* New York: Public Affairs, 1999.

PART III

The Foreign Policy Making Process

S O FAR THIS TEXT has employed the values represented by the three dimensions—community, security, and prosperity—to describe the objectives underlying foreign policies and the differences among people on these values represented by the three dimensions—multilateral–unilateral, coercive–noncoercive, and proactive–reactive—to classify their foreign policy behavior. But in the course of describing these foreign policy objectives and behaviors, the text may have given the impression that this framework for analysis is only useful for describing foreign policy outputs and assessing foreign policy outcomes in terms of the three associated criteria—acceptance, effectiveness, and efficiency, respectively.

In Part III of this book, the framework for analysis is used primarily to describe foreign policy inputs. The framework is especially well suited for studying these inputs because the three basic human motivations it employs— honor, fear, and profit—can largely account for the needs, wants, and desires that lead to the establishment of these objectives and behaviors in the first place.

In order to account for all foreign policy inputs it is essential to think of foreign policy as a process in which a variety of actors simultaneously and continuously make contributions to foreign policy making. Although this process is continuous, it is useful to divide it into a series of stages. This is what John Lovell, a political scientist, has done in his "Imaginary Ideal Policy Making Machine" (IIPMM).

Although such a machine is entirely imaginary, it helps us to identify the eight functions performed by policy makers—

scanning, interpreting, transmitting, storing, analyzing, deciding, implementing, and evaluating. Each of these functions represents a stage in the foreign policy process. The first stage involves **scanning** the world at large because although foreign policy is based on the values and interests of the state, more often than not the need for foreign policy arises because of some disturbance outside the state itself. Thus the machine must monitor both the domestic environment of the actor and the foreign environment of the actor in order to gather all relevant information. Of course, the IIPMM is aware of all these events and performs this task perfectly.

The second stage involves coding or **interpreting** these events. The IIPMM must decide which events are relevant for foreign policy making, it must classify these events appropriately, and it must interpret them correctly. In short, the machine is programmed to distinguish between relevant information and background noise. This information is then coded so that incoming data can be compared with similar data acquired in other places at other times. Since the machine is perfect, it has no biases; it is incapable of misperceptions and misinterpretations.

Once these data have been collected and interpreted in the field, current information needs to be **transmitted** to others. Much of this information will be utilized in the country in which it is collected; but some of it will be conveyed to other locations. After its initial use, much of this information will be sent to Washington, D.C.

After this information has been transmitted, it needs to be **stored** either in individual or central files. It is particularly important that this information be stored in a form that will make it readily accessible if and when it is needed again. Foreign policy actors must not only be able to respond to requests for information but also be able to identify the problems that need attention so that the relevant information can be made available.

The fifth stage is the deliberative or **analyzing** stage. During this stage the machine identifies and prioritizes the values and interests at stake in a given issue and weighs the advantages and disadvantages of all alternative courses of action to secure these values and interests. Since the IIPMM is perfect, it is uncanny in its ability to order these preferences and identify all relevant options. The machine automatically assesses each of these alternatives in terms of the value preferences determined earlier.

During the sixth stage the IIPMM makes the **decision** to commit resources for the purpose of solving foreign policy problems. In most cases the machine is programmed to choose the alternative that maximizes the preferred values at least cost to the state. In a crisis the machine will make quick decisions. But sometimes the machine will ask for additional information before it makes a decision. And in some instances it will even reverse itself if new or better information becomes available.

The actions taken to **implement** the decision occur during the seventh stage of the foreign policy making process. Because a series of actions may have to be taken at different times in various places, the IIPMM has been programmed so that all of these actions are taken at the most appropriate time and place. That is, the plans and procedures developed by the machine are so flexible that the actions taken by the machine always are in sync with its decisions.

The eighth and final stage of the foreign policy making process is the **evaluation** of the policy. In many ways this is the most miraculous feature of the IIPMM because even though the actions taken are entirely in accord with the decisions made earlier, the machine is capable of correcting itself if new data become available that suggest that that the decision needs to be changed. Thus the IIPMM is constantly adjusting itself to do an even better job. By continually evaluating the consequences of its actions, it can reprogram itself to scan for additional information, which can be fed back into the machine. Of course, the machine never tires although it runs continually.

The problem with the IIPMM is that it assumes a kind of perfect rationality that is not produced in the real world. When actual foreign policy makers perform these functions, they introduce a variety of non-rational influences. In Chapters 8 through 14 we identify the individuals and organizations that perform these eight functions and show how we can account for their behavior more realistically.

Source: John P. Lovell, *Foreign Policy in Perspective: Strategy, Adaptation, Decision Making* (New York: Holt, Rinehart and Winston, 1970), 208–211.

CHAPTER 8

The Actors Inside and Outside Government

Although the governments of states are the primary actors in foreign policy, international governmental and nongovernmental organizations also play an important role in international affairs. These organizations have been indispensable in recent years, as the world has faced a series of severe environmental disasters — earthquakes, hurricanes, mudslides, and tsunamis. In this picture, young survivors of the 2005 Pakistani earthquake receive pens and paper to draw as part of a psychological project to aid trauma victims, as parents watch. This workshop was conducted by the UN Save the Children organization in Muzaffarabad, capital of Pakistan-administered Kashmir on October 16, 2005. Although governments have promised assistance, this disaster has not generated the same level of government support as the tsunami that occurred in the Indian Ocean in December 2004.

W HEN AMERICANS THINK of foreign policy making, they invariably reflect on the role played by the president. The president, however, is not the only person involved in making U.S. foreign policy. The Constitution requires that the president seek the approval of Congress on important matters such as the appointment of ambassadors, the making of treaties, and the appropriation of funds for foreign programs. Both Congress and the president rely in turn on a large number of experts both for information on what is taking place abroad and for an assessment of how these events affect U.S. interests at home and abroad. Many of these same experts also are needed to implement U.S. foreign policy.

The president and Congress also need the support of the American people. Since the Enlightenment, political theorists have been aware that what people in society think and do is just as important as what people in government think and do, especially in countries with democratic governments and capitalist economies. Whether they are needed to volunteer for military service, conserve vital resources, or invest in public bonds, the aggregate behavior of ordinary citizens is often crucial to successful foreign policy making.

Government and society can act in concert only if the many different kinds of actors do their part. Government officials must keep abreast of overseas events. The press must inform the public. Societal groups must assess the effects of foreign events on the interests of their members, and so inform the government. Congress must pass the required legislation. The president and the bureaucracy must make the right decisions and implement them in ways that society as a whole can support. In short, all of these actors are engaged in essential aspects of foreign policy making. Although some are more involved than others in various stages of that process, depending on their interests, responsibilities, and areas of expertise, each actor or set of actors makes a distinct contribution to foreign policy making.

Because approaches to the explanation of foreign policy are so closely tied to different actors, this chapter begins with a discussion of actors and then concludes by identifying the approaches most intimately associated with them. Inasmuch as all of these actors are engaged in the same overall process, this chapter emphasizes the organizational context in which they work. Subsequent chapters focus more distinctly on the people involved and the positions they hold as well as the approaches affiliated with the people in these various positions.

Foreign Affairs Organizations

Both governmental and nongovernmental organizations (NGOs) make and influence foreign policy. Most students of foreign policy tend to look chiefly at governmental organizations, but NGOs also have become important. Indeed, the relationship between these two kinds of organizations has become so entwined that it is difficult to understand foreign policy making without taking both kinds into account.

The Role of Government

Only governments can make laws and ratify treaties that have the effect of law. Some laws define the rights and obligations of states toward each other. For example, laws of diplomacy define the beginning and termination of a diplomatic mission, diplomatic ranks, and the functions of diplomatic agents. When these laws were initially formulated, there were less than a dozen states. Now there are almost two hundred. Because almost all of these states have diplomatic relations, about 40,000 separate diplomatic links exist among the governments of these countries, a figure that does not even include the multiple channels that exist between most governments.

Increasingly negotiations among these governments also take place either at any one of the more than 1,000 ad hoc international conferences that the U. S. government attends each year or at regular meetings held at the permanent sites of numerous international organizations. Of the 993 mainline, intergovernmental organizations (IGOs) 245 are either federations of international organizations, universal membership organizations, intercontinental membership organizations, or limited or regionally defined membership organizations, such as the UN, UNESCO, OPEC, and ASEAN, respectively; 748 are organizations having a special form, including foundations and funds, such as the World Bank (WB).[1] If one includes dependent bodies, such as the OECD Development Centre, and organization substitutes, such as the Nordic Customs Cooperation Council, there are an additional 3,923 IGOs. These organizations themselves report almost 50,000 links with each other, that is either formal associate relations, formal consultations, operational links, or financial links. Of course, this does not include the relationships among the individuals and collectives sharing memberships within these organizations. Figure 8.1 diagrams this network of bilateral and multilateral relationships among government officials, often referred to as **track one diplomacy**.

Although the U.S. government has exclusive authority to represent the state as a whole in foreign affairs, it can seldom prevent nongovernmental organizations from simultaneously representing various elements of American society abroad. In the first place, the federal government itself is limited by the Constitution. Specifically, the Tenth Amendment provides that "[t]he powers not delegated to the United States by the Constitution, nor prohibited by it to the States, are reserved to the States respectively, or to the people." Although this clause is not usually interpreted as having a restraining effect on the federal government in the area of foreign affairs, it does underscore the fact that the American people are the final arbiters in a democratic society.

Diplomacy, then, is a two-level game. The first level is the bargaining between the government and society, a relationship often depicted as a pyramid with government at the top and society at its base, as Figure 8.2

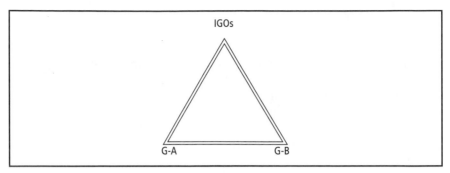

Figure 8.1. Track One Diplomacy
The lines between government G-A and government G-B depict the diplomatic relationships between all pairs of governments. The lines between G-A and G-B on the one
hand and all international organizations (IGOs) on the other represent the diplomatic
relationships between all individual governments and IGOs.

shows. This image of the state suggests that government and society are
unified. Government controls society by word and action. Society influences government by means of elections, public opinion, and pressure
politics. This image of the state also suggests that any differences between
government and society can be resolved. The second level of diplomacy is
the bargaining between the governments of two or more different states.
If a pyramid represents the first level, the second level might be represented as the knot of a bow tie, with the base of the pyramid representing
the bows of the bow tie, as Figure 8.3 shows. Figure 8.3 is not, however,
an accurate view of the role of society in foreign affairs; civil societies also
are in direct contact with one another.

The Role of Civil Society

When Britain's North American colonies declared their independence in
1776, the first emissaries selected by the Continental Congress to represent the new American government abroad were Arthur Lee, a Virginian
already serving in London as a commercial agent of Massachusetts, and

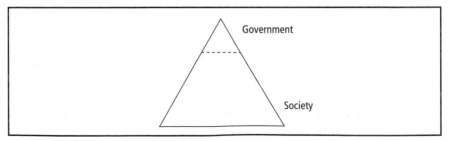

Figure 8.2. Pyramid
Government is represented by the small triangle at the top; society is represented by
the larger trapezoid that makes up the bottom of the triangle.

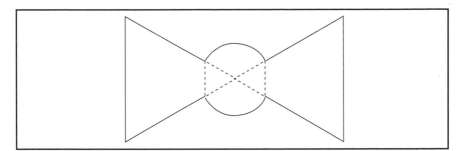

Figure 8.3. Bow Tie
The knot in the center of the bow tie represents the diplomatic relationships between the government of state A and the government of state B; the ends of the bow tie represent the civil societies of states A and B. This pair of states in turn represents the bilateral relations between all states.

Charles William Frederick Dumas in The Hague. Lee's presence as a commercial agent shows that American NGOs have always represented themselves abroad. Thanks to affordable transoceanic transportation and electronic communications, the cross-border ties between American NGOs and their overseas counterparts are today both myriad and persistent. If one wished to represent contemporary ties between American NGOs and those in other countries using the traditional pyramid, one would have to wrap the bow tie shown in Figure 8.3 around an object that resembles the meager neck of Ichabod Crane, the schoolmaster in the *Legend of Sleepy Hollow,* as Figure 8.4 shows, and observe the links that private individuals and groups in one society have with their counterparts in other societies.

As early as 1830, Alexis de Tocqueville remarked upon the large number of private associations in the United States. In 2003 Gale's *Encyclopedia of Associations* listed over 22,000 national associations in the United States,[2] and this figure does not include the even more numerous local and regional associations. Other countries have not always had such well-

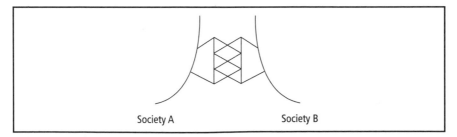

Society A   Society B

Figure 8.4. Cross-Border Contacts
The curved lines depict the back of Ichabod Crane's neck. The trapezoidal figures on either side of Ichabod's neck represent the society of state A and society of state B. The crossed lines that resemble crossed laces represent the numerous contacts between not only society A and society B, but also the contacts between all societies.

organized civil societies, but they are catching up with the United States in this regard. The absolute percentage change in country participation in INGOs from 1993 to 2003 was 44.5 percent in the United States, as compared to 28.4 percent in Kenya, 49.9 percent in Austria, and 5.4 percent in Iraq. Countries that have recently become independent or become more open have shown the greatest percentage change; for example, 563.2 percent in Belarus, 7,850 percent in Slovakia, and 75 percent in China.[3]

In addition, 11,397 international nongovernmental organizations (INGOs) are functioning at the global level—7,261 universal membership organizations, intercontinental membership organizations and limited or regionally defined membership organizations such as Amnesty International (AI), Commonwealth Jewish Council, and Latin American Federation of University Women, respectively; and 4,136 organizations having a special form, including foundations and funds, such as Catholic Relief Services, the Grameen Trust, and the Ford Foundation.[4] These organizations themselves report over 35,000 links, including formal associate relations, formal consultations, operational linkages, and financial linkages. This does not include the relationships between the individuals and collectives sharing memberships in these nongovernment organizations.

The relationship between track one and **track two diplomacy** is shown in Figure 8.5. The bilateral relationships between NGOs in country A and NGOs in country B are represented by the base line of the outer

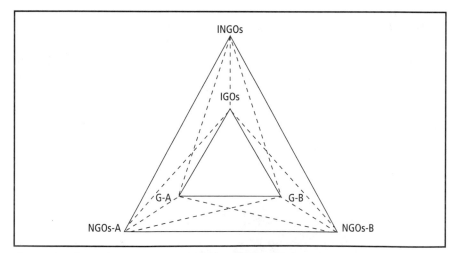

Figure 8.5. The Track Two Setting For Track One Diplomacy
The figure depicts the many layers of contacts among NGOs with the governments in their own state, NGOs in other states, IGOs, global and regional INGOs, and the "boomerang" contacts with governments of other states. These contacts are multiplied many times over, as all of these organizations in turn have contacts with the other governments and organizations.

triangle. The lines connecting these NGOs and the apex of the outer triangle represent the relations between NGOs and INGOs. The total number of possible connections between these organizations boggles the imagination.

But it is not just the connections between NGOs and INGOs that are of concern here; it is also the links between governmental and nongovernmental organizations. The dotted lines in Figure 8.5 show the relationship between NGOs, INGOs, and various governmental organizations. These relationships are important not only because of the *direct* influences exercised by civil society and government on each other, as depicted in the pyramid in Figure 8.2, and between civil societies and governments, as represented in the bow ties in Figures 8.3 and 8.4, but also because of the *indirect* influences that governments and civil societies have on one another. Governments sometimes can influence events in other countries more effectively by funneling their resources through NGOs than they can by using their own resources directly. Similarly, NGOs sometimes can influence foreign policy in their own country more effectively by working through the governments and NGOs of other societies than they can by contacting their own government directly. This **boomerang strategy** has proven effective for various issues such as the environment.[5]

Samples of People in Foreign Affairs Organizations

Although the term "foreign policy maker" is usually reserved for those who make foreign policy decisions—that is, have the authority to commit an organization and its resources—policy makers' decisions would not be very meaningful if they could not depend on those engaged in other stages of the foreign policy-making process. Much of the rest of this chapter is devoted to taking a closer look at the role of all foreign policy makers by examining the findings of the 1984 Transnational Project.[6] Although this survey of foreign policy makers both inside and outside government was conducted over twenty years ago, it tapped attitudes that, if anything, are even more understandable today than they were at the time.

The Transnational Project organizers began by identifying which U.S. government officials listed in the *Federal Yellow Pages* actually make American foreign policy.[7] In addition to the president, vice president, and members of the National Security Council (NSC), a host of other agencies and departments are involved in the policy-making process, including the Departments of Defense, Treasury, and Commerce; members of the House and Senate; and occasionally even the federal courts. Although several thousand of these officials were listed in the *Federal Yellow Pages*, the Transnational Project only surveyed about 750, or 20 percent of them. Just over 50 percent, or 377, of the officials contacted responded to the survey.

Project organizers found it was more difficult to determine which nongovernmental organizations to include in the population of NGO leaders to be sampled and surveyed. Because of the diversity of nongovernmental organizations, several different populations were surveyed. The principal population surveyed was that listed in Gale's *Encyclopedia of Associations: National Associations of the U.S.* In 1981 Gale listed 17,500 nongovernmental membership associations, divided into seventeen categories: trade, agriculture, legal, scientific, educational, cultural, social welfare, health, public affairs, fraternal, religious, veteran, hobby, athletic, labor, chamber of commerce, and Greek letter organizations. Two-thirds of the national associations in the original sample of 1,014 responded to the survey, but only about 40 percent (280) of these associations indicated that they had an interest in transnational affairs. And only slightly less than half of these (135) indicated that "in terms of the objectives, staff-time, and budget" of their organization, transnational affairs were of "prime importance" or of "strong, secondary importance" to them. These associations varied tremendously in size and type of membership, staff, and financial resources. But as Chapter 13 points out, some of the most powerful organizations of this kind have only a few members, small budgets, and little staff.

Four more specialized populations also were included in the survey. Two of these specialized populations were composed of **private voluntary organizations (PVOs).** One population consisted of 123 church-related Protestant, Catholic, and Jewish PVOs that conduct missions or other service activities overseas—for example, the Mennonite Central Committee, Salvation Army, Foreign Mission Board of the Southern Baptist Convention, Wycliffe Bible Translators International, Maryknoll Sisters, and United Jewish Appeal. The other population consisted of 165 PVOs that were registered with the U.S. Agency for International Development so they could distribute government food and other materials overseas—for example, the Cooperative for American Relief Everywhere (CARE), Hadassah, Meals for Millions/Freedom from Hunger Foundation, Volunteer Development Corps, and the World Rehabilitation Fund.[8] About 57 percent of the PVO leaders responded to the survey.

The other two populations were transnational corporations (TNCs). For the first, survey organizers contacted the chief international officers of 165 of the top 200 American firms in terms of total assets.[9] Among these firms were Exxon, General Electric, Dow Chemical, Lockheed, and Alcoa (Aluminum Company of America). For the second population, survey organizers approached the chief international officers of the top one hundred American banks with foreign deposits, as well as twenty-five regional banks with foreign loans in excess of $15 million in 1983.[10] The regional banks included Citizens and Southern Bank in Atlanta, First Tennessee Bank in Memphis, First Security Bank in Salt Lake City, First Wisconsin National Bank in Milwaukee, and Southwestern Bank in Houston. About 42 percent of the TNC executives in both categories responded.

Because little was known about the ubiquitous roles of NGO, PVO, and TNC officials in foreign policy making, the Transnational Project organizers used the eight functions carried out by the Imaginary Ideal Policy Making Machine (IIPMM) described in the introduction to Part III to describe their foreign policy activities. The eight IIPMM functions of scanning, interpreting, transmitting, storing, analyzing, deciding, implementing, and evaluating will be covered in the next several sections. Inasmuch as these functions were initially based on roles attributed to government foreign policy officials, project organizers have included government officials largely for comparative purposes.

Do NGO Leaders Make Foreign Policy?

Project organizers agreed to accept NGO, PVO, and TNC leaders as foreign policy makers only if the organizations they represent could meet three general criteria.

They are:

1. the entity must perform significant and continuing functions, significant in the sense that they have a continuing impact on interstate relations;

2. the entity has some degree of autonomy or freedom in its own decision making; and

3. the entity is considered significant by the foreign policy makers of other nation-states and is given significance in the formation of states' foreign policies.[11]

Are NGO Leaders as Involved as Government Officials in Foreign Policy Making?

This section reports how the respondents in the Transnational Project actually performed the eight basic IIPMM functions.[12] It shows that those who handle foreign affairs in NGOs are as engaged in each stage of the policy-making process as government foreign policy officials.

Scanning.   Government officials everywhere undertake the task of scanning. American satellites collect information on surface activities around the world, but much of the specific information available on foreign countries is collected by officials operating out of one of the some 250 U.S. embassies and missions or 500 military posts located throughout the world. Although each of these installations is different, a typical embassy will have attachés or counselors representing at least a dozen departments and agencies besides the Department of State. Chapter 10 describes more fully how agencies collect a wide range of intelligence.

Representatives of American NGOs are as conspicuous as U.S. government officials in foreign capitals, and they have an especially large presence, compared with government officials, in rural areas. They too have wide-ranging interests in information about the host country. A religious mission may be particularly interested in the growth of churches; an agricultural organization in the types and quality of soils; a bank in capital flows; and a business in local markets and distribution systems. Sometimes the information collected by NGOs may actually be much better than that available to the government. For example, in 1977 early U.S. action in Argentina was largely attributable to the human rights documentation provided by Amnesty International and other NGOs and not to information received through official government channels.[13]

Interpreting.   One of the primary tasks of American officials stationed abroad is to interpret the information available to them. Many of the U.S. officials stationed abroad report directly to their home departments or agencies in Washington, D.C., following the protocol established by their department or agency for collecting and interpreting. The U.S. ambassador seeks to give the Department of State an overall sense of any change underway in the surrounding society, and these reports may require opening up new avenues of inquiry.

Private U.S. activists and organizations also are interested in understanding events overseas. In view of their diverse audiences, however, they must work especially hard to frame transnational issues effectively. For example, in earlier years women's movements in the North and South had such different priorities that they were unable to work together effectively. Not until they began to talk about women's issues in terms of violence did the two movements finally converge in the 1980s.[14]

Transmitting.   Some of the information transmitted by government officials stationed overseas to their home department and agencies is likely to be distorted, either because it is extracted from its local context or because officials in the field and in Washington interpret things differently. At some points, bits of this information are compiled and redistributed. For example, the National Security Agency (NSA) in the Defense Department will translate the radio broadcasts collected worldwide on a daily basis, and the National Reconnaissance Office in the Defense Department will interpret satellite photographs. Some of this information will find its place in the periodic reports prepared by various government offices. For example, the CIA regularly prepares intelligence assessments and estimates.

Although the field officers and traveling representatives of American NGOs also transmit information to their home offices, they are more likely than government officials to share information with others outside their organization. Many of them belong to activist networks both in the host country and around the world. Therefore, what NGOs may lose as a result of less sophisticated methods of transmitting information to their national headquarters, they probably gain by sharing information more broadly both across borders and across organizations.

Storing. Most government organizations store the intelligence received from abroad—in both electronic and hard copy forms—in central files. Despite the sophisticated systems in place for storing intelligence, some government organizations have difficulty retrieving information either because the people most familiar with it have been rotated to other jobs, possibly abroad, or because retrieval technology quickly becomes obsolete. Moreover, with changes in administration some politically sensitive information may become conveniently "lost."

Private activists and NGOs are less likely than government departments and agencies to maintain sophisticated central files for storing information, but they are more likely than their government counterparts to have access to the institutional memory of their staffs. Moreover, the information in the nongovernment networks is more likely to remain in circulation. Indeed, one of the most important functions of those engaged in advocacy in the nongovernment world is to develop the information or "stories" obtained in the field and reframe or recode them so they have more impact on decision makers in other organizations, especially in the media and government.[15]

The difference between governmental and nongovernmental organizations in the foreign policy-making process is particularly salient at this point. Because government is formally responsible for so many things, it often stores information until events force it to act. By contrast, the missions and responsibilities of activists and NGOs are more narrowly defined, so they are constantly utilizing the information they have collected, looking for ways to frame their issue so they can get it on others' agenda.

Analyzing.   Once an issue has been raised, government officials begin to assess their preferences and analyze options in terms of those preferences. Ideally, each relevant government department or agency is given an opportunity to bring its considerations to bear on an issue. But as the fallout from intelligence-sharing snafus preceding the September 11, 2001 attacks indicates, this doesn't always happen. The evidence suggests that the Department of Defense and the White House routinely ignored competing intelligence provided by other departments.

NGO leaders also engage in ordering preferences and analyzing options for foreign affairs issues. Unlike in government, however, fewer people are engaged in the organization's effort, the preferences are often preordained, the range of options is narrower, and the actual process is less transparent. When differences over alternative strategies do arise, however, they can be as contentious as they are within government, in part because the people involved are so much closer to each other personally and may have a high personal stake in the issues.

Deciding.   In government, routine decisions are usually made at lower levels in accordance with standard operating procedures (SOPs). Non-routine decisions that involve different interests may move slowly through the decision process, giving all those with a legitimate stake in the outcome an opportunity to express their views, including NGOs. Many of these decisions also are likely to require congressional action in some form. Non-routine crisis decisions are usually made by the chief executive. Some lower-level officials and even outsiders may have input, but it may be restricted by time and other constraints.

NGOs also have procedures for foreign policy decision making, but theirs are likely to be much simpler than those developed within the government. The Transnational Project found that in 66 percent of cases (135) such non-routine decisions are made by either the top official with consent of a governing board or committee, the head of an international department with approval of a top official or governing board, or an advisory committee with the approval of the membership at an annual or biannual meeting. In 19 percent of cases the president, executive director, or other top official made such foreign policy decisions without the approval of a governing board or committee.

Implementing.   The government officials who make foreign policy decisions are likely to be far removed, in distance and employment level, from those who implement them, including the policies implemented by non-government leaders such as the private voluntary organizations working with the Agency for International Development. For that reason, it is especially important that government decisions be in written form and that all those concerned are aware of the SOPs for implementing various policies. In this way, higher-level officials can anticipate how lower-level officials will carry out foreign policy decisions.

In nongovernmental organizations the same dynamics are at work, but it is more likely that NGO leaders will either implement the policy themselves or at least be personally acquainted with those who do. NGO leaders also encounter the problem of dealing with subordinates over great distances, and they may be at a disadvantage because they are probably less likely than government officials to have good communications in the field.

Evaluating.   In government those who implement foreign policies are expected to monitor the effects of such policies, but special agencies also undertake this task. Within each department or agency, offices such as that of the inspector general of the Foreign Service evaluate performance. Congress also plays an important role in monitoring government actions and policies, as do the staffs of various congressional committees and the Government Accountability Office.

The activists associated with NGOs are in an especially good position to monitor government foreign policies of special interest to them. According to one observer, "Once a government has publicly committed itself to a principle—for example, in favor of human rights or democracy—networks can use these positions, and their command of information, to expose the distance between discourse and practice." [16] But NGOs often do not have the resources or the inclination to monitor their own activities overseas. As a result, the leaders of NGOs are frequently not in a position to correct problems that emerge in their overseas services until it is too late.

This comparison of foreign policy making by governmental and nongovernmental organizations highlights broad similarities as well as important differences among them. Two differences between the two kinds of organizations stand out: differences in authority and in internal constraints. The authority exercised by government officials is usually specified in U.S. statutes in accordance with the Constitution. In carrying out their duties, these officials are able to act within a fairly well-defined sphere of activity on behalf of the government. The leaders of NGOs usually derive their authority from the constitution, by-laws, or papers of incorporation of their respective organizations. Their prerogatives are therefore limited by their organization's scope.

This being said, government officials usually have others at the same or higher levels of authority looking over their shoulders. They also are constrained by the division of labor within the government and by the transparency of public service in a democracy. Although nongovernment leaders have more limited authority, they are somewhat less likely than government officials to be constrained by others within their organization, and their jobs are less transparent from the standpoint of coverage in the news media. For this reason, the government sometimes works through nongovernmental organizations.

Because government officials and NGO leaders perform similar functions, and at times work closely together, it is important to determine to what extent NGOs operate autonomously. This issue is addressed in the next section.

Do NGO Leaders Act Autonomously in Foreign Affairs?

To answer this question the Transnational Project asked both government officials and NGO leaders participating in the survey whether NGOs conduct their own foreign policies. Table 8.1 compares their responses. Over 73 percent of government officials agreed that American NGOs operating abroad frequently conduct their own foreign policies. Interestingly, only 48–54 percent of NGO leaders agreed. On the basis of the written comments of NGO leaders, however, it appears NGOs are more reluctant than government officials to admit that NGOs play an independent role in foreign affairs, because they do not want their overseas activities to be compared with government ones. After all, government officials represent a

Table 8.1. Government Officials and Leaders of NGOs, PVOs, and TNCs on Whether American NGOs Operating Abroad Frequently Conduct Their Own Foreign Policies[a]

	Government Officials	Leaders of NGOs	Leaders of PVOs	Transnational executives
Agree Strongly	**12.9**	**7.4**	**4.0**	**2.8**
Agree Somewhat	**60.3**	**45.9**	**49.7**	**45.3**
Not Sure	9.9	23.7	18.1	18.9
Disagree Somewhat	14.2	17.8	21.7	21.7
Disagree Strongly	2.7	5.2	11.3	11.3
N	373	135	149	106
No Response	4	11	12	17

a. Percentages are based on the values for *N* (total number of respondents) in each column and do not reflect those who did not respond.

Source: William O. Chittick, "State, Society, and Foreign Policy: The Treatment of Non-Government Actors in Foreign Policy Analysis" (paper presented at the annual meeting of the International Studies Association, Anaheim, California, March 27, 1986).

sovereign state, and its actions are not always well received by host countries. Most NGOs claim to represent values or interests that they share with target groups within other countries. In this sense they do not regard themselves as "foreign" in the same sense that a sovereign state would.

These results suggest that NGO leaders operate autonomously abroad, but these results do not specify under what conditions NGO leaders and government officials might work together. When asked whether they confer with the U.S. government when considering new activities abroad, only 4 percent of NGO leaders indicated that they seek formal U.S. government approval as a matter of course. Table 8.2 compares the responses of different types of NGO leaders. Only 11 to 16 percent of NGO leaders stated that they check with appropriate U.S. government agencies as a matter of form. Moreover, from 82 to 85 percent of the PVO and association leaders admitted that either they check with appropriate U.S. government agencies only if there might be a problem or they never ask the U.S. government unless required by law to do so. Two-thirds of business leaders gave similar responses.

But then how do NGO leaders decide whether the foreign policies they undertake are appropriate? After all, some of them carry out government policies, and others use government policy as a primary point of reference even if they do not contact the government directly. When asked what right American NGOs have to make independent decisions abroad, a majority, 54 and 58 percent, of association leaders and PVO leaders, respectively, indicated that their mandate came from their own organization—that is, their activities overseas fall within their normal sphere of operations at home. Another 29 and 30 percent, respectively, contended

Table 8.2. NGOs Conferring with U.S. Officials When Considering New Activities Abroad[a]

When your organization is considering new activities abroad, it:	Percentage of Association Leaders[b]	Percentage of PVO Leaders	Percentage of TNC Leaders
1. Seeks formal U.S. government approval	3.8	3.5	4.2
2. Checks with appropriate U.S. government agencies as a matter of form	11.3	14.6	16.0
3. Checks with appropriate U.S. government agencies only if there might be a problem	34.0	38.2	37.0
4. Never asks the U.S. government unless required by law to do so	50.9	43.8	28.6
5. Not applicable	—	—	14.3
N	53	119	144
No Response	4	4	17

a. Percentages are based on *N*, the total number of those who actually responded to this question.
b. Only 57 of the 161 association leaders who responded actually have offices overseas.

Source: William O. Chittick, "State, Society, and Foreign Policy: The Treatment of Non-Government Actors in Foreign Policy Analysis" (paper presented at annual meeting of the International Studies Association, Anaheim, California, March 27, 1986).

that their mandate arose from the fact that their actions are consistent with general global values and are acceptable to the host country. Table 8.3 compares the responses of association and PVO leaders.

Thus NGO leaders generally derive their authority to act internationally not from the U.S. government per se, but either from their understanding of the rights of organizations such as theirs to operate independently in American society or from the right of organizations such as theirs to pursue cosmopolitan values by means of transnational activities.

Are NGO Leaders Really Important Players in Foreign Affairs?

On the basis of the findings of the Transnational Project, it appears that a majority of nongovernmental organizations act autonomously abroad. But how important are NGO activities abroad?

The View of Government Officials.   To answer this question the Transnational Project asked government officials to rate on a seven-point scale, ranging from very important (7) to not important at all (1), the importance of both governmental and nongovernmental activities in building long-term relationships between peoples and nations. Table 8.4 sets out the responses of the government officials. By giving a rating of 4 or higher, roughly 90 percent of officials indicated that they thought both NGO leaders and government officials were important. Interestingly, over 50 percent

Table 8.3. Justifications for NGO Decision Making Abroad[a]

Many American NGOs enjoy considerable autonomy when they operate within the United States. What right do these same organizations have to make independent decisions abroad?	Percent of Association Leaders	Percent of PVO Leaders
American organizations are free to make their own decisions abroad as long as their activities . . . and are acceptable to the host country.		
1. Have explicit approval of the U.S. government	3.1	3.4
2. Are consistent with U.S. government policies	14.0	8.1
3. Fall within their normal sphere of operations at home	**54.3**	**58.1**
4. Are consistent with general global values	**28.7**	**30.4**
Total	100.0	100.0
N	129	148
No Response	17	13

a. Percentages are based on *N,* the total number of those who actually responded to this question.

Source: William O. Chittick, "State, Society, and Foreign Policy: The Treatment of Non-Government Actors in Foreign Policy Analysis" (paper presented at annual meeting of the International Studies Association, Anaheim, California, March 27, 1986).

of government officials thought that NGOs were as important or more important than the government in building these relationships (these are the percentages on or below the diagonal). Only 23 percent thought that the government was *more* important than NGOs in this regard.

What explains these results? Anyone who reads the newspaper everyday or listens regularly to the news on radio or television is well informed of the international activities of government officials, but the transnational activities of American nongovernmental organizations receive little media attention. News coverage, however, is not a reliable yardstick for measuring the importance of NGO cross-border activity. One possible answer is that NGO activity is so commonplace abroad that it is just not considered newsworthy. Another answer is that the media simply are incapable of covering the activities of all NGOs operating overseas. Still another answer is that the contributions of many individual NGOs are not very significant in themselves. It is only when these activities are aggregated that they become significant. Thus the largely unreported transnational relations of U.S. NGOs are akin to an iceberg, most of it invisible because it is underwater.

Complementary Roles.   Perhaps the real test is whether the government sometimes uses NGOs to implement its most important foreign policies.

Table 8.4. Responses of Government Officials on the Importance of Government and NGOs in Building Long-term Relationships between People and Nations

		Very Important 7	Importance of Government 6	5	4	Not Important at All 3–1	No Opinion 0	Percent
Very important	7	20.7	8.0	6.6	2.4	1.1	0	38.8
	6	5.6	8.8	8.5	5.3	2.9	0	31.1
	5	1.3	3.4	5.0	2.1	0.8	0	7.6
	4	0.5	1.6	2.4	2.6	1.3	0.3	8.7
	3–1	0.3	1.3	1.1	1.3	2.6	0	6.6
No opinion	0	0.3	0.3	0.3	0	0	1.3	2.2
Percent		28.7	23.4	23.9	13.7	8.7	1.6	100.0

(left axis label: Importance of NGOs)

Source: William O. Chittick, "State, Society, and Foreign Policy: The Treatment of Non-Government Actors in Foreign Policy Analysis" (paper presented at annual meeting of the International Studies Association, Anaheim, California, March 27, 1986).

As noted, the government often prefers to give economic assistance through PVOs. And since the 1980s the government also has relied heavily on NGOs to promote democracy abroad. Yet most NGOs zealously guard their independence from the government.

To better determine whether NGOs are any more or less important than government officials in a particular dimension of foreign policy and whether government officials regard NGOs as largely cooperative or competitive, the Transnational Project asked both government officials and NGO leaders what aspects of international and transnational affairs are of most interest to them. Because almost three times as many government officials as NGO leaders were answering this question, a rank-order correlation was used to determine similarities in their interests, and the results are shown in Table 8.5. The respondents were not limited to a certain number of responses, and most indicated about three different aspects of international affairs. The result was a weak positive correlation between the issue foci of the two kinds of organizations.[17] Assuming that the samples are truly representative of the populations concerned, this comparison suggests the

Table 8.5 Government and NGO Interest in Various Aspects of International and Transnational Relations

Aspect of International Relations	Dimension[a]	Government Officials (N = 377)		NGO Leaders (N = 133)	
		Frequency	Rank[b]	Frequency	Rank
Foreign relations generally	S	151	1[c]	21	**6.5**
Economic development	P	100	2	11	**14.5**
Specific country or regional issues	S	93	3	10	**16.5**
Military and security affairs	S	90	4	7	**20.5**
International trade	P	80	5	19	8.5
International comm. and cultural exchange	C	61	6	36	3.5
Human development	C	57	7	36	3.5
International business	C	51	8	17	10.5
Food production and agriculture	P	44	9.5	17	10.5
Human rights	C	44	9.5	19	8.5
Professional-technical exchange	C	41	**11**	37	**2**
International law and organization	S	40	12.5	14.5	
Foreign investment or loans	P	40	12.5	11	14.5
Natural resources and environment	C	33	14	10	16.5
Education	C	31	**15**	51	**1**
Ideology	C	29	17	6	23
Refugees	C	29	17	7	20.5
Community development	C	29	**17**	21	**6.5**
Nutrition and population	C	26	19	7	20.5
Medicine and public health	C	24	**20**	29	**5**
Social welfare	C	21	**21.5**	14	**13**
Disaster relief	C	21	21.5	9	18
Free labor movement	P	13	**23**	4	**24**
Religious activities	C	7	**24**	15	**12**

a. S = security, P = prosperity, and C = community.
b. Spearman's rank-order correlation or r_s = 0.29, where −1.0 is perfectly correlated and −1.0 is perfectly uncorrelated.
c. Rankings are shown in bold if there are differences of five or more ranks.

Source: William O. Chittick, "State, Society, and Foreign Policy: The Treatment of Non-Government Actors in Foreign Policy Analysis" (paper presented at annual meeting of the International Studies Association, Anaheim, California, March 27, 1986).

presence of broad similarities as well as some differences in the issues of interest to these two kinds of actors.

On the one hand, government officials appear to be somewhat more concerned than NGO leaders with security issues, especially military and security affairs and specific country or regional issues. After all, the government is responsible for forming, training, and commanding the country's military forces; NGOs largely play a support role, though some NGOs have a primary interest in military and security affairs. For example, the military-industrial complex includes defense contractors, security lobbies, and study groups that back the military. Some veterans and patriotic groups also have a primary interest in security affairs.

On the other hand, many NGO leaders seem to be somewhat more interested than government officials in certain community issues, particularly medicine and public health, education, religious activities, and community development. The government works closely with such groups, but it cannot replace them. For example, the government may facilitate the relationship between musicians, artists, and other professionals in this country and foreign audiences, but the Department of State does not control these groups. One exception may be in the area of promoting democracy, which will be discussed more fully in Chapter 14.

The complementarity of governmental and nongovernmental organizations is particularly striking in the domain of prosperity. Except for economic development, there does not seem to be much difference between government officials and NGO leaders on prosperity issues. In this area individual companies and banks are usually the primary actors, but government plays a crucial role in both regulating and supporting their overseas activities. When TNCs are doing well, they usually eschew government interference, but when they encounter obstacles they cannot deal with effectively by themselves, they seek government assistance.

Importance Illustrated.   This section focuses mainly on the relations between INGOs and IGOs because Chapters 13 and 14 deal with the role of NGOs in the domestic context.

Only Article 71 of the UN Charter requires a principal organization of the United Nations, the Economic and Social Council (ECOSOC), to establish consultative relationships with NGOs. Although other organizations in the UN family have at some point made their own formal or informal arrangements to consult INGOs and NGOs, most have initially patterned their consultative relationships after those developed by ECOSOC. In the 1990s about 1,500 INGOs had official consultative status with ECOSOC.[18] The importance of INGOs is apparent in all eight stages of policy making at the global level.

The INGO contribution to scanning is best illustrated by the early history of the United Nations Education, Scientific, and Cultural Organization (UNESCO). Its board was initially composed of outstanding persons who represented societies rather than governments. The first director-general of UNESCO, British biologist and author Julian Huxley, personally played a key role in creating some INGOs, such as the International Theatre Institute and the International Council of Museums, because he realized that the broad purposes of UNESCO could not be realized without their help. Eventually though, governments became so disenchanted with the independent spirit of UNESCO delegates that the governments of UNESCO's member states changed the constitution of that organization so that its delegates would better represent governments.[19] Nevertheless, INGOs such as the International Congress of Scientific Unions (ICSU) continue to provide the scientific backing required to deal with many factual issues. For example, ICSU was instrumental in developing the Scientific Committee on Problems of the Environment (SCOPE) that provided much of the scientific data for both the Stockholm Conference in 1972 and the Earth Summit in 1992.

IGOs such as the Commission on Human Rights (CHR) and the Commission on the Status of Women (CSW) regularly depend on INGOs to interpret the needs of special groups such as women and children in the field of human rights. Initially, the CSW focused almost exclusively on the political and legal rights of women in the public sphere. It was INGOs that tied the rights of women to the important issues of education and development and recognized "that women are more likely to experience violations in the private sphere, which are perpetrated by private individuals rather than the state."[20] And it was INGOs such as Save the Children Fund that recognized that the nutrition standards initially set for refugees were not adequate for children, who made up almost half of the refugees that UNHCR deals with.[21]

Some INGOs possess fast and reliable ways of transmitting sensitive information. For example, Amnesty International (AI) has a significant research staff in London as well as over eight thousand adoption groups in seventy countries. AI's central research staff can more than match those available to the relevant IGOs such as the UNHCR. Indeed, the director of the UN Center for Human Rights has acknowledged that "85 percent of our information came from NGOs."[22]

In addition to storing information, INGOs play a crucial role in **agenda setting** for IGOs. For example, in 1991, when preparations had just begun for the 1993 UN World Conference on Human Rights, AI decided to propose the establishment of a UN Office of the High Commissioner for Human Rights. Although this idea had been considered before, it was not one of the ideas being promoted for the 1993 conference. Yet AI pushed the proposal, and despite the fact that INGOs were prevented from participating in drafting the final document, AI succeeded not only in having the proposal included in the document but also in obtaining its acceptance at the conference in Vienna.[23]

Agenda setting by INGOs is even more dramatically illustrated by their successful attempts to convince the World Bank to consult them, even though the Bank has no provision in its charter that it must consult with INGOs. Beginning in the mid-1970s, the Bank organized a specialist workshop involving INGOs. Some progress was made in the 1980s in making the Bank more responsive to the environmental concerns of mainline groups, such as the World Council of Churches. But in the 1990s more radical groups such as the Sierra Club sought the end of World Bank activities altogether. As a result, the World Bank has become more responsive to some of the concerns of INGOs such as "sustainable development," "popular participation," and "people's ownership" and remains resistant to the demands of other INGOs. [24]

INGOs also contribute substantially to the analysis of global problems. For example, in 1983 the INGOs working on what was to become the Convention on the Rights of the Child decided to hold an "[I]NGO consultation." Because the participants in the consultation had more professional experience working with children than the government members of the official Working Group established by the UNHCR's Commission on Human Rights to draft the convention, INGO participants were able to bring new perspectives and insights to bear on those drafting the document, including the controversial provision to bar young children from being recruited into armed forces.[25]

Although much of the influence of INGOs occurs in lower-level working groups and subcommissions of IGOs, INGOs do influence the final decisions of IGOs. For example, in the 1980s the UNHCR was responsible for the legal and political rights of refugees and the World Food Programme was responsible for transporting food to the port of the country in which the refugees were located, but no IGO was deemed responsible for actually feeding the refugees and looking after their other needs. As INGOs are wont to point out, "It is not possible to protect a dead refugee." It was only at the insistence of Save the Children Fund and other INGOs that the UNHCR finally "accepted responsibility for meeting nutrition standards, monitoring food storage and distribution, and monitoring the occurrence of illnesses that result from malnutrition." [26]

INGOs also play a key role in implementing many of the decisions made by IGOs. For example, the Commission on Human Rights has several procedures for investigating accusations that human rights have been violated, including a public procedure for investigating country situations, a parallel confidential procedure, and a mechanism for investigating classes of abuses such as racism and violence against women. Amnesty International maintains offices in New York and Genève for the purpose of supplying current information to the commission, its special rapporteurs, and its various treaty-monitoring bodies. Without this kind of assistance from AI, the commission could not do its job.

Finally, INGOs provide essential feedback to intergovernmental organizations. Although the United Nations has some regional and even local UN Development Programme (UNDP) offices, the UN family of organizations is largely dependent on governments and INGOs to keep it informed and monitors the effects of its policies abroad. For example, the UNDP, the Food and Agriculture Organization (FAO), and the World Bank in conjunction with the World Resources Institute asked the International Tropical Timber Organization (ITTO), which is composed of private producers and consumers of tropical timber, to oversee its Tropical Forestry Action Plan.[27]

Nongovernmental organizations are then involved in every aspect of foreign policy. They generally act autonomously, although they can and do sometimes work closely with government, and they are important, although their importance varies depending on the timing and the nature of the foreign policy issue.

Having described a comprehensive set of foreign policy actors, including NGOs, INGOs and IGOs as well as governments of states, it is time to show how foreign policy analysts attempt to explain foreign policy making with reference to one or more of these actors. Each approach highlights a different set of actors and assumes that these actors play a decisive role in the foreign policy process. None of these approaches denies the possibility that one or more of the other approaches could be operating at the same time.

Approaches to Studying Foreign Policy Making

Because a variety of actors are engaged in foreign policy making, it is not surprising that students of foreign policy employ many different approaches in their analysis. Indeed, in this section the discussion is organized by the link between actors and approaches. Some approaches focus on the government as a unitary actor; others emphasize the many different organizations that compose the government; and still others spotlight the people who come together to make interdepartmental decisions. And then there are approaches that emphasize society as a whole, organizations that make up society, or key persons in society.

This section provides an overview of the seven different approaches by identifying the primary unit of analysis, the basic organizing concepts, and the main inference pattern employed by each approach, as set out in Table 8.6. The approaches are: rational actor model, institutionalism, organizational behavior model, **governmental politics model, majoritarianism, pluralism,** and **elitism**. Additional evidence of the explanatory power of these approaches is provided in later chapters.

In introducing these approaches, most foreign policy analysts begin with the president and the president's advisers and then include increasingly wider sets of participants. The pyramid shown in Figure 8.2 with government at the top and society at the bottom best represents this perspective. Others invert this pyramid and conceive of these foreign policy actors as forming a **funnel of causality** with the general public and society at the top and government officials at the bottom.

Although arguments can be made for both the top-down and bottom-up approaches, it is important to recognize that the flow of influence be-

Table 8.6 Approaches to Explaining Foreign Policy Outputs

	Unit of Analysis	Organizing Concepts	Inference Pattern	Evidence
Rational actor model	Government as a unified actor, representing the state	Preferences, alternatives, consequences, and maximizing choice	If x is chosen, it must be the maximizing means to a given end.	Chapters 5–7
Institutionalism	Characteristics of government as a whole	Separation of power, checks and balances, electoral systems, etc.	If x occurs, it was determined by structural features of the government.	Chapter 9
Organizational behavior model	Organizations within the executive branch	Parochial goals, fractionated power, SOPs, and action-channels	If x is chosen at t_2, then x must have occurred in similar circumstances at t_1.	Chapter 10
Governmental politics model	Individuals in key positions in government	Personality, group dynamics, political bargaining, and compromises	If x is chosen, then x is the result of infighting among these individuals.	Chapter 11
Majoritarianism	Aggregate and collective opinions in society	Elections, public opinion, and political culture	If x is chosen, then x must reflect an effective majority.	Chapter 12
Pluralism	Formal and informal organizations in society	Pressure groups, social movements, struggle for power	If x is chosen, then x must be favored by a coalition of the strongest groups.	Chapter 13
Elitism	Social and power elites in society	Upper social classes, power elites	If x is chosen, then x must be favored by a powerful elite.	Chapter 14

tween these participants is not one-way. Rather, actors are engaged in a continuous, simultaneous, interactive process. This section begins by looking at the government as a whole and then focuses on successively smaller units of analysis within the government. It then looks at society as a whole and then successively smaller units of analysis in society.

Rational Actor Model

In Parts I and II of this book foreign policy actions were explained largely in terms of the **rational actor model.** The basic unit of analysis in this approach is that the state is represented by the government or by officials representing the government. This state actor is supposed to be guided by the national interest—that is, the interest of all the people represented by the state. The national interest is assumed to value security above all other values, because other values cannot be realized unless the state is secure. These security values in turn are determined by reference to the circumstances in which the state finds itself.

In short, this approach assumes that the state is seeking to maximize an accepted order of preference. It further assumes that the alternative courses of action available to the state are defined by the internal and external circumstances in which the state finds itself, and that it is possible for the state to determine the likely consequences of its taking each of these actions under these circumstances. These consequences are assessed to determine which set of them best matches the preferences of the state.

The final component is rational choice. If the goal is to maximize security in a given situation, then foreign policy making consists largely of a rational analysis of the situation. The rational actor model assumes that the state will choose that method likely to maximize its interests in terms of security at the lowest cost.

The problem with this approach is that it assumes that there is a national interest that represents the preferences of a diverse set of actors, that these actors correctly perceive their environment, that they can identify all alternative courses of action, that they have a theory that allows them to predict the consequences of implementing each of these courses of action, and, finally, that there is some agreement on which of these actions will maximize all of their values at minimum cost. Because many scholars question the ability of states and government officials to make all these calculations, they argue that at best these actors pursue a "bounded rationality."

Institutionalism

Institutionalism reflects the belief that the choices of a society are influenced by how that society is organized. This approach is evident in some of the earliest texts such as the Bible, in which separate chapters deal with Israel under judges and kings. This approach became particularly important during the Enlightenment when a new breed of political theorists looked closely at differences in how states were constituted. Even today, whether a state is democratic or undemocratic, or whether it features a free market or a command market, matters greatly.

Historical institutionalism emphasizes a wide range of government institutions, including separation of powers, federalism, checks and balances, majority elections in single-member districts, and judicial review. Neoinstitutionalism combines the influence of these institutional variables with that of variables at the individual and societal level, such as individual and mass identities and perceptions. The argument is essentially that these institutions influence the motivations of people within these structures.

Fully aware of the kinds of structures employed by a government as well as the people involved, institutionalists contend that it is possible to predict the behavior of the people and organizations within that structure—that is, anyone who knows how a government is structured can predict some of the outputs of that government. For example, institutionalists might argue that democratic governments do not go to war with other democratic governments.

But institutionalists are not just preoccupied with the essential characteristics of a government; they also may be interested in the internal structuring of organizations within that government. For example, they may be fascinated by the kinds of specialists employed by an organization, by the way in which those specialists are organized, and by the specific efforts undertaken to coordinate their actions.

Organizational Behavior Model

The **organizational behavior model** focuses on the internal structures of specific organizations. It recognizes that the government is composed of a large number of functional organizations—for example, the Department of State, Department of Defense, and CIA. These organizations are important because they produce most foreign policy outputs.

But these organizations are not all-powerful; they have the power only to do particular things. Each organization hires specialists who are educated and trained to perform certain tasks. Each develops a culture that is particularly suited to addressing the problems assigned to it. Its specialists are organized so that they are proficient at doing certain things. By following standard operating procedures, the specialists are able to produce foreign policy outputs on a timely basis.

Because such organizations are structured to handle certain problems according to an established routine, it is possible to predict the foreign policy outputs of such organizations by recognizing which routine they are following. Thus it is assumed that if an organization produced a given policy at one time, then that same organization will also pursue the same foreign policy at a subsequent time, if the circumstances are similar.

This form of explanation may work well when discrete organizations are left alone to deal with a particular foreign policy problem, but it will not work very well if other organizations become involved or if the problem is given to some interdepartmental committee for a decision. Because the most important foreign policy decisions usually involve more than one department, it is useful to look more closely at the way in which interdepartmental decisions are made at the higher levels of government.

Governmental Politics Model

When foreign policy decisions cannot be made at lower levels in an organization, they are transferred to higher levels, where they are subject to the influence of the executives who operate at the interdepartmental level. These men and women are usually involved in a group decision process. Some of these decision groups, such as the National Security Council, are formally established by statute; others are quite informal, having been created on an ad hoc basis to deal with an issue that had not been anticipated such as President Johnson's Tuesday lunch group that made U.S. Vietnam policy.

Because members of the interdepartmental groups have more latitude in making decisions than the people at lower levels, the personalities of the group members sometimes become as important as the positions they occupy in determining their views on issues. As a result, the collective decisions of these groups are best understood as a compromise among particular individuals in key positions. Of course, the officials engaged in decision groups are subject to many outside political influences, including public opinion and pressure groups.

Majoritarianism

In a democracy, elections are the final arbiters in foreign policy making. If the principal leaders of a government do not represent a majority of the electorate, they eventually will be removed from office. For this reason, both elected officials and those appointed by them are particularly sensitive to the influence of public majorities.

Because an election usually determines who will make foreign policy decisions rather than what decisions will be made, elected officials are especially heedful of public opinion. If the government makes an important foreign policy decision, the president and other officials most likely feel either that a majority of the public supports that decision or that a majority of the public will eventually do so. In fact, presidents invariably claim that their foreign policies have majority support.

However, public indifference to many foreign policy issues suggests that what may really be important is not the active support of a majority of the public, but rather the support of the most powerful groups within the public that take an interest in the particular foreign policy under consideration. The focus of attention therefore shifts from the public at large to those organized interests in society that do pay attention to foreign policy.

Pluralism

Pluralism assumes that society is divided into organized groups, each of which represents a different set of values and interests. Because these nongovernmental organizations are responsible for representing their members' values and interests in both foreign and domestic affairs, foreign policy can be understood in terms of the struggle for power among these organizations.

Indeed, many of these organizations hire expert staffs for the express purpose of bringing pressure to bear on both the public at large and the government to accept their preferred foreign policies. Some organizations may even be able to produce a mass movement that the government can ignore only at its own peril. But usually these organizations must compete with other groups that have quite different views. They often seek private hearings with officials to ensure that the government understands their foreign policy perspective.

If a particular foreign policy is adopted, the policy is presumed to be the result of pressures exerted by competing groups in society. The foreign policy of the government may reflect either the views of a dominant group or the views of a dominant coalition of such groups.

Often, however, there is at least a suspicion that the foreign policy of the state represents neither a majority of the public nor a majority of those groups that are particularly interested in it. Indeed, some suspect that the state's foreign policy really represents the values and interests of a powerful elite that does not represent the public at all.

Elitism

In most societies, even democratic ones, a powerful minority—an elite—controls a majority of society's most valued resources. If this elite controls the most fungible assets of society such as money or oil, it may also control the state's foreign policy.

Although some people claim that particular ethnic or religious groups control U.S. foreign policy, the most common assertion is that a moneyed elite is in control because, after all, the United States is a capitalist society. The latter claim is based on the idea that the upper social classes control both the corporate and public interest sectors of American society. Although many of the people in these upper social classes have no particular interest in foreign policy, the contention is that there is a tightly organized network of members of these classes that actually governs on behalf of these classes as a whole. Thus if the United States pursues a given foreign policy, it is assumed that this policy uniquely serves the interests of this governing class. Because neither the governing class nor the larger upper social classes it represents has the voting power to control the government in a democracy, it must convince the people at large that its foreign policies serve the interests of the nation as a whole—all of which brings this discussion back to the rational actor model. That model posits that the foreign policies of the state are not the work of bureaucrats, elected officials, pressure group leaders, or a few carefully positioned members of an elite, but rather of a unified state and the national interest.

Conclusion

Because this book has already devoted considerable space to rational explanations of foreign policy, especially in Chapters 5 through 7, other approaches will be highlighted in the remainder of the chapters in Part III. (The latter often include rational components, but they do not provide any assurance that the foreign policy selected will represent the best choice under the circumstances.) Chapter 9 considers the institutional approach, and especially whether American institutions, such as the electoral system and the separation of powers at the federal level, so divide the government that the state cannot pursue its national interests. Chapter 10 examines the organizational behavior model and raises the question of whether the large departments of the government provide the quality ingredients needed to produce an effective foreign policy. Chapter 11, devoted to the governmental politics model, explores the extent to which personality and position introduce administrative and psychological factors that prevent the state from making rational decisions.

Chapters 12 through 14 examine societal approaches to explaining foreign policy. Chapter 12, on majoritarianism, considers what measures of public opinion are most consistent with a realization of the national interest and how to discriminate between public opinion and political culture. Chapter 13, devoted to pluralism, looks at the extent to which foreign policy is dictated by organized interests and values, not the national interest. Finally, Chapter 14, on elitism, explores the evidence that a governing class actually makes foreign policy in its own interest rather than the national interest.

Key Concepts

agenda setting   300
analyzing   278
boomerang strategy   287
deciding   278
elitism   302
evaluating   279
funnel of causality   302
governmental politics model   302
implementing   278
institutionalism   304
interpreting   278
majoritarianism   302

organizational behavior
   model   305
pluralism   302
private voluntary organizations
   (PVOs)   288
rational actor model   303
scanning   278
storing   278
track one diplomacy   283
track two diplomacy   286
transmitting   278

Suggested Readings

1. Chittick, William O. *The Group Perspective in Foreign Policy: A Report on U.S. World Affairs Oeganizations (NGOs)*. University of Georgia Library, 1977.

2. DeMars, William E. *NGOs and Transnational Networks: Wild Cards in World Politics.* London: Pluto Press, 2005.

3. Drezner, Daniel W., ed. *Locating the Proper Authorities: The Interaction of Domestic and International Institutions.* Ann Arbor: University of Michigan Press, 2003.

4. Keck, Margaret E. and Sikkink, Kathryn. *Activists Beyond Borders: Advocacy Networks in International Politics.* Ithaca: Cornell University Press, 1998.

5. Ronit, Karsten and Volker Schneider, eds. *Private Organizations in Global Politics.* London: Routledge, 2000.

6. Willetts, Peter, ed. *"The Conscience of the World": The Influence of Non-Government Organizations in the UN System.* London: Hurst and Co., 1996.

CHAPTER 9

Institutionalism:
Congress and the Executive

The framers of the U.S. Constitution built institutions capable of rendering internal checks and balances so that no simple majority could dominate the U.S. government. However, political parties soon emerged whose purpose was in part to provide unity. When one party controls all of the major institutions of government, it is the responsibility of the opposition party to find ways to reassert these checks and balances. In the picture above Senate Minority Leader Harry Reid (D-Nev.), center, flanked by Sen. Charles Schumer (D-N.Y.), left, and Sen. Richard Durbin (D-Ill.), meets with reporters on Capitol Hill after a closed-door Senate session on November 1, 2005. Democrats forced the Republican-controlled Senate into an unusual closed session, saying that Republicans had ignored their pleas for the Senate to question the intelligence that President Bush used in the run-up to the war in Iraq.

T HE FIRST APPROACH to be considered in Part III is institutionalism, because it pervades all of the other approaches to be covered. Institutions are complex sets of rules designed by human beings to guide the choices of current as well as successor generations. These rules assume many different forms, but the most fundamental rules for making foreign policy in the United States are found in the U.S. Constitution—the rules governing the relationship between Congress and the president in foreign affairs.

Institutionalism and Its Limits

Institutionalism is central to the American system of government because the founders wanted a government of laws, not men. They realized that ordinary people in the new government would be asked to make foreign policies under unusual circumstances, so they fashioned institutions that would lead these people to follow rules that incorporated what they regarded as sound principles of community, security, and prosperity. For example, they gave Congress the power to declare war because they thought that only a body representing the people should make such a decision. Although the framers established structures to constrain government officials, this chapter emphasizes individual rules because people can always choose whether or not to follow such rules.[1]

Institutions and Institutionalism

Rules are created by the continual and repeated interaction of people in society. Thus the act of one person, if accepted by another and subsequently practiced by them and others, eventually becomes a rule. In fact, any practice or convention may become a rule if enough people follow it. Although people are free to ignore rules, agents generally choose to follow them because they believe that by following the rules they are more likely to reach their intended goals.

This chapter is concerned with three different kinds of rules: practices, norms, and laws. These rules may be combined in various ways, but it is assumed for the purpose of explication that certain kinds of rules predominate in particular institutions, so that the kind of rules directly affects the character of the institution. Thus an institution based on **practices** would be one in which people adhere to rules because not doing so would violate cause and effect in the physical world. For example, the balance of power is an institution in international relations that is based on the "world of observational facts."[2] If an agent of the state allows another country to gain preponderant power and become a hegemon, the first state can expect to suffer dire consequences. In this sense, the balance of power is an institution based in actual practice.

Norms are rules that establish a standard of what people believe *should* be done. This normative (or ethical) world is "a world of intention and

meaning." [3] For example, a capitalist market is not based on actual physical laws; rather, it is based on rules that are normative in character. A
market cannot ensure that the prices of goods will enhance efficiency unless the prices of these goods are fair. The norm of fairness is not easy to
define, but generally one knows what it is not. For example, the price of
goods being dumped on the market is not fair—that is, the goods are being
sold for less than the cost of producing them and have dire effects on the
producers of similar goods. Likewise, the price of a commodity in the international market is not fair if a cartel can arbitrarily set the price. Thus a
free market is an institution presumably based on the norm of fairness;
the participating states promise to abide by certain rules. One of the problems with international trade is that the world has, at least until now, not
had a very good or reliable mechanism for determining when a state or
states have violated this norm of fairness.

An institution is considered legal if the peoples or states involved have
formally adopted and codified the rules on which it is based. These **laws**
embrace the constitutions, charters, and statutes of organizations within
states as well as treaties among states. Sometimes the distinction between
norms and laws is obscure. For example, the Universal Declaration of
Human Rights is a set of norms, whereas the International Covenant on
Civil and Political Rights and the International Covenant on Economic,
Social, and Cultural Rights are treaties that have been ratified by states,
giving them the force of law. Although the International Court of Justice
and other national and international courts do not always have the power
to enforce these international laws, they are generally supported because
most states have formally adopted them.

These practices, norms, and laws exist at every level of society, but they
are particularly well developed in complex societies.[4] In the case of the
new American republic the framers wanted an open foreign policy-
making process, and so they established a procedure that required elected
officials in several branches of government to cooperate on key foreign
policy decisions. Because these officials were to be chosen by majorities or
pluralities in various states and districts, they could be expected to have
different incentives. Yet under this system, separate institutions staffed by
officials with different priorities and interests were expected to arrive at
suitable compromises.

Thus the institutions of American government and society were inserted between the preferences of individual citizens and the domestic
and foreign policies of the country in order to temper those policies. By
identifying the effects of various institutions on the motivations of officials, this chapter will show these rules are transformed into predilections
for various foreign policies. Although officials may be quite conscious of
these institutional influences on their foreign policy stances, they need
not be.

In this context it may be useful to distinguish between the old institutionalism and the new institutionalism. The **old institutionalism** emphasizes the "vested interests" of those who hold particular positions in government.[5] For example, the secretary of state usually wants to give diplomacy a chance because the State Department conducts diplomacy. Thus the secretary of state has a vested interest in diplomacy because the secretary controls it. The **new institutionalism** stresses the power of common understandings that certain actions are more appropriate than others for officials in particular positions.[6] For example, officials in the State Department may emphasize negotiations because they believe that mutual acceptance is the only real solution to international conflicts of interest. By emphasizing the effects of socialization, the new institutionalism emphasizes the importance of values as well as interests in shaping foreign policies.

This emphasis on the immediate context in which officials make foreign policy enables institutionalists to explain much of the continuity of foreign policy. It shows how different officials even under varying circumstances are likely to make the same decisions. However, these institutional factors are not as adept at explaining changes in foreign policy unless it can be shown that the institutions also changed. Some of these limits are examined in the next section.

The Limits of Institutionalism

Two groups tend to dismiss the importance of institutions: rationalists and political behavioralists. Rationalists generally assume that the preferences of foreign policy makers are a given, because these preferences can be deduced from the circumstances that those officials face in the real world. For example, one kind of rationalist, political realists, generally discounts the importance of institutions, arguing that it does not really matter how an official was elected or even what office that official happens to hold because all officials will give priority to the immediate security interests of their country regardless of those institutional influences. Thus events account for shifts in foreign policy that cannot be explained by institutional factors.

Political behavioralists believe it is more appropriate to focus on the observable behaviors of officials than institutional factors, because they favor universal explanations over country-specific ones. For example, behavioralists would rather show that individuals with particular attributes, such as gender or age, behave in a certain way rather than demonstrate that this behavior is the result of holding the office of president. They too discount institutional explanations, because they cannot account for differences in foreign policy when these structures do not change.

Although both rationalists and behavioralists make valid points, institutionalism is emphasized in this and subsequent chapters because institutional rules have independent effects on foreign policy decisions. Moreover, these rules often perform different functions in the foreign policy process. Some rules are designed to enhance the acceptability of foreign policies by providing for better coordination; other rules, the efficiency of foreign policies by providing for greater specialization; and still other rules, the effectiveness of foreign policies by providing for greater control. Thus the next three chapters emphasize different sorts of rules: Chapter 9 emphasizes coordination; Chapter 10, specialization; and Chapter 11, control.

As rationalists note, the coordination of foreign policy within the U.S. government is greatly affected by outside forces. Thus the foreign policy analyst needs to distinguish between crisis, strategic, and regular foreign policies.[7] **Crisis foreign policies** are those in which there is little or no time to deal with a serious threat, such as the September 11, 2001 attacks on New York and Washington.[8] **Strategic foreign policies** are those in which there is a serious threat but foreign policy actors need to take time to address it in part because of the need to mobilize new resources to deal with the threat. For example, it will take some time to decide how to deal with the proliferation of nuclear weapons in Iran and North Korea.[9] **Regular foreign policies** are those in which the threats and opportunities facing society are less compelling, and therefore much or little time may be devoted to them.[10]

The distinctions between these three kinds of foreign policy are very important because the rules governing the relationship between Congress and the president change depending on what practices, norms, and laws are considered appropriate for each type of foreign policy. The distinction between a crisis and a strategic foreign policy became particularly controversial with respect to the Iraq War in 2003. The George W. Bush administration considered the need to change the regime in Iraq as a crisis because they argued that there were direct links between al Qaeda and Iraq and that Iraq's reconstituted WMD would soon be shared with al Qaeda. Opponents argued at the time, however, that these links had not been proven and that the Bush administration was misusing the available intelligence (if not manufacturing it) to magnify both the threat and its urgency.[11] Congress largely bought the idea that Iraq represented a crisis; the UN Security Council did not.

The coordination of these three kinds of foreign policies is discussed separately in this chapter because the differences between them significantly affect how these different kinds of foreign policy are made. The institutions most relevant to each kind of foreign policy will be introduced first.

The U.S. Constitution and Crisis Foreign Policies

The United States is governed under one of the oldest written constitutions in the world. Its longevity is a testament both to the authority of the Constitution in American political culture and the value attached to the specific institutions it set out. Even today institutionalists study the mechanics of the U.S. government to determine how these rules shape political behavior. If foreign policy actors behave appropriately, and especially if they behave inappropriately, institutionalists are usually prompted to ask what rules, norms, or laws led to this behavior. For example, these concerns led to the creation of the special commission to study the attacks of September 11, 2001.[12]

The Formal Institutions of Government

The framers fashioned a Constitution that employed two devices: (1) checks and balances, which had been employed in the mixed constitutions of ancient Greece, and (2) a more modern device, separation of powers, which had evolved in the English constitution. But whereas the English began with a mixed constitution and gradually developed separate powers, the Americans started with the separation of powers and then grafted checks and balances onto it.[13]

Separation of Powers.   Because the citizens of the new American republic feared both the tyranny of the many and the tyranny of the few, they devised institutions with **separate powers** to protect themselves from their own government. They began by separating the new federal government from the governments of the states (the thirteen former colonies).[14] This federal principle directly contradicted the indivisibility of sovereignty under the absolutist state system. Although the framers established and strengthened the federal government in part to ensure unity in the foreign policy of the United States, the citizens of individual states as well as the states themselves continued to engage in a wide variety of foreign activities.

The framers then separated the three functions of government and assigned each to a different branch of the federal government. The legislative power was granted to Congress in Article I of the Constitution; the executive power to the president in Article II; and the judicial power to a Supreme Court in Article III. Because the executive and judicial functions depend on the legislative function, the legislature generally takes precedence over the executive and judicial branches of government in most countries. For that reason, the chief executive is chosen by the legislature in parliamentary systems of government. But because the framers feared the ascendancy of the legislative branch of government, they separated the legislative and executive branches by means of an electoral system that made them even more independent of one another. That is why America has a presidential system of government.

Electoral System.   In the American presidential system pluralities or majorities in single-member districts and states elect members of the House and the Senate respectively.[15] The president is elected by an Electoral College, which is composed of electors chosen by states according to their total number of senators and representatives. The winner of the presidential contest must receive an absolute majority—268 votes—of the total number of electoral votes, 535. If no one receives a majority, the House of Representatives selects the president. In that case, each state delegation in the House receives one vote, and a majority of states is required for election.

This complicated system ensures that House members, senators, and the president represent different constituencies. Representatives in the lower house represent smaller districts and therefore more diverse local interests; senators represent states as a whole and therefore more aggregated interests; and the president, who must have the support of either a majority of the Electoral College or a majority of states in the House of Representatives, represents something approaching the national interest.

These institutional differences shape the beliefs of those who hold these positions. For example, the Chicago Council elite foreign policy survey of 1998[16] found that members of the House of Representatives were more likely than other elites to favor MCA foreign policy choices: unilateral, noncoercive, and reactive; members of the Senate to adopt MCA foreign policies: unilateral, coercive, and reactive; and political appointees in the executive branch to favor MCA foreign policies: multilateral, coercive, and proactive.[17] These differences in foreign policy preferences, which are illustrated in Table 9.1, support the separation of powers. The checks and

Table 9.1. Dimensions of Foreign Policy: Policy Stances of Government Officials in the Executive and Legislative Branches

	Multilateral		Unilateral	
	Coercive	Noncoercive	Noncoercive	Coercive
Proactive	Executive political appointees			
Reactive			Members of the House of Representatives	Members of the Senate

Note: The table is based on a regression analysis of individual factor scores on the foreign policy goal questions used in the 1998 CCFR elite survey. These three groups of officeholders were compared with seven other elites: business, education, interest group, labor, media, religious, and think tank leaders. The analysis was conducted by the author.

Political appointees in the executive are generally more multilateral than House and Senate members because they represent a broader constituency and more proactive because they are more positive about current government policies. Executive appointees and even members of the Senate are more coercive than members of the House because the latter have two-year terms and are closer to the people.

balances between the branches of government provoke specific conflicts between them, which can force them to arrive at consensus policies.

Checks and Balances.   Although each branch of government is given a distinctive function, it cannot fully execute that function without the assistance of other branches. Thus the power of the legislature to pass laws is checked by the right of the president to veto such legislation. To overturn a veto, both houses must muster a two-thirds vote—something that happens infrequently. Similarly, the right of the president to negotiate treaties and to appoint and receive ambassadors is balanced by the requirement that the Senate consent to treaties and confirm appointments. Even the power to make war is **balanced** in the Constitution. The president is acknowledged to be commander in chief of the nation's armed forces, but only Congress has the constitutional power to declare war.

The Constitution is less explicit about the powers of the judicial branch of the government. But one of the most important duties of the Supreme Court and various inferior courts is to interpret the Constitution and other laws of the land. These courts are specifically charged with resolving disputes involving the constitutional interpretation of the relationship between the federal government and the several state governments as well as the relationship between the congressional and the executive branches of government. The courts also have the responsibility for interpreting the relationship specified in the Constitution between these government institutions and ordinary citizens.

Whereas the separation of powers appears to assume that the branches of the federal government are highly specialized and largely autonomous, the checks and balances incorporated into the Constitution appear to assume "interaction between necessarily homogeneous and coequal entities." [18] This combination seems to produce three advantages: (1) the executive is more stable because it is not responsible to the legislature; (2) the executive is more democratic because the president is elected directly by the people; and (3) the government as a whole is more limited because power is thoroughly divided among its branches. [19] But there also are some disadvantages. For one thing, the system is prone to deadlock when the president and Congress are politically divided on foreign policy issues. For another, the system is subject, at least temporarily, to rigidity whenever the president loses the confidence of the legislature. And finally, the system generally encourages officials to view politics as a zero-sum game, because those who are chosen in plurality elections from single-member districts represent only part of the people in these districts. [20]

The next section further examines how the **presidential system** works by describing the relationships that have evolved among the three branches of the federal government, and especially the one between Congress and the president.

Congress, the President, and Foreign Policy

Constitutional scholars frequently note that the U.S. Constitution was an open invitation for struggle between the president and Congress over foreign policy.[21] And indeed, the contest between these two branches has persisted over the years. The country's earliest leaders—George Washington, Alexander Hamilton, Thomas Jefferson, and James Madison—had very different ideas about the relationship between the president and Congress. For example, when President Jefferson became aware that France might be willing to sell the Louisiana Territory, he was uncertain how to proceed. As a strict constructionist of the Constitution, he recognized that there was no provision in that document for making such a purchase. Despite his misgivings, he eventually decided to go ahead with the purchase, knowing that Congress or the courts might overturn his action.[22]

From Washington to World War II: 1789–1944.   Other strong presidents also extended the implied powers of the president in foreign affairs. Abraham Lincoln, Theodore Roosevelt, Woodrow Wilson, and Franklin D. Roosevelt all assumed extraordinary powers, especially as the commander in chief; but invariably they recognized that Congress and the Supreme Court had the right to review and possibly rescind their actions.[23] Although Congress often acquiesced in these executive actions in wartime, it usually reasserted its interests in the periods of peace that followed.

In the early years the need for legislation in foreign affairs was minimized by the fact that the United States more often than not pursued a **declarative foreign policy**—that is, a policy based on statements of intent that did not require any additional actions, such as the original Monroe Doctrine and the Stimson Doctrine. The treaty-making power was also important. Although the Senate seldom failed to consent to the treaties negotiated by the president, it did revise some of them, and the president sometimes held back agreements with other countries, anticipating that there might be some difficulty in getting the two-thirds vote required for Senate approval.

The executive branch of the government was quite small during the nineteenth century; and prior to civil service reform Congress controlled patronage in the executive branch. This sometimes made it difficult for the president to take initiatives in foreign policy.

The Supreme Court generally treated most foreign affairs issues that arose between the two political branches of the government as political questions—that is, questions not suitable for adjudication. When the Court did speak out, it strengthened the power of the federal government as a whole in foreign policy, not one branch at the expense of another. For example, in *Missouri v. Holland* (1920) the Court established the primacy of the federal government over the states by upholding a Migratory Bird Act that was being challenged by states' rights advocates.[24] Justice Oliver Wendell Holmes, speaking for the Court, recognized the implied powers of the president in foreign policy by ruling that even though the Constitution does not give Congress the power to regulate migratory birds, a 1816 treaty between the United States and Britain negotiated by the president and approved by the Senate can do so.

The Supreme Court also upheld the implied powers of the executive in *United States v. Curtiss-Wright Export Corp.* (1936).[25] In this case the Court found that President Franklin D. Roosevelt was within his rights to prevent the Curtiss-Wright Corporation from selling machine guns to Bolivia through an executive order without specific congressional authorization. According to Gordon Silverstein, Justice George Sutherland, speaking for the Court, argued that "the national government's authority in foreign affairs did not require 'affirmative grants' of power from the Constitution because they were derived from a source outside of the Constitution," that is, international sovereignty.[26] Then in two cases decided just prior to and during World War II, *United States v. Belmont* (1937) and *United States v. Pink* (1942), the Court established that an executive agreement had the same effect as a treaty.[27]

From World War II to the Vietnam War: 1945–1972. Presidential power underwent significant changes during and after World War II. The war was important in two respects. First, the United States played a more active role in the international arena, undertaking programs and activities that required significant legislation. Most of this legislation took the form of ordinary statutes, such as the National Security Act of 1947.[28] Other measures were in the form of executive orders and treaties. Presidents often preferred executive orders because they had the same effect as treaties but avoided the prospect of an open debate that might not result in the two-thirds support needed for formal Senate consent. For example, when Eisenhower wanted military bases in Franco's Spain, he treated the 1953 Pact of Madrid as an executive agreement, in order to avoid any problems in the Senate. When this base agreement was renegotiated in 1976, Spain was a young democracy, and so it was submitted to the Senate as a treaty.

Second, the war stimulated the development of the first atomic weapons, such as those used on Hiroshima and Nagasaki, and then nuclear weapons with delivery means that drastically reduced time requirements. Now international threats were omnipresent and defense considered impossible. To deter nuclear attacks, the Eisenhower administration developed the doctrine of massive retaliation. And when the Soviets later reached nuclear parity with the United States, some proponents of executive prerogative in foreign affairs even claimed a presidential right to initiate a first strike nuclear attack if it were determined that American national security was at stake.[29] Such a foreign policy prerogative not only ignored the right of Congress to declare war, but largely discounted the relevance of the Constitution itself in the face of a nuclear crisis.

Congress did not accept this extension of presidential power without a struggle. In 1953 Sen. John W. Bricker, R-Ohio, tried both to give power back to the states by proposing a constitutional amendment rescinding *Missouri v. Holland* and giving "Congress the power to regulate all executive agreements." [30] The Bricker Amendment failed to receive the necessary two-thirds majority in Congress by one vote, and Congress generally seemed content to allow the president to shoulder most of the responsibility for dealing with international crises during this period.

However, in several important cases the Supreme Court itself placed limits on the president's foreign policy power. In *Youngstown Sheet and Tube Co. v. Sawyer* (1952) the Court held that President Harry S. Truman had acted unconstitutionally in seizing control of the nation's steel mills to prevent a national strike and protect national security. [31] In *New York Times Co. v. United States* (1971) the Court ruled that the Nixon administration could not prevent the publication of the *Pentagon Papers* on national security grounds. [32]

Nevertheless, throughout this period presidents took the initiative in foreign policy. In fact, Aaron Wildavsky has argued that there were actually two presidencies: one dealing with foreign affairs, the other with domestic affairs. [33] According to Wildavsky, presidents were much more powerful in foreign than domestic affairs because they were able to convince Congress to accept most of their foreign policy initiatives. Although some observers believe that this contrast between the two presidencies is overdrawn, it makes sense to others. [34]

From the Aftermath of Vietnam to the Present: 1973–2005. In the wake of the Vietnam War, in 1973 Congress passed the **War Powers Resolution** that sought to restrict the ability of the president to put troops in combat situations without congressional consent. The original Senate version placed specific reporting requirements on the president and allowed Congress to halt executive military action if the president did not receive explicit congressional authorization to keep troops overseas after sixty days—or ninety if the president certified that further military action was needed to disengage U.S. troops from a conflict safely. A conference committee weakened this original version, however, and the final resolution did not include the kind of operative language that would compel presidents to inform Congress when they deployed troops into combat situations, nor require them to withdraw those forces after sixty to ninety days if they did not receive explicit authorization from Congress.

In practice, both presidents and Congress have glossed over the War Powers Resolution when it has seemed most relevant. On every occasion since 1973 in which American troops have been sent abroad, the president has bypassed application of the resolution, and although presidents have provided some of the information desired by Congress and although they have often withdrawn these forces before the sixty-day limit, they have not acknowledged having done so because of the resolution.

For example, within days of the 1990 Iraqi attack on Kuwait President George H. W. Bush sent U.S. forces into the Persian Gulf area without reporting to Congress as required by the War Powers Resolution. Although he occasionally informed Congress and the public about his actions, he did so on his own timetable without regard for any statutory requirements. This was especially true shortly after the midterm elections in November 1990, when he virtually doubled U.S. forces in the Gulf area and thus changed the posture of American forces from defensive to offensive.

In fact, he did not ask Congress for a vote on his plan to use force against Iraq until early January—again without reference to the resolution. And when Congress finally voted in favor of the troop commitment in mid-January 1991, it too did so without any reference to the requirements of the War Powers Resolution. By that time it was too late for any real dialogue to take place. Not only were more than 500,000 U.S. troops set to launch an invasion in a matter of hours, but also Bush had coopted the Democratic opposition by persuading the UN Security Council to legitimize American action once the January 15 deadline had passed. In effect, Bush's strategy deflated the main Democratic argument, which was that the effort to combat Iraq should be a more multilateral one.[35]

The provisions of the War Powers Resolution were even less in evidence when President Clinton committed American troops to Balkan peace keeping as part of the Dayton accords in late 1995. He did not seek formal approval from Congress because it generally opposed his policy in Bosnia. Yet Congress was reluctant to take a stand on the matter, and so, as James M. McCormick points out, "the House and Senate could do little but pass a resolution supporting the troops, even as they opposed the overall Clinton administration policy."[36]

A similar situation arose in early 1999 when Clinton had U.S. forces take the lead in NATO air strikes against Yugoslavia because of its persistent efforts to persecute Kosovars with Albanian background. Clinton did not seek a positive congressional vote on his decision. The evidence suggested that there was a partisan division in Congress over the decision and that the public also was divided, with only a slim majority, if any, supporting the president's action. Although NATO apparently expected these air strikes to last only a few days, they continued for seventy-eight days, and during that time the president made no effort to consult with Congress.

The War Powers Resolution did not really become an issue either in the case of U.S. military action against al Qaeda and the Taliban in Afghanistan in October 2001 or the Iraq War in March 2003 because President George W. Bush got congressional approval before he committed large numbers of U.S. forces to those areas. Although it can hardly be said that the War Powers Resolution has no effect, the truth is that neither branch has consistently acted in accord with it. Indeed, members of Congress have twice attempted to repeal the resolution, arguing that it does more harm than good. After all, the resolution does explicitly acknowledge that the president has the right to send military forces into conflict situations without congressional authorization.

But the War Powers Resolution has served as a model for other efforts by Congress to limit presidential prerogatives in foreign affairs. For example, in the 1970s Congress was particularly eager to bring covert intelligence activities under control after it learned that U.S. intelligence operatives were not only conducting covert activities abroad but also spying on citizens at home. In an effort to restrict these activities, Congress passed in 1975 the Hughes-Ryan Amendment to the National Security Act of 1947, which explicitly required the president to authorize and report covert actions.[37] The Intelligence Oversight Act of 1980 represented an additional effort to strengthen these reporting requirements.

Yet in 1986 it became public knowledge that the National Security Council and the CIA under Ronald Reagan had arranged covert arms sales to Iran in part to raise funds for the Contra forces fighting in Nicaragua. The Reagan administration had consistently denied selling arms to Iran, and the 1982 Boland Amendment had explicitly prohibited providing any military assistance to the Contras. The Reagan administration officials most closely involved—national security adviser John Poindexter and his aide Lt. Col. Oliver North—defended their actions on the grounds that the president had the authority under the Constitution to do whatever he thought was necessary despite any prior assurances and denials.

But once again Congress failed to produce any legislation that would remedy the situation. In the Intelligence Authorization Act of 1991 Congress did require the president to provide advance written "findings" for all covert actions. When prior notice was not possible, it could be provided no later than forty-eight hours after the decision was made. But to ensure passage Congress eventually provided an escape clause allowing such reports "in just a few days" when they could not be made beforehand.

In its efforts in the mid-1970s to reassert its own prerogatives in foreign affairs, Congress demanded a role in approving arms sales, which originally were regarded as a normal part of international trade. Accordingly, Congress provided in the International Security Assistance and Arms Export Control Act of 1976 a right to review military sales on a case-by-case basis. Although Congress has seldom exercised the power to veto particular arms sales, it has had an influence.

Congress also asserted its prerogatives in the area of arms control. In 1987 Reagan announced a reinterpretation of the Antiballistic Missile Treaty that would allow the United States to develop his Strategic Defense

Initiative (SDI). The Senate objected to the idea that the executive could reinterpret a treaty after it had won Senate approval. But when the administration gave private assurances to Georgia senator Sam Nunn, chair of the Senate Armed Services Committee, and others that it would proceed cautiously and in consultation with legislators, Congress chose not to put restrictive language in the National Defense Authorization Act for Fiscal Years 1988 and 1989.

This brief history of the relations between Congress and the president and the failure of Congress to institutionalize the constraints it has occasionally passed suggest that the president does have the right to act in certain crisis situations.

The President and Crisis Foreign Policies

Since the cold war the United States has faced various military, economic, and humanitarian crises. Generally speaking, presidents have been more likely than the opposition in Congress to favor proactive and coercive foreign policies. Democrats have been more supportive of multilateral norms than Republicans. Despite these differences, most members of Congress concede that it is the prerogatives of presidents to take the actions they feel are necessary to defend the security of the country. It makes little or no difference who is president or to which party the president belongs. It also makes little or no difference whether there is a **united** or a **divided government**.

The willingness of Congress to surrender power to the president in a crisis has increased the possibility that a president might engage the country in a preventive war. This scenario is particularly relevant since President George W. Bush released his National Security Paper in September 2002.[38] Bush has argued that the threat posed by the nexus between terrorism and rogue states is so great that preemptive action may be justified in a number of cases. Critics view this foreign policy doctrine as particularly frightening, especially if it were to involve the "first use" of nuclear weapons.

Divided Government and Strategic Foreign Policies

The role of Congress is limited in crisis situations because it never has sufficient time to consider the development of new resources. But in making strategic foreign policy choices the government must determine not only what objectives it will pursue but also what resources it will need to achieve those objectives. This need to generate new resources compels the president to seek congressional support. Strategic foreign policies emerge when what Marie Henehan calls critical issues face the country.[39] (Critical issues are considered synonymous with strategic issues here. The latter terminology is used rather than the former because there is less likelihood that it will be confused with crisis issues.) Strategic issues are discrete problems that are so important that they tend to dominate all other issues until they are resolved, which may take several years.

Strategic Issues

Using independent historical sources, Henehan identifies three such issues in the eighty-eight years between 1896 and 1985: (1) American imperialism at the close of the nineteenth century; (2) U.S. involvement in Europe, beginning in 1914; and (3) the communist threat after World War II.[40] (Although Henehan's study does not encompass the threat of terrorism, especially since the September 11, 2001 attacks, that is another example of a critical issue.) In each case foreign policy was considered critical because the president and the nation could not proceed without having consensus on Capitol Hill and in the White House on what stance to take.

Henehan found that Senate involvement was high in 1897, 1917–1920, and 1947–1950 when the three issues mentioned above were first introduced, and declined once a consensus was reached that allowed the executive to implement the policies developed.[41] But there were some exceptions to this pattern. In 1978 the Panama Canal treaty again raised the old issue of imperialism. Also, in the mid-1930s and early 1940s the issue of U.S. involvement in Europe arose in a new context. But the primary exception occurred in the 1970s and 1980s when the U.S. defeat in Vietnam led to a basic reappraisal of American policy toward the communist threat. Figure 9.1 shows the Senate roll-call votes on critical foreign policy issues.

Henehan demonstrates that the Senate was fully engaged when these issues arose by showing that a higher percentage of the roll-call votes during these peak periods involved amendments or procedural votes rather than votes on actual bills and conference reports. The increased activity stemmed from disagreements within the Senate; when the Senate was less involved—that is, when the number of roll-call votes was lower—there was less disagreement.

This cyclical pattern is interesting for several reasons. First, it seems to confirm the rationalist argument that international events determine congressional involvement, not domestic institutions. Second, it helps to explain why the president seemed to dominate Congress in the 1950s and 1960s after Congress had authorized the formation of a series of alliances to prevent Soviet expansion and had turned over implementation of this containment policy to the executive, and why Congress reasserted itself in the 1970s and 1980s when it felt that the policy needed to be reexamined.

But the fact that international events rather than domestic institutions trigger such issues does not mean that domestic institutions are not important in their resolution. In fact, the nature of domestic institutions helps to explain how the government deals with strategic issues. Because these is-

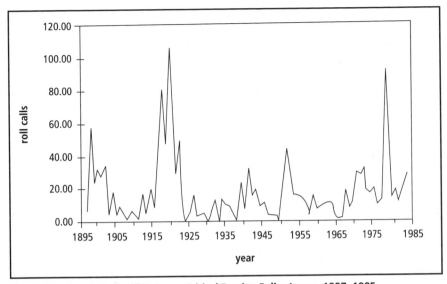

Figure 9.1. Senate Roll-call Votes on Critical Foreign Policy Issues, 1897–1985.
Source: Marie T. Henehan, *Foreign Policy and Congress: An International Relations Perspective* (Ann Arbor: University of Michigan Press, 2000).

sues require the involvement of the government as a whole, the president acting alone cannot resolve strategic issues. Both political branches and both political parties in Congress must address strategic issues.

Political parties are only indirectly involved in making crisis policies because presidents, regardless of their party identification, determine those policies. Yet even though presidents take the initiative in resolving strategic issues, they cannot implement these policies without the support of Congress, which usually means some accommodation with the opposition party in Congress. Therefore, the role of political parties in making strategic foreign policies must be taken into account.

Political Parties and Elections

The framers quickly discovered that "separate institutions sharing power"[42] required some kind of unifying device by which those in government as well as those in the public could impose collective responsibility on office holders. Although the founders, particularly James Madison, opposed "factions," they quickly turned to the political parties because they were the most efficient way to build both government and electoral coalitions over time. Since parties, like all institutions, are shaped by the needs of those who create them, this section will distinguish between the need for parties in government and parties in the electorate.

Parties in Government.   Of the many issues facing George Washington's administration, the principal one was how much power would be vested in the federal government as opposed to the state governments.[43] In retrospect, the division among members of Congress on this critical issue seems obvious, but at the time it was obfuscated by the kinds of ad hoc compromises that were reached on individual issues. Finally, though, Alexander Hamilton was able to develop in Congress a coalition of Federalists who supported a strong federal government. By the end of the Second Congress Thomas Jefferson and James Madison realized that they also would have to develop an "electoral party" in order both to block the coalition formed by Hamilton and to gain sufficient strength to become the strongest party in government in the future.[44] They founded the Republican Party, which later evolved into the Democratic Party. Through affiliation with the first parties, the Federalists and Jefferson's Republicans, those in government took a particular stance on public issues. The parties also served as the vehicle through which these officials could identify themselves and seek public support at election time.

Jefferson's Republican Party won control of the presidency and Congress in 1801 and remained an active party in government for the next twenty-four years. But the Federalist Party took the wrong position on the War of 1812 and gradually faded away. By 1820 Jefferson's Republicans were inviting all congressmen to participate in the renomination of President James Monroe. However, an economic downturn resulted in the emergence of five candidates for president in 1824: William Crawford, John Quincy Adams, Andrew Jackson, Henry Clay, and John C. Calhoun. Jackson received the most popular votes, but he did not receive a majority of votes in the Electoral College. When the House of Representatives chose the second highest vote getter, John Quincy Adams, as president, Jackson was so upset that he, with the help of Martin Van Buren, developed the Jackson-Calhoun faction of the Republican Party into a separate party.

Jackson's Republicans emerged as a North–South alliance between state and local supporters of the Jackson–Calhoun faction and radicals in New York, Virginia, and Georgia. Van Buren also organized a caucus in Washington, D.C. that provided national support to affiliates of the alliance and others. This alliance and caucus became the first American political party organized nationally at the state and local level. Van Buren thought of it as a "mass party" in the sense that it did not belong to one popular figure but to its members as a whole. Jackson used the alliance and caucus to confront the Adams-Clay faction that now controlled the executive branch of the government.[45] This was the first time in American history that a Congress was organized to confront the president.[46] The Tocqueville prediction that a democracy could not persevere in difficult foreign policy undertakings was partly based on Adams's experience with Congress during this period.

Parties in the Electorate.   By 1830 this Republican alliance and caucus was renamed the Democratic Party. The new Democratic Party was different from Jefferson's Republican Party and the Federalist Party in that it was not only a party in government but also a party organized at the grass-roots level in society. In the meantime the Adams–Clay faction of Jefferson's Republican Party also began to organize nationally at the state and local level. In order to accommodate all the anti-Jackson factions they could the Adams-Clay faction or national Republican Party became the Whig Party in 1836.

Both the Democratic Party and the Whig Party were national parties. Because the North was growing faster than the South, the North had a significant advantage in the House of Representatives. The South depended upon an equal division of slave and free states to protect themselves in the Senate. Both parties tried to bridge the gap between North and South by offering balanced tickets. For example, Democrats required a two-thirds vote to nominate a president and a vice president so that the South could protect itself in the Senate where the vice president could caste a tie-breaking vote if necessary. Although the Whig Party was able to nominate candidates for president and vice president by simple majority vote, it also offered balanced tickets during this period.[47]

However, the population was growing, especially in the North, and moving West. It became increasingly difficult for the two national parties to grapple with the changes taking place in various sections of the country. Slavery was a dominant interest among the cotton-planters in the South. Opposition to new immigrants, or nativism, represented by the American, or Know-Nothing, Party became very important in the Northeast. The abolition of slavery and the Free Soil Party became particularly popular in the Northwest. The Whig Party was largely responsible for the Great Compromise of 1850 but failed to consolidate its position in 1852 when General Winfield Scott, its presidential candidate, lost in a landslide to the Democrats' Franklin Pierce. As a result, the Whig Party collapsed, and the Democratic Party fought unsuccessfully to maintain its strength in both the North and the South. In the interim, a new Republican Party became more adept than other parties at uniting Whig and Democratic elements in the more populous northeastern and northwestern sections of the country. Thus a Republican Party centered largely in the North was able to defeat the national Democratic Party in 1860 with Abraham Lincoln's election.

Although the party system failed to prevent the Civil War, a national Republican Party and a national Democratic Party gradually emerged after that war to serve their unifying function both as parties in government and as parties in the electorate. Today, some consistent themes differentiate the two major parties, although both have undergone significant changes in their general platforms. John Gerring contends that first the

Whig Party and then Lincoln's Republican Party embraced a similar set of beliefs from the 1830s until the 1920s, when the Republicans reassessed its stance.[48] As state builders and economic nationalists, the Whig–Republican Party believed that a strong federal government was essential to preserving the Union, gaining prosperity, and maintaining the fabric of American society. The older generation of American conservatives also sought freedom from civil disorder and from intrusions by foreign goods, foreign peoples, and foreign ways. But in the 1920s the Republicans reassessed the situation and came to the conclusion that whereas the government was once necessary to contain the passions of the masses, it was now time to set citizens free from the machinations of their government.

Gerring divides the ideological history of the Democratic Party into three periods. From Andrew Jackson in the 1830s through Grover Cleveland in the 1890s, the Democratic Party was basically the party of Jefferson— that is, a party in favor of "limited government, libertarianism, minority rights, civic virtue, and an adherence to tradition." [49] But in the 1890s the Democratic Party became a populist party. It actually sought government intervention and regulation both as a means of redistributing wealth and as a means of dealing with the growing power of monopolies and big business. By the 1950s the Democratic Party had changed again. It became less class-oriented and leaned toward a more universalist perspective— that is, it wanted to extend rights to all aggrieved claimants and promote inclusion.

Although Gerring argues that both parties have undergone major ideological changes, they each have core beliefs that have not changed. Over the years Republicans have been unified by the goals of prosperity, social order, and patriotism; the Democrats have sought equality.

American parties continue to be a strong source of belief in the American political system, as the 2004 presidential election clearly demonstrates. Table 9.2 contrasts the core beliefs of each party, based on data from 1998: Republican elites tend to favor foreign policies that are more unilateral, coercive, and proactive, or MCA; Democratic elites generally embrace those that are more multilateral, noncoercive, and reactive, or MCA.[50]

With the exception of the Civil War the two major parties in the electorate have united the country despite the sometimes bitter campaigns between them. At the same time, competition between the two parties in government has increasingly divided the national government. A divided government exists when a party different from the party controlling the White House controls one or both chambers of Congress. Table 9.3 lists each Congress since World War II and indicates whether it is a united or divided government. Because strategic foreign policies require joint action by both the president and Congress, some observers, such as Tocqueville, argue that these policies may be impaired by excessive partisanship in government.

Table 9.2. Dimensions of Foreign Policy: Party Elites in 1998[a]

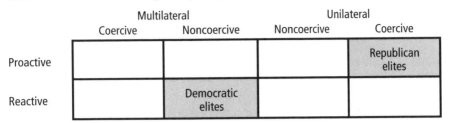

| | Multilateral | | Unilateral | |
	Coercive	Noncoercive	Noncoercive	Coercive
Proactive				Republican elites
Reactive		Democratic elites		

Republican elites are generally more unilateral than Democrat elites because they place more emphasis on the values of liberty, freedom, and independence, more coercive because they place more emphasis on order, and more proactive because they believe that the United States must exert its influence abroad.

Democrat elites are generally more multilateral than Republican elites because they emphasize equality and universality, more noncoercive because they believe that force should be used as a last resort, and more reactive because they are more reticent about foreign policy initiatives.

a. This comparison is based on a regression analysis of individual factor scores on the foreign policy goal questions in the 1998 CCFR elite survey, using differences in party identification. The analysis was conducted by the author.

Effect of Elections and Partisanship on Strategic Foreign Policies

Presidential elections have two effects on strategic foreign policies, which are quite independent of the international situations that these policies are designed to address. First, the United States tends to act more combatively or coercively than it would otherwise. For example, the 1948 election stressed cold war themes; the 1952 election, the East–West struggle; the 1960 election, the so-called missile gap; the 1976 primary election, an attack by Reagan on détente; the 1980 election, military spending; the 2000 election, military preparedness; and the 2004 election, the war in Iraq.[51]

Second, depending on their outcome, presidential elections foster discontinuities in U.S. foreign policies. For example, after the 2000 election President George W. Bush signaled that U.S. foreign policy on the Middle East peace talks, Russia, China, North Korea, the environment, and other issues was changing. Whatever merit there may be in changing some or all of these policies, these abrupt shifts are clearly disconcerting to other countries.

The actual outcome, however, may be quite different from the pre-election rhetoric, because it depends on the ability of the president to muster enough votes in Congress to sustain a strategic foreign policy. Although this task may seem to be much easier if the government is united, that is not always the case. Charles O. Jones identifies four possible outcomes: (1) bipartisanship, (2) cross-partisanship, (3) co-partisanship, and (4) partisanship. **Bipartisanship** occurs when the party of the president

Table 9.3. Democratic and Republican Party Control of the Presidency and Congress since World War II

Congress	Years	President	Party	Senate	House	Divided or United
				\multicolumn{2}{c}{Congress}		
79th	1945–1947	Truman	D	D	D	United
80th	1947–1949	Truman	D	D	R	Divided
81th	1949–1951	Truman	D	D	D	United
82nd	1951–1953	Truman	D	D	D	United
83rd	1953–1955	Eisenhower	R	R	R	United
84th	1955–1957	Eisenhower	R	D	D	Divided
85th	1957–1959	Eisenhower	R	D	D	Divided
86th	1959–1961	Eisenhower	R	D	D	Divided
87th	1961–1963	Kennedy	D	D	D	United
88th	1963–1965	Kennedy	D	D	D	United
		Johnson	D			
89th	1965–1967	Johnson	D	D	D	United
90th	1967–1969	Johnson	D	D	D	United
91th	1969–1971	Nixon	R	D	D	Divided
92nd	1971–1973	Nixon	R	D	D	Divided
93rd	1973–1975	Nixon	R	D	D	Divided
		Ford	R			
94th	1975–1977	Ford	R	D	D	Divided
95th	1977–1979	Carter	D	D	D	United
96th	1979–1981	Carter	D	D	D	United
97th	1981–1983	Reagan	R	R	D	Divided
98th	1983–1985	Reagan	R	R	D	Divided
99th	1985–1987	Reagan	R	R	D	Divided
100th	1987–1989	Reagan	R	D	D	Divided
101st	1989–1991	G. H. W. Bush	R	D	D	Divided
102nd	1991–1993	G. H. W. Bush	R	D	D	Divided
103rd	1993–1995	Clinton	D	D	D	United
104th	1995–1997	Clinton	D	R	R	Divided
105th	1997–1999	Clinton	D	R	R	Divided
106th	1999–2001	Clinton	D	R	R	Divided
107th	2001–2003	G. W. Bush	R	D	R	Divided
108th	2003–2005	G. W. Bush	R	R	R	United
109th	2005–2007	G. W. Bush	R	R	R	United

Source: //ustudies.semo.edu/ui320-75/course/presandcongress.asp

and the opposition party in Congress agree on the substance of foreign policy issues.[52] This is probably the best possible outcome. The second-best outcome is **cross-partisanship**—when the president is able to convince a sufficient number of opposition party members to cross over and support his policy. The third-best policy outcome is **co-partisanship**—that is, the opposition party in Congress accepts the president's policy at the last moment. This is how a crisis policy is often made. The worst policy outcome, at least from the standpoint of the president, is **partisanship,** which occurs when the opposition party continues to pursue a partisan course and deadlocks the government. Each of these outcomes has occurred in response to strategic issues.

Bipartisanship.   When the communist threat emerged after World War II, President Truman sought the support of both political parties for his containment policy. His predecessor, Franklin D. Roosevelt, initiated efforts by offering to meet with Republican senator Arthur H. Vandenberg of Michigan, the influential chair of the Senate Foreign Relations Committee and an isolationist who changed his thinking at the close of World War II.[53] Truman often consulted with Vandenberg before making foreign policy decisions, and, with Vandenberg's help, he was able to develop bipartisan positions on some of his containment policies. The genuine system of advance consultation that Truman established is sometimes known as **procedural bipartisanship.**

Although Truman campaigned in the 1948 election against that "do-nothing Eightieth Congress," that Congress did provide the support needed for both the Marshall Plan and the Truman Doctrine.[54] The Marshall Plan provided the economic funds necessary to reconstruct Europe; the Truman Doctrine provided the military assistance thought necessary to confront Soviet ambitions in Greece and Turkey. These policies actually represented a compromise; the administration was allowed to take these initiatives in Europe with the understanding that it would keep expenditures for military defense and foreign policy within reasonable bounds. Table 9.4 illustrates the dimensions of this compromise.

Cross-partisanship.   International events rapidly overtook the bipartisan agreement Truman had worked out. Faced with the Soviet explosion of an atomic device and the severity of the economic situation in Europe, Truman had to abandon most of his domestic political program in favor of a military buildup in Europe. At the same time, the loss of China to the communists prompted most Republicans to question the administration's commitment to defense against communism. Unfortunately, Senator Vandenberg had become ill, and so Truman had no one on the Republican side to rally liberal Republicans around his new policy. Benjamin O. Fordham contends that Truman made a tacit bargain with Republicans.[55] If they would support increased defense expenditures, he would allow them to pass the Internal Security Act and lay the groundwork for the McCarthy-type investigations of subversives in government and society whom they blamed for recent communist gains in Asia. In this case, the president still had the initiative and Congress responded. But because there was no established bipartisan procedure by which Truman could develop substantive agreement, he had

Table 9.4. Dimensions of Foreign Policy: Bipartisanship in the Eighty-first Congress

| | Multilateral | | Unilateral | |
	Coercive	Noncoercive	Noncoercive	Coercive
Proactive		Truman and liberals in Congress favored Marshall Plan		Truman and liberals in Congress favored Truman Doctrine
Reactive			Conservatives in Congress agree to both Truman Doctrine and Marshall Plan so long as Truman kept defense and other expenditures down	

This table shows the character of the bipartisan compromise encompassed by the containment policy. Although there were other differences between the two most prominent foreign policy instruments associated with the containment policy, the Truman Doctrine and the Marshall Plan, the main compromise was on the proactive–reactive dimension. Conservatives accepted the containment policy favored by liberals as long as liberals agreed with conservatives to keep military and other international expenditures down.

to accept outcomes he did not want to get something he did want. Table 9.5 illustrates the cross-partisanship that replaced the bipartisanship of the early years of the Truman administration.

Partisanship.   After the Vietnam War many Democrats were disillusioned with the containment policy as it had developed under a succession of Democratic and Republican administrations. They questioned whether coercive measures could be very effective in dealing with wars of national liberation throughout the developing countries. In the late 1970s a small rebel group, the Sandinistas, were about to topple the Nicaraguan dictator Anastasio Somoza, whom the United States had supported over the years. In response, President Jimmy Carter decided to employ a new strategy. Rather than support an unpopular dictator, he would try to establish a moderate regime that might be more acceptable both to the Nicaraguan people and to the leaders of other Latin American countries. When that failed, he decided to work with the conquering Sandinistas, with the hope that the United States could have a positive influence on the new regime because the Americans had the resources the Sandinistas needed to rebuild Nicaragua.

This new policy was bitterly opposed by Republicans in Congress who expected the United States to treat the Sandinistas the same way that the United States had treated Castro in Cuba. Initially, Carter was able to secure passage of a $75 million bill for economic assistance to Nicaragua, mainly for moderate groups in that country, but the Republican minority in Congress used every device at its disposal to prevent this policy from being effectively implemented. Table 9.6 illustrates the partisanship be-

Table 9.5. Dimensions of Foreign Policy: Cross-partisanship between Truman and Senate Republicans

| | Multilateral | | Unilateral | |
	Coercive	Noncoercive	Noncoercive	Coercive
Proactive				Truman, liberal Democrats, and key Republicans in Senate agree to major increase in defense expenditures
Reactive				Truman remains silent while conservative Republicans and some Democrats pass the Internal Security Act

This table illustrates cross-partisanship between Truman and the Senate Republicans. On the one hand, Truman and the liberals in Congress in 1950 wanted to increase defense expenditures in order to better implement the containment policy abroad, but the conservatives in Congress wanted to contain costs. On the other hand, conservatives in Congress were willing to acquiesce in these larger defense expenditures if Truman would allow them to pass the Internal Security Act that permitted the pursuit of the communist threat inside the United States; neither Truman nor the liberals in Congress wanted to do so.

tween Carter and House Republicans that marked Carter's policy in Nicaragua.

When Ronald Reagan defeated Jimmy Carter in late 1980 for the presidency, he reversed American policy toward Nicaragua. He opposed the Sandinistas and eventually created a Contra army in Honduras for the purpose of overthrowing the Sandinista regime in Nicaragua. But Reagan faced a Democratic majority in the House of Representatives that vigorously opposed his efforts to militarize the conflict in Nicaragua. Indeed, Speaker Jim Wright became personally involved in helping the Central American leaders negotiate an end to the conflict. Table 9.7 illustrates the partisanship between Reagan and Congressional Democrats that marked Reagan's policy in Nicaragua.

In both of these cases strong partisanship in Congress prevented presidents from implementing their preferred policy in Nicaragua. President Carter failed to work with the Sandinista government effectively in part because Republicans in Congress blocked the funding. Later, President

Table 9.6. Dimensions of Foreign Policy: Partisan Differences between Carter and House Republicans

| | Multilateral | | Unilateral | |
	Coercive	Noncoercive	Noncoercive	Coercive
Proactive		With support of Latin American goverments and a Democratic majority in Congress Carter offers a $75 million aid package to Nicaragua		Republicans in Congress oppose the $75 million loan
Reactive				

The purpose of this table is to illustrate the partisan differences between President Carter and the Republican opposition in the House over a $75 million loan package to Nicaragua in 1980. Carter favored a loan package that might persuade the Sandinistas to cooperate with the United States, a foreign policy initiative that had wide support among Latin American countries. The Republicans in the House opposed the loan package, preferring to force a change of government in Nicaragua.

Reagan failed to defeat the Sandinistas because Democrats in Congress limited funds for his Contra forces. At first blush, one could argue that foreign policy wasn't the issue, politics was. In fact, partisanship prevented both presidents from conducting an effective foreign policy. But one also could argue that although partisanship undermined official policy, the eventual outcome—an election in Nicaragua—was probably better than one could expect under the policy preferred by either Carter or Reagan.

Table 9.7. Dimensions of Foreign Policy: Partisan Differences between Reagan and Congressional Democrats

| | Multilateral | | Unilateral | |
	Coercive	Noncoercive	Noncoercive	Coercive
Proactive		Speaker Wright and House Democrats support negotiations		President Reagan and Republicans try to oust Sandinistas
Reactive				

The purpose of this table is to illustrate partisan differences over U.S. foreign policy toward Nicaragua during the first Reagan administration. President Reagan's Nicaragua policy was unilateral because it was promulgated largely by the United States, coercive because it relied upon a Contra force to dislodge the Sandinistas who controlled Nicaragua, and proactive because it emphasized the benefits of overthrowing the Sandinistas. However, the Democratic Speaker of the House, Jim Wright, actively sought to support international efforts to negotiate a settlement of the dispute.

This pair of incidents suggests that if presidents cannot sell their foreign policy to the American people or Congress, a proactive foreign policy is probably contraindicated and impossible.[56]

These illustrations suggest that both elections and partisanship significantly affect strategic foreign policies. And yet one cannot conclude that either elections or partisanship prevent the United States from pursuing a consistent foreign policy. Much depends on the political and diplomatic skills of the people involved. Despite the vagaries of the political system, the United States has generally been able to pursue a consistent foreign policy. Once strategic policies have been established, they become routinized, which means that they resemble regular foreign policies.

Congress and Regular Foreign Policies

When there is no overwhelming international threat—that is, when there is no apparent reason to give international exigencies priority over domestic considerations—the executive and legislative branches of the U.S. government are equally involved in foreign policy making. Under these circumstances, foreign policy making resembles domestic policy making.

Regular Issues

In her survey of Senate votes on foreign policy issues, Henehan identified at least six kinds of foreign policies that she called regular: tariff, immigration, foreign aid, defense, regular diplomatic, and miscellaneous. Each of these issues presented a different pattern.[57] The tariff issue was the most persistent partisan issue in the Senate until passage of the Reciprocal Trade Act of 1934. Although Congress still has the final say on trade matters, Congress has reduced the persistent partisanship on the trade issue by allowing the executive branch to take the initiative on reciprocal trade agreements, especially under fast-track provisions between 1974 and 1994 and again in 2002. By contrast, the immigration issue has periodically attracted Senate attention. Military expenditures are associated with strategic issues because they involved preparation for war. Foreign aid also was associated with the cold war, when it served as the carrot that accompanied the military stick. In the 1960s, however, public support for foreign aid began to slip as Europe and Japan recovered and the U.S. economy began to falter. After the end of the cold war, the use of foreign aid as a carrot declined even more.

With the exception of the tariff prior to 1934, regular foreign policy issues were less contentious than those involving international threats. As a consequence, these issues are usually handled at lower levels in Congress and the executive. Because Congress is heavily engaged in regular foreign policy issues and because Chapter 10 deals exclusively with the executive branch, the remainder of this chapter focuses on how to explain congressional behavior on regular foreign policy issues.

Four explanations are considered. First, differences between the two chambers explain congressional behavior because majorities in each chamber determine foreign policy outputs. Second, majorities in the majority party explain congressional behavior because each chamber is organized on a partisan basis. Third, seniority in party in committees determines congressional behavior because senior members have special prerogatives in the committees dealing with specific issues. And, forth, individual issue advocates determine congressional behavior because they can outmaneuver less interested members, using some or all of the factors just noted.[58]

The Two Chambers

There are 435 members in the House of Representatives and 100 members in the Senate. In view of the difference in size of the two chambers, it follows that House members specialize more than Senate members. For example, in 1996 the average House member served on 1.8 committees, and the average senator served on at least 3.2 committees. Because most House incumbents choose to retain their committee assignments year after year, House members tend to become experts on specific aspects of the government. By contrast, members of the Senate tend to grandstand as generalists although they also can become experts through specialization.

The size of the two chambers also affects the rules they employ. Generally, the House uses stricter rules than the Senate in order to facilitate the flow of bills to the floor of the House and to ensure their swift consideration once there. The House Rules Committee monitors the progress of bills in committee, determines when those bills will come to the floor of the House, and decides what rules will govern their consideration such as time limits for the debate and what, if any, amendments will be allowed. The Speaker of the House has some discretion in dealing with independent or recalcitrant committees such as referring bills to multiple committees and setting time limits on committee action. Multiple referrals allow the Speaker to bypass a committee that may not report a bill the Speaker wants passed. Time limits ensure that the bill will be reported out on a timely basis. Though rarely used, the House majority can sign a discharge petition, which, if passed, has the effect of bringing a bill out of a recalcitrant committee.

Senate rules provide greater latitude both to the majority and to individual members. Although the Senate, like the House, has a procedure for discharging a bill from a recalcitrant committee, it is seldom used because senators can easily sidestep the problem by offering amendments to other bills—amendments that duplicate the bill they wish to extract from a committee. The majority leader of the Senate usually employs unanimous consent agreements to control the flow of legislation in that body. The majority leader can also, at the request of individual members of either party, "hold" committee bills scheduled to come to the floor for debate. That privilege is granted to individual members because Senate rules allow senators to filibuster legislation on the floor unless a supermajority votes for cloture. These rules encourage senators to develop bipartisan coalitions in order to obtain the majorities or supermajorities they need to control the flow of legislation in that body.

Finally, differences between the two chambers affect their roles in the overall legislative process. For example, members of the House Appropriations subcommittees usually go through agency budgets with a fine-tooth comb, paying special attention to any proposed increased spending. They identify the most questionable areas of the expenditure and often cut the proposed agency budgets accordingly. The relevant Senate Appropriations subcommittees then have the task of reviewing these problem areas, like an appellate court reviewing the decisions of a lower court, and of restoring or not restoring some of the funds cut by the House subcommittees. A conference committee that resubmits its recommendations to both chambers then works out the differences between the House and Senate appropriations bills.

Although House members are better able to specialize in the subject areas addressed by authorization committees, they do not necessarily play a more active role in the foreign policy process than their counterparts in the Senate. For example, the Senate Committee on Foreign Relations has often assumed a lead role in authorizing foreign policies because of the special role of that committee in consenting to treaties and confirming appointments. Since the mid-1970s, however, House authorization committees such as the Committee on International Relations have become at least as active as their counterparts in the Senate.

These institutional differences between the House and Senate chambers can affect the foreign policy outputs of Congress. Such differences in output also can sometimes be explained by differences between parties in each chamber.

Parties in Congress

For over two centuries political parties have organized the House of Representatives and the Senate. The House as a whole elects its presiding officer, the Speaker of the House, and the majority party in the Senate elects a president pro tempore who chairs that chamber in the absence of the vice president of the United States. In addition, the majority and minority parties in each chamber elect floor leaders and whips. The Speaker of the House and the Senate majority leader, to a lesser degree, play the most important role in their respective chambers.

Parties in the American Congress are not as powerful as their parliamentary counterparts in Europe. Only something over half of the roll-call votes in both chambers are party leadership votes in which the leaders and whips of both parties attempt to impose party discipline on their members. It is generally difficult to measure the effectiveness of party leadership because the party's position on many of these votes closely corresponds to the individual preferences of the party's members. Nevertheless, there are always instances in which a party member's individual interest in voting with the party is less compelling than the collective interest of the party and its leadership. As a consequence, the leadership of both parties has used its influence on committee assignments and the legislative agenda to enforce party loyalty.

In 1974 the Democratic Caucus assumed a stronger leadership position in the House. Among other things, it insisted on regular meetings of the caucus so it could instruct party leaders. It also strengthened the role of the party in the House by giving the Speaker of the House more influence over committee assignments and key committees such as Rules and Ways and Means. The Democratic Caucus continued to dominate the House until 1994, when the Republicans finally gained the majority in that chamber and the Republican Caucus gained the right to control committee assignments for the majority party. By inserting the most loyal party members into the most prestigious committees, the party leadership was able to control key committees such as Rules, which determines the fate of most bills in the House.

Similar processes of committee assignments take place in the Senate; but both parties have limited the leadership's discretion in making assignments. Senate Republicans make assignments strictly on the basis of seniority. Senate Democrats have such a large Steering Committee that it would be difficult for the leadership to exercise much discretion.[59] Thus, in the House at least, the majority party can control the most prestigious committees such as Rules, Ways and Means, and Appropriations. But party managers, even in the House, are limited in their ability to completely control the congressional agenda. Most of the work of Congress is actually done in committee rather than in the House or the Senate as a whole, although legislation can change significantly on the Senate floor.

Committees

Each chamber has over a dozen major committees, most of which are divided into subcommittees. General foreign policy is addressed by the International Relations Committee in the House and the Committee on Foreign Relations in the Senate, military policies by the National Security Committee in the House and the Armed Services Committee in the Senate, and international trade by the Ways and Means Committee in the House and the Finance Committee in the Senate. Table 9.8 lists the House and Senate committees with primary jurisdiction in foreign policy.

From the 1920s to the 1970s chairs of House and Senate committees conducted much of the business of Congress without regard for party

Table 9.8 Senate and House Committees with Jurisdiction in Foreign Policy, 2005–2006

Senate	House
Agriculture, Nutrition, and Forestry Marketing, Inspection, and Product Promotion	**Agriculture** Specialty Crops and Foreign Agriculture
Appropriations State, Foreign Operations, and Related Agencies Defense Military Construction	**Appropriations** Science, Depts. of Commerce, Justice, State, and Judiciary Foreign Operations, Export Financing and Related Programs Military Construction National Security
Armed Services Airland Emerging Threats and Capabilities Personnel Readiness and Management Support Seapower Strategic Forces	**Armed Services** Tactical Air and Land Forces Terrorism, Unconventional Threats and Capabilities Military Personnel Military Procurement Readiness Strategic Forces
Banking, Housing and Urban Affairs International Trade and Finance	**Small Business** Tax, Finance, and Exports
Budget	**Budget**
Commerce, Science, and Transportation Trade, Tourism, and Economic Development Technology, Innovation, and Competitiveness Global Climate Change	**Energy and Commerce** Commerce, Trade, and Consumer Protection Energy and Air Quality Telecommunications and the Internet
Energy and Natural Resources	**Resources** Energy and Mineral Resources Fisheries and Oceans
Environment and Public Works	
Finance International Trade	**Financial Services** Domestic and International Monetary Policy, Trade, and Technology
Foreign Relations African Affairs East Asian and Pacific Affairs	**International Relations** Africa, Global Human Rights, and International Operations Asia and the Pacific

continues on next page

Table 9.8 continued[a]

Senate	House
European Affairs	Europe and Emerging Threats
International Economic Policy, Export & Trade Protection	
International Operations and Terrorism	International Terrorism and Nonproliferation
Near Eastern and South Asian Affairs	Middle East and Central Asia
Western Hemisphere, Peace Corps, and Narcotics Affairs	Western Hemisphere
	Government Reform
Health, Education, Labor and Pensions	Criminal Justice, Drug Policy, and Human
Bioterrorism and Public Health Preparedness	Resources
	National Security, Emerging Threats, and International Relations
Judiciary	**Judiciary**
Immigration, Border Security, and Citizenship	Immigration, Border Security, and Claims
Terrorism, Technology and Homeland Security	Courts, the Internet, and Intellectual Property
	Crime, Terrorism, and Homeland Security
Veterans Affairs	**Veterans Affairs**
Select Committee on Intelligence	**Permanent Select Committee on Intelligence**
Joint Economic Committee	**Joint Economic Committee**

a. These committees and subcommittees were selected because they have the most obvious jurisdiction in foreign affairs.

Sources: U.S. Senate website—www.senate.gov—accessed Nov. 8, 2005; U.S. House of Representatives website—www.clerkweb.house.gov—accessed Nov. 8, 2005.

majorities. This system allowed members of both parties to vote in accordance with their districts—a help when election time rolled around. Meanwhile, the seniority system allowed them to bide their time with the assurance that they would eventually obtain one of these coveted positions of power.[60]

Beginning in 1974, however, the seniority system broke down because the liberal northern Democrats outnumbered the conservative southern Democrats who held most of these senior positions. At that point the Democratic Caucus replaced three Democratic committee chairs with seniority with members more acceptable to the caucus as a whole. This action served as a warning to all committee chairs that they owed their positions to the Democratic Caucus and not to their own seniority on the committee. When the Republicans gained control of the House in 1994, their leaders made similar changes.

Although the absolute power of seniority has diminished in Congress, however, the chairs of congressional committees and even subcommittees are still important. For one thing, they usually control committee budgets and staff. This often allows them to exert great personal influence in foreign policy making. Such members may also serve as surrogates for different groups in government or society. In short, congressional committees provide opportunities for a wide variety of outside influences, including executive departments and agencies, special interest groups in society, and public majorities.

The influence of some of these chairs has been quite phenomenal. For example, former senator Jesse Helms (R-N.C.) was able to use his position as chair of the Senate Foreign Relations Committee to block confirmation of many nominees for various foreign affairs posts. Helms also worked in tandem with the Appropriations Committees to reduce the strength and autonomy of three independent agencies associated with American foreign policy: the Arms Control and Disarmament Agency (ACDA), the U.S. Information Agency (USIA), and the Agency for International Development (AID). ACDA and USIA have now been incorporated into a smaller State Department, whereas AID has lost much of its funding.[61]

Individual Issue Advocates

By the 1960s American political parties were clearly in transition. Relying on more sophisticated opinion polls and methods of political advertising and fund raising, candidates sought to appeal to voters on the basis of their own voting records and personalities and rely less on party-centered campaigns. According to National Election Surveys, one result of this phenomenon was that strong party identification, especially among younger people, declined.[62] Although there is evidence that some of these younger voters later assumed stronger party identifications and although there is no good evidence that those who have strong party identifications have become any less prepared to vote for their preferred party, a much larger number of people now claim to be independents—that is, they claim not to have a preference for either party.[63]

Moreover, the incidence of split ticket voting has increased since the 1960s. Political scientists note that as many as 25 percent of voters now vote for the presidential candidate from one party and a representative or senator from another party. Morris Fiorina estimates that as many as 8 percent of the electorate may do this purposively to achieve divided government.[64]

Because regular foreign policy issues may affect congressional constituencies differently, members do not always vote strictly along party lines. They increasingly look at the interests and values of their individual constituencies. And some members of Congress are **individual issue advocates** because they have strong positions on specific issues assume quite independent roles while serving in that body.

For example, in the mid-1990s Senator Paul Sarbanes, a Greek American member of the Senate Committee on Foreign Relations, was able to hold up the transfer of three frigates to Turkey for almost three years because the Clinton administration was sensitive to his concerns, and possibly the concerns of other Americans of Greek descent. In the absence of preponderant support for regular foreign policies, it is relatively easy for a few committed advocates to exercise disproportionate influence over those policies.[65]

Because Congress is more open than the executive to organized pressures, individual committees and even individual members may represent particular groups in government and society. As one analyst explains, "Today's committee chairs have enough trouble persuading their own panel members to hold ranks, much less being able to sway other members of this highly individualistic Congress." [66] Thus members who are fulfilling their own conceptions of their roles in the government drive much of the day-to-day work of Congress.

Conclusion

Because the framers institutionalized the separation of power laced with checks and balances for the federal government, they put a premium on developing unified positions on foreign policy. This chapter shows how those in Congress and the executive branch attempt to achieve unity under different circumstances. When the country faces a foreign policy crisis, the president takes control and Congress acquiesces. Both Congress and the president are heavily involved in the formation of strategic foreign policies. Once such policies are established, however, the president tends to play a more dominant role than Congress in their implementation. Congress tends to play a significant role in regular foreign policy issues.

This description of U.S. foreign policy making is accurate insofar as the relationship between Congress and the president is concerned. But it does not take into account the influence of the foreign policy bureaucracy. This is the subject of the next chapter.

Key Concepts

balanced (powers)   317
bipartisanship   329
co-partisanship   330
crisis foreign policies   314
cross-partisanship   330

declarative foreign policy   318
divided government   323
individual issue advocates   342
laws   312
new institutionalism   313

Suggested Readings

1. Fordham, Benjamin O. *Building the Cold War Consensus: The Political Economy of U.S. National Security Policy, 1949–1951.* Ann Arbor: University of Michigan Press, 1998.

2. Henehan, Marie T. *Foreign Policy and Congress: An International Relations Perspective.* Ann Arbor: University of Michigan Press, 2000.

3. Maltzman, Forrest. *Competing Principals: Committees, Parties, and the Organization of Congress.* Ann Arbor: University of Michigan Press, 1997.

4. Silverstein, Gordon. *Imbalance of Powers: Constitutional Interpretation and the Making of American Foreign Policy.* Oxford: Oxford University Press, 1997.

CHAPTER 10

Organizational Behavior Model: The Foreign Affairs Bureaucracy

Bureaucracies are formed when specialists are organized and coordinated to perform tasks more efficiently than they could accomplish otherwise. The foreign affairs bureaucracy of the United States consists of tens of thousands of experts located in sixty-five departments and agencies spread throughout the world. One of the functions of the foreign affairs bureaucracy is intelligence gathering. In the picture above two photo interpreters, Master Sergeant Barclay A. Trehal and Staff Sergeant Sheryle Pearson, review reconnaissance film taken by an RF-4C Phantom II aircraft belonging to the 152nd Tactical Reconnaissance Group of the Nevada Air National Guard. The interpreters are wearing protective gloves so that they will not leave any residue on the film.

T HAT DEADLOCK BETWEEN THE TWO most political branches of government—the president and Congress—is increasingly characteristic of foreign policy making in the United States does not mean that the United States cannot have an active foreign policy. After all, Congress and the president have created a complex bureaucracy with thousands of foreign policy experts who are quite capable of making foreign policy decisions. Indeed, these experts probably make 99 percent of these decisions even when the government is not deadlocked. This chapter describes the lower levels of the foreign affairs bureaucracy and explains how it affects American foreign policy. From the standpoint of institutionalism this chapter emphasizes specialization.

Organizational Behavior Model

The foreign affairs bureaucracy encompasses all those federal departments and agencies with a primary or strong secondary interest in some aspect of foreign policy. Sixty-five separate departments and agencies in the federal government have an interest in certain aspects of foreign policy, even if most of them are not interested in general foreign policy. For example, the federal Centers for Disease Control and Prevention (CDC) in Atlanta will only become an active participant in foreign policy decision making when infectious diseases such as Severe Acute Respiratory Syndrome (SARS) endanger the health of U.S. citizens.

Is it possible to have a coherent foreign policy when so many departments and agencies are involved in making foreign policy decisions? And how can those decisions be explained with reference to a single, coherent actor if different experts in such a wide variety of organizations actually make foreign policy? The **organizational behavior model** provides an alternative approach.

The Model

The organizational behavior model is based on the supposition that most decisions are made by lower-level officials in a constellation of loosely allied organizations. Each organization or subunit is structured in such a way that it can perform its specific function efficiently. This efficiency is achieved by getting hundreds of people to respond to basic cues, or **standard operating procedures** (SOPs), that are simple enough to be learned and applied easily. Because these procedures are standardized, it is possible to predict an organization's behavior from one time to the next so long as the task remains the same.[1]

The explanatory power of the organizational behavior model is based on **specialization,** that is, the consistent manner in which organizations perform their special functions. But the division of labor that allows such specialization produces a countervailing need for **coordination.** After all, if the output of one unit did not mesh with the outputs of other units, the efficiency derived from specialization would not be very meaningful. The requirement for coordination reinforces the need for SOPs so that each unit within the bureaucracy can anticipate what every other unit is doing. That coordination, in turn, is not possible unless a degree of central **control** is exercised so that the programs and routines performed by these different organizations remain on track.

A more complete understanding of how the bureaucracy works depends therefore on a more in-depth examination of four aspects of the organizational behavior model. Specifically, how do organizational autonomy, career service, and organizational culture influence standard operating procedures, and how do these SOPs, in turn, provide for a modicum of coordination and control?

Organizational Autonomy.   All large organizations take advantage of a division of labor to perform specific tasks more efficiently. By having a group of people specialize in one element of the production cycle, organizations are able to produce many more goods and services than the same number of people could produce if working separately. But it is important to distinguish between nongovernmental and governmental organizations. Most nongovernmental or private organizations, such as corporations, are able to focus almost exclusively on producing a product or providing a service. By contrast, government organizations are often more concerned with processes than outcomes—that is, they are more concerned with *how* things get done than they are with *what* gets done. Especially in a democratic government, public organizations are responsible to a host of outside parties in a way that private organizations are not.

Indeed, government departments and agencies are responsible not only to the president—who is also their chief executive officer—but also to Congress and the public. They are required to follow the laws, norms, and practices set forth in executive orders, congressional statutes, and understandings they have with specific congressional committees, pressure groups, and the other departments with whom they deal on a regular basis. Ironically, the fact that they are responsible to such a range of outside institutions gives them a degree of autonomy from any one outside group.

The independent behavior of many departments and agencies in the foreign affairs bureaucracy is further strengthened by the fact that some of these agencies have their own career services. The next section looks at three of the most important career services in the federal bureaucracy.

Career Service.   A **career service** is one in which employees enter an organization at a very junior level and seek regular promotions to the most senior levels.

The U.S. Foreign Service, with its some twelve thousand members, is one example. The Rogers Act, by uniting the consular and diplomatic services of the United States, created the Foreign Service in 1924. The officers in this career service are recruited on the basis of competitive written examinations, which are followed by oral interviews. Early in the process applicants are asked to indicate which of several career paths they would like to follow, such as political, economic, consular, and administrative work. Because the Foreign Service admits only a portion of those who pass these exams and interviews, several years usually pass between a successful applicant's first contact with the Foreign Service and a job offer.

After a short stint at the Foreign Service School in Washington, D.C., new officers are usually assigned to posts abroad where they are schooled in the art of political reporting and negotiating, which are the primary tasks of America's diplomats. Because the number of top jobs—ambassadorships abroad and assistant secretary positions in the Department of State—are in very limited supply, these officers are rotated every three years to ensure opportunities for the varied training and experience needed for promotion. Traditionally, foreign service officers have been promoted on the basis of their political reporting and the ratings of their superiors. Box 10.1 describes the career path of one such officer.

Other departments with significant international interests also have developed small career services; for example, 400 attachés with Treasury, 250 employees of the Commerce and Agricultural foreign services, and smaller numbers representing other departments and agencies serve overseas.

The U.S. military is another example of a career service. Roughly 250,000 active-duty officers serve in America's armed services. Most of these officers hold junior ranks and are stationed at key military bases throughout the United States and at some ninety U.S. military bases overseas. Although only a very small fraction of these officers are assigned to commanders in the field, the offices of the Joint Chiefs of Staff, or the office of the secretary of defense where they become involved in making general foreign policy, many are engaged in implementing those policies, particularly when the United States employs military force abroad.

The military officer corps is larger than one might expect for an active duty force of just over 1.4 million troops, largely because after World War II U.S. leaders thought they could mobilize a much larger force more quickly if they retained a large, experienced officer corps. As a result, relatively few military officers command troops for any considerable period of time because there are more officers than troops to command. In lieu of command positions, military officers often serve in staff positions that otherwise might be filled by civilians. Because most officers seek troop commands in order to compete for promotions, tours of duty in these command positions are kept very short so that as many officers as possible have a fair chance at promotion. Indeed, during the Vietnam War and the

BOX 10.1

Profile in Action: Martin J. Hillenbrand

As a young boy growing up in Chicago, Martin J. Hillenbrand had demonstrated a drive to excel. He received a full scholarship to the University of Dayton and then pursued almost two years of coursework toward a doctorate in political science at Columbia University in New York City before entering the Foreign Service in 1939, in the early days of World War II.

In the spring of that year Hillenbrand was appointed vice consul at the American consulate general in Zurich, where he received first-hand experience dealing with the flood of U.S. visa requests from Jews fleeing Austria and Germany. After a brief stint in 1940, at the Foreign Service Officers' Training School in Washington, D.C., he was assigned to the consulate general in Rangoon, Burma, where, as vice consul, he worked with the small, transient American community there. He assisted the American merchant marine, missionaries, businessmen, and those engaged in the Lend Lease program for China, those traveling over the Burma Road to China, and the American-manned Chinese Air Force under Colonel Claire Chennault, best known as the Flying Tigers.

As Japanese forces closed in on Burma in the late summer of 1941, a mad dog bit Hillenbrand, but he escaped to Calcutta, where he received medical attention. Because he lost the doctoral dissertation he had been working on in Zurich and Rangoon, he began to write another in Calcutta, where he was a vice consul, serving the Americans fleeing the Japanese in that part of the world. In the early summer of 1944, just as the war was winding down, Hillenbrand arrived at the consulate general in Mozambique, a neutral Portuguese colony where there was a strong German presence.

In June 1946 Hillenbrand was assigned to the post of U.S. consul at Bremen, Germany, which was serving as the American seaport in the British sector of Germany. There he acted as the U.S. liaison with the British military government and became the American contact with leading Germans in the British zone of occupation, including Konrad Adenauer, the future German chancellor. Hillenbrand served almost three and a half years in Bremen but did manage to return briefly to the United States in 1948 to defend his doctoral dissertation at Columbia. While in Bremen, he also served as an intermediary for drafting the new German constitution.

As the overall military government of occupation ended in 1949, he returned to the United States, where he spent a year taking advanced courses in economics at Harvard University. In the summer of 1950 he became chief of the Division of German Government in the Bureau of German Affairs in the State Department.

In 1952 Hillenbrand was assigned to the headquarters of the North Atlantic Treaty Organization (NATO) in Paris. The next year he was detailed to work with Ambassador David Bruce on the proposed European Defense Community (EDC) treaty. When the EDC failed in 1954, Hillenbrand stayed on as U.S. observer during the "Eden initiative," which succeeded in drawing up the six-power (seven including Britain) and fourteen-power agreements that brought Germany into the Western defense system.

Soon after Hillenbrand was assigned as political adviser to the U.S. military government in Berlin in 1956, his former boss, David Bruce, was named U.S. ambassador to the Federal Republic of Germany. As political adviser, Hillenbrand worked with his counterparts from Britain, France, and the Soviet Union to oversee relations between the Western sectors of Berlin and the Soviet sector and to deal with the political aspects of the relationship between the city of Berlin and the West.

In October 1958 Hillenbrand was asked to return to Washington as director of the Office of German Affairs (the former Bureau of German Affairs), just as Ambassador Bruce was confronted by the Berlin crisis in Germany, which was instigated by Nikita Khrushchev when he threatened to turn the functions still performed by the Soviet government in Berlin over to the East German government. Hillenbrand formally held this position until the end of the Berlin crisis in 1963. He headed the American representation to the "Four Power Working Group," which provided guidance to the principals engaged in the Geneva, Camp David, and Vienna Conferences. He also chaired all of the meetings of this group in Washington.

In 1963 Hillenbrand was assigned as minister and deputy chief of mission to the U.S. embassy in Bonn, Germany, where he renewed contacts with Chancellor Adenauer. He also became a close friend of the future German chancellor Helmut Kohl. In 1967 he was appointed U.S. ambassador to Hungary, where he dealt with the liberal movement in that country after the Soviets repressed the liberalization in Czechoslovakia known as the "Prague Spring."

In early 1969 Hillenbrand returned to Washington as assistant secretary of state for European affairs. Although he was now responsible for U.S. relations with some thirty countries, he played a major role in the negotiation of the Four Power Agreements on Berlin with the Soviet Union. Almost three and a half years later he became U.S. ambassador to West Germany. As ambassador, he worked with Chancellor Willy Brandt and the new Social Democratic Party leadership of Germany with whom he had earlier established close ties in Berlin. Hillenbrand retired from the Foreign Service in 1976.

Second Gulf War the average tour of duty for regular active-duty troops in the combat zone was often less than one year.

The service academies of the army, air force, and navy produce a steady flow of college-educated officers for the military services. Marine Corps officers are trained at the U.S. Naval Academy. Other sources of military officers are the ROTC (Reserve Officers Training Corps) programs in many public and private colleges and universities and the individual programs that cater to those with college degrees who do not have access to ROTC programs. Many of these officers attend special officer training schools run by the military services. Each of the three main armed services also maintains a war college to provide advanced training to senior officers.

Finally, tens of thousands of specialists in the federal civil service deal with various aspects of foreign affairs. Once in government, economists, political scientists, sociologists, geographers, engineers, scientists, managers, and writers become government economists, intelligence analysts, budget specialists, communications experts, and administrators. They provide the primary staff in the departments that deal with foreign policy such as Treasury, Commerce, Agriculture, Health, Labor, and Education, and in the various agencies that do the same, such as the CIA. They supplement foreign and military service personnel in the Departments of State and Defense.

These jobs are classified according to the level of training, experience, and skills required. Applicants are initially screened by an open, competitive examination that varies somewhat by agency and the character of the job. At lower levels of the civil service the process is highly centralized, whereas at higher levels it is increasingly decentralized. Once candidates are rated and scored on this basis, those who will serve as their supervisors select them.

The existence of separate career services strengthens the autonomy of key departments in the foreign affairs bureaucracy. Although not all departments have a separate career service, most departments and agencies do have their own cultures.

Organizational Culture. The formal structure of each department and agency is usually the result of compromises between the president, Congress, and those elements of the public most interested in these organizations. Their informal structure, however, is largely determined at the operational level—that is, at the lower levels in the bureaucracy. This informal structure consists of rules that "both define and grow out of a distinctive organizational culture. **Organizational culture** is thus the set of beliefs the members of an organization hold about their organization, beliefs they have inherited and pass on to their successors." [2]

Cultural identity is particularly important to the Marine Corps, because of all the military services, its status as a separate service is most in doubt.

(The Marine Corps actually comes under the Department of the Navy.) Although the Marine Corps has a distinctive function—to conduct amphibious landings—it must have a sense of mission that goes beyond that particular task. As a result, every marine is trained to be a superior, disciplined soldier—that is, marines are members of an elite corps, distinguishable from the other services and perhaps best characterized by the saying "there is the Marine way, and the wrong way." This cultural value influences the kinds of people who are recruited for the marines; it dictates how they are trained; and it determines who will be promoted. In short, it influences everything marines do.

It seems as though most organizations would develop SOPs solely devoted to undertaking their specific tasks as efficiently as possible. But this brief look at organization culture reveals that the SOPs developed by these organizations have as much to do with maintaining the legitimacy and status of the organizations as with performing efficiently.

Indeed, these organizational cultures are often so transparent that it is not at all uncommon for outsiders to adopt stereotypic views of organization members. For example, the officials who work for the U.S. Agency for International Development (USAID) might be stereotyped as liberal do-gooders, whereas those who work for the military are often labeled cautious conservatives. But when these stereotypes are applied to individuals, they may or may not be true. If one carefully considers a range of factors such as job description, career service, previous service, and length of time in service, it may well be true that "where you sit, determines where you stand" on issues.[3]

Presidents often try to overcome what they regard as "grooved" thinking on the part of lower-level bureaucrats by appointing their own people to supervisory positions. In this context it is useful to distinguish between **career executives** and **political executives**. Both kinds of executives are appointed by the president and confirmed by the Senate, but career executives are promoted from within their career services, and so they generally share the same organizational culture as lower-level officials. Only a small fraction of the nearly 5,000 career executives in the government is involved in foreign policy making. Although career executives are expected to serve the administration in power regardless of their political preferences, they have gradually become more politicized because promotion from within the bureaucracy depends more and more on political orientation.

Nevertheless, the distinction between career and political executives remains relevant. Political executives, who today number about seven hundred, are usually appointed from sources outside the bureaucracy and commonly have very close political ties to the president. In fact, every secretary of state in the nation's history has been a member of the president's party. And President Clinton created a series of new positions for undersecretaries and deputy undersecretaries to watch over the permanent bureaucracy in the State Department.

Now that this chapter has defined some of the formal and informal institutions that influence members of the bureaucracy, the next section shows how these institutions affect organizational processes.

Organizational Behavior. The standard operating procedures (SOPs) developed by government organizations often give decision makers choices they would not have otherwise. After all, these programs and routines determine not only what actions will be taken but also what information is available to these organizations, what options they will consider, and how these options will be implemented. For example, the 9/11 Commission Report shows that the September 11, 2001 attacks "fell into the void" between U.S. agencies dealing with foreign and domestic threats. The CIA, organized on a foreign-area basis, developed a "zone defense," where one protects an area. The FBI, organized to investigate individual suspects, developed a "man defense," where one defends against another person. Had the two agencies shared information, a combination of the two approaches might have been productive.[4]

Operational procedures are often so complex that each organization can reasonably be expected to develop only a limited number of them. As a consequence, organizations are seldom able to offer the best possible method of achieving any given objective. Instead, they provide decision makers with a choice among the programs or routines available at the time for a given purpose. Because decision makers' choices are almost always severely restricted, they are governed by the *logic of appropriateness* rather than the *logic of consequences* preferred by rational actors.[5] Both the logic of efficiency and the logic of efficiency, previously discussed in chapter 1, emphasize the results of an action.

For example, in his preparation for the Gulf War in 1991, field commander Norman Schwarzkopf assumed that Iraq would use fixed launchers for its SCUD missiles, and American forces had appropriate plans for eliminating those fixed sites at the beginning of the conflict. But Iraq employed SCUD missiles on mobile launchers. So the United States did not find and destroy Iraq's launchers.[6] When Secretary of Defense Richard B. Cheney subsequently ordered Schwarzkopf to do so because Israel was under attack, Schwarzkopf had no appropriate plan for implementing such a policy.[7] Cheney, thinking in terms of the logic of consequences, quickly lost his cool. According to an eyewitness, he said, "As long as I am Secretary of Defense, the Defense Department will do as I tell them. The number one priority is to keep Israel out of the war."[8] Unfortunately, Schwarzkopf did not have an appropriate routine for dealing with such elusive targets. Although he increased the number of sorties (a single plane set out to engage targets and return) directed against Iraqi

SCUD launchers and although he had American and British special operations harass the Iraqi missile crews, neither measure was successful.[9] As much as the commander may have wanted to be more responsive to Cheney's directive, he could not improvise a more satisfactory routine in the time available.

Often SOPS are needed to permit several different departments to work together. The "rules of the game" will usually prescribe which officials are to be involved and how much discretion each will have in making particular decisions. These rules may be established by congressional statute, by executive order, or simply by practice.

For example, in the Export Administration Act of 1969 Congress granted the primary responsibility for approving export licenses for **dual-use goods** to the Department of Commerce. A dual-use good is one that has both a civilian and a military use. However, before approving such sales the Commerce Department must, by statute, consult with both the Departments of State and Defense to determine whether there are any security or other reasons why these particular goods should not be sold abroad. Yet even if these departments object to the sale, the Commerce Department can approve it unless one or both of these departments successfully appeal the decision to the White House.

The Commerce Department's authority to make such decisions is a good example of an **action channel**. In this case, the action channel runs from the lowest-level official in Commerce who initiates the approval process to the upper-level official who eventually approves or disapproves the export license. Commerce officials in this channel control the action in the sense that officials at their level in other departments who want to influence this decision must direct their influence toward these Commerce officials. Because the Commerce Department is primarily responsible for building relationships between the U.S. government and the American business community, its officers will naturally approve these licenses unless there is a compelling reason not to do so.

Thus between March 1985 and August 1990 the Commerce Department approved without condition nearly 800 export licenses for the sale of dual-use technology and materials to Iraq. The State Department seldom objected to any of these licenses because it was its policy to maintain close relations with Iraq, which was currently engaged in a conflict with Iran, a government that was unfriendly to the United States. The Defense Department, however, objected to over 40 percent of these requests on the grounds that they endangered national security. Nevertheless, the Commerce Department approved these licenses, arguing that if U.S. businesses did not sell these technologies or materials to Iraq, other U.S. allies would be happy to do so. Only one of these sales was successfully appealed to the White House—a request to sell industrial furnaces to Iraq.[10] Table 10.1 illustrates the dimensions of the different agency stances to the sale of dual-use

Table 10.1. Dimensions of Foreign Policy Inputs: Organizational Stances on the Sale of Dual-use Goods

	Multilateral		Unilateral	
	Coercive	Noncoercive	Noncoercive	Coercive
Proactive			Departments of Commerce and State	
Reactive				Department of Defense

Because the Commerce Department is the action channel for the approval of dual-use exports, it plays the central role. Commerce's export-control policy is generally <u>MCA</u>—unilateral because it is primarily concerned with U.S. business interests, noncoercive because it is predisposed to approve these business requests, and proactive because it wants to help U.S. businesses capture foreign markets.

The State Department's export-control policy is generally <u>MCA</u>—unilateral because it wants to serve U.S. interests, noncoercive because it wants to support foreign sales unless there is a good policy reason for not doing so, and proactive because it favors trade with most other countries.

The Defense Department is <u>MCA</u>—it is also unilateral because it gives priority to U.S. defense interests, more coercive than other departments because it is anxious to prevent these goods from reaching the wrong parties, and more reactive than other involved agencies because it wants to prohibit the sale of these goods to certain countries.

goods. Not all foreign policy decisions can be explained in terms of the organization process model, however. There are definite limits.

Limits of the Model

Although experienced bureaucrats frequently rely upon the organizational behavior model to account for foreign policy decisions, this model is not as usable to those who are unfamiliar with the routines of various organizations. Moreover, to the extent that this model depends on unique features of U.S. organizations at a particular time, it cannot explain behavior in those same organizations at other times or the behavior of organizations in other countries. Despite these deficiencies, the organizational behavior model provides a powerful explanation for most decisions made by lower-level organizations. Because organizational behavior varies somewhat from one organization to another, this chapter explores some of the features of four different kinds of organizations that have an important impact on American foreign policy: the State Department, the Defense Department, economic organizations, and intelligence agencies.

Diplomatic Organizations

New foreign service officers are usually sent abroad to various embassies and consulates early in their training to develop the skills they will need to report on political activities abroad, coordinate the basic policy decisions in Washington, and then implement these policies overseas.

Embassies

Senior career foreign service officers hold about two-thirds of U.S. ambassadorial posts, and non–foreign service officers hold a third. Indeed, political appointees hold some of the major ambassadorial posts such as France and Great Britain. Many of these non–foreign service officers have made significant financial contributions to the president and the president's party. Invariably, however, the deputy chief of mission (DCM) is a foreign service officer. The ambassador relies on foreign service officers to head the embassy's political, economic, consular, and administrative divisions, but the bulk of the embassy staff is made up of officers assigned by other government departments and agencies, including Agriculture, Commerce, Defense, Treasury, the CIA, the U.S. Information Agency, USAID, and the Peace Corps.

In the host country the ambassador usually tries to coordinate U.S. efforts at the local level through a **country team** made up of the embassy's principal officers. Although the ambassador is the titular head of this country team, many of the officers involved receive instructions from and make reports to their parent organizations in Washington. For this reason, it is not always easy for the ambassador to give coherence to American efforts in the host country, especially if there are major policy differences between the State Department and the other departments and agencies represented on the country team.

Although the Foreign Service encourages its officers to become familiar with local customs and languages, most of those assigned to an embassy will be policy generalists. The size and organization of the Foreign Service are simply not conducive to a career that revolves around specialization in the affairs of one country. Besides, the State Department usually rotates its officers to different countries to protect itself from the accusation that its officers are better representatives of the host country than they are of the United States.

After the departing and newly arriving embassy officers exchange essential information, the new ambassador assumes the responsibility for signing off on all important cables between the field and Washington, except perhaps for those originating with intelligence groups such as the CIA, which, to protect its sources, acts as secretly and autonomously as possible. Because of strong differences within the Foreign Service over Vietnam policy in the 1960s and 1970s, younger foreign service officers demanded alternative means of communication so that they could get their views back to Washington. This "dissent" channel proved very important in places such as Nicaragua in the late 1970s where non–foreign service ambassadors developed cozy relationships with local dictators and essentially hid the negative aspects of the local regime in their reports. In some cases foreign service officers have used these supplementary channels to keep Washington abreast of a situation in which the ambassador was not providing objective reports on the host country.

The tasks performed by an embassy's political officers are really the heart of the traditional Foreign Service and State Department activities abroad. One of the primary responsibilities of such political officers is to gather information on the internal and external politics of the host country—a task that usually entails contact with opposition groups. Because host governments often resent such efforts, the United States occasionally has halted them, only to learn the hard way how important these contacts are—for example, in Iran in 1978 and in Nicaragua in 1979. Even when an embassy is acutely aware of changes taking place within a society, it may be difficult to project the consequences of any new initiatives. For example, in the mid-1980s embassy officials found it difficult to report objectively about Mikhail Gorbachev's new policies in the Soviet Union because the administration in Washington was fond of referring to the Soviet Union as the "evil empire." [11]

Embassy officials are responsible not only for analyzing information but also for reporting it back to Washington concisely and clearly. Political officers must overcome any cultural barriers to understanding the local politics. For example, a junior officer in the Côte d'Ivoire may find it difficult to explain why a one-party regime in that country actually represents a positive political development even though Americans believe that party competition is essential to democracy. [12]

The embassy also may become heavily involved in implementing U.S. foreign policy at the country level. For example, when President Jimmy Carter sought to implement his human rights policies, he discovered that there was much resistance to these policies both in the U.S. government and in American embassies overseas. Lawrence Pezzullo, the U.S. ambassador to Paraguay during the Carter administration, realized that his embassy was not united behind Carter's new human rights policy. But rather than attempting on his own to apply that policy to Gen. Alfredo Stroessner Mattiauda, the local dictator, he spent many months discussing the new policy with his country team so that his embassy could present a united front before trying to convince Stroessner that the United States was serious about human rights. The preparatory work within the embassy proved worthwhile. Once Stroessner and his henchmen realized that all their contacts with the U.S. embassy were emphasizing the importance of human rights in America's relations with Paraguay, they made some concessions.

Sometimes the embassy must call in outside help to convince the host government to pay attention to its new policy. For example, shortly after the assassination of opposition leader Benigno Aquino Jr. in the Philippines in 1983, the American government decided that either President Ferdinand Marcos would have to accept reforms or the U.S. government would have to work toward his replacement by strengthening those Filipino institutions that could provide the basis for a more democratic government in the future. Yet the American embassy in Manila found it difficult to convince Marcos that he must implement reforms because he believed he had a close personal relationship with President Ronald Reagan. When it became evident that Marcos did not intend to undertake reforms, the embassy brought in Senator Paul Laxalt, a close friend of President Reagan, to convince Marcos that he must allow reforms or lose American support. He responded by calling a snap presidential election to renew his political mandate—an election that eventually resulted in his removal from office.[13]

Because they deal with the host government on a daily basis, embassy officers may convince themselves that they are in the best position to know what foreign policy the United States should pursue in relation to that country. These officers sometimes perceive people in Washington as meddling in their affairs. Often, however, it is equally important to reconcile U.S. interests in a particular country with America's worldwide interests. In some instances, Washington may send in an experienced special negotiator and team of experts to join the political officers in the embassy so that American interests are represented more fully in specific negotiations.[14] In other instances, an assistant secretary of state in charge of American policy toward a particular region may hold meetings with the relevant chiefs of missions (ambassadors) to explain the nuances of some of Washington's newer policies. Such meetings also give ambassadors an opportunity to express their collective views on policies being pursued by Washington.

State Department

At the headquarters of the State Department in Washington, D.C. the emphasis tends to be on policy analysis, decision making, and policy evaluation. Traditionally, the lowest-level decision maker in the State Department is an assistant secretary of state or a deputy assistant secretary, but, with few exceptions, most of their choices are shaped by lower-level officers. In this sense, the old adage that " 'the buck stops here' ignores the reality . . . that every 'buck' is forged, shaped and framed by immediate subordinates." [15] Or, as former secretary of state Dean Acheson has noted, "The springs of policy bubble up; they do not trickle down." [16]

Indeed, so much is going on in the world that the secretary of state and other high-level officials must devote most of their attention to the most urgent matters. However, the most urgent matters are not necessarily the most important ones. Urgency is sometimes determined by events abroad, but it is just as likely to stem from domestic events that may not seem that important in retrospect. For example, top officials may have to deal with a specific issue because a congressional committee will be taking it up next week, or the president wants to include something about it in an upcoming speech, or a visiting foreign dignitary is expected to raise the issue with either the president or the secretary of state.

Because embassies are the eyes and ears of the Foreign Service, the State Department is largely organized on a regional basis. The most important bureaus are those dealing with European and Canadian Affairs, East Asian and Pacific Affairs, African Affairs, Near Eastern Affairs, Western Hemisphere Affairs, South Asian Affairs, and International Organization Affairs.[17] Although the department emphasizes these bilateral relationships, in view of global communications, it must to do so in a way that will not cause unfavorable global repercussions. The Department of State also houses a large number of functional bureaus, including Economic and Business Affairs; Political-Military Affairs; Consular Affairs; Democracy, Human Rights and Labor Affairs; International Narcotics and Law Enforcement Affairs; Oceans and International Environmental and Scientific Affairs; Population, Refugees, and Migration Affairs; Intelligence and Research; Public Affairs; and Legislative Affairs.

Paper Trail.   All of these bureaus and the subordinate offices and desks associated with them must coordinate their information reporting process. For example, a message about an event in South Asia arrives at the Department of State from the U.S. embassy in India. An operations officer in the communications center then sends the **action copy** of the message to the Bureau of South Asian Affairs, because it is the unit primarily responsible for responding to the message. The communications officers also send **information copies** of the same message to other geographical and functional bureaus in the department, to the secretary of state and other top officials, and to other appropriate departments and agencies of the government, including the White House, the Department of Defense, and the CIA.

Once the action copy arrives in the communications center of the Bureau of South Asian Affairs, it is sent on to the Office of Indian, Nepal, and Sri Lanka Affairs, and most likely to a desk officer in charge of some specific aspect of U.S. relations with India. In the meantime, the bureau's communications center is churning out information copies of the same message to other officials throughout the Bureau of South Asian Affairs. Because this process is repeated in message centers throughout the government, in theory every government official who has a legitimate interest in this message will get a copy. On the basis of past policy, many of those who receive the message will think they know how the government should respond to it, but it is the job of the officials who receive the action copy to initiate this response. Even though higher-level officials may be prepared to act, the action is usually initiated by lower-level officials.

The initial response to the incoming message, usually drafted by the lowest-level officer in this action channel, is forwarded up the channel until someone designated to sign off on this policy for the secretary approves it. (Only a small percentage of these outgoing messages are actually signed by either the secretary of state or the president.) At each stage of the approval process the lower-level official will consult with his or her superiors as well as anyone outside the State Department who is expected to sign off on the response at his or her own level. In most instances, those initially responsible for taking action will try to get a consensus at the lowest level possible. That way, they can exercise some control over the matter.

Deadlines.   **Deadlines** are important in this process, because officials at a given level can have the most direct influence on a response when the paperwork is on the desk of an action officer at their level even if he or she is in a different bureau. Deadlines are just one example of the kinds of rules that govern the way decisions are made. These rules may vary, however, depending on the type of policy, its urgency, and the personalities of those involved, among other things. Most people in the bureaucracy probably prefer a policy response that is in tune with established instructions. But if a group of officials wants to change the policy, differences of opinion may emerge at every level until the policy has been signed off either by the secretary of state or by the president.

Many of the issues that arise may involve minute details. But even the smallest details can be very important in diplomacy, and efforts to change policies are often initiated over what might seem to be trivial matters at the time. For example, during the Carter administration a dispute arose between the Bureau of Western Hemisphere Affairs and the new Bureau for Human Rights and Humanitarian Affairs over the question of whether the United States should provide the Nicaraguan national guard with "sling swivels" for their rifles.[18] This issue became important because the two bureaus had very different ideas about what stance the United States should take toward the regime of Nicaraguan leader Anastasio Somoza. The Inter-American bureau was prepared to let the national guard have U.S. swivels on their rifles because at the time it thought the guard could still play an important role in denying victory to the left-wing opposition group, the Sandinistas. The Human Rights bureau wanted to deny the request for swivels to signal American dissatisfaction with Somoza's policies. Although the swivels cost only a few cents each, the secretary of state eventually had to make the decision. He denied the sale.[19]

When the United States later tried to get Somoza to give up power in Nicaragua in 1979, he refused, offering instead to hold a plebiscite to legitimize his rule. The Carter administration was divided over how to deal with this offer. The assistant secretary of state for the Latin American bureau, a career executive, felt that Somoza had proposed the plebiscite as a delaying tactic and wanted to threaten Somoza with a series of economic and political measures if he did not resign immediately. The NSC expert on Latin America, Robert Pastor, a political appointee, generally agreed with this analysis of Somoza's motives, but did not feel that the United States, being a democratic country, could oppose the idea of holding a plebiscite. Carter decided to proceed with a plebiscite, but the effort to negotiate a plebiscite eventually failed, probably because Somoza knew he would lose.[20] By the time this occurred, the opportunity to create a reform government to replace Somoza had run out because Sandinista forces were taking over the country. As in this instance, political executives are often tempted to abide by the logic of general policies rather than predict how particular situations will turn out because, although they may have more general experience, they may not have the best available information on the situation abroad. Table 10.2 shows the differences in dimensions between political appointees and career executives in their policy recommendations for Nicaragua.

The conflicts between officials in different bureaus and at various levels in the State Department occur in other departments and agencies of the government as well. But the issue of control is particularly interesting in the Department of Defense because each of the three main military services (four if the Marine Corps is included) is a separate department, and each of these military services has its own constituency both in Congress and in society as a whole. Moreover, the problem of control in the Department of Defense is compounded by the fact that both the president and the secretary of defense are charged with the responsibility of maintaining civilian control over the military.

Military Organizations

The State Department is a large, complex organization, but it is not nearly as large or as complex as the Department of Defense. Whereas the State Department employs about 25,000 people (half of whom are serving abroad at any given time), the Defense Department has about 4 million employees. Of those, over 1.4 million are in the uniformed services and another 2.6 million are civilian employees. About one-fourth of U.S. active-duty personnel are stationed at some ninety bases located abroad. The Department of State has a budget of several billion, whereas the Defense Department's budget is about $455 billion, which makes up over 50 percent of the discretionary portion of the U.S. federal budget. Indeed, the Defense Department probably wastes more money than the State Department spends altogether.

The rest of this section on military organizations and processes focuses on just two aspects of the Defense Department: the inter-service rivalry and civil–military relations. Both of these topics raise the central issue of control.

Table 10.2. Dimensions of Foreign Policy Inputs: Positions Taken by Various Government Officials on Nicaraguan Dictator Anastasio Somoza, 1978–1979

| | Multilateral | | Unilateral | |
	Coercive	Noncoercive	Noncoercive	Coercive
Proactive				Career executives (specialists) in Bureau of Inter-American Affairs want to "force Somoza out."
Reactive		Political executives (generalists) in the State Department and White House favor international mediation/ plebiscite.		

The political executives inside and outside the Department of State wanted to transform the plebiscite idea into a vote on Somoza's staying in power and negotiate terms that would ensure a free election, an MCA policy. They were multilateral because they did not feel that they could oppose the democratic idea of holding a plebiscite or a free election to resolve the issue, noncoercive because they hoped to reach an agreement, and somewhat reactive because they were not prepared to pay the costs of forcing a change in Nicaragua.

The career executives in the Bureau of Inter-American Affairs (later known as Western Hemisphere Affairs) wanted to dismiss the plebiscite and apply pressure on Somoza to bring about his departure, an MCA policy. These career executives were unilateral because they were thinking mainly of U.S. interests, coercive because they were prepared to employ a full list of sanctions, and proactive because they wanted to get Somoza out of Nicaragua as rapidly as possible.

Inter-service Rivalry

By the end of World War II, U.S. military forces could no longer function effectively under separate Navy and War Departments. The development of an air force and the need for joint air-land-sea operations led to the creation of a single Department of Defense in 1947. Because the new air force asserted that it could deliver a knock-out blow to the enemy more cheaply than the army and that it could project U.S. power abroad more effectively than the navy, both of these traditional services were scrambling to maintain their traditional military missions. The competition between the three main services and the Marine Corps was particularly intense from about 1944 until 1953. But in this period each of main services received roughly equal funding.

In the 1950s, however, the air force gained a decisive advantage because President Dwight D. Eisenhower's "new look" emphasized a policy of massive retaliation based on strategic air capabilities. At this point, the air force was receiving about 47 percent of the Defense Department budget, and the army and navy were receiving 22 percent and 29 percent, respectively.[21] In the 1960s the army and the navy (including the Marines) stressed their greater capacity for fighting limited wars, and the navy was bolstered by its strategic nuclear submarine capability. But the air force continued to maintain its budget advantage, insisting that air force missiles and bombers were essential for strategic deterrence and that air force bombers and fighters were the best means of fighting conventional wars without sustaining large numbers of casualties.

The competition among the military services also spilled over into the political realm. Each of the services developed a special relationship with the relevant congressional committees, with the industrial sectors that would benefit the most from its purchases, and with veterans and other support groups. These coalitions among the military services, congressional committees, and particular industrial sectors—the so-called **iron triangle**—made it exceedingly difficult for Congress and the president to deny any of the military services the expensive weapons and bases they needed to sustain their missions.

After the Vietnam War, each of the military services recognized that it needed more flexibility—that is, some capability to operate in the air, on land, and at sea. These expanded capabilities led, however, to some duplication. Gradually, the president and Congress allowed such duplication because it strengthened the individual services and lessened the rivalry between them. That rivalry might have been even worse had it not been for the competition among different divisions within each of the military services. For example, the bomber troops in the air force would have pushed their advantages over fighter troops in other services even further had such a step not had the potential to undermine the position of fighter troops in the air force.

The organization of the Department of Defense reinforced the autonomy of the individual military services. A chief headed each of the services, and these chiefs, in turn, formed the Joint Chiefs of Staff (JCS). The commandant of the Marine Corps joined the chiefs of the other services on the JCS when that was appropriate. The chairman of the Joint Chiefs of Staff (CJCS) was simply one among equals; he did not have any more formal power than the chiefs of the other services. Thus each chief felt primarily responsible for his own military service, and most decisions by the JCS represented the lowest common denominator of what these individual chiefs could agree on. This organization fostered several military fiascos, including the failed attempt to rescue the hostages in Iran during the Carter administration.[22]

In 1986 Congress moved to create a more effective central military command by passing the Goldwater-Nichols Act. This act gave the JCS chairman and the chairman's special deputy exclusive access to the president and a larger staff. The idea was that the JCS chairman would develop a unified staff that would serve him and the country as a whole rather than the separate service chiefs. In addition, the new act provided for a commander in chief in each theater of war with similar authority over all of the service elements under that commander's control.

The 1991 Persian Gulf War provided the first good opportunity to assess the affect of this new legislation on strategic policy making both in the field and in Washington. General Colin Powell was chairman of the Joint Chiefs of Staff, and General Norman Schwarzkopf was commander in chief of the Central Command (CENTCOM). All three services and the Marines were under the command of Powell and Schwarzkopf.

Schwarzkopf gave primary responsibility for planning various aspects of the war to the individual services—that is, he gave them autonomy. The air force was primarily responsible for the first phase of the conflict, the air war; the army, for the second phase of the conflict, a single envelopment around the enemy in the western desert to enclose retreating Iraqi forces; and the marines for a "fixed" assault on Iraqi troops in the eastern desert on the Kuwaiti-Saudi border. The navy was not given as decisive a role as the other main services because both the air force and the army had access to adequate land bases from which to launch their attacks.

One of the first issues of control in the Gulf War was how to distinguish between friendly and unfriendly aircraft. The air force's F-15C fighter planes had systems that could separately identify friend and foe. But navy fighter planes were only equipped with technology that could identify one or the other, not both. Because the air force was the action channel, the air force defined the rules of engagement; and it decided that U.S. planes could take action against other planes in the combat zone only if they had two independent means of verification—that is, U.S. planes would have to both confirm that they were dealing with an enemy plane and confirm that they were not dealing with an allied plane.[23] The navy, unlike the air force, did not have this capability, and it complained that its fighter pilots would not be able to get as many "kills" as air force pilots under these rules of engagement. The air force prevailed, however.

The relations between the marines and the army in the Gulf War posed another large control problem. The marines were unhappy to learn that they were being asked to engage in a fixed assault. The whole idea that they were supposed to hold the enemy in place and not advance on the enemy was alien to the marines. They had tested the ability of the Iraqi forces opposing them during the Khafji battle in late January 1991,[24] and they were convinced that they could defeat these forces and take Kuwait

City in a matter of three days. Schwarzkopf didn't listen to the marines very carefully and approved their plan for a **fixed offensive** without understanding what would happen if the marines were as aggressive as they are trained to be.

Unfortunately Schwarzkopf focused his attention on the Seventh and Eighteenth Army Corps, which he had positioned in the western desert in Saudi Arabia for what he thought would be the knockout blow against Iraq. The Seventh Corps, which had been transferred from Germany to CENTCOM, was to rapidly envelop Iraqi forces, a move that would cover hundreds of miles of desert. The army generals wanted to take their time both so that they could maintain a "tight fist" and so that they would not outrun their supply base. Unfortunately, the army and marine components of the attack were not well coordinated. An aggressive marine attack forced an Iraqi retreat before the army could complete its wide maneuver in the western desert and trap Iraqi forces in southern Iraq and Kuwait. Thus although CENTCOM was intended to be a joint command under a single commander, it did not fight as a unified command.

Although it is too early to assess the effectiveness of CENTCOM in the Iraq War, it seems that the combined forces operated more effectively than they did in the Persian Gulf War.[25] Rather than having an air war followed by a ground war, the air–ground–sea attack occurred simultaneously. Although CENTCOM seemed to demonstrate more flexibility in the actual conduct of the Iraq War than the Persian Gulf War, it was largely unprepared for the post–war situation that emerged.

Since the end of the cold war, the United States has substantially reduced the size of American military forces, but it has not required "significant changes in basic force structure or doctrine."[26] Five reviews—the 1990 Base Force, the 1993 Bottom Up Review, the 1995 Commission on Roles and Missions, the 1997 Quadrennial Defense Review (QDR), and the 2001 QDR—have reduced nuclear forces, except for SLBM, by about 50 percent; total active duty forces, except for marines, by almost 40 percent; and Ready Reserves, except for air force and marines, by 20 to 40 percent.[27] Under Clinton's bottoms-up-review (BUR) the air force was slated to organize some 400,000 troops into twenty tactical fighter wings and other units; the army was to have an active-duty force of about 450,000 troops organized into fourteen divisions, including five infantry divisions, four mechanized divisions, three armored divisions, one airborne division, and one air assault division; the navy was to have nearly 420,000 troops, as well as twelve carriers and 340–350 surface ships and a submarine-based strategic nuclear missile force; and the marines were to have approximately 180,000 troops divided into three expeditionary forces.[28] As a result of the September 11, 2001 attack and the Iraq war, there have been some adjustments, particularly the decision to organize ground forces into brigade-sized units rather than divisions. By the end of fiscal year 2005, Congress authorized the air force to have 359,700 active-duty troops; the army, 502,400 troops; the navy, 365,900 troops, and the marines, 178,000 troops.

In September 2003 the United States had committed roughly 180,000 to the occupation of Iraq, 150,000 troops of whom were actually deployed in Iraq itself. Of these, approximately 120,000 were army troops. However, the army itself could only sustain an occupation force of 38,000 to 64,000 troops indefinitely, using units from the army's active components.[29] It has had to activate army reserve and National Guard troops in order to meet the overall requirement in Iraq. Given the problems that the army and even the marines have had in recruiting people to replace those who are leaving these services, especially the recruitment of replacements for the most dangerous specialties, such as detecting and disarming homemade bombs, this commitment has undermined the ability of U.S. forces to deal with other security requirements. Whether the United States will be able to meet its force requirements under the all-volunteer system will depend in part on how well the Department of Defense deals with another issue: civil–military relations.

Civil–Military Relations.

According to Max Weber, the ideal relationship between a democratic society and the military would be one in which (1) all those in the military are citizens; (2) the military is representative of civil society; (3) the military is integrated into civil society, except when it is absolutely necessary for it to be separate to perform its military function; and (4) the military is subordinate to civil authorities.[30] Because the United States has a citizen army, both the similarities and differences between the military and civil society, as well as the relations between the military and civil society, are causes for concern. Three social issues have created special problems for the military: homosexuality, women in combat, and sexual harassment.

In 1992 presidential candidate Bill Clinton promised he would end the ban on homosexuals in the military if elected. But when he attempted to do so early in his first term, many in the Defense Department and Congress objected. He then delayed the implementation of his decision for six months while a committee advised him on the policy, and then reversed himself by announcing a "don't ask, don't tell, don't pursue" policy instead. That policy continued to be controversial both among those supporting gay rights in the military and society and those opposing homosexuality in the military and society.

The Clinton administration was more successful at creating equal opportunities for women in the military. Whereas women were once barred either by law or by policy from serving in a variety of combat positions, they are now able to fly combat missions and to serve on combat ships. The army and the Marine Corps also have opened some combat positions to women, but they have been reluctant to make all such positions available. "One in every six GIs (one in five in the Air Force) on active duty today is female;" however, women are not assigned to elite units like the Rangers, SEALs, Green Berets, and the secretive Delta Force, all of whom emphasize male-chauvinist thinking.[31]

As women become more numerous in the military services, they are calling attention to the continuing problem of sexual harassment. The issue finally received national attention in 1991, when male naval aviators at a Las Vegas convention engaged in gross sexual misconduct against some of their female colleagues. After the Tailhook scandal, the military command took actions to eliminate the problem, but it continues to afflict the military. In 2003, 579 of 659 female cadets at the Air Force Academy responded to a survey, 70 percent of whom reported sexual harassment, 22 percent had been pressured for sexual favors, and 19 percent were victims of rape or attempted rape.[32]

The military services are not so representative of American society in other ways as well. For example, the military is far more conservative and Republican than the American population as a whole, making Weber's fourth factor—civilian control over the military—even more important.

The U.S. Constitution directs the president to serve as the nation's commander in chief, and the National Security Act of 1947 stipulates that the secretaries of defense, army, navy, and air force must be civilians. Indeed, each of these civilian secretaries has a separate staff and is expected to oversee the operation of his or her respective departments, including military chiefs. However, the military staffs of the service chiefs have traditionally been much stronger than those of the individual department secretaries. The Goldwater-Nichols Act has tried to strengthen civilian control by enhancing the power of the service secretaries. The act also reiterated that the service secretaries have the *sole* and *ultimate* power within the Department of Defense on *any* matter on which they choose to act.[33]

As noted earlier, it is probably too early to assess the effects of this measure. President George H. W. Bush and Secretary of Defense Cheney tried to leave their commanders (Powell and Schwarzkopf) alone once the war began, but civilian leaders made the crucial decision on when to end the war. Unfortunately, this decision was not carefully coordinated at all levels. General Schwarzkopf did not object, but he seemed unsure whether General Powell was speaking for the president, the secretary of defense, or himself as JCS chairman. When Schwarzkopf informed his immediate subordinates, they were shocked because the gate had not yet been closed on Iraqi forces. Table 10.3 illustrates the degree to which the coordination between civilian and military commanders at the end of the Persian Gulf War was not well worked out.

Table 10.3. Dimensions of Foreign Policy Inputs: Civilian Control over the Military at the End of the Persian Gulf War

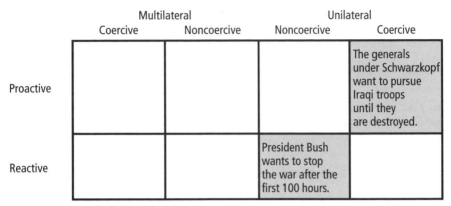

| | Multilateral | | Unilateral | |
	Coercive	Noncoercive	Noncoercive	Coercive
Proactive				The generals under Schwarzkopf want to pursue Iraqi troops until they are destroyed.
Reactive			President Bush wants to stop the war after the first 100 hours.	

At the end of the Persian Gulf War, the army generals under Schwarzkopf advocated an MCA policy—unilateral because they wanted to act regardless of the fact that coalition partners might raise questions, coercive because they wanted to continue the use of force, and proactive because they emphasized the benefits of completing the mission.

President Bush advocated an MCA policy—unilateral because although he may or may not have been concerned with the views of coalition forces, he was prepared to act on his own, noncoercive because he wanted to end the hostilities, and reactive because he was concerned with the costs of extending the war into Iraqi territory.

President Bush has consistently argued that he had the full support of his generals in the field with respect to both force levels and strategies during and after the Iraq War. However, Representative John P. Murtha's proposal in November 2005 to pull American forces out of Iraq in six months raises some questions about the relations between the president and his generals, because as a decorated marine and long-time member of the House Armed Services Committee Murtha has had ready access to many of the same generals.[34]

Problems of control almost always raise issues of coordination. Coordination problems figure more prominently in the discussion of U.S. international economic policy than diplomatic and military policy because so many different departments and agencies are involved.

Economic Organizations and Processes

The primary government organization in the economic field is the Treasury Department, one of the three original cabinet departments. The State Department has a primary interest in international economic issues, and over the years other departments and agencies have developed significant interests in various aspects of the international economy, including the Departments of Agriculture, Commerce, Energy, Labor, and Transportation.

Each of these departments has at least one bureau or office devoted exclusively to some aspect of the international economy. Congress also has established special agencies to administer various international economic programs such as the Export–Import Bank, the Overseas Private Investment Corporation, and the U.S. Agency for International Development.

Interagency Committees

When international economic issues arise in the American government, they are usually addressed by interagency committees composed either of the principal heads of each of the concerned departments and agencies or their deputies. Early in the cold war either the secretary of state or his deputy would usually chair such committees, because the Department of State was pressing claims made by foreign countries on the robust U.S. domestic economy.

For example, even as late as 1974, when the Group of 77 first proposed a new international economic order to obtain trade and other concessions from the developed world, the State Department chaired the meeting in which representatives of State and the Department of the Treasury addressed the issues. The State Department was no more prepared than Treasury to interfere with market forces in order to satisfy the demands of the Group of 77(G-77), but the State Department was prepared to discuss new arrangements for various commodities on a case-by-case basis. Senior officials at the Treasury Department insisted, however, on "keeping the lid on the extent and costs of commodity agreements." [35] Table 10.4 illustrates the differences between the State and Treasury Departments' positions on the demands of the G-77.

The reticence of these departments to make concessions to developing countries stemmed in no small part from the fact that by the 1970s the economies of Europe and Japan had recovered from World War II to the point that international economic issues were beginning to negatively affect the U.S. economy. Meanwhile, the State Department no longer chaired the interagency committees. Some observers argued that the more domestically oriented government departments and agencies were no longer willing to allow the State Department to carry out that role because they believed the State Department was too biased in favor of foreign interests. Others contend that the State Department surrendered this role because the secretaries of state did not always assert themselves enough. Today a wide variety of interagency committees are used to coordinate international economic policy. For example, during the Clinton administration, an assistant to the president, aided by two senior officials from the State and Treasury Departments, provided informal U.S. economic policy coordination for meetings of the Group of Seven (G-7) industrialized countries.[36]

Some of this coordination is now done by the National Economic Council (NEC), which President Clinton created in 1993 to perform the

Table 10.4. Dimensions of Foreign Policy Inputs: Departmental Positions on the New International Economic Order in 1974

| | Multilateral | | Unilateral | |
	Coercive	Noncoercive	Noncoercive	Coercive
Proactive			Treasury is unresponsive to developing countries.	
Reactive			Department of State wants to be responsive to developing countries.	

In response to the demands of less developed countries for a new international economic order the U.S. Treasury was <u>MCA</u>—unilateral because it focused on American economic interests, non-coercive because it did not feel that threatened, and proactive because, favoring the existing system, it was unwilling to make any concessions to less developed countries.

The State Department was largely <u>MCA</u>—unilateral because although the department wanted to discuss the issues raised by the G-77, it was not prepared to make many concessions, noncoercive because the department felt that these issues should be negotiated, and (at least compared to Treasury) reactive because the department felt that some effort ought to be made to satisfy the demands for fairness raised by these countries.

same function in economic affairs that the National Security Council has performed for almost fifty years in the security area.[37] Although it is as yet too early to assess the overall effectiveness of this new institution, the NEC did play a key role in the negotiations among various executive agencies over the North American Free Trade Agreement (NAFTA), the Uruguay Round of the General Agreement on Tariffs and Trade (GATT) negotiations, and the Asia Pacific Economic Conference (APEC), particularly as it applies to Japan.[38]

The range of international economic issues that various government departments and agencies must address has grown steadily. The issues include problems involving exchange rates, food policy, environmental policy, science policy, and trade policy. The remainder of this section will focus on trade policy, because it highlights the conflict between domestic and international economic concerns better than any other issue.

Trade Policy

The Constitution gives Congress the primary responsibility for regulating commerce between the United States and foreign countries. Indeed, for the first 150 years of the nation's history, it was Congress, not the executive, that determined what duties the United States would place on various goods and services entering the country.

All this changed, however, when Congress passed the Reciprocal Trade Agreements Act of 1934. In that act Congress authorized executive branch officials to negotiate reciprocal tariff reductions.[39] What is not so commonly understood is that Congress granted this power to the executive largely to at least partly escape the imbalance of political pressure that had persistently plagued Congress over trade arrangements. Most Democrats favored liberal or free trade but found it difficult to sustain such a policy because those industries that stood to be hurt by foreign imports always put great pressure on Congress to raise duties on these imports. The only way Congress could effectively reduce the tariffs that were, among other things, responsible for the Great Depression was to give the president the power to use possible reductions in tariffs to bargain with other countries to reduce their barriers to U.S. goods and services.

Congress, by itself, could not do this effectively. Not only was it in no position to bargain with foreign countries directly, but also it was at a distinct disadvantage in bargaining with domestic groups. According to I. M. Destler, Congress faced the "chronic imbalance between those who benefit from trade protection and those who pay the costs." Those who benefited from trade protection had an advantage both in "intensity of interest and, as a result, in political organization" that could not be matched by those who benefited from free trade.[40] All too often those who benefit from free trade—industrial users of imports, retailers, exporters, and foreign governments—take their good fortune for granted and see no need to organize in order to realize or maintain these benefits. As a result, individual members of Congress and the key congressional committees are subject to enormous pressures to provide relief to a few businesses, and little countervailing pressure to protect free trade, even though more people are likely to benefit from free trade.

From 1934 to 1962 the State Department took the lead in arranging reciprocal trade agreements and in chairing the interagency committees that resolved particular international economic issues. At this point Congress established a special trade representative as part of the Trade Expansion Act of 1962, because it suspected that the State Department did not give equal weight to international and domestic interests. Because the U.S. trade representative (USTR) was not a cabinet officer and was not necessarily close to the president, he or she did not always have the clout required to play the "brokering" role envisaged by congressional leaders, but the most effective USTRs have been astute political managers who have used their political know-how to broker deals both between the executive and Congress and between the United States and foreign countries.

By 1974 it had become clear that to further reduce trade barriers, the administration would have to address the problem of non-tariff barriers. Non-tariff barriers refer to a variety of domestic policies that restrict trade, such as health and safety standards. Congress was not prepared to grant this kind of authority to the administration, so the two branches developed a new procedure, **fast-track authority,** which requires Congress, within a fixed period of time, to take a simple yes or no vote, with no amendments permitted, on trade agreements specifically concluded under this negotiating authority.[41] This procedure lapsed in 1993, but it was renewed in 2002.

Congress has provided remedies for businesses that believe they have been treated unfairly. The Antidumping Act of 1921, the most commonly used measure, allows a business to petition the government to impose a countervailing duty if it can show that a foreign country is unfairly unloading goods in the U.S. market. Section 201 of the Trade Act of 1974 also allows a business to appeal for temporary relief if it can show injury as a result of trade concessions by the United States. Section 301 of the Omnibus Trade Act of 1988 requires the USTR to "investigate countries determined to have a history of violating existing laws and agreements dealing with intellectual property rights." And an amendment to Section 301, the so-called Super 301, required the USTR in 1989 and 1990 to designate "priority foreign countries" that were impeding U.S. exports and to provide retaliation if foreign action was insufficient or not forthcoming.[42]

Some of these remedies may make it too easy for inefficient businesses to seek relief. For example, only 5 percent of the 539 antidumping cases pursued since 1980 have failed.[43] But Section 301 has actually served to promote more liberal trade because it calls for the USTR to negotiate trade concessions with the offending country. Thus the USTR can use the complaint by a domestic producer to negotiate an arrangement that would provide opportunities for producers in both countries. The object of these provisions is not only to provide relief where it is most needed, but also to ensure that these measures do not prevent trade liberalization as a whole.

International economic policy is especially interesting because it requires not only the coordination of economic and political issues but also a balance between domestic and international concerns. The next section turns to another function of government—intelligence gathering. Because intelligence gathering is concerned primarily with the collection and analysis of information, it calls into question the relationship between those who are engaged primarily in those early stages in the foreign policy-making process and those who are mainly decision makers.

Intelligence Organizations and Processes

U.S. leaders have recognized the importance of gathering intelligence in foreign policy making since the very beginning of the republic. Gen. George Washington ran an intelligence operation during the Revolutionary War, and Congress granted him the authority to develop an intelligence capability during his first term as president. Eventually, the State,

Navy, and War Departments, as well as other agencies, also developed their own intelligence-gathering capabilities.

Early in the cold war, the State Department largely handled collecting intelligence on cultural, political, and economic activities abroad, and the Department of Defense concentrated on military intelligence. For example, the secretary of defense became responsible for most of the more technical means of intelligence gathering: the National Security Agency (NSA) conducts electronic intelligence, the National Geospatial-Intelligence Agency (NGA) performs imagery collection and analysis, and the National Reconnaissance Office (NRO) provides satellite intelligence.

The National Security Act created the Central Intelligence Agency at the same time that the Department of Defense and the National Security Council (NSC) were formed in 1947. But this legislation did not create a strong central intelligence organization. It provided no explicit authority to collect intelligence or to conduct clandestine activities, although it did contain some vague language to the effect that the NSC, to which the CIA reported, could assign various tasks to the CIA. And indeed, the initial meeting of the NSC established a new intelligence operation in Eastern Europe, where the chaotic situation after the war created a rich opportunity for developing human intelligence sources.[44]

Once it was established, however, the CIA was aggressive in developing its intelligence activities. Although it never really was able to displace the collection and analysis capabilities of the intelligence bureaus in other departments, it did develop Directorates of Intelligence and Operations. The Directorate of Intelligence was largely devoted to analyzing intelligence information provided by other agencies, but the Directorate of Operations became the primary vehicle of clandestine intelligence activities for the U.S. government.

Intelligence Collection and Analysis

Approximately 90 percent of the $40 billion budget for all foreign intelligence activities in the government is spent on intelligence collection. During the cold war, about three-fifths of the overall budget and as much as 90 percent of the CIA's own effort was directed at the Soviet Union.[45] Because the Soviets were the main enemy of the United States, the CIA was concerned primarily with answering puzzles about the Soviet economy and military capability: How large was the Soviet economy? How many ballistic missiles did the Soviets possess? These questions put a premium on espionage, because the Soviets would not provide such information voluntarily. Although public sources might be used to assess the validity of such intelligence, secret sources were usually required in order to come up with the definitive answers desired.

Once the cold war was over, only about one-fifth of the overall intelligence budget was devoted to Russia. Intelligence agencies explored a wide range of new questions, including the widening ethnic conflicts; the ability of rogue states to destabilize entire regions; the spread of weapons of mass destruction; and the extent of already large-scale environmental degradation.[46] Many of these new topics could be better characterized as mysteries than puzzles.[47] They involve questions for which there are no concrete answers, even though they may be terribly important in terms of policy planning. Much of the information required to answer these types of questions is from publicly available sources.

Thus the end of the cold war marked the beginning of a new era of intelligence—one likely to involve the intelligence community in a broader range of research questions and one likely to require it to master a much wider array of sources. Many of these sources will be found in government departments and agencies with whom the CIA has not developed close working relationships in the past, and many will involve nongovernmental organizations. Thus the intelligence community will have to learn to work more effectively with academics, U.S. NGOs, INGOs, and IGOs. For the CIA, this will involve an entirely different *modus operandi* requiring new subject specialists and new technical means.

The intelligence community had barely begun to meet these challenges when, as a result of the September 11, 2001 attacks, it was confronted with the overarching need to provide timely information on groups such as al Qaeda. The terrorism issue poses both puzzles and mysteries, and the 9/11 Commission provides the best guide to both the problems and the remedies that need to be considered. The failure of the nearly fifteen agencies that now make up the intelligence community to identify the nineteen al Qaeda operatives who entered the United States beginning in January 2000 for the purpose of flying commercial jets into key buildings, with symbolic value both domestically and abroad, underscored the weakness of U.S. intelligence agencies.

These weaknesses are too extensive to catalogue here, but they encompass breakdowns in specialization, coordination, and control. There were not enough linguists in all these agencies to translate the information coming to this country about al Qaeda activities. Moreover, the key agencies had no coordinated purpose or mission, so they could not effectively share the intelligence they did have. And no one at the top really assumed the responsibility for taking action in the short run.

The 9/11 Commission has made a number of recommendations to deal with these and other problems. Two of these recommendations will be discussed here. One recommendation is to unify the intelligence community under a new national intelligence director who has budget and hiring authority over all of the key intelligence agencies and who oversees the work of intelligence centers dealing with specific topics.[48]

The second recommendation deals with the relationship between intelligence analysts and policy makers in other departments and agencies of the government. The problem here is that intelligence analysts and policy makers are such different kinds of people. Generally speaking,

> Intelligence analysts still work in a world of paper, while policy relies mostly on discussion. Analysts analyze what can go wrong, while policy types think wishfully of what might go right. Analysts, focused on events abroad, take a long-term view and tend to presume that the world is largely impervious to U.S. action. Indeed, they may understand the inner machinations of Bonn or Tokyo better than they know the workings of Washington.
>
> Policy officials, by contrast, see foreign policy issues through the prism of domestic consequences. Their time horizon is short, and they are prone to overstate the potential impact of decisions made in Washington. The average tenure of assistant secretaries is little more than a year.[49]

The traditional view is that intelligence analysts should be kept separate from policy makers, such as those in the Defense Department, to ensure that the analysts maintain an independent perspective. If analysts do not maintain their independence, they are all too likely to confirm what policy makers want to hear, as was apparently the case with intelligence officers in many areas of the government prior to the Iraq War. The Bush administration was so intent on finding evidence of WMDs in Iraq that they failed to consider that Saddam Hussein had gotten rid of those weapons before the war began.[50]

On the other hand, the separation of intelligence analysts and policy officials may ensure that the intelligence collected by analysts is largely irrelevant to policy officials. To enhance the relevance of intelligence, the 9/11 Commission recommends that intelligence analysts in specific national centers assume responsibility for joint operational planning as well as joint intelligence collection. Of course, this operational planning would follow the policy direction of the president and the National Security Council, and the implementation of these plans would be the responsibility of regular departments and agencies of the U.S. government.[51]

Covert Actions

Eisenhower and other presidents have found covert intelligence actions attractive because they appear to be an effective means of accomplishing difficult tasks at relatively little cost and without assuming much responsibility. However, the claims of success in Iran in 1953 and Guatemala in 1954 have to be weighed against the subsequent disastrous relationship between the United States and each of these countries. In Iran, the CIA was able to install the shah to power simply by organizing street mobs in the capital of Tehran. But the shah was overthrown in 1979, and the United States has not been able to establish normal relations with that strategically important country since then. In Guatemala, the CIA was able to convince that country's government that it was under attack when it was not. But the social revolution that the United States aborted in 1954 degenerated into a guerrilla war that consumed Guatemala for over forty years. Thus the long-term consequences of these covert actions were very costly indeed.

In the short run at least, covert actions do offer the advantages of surprise and deniability. In the long run, however, the secrecy that characterizes covert actions carries operational risks. For example, to ensure secrecy and deniability, the CIA often has to obtain older, less reliable equipment. Thus the planes, landing craft, and motors that the CIA used for the 1961 Bay of Pigs invasion of Cuba were marred by equipment failures. The planes could barely reach their target before they had to return to their bases in Guatemala, and the motors used in some of the landing craft did not work.

The need to maintain secrecy also undermined the intelligence effort at the Bay of Pigs. For example, the image interpreters who evaluated the photos of beaches at three different sites were not told that they were doing so for an amphibious landing. If they had, they might have realized that what they took for seaweed off the Bay of Pigs was actually a reef that seriously delayed the operation and therefore provided Castro with an early warning of the invasion.

The penchant for deniability also can deprive covert actions of the political support or crucial information needed at critical moments. In 1961 President Kennedy denied the intelligence agents running the Bay of Pigs attack the air strikes they needed to protect the Cuban exiles caught on the beach. In 1973, when Secretary of State Henry A. Kissinger decided to call off both the overt attempt to influence the Chilean election and the covert plan to get rid of Chilean president Salvador Allende, word about Kissinger's decision to call off the covert plan did not reach the operators in Chile. Once started, a secret operation is not so easy to stop.

The use of covert methods also presents another dilemma for democratic states. Can the United States employ covert actions abroad without incurring a high risk that these same methods will be used internally? That is precisely what happened in the Watergate scandal in the early 1970s. Richard Nixon's White House staff hired G. Gordon Liddy and former CIA operatives to break into the Democratic Party headquarters in Washington, D.C. As a result of this and other actions, Nixon was forced to resign in 1974 to avoid impeachment by the House of Representatives. Many believe that the American Patriot Act of 2001 magnifies the likelihood of similar intrusions on the rights of ordinary Americans as a result of the war on terrorism.

It is increasingly difficult to draw the line between foreign and domestic affairs. In earlier days the FBI was occupied with domestic intelligence as a means of fighting domestic crime, and the CIA devoted itself exclusively to international intelligence as a means of dealing with external threats to the

United States. Indeed, when President Clinton's first national security adviser, Anthony Lake, met with officials from both the CIA and the FBI to propose that the FBI assist the CIA in dealing with the mounting crime problem in Russia, the CIA official responded, "Russia is ours." [52] As a result of the September 11, 2001 attacks the FBI is now heavily involved in U.S. embassies abroad and the CIA is heavily engaged in homeland security.

Although the 9/11 Commission did not deal very explicitly with covert activities, it did urge the intelligence community to be as transparent as possible. For example, it recommended that the overall budget for intelligence activities be made public. The commission noted the extent to which key information was not as widely shared within the intelligence community because of the overuse of the "need to know" restriction. The 9/11 Commission also recommended that primary responsibility "for paramilitary operations, whether clandestine or covert, should shift to the Defense Department." [53]

Conclusion

In order to take advantage of the benefits of specialization, foreign affairs organizations employ SOPs. When these procedures are appropriate for dealing with the foreign policy problem at hand, these organizations not only operate efficiently but also consistently, which makes their behavior quite predictable. However, these organizations are limited in the number of such routines they can master at a given point in time, and so they usually lack both the authority and standard procedures for dealing with new problems. Moreover, many different organizations—diplomatic, military, economic, and intelligence—are involved, and so their outputs need to be carefully coordinated in order to ensure beneficial outcomes.

When new demands are placed on these organizations or when they cannot resolve the differences between them, higher-level officials are usually called upon to make foreign policy decisions. The next chapter focuses on how both the personalities and positions of these higher-level decision makers affect U.S. foreign policy.

Key Concepts

action channel   353
action copy   358
career executives   351
career service   346
control   346
coordination   345
country team   355
deadlines   359
dual-use goods   353
fast-track authority   371

fixed offensive   364
information copies   358
iron triangle   362
organizational behavior
   model   345
organizational culture   350
political executives   351
specialization   345
standard operating procedures
   (SOPs)   345

Suggested Readings

1. Allison, Graham and Philip Zelikow. *Essence of Decision: Explaining the Cuban Missile Crisis.* 2d ed. New York: Addison-Wesley Longman, 1999.

2. Cohen, Stephan D. *The Making of United States International Economic Policy: Principles, Problems and Proposals for Reform.* 5th ed. Westport, Conn.: Praeger, 2000.

3. Gordon, Michael R and General Bernard E. Trainer. *The Generals' War: The Inside Story of the Conflict in the Gulf.* Boston: Little, Brown, 1995.

4. Lake, Anthony. *Somoza Falling.* Boston: Houghton Mifflin, 1989.

5. Zegart, Amy B. *Flawed Design: The Evolution of the CIA, JCS, and NSC.* Palo Alto: Stanford University Press, 1996.

CHAPTER 11

Governmental Politics Model: The President and His Advisors

President Bush meets with his war council at Camp David, Saturday, March 22, 2003. Present at the table with the president are, from left, Vice Chairman of the Joint Chiefs of Staff Peter Pace, Chairman of the Joint Chiefs of Staff Richard B. Meyers, Secretary of State Colin Powell, Secretary of Defense Donald Rumsfeld, Vice President Dick Cheney, Deputy Secretary of Defense Paul Wolfowitz, Chief of Staff to the Vice President Lewis Libby, Chief of Staff Andy Card, National Security Advisor Condoleezza Rice, CIA Director George Tenet, and Alberto Gonzales, counsel to the president. It is noteworthy that no bureaucratic experts were included in this meeting, except perhaps for those with military experience.

FOREIGN POLICY MAKING in large organizations requires effective specialization, coordination, and control. In the last chapter, specialization was a predictor of organizational behavior. Sufficient control and coordination in the form of SOPs were built into lower-level organizations. However, at higher levels in the bureaucracy the problems of control, specialization, and coordination are so manifest that we can only predict the outputs of government as a whole as the resultant of governmental politics.

Governmental Politics Model and Its Limitations

The governmental politics model emphasizes the individuals who represent the various departments and agencies of the foreign policy bureaucracy in interdepartmental groups, especially those "who sit atop these organizations." [1] These individuals are the central players in the game of **governmental politics**. Governmental politics refers to the bargaining among individuals representing various departments, agencies, and offices at different levels of the government." [2] The model conceives of foreign policy decisions as the political resultant of interactions among these individuals.

Specifications of the Model

The governmental politics model is best understood as a rejection of the rational model of decision making. Thus it is appropriate to restate that model before delineating the governmental politics model. The rational model conceives of foreign policy decisions as the result of calculations by a single actor (individual or organization). It posits that this actor has a coherent set of foreign policy preferences, considers a wide range of alternative methods of achieving these preferences, and chooses the best method of achieving these preferences.

By contrast, the governmental politics model notes that there is not one single actor but rather a host of such actors. This description by Strobe Talbott of the multiple actors involved in Bosnia policy provides an example of the governmental politics model:

> In Bosnia, nine agencies and departments of the U.S. government are cooperating with more than a dozen other governments, seven international organizations, and 13 major NGOs—from the Red Cross to the International Crisis Group to the American Bar Association—to implement the Dayton Peace Accords.[3]

As this example suggests, any given issue will involve many different individuals and organizations, and these parties will all see "different faces of issues." [4] As a result, these individuals and organizations will not be able to agree on a single set of preferences. Instead, they will have conflicting preferences based on varying "conceptions of national security, organizational, domestic, and personal interests." [5]

Moreover, the model assumes that none of these individuals or organizations is capable of dominating the decision.[6] Specifically, this means that neither the president nor any other interested party is able to impose its own preferences on the other parties involved. Since the parties cannot agree on a single set of preferences, the final decision cannot be rational because there is no common standard by which to determine which of the alternatives being considered best meets that standard.

In lieu of such a standard, the governmental politics model assumes that the final decision will simply be the political outcome of bargaining among the parties involved in the decision. Since that resultant comes out of "pulling and hauling" among individuals representing diverse organizations in the government, it is often a compromise that is the "lowest common denominator" of the preferences represented by the participants.

In contrast with the optimizing model that suggests a fairly comprehensive, logical process, advocates of the governmental politics model argue that foreign policy "problems are too difficult and time is too short for rational analysis."[7] They envisage a chaotic process in which there are so many different issues clamoring for the attention of high-level officials that they rarely focus on one issue at a time. As a result, they contend that foreign policy preferences are never completely worked out, and all the possible options are never systematically developed. At best the choice boils down to the status quo option and a single alternative, the satisficing model.

In order to predict such resultants, the personalities, positions, and bargaining strategies of all those involved have to be taken into account. This requires detailed information both about the context in which the decision is made and about the participants in the decision-making process.[8]

Since proponents of the governmental politics model speak of a resultant rather than a decision, the model suggests that the bargaining among these participants may continue even after a tentative outcome has been achieved. An issue may never be fully settled, and individuals and organizations will feel free to reopen the issue when their bargaining position improves. This is particularly true if we distinguish between the initial decision and the various actions that may be taken in order to implement a decision.

There are numerous examples of messy decisions that may reflect this kind of process in the history of American foreign policy. The failure of the hostage rescue mission in Iran in 1980 is one possible example.

Failure of the Hostage Rescue Effort in Iran

In the spring of 1980, the military and the CIA devised a plan to rescue the 53 American hostages still held in Iran. Initially President Carter had hoped that he could negotiate the release of these hostages, but when diplomatic efforts appeared to collapse, Carter turned to the military. As a result of the inter-service rivalry discussed in Chapter 10, each of the four services insisted on a prominent role in the rescue mission. Predictably a plan emerged in which each service was given its customary role: The navy provided ships; the air force, planes; the army, rangers; and the marines, the helicopter pilots.[9]

Unfortunately, this compromise did not produce a very workable plan. Although the plan had many problems, the primary difficulty was that six helicopters were required to carry out the mission. The rescuers started out with eight helicopters but abandoned one when a warning light appeared early in the mission. Then the seven remaining helicopters encountered a dust storm in the desert and became disoriented. The Marine commander flew out of the storm and landed, expecting the others to follow. But only one of the remaining helicopters returned to the carrier, while the other five fought their way through the storm. When the Marine commander realized that most of the others were trying to fly through the storm, he followed them.[10] By the time all six helicopters had arrived at Desert One—an hour and 25 minutes late—one of the six helicopters needed to return to repair a hydraulic pump that could not be repaired on site. As a result, the mission was aborted since all six helicopters were required. To make matters worse, one of the helicopters, in the process of repositioning itself in the desert, hit a C-130 cargo plane, which exploded, killing and injuring a number of the rescue party.

This disaster partly resulted from the insistence of every service on participating, even though they were not equally prepared to carry out the mission. Navy helicopters were not as well equipped as army helicopters for operations in the desert; and marine pilots did not have as much experience as army pilots in flying in sandstorms.[11] But the disaster was also created by the lack of coordination among the participating services. In order to maintain secrecy and avoid inter-service bickering, there was no written plan for the operation, and all of the parties had not formally rehearsed together.[12] As a consequence, the Marine pilots did not have some of the information available to others on the mission. The first Marine pilot to turn back did not realize that his malfunction was not that serious.[13] And those who confronted the sandstorm did not realize that they could have safely climbed to 400 feet and avoided the storm without being picked up by Iranian radar. Had they done so, they might have reached Desert One without damaging a hydraulic pump on the sixth helicopter. Unfortunately, no one had told them.[14]

Of course, it would be unfair to characterize every important decision made by the U.S. government as a compromise of this sort. There are many who contend that the governmental politics model is a distortion of decision making in the highest levels of the foreign policy bureaucracy.

Limitations

Perhaps the most common criticism of the governmental politics model is that it ignores the fact that the president appoints the top executives in his administration and is in a position to coordinate and control their activities.[15] Since the president has a stake in developing the most effective foreign policies possible, he has every reason to ensure that his preferences guide foreign policy decision making at every level in the administration. Some presidents and their advisors may assume that the foreign policy bureaucracy produces reasonable, if not rational, decisions, but if they don't, the president has every reason to exercise effective leadership. For example, both President Nixon and National Security Adviser Henry Kissinger believed that they could cut through the red tape, the status quo biases, and other shortcomings of the bureaucracy by centralizing foreign policy decision making in their own hands.[16]

Another limitation of the governmental politics model is that it requires analysts to have very detailed information about the decision context and decision participants in order to predict outcomes. This information may be readily available to some insiders, but it is difficult for outsiders to gain access to information and employ the kind of analysis required to make these predictions.

This chapter presents some of the details required to employ this model effectively. Graham Allison and Morton Halperin identify three categories of things that such an analysis must cover: (1) who plays; (2) what determines the stands of each; and (3) how these stands are aggregated.[17] Accordingly, this chapter first identifies the players, then examines the influence of individual and organizational factors on them, and finally shows how these influences are aggregated in small decision-making groups.

Players

There are three different kinds of players (chiefs, staffs, and career bureaucrats) involved in decision making at the top of the executive branch of the U.S. government. Although the president appoints all three kinds of players, the character of these appointments and the conditions of their service are very different.

Chiefs

The president and those cabinet officers or senior advisors who have fairly frequent, direct contact with the president on foreign policy matters are all chiefs. As the number of federal departments and agencies reporting to the president during the Great Depression increased, even Franklin Roosevelt realized that the presidency had grown beyond his **span-of-control**, that is, beyond the number of individuals that any one person can control effectively. The establishment of the Executive Office of the President (EO) in 1939 allowed Roosevelt to delegate to his senior White House staff some of the responsibility for overseeing the affairs of the government.

Although the president appoints both the heads of the main departments and senior White House staff, there are important differences between these two kinds of chiefs. (Senior White House staff members are considered chiefs so as not to confuse them with regular White House staff.) The secretaries of State, Defense, and other department or cabinet chiefs are usually older, more experienced individuals. Although many cabinet officers are not known personally by the president until they are appointed, they are potentially very valuable to him both because they represent independent sources of advice and because they oversee the organizations that carry out most foreign policies.[18] The Senate confirms cabinet chiefs, and so these individuals are directly responsible to Congress as well as the president.

The national security advisor and other White House chiefs are usually younger and less experienced than cabinet chiefs. They have often known the president for some time and are very loyal to him as a person. They usually know what the president wants, but they may lack the government experience or operational knowledge to assist him at first.[19] White House chiefs are not subject to Senate confirmation, and they usually are not subject to appear before congressional committees.

The relative importance of the experienced cabinet chiefs on the one hand and the loyal White House chiefs on the other has changed over time. Although the White House is only involved in a small fraction of the foreign policy issues that are dealt with by the foreign affairs bureaucracy, with respect to developing those issues in which the president takes a special interest, White House chiefs are clearly more important than cabinet chiefs. A succession of relatively weak cabinet chiefs may have contributed to this shift in importance, but it basically stems from persistent efforts by presidents themselves to centralize foreign policy decision making on those issues for which they assume personal responsibility.[20] Although White House chiefs are generally in a better position than cabinet chiefs to work with the president in developing these foreign policies, cabinet chiefs remain in a better position than their White House counterparts to implement most foreign policies.

No matter what a new president may say about his cabinet chiefs, their status will evolve, depending upon their personal relationships with the president himself. The competition among chiefs, especially those who hold cabinet positions, can create friction. For example, when President Kennedy appointed Dean Rusk as his secretary of state in 1961, Rusk, who had been an assistant secretary under Dean Acheson and George Marshall, expected to be treated with the same deference that Acheson and Marshall had received under President Truman. But President Kennedy was not comfortable with this degree of formality and invited his national security adviser, McGeorge Bundy, to participate fully in foreign policy decisions. Rusk often held back, expecting to be consulted in private, while Bundy and the secretary of defense, Robert McNamara, participated fully in the discussion of all foreign policy issues.[21]

Staffs

When the EO was created, a number of bureaus and offices were taken from other departments and placed in this office, which also included the Office of the White House. The largest of these units was the Budget Bureau, which had been part of the Treasury Department. Over the years additional offices have been added, including the Council of Economic Advisers (1946), the National Security Council (1947), the Office of Special Assistant to President for Science and Technology (1957), the Office of the United States Trade Representative (1974), the Federal Emergency Management Agency (1979), and most recently the National Economic Council (1993). There are now as many as ten distinct offices in the EO, totaling about 1,600 people.

Although Congress has created some of these, it is the president who decides if and how the staff associated with these offices will be used. Thus the EO may change with each president. The one constant is that these staff positions are mostly filled by **in-and-outers**—the staff that comes in with the president or his party and leaves when that president or party leaves the White House. These individuals may be ideologues who are committed to the programs of the president and his administration or they may be rising stars on loan from the relevant departments and agencies involved in foreign affairs.

Many of these individuals have considerable expertise in areas relevant to their staff position, but their primary job is to support the chiefs in the White House. As a consequence, they must often jump from one issue to the next as the focus of top-level decision making changes. These individuals draft the speeches, memos, plans, and even legislation attributed to the president, the administration, or the principal advisors for whom they work. In many ways these individuals are facilitators; they are expected to accomplish what the principals want even if they are not fully briefed on the matter.

Originally the staff performed three broad functions: coordinating, gate-keeping, and promotion. For example, the National Security Council staff traditionally has been involved in writing speeches, preparing for press conferences, and dealing with the president's correspondence with individual private organizations and individual congressmen. But increasingly the staff has assumed major responsibility for making policy because presidents rely upon this staff to formulate options and to control policy implementation.

Career Bureaucrats

Finally, there is a much larger group of individuals who are members of the permanent bureaucracy. Most of them have no direct contact with the White House, but individuals at the assistant secretary level or higher in the bureaucracy are occasionally called on to share their expertise with Congress and the president. These high-level career bureaucrats are usually senior members of one of the career services: civil service, foreign service, or military service, and they generally have more experience and expertise in their areas of responsibility than White House staffers. These individuals may have had some experience in other departments and agencies, but usually they have spent the vast majority of their time in one of the main departments, such as the State, Defense, or Treasury Department, etc.

Career bureaucrats are particularly active in the phases of foreign policy making that proceed and follow final decision making, analysis, and implementation, respectively. At lower levels these individuals scan for new information, and then code and store that information until it is ready for analysis. They initially frame issues for decisions and largely determine what information government will have, and how that information will be interpreted. At higher levels these individuals make most routine foreign policy decisions and provide expert advice to those who are involved in making decisions at even higher levels.

These are also the individuals who implement government policies at all levels. They establish SOPs, which they are usually reluctant to change in part because these procedures represent hard-won compromises. Of course, the career bureaucrats also interpret the statements of the president in the absence of more specific instruction. Generally speaking, they will seem less than responsive to the president partly because they are as responsible to Congress as to the president, since presidents come and go while congressmen may stay on for decades. The career bureaucrats try to solve as many issues at their level as possible both because they have the expertise for making such decisions and because they want to be sure that such decisions be made correctly.

Although much of the work of these top-level career diplomats involves coordinating their activities with counterparts at similar levels within their own departments as well as with those in other agencies, they are sometimes involved in decisions at the highest level. For example, Martin Hillenbrand, the foreign service expert on Berlin and U.S.-German affairs profiled in Chapter 10, was repeatedly included in ministerial meetings and White House conferences when those issues were discussed.[22] At the same time, some career officers who have expertise to offer on key issues are locked out of these decisions.[23] This type of exclusion will be covered later in this chapter.

Influences on Players

Governmental politics places an emphasis on **individuals in positions.** This phrase refers to the interactions between two kinds of variables: differences among individuals in personality, belief, perception, and style and differences in the positions these individuals hold in an organization.

Differences among individuals will be considered first. Then differences in the positions held by these individuals will be considered.

Differences among Individuals

Cognition deals with what people know and how they know it. Political psychologists discuss cognitive differences among individuals in terms of **schema.** Schema refers to the structure of knowledge or cognitions that individuals hold in their minds. Such schema can take the form of whole belief systems. But many individuals only hold isolated fragments of these structures in the form of "specific instances, exemplars, or analogies." [24] Most scholars prefer to study these fragmentary thoughts rather than the whole belief systems because it is easier to show how these fragments are connected in the brain.[25] The purpose of the framework employed in this book, however, is to encourage students and practitioners to use the underlying belief system—the three dimensions—that most of them already possess in their analysis of foreign policy.

Political psychologists have developed a number of theories based on studies showing how individuals employ such fragmentary thoughts, and not necessarily in a rational way. According to the **cognitive miser theory**, individuals employ such fragments as shortcuts in order to simplify some of the steps required to reach a rational decision. For example, Yuen Khong has shown how Dean Rusk, who was secretary of state during the first part of the Vietnam War, used the Korean analogy as the basis for assessing the Vietnam situation in the 1960s.[26] The Korean case must have been particularly salient to Rusk because he had been assistant secretary for Far Eastern Affairs during the Korean conflict and actually played a role in establishing the thirty-eighth parallel as the dividing line between North and South Korea.[27] Because Rusk perceived the two Koreas as independent states, he naturally envisaged South Vietnam as an independent country when North and South Vietnam were divided along the seventeenth parallel in 1954. In defining South Vietnam as a separate state, Rusk naturally perceived the presence of North Vietnamese troops in South Vietnam in the mid-1960s as evidence of interstate aggression.

Moreover, Rusk perceived China as a threat—perhaps the main threat—in the Vietnam War because China had nearly defeated U.S. forces when Chinese troops entered the Korean War. Rusk himself must have been particularly sensitive to the danger of Chinese intervention in the Vietnam War because he was one of those in the State Department who had argued that the United States should pursue its attack across the thirty-eighth parallel in Korea. That decision turned a quick victory into a near defeat, and the resulting stalemate in Korea was one of the reasons that the Democrats lost power in 1952.

The problem with Rusk's dependence on the Korean analogy to guide his thinking about the emerging situation in Vietnam is that it led him to draw erroneous conclusions about the war. Rusk assumed that the conflict was essentially international rather than domestic, and he assumed that the North Vietnamese would open things up for the Chinese. The fact that Rusk relied so extensively on the Korean analogy in his thinking about the Vietnam War even though he had a great deal of information about both Korea and Vietnam shows that it is not enough to know what information is available to a person. It is also essential to know how that person uses that knowledge.

But the cognitive miser theory is only one of several examples of nonrational ways of thinking about foreign policy. Another is the **cognitive consistency theory**, which holds that individuals simplify reality by assuming consistency or balance among factors when there is no such consistency or balance. For example, supporters of the Bush administration in 2004 recognized both Osama bin Laden, the head of the al Qaeda terrorist network based in Afghanistan, and Abu Musab al-Zarqawi, the Jordanian militant who is thought to lead the main group of insurgents in the center of Iraq in 2004, as international terrorists. Bush supporters also knew that Iraq's Saddam Hussein had offered cash payments to Palestinian suicide bombers. They tried to associate the unpopular Saddam Hussein with these terrorists by pointing to the fact that al-Zarqawi had been reported in Afghanistan in 1990 and 2000 and in Iraq in May–July 2002 and 2003. But prior to the American invasion there was no reliable evidence that al-Zarqawi was associated with either Hussein or bin Laden.

The problem with assuming structural balance or consistency is that it may become so ingrained in one's thinking that one persists in believing it even when the evidence points in the opposite direction. Al-Zarqawi had been in Afghanistan, but there is no evidence that he was tied to bin Laden at the time. Al-Zarqawi had also been in Iraq when Hussein was in power, but he was helping a group of militants in the Ansar al-Islam camp in Kurdish northern Iraq who opposed Hussein. The alleged ties between Hussein and bin Laden through al-Zarqawi could not be proven, yet it was one of the Bush administration's main justifications for the war in Iraq. This irrationality is the main reason that cognitive consistency is one of the least rational theories of decision making.[28]

Yet another nonrational theory of decision making is **attribution theory**. It refers to the tendency of individuals to attribute outcomes to a single cause. For example, a **fundamental attribution error** occurs when an individual assumes that another person is primarily motivated to do something out of mean-spiritedness, without considering the circumstances that may have led that person to take such an action. This presumption is irrational since most individuals overlook their own propensity to take such actions by explaining their own behavior in terms of other exigencies.

Attribution theory nourishes the probability that a particular theory is true without actually attempting to falsify it. For example, President

George W. Bush assumed that Saddam Hussein was hiding WMD because the Iraqi leader did not provide ready access or complete information to UN inspectors. But the Duelfer Report concludes that Saddam Hussein actually misguided the United States and the United Nations about the status of WMD in Iraq because he was concerned that Iran, a more powerful country on his eastern border, might attack Iraq if it knew for sure that Iraq did not possess WMD.[29] Apparently the Bush administration did not consider this alternative when it argued that the only reason Hussein did not cooperate with UN inspectors was that he had WMD.

The framework employed in this text attempts to overcome the kinds of errors caused by relying on various mental shortcuts by emphasizing a more general schema or belief system based on logic grounded in the three basic human motivations. This framework employs three distinct kinds of logic in thinking about foreign policy: the logic of acceptability, the logic of effectiveness, and the logic of efficiency. Chapter 1 shows that individuals differ on what constitutes the most acceptable, effective, or efficient policy on these three motivated dimensions. The next two sections consider some of the perceptual and stylistic factors that may help explain these personal differences.

Personality and Perception.   One connection between personality and cognition is largely based on perceptions. Individuals prefer "certain kinds of environments, tasks and cognitive patterns." [30] The most widely used and tested instrument in use today for measuring the effect of personality on perception is the Myers-Briggs Type Indicator (MBTI). It measures personality differences on four distinct dimensions: (1) Introversion versus Extroversion, (2) Sensing versus Intuition, (3) Thinking versus Feeling, and (4) Judging versus Perceiving.

The **Introvert–Extrovert scale** measures whether individuals are more introspective and reserved on the one hand or more expressive and gregarious on the other. Many consider President Carter an Introvert (I) because he liked to read and valued the time that he spent by himself going over important papers. President Clinton is thought to be an Extrovert (E) because he likes to talk to a wide range of people and his favorite way of getting information is through discussions with others.

The **Sensing–Intuition scale** is based on different kinds of perception. This distinction is similar to the biological research that features the different functions of the left and right halves of the human brain. Cognitive neuroscientific research shows that "the left hemisphere of the brain engages in linear, verbal, and computational thought," which correlates to Sensing (S), whereas "the right hemisphere of the brain visualizes spatial relationships and other impressionistic abstractions," which correlates to Intuition (N).[31] A sensation type is someone who uses the five senses—seeing, touching, smelling, hearing and tasting—to experience things. Such an individual is likely to focus on the individual trees in a forest. For example, John Foster Dulles, Eisenhower's secretary of state, was very interested in factual details; he was a sensation type. The intuitive type uses his or her imagination to perceive possibilities. This type is more likely to see the forest as a whole. Both Carter and Clinton are viewed as examples of intuitive types.

The **Thinking–Feeling scale** involves different kinds of judgments. Thinkers (T) assume an objective perspective; they tend to emphasize logical decision making. Feelers (F) are more likely to make decisions on a subjective, value, or emotional basis. President Carter is usually regarded as a thinking type; he wanted to arrive at the logical answer. Clinton is more adept at feeling; he is especially gifted at empathizing with others. "In sample populations, about 60 [percent] of all males are Thinkers; about 65 [percent] of all females are Feelers." [32]

The **Judging–Perceiving scale** involves two orientations toward the outside world. People who seek order in the world and like to resolve matters quickly are considered Judging (J) types. Those who prefer to live in a more flexible or spontaneous way and are willing to tolerate a considerable amount of disorder are Perceiving (P) types. Carter is more judging; he likes things to be orderly. Clinton places more emphasis on perception; he is constantly trying to determine what opportunities are available.

Individuals do not necessarily prefer one polar position more strongly than the other on these four scales. For example, the same individual might be both a thinker and a feeler. However, many individuals do have distinct tendencies. Former president Carter is generally regarded as an Introvert–Intuitive–Thinking–Judging person, a INTJ type; former president Clinton, a Extrovert–Intuitive–Feeling–Perceiving person, a ENFP type.

The rational actor model places particular emphasis on Sensation (S) and Thinking (T) because rationality stresses observation and reasoning. However, it should be clear that many individuals rely on Intuition (N) and Feeling (F) in making foreign policy decisions. Does the fact that some people rely more on one kind of perception than another mean that they make poor decisions? Not necessarily.

Miriam Steiner makes this point nicely by contrasting the ability of a U.S. diplomat and a Brazilian diplomat to settle a 150-year-old dispute between Ecuador and Peru in 1941.[33] The military dispute arose over possession of territory around the Maranon River that would give Ecuador access to the Atlantic Ocean. The American diplomat, Sumner Welles, wanted Peru to give Ecuador access to the ocean even though Peruvian forces had prevailed in the conflict. He failed. Then the Brazilian diplomat, Oswaldo Aranha, took his turn, and was able to settle the same dispute quickly. Aranha came up with a solution that got Peru to make the maximum concessions it could under the circumstances and got Ecuador to accept them. Steiner concludes that Aranha was more adept than Welles in assessing the "complex mixes of passion and calculation" involved in the conflict.[34]

A similar validation of intuition in foreign policy making took place at the Reykjavík Summit in Iceland in 1985. On that occasion President Reagan, who was regarded by some as "intelligent but intellectually lazy," [35] was able to intuit that Mikhail Gorbachev was really serious about arms control. Reagan's advisers at Reykjavík were shocked when Reagan agreed to embrace Gorbachev's offer of total nuclear disarmament because he was ignoring the whole rationale behind U.S. nuclear deterrence policy. Yet Reagan's intuitive leap may have been an important opening in paving the way for a peaceful end to the cold war.

Differences in perception are often crucial in determining one's stance on foreign policy issues. For example, "the president's work habits, the ways he likes to receive information, the people he prefers around him, and how he makes up his mind" are all important in determining how the president organizes the White House.[36]

Personality and Cognitive Style.   Individuals have very different ways of learning. Five differences in cognitive style may be particularly helpful in differentiating among the leadership styles of individuals. First, one needs to distinguish between individuals who are **open-minded** and **closed-minded**. Individuals who are open-minded believe that they can use additional information to make decisions; those who are closed-minded believe that they already have enough information to make a decision. President Eisenhower was open-minded. He wanted thorough staff work so that he would have as much information as possible. President Reagan is a classic example of a closed-minded person because he usually depended on a few basic principles to make decisions. He was not always eager to get more information.

There are also differences in level of **cognitive complexity**. Those with high complexity employ more dimensions and need more rules for integrating these dimensions because they have a need to make more discriminating judgments; those with low complexity tend to employ fewer dimensions and need fewer rules to integrate these dimensions. The latter are often referred to as concrete. President Clinton's cognitive style is generally thought to be of high complexity because he constantly looked for more discriminating information. President Truman's style is usually characterized by low complexity because he used just a few key distinctions. (The framework employed in this text is more complex cognitively than other frameworks because it requires a foreign policy analyst or student to take all three dimensions into account continuously.)

The cognitive processing of information by individuals is also affected by **stress.** Stress occurs when individuals believe that they must arrive at an important decision in a short period of time. Although a modest amount of stress may actually improve cognitive functioning, severe stress makes cognitive processing more difficult.[37] Of course, some individuals are better at dealing with stress than others. George H. W. Bush is a good example of the negative effect of severe stress on a decision maker because under normal circumstances he was quite good at processing information, but when he perceived a threat to his position, he was less effective in processing information.[38]

Moreover, there are differences among individuals with respect to the **locus of control**, that is, do individuals believe that they are in control or do they feel that events control them? If individuals have a high (internal) locus of control, they want as much information about a situation as possible because they believe they can use that information to influence outcomes. If individuals have a low (external) locus of control, they are much less interested in information about their environment because they believe that both events and subsequent outcomes are largely beyond their control.

Finally, there is an important difference among individuals in the extent to which they are **self-monitors**. High self-monitors are always looking for cues from their environment as to how they should act whereas low self-monitors usually respond to their own inner sense of direction in deciding how to act. High self-monitors are hungry for new information; low self-monitors are not. Clinton is regarded as a high self-monitor; George W. Bush is a low self-monitor.

As shown below, political psychologists Margaret Hermann and Robert Preston combine a number of these factors to describe three basic elements of cognitive style. They are: (1) sensitivity, (2) control, and (3) involvement.[39] These three elements are particularly useful because they tap the three motivated criteria underlying the three dimensions employed in this text. Sensitivity is closely related to the acceptability criterion (social affiliation); control is closely related to the effectiveness criterion (power); and involvement is closely related to the efficiency criterion (achievement).

Individuals who have a high need for affiliation are more likely to show sensitivity. They are more likely to solicit feedback because they want their foreign policies to be well received by others. These individuals are likely to be open-minded, cognitively complex, high self-monitors, intuitive (N), feelers (F), perceivers (P), and perhaps extroverts (E). They frequently engage in policy discussion and debate before arriving at a decision. Those who are less driven by the need for affiliation are satisfied if they have the support of their immediate advisers. They do not place as much emphasis on interpersonal relationships, particularly with outsiders. They are often closed-minded, concrete, judging (J), and low self-monitors. Their search for information may be limited to what is supportive of what they already want to do because they are cognitive misers who rely on analogies. They often put a premium on being decisive.

Individuals who are strongly motivated by power generally want to control foreign policy decisions; they generally prefer very formal, highly structured decision-making processes. They are also likely to be judging (J) types. They often have a high (inner) locus of control. Those who are less driven by power considerations are more willing to work with others to arrive at a consensus or majority decision. They prefer more informal, less tightly organized structures for making decisions. And they are likely to be perceiving (P) types with a low (external) locus of control.

Individuals who are strongly motivated by achievement are generally **problem-oriented** or **task-oriented**; they want to be involved in foreign policy decisions.[40] Such individuals are more likely to emphasize perception, open-mindedness, high cognitive complexity, and a high (internal) locus of control. They are also more likely to tolerate differences of opinion because they believe that the expression of such differences may improve the quality of the overall solution. Generally speaking, the more intelligent and more experienced an individual is in foreign affairs, the more likely that person will become involved in finding the best solution to a foreign policy problem. On the other hand, individuals who are less experienced in foreign affairs, less inclined to think things through, and less interested in foreign affairs generally and who are closed-minded, are concrete (rather than highly complex), have a low (external) locus of control, are judging (J), and under extreme stress, are more likely to be **process-oriented**.[41] Their emphasis is on getting others to accept a solution already arrived at.

By integrating many of these psychological factors into one of three basic elements—sensitivity, control, and involvement—Hermann and Preston have made it much easier to categorize foreign policy makers because each of these elements is associated with one of the three basic motives employed in this text. This makes it possible to classify the personal styles of decision makers according to the same matrix tables used to describe foreign policy outputs in Parts I and II of this text. Table 11.1 shows the styles of decision making preferred by Presidents Clinton and Bush. Clinton is considered high on sensitivity (social affiliation), low on control (power), and low on involvement (achievement). President George W. Bush is considered low on sensitivity (social affiliation), low on control (power), and low on involvement (achievement).

Of course, one has to be very careful in typing these individuals. Both Clinton and Bush are considered low on involvement, but there are some situations in which they were more involved than they were in other situations. For example, Clinton was very involved in the Middle East peace talks in 2000; and Bush was more involved in the fight against terrorism immediately after the September 11, 2001 attacks. As these examples

Table 11.1. Dimensions of Foreign Policy Inputs: The Cognitive Styles of Individuals

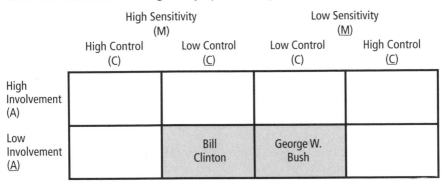

| | High Sensitivity (M) | | Low Sensitivity (M) | |
	High Control (C)	Low Control (C)	Low Control (C)	High Control (C)
High Involvement (A)				
Low Involvement (A)		Bill Clinton	George W. Bush	

Bill Clinton's preferred operational style is MCA—high sensitivity because he is open-minded, shows a high level of complexity, and is a high self-monitor; low control because he prefers an informal, nonhierarchical advisory structure and; low involvement because he did not consistently maintain a high level of interest in international affairs. George W. Bush's preferred style is MCA—low sensitivity because he is a low self-monitor; low control because he has low power needs; and low involvement because he delegates policy formulation and implementation to subordinates.

Source: See Thomas Preston and Margaret G. Hermann, "Presidential Leadership Style and the Foreign Policy Advisory Process," in *Domestic Sources of American Foreign Policy: Insights and Evidence,* ed. Eugene R. Wittkopf and James M. McCormick (Lanham, MD: Rowman and Littlefield, 2004), 373–377.

show, foreign policy decisions are often triggered by outside events. Such events often have an independent affect on these decisions. But this chapter is less concerned with events than it is with the effect of individuals-in-positions. Having discussed some of the most important variables in individual personality, it is now time to deal with some of the organizational factors that affect high-level decision makers.

Differences among Position-holders

Earlier a distinction was made between three kinds of position-holders—chiefs, staff, and career bureaucrats—at higher levels in the foreign policy bureaucracy. Now it is time to show how these different position-holders interact both with the president and with each other. These interactions are important for understanding foreign policy because these three types of position-holders are the individuals who link the president to the foreign affairs bureaucracy as a whole. Because the bureaucracy was discussed in terms of coordination, centralization, and specialization, it might be useful to reintroduce these terms into the discussion at this point. After all, the centralization of decision -making in the White House does not negate either the need for specialization or the need for coordination. How are these three organizational functions—coordination, centralization, and specialization—performed at the highest level in the government? Staff generally provides coordination; chiefs, centralization; and career bureaucrats, specialization.

Coordination. The president's desire for social affiliation and willingness to engage others in the decision-making process will determine how sensitive the president will be to the opinion of other players and what kind of interpersonal relationships will develop within decision-making groups. If the president is highly motivated toward affiliation, that is, if he wants the approval of a broad range of people, then the president will use his advisors as sources of important information with respect to the various constituencies they represent. He may even encourage them to express reservations about the policies being considered so that he will appreciate some of the obstacles that he will have to overcome to build support for his foreign policy. If the president has low motivation toward affiliation, he is less interested in having information about what others have to say about the policy being considered. He is certainly unlikely to seek out negative information that would cause him and others to question their own thinking about what should be done.

Coordination is required in order to ensure that all aspects of a foreign policy will be considered both in making a commitment to act and in implementing such actions. The problem of insufficient coordination is illustrated by the ill-fated decision of the United States to cross the thirty-eighth parallel into North Korea during the Korean War. In the late summer of 1950, differences of opinion emerged within the State Department as well as between the State and Defense Departments over the issue of whether to pursue the retreating North Korean forces over the thirty-eighth parallel. Paul Nitze, who was the director of the policy planning staff in the State Department at the time, questioned the wisdom of going beyond the thirty-eighth parallel, whereas Dean Rusk, who headed the Far Eastern Division of the State Department, favored it. The Defense Department and the individual services also favored going beyond the thirty-eighth parallel.

The language used by these two departments at the time reflected these policy differences. The State Department draft of August 23, 1950, "while recognizing the growing public and congressional sentiment favoring action north of the parallel," emphasized that the United States had "no commitment to use armed force in the effort to bring about Korean independence and unity and that decisions regarding whether to cross the [t]hirty-eighth [p]arallel should be deferred." [42] The next day, military representatives "emphasized that the postponement of the decision recommended by the State Department would delay the lengthy buildup of forces necessary if a decision to cross the parallel were taken." [43]

On August 25 several decisions were made by the NSC senior staff that altered the previous State Department position. First, the State Department agreed to military operations north of the [t]hirty-eighth [p]arallel, so long as UN forces kept well clear of the Russian frontier." Second, the NSC senior staff decided that in the absence of Chinese Communist or Soviet participation, UN forces should not stop at the thirty-eighth parallel. Finally, the NSC senior staff noted it to be " 'politically desirable, if military feasible' for South Korean forces to be used primarily in actions beyond the parallel and that the participation of American forces should be minimized." [44]

As was his custom, Truman received the NSC report without a full discussion of differences that had been worked out among the NSC senior staff. When Truman reviewed NSC 81 with the NSC on September 7, 1950, JCS Chairman Omar Bradley objected that it was not clear, and so the document was amended by Secretary of State Acheson to allow MacArthur to carry out his plans to use troops in the north as long as he did not provoke Chinese or Russian intervention. But Acheson also insisted that Washington make the final decision. President Truman subsequently signed the amended version, NSC 81/1, even though he may not have been fully aware of the debates that had been taking place at the senior staff level.

General MacArthur later sent American troops north of the thirty-eighth parallel without getting Washington's final approval. Truman subsequently fired MacArthur for acts of disobedience, and China entered the Korean War when American forces drew close to the Chinese border. In this case President Truman would have had to control both the movement of American and allied forces in Korea as well as the communication of American intentions with regard to China in order to have avoided Chinese intervention. Even then, it might not have made any difference.

Problems of coordination also extend to other branches of the government and other situations. For example, in conjunction with the situation in Dien Bien Phu, Vietnam, in 1954, President Eisenhower had at one point responded to an urgent French request to send aircraft and 400 technicians to Indochina by sending approximately 200 uniformed technicians to that country.[45] But when word of this unilateral action got out, former senator John Stennis and his colleagues on the Armed Services Committee were upset. Eisenhower immediately sent his associate, Walter Beatle Smith, to the Senate and eventually agreed to replace the uniformed technicians with civilians.[46] In this and other instances Eisenhower demonstrated his sensitivity to others even when he had already made a decision.

Eisenhower's sensitivity on this occasion can be contrasted with the insensitivity of former president Reagan to opposing opinions. Although Reagan was cordial in person and although he was quite popular with many in the general public, he was not particularly concerned with public acceptance of his foreign policies. Indeed, one of the foreign policies closest to his heart was the development of a Contra force to oppose the

Sandinista government in Nicaragua in the 1980s. This policy never had more than about 30 to 40 percent support among the American people, to say nothing of the opposition it raised in many foreign governments.[47] Yet Reagan persisted in advocating this policy in public and especially in the U.S. Congress to the point that his advisors actually tried to implement his policies covertly—a course of action that resulted in the Iran-Contra scandal—despite the opposition of a majority in Congress and the American public. Even Reagan's cabinet secretaries, George Shultz and Caspar Weinberger, were opposed to the arms-for-hostage policy, but they too were kept largely in the dark as to what was going on.

Centralization. The ability of the president to control the administration's foreign policy is based on historical precedents under the U.S. Constitution and the mandate he receives from the electorate. Presidents usually have great latitude in defining their relationships with those whom they appoint to executive positions. If the president wants to dominate the decision-making process, he can organize cabinet chiefs into a formal hierarchy and manage the flow of information between himself and cabinet chiefs in such a way that he controls all the important decisions himself. If the president wants the input from cabinet chiefs to help make decisions, he can encourage a freewheeling discussion of foreign policy issues among them.[48]

The power of the president is affected by the election cycle. When a new president from a new party (the party previously out of power) is elected, he becomes the principal foreign policy decision maker only after winning a highly contested domestic election. This often means that the president's fortunes are so tied to the outcome of the election that he has neither the time nor the staff to develop a detailed foreign policy prior to assuming office, as was the case with George W. Bush in 2001 and Bill Clinton in 1993. (Of course, a president seeking a second term or a new president representing a party already in power will not face the same degree of difficulty.)

The transition from the election campaign to governance is particularly difficult in the foreign policy arena because domestic campaigning rarely brings a new president into contact with those on whom he will depend to carry out his foreign policy. Indeed, if he is running as a governor or even as a senator or representative, he is likely to have had relatively little contact with foreign policy experts. Thus a new president usually has no more than the two and a half months between his election and his inauguration to select his foreign policy team and to formulate a foreign policy program.

As a consequence, unless the new president has broad interests and experience in foreign affairs, he must spend most of his first year in office just getting to know his foreign policy team and learning how foreign policy works. This was certainly true of Bill Clinton who did not even attempt to articulate his overall foreign policy for some nine months. (It was somewhat less true of George W. Bush because he brought so many people who had served under his father into executive positions.) The opportunity to develop foreign policy leadership is usually much shorter than generally thought because by the end of the second year, the new president is embroiled in mid-term congressional elections and looking ahead to the possibility of running for a second term.

Even a second-term president may find it difficult to undertake new initiatives since there may be new foreign policy personnel to integrate into the administration as well as a new Congress to work with. Yet this fifth and sixth year probably offers the president the best opportunity to take new initiatives, because in the seventh and eighth year he becomes a "lame duck," as everyone's attention is focused on the election of the next president.

Although the president's personality and style determine the basic structure of groups in the White House, other members will also attempt to exercise authority when given the opportunity to do so. Generally speaking, White House chiefs have often become more influential than cabinet chiefs because they have closer contact with the president himself. For example, Condoleezza Rice, when she was national security adviser during George W. Bush's first term, not only chaired meetings of the principal cabinet chiefs during preliminary discussions but also served as the main liaison between these principals and the president between meetings.[49] Vice President Cheney is believed to have extraordinary influence in his position. Many believe that Cheney, who has higher power needs than the president, is responsible for the more hierarchical, secretive advisory system in the Bush White House than one would expect of a low power president.[50]

White House chiefs have considerable latitude in determining which players are to be directly involved in interagency discussions. For example, Zbigniew Brzezinski, Carter's national security adviser, repeatedly attempted to influence the composition of the group that would be deciding policy toward Iran during the imminent collapse of the Shah's government in late 1978.[51] Since the United States belatedly recognized the problem, there was considerable pressure to reach a decision. Brzezinski felt that quick action could save the Shah, but the State Department disagreed, so Brzezinski tried to change the composition of the decision-making group. He began to rely on Ardeshir Zahedi, Iran's ambassador to Washington, and special emissaries that he sent to Iran rather than on the reports of William Sullivan, the U.S. ambassador to Iran. In addition, Brzezinski was successful in excluding Henry Precht, the State Department's country director for Iran, from these meetings.

So far we have emphasized the importance of centralization. Centralization of power is important, but the centralization of power in the hands of a president or White House chiefs also can be dangerous if they do not involve the foreign affairs bureaucracy (specialization) and if they are not sensitive to other points of view (coordination).

Specialization.   Motivation toward achievement determines whether a president will focus on the more specialized task of finding the best possible solution to a foreign policy issue or problem or whether he will be satisfied with simply developing support for an acceptable solution. If the president ranks high on achievement, he is more likely both to look for additional options and to consider these options more carefully. Moreover, his desire to develop the best policy will lead him to tolerate a significant amount of disagreement among his advisers. He may even encourage such disagreements in order to have the ideas and information needed to make the best choices. If the president's motivation is low on achievement, then he is more likely to accept the first acceptable solution that comes to his attention. Since it will take less time to identify a solution, he is much more likely to focus the attention of the group on building support for this solution. Hence the emphasis is on the political process.

For example, President Eisenhower was strongly motivated to make good foreign policy decisions. When the French asked the United States to assist them in Vietnam in early 1954, Eisenhower consulted with a wide range of advisers.[52] The United States was already paying a high proportion of the financial cost of the French military effort in Indochina, and French forces in Dien Bien Phu were in a very precarious situation. Although Eisenhower was determined "to face issues and resolve them," he was cautious about making premature commitments.[53] Eisenhower did not favor the United States taking unilateral action in Vietnam, but he was open to the possibility of multilateral intervention if France agreed to eventually pull out of Vietnam and grant Indochina its independence. The French refused, and Eisenhower allowed the Vietminh to take the French fort at Bien Dien Phu.

Just a little over ten years later, President Johnson faced a similar situation in what was now South Vietnam. But by this time Kennedy had put thousands of U.S. military advisers in South Vietnam, and the United States had signed protocols to the Southeast Asia collective defense treaty, which generally committed the United States to consider at least taking action if the former states of Indochina came under attack. When U.S. forces were attacked in the highlands of South Vietnam, all the members of the NSC called for retaliation.[54] Johnson quickly decided to retaliate, a decision largely made on the advice of McGeorge Bundy, Johnson's national security adviser, who was touring Vietnam at the time.

One could hardly argue that the situation in Vietnam may not have been any more desperate in 1965 than it was in 1954, although American military personnel were more directly involved in 1965 than in 1954 and the president in office had a different leadership style. Eisenhower, an experienced military commander, took the time and made the effort to reach a rational decision; Johnson, who had little executive and no military experience, felt compelled to act immediately. Eisenhower took the time to look for the best solution to the problem; Johnson just went ahead and did what he thought was expected of him.

In many instances the president will actually have to demonstrate an intense interest in getting unwelcome information because if he does not do so, his advisers may not share it with him. For example, President Jimmy Carter may not have undertaken the hostage rescue mission discussed earlier if he had known what his director of central intelligence, Stanfill Turner, knew at the time. But Turner himself favored the rescue attempt, so he did not share with the president a special CIA report that estimated that "the rescue plan would probably result in the loss of 60 percent of the hostages during the mission." [55] If President Carter and other advisors had received this "best estimate," they might have called off the rescue mission altogether.

This problem of unshared information becomes particularly serious when the president and White House chiefs do not trust career bureaucrats to implement their decisions and attempt to carry out these actions with their own staff. This is essentially what happened when Marine colonel Oliver North, a staffer on the National Security Council, sold weapons to Iran to obtain money for the Contra forces operating against the Sandinistas in Nicaragua in the mid-1980s. Such machinations are more likely when key cabinet chiefs are closed out of decisions. In the Iran-Contra example, neither Secretary of State George Shultz nor Secretary of Defense Casper Weinberger knew what Oliver North was doing.

White House chiefs and their staff are also in a position to make policy indirectly. For example, they can sometimes maneuver the president into making a commitment when career bureaucrats are not in the picture. In late 1993, when the Clinton administration was considering whether NATO should expand to accept former members of the Soviet bloc such as Poland, Czechoslovakia (now the Czech Republic), and Hungary as regular members despite Russian opposition, there were strong differences of opinion within the U.S. government. A small group within the State Department wanted to pursue NATO expansion as quickly as possible, as did the Pentagon.[56] But a number of others, especially experts in the Bureau of European Affairs, felt that the United States should adopt a more cautious approach, emphasizing the Partnership for Peace (PFP) plan that allowed the states in Eastern Europe to operate jointly with NATO without actually becoming full-fledged members of NATO. Table 11.2 illustrates the dimensions of the different opinions on NATO expansion.

The issue had not been resolved when Anthony Lake, Clinton's national security advisor, persuaded Clinton to include a key statement

Table 11.2. Dimensions of Foreign Policy Inputs: Institutional Factors and NATO Expansion

	Coordination			
	High (M)		Low (M̲)	
	Centralization		Centralization	
	High (C)	Low (C̲)	Low (C̲)	High (C)
Specialization High (A)		Careerists in the Bureau of European Affairs were cautious about NATO expansion		
Specialization Low (A̲)				National security advisor Anthony Lake and others favored NATO expansion

Career bureaucrats in the Bureau of European Affairs were MC̲A—high coordination because they knew in some detail how various East European countries would assess their NATO prospects, low centralization because they do not normally have direct contact with the president, and high specialization because they dealt with these issues every day. National security advisor Anthony Lake was M̲CA̲—low coordination because he had an agenda, high centralization because he had almost daily contact with the president, and low specialization because European affairs was just one of many issues he dealt with every day.

about the relationship of PFP membership to NATO membership in a speech delivered in Prague, the capital of the Czech Republic, in January 1994. Clinton in effect declared that, "[w]hile the Partnership is not NATO membership, neither is it a permanent holding room." That statement changed the NATO dialogue from "whether NATO will take on new members [to] when and how." [57] Once Lake had gotten Clinton to make that statement in public, those who favored a "fast-track" approach to NATO expansion had won the bureaucratic war because the statement offered an interpretation of PFP that favored NATO membership.

The danger for the president and the country when White House chiefs are the driving force behind foreign policy is that the president will be led to make a commitment without fully understanding the issues involved. When the most sensitive issues gravitate to the White House for decision, "senior generalists" replace "the experts." [58] Thus White House chiefs or staffers who are often " 'can-do guys,' loyal and energetic fixers unsoured by expertise," often replace expert career bureaucrats who tend to be cautious about new initiatives.[59] To a lesser extent this may even be true of cabinet chiefs who are generalists even if they can seldom be described as "can-do guys."

The NATO enlargement example is a good illustration of this divide. The careerists in the Bureau of European Affairs were high coordination because they were reluctant to enlarge NATO when Russia opposed it; low control because they were long-term bureaucrats; and high specialization because European problem were their main specialty. Anthony Lake and others were low coordination because they were uninterested in Russia's attitudes, high control because they had access to the president, and low specialization because they only occasionally dealt with European affairs.

Because the functional prerequisites for policy making in large organizations—coordination, control, and specialization—also line up with the three motivational criteria employed in this text, it is possible to combine both differences in individual perception and cognitive style and differences in foreign policy orientation in studying small group decision making. The remainder of this chapter focuses on decision making in small groups because that is where these considerations come together to influence foreign policy decisions.

Small Group Decision Making

In the United States, small informal groups throughout the foreign policy bureaucracy often make key foreign policy decisions. If and when these decisions cannot be made elsewhere, the president not only chairs the group but also leads the discussion. Although all members of such groups have some influence on decisions, the president has the most influence because he appoints most of the other participants and often determines which advisors will deal with which decisions. Thus presidential leadership style is a crucial factor in explaining how high-level foreign policy decisions are made throughout the government, and especially in the White House.

Such groups need to be studied separately because they may either enhance the rationality of foreign policy decision making, or they may subvert it. In order to assess these possibilities, one needs to consider how such groups function both in theory and in practice.

Theory

Each of the leadership styles—sensitive, controlled, and involved—developed by Margaret Hermann and Robert Preston deal with a different aspect of the way in which groups function.[60] Differences among individuals in sensitivity determine how information will be coordinated among members of the group. Differences among individuals in the desire for control determine how much centralization there is in the group. And differences in involvement, and particularly differences in the substantive focus of the group, determine the type of specialization within the group. Each of these factors will be considered in defining various groups.

It is important to recognize that there is a correspondence between the leadership styles of individuals—sensitivity, control, and involved—the functions performed by small groups—coordination, centralization, and specialization—and the three criteria employed in the framework in this text—acceptability, effectiveness, and efficiency, respectively. This allows one to classify the small groups established by leaders with these personal styles, according to the motivationally derived types of foreign policies employed in earlier chapters. That is, the motive of affiliation provides the incentive for both multilateralism and coordination; motive of power provides the incentive for both coercion and centralization; and the motive of achievement, the incentive for both involvement and specialization. Thus the eight types of small groups in Table 11.3 are shown in the same matrix format used to describe foreign policies in this text, because these foreign policies are in part the outcome of these particular decision-making groups.

The groups are labeled in terms of the kinds of foreign policies they are likely to produce. Thus groups that feature high coordination, centralization, and specialization tend to produce MCA foreign policies. Each member of such a group represents an important constituency that the president wants to take into account in making decisions. They serve as a sounding board for the president. They spend their time anticipating problems, considering new options, and studying the likely consequences of those options. Since these groups are sensitive to their environments, well led, and problem-focused, they are likely to make rational decisions. Eisenhower's decision not to aid the French in Dien Bien Phu and Kennedy's decision to quarantine Cuba are examples of foreign policies that might be expected from this kind of group.

Groups that rate high on coordination, low on centralization, and high on specialization tend to produce MCA foreign policies. In such groups each adviser's input is valued because the leader is interested in the reactions of those inside as well as outside the advisory system. Such groups usually try to reach a consensus because everyone is accountable for the decisions made. And since the leader is highly involved, he or she is likely to know his or her advisers quite well. Unfortunately, if the group is relatively new and if the leader does not give sufficient direction to its members, they may not feel as free to speak their minds. This can lead to a phenomenon called **new group syndrome**.[61] This may well have been part of the problem with discussions of the Bay of Pigs invasion in the early Kennedy administration. Fortunately, Kennedy had addressed this problem by the time of the Cuban missile crisis.

Groups that rate low on coordination and centralization but high on specialization tend to produce MCA foreign policies. The members of these groups are not particularly interested in different points of view. The group strives to reach a consensus, and the leader looks to group members for psychological support. The members of this type of group are mainly interested in shaping options and in implementing their chosen option. This type of group is especially susceptible to the phenomenon of **groupthink**. According to Irving Janis, groupthink occurs when a group has a strong tendency to seek concurrence under stress.[62] It is the need for affiliation under stress that causes concurrence-seeking or group cohesion. Janis himself uses the Vietnam and other instances to illustrate the operation of groupthink.[63]

Groups that rate low on coordination, but high on centralization and specialization tend to produce MCA foreign policies. In this type of group the leader does not encourage disagreements except on implementation. The leader is especially interested in framing the policy agenda, and so the group focuses on important decisions. In such groups the procedures for making policy are well defined and highly structured. The danger associated with this kind of group is over-centralization. The fact that information is not processed effectively throughout the whole foreign policy bureaucracy means that this type of group can easily go astray. Nixon's decision to invade Cambodia may have been a result of the decision process of this kind of group.

Groups that rate high on coordination and centralization, but low on specialization tend to produce MCA foreign policies. These groups are especially interested in solutions that will be accepted politically. Members of the group are viewed as part of a team, and policy is largely made by discussion among them. Since the leader of these groups is not always involved, he depends upon expert advisers to propose and delineate problems and options. The problem with this kind of group is indecision. The leader may unwittingly take on too much responsibility, especially given his level of involvement. Carter's failure to take more decisive action in Iran in 1979 may reflect this kind of decision-making group.

Groups that rate high on coordination, but low on centralization and specialization tend to produce MCA foreign policies. The members of such groups are expected to act more or less independently. Since such groups are prone to take into consideration a wide range of factors and have little coherence, they are likely to arrive at compromises that represent the lowest common denominator of the policy positions represented. They are expected to have the skills to see that the policies they develop are effective. This is the classic description of governmental politics. This kind of decision-making group may have been responsible for Clinton's failure to deal more effectively with the genocide in Rwanda in 1994.

Groups that rate low on coordination, centralization and specialization tend to produce MCA foreign policies. One or two advisors in this kind of group often play the role of gatekeeper for information and access to the leader. Even if the leader has strong ideas about some aspects of the policy, he is not very interested either in developing the policies or in implementing

Table 11.3 Dimensions of Foreign Policy Inputs: Types of Small Decision Groups

MCA

High Coordination (M)
Advisers represent important
constituencies
Willingness to tolerate conflict

High Centralization (C)
Advisers used as sounding board
Coherence in policy is valued

High Specialization (A)
Time spent considering options and
consequences
Interested in planning and anticipating
problems

MCA

High Coordination (M)
Advisers' input is valued
Interested in reactions inside and
outside advisory system

Low Centralization (C)
Sharing of accountability
Consensus is valued

High Specialization (A)
Seek advisers who demonstrate interest in
noncontroversial policy

MCA

High Coordination (M)
Seek experts as advisers
Seek doable solutions that will sell
politically

High Centralization (C)
Advisers seen as part of team
Policy by discussion
Compromise is valued

Low Specialization (A)
Advisers propose and delineate problems
and options

MCA

High Coordination (M)
Seek advisers with skills that match
position

Low Centralization (C)
Advisers have leeway to decide policy

Low Specialization (A)
Seek advisers who are interested in acting
independently

Source: Adapted from Margaret Hermann and Thomas Preston, "Presidential Leadership Style and the Foreign Policy Advisory Process," in *The Domestic Sources of American Foreign Policy,* ed. Eugene R. Wittkopf and James M. McCormick (Lanham, MD: Rowman and Littlefield 2004), 372.

---

them. He is only responsible for overseeing these policies. The members of these groups may be expected to follow general guidelines in developing policies in their areas of specialty. Such a group is susceptible to a whole range of group effects, most notably the **risky-shift**. The risky-shift refers to the tendency of a group to either take more or fewer risks than the

MCA

Low Coordination (M)
  Seek advisers with similar vision
  Little willingness to tolerate conflict

Low Centralization (C)
  Advisers provide psychological support
  Groupthink is possible

High Specialization (A)
  Interested in shaping option
  Discussion focuses on how to coordinate
  policy

MCA

Low Coordination (M)
  Disagreements allowed on means but not
  ends
  Interested in focusing on important
  decisions

High Centralization (C)
  Loyalty is important
  Interested in framing policy agenda

High Specialization (A)
  Procedures well-defined and highly
  structured

MCA

Low Coordination (M)
  One or two advisers play gate keeper role
  for information and access

Low Centralization (C)
  Just Interested in overseeing policy

Low Specialization (A)
  Seek advisers who can act on own within
  particular framework

MCA

Low Coordination (M)
  Select advisers with similar policy
  concerns

High Centralization (C)
  Decision shaped by shared vision

Low Specialization (A)
  Advisers viewed as implementers and
  advocates of policy
  Interested in evaluating not generating
  options

members of the group would take individually. There are a number of different explanations for such polarization. It generally happens when "members of the policy group were intensely motivated toward self-censorship, isolated from dissonant views through strict secrecy, and the elimination of dissidents from the group."[64] The Iran-Contra scandal that occurred during the Reagan administration may have been an example of the outcome of this kind of decision-making process.

Groups that rate low on coordination, high on centralization and low on specialization tend to produce MCA foreign policies. Since the members of this kind of group have similar concerns, there is limited interest in exchanging information among them. The decisions of this kind of group are based on a shared ideology. Because the general outline of these policies has already been formulated or because circumstances are allowed to define these policies, the members of such groups are implementers and advocates of this policy. The leaders of such groups are usually considered decisive, but they are prone to make nonrational decisions. Johnson's failure to consider any change in strategy in Vietnam may have been the result of this kind of decision-making process.

Having identified the universe of group-types based on the performance of these three functions, we can now look at the actual groups formed by various presidents since World War II. By describing the sensitivity, control, and involvement of each of these presidents, we can characterize the decision groups under their leadership.

Praxis

In describing the actual practice of foreign policy decision making in the White House, the discussion will focus on the National Security Council (NSC). Although Amy Zegart argues convincingly that American presidents have reshaped the NSC to serve their need to centralize foreign policy decision making in the White House by upgrading the NSC staff, converting the NSC executive into their national security advisor, and calling very few meetings of the formal NSC,[65] we will focus our discussion on this body because it remains the formal structure for making such decisions, even though it is seldom used.

Evolution of the National Security Council.   In addition to the president and the secretaries of State and Defense, the original NSC included the chairman of the now defunct National Security Resources Board (NSRB) and all three military service secretaries. The service secretaries and the chairman of NSRB were dropped in 1949, in favor of the vice president.[66] President Truman downplayed the role of the NSC in decision making, beginning in 1947, because he was determined to make all important decisions himself. He did not even attend the first NSC meetings lest some think that the NSC actually made the decisions rather than the president. Truman expected his chief advisors to recommend policy actions in their areas of responsibility, so the head of the NSC did not have an advocacy role. Moreover, Truman did not like to have his advisors engage in conflict at NSC meetings. He asked the staff to work out these differences beforehand, so that he and his chief advisors could make a clear choice. When conflicts did occur either between Truman and one of his advisors or between two of his advisors, these conflicts were settled quickly between the individuals involved.[67]

As a result of his extensive experience both as a military staff officer and as a high-level decision maker in the Second World War, Dwight

Eisenhower took a special interest in managing national security affairs when he became president in 1953. Unlike Truman, Eisenhower participated actively in NSC discussions and appointed a national security advisor to assist him in running this decision-making system. He established a Planning Council for developing foreign policy options and an Operations Coordinating Board for implementing NSC decisions. Although Eisenhower made the final decisions himself, he encouraged chiefs to bring other players to NSC meetings in order to ensure that he had all the requisite expertise on the issues to be dealt with at the meeting. Eisenhower welcomed conflicting points of view and wanted to resolve conflicts himself. For example, he required interagency staffs to identify in writing all the differences that emerged in discussions at lower levels.

When President Kennedy replaced Eisenhower in 1961, he dismantled both the Planning Council and the Operations Coordinating Board, despite Eisenhower's advice not to do so. Like Eisenhower, Kennedy was problem-focused, but he thought that the Eisenhower system was too unwieldy. He wanted a more flexible system such as the one Roosevelt had used in the Second World War. Kennedy wanted to make decisions in a less structured context, and so he did not distinguish among his advisers on the basis of the positions they held. He allowed anyone to make substantive contributions to the issues being discussed. Indeed, McGeorge Bundy, Kennedy's national security advisor, participated as equally as a policy advocate and as a facilitator in these discussions. Like Eisenhower, Kennedy relied upon the permanent bureaucracy to help him develop and implement his policies, so he occasionally contacted lower-level officials personally in order to check facts and get opinions.

Lyndon Johnson kept the Kennedy chiefs in place when he succeeded the assassinated president in 1963. Johnson's expertise was in domestic, not foreign, policy, however, and so he relied upon his advisors to generate options. Johnson often met with his chief advisors in a "Tuesday Luncheon" group rather than the NSC so that he could keep his vice president, Hubert Humphrey, out of the deliberations. Johnson preferred smaller groups so that he could control the participants, although he often allowed majorities to make decisions. These meetings were often so poorly staffed that there was no formal agenda, or even a formal record of the decisions made. In 1967 Johnson finally established a Senior Interdepartmental Group "both to review the options that were presented to the NSC and to follow up on decisions reached by the Council." [68] An undersecretary of state chaired these meetings.

When Richard Nixon replaced Johnson as president in 1969, he was determined to reestablish a more formal NSC process, but he did not want the large, deliberative NSC that he had experienced as Eisenhower's vice president. Given his interest in foreign affairs and his previous experience as vice president under Eisenhower, Nixon wanted to be his own secretary of state. With the assistance of Henry Kissinger, his national security advisor, Nixon fashioned an NSC system that centralized foreign policy decision making in the White House to an unprecedented degree. He abolished the Senior Interdepartment Group established by Johnson, and replaced it with a Senior Review Group chaired by Kissinger. Under Nixon the main departments initially produced some fifty National Security Study memoranda in the first year from which the Senior Review Group developed policy options for the president. Kissinger virtually replaced William Rogers, Nixon's first secretary of state, as the primary spokesman for the administration's foreign policy. Eventually Kissinger succeeded Rogers as secretary of state, and at the same time retained his position with the NSC.

When President Nixon resigned as a result of the Watergate scandal in 1974, Gerald Ford replaced him. Ford initially kept most of Nixon's chief foreign policy advisors in place, but since he was less interested in foreign affairs than Nixon, he depended more upon his advisors to develop options. He also loosened the tight control that Nixon and his White House staff had developed over foreign policy. Eventually Ford asked Kissinger's assistant in the NSC, Brent Scowcroft, to replace Kissinger as his national security advisor, leaving Kissinger in his position as secretary of state. Since Ford had to campaign for office if he wanted to stay in power, he was particularly interested in the political fallout of the foreign policies being pursued by his administration.

Like most of the newly elected presidents before him, Jimmy Carter sought to overcome what he perceived as the major problem with the NSC system used by his predecessors prior to 1977. Although Carter did not have previous experience in foreign affairs, he did take a personal interest in decision making. He was convinced that if his advisors carefully laid out all the facts, the best policy would emerge. He preferred a far more informal system than that established by Nixon, one in which foreign policy making would be decentralized. Accordingly, Carter announced that Cyrus Vance, his secretary of state, would be his primary foreign policy advisor and that Zbigniew Brzezinski, his national security advisor, would largely play a management role. However, Brzezinski differed with Vance on most foreign policy issues and eventually he, not Vance, became the chief foreign policy spokesman. Indeed, the actual operation of the NSC under Brzezinski was more similar to Kissinger's NSC than Carter would like to admit. Carter studied policy issues in detail but often became so involved in attempting to satisfy various interests that he was indecisive. President Carter often had considerable dissent within his decision-making group because of the differences of opinion between Brzezinski and Vance. However, when these differences did occur, Carter discouraged others from joining the fray.[69]

When Ronald Reagan became president in 1981, he too announced that his secretary of state, Alexander Haig, not his national security advisor would be his chief advisor on foreign policy, and Reagan appointed a number of relatively weak NSC advisors to make that point stick. But although Reagan had little experience in foreign affairs, he was ideologically committed to certain policies. He thought that he could accomplish what he set out to do by appointing people he trusted and then leave them alone so they could get the job done. But Reagan's ideologically driven, hands-off approach got him into trouble. His White House chiefs did not have the requisite foreign policy knowledge or experience to effectively exercise that power. In time some members of the NSC staff became so suspicious of the permanent bureaucracy that they began to conduct their own operations. One reason Reagan lost control of his foreign policy is that he paid little attention to what people outside his immediate circle said about it.

Reagan's vice president, George H. W. Bush, was elected to succeed him in 1989. Unlike Reagan, Bush had considerable experience in foreign affairs, and he was a very active participant in foreign policy decision-making groups in his administration. By appointing cabinet secretaries with extensive White House experience to foreign affairs departments, he ensured that these departments had more to say about foreign policy decisions than they had for some time. Although Bush formed a very collegial group of foreign policy advisors, who worked well together, he and they did not function very well under stress. When Bush felt personally challenged as he did with respect both to Panama and to the Persian Gulf War, he did not seek contrary points of view.[70] For example, in the Persian Gulf War Bush was so adamant about taking military action against Iraq in 1990 that neither his secretary of state, James Baker, nor the chairman of his Joint Chiefs of Staff, Colin Powell, even raised their doubts. The only issue discussed at the time was how the war should be conducted.

President Clinton replaced Bush after Bush's first term. Clinton did not initially have a strong interest in foreign affairs. He had hoped that his first national security advisor, Anthony Lake, could manage foreign policy for him. When that proved impossible, Clinton became more active. Since Clinton likes to be at the center of things, he prefers to make policy in the context of a wide-ranging discussion. But his desire to hear all sides of every issue often makes it difficult for him to make a decision.

George W. Bush was elected in 2000. As a new president of a new party, he appointed a number of cabinet chiefs who had previously served in high positions in his father's administration. He allowed his national security advisor, Condoleezza Rice, to chair the meetings of his principal cabinet chiefs. Once they had developed a clear option, he weighed in to make the final decision. President Bush put great emphasis on sticking to his decisions and depended largely on his advisors to implement these decisions.

Having described the leadership style of each post–World War II president in the NSC, it is now possible to assign each of them to one of the eight group-types associated with various foreign policies.

Presidents by Group Type.   Our confidence in these assignments is enhanced by the pioneering work of Margaret Hermann, who has typed some 120 world leaders according to the criteria of sensitivity, control, and involvement.[71] According to Hermann and Preston, nine post–WWII presidents represent six of these eight types. Eisenhower and Kennedy are MCA; George H. W. Bush, MCA; Nixon, MCA; Carter, MCA; Clinton, MCA; Reagan and George W. Bush, MCA; and Truman and Johnson, MCA.[72] Earlier Hermann had classified Nixon as an MCA type. Hermann does not classify President Ford because she says there is insufficient data to type him, but using her categories, President Ford could be classified as MCA because he seems to be the exact opposite of Nixon on all three dimensions. Table 11.4 illustrates the placements of each of these leaders on the three dimensions.

Because of the systematic way that the three-dimensional framework is applied in this text, it is easy to show the number of dimensions on which any two types of decision makers differ from one another. If two types are in adjoining cells of the matrix table, there is only one dimension of difference between them. If two types are touching at just one point, that is, diagonal, there are two dimensions of difference. And if the two types are not touching at all, there are three dimensions of difference. For

Table 11.4. Dimensions of Foreign Policy Inputs: Classification of Post–World War II Presidents by Leadership Style

		Coordination			
		High (M) Centralization		Low (M) Centralization	
		High (C)	Low (C)	Low (C)	High (C)
Specialization	High (A)	MCA Eisenhower Kennedy	MCA George H. W. Bush	MCA George H. W. Bush[a]	MCA Nixon[b]
	Low (A)	MCA Carter	MCA Clinton Ford[c]	MCA Reagan, George W. Bush	MCA Truman, Johnson

a. George H. W. Bush scored at the mean on coordination (sensitivity). Hermann and Preston classify him as MCA, but he is also classified MCA here because he did not demonstrate sensitivity in his major decisions on the Persian Gulf War and Panama.

b. Hermann and Preston do not classify Nixon in their 2004 study, but they considered him MCA in "Presidents, Leadership Style, and the Advisory Process," in Whittkopf and McCormick, *Domestic Sources*, 1999, 357.

c. Hermann and Preston do not present scores for Gerald Ford. However, he is classified here as MCA because he appeared to be the exact opposite of Nixon on all three dimensions

Source: Adapted from Margaret Hermann and Thomas Preston, "Presidential Leadership Style and the Foreign Policy Advisory Process," *The Domestic Sources of American Foreign Policy,* ed. Eugene R. Wittkopf and James M. McCormick (Lanham, MD: Rowman and Littlefield, 2004), 369.

example, Table 11.4 shows that Truman and George W. Bush and Eisenhower and Carter differ on one dimension, centralization and specialization respectively. Clinton and Kennedy, George H.W. Bush and Reagan, and Nixon and George W. Bush all differ on two dimensions, that is, specialization and centralization, specialization and coordination, and specialization and centralization, respectively. Finally, differences between Eisenhower and Reagan, Kennedy and George W. Bush, and Nixon and Clinton exist on all three dimensions.

Conclusion

All of the factors that influence foreign policy impinge directly on the president and his principal advisors. These influences are so extensive that scholars usually focus on one or two factors while they control for the others. Depending on what influences they emphasize, some conclude that top-level decision making in the White House is rational; others assume that the outcomes of these White House deliberations are largely resultants of the political process and not necessarily rational.

To acknowledge that foreign policy making is both rational and non-rational is disconcerting, for most people assume that the rational is preferable to the nonrational. Yet nonrational considerations may be positive as well as negative for decision making. The nonrational influences depicted by cognitive consistency, cognitive miser, and attribution theories exhibit faulty observation or logic. At the same time, the non-rational contributions of those who use feeling and intuition to make decisions are essential to any comprehensive approach to foreign policy decision making. But to exclude the former and to include the latter in foreign policy decision making places extraordinary demands on the individuals and groups making these decisions.

Three conclusions might be drawn from this discussion. First, the quality of individual decision making matters. Those who have previous experience with foreign policy and those interested in foreign affairs not only become more engaged in foreign policy decision making but also are more likely to focus on the task of selecting the best possible policy. However, intelligence, previous experience, or interest do not guarantee that such individuals will not fall prey to dehabilitating practices that can have negative consequences. For example, Kennedy and Johnson's secretary of state, Dean Rusk, was intelligent, experienced, and interested in East Asia, but he apparently relied upon a Korean analogy that led him to advocate military intervention in the Vietnam War. Likewise, George H. W. Bush, one of our more experienced presidents in foreign affairs, insisted that the United States take military action against Iraq in 1990–1991 without giving those in his inner circle who questioned his actions a real opportunity to be heard.[73] At the same time, we need to recognize that individuals without extensive experience or interest in foreign affairs may have faculties that are important in making foreign policy decisions. For example,

Reagan's intuitive ability to see the possibility of complete nuclear disarmament between the United States and the Soviet Union may have been an important step in bringing about a peaceful end to the cold war. By the same token Truman's penchant for being decisive may have been important in getting us into the cold war in the first place.

Second, the quality of group decision making matters. The world is too complex for any one individual to assemble all the information that is relevant for making foreign policy decisions. Individuals can compensate for known weaknesses by joining with others whose strengths compensate for their weaknesses. Thus the group as a whole can be stronger than the individuals who compose it. But this does not happen automatically. All the players need the confidence that the president will be able to make decisions and stick to them. If the president goes along with the last person that talks with him, real decisions never get made. The result is likely to be chaos. At the same time, the president depends on his advisors—chiefs, staff, and career bureaucrats—both for the development of options and for implementation. But if the president is focused on the political process rather than the problem, it is difficult to keep the lines of communication open. Moreover, the president and his chief advisors cannot do everything themselves. They depend on each other and the departments they represent to follow through on their commitments to each other. If they do not have that kind of unity, they cannot perform well.

Third, individuals can learn from their mistakes. Kennedy's decision on the Bay of Pigs has been referred to as "the perfect failure." [74] In the weeks prior to the invasion Kennedy assumed that some Cubans would be prepared to rise up against Castro because that is what he expected in a communist regime. The fact that the CIA told him that the United States could not count on any domestic resistance in Cuba to help them oust Castro did not seem to register with Kennedy. He simply ignored such statements because in his mind popular unrest went with communism, so if Castro had a communist government, there would be popular opposition to the Castro regime.[75] Kennedy substituted his own sense of cognitive consistency for the facts in this case, and he failed to listen carefully to those who could correct his errors.

Yet Kennedy was able to improve his decision process. His decision to quarantine Soviet ships carrying missiles and other military supplies to Cuba in 1962 is generally regarded as a rational one because he was able to remove Soviet missiles from Cuba without causing a world war fought with nuclear weapons. In this case Kennedy carefully prioritized his objectives and then considered the pros and cons of at least six different courses of action before actually choosing an action which would preserve the president's authority, maintain America's freedom of action, and yet avoid World War III.[76]

Even Johnson, who preferred to deal with chiefs on a one-to-one basis and had largely closed out the rest of the bureaucracy during key decisions on Vietnam, realized his errors. Under President Johnson, the "Tuesday Luncheon" meetings between the president, his national security advisor, and his secretaries of state and defense were so disorganized and unprepared, that the only records kept were McGeorge Bundy's notes.[77] This clearly prevented lower-level experts from having any direct influence on these decisions. In the closing months of his administration Johnson corrected his mistake by establishing an interdepartmental review committee that could prepare options for his decision-making group.

Key Concepts

attribution theory   387

closed-minded   390

cognitive complexity   390

cognitive consistency theory   387

cognitive miser theory   386

fundamental attribution
   error   387

groupthink   403

governmental politics   379

in-and-outers   384

individuals in positions   385

Introvert–Extrovert scale   388

Judging–Perceiving scale   389

locus of control   391

new group syndrome   402

open-minded   390

problem-oriented   392

process-oriented   393

risky-shift   404

schema   386

self-monitors   391

Sensing–Intuition scale   388

span-of-control   382

stress   390

task-oriented   392

Thinking–Feeling scale   389

Suggested Readings

1. Burke, John P. and Fred I. Greenstein. *How Presidents Test Reality, 1954 and 1965.* New York: Russell Sage Foundation, 1989.

2. Khong, Yuen Foong. *Analogies at War: Korea, Munich, Dien Bien Phu, and the Vietnam Decisions of 1965.* Princeton, N.J.: Princeton University Press, 1992.

3. Mitchell, David. *Making Foreign Policy: Presidential Management of the Decision-making Process.* Burlington, Ver.: Ashgate, 2004.

4. Moens, Alexander. *The Foreign Policy of George W. Bush: Values, Strategy, and Loyalty.* Burlington, Ver.: Ashgate, 2004.

5. Wittkopf, Eugene R. and James M. McCormick, ed. *Domestic Sources of American Foreign Policy: Insights and Evidence* 3d ed. Lanham, MD: Rowman and Littlefield Publishers, Inc., 1999.

6. Yetiv, Steve A. *Explaining Foreign Policy: U.S. Decision-Making and the Persian Gulf War.* Baltimore: Johns Hopkins University Press, 2002.

CHAPTER 12

Majoritarianism: Political Culture and Public Opinion

WITH LEE ANN PINGEL

Between elections the American people rely on political culture and public opinion to keep elected officials in line. But occasionally there are circumstances in which these traditional constraints on executive power do not work. When that happens, Americans are prepared to take to the streets in order to protest government policies. In this picture, Americans opposed to the Vietnam War flood Pennsylvania Avenue in Washington, DC, in April 1971 in order to conduct a peaceful protest. Two years later President Nixon withdrew American forces from Vietnam.

IN DEMOCRATIC THEORY the foreign policy of a country should be shaped by the views of its citizens. Typically, political scientists have not considered the public to have much impact on a state's foreign policy, but this is not actually the case. In fact, the American public influences foreign policy in two ways: first, by helping to formulate it; second, by evaluating its implementation. Although foreign policy is usually a response to external events, the character of domestic society determines the internal rejoinder. In that the creators of U.S. foreign policy arise out of the general populace, they are products of American society and culture. Thus a subjective cultural bias is brought to bear on those who make foreign policy decisions. The public draws upon the same culture in forming its opinions on current events. This is only one of the ways that the public helps to formulate foreign policy. The public also evaluates the foreign policies of the government and society. One way the public expresses its judgment is by voting. In a democracy policy makers are ultimately answerable to their constituents for the policies they implement. Although public satisfaction and dissatisfaction are expressed most clearly in elections, most politicians want to keep their jobs and be reelected, and so they also pay close attention to public opinion between elections.

Examining these two phenomena, "political culture" and "public opinion," can help to explain developments in foreign policy. **Political culture** refers to the core beliefs that distinguish the people in one society from another. It is what most people assume others in their society believe and what allows them to identify with others in their society. Political culture influences the opinions and actions of members of a society. Opinions are conclusions thought out, yet open to dispute. When these individual opinions are aggregated, they are referred to as **public opinion**. This chapter first introduces American political culture and public opinion; and then discusses the relationship between the two.[1] But in order to understand fully the significance of political culture and public opinion, one first needs to understand more fully what majority rule means in the American system of government.

Majoritarianism and Its Limits

As the Age of Absolutism was giving way to the Age of Enlightenment in the late eighteenth and early nineteenth centuries, most political theorists thought that a just government depended upon the consent of the governed. In theory that meant government by unanimous consent, but most commentators realized that the rule of unanimity was impractical. So **majoritarianism** emerged as the *minimum* basis for claiming that a given government was ruled by the consent of its citizens.

The only way of ensuring true **majority** rule was by a direct majority vote in which the people as a whole would vote on every issue. But a direct system of democracy was also impractical, so the founders settled on an indirect system, a republic, in which citizens would first elect representatives by majority vote and then these representatives in turn would vote on individual issues. Thus a republic was an indirect way of realizing democracy.

Because democracy really meant consensus—not majority rule or republicanism—the founders strived for other ways to achieve a "just majority system." [2] They developed a number of institutions—federalism, separation of powers, checks and balances, super-majorities, and an electoral college—to ensure that government would serve a popular consensus rather than a simple majority of the people. Eventually a winner-take-all system of elections in single-member districts emerged that favored two competitive parties so that the person elected from a district would have to represent the political center or median voters in the district in order to better realize consensus. (Incidentally, this system has been largely thwarted in the election of members of the U.S. House of Representatives because virtually all House districts have been scientifically designed by state legislatures to ensure that one party dominates each district. House incumbents rarely lose an election because their party has a stable majority in the district, leaving those who support the candidate of the other party without effective representation.)

Finally, the founders tried to ensure a just majority system by prohibiting the government from interfering with fundamental human rights (minority rights) as expressed in the Bill of Rights. Although the founders relied primarily on the formal law of the Constitution to ensure just rule, they hoped that the informal norms and practices incorporated in political culture and public opinion would also ensure a just government. This chapter explores some of the ways in which these informal checks operate in the American system of government.

Political Culture and Foreign Policy

It's been said that the most important thing we can know about a people is what they take for granted.[3] A society's underlying beliefs are often taken for granted, having become so integrated into the structure of the society that people are no longer fully cognizant of them, which is why a key to understanding U.S. foreign policy is an understanding of the basic beliefs of the American people.

Obviously, no two people in American society will share exactly the same set of values. There does not have to be complete agreement among society's informal organizations, for example along cultural, racial, or gender lines, for there to be beliefs that are widely shared and deeply felt by a majority of Americans. These core beliefs comprising American political culture constitute the often-hidden structure guiding U.S. foreign policy, so exposing these beliefs allows us to better understand the American decision-making process in general, and the role of U.S. citizens in that process in particular.

Freedom and equality are the two most important values in American culture. Of the two, freedom, or liberty, sometimes seems to carry the most weight because both capitalism and democracy are based in part on the concept of freedom. "Capitalism pre-supposes freedom of competition and freedom of exchange between producers and consumers, buyers and sellers"; and democracy is based on the free exchange of information and ideas.[4] Although the public seems to have embraced equality more slowly, this concept is firmly rooted in written documents such as the Constitution and is gradually making more of an impact.

Another set of core values is based on the Protestant work ethic. The idea that the virtuous life requires hard work buttresses capitalism by supporting "the deliberate pursuit of wealth and material goods" and reinforces the radical individualism that Tocqueville saw permeating American society and that underlies the notion of freedom.[5]

Still another core belief is **American exceptionalism**, the idea that Americans are a unique and exemplary group of people. This idea can be traced back to the eighteenth-century English political philosopher John Locke, who greatly influenced the American founders and who is often seen as the intellectual father of the Constitution.

Until the creation of the United States, however, Locke's social contract theory of limited government was untested. For although the concept of individual freedom was already fairly common in seventeenth-century Europe, the American concept of freedom was unique because, unlike other societies, Americans did not have to construct their "new society on the ruins of an old one."[6] They were, as Tocqueville wrote, "born equal" rather than having to fight for their equality by first having to dismantle a society built on a divisive class structure.[7] This difference led to much romanticizing of the American example, so that even European thinkers regarded America as the fulfillment of the liberal political dream of the Enlightenment period.

There are three aspects of American exceptionalism that are particularly important: (1) America's image of itself as a uniquely democratic nation; (2) America's preoccupation with the moral and legal justifications for the use of force; and (3) America's expectation of success in foreign policy. Each of these aspects of American culture also highlights American beliefs in one of the three dimensions of foreign policy: America's self-image as a unique democracy provides Americans with their primary identity within the international community; America's emphasis on legality and morality define the approach of Americans to security; and America's expectation of success explains why Americans embraced internationalism and involvement as a route to prosperity as the nation became more powerful. We will now deal in more detail with each of these aspects of American culture.

American Community as Democracy

Few Americans question the intrinsic value of the democratic institutions envisaged by Locke and incorporated into the Constitution by the founders. Even if their vision is yet imperfectly fulfilled, most Americans feel that abandoning the original prescriptions rather than trying to improve their functioning would be "throwing the baby out with the bath water." These democratic institutions back up the familiar concept of American individualism by providing a basis for other concepts of American government, such as natural rights, the rule of law, the protection of private property, limited government, federalism, the separation of powers within government, due process, regular elections, majority rule, and minority rights. Many Americans are so convinced of the universal value of these institutions that they assume that other states would benefit from developing similar institutions.

Throughout U.S. history, Americans have contrasted the foreign policies of "good" democratic societies with the foreign policies of "bad" societies, alternatively monarchical, fascist, or communist governments. The American distinction between the "bad" governments of those states and the "good" people that comprise those societies is the basis of their belief that many of these societies, if given a choice, would prefer a government just like the American example. Certainly the United States seeks to increase the world's total of democratic governments under the conviction that democratic states get along better and can more easily form large security communities. The assertion that democracies do not make war against one another has now become a cornerstone of contemporary American international relations theory and American foreign policy under President George W. Bush, particularly in the Middle East.[8]

Although Americans have never wavered in their belief in democratic values, there have been persistent concerns about the efficacy of democracies in foreign affairs. This dubiousness reflects a lack of trust in the public's ability to make timely and informed decisions about international situations and events. Even John Locke provided for foreign affairs to be handled differently than domestic affairs by designating a separate federal power for dealing with foreign affairs.

Despite these reservations, however, many Americans believe that the methods employed in domestic decision making are equally workable for decision making in foreign affairs. Indeed, Americans often place so much trust in democratic government that the United States invariably recommends that any troubled country hold free elections as the first step toward solving its problems. Because U.S. society accepts the results of such elections, it readily assumes that elections will bring stability to other societies. Woodrow Wilson's penchant for "open covenants openly arrived at" and "self-determination for all peoples" are examples of this democratic methodology applied internationally. Indeed, U.S. enthusiasm for intervention in the name of democracy abroad, an enthusiasm that was tempered by its weakness in earlier years, has become increasingly active in the effort to extend democracy abroad, most recently to Afghanistan and Iraq.

Yet the belief that American values were universal also imposed a theoretical restraint on the use of U.S. force abroad, because of the recognition that other countries had the right to pursue their own values and interests. If the United States were to intervene in the affairs of others, it would have to do so in terms of their rights, not just our own. This sense of a global community is the basis for a series of moral and legal restraints on the use of force, restraints that bind all states.

Morality in American Security Policy

From the beginning, American society has been based on the conception of natural rights, and has relied heavily on law and morality to constrain intrusions on these rights. These constraints, embodied in the Bill of Rights, are particularly designed to keep government from infringing on the rights of individuals. Because the international legal system is not as well developed as the domestic one, moral constraints have been even more necessary in the conduct of international affairs. Forceful action outside the United States is constrained by international law and morality.

Historically, there has been a split in political theory regarding the use of force. In Europe, foreign policy actors traditionally viewed the balance of power as a "zero-sum game." They believed that the requirements of power and morality were in constant conflict; and they could ill afford the luxury of taking stances largely or solely on the basis of international law and morality. In the United States, the balance of power was not viewed as a zero-sum situation, and the choice surrounding intervention was always a profoundly moral and legal question.

Following from the peaceful conduct of domestic affairs is the assumption that democracies would also pursue their relations with other countries by peaceful means, especially if the other country is also a democracy. Americans believed that if peaceful means of dispute resolution were possible, then the use of force could only be justified after a careful assessment of whether it was in accord both with a democracy's obligations under international law and with moral principles. The use of force in self-defense was considered automatically justifiable; more deliberation was required to justify using force offensively.

Ironically, the September 11, 2001 attacks have reversed these sentiments. Now the United States under the Bush administration feels compelled to undertake preventive wars to quell possible terrorist threats. Europeans generally, especially France and Germany, feel that such actions must be held to a higher standard of moral and legal constraint. The

United States has apparently succumbed to "jealous nationalism" or what the late international scholar Hans Morgenthau referred to as **nationalistic universalism**, that is, the assertion that one's national values are truly universal.[9]

American idealism often has led the United States to engage military force on behalf of moral principles, such as Wilson's campaign "to make the world safe for democracy" or Reagan's efforts to thwart the tactics of the Soviet Union's "evil empire." In these instances, the use of force has been deemed justified when the United States determines that it, or another state, has been the victim of aggression, even if the aggression is largely ideological.

Exceptionalism in the service of morality can become dangerous, even hypocritical. A persistent self-image as the "good guy" or "global policeman" may lead American society to think that all of its policies are automatically good, and an unquestioning belief in one's innocence and benevolence may dull the appetite for critical self-reflection and evaluation of one's moral assumptions.

The Expectation of Prosperity

Whether because of the uniqueness of its democratic institutions, its sense of innocence and morality, or its phenomenal growth, the United States has little experience in dealing with other states on the basis of equality. For most of America's recent history it has dealt with others from a position of superior power. America's success as a country naturally leads to the assumption that following the American example would do much to alleviate other countries' political and economic troubles.

In truth, America's success is partly based on the fact that this country throughout much of its history was especially well endowed with all of the factors needed for economic growth. It experienced extremely rapid population growth over an extended period of time, substituting intensive immigration when the birth rate began to decline. America's large size provided a wide variety of important natural resources and also fostered industrial growth by attracting vast amounts of overseas investment capital.

As important as these advantages were, however, American success has been based to an even larger extent on the ideas that permeate American society. Certainly, racism and other widespread negative stereotypes limited access to the "American Dream" for many people, but the existence of a country with this sort of dream of individual success at all was remarkable—even if many people were able to improve their standard of living only slightly, this was often more than was possible in any other society. The American value of equality boosted the level of prosperity generally by creating a mass market that drove the development of mass production. For example, Henry Ford, the founder of Ford Motor Company, could not have produced his economy cars in an unequal society; he needed a socioeconomic structure in which a large number of people could afford a car.

Thus Americans naturally associate the ideas of free enterprise capitalism with democracy. Equal opportunity to engage in a free market is readily identified with equal participation in the political process. Even though many Americans see in their own lives how capitalism creates wide disparities in income levels between, for example, company owners and company workers, they remain reluctant to accept the fact that such inequalities can easily vitiate the democratic process. Americans remain convinced of the possibility of "rags to riches," that the "wheel of fortune is in constant revolution, and the poor, in one generation, furnish the rich of the next." [10]

This optimistic attitude is buoyed by an essentially ahistorical and simplifying approach to problem solving. The long, intricate, historical roots of international problems seldom discourage Americans. Although American interventions in Vietnam in 1973, Lebanon in 1983, and Somalia in 1993 have been disasters, these negative experiences never seem to hold this country back very long. When the United States does fail abroad, Americans tend to blame such failures on particular leaders or groups rather than to question America's ability to bring about the kinds of changes it believes are necessary.

The beliefs associated with these three aspects of American exceptionalism are constantly changing as Americans reinterpret their shared political culture. Indeed, on the morning after the 2004 presidential election Thomas Friedman, the liberal *New York Times* columnist, awoke to discover that the people who supported the other man "don't just favor different policies from me—they favor a whole different kind of America from me. We don't just disagree on what America should be doing; we disagree on what America is." [11] The stark contrast in the way American exceptionalism is interpreted by a majority of Republicans and Democrats makes it easier to understand changes in American political culture over time.

The truth is that there are important conflicts between some American core values. For example, democracy emphasizes the essential equality of individuals; capitalism produces marked economic inequalities among individuals. "Democratic doctrine presumes that citizens have the right to control their own lives and, indirectly at least, the institutions (including economic institutions) that shape their lives." But capitalist doctrine holds that "owners and managers of private enterprise must be free to set wages and prices, accumulate capital through savings, decide on how to invest their wealth, and organize the workplace." [12] Thus the exigencies of capitalism limit the rights that democracy extends to the people. As the circumstances of individuals change in society over time, they interpret their rights differently. These differences in interpretation help to explain the cyclical moods that occur in American society.

Mood Cycles

Although American belief in its democracy, morality, and success has seldom faltered, it is important to realize that the strength of particular beliefs does wax and wane over time. Political scientist Frank Klingberg has identified three general mood cycles in American history—a union–liberty cycle, an idealist, realist, and rationalist cycle, and an extroversion–introversion cycle—that generally correspond to the three dimensions—community, security, and prosperity, respectively—used in this text.[13]

Although Klingberg's regular cycles are controversial, they underscore an important point: American political culture is constantly being reinterpreted by Americans themselves. At various times American culture can support any of the eight different types of foreign policies delineated by the three dimensions employed in this text. On the community dimension, American policy has ranged from the unilateralism of Washington's "no entangling alliances" to the multilateralism of Lincoln's Union Party. On the security dimension, American foreign policy has embraced both Jackson's militarist policy of "Indian removal" and Lincoln's nonmilitarist policy of "reconstruction." And on the prosperity dimension, American policy has incorporated both the perceived isolationism of the 1920s and 1930s and the internationalism of the 1950s and 1960s.

Although American political culture characterizes the beliefs of most citizens, one cannot forget that American society is composed of many different subcultures and individuals. Like a painting by Georges Seurat, political culture presents a coherent picture from a distance, but at close range that picture dissolves into separate dots of color. In the same way, American political culture is an amalgamation of individuals who have distinct personalities and unique experiences, and rely on different sources for information about government, society, and the international system. Thus, in order to determine what Americans are thinking about foreign policy at a particular point in time, one needs a different measure of agreement—that of public opinion.

Public Opinion and Foreign Policy

Once elected, the authority of American officials is based on the fact that they were either elected by a popular majority or appointed by someone who was. But since the public is responsive to current events, opinions change, and officials need other measures of public opinion to guide them between elections. Individual officials may rely on a variety of different sources for information on public opinion, but increasingly they look to the opinions of a representative sample of the adult population of the United States.[14] The advantage of specifying a fixed population is that, using modern sampling techniques, public opinion pollsters can obtain a reasonably accurate and reliable measure of public opinion about any particular foreign policy issue at a given time.

How Are Public Opinion Polls Conducted?

Academic, commercial, media, and political pollsters collect the most accurate data on public opinion. (Government polls are usually conducted by commercial polling organizations, such as Gallup or Harris.) Whether these polls are based on face-to-face interviews, the telephone, or the Internet, the responses are from a representative sample of adults in the population being surveyed. Anywhere between 600 and 1,500 individuals are usually surveyed in a national poll. These individuals are randomly selected from various strata in the population so that those elements in the population will be represented in the sample. Depending on the size of the sample, these polls can accurately predict the opinions of the larger population within, plus or minus, a few percentage points.

There are differences in outcomes, depending on the method employed. Telephone respondents are apparently more likely than others to go for the first option given. Since the individuals to be contacted by phone are not always at home, interviewers may have to call back a number of times to ensure that they get the right person. If some of these individuals cannot be contacted by phone, the pollsters will weight the responses of those in that strata who have been contacted, so that element in the overall population will be accurately reflected in the sample. Generally speaking, there is more difference between face-to-face interviews and telephone interviews than there is between face-to-face interviews and Internet surveys.[15]

The consumers of polls need to be aware of some of the factors that affect the reliability and validity of information gleaned from polls. It is important to realize that commercial polling is a business, and foreign policy questions are usually included in polls either when there is a hot foreign policy topic or when a sponsor is willing to pay for the inclusion of a few such questions. Media pollsters in particular are likely to conduct foreign policy polls when there is a great deal of uncertainty about a given foreign policy situation. Isolated questions on foreign policy are most characteristic of various commercial polls. In both cases the value of the results may be contaminated by the context in which the questions are asked. Unfortunately, the consumers of information from polls do not always realize what some of these contaminants might be.

Although these pollsters adhere to scientific standards in developing their questions and samples, their clients do not always present the results of these polls in the most objective manner. Thus the form in which the general public receives the results of these polls may have been manipulated to produce a desired slant. This places the responsibility for interpreting polls largely on consumers, who have to judge the results on the basis of what is and is not reported. When such polls are cited, the consumer may be able to determine sample size or margin of statistical error, but he or she is seldom told how many "callbacks" were made to get the opinion of the "right" person (say, white male blue-collar workers, or Southern African-Americans), or what kinds of "weights" had to be given to a few respondents in order to make the sample representative of various groups. More significantly, the consumer is seldom told whether or not those respondents who initially said, "don't know" were probed according to some pre-programmed system to lower this response category.

Since relatively few foreign policy questions are asked in any one poll, the consumer should actually compare the responses of people to the questions asked by different pollsters about the same issue at the same time in order to interpret the results properly. Such comparison is important because it is difficult to determine how much bias is being introduced by question wording unless you can compare responses to several different questions. For instance, at the time that the United States was seriously considering the use of force against Iraq in 1990, several different polling agencies happened to ask very different questions, as Table 12.1 shows. The responses to these questions could lead an analyst to conclude that two-thirds of Americans at the time supported going to war or that two-thirds of Americans opposed military action. It is only when one sees these questions and the responses together that one realizes how sensitive public opinion is to question wording, and how useful it is to have multiple questions asked. As Table 12.1 illustrates, there is a lot of difference in how people regard the use of force in conflict and war. People respond quite differently to the idea of threatening to use force (as deterrence), defense, and initiating conflict.

Most opinion analysts focus on marginal differences between those who respond one way or another on individual questions. But the tendency to analyze public opinion in this way reduces the likelihood that one will fully appreciate either the connectivity between answers or changes in opinion. Even when one compares marginal differences to two identical questions given at two different times, one can only get a sense of gross change. In order to determine the degree of individual change, one must conduct panel studies, polling the same people over different points in time. Multi-question analyses, using panel designs, are essential if one wants to get at the reasons why opinions are changing and perhaps even to determine whether real change has occurred.[16]

What Impact Do Opinion Polls Have?

The relationship between public opinion and foreign policy is more complicated than most people realize. Political scientist Bruce Russett says that though some analysts contend that the public makes policy, others contend that policy makers create public opinion, and still others contend

Table 12.1. Public Support for U.S. Forces in the Persian Gulf, 1990

1. **ABC News/*Washington Post:*** Do you agree or disagree that the United States should take all action necessary, including the use of military force, to make sure that Iraq withdraws its forces from Kuwait?

	Agree, Use Force	Disagree	Don't Know	Number
1990, November 14–15	65%	26%	8%	(515)

2. **Gallup**: Now that the U.S. forces have been sent to Saudi Arabia and other areas of the Middle East, do you think they should engage in combat if . . . Iraq refuses to leave Kuwait and restore its former government?

	Engage In Combat	Do Not Engage In Combat	Don't Know	Number
1990, November 15–16	46%	40%	14%	(754)

3. ***Los Angeles Times:*** Overall, taking into consideration everything you heard or read about the Mideast crisis, do you think the United States should go to war against Iraq, or not?

	Go to War	Do Not Go To War	Don't Know	Number
1990, November 14	38%	53%	9%	(1,031)

4. **Gallup**: All in all, which of these courses of action do you agree with:

The United States should keep troops, planes and ships in and around Saudi Arabia as long as is necessary to prevent Iraq from invading Saudi Arabia, but without initiating a war.

The United States should initiate a war against Iraq in order to drive Iraq out of Kuwait and bring the situation to a close.

	Initiate War	No War	Don't Know	Number
1990, November 15–18	28 %	65 %	7 %	(1,018)

Source: Adapted from John Mueller, "The Polls—A Review," *Public Opinion Quarterly* 57 (1993): 86–87.

that policy makers and public opinion are essentially irrelevant to one another, he himself feels that policy makers and public opinion interact with one another.[17] Those employing Russett's approach have shown that there is congruence between changes in public opinion in one year and changes in foreign policy in the next. Over 60 percent of the time a change in one brings about a change in the other, and more often than not, changes in opinion precede changes in policy.[18] A later study confirms that foreign policy outcomes are consistent with the preferences of a majority of the public in over 67 percent of the foreign policy cases studied.[19]

Other evidence suggests that the relationship between public opinion and foreign policy is proportional: the more agreement there is among people, the more public opinion influences foreign policy. Using information obtained through the Freedom of Information Act, Thomas Graham has traced what key officials knew about public opinion during the early cold war period and how that information influenced their arms control decisions.[20] His analysis suggests that officials may consciously or unconsciously employ five levels of public support, listed in Table 12.2, to measure the wisdom of implementing a policy.

If the relationship between public opinion and foreign policy is proportional, it would obviously be risky for presidents to pursue foreign policies that have only the support of a **plurality**. One example of such a policy was Reagan's decision in the early 1980s to covertly arm the Contras as a means of overthrowing the Sandinista government in Nicaragua, since he rarely had more than 40 percent support for an open policy. Elliott Abrams, assistant secretary for Inter-American Affairs at the time, notes that, "had public support been generally sixty–forty in the president's favor [rather than the reverse], the administration would have probably put forward a more forceful policy." [21] As it was, the administration operated clandestinely, with the help of national security advisor Poindexter and staffer Oliver North, only to be faced with the enormous Iran–Contra scandal when information about the government's activities filtered out into the public.

Even with public support at the majority level, Graham thought the president must be cautious because the opposition may challenge his policy. If support reaches a **consensus** level, he thought the policy was in a much stronger position. If there was preponderant support, Graham thought it would actually deter political opposition. And if public support was virtually unanimous, Graham maintained it "dominated the entire political system and swept all political opposition away." [22]

These guidelines are generally helpful, but there are situations in which the American public is so conflicted that the guidelines are not that relevant. For example, in mid-February of 2003, the UN Security Council was divided on whether or not to continue inspections for WMD in Iraq. At the time the United States was threatening to invade Iraq on its own,

Table 12.2. Levels of Public Support for Foreign Policy

Categories	Level of Support
Plurality	less than 50% but more than other options
Majority	50% to 59%
Consensus	60% to 69%
Preponderance	70% to 79%
Virtual Unanimity	80% and above

Source: Thomas Wallace Graham, "The Politics of Failure," PhD. diss. Massachusetts Institute of Technology, June 1989, 57.

without the support of key allies. In a poll taken by the Program for International Policy Attitudes (PIPA) at the time, 67 percent of the public was very pessimistic about the success of the inspections. Nevertheless, 56 percent of Americans said it was necessary to get UN approval. PIPA found that respondents reacted positively to arguments made on both sides of the issue at either the plurality level or the **preponderance** level. When respondents were finally asked how they would feel if the president decided to act on his own without UN approval, 37 percent said they would agree, 36 percent, would not agree, and 25 percent, would not agree, but would still support the president.[23] Given this level of ambiguity, one might ask whether public opinion polls should be taken seriously.

Should Public Opinion Polls Be Taken Seriously?

Among those who acknowledge the interaction between public opinion and foreign policy a further distinction must be drawn between **traditionalists** and **revisionists**. Traditionalists generally believe that policy officials must do what they think is best regardless of current public opinion; revisionists believe that policy officials would be wise to consider seriously public opinion in policy making. They differ on two main issues: simplicity versus complexity and instability versus stability.

Simplicity versus Complexity. Traditionalists argue that little weight should be given to the current level of public opinion because the general public is generally apathetic about foreign affairs and lacks the knowledge and experience to make a meaningful contribution to foreign policy. There is, in fact, solid evidence that a shocking percentage of the American people lack specific factual information about current foreign policy. For example, only about one in four individuals in the general public is usually able to recall the name of the secretary of state or locate on a map countries that are in the news at the time. In 2004 only 22 percent of the American public could name the secretary-general of the United Nations, Kofi Annan.[24] Traditionalists usually attribute this lack of information to the fact that the American people are so caught up in their daily lives that they do not pay much attention to foreign affairs.

Moreover, even when members of the public pay attention to foreign affairs, traditionalists believe that they often get it wrong. After all, people are quite capable of misperceiving facts to fit their predispositions. For example, in the 2004 presidential campaign 72 percent of Bush supporters said that they believed, just before the war, that Saddam Hussein either had WMD or a major program for WMD while only 26 percent of Kerry supporters did; and 75 percent of Bush supporters believed that Iraq had ties with al Qaeda while only 30 percent of Kerry supporters did. These differences in perception persisted throughout the campaign even though a series of government reports later showed that neither claim was true.[25]

Revisionists readily acknowledge that the public often lacks specific and important details, but they argue that the public usually knows the essentials of any given issue and is quite able to make independent assessments of the country's foreign policy. Traditionalists also argue that public opinion on foreign policy is largely unintelligible because there are no underlying principles or tenets that structured these opinions. This conclusion is based on the idea that there is no ideological consistency or structure to foreign policy opinions because party identification or a liberal–conservative orientation is not consistently associated with many foreign policy opinions.[26] However, revisionists have demonstrated, as Chapter 1 shows, that public opinion on foreign policy is structured along three broad dimensions: community, security, and prosperity. This structure also has implications for another aspect of the controversy, the stability of public opinion on foreign policy.

Instability versus Stability.   Traditionalists also contend that public opinion is often invalid because it fluctuates so much over time. They characterize public opinion as emotional, moody, and irrational.[27] In fact, there are a number of instances in which public opinion has shifted widely on key foreign policy issues. For example, during the 1980s American opinion on the character of the Soviet threat varied by as much as 50 percent over a ten-year period, as Figure 12.1 shows.[28] Most traditionalists conclude

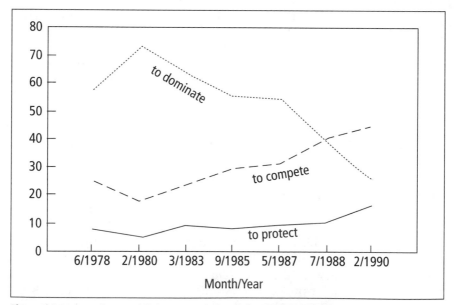

Figure 12.1. American Public's Perceptions of the Soviet Union's Primary Objective in World Affairs
Source: H. Hinckley, *People, Polls, and Policymakers: American Public Opinion and National Security* (Lanham, Md.: Lexington Books, 1992), 49.

that in view of these instabilities, policy makers would be unwise to consider seriously public opinion in making day-to-day policy decisions.

Revisionists argue, however, that multidimensionality actually ensures stability. If one could explain public opinion on foreign policy with reference to just one dimension, say proactive–reactive, then a change in public opinion on that dimension could cut across all issues. If opinions vary on multiple dimensions, however, a change on one dimension may not affect public opinion as a whole very much on any given foreign policy issue.[29]

By examining virtually all of the public opinion data on foreign policy questions repeated over time revisionists have found that at least 50 percent of the time there is no significant change (of six percentage points or more) in public opinion.[30] Moreover, when public opinion does fluctuate more than 6 percent, there are often good reasons for these changes. For example, they might note that although public belief that the Soviet Union was trying to dominate global dynamics fell from 73 percent in 1980 to only 25 percent in 1990 (see Figure 12.1), but there is nothing remarkable in that, given the changes in the Soviet Union's domestic and foreign policies due to first *perestroika* and *glasnost* and then the fall of the communist government.

Table 12.3 shows the consistency of public opinion on foreign policy in the public opinion data collected by the Gallup and Harris organizations for the Chicago Council on Foreign Relations on U.S. foreign policy goals on a quadrennial basis from 1974 to 2002. A cursory glance at the percentages of those who responded "Very Important" each year shows that there is broad consistency in these responses over time. The main exceptions (in bold print) are the polls for Oct. 23–Nov. 15, 1990, the collapse of the Soviet empire, and 2002, after the September 11, 2001 attacks.

Because revisionists have more confidence in the validity of public opinion polling, some of them have developed a more **"deliberative"** style of **polling**. As one key proponent of this method explains:

> An ordinary poll models what the electorate thinks, given how little it knows. A deliberative opinion poll models what the electorate *would* think if, hypothetically, it could be immersed in intensive deliberative processes. The point of a deliberative opinion poll is prescriptive, not predictive.[31]

This new form of polling attempts to refine the crude results of traditional polls by bridging the gap between what the public thinks at the moment and what the public would be likely to perceive as its interest if it were provided with all the facts.

"Public Interest" Polling. In order to correct for public misinformation and misperception, **public interest polls** provide respondents with "sufficient factual information so that the public has a basis for the values, judgments, and opinions that it expresses." [32] Of course, there are limits to the amount of information that pollsters can provide over the telephone.

Table 12.3. Percentage of the General Public Who Believe Various Foreign Policy Goals Are "Very Important"[a]

Foreign Policy Goal Questions:	1974	1978	1982	1986	1990	1994	1998	2002
Community								
Combating world hunger	61	59	58	63	n/a	56	62	61
Helping to improve the standard of living of less developed nations	39	35	35	37	33	**22**	29	30
Improving the global environment	n/a	n/a	n/a	n/a	73	**58**	53	**66**
Promoting and defending human rights in other countries	na	39	43	42	**58**	**34**	39	47
Strengthening the United Nations	46	47	48	46	52	51	45	**57**
Strengthening international law and institutions	n/a	n/a	n/a	n/a	n/a	n/a	n/a	43
Security								
Defending our allies' security	33	50	50	56	61	**41**	44	**57**
Maintaining superior military power worldwide	n/a	n/a	n/a	n/a	n/a	50	59	68
Helping to bring a democratic form of government to other nations	28	26	29	30	28	25	29	34
Preventing the spread of nuclear weapons	n/a	n/a	n/a	n/a	84	82	82	90
Combating international terrorism	n/a	n/a	n/a	n/a	n/a	n/a	79	**91**
Protecting weaker nations against foreign aggression	28	34	34	32	32	24	32	41
Prosperity								
Protecting the jobs of American workers	74	78	77	77	84	83	80	85
Securing adequate supplies of energy	75	78	70	69	76	**62**	64	**75**
Promoting market economies abroad	n/a	n/a	n/a	n/a	n/a	n/a	34	36
Controlling and reducing illegal immigration	n/a	n/a	n/a	n/a	n/a	72	**55**	**70**
Stopping the flow of illegal drugs into the U.S.	n/a	n/a	n/a	n/a	n/a	85	81	81
Reducing our trade deficit with foreign countries	n/a	n/a	n/a	62	56	59	50	51
Safeguarding against global financial instability	n/a	n/a	n/a	n/a	n/a	n/a	n/a	54
Reducing our trade deficit with foreign countries	n/a	n/a	n/a	n/a	n/a	n/a	n/a	51

a. Differences in the order of 10 percentage points or more in successive years are put in bold type.

Source: Chicago Council on Foreign Relations, *Worldviews 2002,* October 2002, 106–115.

In order to test for the stability of public opinion public interest polls sometimes employ "experts on opposite ideological sides of an issue to ensure that the person polled is presented with objective questions." One technique is first to ask a question, then provide a few "pro" and "con" arguments before asking the question again. In this way "public interest" pollsters can gauge, even if only roughly, the effect of new information on the public's thinking.

Moreover, public interest polls recognize the multidimensional character of opinions. They ask enough questions so that if the answers to individual questions seem nonsensical, analysts can try to determine what individuals are thinking by examining their responses to other questions probing different aspects of the issue. Since public interest polling expands the understanding of public opinion, it forces a reconsideration of the relationship between public opinion and political culture.

Public Opinion and Political Culture

This section is divided into two parts. The first part shows what the public would think about international community, security, and prosperity after the public has been provided with factual information. The section features a series of public interest polls by Americans Talk Issues (ATI) between 1990 and 1995.[33] Box 12.1, Individuals in Action, profiles ATI's founder. The ATI data are supplemented by findings from a more recent poll by the Chicago Council on Foreign Relations. The second part of this section shows how these public interest results are related to a measure of political culture.

Public Interest Poll Findings on Community

ATI surveys show that public opinion generally believes that functions should be performed at the lowest possible level, that is, if an issue can be handled locally, it should be dealt with locally; if an issue cannot be handled successfully at the local, state, or national level, then it should be handled at the regional or global level. Of course, regional and global organizations cannot be expected to handle such problems unless they have the authority to do so. This means that societies and governments must be prepared to surrender some sovereign powers in order for these organizations to solve such problems.

Among the findings of the Americans Talk Issues poll is that the public's level of support differed depending on how the granting of authority to the UN was characterized:

[S]upport for "this pooling of sovereignty" ranges from 27[percent] to 93[percent] depending on the issue and on how the proposal is worded. . . . Support is higher for UN authority when limited to the specific areas of global security, environment, and sustainable development. It is higher if the survey

BOX 12.1

Profile in Action: Alan F. Kay

After serving as a Japanese interpreter in the U.S. Army from 1944–1946, Alan F. Kay received a BS in mathematics from MIT in 1948 and a PhD in mathematics from Harvard University in 1952. Dr. Kay was cofounder of a military research and development firm (1954–1963) and CEO (1966–1979) of AutEx, Inc., a supplier of computerized communications networks to industry, including the first commercially available e-mail service. Following a career as an inventor, Dr. Kay became interested in investing and became a board member in several start-up companies pioneering energy efficiency and pollution clean-up technologies. He also turned to social innovation in 1979. He became interested in nuclear issues, and cofounded Business Executives for National Security (BENS) and served as a board member of the Center for Defense Information.

Then, in 1987, he returned to something he had done as part of the army of occupation in Tokyo in 1946. As a Japanese language interpreter, he had conducted person-on-the-street interviews for General Douglas MacArthur who used the feedback to help turn the one-time military empire into a market-oriented democracy. Many years later, working for his data communications company, he had market research firms conduct telephone surveys to find the most cost-effective way to develop and sell industry-specific products. In 1987 he began to conduct a dozen surveys on security issues over a fifteen-month period during the presidential campaign. Although none of the original thirteen presidential candidates who cooperated with his project seemed to use any of his findings, he himself was astounded by the "common sense and collective wisdom" of the public.

So using his own resources, he created his own polling organization, Americans Talk Issues, to see if he could get Congress and other public officials to take the views of the American public more seriously. His object was to identify "policy positions that have broad support from both the public and bipartisan teams of experts." Over the next eight years he conducted a series of national surveys to explore an even wider array of public issues. Some of the results of these surveys have been included in this chapter.

shows that due process of law and principles of accountability, transparency, and democracy will be observed. It is still higher if granting the authority will not require an amendment to the U.S. constitution. It is higher if the UN itself is the entity granted the authority. It is higher if the proposal is not described as giving the UN authority but as making the UN more effective.[34]

These earlier findings are corroborated by a poll conducted by the Chicago Council on Foreign Relations (CCFR) in 2004. In that poll 66 percent of the public agreed that "when dealing with international problems, the [United States] should be more willing to make decisions within the United Nations even if this means that the United States will sometimes have to go along with a policy that is not its first choice." And 59 percent of the public even favored or somewhat favored "changing the veto right of the five permanent members in the UN Security Council so that if a decision was supported by all the other members, no member, not even the United States, could veto the decision." Moreover, 57 percent of the public thought that "the United States should make a general commitment to accept the decisions of the World Court rather than deciding on a case-by-case basis whether it will accept the court's decision." [35]

What is particularly impressive about Americans' perception of the United Nations as a vehicle for providing solutions for global problems is that the public is apparently willing to give the organization the necessary enforcement power. In 1993 ATI found that 72 percent of Americans favored the following proposal:

> In order to protect and preserve the world's environment, United Nations resolutions on polluting the atmosphere and dumping toxic wastes in the ocean should have the FORCE OF LAW and rule over the actions and laws of individual countries with weaker environmental protection laws, even the laws of the United States when our environmental protection laws are weaker.[36]

Again, in two separate ATI surveys in March and April 1993, 82 percent and 87 percent of Americans, respectively, were "in favor of the UN, with due process of law, arresting individuals, including heads of state, accused of certain serious crimes and trying them before an International Criminal Court." [37]

Public Interest Poll Findings on Security

ATI polls also show that the American people are prepared to approve the use of force for a wide variety of purposes. These earlier results are also corroborated by a recent CCFR poll. The data from the CCFR poll, presented in Table 12.4, show that there is 15 to 20 percent more support for forceful action taken with UN Security Council approval than there is for individual countries taking forceful actions without UN approval. Asked "if they have strong evidence that the other country is acquiring weapons of mass destruction that could be used against them at some point in the future," only 17 percent of the public believed they would have the right to go to war. Fifty-three percent of respondents felt that they would only have that right "if they have strong evidence that they are in imminent danger of being attacked by the other country." [38]

Table 12.4. Public Support for Forceful Action with and without UN Security Council Approval

Use of Force for Various Purposes	Percent supporting use of force with UN approval	Percent supporting use of force without UN approval
1. To prevent severe human rights violations such as genocide	85	70
2. To stop a country from supporting terrorist groups	81	61
3. To defend another country that has been attacked	77	59
4. To prevent a country that does not have nuclear weapons from acquiring them	70	50
5. To restore by force a democratic government that has been overthrown	60	40

Source: Adapted from Chicago Council on Foreign Relations, Global Views 2004: American Public Opinion and Foreign Policy (Chicago: CCFR, 2004), 24, Fig. 2-1.

Only when terrorism is mentioned specifically is the public more willing to support U.S. unilateral action. Eighty-three percent support "U.S. air strikes against terrorist training camps and other facilities." Seventy-six percent approve "attacks by U.S. ground troops against terrorist training camps and other facilities." But only 20 percent believe "the United States has the responsibility to play the role of world policeman, that is, to fight violations of international law and aggression wherever they occur." And 80 percent believe that "the U.S. is playing the role of world policeman more than it should be."[39]

Moreover, a 45 percent plurality of the American public believe that in the future, compared with what it has been doing, the U.S. government should put more emphasis on diplomatic and economic methods in the effort to fight terrorism.[40] The public's reservations about using military force abroad also show up in their opinions on defense expenditures. In an ATI report in 1995 the public was "split almost evenly" between those who thought the United States was spending too much (42%) and those who thought current levels of funding were about right (40%). In the twenty-five previous years, the responses to this question had fluctuated widely with a slight majority (51%) saying that we were "spending too little" in 1980, as Figure 12.2 shows.[41] In 2004 the CCFR found that only 29 percent of the public felt that U.S. government spending for defense should increase; 44 percent felt that it should be kept about the same.[42]

Public Interest Poll Findings on Prosperity

The American public is apparently ready to support international agreements to regulate a wide range of global activities relating to prosperity. ATI data show that support ranges from "consensus" to **virtual una-**

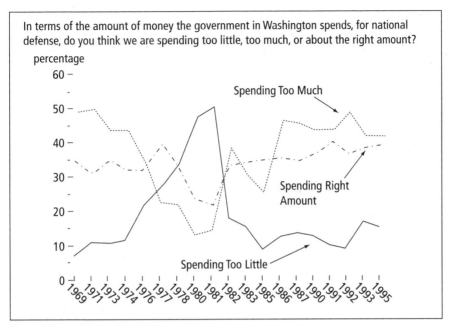

In terms of the amount of money the government in Washington spends, for national defense, do you think we are spending too little, too much, or about the right amount?

Figure 12.2. American Public's Perceptions of Defense Spending
Source: ATI #28 (1995).

nimity for moderate to strict international regulation of the first five of the following activities:

1. Cross-border pollution (90%);

2. Global arms sales (85%);

3. Manufacturing plants moving to countries of cheap labor (73%);

4. 24-hour securities and currency trading (66%);

5. Multinational companies dividing the design, manufacturing, and marketing of products (64%);

6. Workers seeking better jobs in different countries (52%);

7. Global information/entertainment flows (34%).

Three of these activities (questions 3, 5, and 6) present complicated global issues that are usually dealt with in the context of "free trade versus protectionism." The public's approval of global regulation in these cases stands apart from the nationalist measures promoted by many politicians, such as "unilateral protectionism" or "fair" trade agreements.[43] The large percentages of the public willing to recommend "strict controls" for questions 1 through 3 above shows that the American people are prepared to accept international solutions. Only a third of the public is supportive of regulating information/entertainment flows, however.

In the 2004 CCFR poll 64 percent of the public thought globalization, especially the increasing connections of the U.S. economy with others around the world, was mainly good for the United States, but 64 percent of the public recognized that international trade was bad for the job security of American workers. 93 percent of the public felt that countries that are part of international trade agreements should be required to maintain minimum working conditions, and 91 percent thought that countries that are part of international trade agreements should be required to protect the environment.[44]

Americans also want to cut government spending on economic assistance in general. When asked about economic aid, 64 percent want to cut it back, 26 percent indicate they want to keep it the same, and just 8 percent want to expand it.[45]

In short, public interest polls indicate that the public is more multilateral than one might expect. After all, American exceptionalism places a strong emphasis on unilateralism. In this context it is important to remember that public opinion is an aggregation of individual opinions; it shows to what extent individuals hold **common** or disparate **opinions**. Political culture, on the other hand, is what individuals assume other people in society think about things; it represents what individuals perceive to be **shared opinions**.

Why Is Public Opinion So Different from Political Culture?

The relationship between public opinion and political culture may be illustrated by one series of questions asked in the CCFR survey. In addition to asking both members of the general public and foreign policy elites about their attitudes toward certain international policy issues, foreign policy elites were asked to estimate public opinion on these same issues. These estimates give one a rough measure of what these elites perceive to be the opinions *shared* by members of the public, that is, the political culture.[46] The results are shown in Table 12.5.

The first two numbered columns of Table 12.5 show that the general public and foreign policy elites generally favor multilateralism on the first seven questions asked. This result is not that surprising because one could argue that both groups are influenced by the same political culture. But the third numbered column shows that the elites' estimates of public opinion on six of the first seven questions are, on an average, forty percentage points lower than the opinions reported by the public sample in the first numbered column. This shows that elite perception of public opinion, and thus the political culture, is much less supportive of multilateralism than public opinion actually is. (Elites do not misperceive public opinion on the last four questions because actual public opinion is not that multilateral). The last column in Table 12.5 suggests the consequences of this disparity; it presents a brief description of the actions that the administration and Congress have taken on these same questions.[47] Careful examination reveals

Table 12.5. Contrasting Public and Elite Opinion with Elite Perception of Public Opinion on Various Actions

	Percentage of public in favor of action	Percentage of elite in favor of action	Percentage of elite perceiving that public is in favor of action[a]	Presidential and Congressional Action
1. United States participating in UN peacekeeping	78	84	39	Varies on a case by case basis
2. United States participation in International Criminal Court	76	70	30	George W. Bush abrogated signing; Congress passed a hostile Nethercutt Amendment
3. Using U.S. troops to stop genocide	75	86	55[b]	Varies on a case-by-case basis
4. United States not taking sides in the Israel–Palestinian conflict	74	77	32	Most observers recognize that the United States favors Israel.
5. Adopting Kyoto Protocols on global warming	71	72	38	Bush opposes; Senate voted against McCain-Lieberman.
6. Accepting adverse WTO decisions	69	85	29	Bush accepts; both houses of Congress amend tax code
7. Willing to make decisions within the United Nations	66	78	26	President opposes; Congress doesn't act.
8. Use of U.S. troops to ensure oil supply	54	36	37	It is difficult to separate this reason for U.S. troops from other reasons
9. Decreasing legal immigration levels	54	10	50	U.S. government has tightened its control as part of its anti-terrorism effort
10. Financing the UN via a tax on oil and arms sales	49[c]	46	31	Neither the president nor Congress has acted
11. Favors increasing defense spending levels	29	15	13	President and Congress have steadily increased spending

a. The sample size of leaders was expanded to include one hundred congressional staffers.
b. Only 40 percent thought more than 60 percent of Americans would favor using U.S. troops to halt genocide.
c. A plurality of the public actually supports such a tax; a plurality of elites does not.
Source: See Chicago Council on Foreign Relations and Program on International Policy *Attitudes* (PIPA), "The Hall of Mirrors: Perceptions and Misperceptions in Congressional Foreign Policy Process," October 1, 2004, 5–19.

that government action is more in accord with political culture, or the elite perceptions of public opinion, than it is with the opinions of either the public or the elites themselves. In effect, a comparison of these different measures shows that political culture "trumps" public opinion.

Why is this the case? It could be argued that these results show that elites do not know what the public thinks. That may be, but the disparity is just too large to be explained entirely by elite ignorance of public opinion. It is much more likely that these elites, most of whom have considerable experience dealing with the public on such issues over time, are heavily influenced by what they perceive to be *shared* opinions even if those opinions are not held in *common* by a large number of citizens. In effect, elites are anticipating the kinds of public opposition to multilateral measures that can be invoked by a single, self-willed icon of American culture, such as former senator Jesse Helms of North Carolina. Helms, a vigorous critic of the United Nations, frequently called attention to his ability to be reelected to the Senate four times, despite polls showing that two-thirds or more of the public supported the United Nations.[48]

This analysis demonstrates why political leadership must be especially concerned with how people (both the public and elites) *perceive* public opinion because perceived public opinion (political culture) is not usually the same as *actual* public opinion, even though the latter is partly based on the former. This distinction can also explain why politicians resist public interest polling and why public interest polling is so important. Because public interest polling is prescriptive, the contrast between political culture (perceived public opinion) and public opinion (as measured by public interest polling) is even sharper than the distinction between political culture and public opinion.

Given the three-dimensional structure of public opinion (and political culture), this analysis also implies that political leadership cannot generally rely on the marginal "yes" or "no" responses to any one question (whether it measures public opinion or political culture) to assess a foreign policy issue. Political leaders should think in terms of all three dimensions simultaneously. Although three-dimensional thinking will not guarantee success, it may mitigate serious errors.

For an example of a success or missed opportunity, depending on one's point of view, it is instructive to look at the handling of the control of international atomic energy in the mid-1940s. At the close of World War II, President Truman had little difficulty in making the decision to use atomic weapons against Japan. But once the destructive capacity of these weapons became general public knowledge, the public began to push for international control of atomic weapons. Since public pressure for the control option was at the level of virtual unanimity, Truman may have had little choice but to establish the Acheson-Lilienthal Committee to consider what proposals the United States might make in this regard. Truman appointed Bernard Baruch, a highly competent bureaucrat in the Truman administration, to devise a suitable plan.

Of course, Baruch knew that there was popular support for a proposal that was both noncoercive and proactive, but he also knew that the administration did not favor such a plan because it wanted to rely extensively on atomic weapons in the postwar period. Baruch also perceived that the American public for cultural reasons and the Soviet Union for very practical reasons would not support an agreement on the control of atomic weapons that was truly multilateral. So Baruch was able to fashion a multilateral proposal that would satisfy American public opinion but invite a Soviet veto, therefore absolving the U.S. government of the need to abide by what appeared to be the dictates of public opinion.[49] If Truman had wanted the Baruch plan to succeed, he would not only have had to convince the Soviets that the Baruch plan was in their interest but also the American people that such a plan was consistent with American political culture—a difficult but not an impossible task.

One reason for devoting Part I of this book to the history of American foreign policy is to show how American leaders have been able to interpret American political culture in so many diverse ways. For example, the unilateral character of American political culture is strongly represented by the idea of American exceptionalism. Although it is true that exceptionalism is an enduring feature of American culture, this does not mean that there is no basis in American culture for multilateral action. In some ways multilateral action is at the very core of American exceptionalism. After all, the purpose of the American Constitution was to create a "more perfect union" out of thirteen separate colonies. In order to do so, the founders had to establish principles, norms, and procedures that would enable the federal government to function as a unified actor while respecting the rights of state governments. With the emergence of new problems at the regional and global level, contemporary multilateralists are simply asking the United States to do what the colonies were asked to do over two hundred years ago.

With respect to the use of force, it must be recognized that in the early years of the republic, Americans were quite ambivalent about the use of force. Some founders did not want a large standing army, but others were energetic in their efforts both to acquire new territory and to redress grievances with foreign countries. Even today there is both a readiness to use force and a reluctance to do so. The United States has a long history of international involvement, but Americans are particularly sensitive to the costs of international engagement. They are prepared to pay their fair share, but they do not want to be the world's financier or policeman.

To the extent that the American public shapes U.S. foreign policy, it is the responsibility of American leaders to interpret political culture in ways that will best serve the interests of the American people. In recent years such political leadership has been most evident in the effort by various presidents to overcome what has been described as the "Vietnam Syndrome," the idea that the American people do not have the will to undertake sustained military operations abroad.

Political Leadership and Public Opinion

American foreign policy in Vietnam under President Lyndon Johnson can best be described as MCA: unilateral, coercive, and proactive. Public opposition to the Vietnam War was MCA; it was based on the beliefs (1) that America's involvement in the war was immoral (multilateralism), (2) that the United States had overemphasized the utility of force (noncoercive), and (3) that the United States was overextended (reactive). Table 12.6 illustrates the contrasting dimensions between the administration and the public over the Vietnam War. During the Vietnam War, whatever elite and public consensus existed on U.S. foreign policy fell apart.[50] Each of Johnson's successors attempted to rebuild the shattered consensus behind American foreign policy, particularly with respect to security policy. This section examines the efforts of four of those presidents: Nixon, Carter, Reagan, and George W. Bush.

Nixon and Détente

Richard Nixon won the 1968 election in part by claiming that he had a plan for getting the United States out of Vietnam. His objective of "peace with honor" required very adroit management because he had to pretend that he was winning the war in order to disguise his withdrawal from Vietnam. Nixon's main effort to build public consensus around his Vietnam policy was on the coercive–noncoercive dimension. Figure 12.3 illustrates Nixon's basic Vietnam strategy.

Table 12.6. The Vietnam Policies of Johnson and the Antiwar Opposition

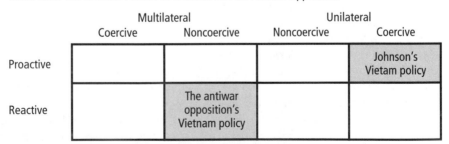

| | Multilateral | | Unilateral | |
	Coercive	Noncoercive	Noncoercive	Coercive
Proactive				Johnson's Vietam policy
Reactive		The antiwar opposition's Vietnam policy		

President Lyndon Johnson was MCA—unilateral because the United States alone made the decision to go to war, coercive because force was used, and proactive because the administration thought it could defeat the North Vietnamese. Public opposition to the Vietnam War was MCA—multilateral because it objected on moral grounds, noncoercive because it wanted to bring the troops home, and reactive because it perceived the war as very costly.

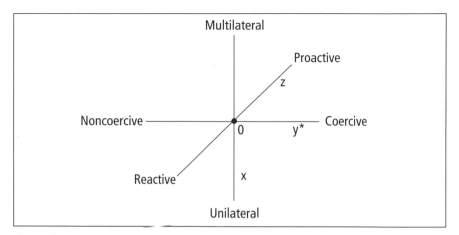

Figure 12.3. Nixon's Basic Strategy for Obtaining Consensus on Vietnam Policy
Nixon's détente policy is on the y axis.

Nixon thought that he could develop a consensus on that dimension by attracting more support from those in the middle of this dimension as part of his policy of détente. He reasoned that the militarists largely on the right would continue to support him because of his well-established anticommunist credentials. He hoped his policy of détente would attract more support from those in the middle who had previously opposed him. Ultimately, he failed both because militarists were not prepared to abandon their anticommunist policies and because many of those in the middle, who belonged to the opposition party, were already alienated by him on the other two dimensions.

One reason Nixon alienated those in the middle of the coercive–noncoercive dimension was that he accused them of being isolationists. Nixon himself was sensitive to that charge because his own policy called for the withdrawal of American forces from Vietnam as soon as Vietnamization could be implemented and South Vietnamese troops could be trained to adequately replace American forces. Since Nixon wanted to negotiate with the North Vietnamese from a position of strength, however, he had to increase pressure on North Vietnam before negotiations could begin. Of course, many of those in the middle of the coercive–noncoercive dimension were proactive and became increasingly impatient with this delay. Realizing himself that most Americans were internationalists, Nixon pejoratively accused these opponents of being isolationists (confounding a noncoercive with a reactive stance.). That way he could then argue that "the silent majority" opposed the "isolationist" position of his opponents.

"Peace with honor" not only delayed negotiations; it also meant that Nixon had to bring pressure on the North Vietnamese by increasing the bombing in North Vietnam, Laos, and Cambodia and to conduct an incursion into Cambodia. But he had to implement this more aggressive aspect of his policy in secrecy because it violated international law. As this part of his policy became more apparent, he alienated many of those in the middle of the coercive–noncoercive dimension because they were also multilateralists. Nixon "tried to find a simple moral category" that would give some significance to his policy, but he was never able to attract much support on the multilateral–unilateral dimension.[51] He could not admit that his real mission was to establish a balance of power, because balance of power politics were anathema to multilateralists. So he made no systematic effort at public education, relying instead on slogans and clichés. His image of a "full generation of peace" never caught on and was supplanted by negative images of My Lai and Watergate. Nixon's foreign policy, which could be classified as <u>MCA</u>, initially received support, but it was eventually overtaken by contradictory events and internal criticism from both the left and right.

Carter and Human Rights

When President Carter took office, he was convinced that America's biggest problem was the lack of public trust in government. He hoped to fill the moral void created by Nixon's predilection for secrecy by giving his foreign policy a strong moral orientation. One of the problems with the American policy of "containment" during the cold war was that it was basically negative, always reacting to Soviet initiatives rather than taking initiatives for peace. Thus "Carter tried to restore public trust by articulating a foreign policy that reflected the character, values, and experience of the American people." [52] In short, Carter placed his attempt to build a foreign policy consensus almost entirely on the multilateralism–unilateralism dimension, as Figure 12.4 shows.

But by emphasizing America's commitment to human rights in the foreign as well as the domestic arena, Carter largely ignored the difficulties in integrating these existing standards into the mix of principles used to conduct the country's foreign policy. The system he envisaged, entailing multilateral cooperation to deal with the emergent problems of development, disarmament, human rights, and the environment, was introduced as if the idea of a cooperative global community was entirely new. This innovative posture placed an enormous burden of proof on the president. By putting himself in the position of having to demonstrate that these innovative policies would actually work, he allowed his opponents to use real or apparent conflicts between old and new ways of doing things to undermine support for his foreign policies.

Like Nixon, Carter also failed to effectively incorporate the other two dimensions into his overall strategy. His opponents often rejected Carter's untried methods as a new form of isolationism. He "emphasized the 1970s as a decade of limits: limits to what the U.S. could do . . . unilaterally in the

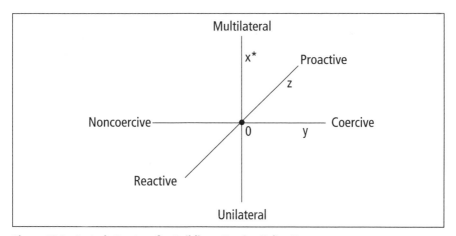

Figure 12.4. Carter's Strategy for Building a Foreign Policy Consensus
Carter's human rights policy is located on the x axis.

world." [53] For example, the decision to return control of the Panama Canal to Panama, which might have been cast largely in terms of cooperative internationalism, was widely viewed as a reactive policy.

More important, Carter failed to convince the public that his policies on the coercive–noncoercive dimension were sound. His efforts to build a better global society highlighted his noncoercive stance. He wanted genuine disarmament, rather than arms control, and he wanted to curtail U.S. arms sales. Of course, this made Carter seem naive to most traditional cold war strategists, and Eugene V. Rostow and Paul H. Nitze quickly reorganized the Committee on the Present Danger to deal with the threat they perceived Carter to be ignoring. Carter's foreign policy can be classified as M<u>CA</u>.

Although his grand design failed in the short run, his campaign on behalf of human rights enhanced America's image among the citizenry of many countries and must be given some credit for the democratization that occurred throughout the world in the 1980s and 1990s. Carter's failure to achieve this in office can largely be attributed to his inability to communicate how his multilateral policies, especially human rights, could contribute to domestic perceptions of American security and prosperity. In the end, Carter had to abandon his noncoercive focus due to events such as the hostage situation in Iran and the war in Afghanistan.

Reagan and Rearmament

Reagan reverted to traditional cold war thinking in developing his design for building public consensus on foreign policy. He argued that the United States had to rebuild the kind of military superiority that had earned it the respect of other countries in the 1950s and 1960s. Extolling the virtues of coercion in the period from 1947 through the mid-1960s, Reagan was an unabashed militarist. Indeed, his militarist rhetoric was so blatant that it triggered a significant antiwar movement in support of a nuclear test ban.

Reagan also assumed a more proactive posture than his predecessors. It was not enough just to contain the Soviet threat, the Reagan Doctrine required the United States to assist anti-Soviet freedom fighters. Also, "Reagan took advantage of favorable trends in Latin America and later in Eastern Europe and the Soviet Union to proclaim a new age of democratic revolutions." [54] Although Reagan's rhetoric often outdistanced his actions, he clearly favored a proactive foreign policy.

Finally, it is important to realize that Reagan was a unilateralist. He was quite prepared to pursue policies in Grenada, Libya, and Central America that America's allies openly opposed. He was also instrumental in pulling the United States out of UNESCO and shifting foreign aid from multilateral to bilateral programs. Reagan, like Carter, portrayed American foreign policy in highly moral terms, but Reagan was eventually more successful than Carter in integrating his moral values into his security policies. Reagan's foreign policy can be classified as MCA, as Table 12.7 illustrates.

Although Reagan's foreign policy did not produce the broad consensus he was seeking, many Americans believe that he forced the Soviet Union to spend itself into bankruptcy and out of existence. Others believe that the Soviet decline began much earlier and was more due to its internal than its external circumstances. Whatever position one takes on this issue, however, it is clear that Reagan was able to benefit enormously from the

Table 12.7. Dimensions of Foreign Policy: Stances of Nixon, Carter, Reagan, and George W. Bush

	Multilateral		Unilateral	
	Coercive	Noncoercive	Noncoercive	Coercive
Proactive				Reagan, George W. Bush
Reactive		Carter	Nixon	

Nixon was MCA—unilateral because he served national interests, noncoercive because he favored détente, and reactive because he wanted to reduce the costs of American foreign policy.

Carter was MCA—multilateral because of his emphasis on universal norms, noncoercive because of his preference for arms control, and reactive because he wanted to reduce costs.

Reagan was MCA—unilateral because he pursued national interests, coercive because of his emphasis on military strength, and proactive because of his attempts to undermine communist governments.

George W. Bush is MCA—unilateral because he often ignores key allies, coercive because he emphasizes the use of force, and proactive because he expects to achieve benefits.

changes in Soviet foreign policy under Gorbachev, so that in his second administration Reagan was actually able to push for disarmament under a new period of détente.

George W. Bush and Unilateralism

President George W. Bush looked to Reagan rather than his own father for inspiration in foreign policy. George W. Bush's foreign policy was largely shaped by his response to the September 11, 2001 attacks. He grounded his active, militarist foreign policy on Franklin Roosevelt's successful efforts to engage the American people in a military crusade against the Nazi threat in World War II. But unlike Roosevelt, who was a multilateralist, Bush took advantage of America's position as the sole superpower in the world to launch the country's most audacious, unilateral foreign policy. The most striking thing about the Bush foreign policy is the notion that the United States was so dominant in the world that it could create its own reality.

Although Bush won a second term largely on the basis of his reputation as a strong anti-terrorist, the country is sharply divided on his foreign policies. Bush's success in dealing with the Vietnam Syndrome will depend largely on events in Iraq. If that country descends into a full-fledged civil war or stalemate, Bush will have unwittingly rejuvenated the Vietnam Syndrome. If Iraq emerges as a semi-democratic country, Bush will have demonstrated the capacity of the United States to act alone in foreign affairs.

These illustrations are instructive because they show how important all three dimensions are in creating consensus. Indeed, most of these strategies failed because the presidents and their advisors neglected the multidimensional character of public opinion on foreign policy. Nixon's plan was to build a consensus by finding the right balance between supporters and opponents on the coercion–noncoercion dimension. He failed because he did not recognize that he also needed to build support on the other two dimensions. Carter's plan was to shift the country's attention away from coercion by emphasizing the positive values of human rights on the multilateralism–unilateralism dimension. He failed because he could not effectively integrate this new element into the other two dimensions. Reagan's plan was to return to the old formula based on an MCA foreign policy. That policy also failed because it did not recognize sufficiently the changes in opinion that had occurred in the meantime and which had at least partly been a result of the policies undertaken by his immediate predecessors. By late November of 2005, a majority of the public opposed the Iraq War, and President Bush's approval rating was at about 34 percent.

What we have learned from these four brief case studies is that public opinion is more complex than our political leadership often acknowledges.

Thus, in order to assess current prospects for achieving consensus on foreign policy, we need to examine public opinion in all its complexity. In fact, the multidimensionality of public opinion opens all kinds of "strategic opportunities" for the country's political leadership.[55] But in order to take advantage of these opportunities, political leaders must not only take into account the multidimensionality of opinion but also the relationship between public opinion and political culture.

Conclusion

This chapter shows that the impact of the American public on U.S. foreign policy is subtler than often thought. Democracy in America has never meant simple majoritarianism. The founders went to great lengths to see that American domestic and foreign policies would be based on a "just majority."

Although the relationship between public opinion and foreign policy is generally proportional, that is, the broader the public's support, the more legitimate the policy, public opinion is often held hostage to popular myths about American political culture. In order to develop a just majority, political leaders not only need to refine public opinion but also to interpret contemporary political culture in ways that support those opinions.

Key Concepts

American exceptionalism 417
common opinions 436
consensus 426
deliberative polling 429
majoritarianism 415
majority 415
nationalistic universalism 420
plurality 426

political culture 415
preponderance 427
public interest polls 429
public opinion 415
revisionists 427
shared opinions 436
traditionalists 427
virtual unanimity 434

Suggested Readings

1. Holsti, Ole R. *Public Opinion and American Foreign Policy.* rev. ed. Ann Arbor: University of Michigan Press, 2004.
2. Kay, Alan F. *Locating Consensus for Democracy: A Ten-year U.S. Experiment.* St. Augustine: Americans Talk Issues, 1998.
3. Page, Benjamin I. and Shapiro, Robert Y. *The Rational Public.* Chicago: The University of Chicago Press, 1992.
4. Melanson, Richard A. *Reconstructing Consensus.* New York: St. Martin's Press, 1991.
5. Sobel, Richard. *The Impact of Public Opinion on U.S. Foreign Policy: Since Vietnam.* New York: Oxford University Press, 2001.

CHAPTER 13

Pluralism: Organized Pressure

Individual sectors of the American public can sometimes have an impact on foreign policy far beyond what one would expect, given their numbers, because they are willing to put one issue above all others. The intensity of group pressure can sometimes control a foreign policy, even one that is contrary to the interests of a large proportion of the American public. This picture shows the intensity of feeling among some Cuban Americans on April 1, 2000, the morning after President Clinton decided to return Elián González to Cuba. Elián was a young Cuban boy whose mother died bringing him by boat to American shores to escape the Castro regime. Despite protests, Clinton thought that the boy should be returned to his father in Cuba. An unidentified protester, wearing a President Clinton mask, joins others in protesting that decision.

DEMOCRATIC THEORY CONTENDS that the people as a whole should determine their country's foreign policy. The last chapter shows that a majority of the American people usually support the foreign policies of the United States because they generally share an ethos of democracy and capitalism that has a continuing impact on public opinion with respect to current foreign policies. But the broad consensus that Americans reach on many foreign policy issues can cover up differences between various categories of individuals in American society. After all, the American people have come from all corners of the earth; and once here they experience many different things, work in various sectors of the economy, and hold a variety of values. Thus within this broad consensus one would expect to find systematic differences as well as similarities of opinion.

These differences of opinion are generally less important when people are informally organized into demographic categories such as men and women, young and old, and rich and poor. People in these **informal organizations** usually have small but fairly consistent differences among them on foreign policy issues. For example, women are generally less coercive than men, young people are usually more coercive than older people, and those with higher incomes are more likely than those with lower incomes to be proactive. But these differences do not usually create major schisms in American society for two reasons. First, these differences are usually quite stable over time, that is, when one plots such differences on a graph over a series of time-points, they show up as **parallel publics.** That is, "all segments of the public generally move in the same direction, and usually at about the same time." [1] Second, the differences of opinion between informal organizations are not usually mutually reinforcing, and so in the aggregate they tend to be distributed on either side of a center point that generally resembles a normal curve.[2] (A distribution resembles a normal curve if it is smooth, symmetrical, and unimodal, that is, bell-shaped.) Thus there is usually a majority in favor of American foreign policies despite differences among informal organizations in society.

However, if one looks at the **formal organizations** in American society, then these differences of opinion may be very stark. (A formal organization has a charter or by-laws that define members, officers, and the rights and duties of each of them toward the other.) The reason for this is that the leaders and most active members of formal organizations often hold very strong positions on some foreign policy issues. And since their opinions on the specific issues of greatest importance to them are likely to dominate their overall outlook on American foreign policy, these differences of opinion may not only be mutually reinforcing but also diametrically opposed to the positions of leaders of other formal organizations. For example, the leaders of the United Automobile Workers of America and the Ford Motor Company have different economic interests, therefore the leaders may clash on a whole series of foreign policy issues because labor and management will have different interpretations as to how these issues will affect their economic interests. Thus even though there may be majority public support for most foreign policies, in order to understand foreign policy making in American society one needs to examine the relations among these formal organizations. The most appropriate framework for explaining foreign policy in terms of these competing organizations is **pluralism.**

Pluralism and Its Limitations

Pluralist theory assumes that society is divided into many different organizations, each with some capacity to influence public policy. It further assumes that the interests and values of this diverse set of organizations establish an equilibrium. Thus the mere existence of these interests and values does not give any particular organization or set of organizations an advantage over the others. Policies favoring one or more organizations develop when these organizations gain better access and exert more pressure than competing organizations. Thus government acts as an umpire that adjudicates among these competing pressures. If a given foreign policy is adopted, according to pluralist theory, it represents a compromise among the competing pressures that various organizations have brought to bear upon the government.

Pluralism does not explain what strategies or tactics these organizations will pursue. Most organizations will attempt to influence government officials directly—the **inside strategy**. But organizations also have the option of attempting to influence the government indirectly by going public—the **outside strategy**. Organizations representing various sectors of the economy, that is **sectoral interests**, are **interest-promoting organizations**. They usually pursue an inside strategy because they represent concrete interests and have the economic resources to gain access to officials; **value-promoting organizations** such as environmental organizations, often pursue an outside strategy because the values they represent may resonate with the larger public.

Although the distinctions between interest-oriented organizations and value-oriented organizations and between the inside strategy and the outside strategy are often useful, they are not infallible. An organization's interests may determine its values and vice-versa, and formal organizations often pursue multiple strategies. For example, the American Israel Public Affairs Committee (AIPAC), which would generally be classified as a value-promoting organization, has ample resources and is very effective at pursuing an inside strategy partly because it fears the opposition of American business and oil interests in the Middle East. Likewise, organized labor—a sectoral interest—sometimes pursues an outside strategy both because it has a large membership and because it may fear being out-maneuvered on the inside by business interests.

Prior to the 1980s it was assumed that organizations that pursued an inside strategy had an advantage because it was the most direct approach; but an outside strategy can be equally effective. This is especially true if the outside strategy can produce a political **movement**. A movement is different from a formal organization in that the individuals caught up in it are not formal members of a single organization or even a group of organizations. Movements represent the more or less spontaneous actions of individuals who are only loosely organized. Yet political movements can exert great pressure as evidenced by the successful movements throughout Eastern Europe that brought down a series of communist governments and indeed even the Soviet Union at the end of the Cold War.[3]

Although such movements are not the same as formal organizations, the latter usually play an important role in the creation of such movements. According to the literature on social movements, they emerge as a result of three factors: (1) the occurrence of events that represent new opportunities or dangers, (2) the existence of "carrying" organizations, and (3) the activation of a leadership group that can use extant organizations to mobilize people to address the new concerns.[4] Thus the structure and communications provided by formal organizations are essential in the formation of new social movements, like anti-globalization, because the networks that exist within and among these organizations create connections among the activists who form these movements. In short, formal organizations house the activists that new leaders can mobilize to create the movements needed to address new problems.

Before illustrating the workings of this pluralist model, one needs to recognize some of its limitations. One such limitation is that pluralism "lumps all lobbying strategies into the generic category of pressure; it is not able to discriminate among different kinds of pressure."[5] Thus pluralism does not explain when organizations will switch from one form of pressure to another.

Another limitation is that pluralism assumes that most actors are willing to compromise. But that is not always true; some organizations will not readily compromise. When compromise isn't forthcoming, either one group dominates or there is deadlock. When one group is able to dominate all the others, it is elitism, not pluralism. When there is deadlock, then bureaucrats are often able to ignore opposing interests and do what they think is best.

Yet another limitation of pluralism is the idea that organizations do not actually compete with each other very often. Rather, they each establish a relationship with particular government organizations and conduct their lobbying activities with these separate organizations, for example, the military-industrial complex. Since such organizations do not compete directly with each other, there is no need to compromise.

Because NGO leaders choose the strategies pursued by nongovernmental organizations (NGOs) in their relations with government organizations, it is important to know what these leaders generally think about American foreign policy, as the next section will show.

Foreign Policy Attitudes of Organization Leaders

Chapter 12 presents the foreign policy attitudes of the general public toward twenty foreign policy goal questions asked by the Gallup or Harris polling organizations for CCFR from 1974 to 2002. This chapter offers a comparable summary of the attitudes of organization leaders to the same set of twenty foreign policy goal questions. Table 13.1 lists which goals organization leaders ranked as "the most important," based on interviews with ten kinds of organization leaders: (1) members of the U.S. House of Representatives, (2) members of the U.S. Senate, (3) assistant secretaries and other senior staff of the administration, (4) vice presidents in charge of international affairs for top industrial corporations, (5) television and radio news directors, network newscasters, and newspaper editors and columnists, (6) presidents of the largest labor unions, (7), presidents of universities, (8) religious leaders representing all faiths, (9), presidents of large special interest groups, and (10) presidents of private foreign policy organizations (think tanks).[6]

As in the case of the general public, the aggregate data for organization leaders show a great deal of continuity over time. There are two or three exceptions. One is the extent to which attitudes toward "securing adequate supplies of energy" seem to be very responsive to oil prices. Another arises from the data for the year 1994, in which leaders were asked to answer only half of the questions, thus making their responses even less reliable as a guide to their aggregate opinions. And finally, the extent to which leaders seemed to give less priority to some prosperity goals after the attacks of September 11, 2001.

However, it is important to recognize that these interviews with organization leaders are not really a sample of all organization leaders because there is no agreement with respect to the population of such leaders. For this reason the real value of the data is showing the differences between different types of organization leaders, as can be seen in Table 13.2, using data from 1998. The data define attitude differences between officials in the executive branch of the government and members of the House of Representatives on all three dimensions. Executive officials are generally multilateral, coercive, and proactive, or MCA types; members or staff of the House of Representatives are unilateral, noncoercive, reactive, or MCA types. Senators differ from executive officials on just two dimensions. Executive officials are multilateral, coercive, and proactive, or MCA types; Senators are unilateral, coercive, and reactive, or MCA types. There is also a wide difference between think tank leaders on the one hand and

Table 13.1. Percentage of Organization Leaders Who Believe Various Foreign Policy Goals Are "Very Important"[a]

Foreign Policy Goal Questions:	1974	1978	1982	1986	1990[b]	1994[c]	1998	2002
Community								
Combating world hunger	76	67	64	61	na	**41**	**56**	59
Helping to improve the standard of living of less developed nations	62	64	55	46	42	**28**	36	42
Improving the global environment	na	na	na	na	**72**	49	46	43
Strengthening the United Nations	31	26	25	22	39	33	32	28
Strengthening international law and institutions	na	na	na	na	na	na	na	49
Security								
Defending our allies' security	47	**77**	82	78	**56**	60	58	55
Maintaining superior military power worldwide	na	na	na	na	na	54	58	52
Helping to bring a democratic form of government to other nations	13	15	23	29	26	21	27	33
Preventing the spread of nuclear weapons	na	na	na	na	94	90	85	89
Combating international terrorism	na	na	na	na	na	na	74	**87**
Protecting weaker nations against foreign aggression	53	**30**	**43**	**29**	28	21	29	27
Prosperity								
Protecting the jobs of American workers	34	34	43	43	39	**50**	45	**35**
Securing adequate supplies of energy	77	**88**	**72**	72	**60**	67	**55**	51
Promoting market economies abroad	na	na	na	na	na	na	36	27
Controlling and reducing illegal immigration	na	na	na	na	na	28	21	22
Stopping the flow of illegal drugs into the U.S.	na	na	na	na	na	57	57	**45**
Reducing our trade deficit with foreign countries	na	na	na	na	na	62	**49**	**34**
Protecting the interests of American business abroad	na	na	na	na	na	na	na	23
Safeguarding against global financial instability	na	na	na	na	na	na	na	49

a. Differences of 10 percentage points or more every four years are put in bold type.

b. The leadership sample was conducted between October 19 and November 16, 1990.

c. Unfortunately, the percentages for 1994 are suspect because each respondent answered only about half the questions.

Source: Chicago Council on Foreign Relations, "Worldviews 2002: U.S. Leaders Topline Report," October 2002, 33–41.

Table 13.2. Dimensions of Foreign Policy: The Location of Various Organization Elites in the Framework[a]

| | Multilateral | | Unilateral | |
	Coercive	Noncoercive	Noncoercive	Coercive
Proactive	Officials in the executive branch		Education leaders	Think tanks leaders
Reactive		Media, religious interest group, labor leaders	Members of the House of Representatives	Business leaders; senators

Think tank leaders are M<u>C</u>A—unilateral because they focus on national interests, coercive because they are mostly realists interested in security, and proactive because they accept the goals of American foreign policy.

Education leaders are M<u>C</u>A—unilateral because they focus on national interests, noncoercive because they are more interested in diplomacy, and proactive because they accept the goals of American foreign policy.

Business leaders are M<u>C</u>A—unilateral because they focus on national interests, coercive because they want stability, and reactive because they are somewhat more skeptical of the goals pursued by official American foreign policy.

Media, religious, interest group and labor leaders are M<u>CA</u>—multilateral because they take a broader view than other private groups, noncoercive because they emphasize diplomacy, and reactive because they are usually more skeptical of the goals pursued by official American foreign policy. (These various groups were treated separately in the analysis.)

The officials in the executive and Congress were discussed in chapter 9.

a. Based on a regression analysis of individual factor scores on the three dimensions, using 1998 CCFR data.

media, religious, interest group, and labor leaders on the other hand. The former are unilateral, coercive and proactive, or M<u>C</u>A types; the latter groups, multilateral, noncoercive and reactive, or M<u>CA</u> types. Finally, education and business leaders differ on two dimensions. Education leaders are unilateral, noncoercive, proactive, or M<u>C</u>A types; business leaders are unilateral, coercive, reactive, or M<u>CA</u> types.

As interesting as these findings are, however, it is important not to take these results too seriously because some of these categories of organization leaders are likely to encompass leaders with a wide range of attitudes on foreign policy goals. This is particularly true of the general categories of interest group leaders and business leaders. The only way to give a more accurate picture of the foreign policy attitudes of some of these organization leaders is to look at specific organizations. The next three sections examine the foreign policy stances of specific organizations on community, security, and prosperity dimensions.

Organizations Based on Community Values

Although Americans are divided into various geographic areas, ranging from a handful of regions, to the fifty states that compose those regions, to the hundreds of thousands of urban and rural communities within those states. Communities of value based on ethnicity, race, and religion in turn crosscut these geographic communities. Cultural communities have the potential either to bind the nation together or split it apart. Although all three of these kinds of cultural organizations have been important in the formation of American foreign policy, this section deals with ethnicity first since it is usually the most exclusive. Subsequent sections deal with the more inclusive communities of race and religion.

Ethnicity

The British, French, and Spanish who first immigrated to this country encountered many different tribes of Native Americans. As the number and variety of immigrants grew, the multi-cultural character of American society also expanded. The one thing that virtually all the individuals belonging to these groups share is an intense feeling of identity with those who share the same ethnic or national heritage. It is the intensity of this feeling that potentially makes these organizations so influential in foreign policy, even though each represents only a small portion of the population as a whole. Since many of the members of these organizations are geographically concentrated, they can exercise inside influence on local politicians. And since some of these organizations have suffered in ways that allow them to appeal to the broader American public, they can also pursue an outside strategy.

The best example of sustained ethnic influence on foreign policy in the post–World War II period is that of the Jewish diaspora. Although the Jewish people share many cultural and ideological bonds, they usually operate more like an ethnic group than a religious group with respect to the state of Israel. American Zionists first organized in the late 1930s and eventually established the American Israel Public Affairs Committee (AIPAC) that is the preeminent religious-ethnic organization of the twentieth century.

"AIPAC's general mandate of maintaining and enhancing [United States]–Israeli relations" is carried out by a professional staff of about sixty-seven people, which reports to a large executive committee composed of representatives of some thirty-eight national and local Jewish organizations.[7] The lay leadership of this staff works with these Jewish organizations to raise funds and disseminate information, but AIPAC is the only official Jewish lobby. The AIPAC staff has developed a symbiotic relationship with key congressmen and senators on Capitol Hill as well as important officials in the executive branch. It or its predecessors have been involved in every foreign policy issue that has arisen between the United States and Israel since 1948. In the 1950s AIPAC was apparently so influential on the Hill that at least one lobbyist working for a new Arab organization found that it was counter-productive to engage in "inside" lobby activities against it.[8]

Indeed, AIPAC's lobbying reputation has been so strong that the Cuban American National Foundation (CANF) of Miami, which was organized in 1980, actually sought AIPAC's help in training its new staff. If there is an ethnic organization that could match AIPAC's effectiveness in the 1980s, it was CANF. One reason why CANF was so effective was that key figures in the incoming Reagan administration actually encouraged the formation of this lobbying organization in the first place. The new administration believed that it would be very helpful to have an NGO that could confront Castro in the domestic arena since Reagan believed that most U.S. problems in Central America were caused by Cuba in the first place. The relationship between the Reagan administration and CANF was so close in the 1980s that CANF virtually ran the U.S. government radio station, Radio Marti, as well as other government programs such as the one for the processing of Cuban exiles coming into the United States during that period.[9]

But CANF's experience in the 1990s underscores another truth about inside lobbying activities in Washington, and that is the need to be in a position to influence both the executive and congressional branches of the government. Although CANF initially thought they had a special access into the Clinton White House, they soon discovered that the new administration could not afford to admit an increasing number of Cuban exiles into the United States. Therefore, CANF began to build closer ties with Congress. At first CANF was discouraged because it appeared that the executive controlled policies toward Cuba, but when Castro's air force shot down two private "Brothers to the Rescue" planes near Cuba, Congress supported the hard-line Helms-Burton bill designed to punish those who were trading with Castro's Cuba. (Brothers to the Rescue is a small private organization in south Florida formed to free Cuba from Castro.) Although the Clinton administration initially vetoed the legislation, it could not sustain its veto, especially with the 1996 election approaching.[10] Thus CANF was able to maintain some influence in the 1990s even though it had lost its special access to the executive branch.

The efforts of AIPAC and CANF are reproduced by other ethnic organizations whenever events bring the relationships between the United States and their homelands into the limelight. Although the relatively large Irish American, Greek American, and Polish American lobbies in this society periodically influence American foreign policies toward their respective countries of origin, smaller ethnic organizations such as those representing the Kurds, Kosovars, Lithuanians, and Slovaks also can have an impact. Some of these ethnic organizations are not very large, but they can act with the kind of single-mindedness that is seldom matched by other kinds of organizations. Ethnic groups are most influential when they possess "(1) an electoral threat, (2) a lobbying apparatus, and (3) a successful appeal to the symbols of American nationhood." [11] Although the foreign policies of AIPAC, CANF, and other ethnic groups often feature unilateral actions, these groups also engage in multilateral activities, particularly when neighboring countries or other ethnic groups are threatening or exploiting their compatriots.

Although ethnic organizations have consistently influenced the foreign policies most relevant to their countries of origin, race-based and especially religious organizations have the capability of playing an equally important role in making foreign policy. The next section deals with race-based organizations.

Race

In the colonial period, English settlers dominated both Native Americans and African Americans. And in the nineteenth century this Caucasian racial bias might have led to expansion into Central America, the Caribbean, the Pacific Islands, and East Asia if it hadn't been for what many perceived as a prohibition against colonies in the U.S. Constitution. But immigration in the late nineteenth and twentieth centuries from Africa, East and South Asia, Latin America, and even the Middle East, as well as Southern and Eastern Europe, gradually changed the racial and religious composition of the United States, so that by 2000, census projections suggested that almost 13 percent of Americans would be of African American origin, about 11.4 percent of Hispanic origin, around 4 percent Asian American, less than 1 percent Native American, and about 70 percent Caucasian and non-Hispanic. It is estimated that by 2050 the non-Hispanic Caucasian population will be less than 50 percent of the total U.S. population.

The racial differences in this country become especially relevant when you realize that in the 2000 election George W. Bush essentially won the racially homogeneous regions in the West and the South, whereas Al Gore's support came from the multiracial areas in the Northeast, the Midwest, the far West, and selected areas of the South. If the parties continue to divide along race-based lines, this could become very significant in terms of foreign policy.

Although the increasingly multiracial character of American society has great potential not only for enabling the United States to become a more harmonious society but also for leading this society to deal more fairly with all groups in the larger world, it also has the potential for division. The United States will have a more difficult time pursuing a Eurocentric foreign policy as Africans, Asians, Latinos, and Middle Easterners begin to push for more even-handed treatment of their homelands, and American foreign policy will have to try to ameliorate whatever clashes of civilizations occur both internally and externally.[12]

In the meantime, race-based organizations, just like other types of issue organizations, work to promote the values and interests they shared with their compatriots around the world. An example is the involvement of African Americans during the 1970s and 1980s in the effort to end apartheid in South Africa. Although African Americans have had a continuing presence in Congress since the Second World War, their representatives concentrated more on issues of justice at home than foreign policy abroad, though African American leaders, such as Martin Luther King Jr. and Malcolm X, began to speak out in opposition to American involvement in the Vietnam War in the late 1960s. The participation of African Americans in foreign policy making, especially anti-apartheid efforts, increased significantly after the 1976 election when African American voters may have provided Carter with his margin of victory.[13] TransAfrica, the African American lobby on foreign policy issues, was formed in 1977.[14] African Americans along with other ethnic and religious organizations played an important role in countering business interests over U.S. foreign policy toward South Africa. As in the case of the close relationship between CANF and the Reagan administration in the 1980s, African Americans found that their values and interests meshed with those of the Carter administration in the late 1970s.[15] TransAfrica continued to press for economic sanctions under the less favorable atmosphere of the Reagan and Bush administrations in the 1980s. Then when Clinton became president, Randall Robinson, who heads TransAfrica, went on a hunger strike and persuaded Clinton to help restore Aristide to power in Haiti.[16] These examples show that although race-based groups may be ideologically less inclusive than religious groups, at the same time they may espouse cosmopolitan causes.

The growing population of Latinos both in the southern United States and in large cities across America suggests that in the near future Latinos will exercise similar influence in foreign policies toward the Caribbean, Central America, and South America. NAFTA has given Latinos a focal point that they did not have before. There is also evidence that Asian Americans, Arab Americans, and even Native Americans are beginning to put their stamp on American foreign policy. One of the things that prevents these race-based organizations from influencing foreign policies in their areas of special interest is that people often identify more closely with their country of origin or specific ethnic group than they do with their larger race-based groups. Thus people will think of themselves as Mexican, Columbian, or Cuban rather than Latinos, or Chinese, Japanese, or Filipino rather than Asian.

Religion

Many of those who first came to the New World did so for religious reasons, and even today two-thirds of Americans say that they belong to a religious organization. Although religion is one of the most inclusive organizations in America, it is also important to realize that America is probably the most religiously diverse country in the world.[17] For the purpose of this analysis American religions will be divided into four broad categories: (1) main-line Protestants who are affiliated with churches belonging to the National Council of Churches (NCC), (2) Catholics who are represented by the U.S. Catholic Conference of Bishops (USCC), (3) evangelical Protestants, many of whom identify with the Moral Majority and the Christian Coalition (the evangelical African American churches are included in this category even though they are different), and (4) a variety of smaller religious groups including Jews and peace Protestants such as the Quakers. Although the first three categories are the largest, the fourth category includes important organizations that can have an influence far beyond their actual membership.

Religious organizations are unique to the extent that they explicitly take "moral and ethical teachings" into account in their foreign policies.[18] Generally speaking, the Catholic Church has taken the lead in opposition to nuclear weapons, and its position is widely supported by main-line Protestants, Jews, and peace Protestants. These organizations have also questioned the use of conventional and unconventional force in many circumstances, whereas evangelical white Christians have generally supported defense expenditures and the use of force abroad. The main-line Protestant churches, along with peace Protestants, Catholics, and Jews, have been especially active in providing refugee assistance. Main-line Protestants have been more suspicious of the government than Catholics and Jews. White evangelicals have become more involved in refugee assistance since Vietnam, although evangelism is still their main priority. Evangelicals have also been more supportive than other religious groups of the cold war policies of the Reagan and George W. Bush administrations.

Of course, not everyone who identifies with a religion can be considered a church member. The distinction is important because only those who are active church members are likely both to be aware of and to accept the positions of church leaders. In theory religious organizations are advocates of radical change.[19] This means that most religious lobbies act as "outsiders" in the policy-making process, that is, they attempt to influence policy by lobbying the public rather than lobbying the government directly. Of course the tactics of religious lobbyists depend on the character of the foreign policies they support. Most church lobbies have accepted the notion that the prime objective of American foreign policy is to serve the national interest and national security, but if they ever got serious about the reduction of poverty in the world, they would represent a major challenge to contemporary American foreign policy because they would be less likely than other lobbyists to compromise on foreign assistance, human rights, and other moral issues.[20] Main-line Protestant and Catholic organizations are the most likely to take this position because they generally oppose wealthy elites in society; evangelicals are probably the least likely to take this position because they usually do battle with cultural elites rather than moneyed elites in this country.

Since religious lobbies have the potential of spawning mass movements, this section examines the role of religious activists in the peace movements in Central America incited by U.S. foreign policies in the 1980s. The United States had established a strong presence in Central America by the mid-nineteenth century. After the Second World War, the economic situation in this area became increasingly desperate because the population was growing rapidly while the availability of land and food was becoming scarce. Unfortunately, the United States government contributed to the region's economic problems by encouraging the governments of these countries to participate in cold war alignments. By the 1970s the situation in Central America had deteriorated to the point where Sandinista rebels could easily overthrow Somoza's U.S.-backed regime. The government of El Salvador, facing a similar fate, sought American help in resisting its own popular revolution. Of course, Guatemala had been engaged in a similar conflict since the American intervention in the 1950s.

American religious leaders were also fully engaged in Central America. Indeed, by the 1960s several hundred Protestant and Catholic missionaries, from dozens of missionary agencies and religious orders, were sent to live and work in Central America.[21] So when the wars in Nicaragua and El Salvador became headline news in 1979 and 1980, respectively, American religious organizations were already on the scene. The U.S. government and American religious organizations clashed with respect to the use of force and the treatment of refugees.

Use of Force in Central America. When the Reagan administration began to develop a Contra military force in Honduras to drive the Sandinistas from power in Nicaragua, there were American religious leaders working with the local people throughout Nicaragua. Early in the conflict, Contras attacked the village of El Porvenir just inside the Nicaraguan border. The attack took place the same day that a church group from North Carolina visiting Managua, the capitol city of Nicaragua, took a busload of Americans to visit the remains of the village. When the group arrived at the village and talked to the survivors, they realized that the Contra soldiers were only a few hundred yards across the border and would probably resume the attack once the bus left. The locals pleaded with them to stay. Although the church group left, the group was so shocked by what they had seen in Nicaragua that the leaders of the group began to organize an appropriate response.

Witness for Peace engaged in two kinds of activities. First, it organized additional tours to Nicaragua so that other concerned persons in the United States could see first hand what their government was doing there. By 1986 it is estimated that Witness for Peace and similar organizations had brought over 100,000 Americans to Nicaragua while the war between the Contras and the Nicaraguans took place.[22] In terms of the framework employed in this text, these visits are an MCA foreign policy activity: multilateral, noncoercive and proactive. Second, Witness for Peace became an important news source back in the United States. These non-government witnesses could provide first-hand accounts of what was happening in remote areas of northern Nicaragua, and so the American news media, which seldom taps local, non-government sources for national or international news stories, were interested in their reports. Since these witnesses presented a much different perspective than that provided by the government, Witness for Peace helped to sustain the debate on the use of force in Central America. The sustained domestic debate is an MCA foreign policy activity: multilateral, noncoercive, and reactive.

The use of force by the United States government in Grenada in 1983 also incited other religious groups to action. Shortly after Reagan's invasion of Grenada, a group of church activists were meeting for fellowship, prayer, and Bible study when some of them expressed their fear that Reagan would invade Nicaragua next. After discussing the issue they drafted "A Promise of Resistance" that pledged the signers to resist this possible invasion. The movement spread, and by 1985 there were more than 200 groups gathering signatures all across the country for the "Pledge of Resistance." Over 50,000 people actually signed this pledge. This may be the first time that a resistance movement has been organized in advance of the use of force, and approximately more than ten thousand activists were jailed for civil disobedience.[23] This domestic protest movement is another example of an MCA foreign policy activity: multilateral, noncoercive, and reactive. Although Reagan did not officially use American forces in Central America except in an advisory role, the war did create a significant refugee problem that affected the United States directly.

Central American Refugee Policies. Most of the refugees from Central America came from El Salvador and Guatemala. There were relatively few refugees from Nicaragua because the Sandinistas consciously attempted to address some of the needs of the poorest segments of the population there. The refugee problem was particularly critical in Western Honduras. The rebels in El Salvador had started their offensive in late 1980, in order to make as much progress as they could before Reagan took office in January of 1981. But President Carter quickly sent arms and other forms of assistance to the government of El Salvador, and the government diffused the initial rebel attacks, sending a large number of El Salvadoran refugees into Western Honduras. Unfortunately, these refugees were not welcome in Honduras. The antagonism had exploded between the two countries during a previous conflict, the so-called soccer war ten years before, was still perceptible.

Most of these refugees were located in three large camps in Western Honduras, close to the El Salvadoran border. But since both the Honduran and El Salvadoran armies as well as the U.S. embassy officials in Honduras considered some of them subversives, all three governments wanted to move the refugees away from the border.[24] Unfortunately for the refugees, the relocation areas were some of the same areas involved in the clashes between Honduras and El Salvador ten years earlier. The safety of the refugees became an issue for religious organizations assisting the refugees when soldiers for the governments of El Salvador and Honduras harassed the refugees on the border.

From a security standpoint all the governments immediately involved wanted to move the refugee camps away from the border. But the refugees refused to leave. The UN High Commissioner for Refugees was prepared to move the refugees, but the UNHCR did not actually run the camps. The camps were run by relief agencies, many of whom were affiliated with main-line Protestant, peace Protestant, and Catholic organizations.[25] Because of the resistance of these religious leaders and the refugees, the UNHCR finally had to assume overall responsibility for the camps. This struggle between governments and religious organizations continued throughout the war period. The attempts by American religious organizations to resist government efforts to move the refugees are a good example of MCA foreign policies: multilateral, noncoercive, and proactive.

While American churches were dealing with the refugee problems in Honduras, an even larger refugee problem was taking place in the United States itself. For every El Salvadoran refugee that was seeking refuge in Honduras, "ten or twenty simply headed north to the United States." [26] There was also a steady stream of Guatemalans seeking refuge in the United States. Since the Reagan administration sided with both the El Salvadoran and Guatemalan governments, it would not accept these individuals as political refugees.[27] The INS, as well as the FBI, made every effort to return these refugees to their home countries, arguing that they were economic, rather than political, refugees.[28]

American churches, especially those on the southern border of the United States, began to provide sanctuary to these refugees. Churches near the border provided security and shelter for the refugees until they could be sent to sanctuary churches and communities in the North. At the height of the endeavor it is estimated that there were 400 churches openly participating in the movement; they included churches from all religious groups.[29] This network operating within the United States to deal with the refugee issue is another good example of an MCA foreign policy activity: multilateral, noncoercive, and reactive, at least insofar as taking factors other than security into account. For a summary of the policies of the religious groups toward the use of force and the refugee problems in Central America, see Table 13.3.

Table 13.3. Diimensions of Foreign Policy: Positions of Government and Religious Organizations in Central America during the 1980s

	Multilateral		Unilateral	
	Coercive	Noncoercive	Noncoercive	Coercive
Proactive	UNHCR policies in Honduras	"Witness for Peace" trips to Nicaragua		Foreign policy actions of the State and Defense Depts. in Central America as well as the policies of the INS and FBI
Reactive		Local U.S. press coverage by "Witness for Peace;" the policies of "Pledge of Resistance;" and the "Sanctuary Movement" in the United States		

UNHCR was MCA—multilateral because this office represents all nations, coercive because it supported the requests of the governments concerned to remove the refugees by force if necessary, and proactive because it emphasized the aims of the governments involved.

The "Witness for Peace" trips were MCA—multilateral because they emphasized human rights, noncoercive because they wanted to end hostilities, and proactive because they emphasized the benefits of the international position they supported.

U.S. Departments of State and Defense, INS, and FBI were MCA—unilateral because they emphasized national interests, coercive because they favored the use of force in these situations, and proactive because they thought that their policies were beneficial.

The "Pledge of Resistance" was MCA—multilateral because it emphasized universal values, noncoercive because it opposed war, and reactive because it wanted the United States to take into account other values.

The "Sanctuary Movement" was MCA—multilateral because of the emphasis on the rights of asylum, noncoercive because it did not employ force, and reactive because it thought that official U.S. policy abroad ignored important values.

Whereas those who are primarily engaged in community issues define problems either in more exclusive or more inclusive terms than the nation itself, those who are mainly concerned with security issues invariably define them in terms of the nation-state. Indeed, according to traditional realist theory, one should not expect many differences of opinion on security issues because the preferred foreign policy is always the one that is most likely to preserve the state. Nevertheless, there are differences of opinion concerning both the character of the threat and the best means of dealing with it. These differences of opinion are considered next.

Organizations Based on Security Values

As in the case of informal community organizations, there are also differences of opinion among those informal organizations that are most concerned with security. Generally speaking, younger persons are more coercive than older persons. That is one reason why so many countries rely upon people between the ages of 17 and 24 to serve in the armed forces. Older adults, especially those over 60, are usually not able to assume the most physically demanding military roles, and they are generally less supportive of military ventures. Of course, this age variable is often confused with **generational data** that attempt to account for differences in foreign policy opinions on the basis of the most salient experience each cohort has had at its most impressionable age. Thus, one can identify a Vietnam War generation, the Gulf War generation, and so on.

There is also evidence that women are less likely than men to favor the use of force, although this relationship does not always hold. In situations such as Bosnia and Kosovo where ethnic cleansing involved well-publicized attacks on women, some polls found that women are as likely as men to favor sending troops in order to deal with the situation.[30] There is also some evidence that women are more willing to employ negotiations as a means of resolving conflicts.

Education is another distinction that is frequently employed to identify differences in opinions on security issues although the variable of education may simply be a substitute for variables such as intelligence levels or awareness of foreign affairs that are more difficult to measure. Generally speaking, individuals who are more intelligent, more aware of foreign affairs, and more educated are likely to favor negotiations although those who are more aware may also be more likely to support the position of dominant groups. But as in the case of other demographic variables, these differences are not very pronounced and fairly stable over time. They represent one more example of parallel publics. But none of these demographic factors seem to be as important as party identification or ideology in shaping opinions on security policy. These factors are discussed next.

Political Parties and Ideology

Political scientists have had more luck in associating differences of opinion on security issues with differences in party identification and ideology. Indeed, the American party system largely emerged over a foreign security issue: how to deal with the conflict situation in Europe following the French Revolution. Since the United States was formally allied with France, the revolution in France threatened to involve America in new wars in Europe—something that all the country's leaders wanted to avoid. Throughout the nineteenth and twentieth centuries differences between the parties often emerged over questions of war or peace. Recent public opinion polls suggest that Republicans are generally more coercive than Democrats although the main difference between Republicans and Democrats is on the unilateral–multilateral dimension.[31]

Since political parties are primarily interested in winning elections, however, it would seem that parties might readily switch positions on political issues in order to win. Thus the differences between party members on security issues might reflect calculations designed to take an opportune position on the issue rather than to take the right or even a consistent position on an issue. And indeed there is evidence that political parties do reverse their positions on the use of force, depending on which party happens to control the White House when force is being employed. It is not uncommon, when there is a change of party in the White House, for the party of the departing president to oppose the war policies of the new incumbent and the party of the incoming president to support forceful measures that they opposed under the former president.

But if parties are not reliable guides to attitudes toward the use of force, then ideology may provide better guidance. Indeed, most analysts find that ideology is a better predictor of opinions on the use of force than party identification.[32] Generally speaking, one expects conservatives to be more likely than liberals to support coercive measures. The two major parties have traditionally had a more conservative and a more liberal wing. But recently the parties have become more ideological, and there are fewer liberals in the Republican Party and fewer conservatives in the Democratic Party. But even this relationship is not consistent over time as ideologues sometimes modify their positions in order to fit their party preferences.

If neither political parties nor ideology provide a more consistent guide to opinions on the use of force, then how can one explain such changes? Pluralists would argue that changes in security policy are the result of competing pressures among public affairs organizations. And indeed beginning in the 1960s, there has been evidence of a growing number of such public affairs organizations. Although many of these groups employ inside strategies, some of the most successful lobbying efforts by these groups have involved the creation of new political movements.

Political Movements and Organizations

Although religious organizations have potential for building political movements, most of the actual political movements in this country are secular in character. Public affairs organizations have been particularly important in the environmental movement, the women's movement, and the antinuclear movement. One of the first such movements to come about in relation to nuclear weapons was Women's Strike for Peace, which developed to protest Kennedy's initial opposition to nuclear test bans. Box 13.1, Individuals in Action, profiles the founder of Women's Strike for Peace.

Although formal public affairs organizations do not appear to have played a very important role in the development of Women's Strike for Peace, formal organizations generally play an important role in defense policy. In his farewell address to the nation, Eisenhower warned Americans that the need for permanent mobilization for war would create a military-industrial complex that would generate ever-increasing defense expenditures. During the 1970s and 1980s political scientists attempted to demonstrate the existence of such a complex by showing the connections between defense contractors, retired military officials, and government officials. Most of these efforts failed to suggest a strong link between the military-industrial complex and congressional votes on military expenditures.[33] Ironically, the best evidence of organized pressure for defense expenditures involves groups such as the extraordinarily successful Committee on the Present Danger (CPD), a public affairs organization whose values were as important as their interests in demanding more emphasis on defense. The foreign policy dimensions of this and other similar organizations are shown in Table 13.4.

Committee on the Present Danger

The CPD first emerged in 1950, then reemerged in 1976, in the aftermath of the Vietnam War. By the time American forces had pulled out of Vietnam, many people in the country questioned the value of relying mainly on American military forces overseas. This attitude, which is often referred to as the Vietnam Syndrome, became an issue in the 1974 congressional elections, and again in the 1976 presidential election. Since George McGovern's unsuccessful presidential campaign as an antiwar Democratic candidate in 1972, a number of former Democratic officials who were very concerned about the future security policy of the country, especially under a Democratic president, resurrected the CPD.

This newly formed organization was particularly alarmed when Jimmy Carter, who favored disarmament, became the Democratic nominee. Leading members of the CPD approached George Bush, who was at that time CIA director under Republican president Gerald Ford. Because the

BOX 13.1

Profile in Action: Dagmar Wilson

Dagmar Wilson, an illustrator of children's books, had been raised abroad as the daughter of a foreign correspondent. In the 1960s she lived in Georgetown in Washington, D.C. She was wealthy and had many friends in large cities across the country. In September of 1961 she was shocked to learn that President Kennedy planned to resume nuclear tests. She was convinced that his foreign policy did not represent the way she and her friends felt about the need for nuclear disarmament. So she contacted her friends around the country, and by November 1, 1961, about 50,000 women turned out in 60 cities to protest America's plan to resume nuclear testing.

As a result of that success, Wilson and other women organized the movement now known as Women's Strike for Peace. This movement has stationed at least one protester outside the White House every day of the year, in all weather, during the Vietnam War. It also persuaded women to lie down in front of trains bringing troops and other materials, including chemicals, to the West coast for shipment to Vietnam.

Although Wilson insisted that her group was not a formal organization, a considerable amount of organizational ability and dedication was required to get even one person to protest in front of the White House every day of the year. Of course, Wilson did not limit her activities to stopping troop trains and protesting outside the White House. She also rented space in Geneva to lobby those who attended the UN's annual disarmament conferences. Wilson's efforts on behalf of disarmament did not go unnoticed. Because she opposed American insistence on on-site inspections as a condition for a nuclear test ban treaty, she was required to testify before the House Un-American Activities Committee in December of 1962. When she later refused to testify before a closed session of the same committee, she was convicted for contempt of Congress, a conviction that was later overturned by a U.S. court.

Wilson represents a small but important group of private individuals who play a significant role in international affairs. Because of the intensity of her efforts, she had an influence on foreign policy making, and as the founder of Women's Strike for Peace, a mass movement, she was able to magnify her personal influence many times. In 1967 Dagmar Wilson was arrested during an antiwar protest at the Pentagon. In later years she continued to work with the peace movement but withdrew as leader of Women's Strike for Peace.[a]

a. Joseph M. Siracusa, *Political Profiles: The Kennedy Years* (New York: Facts on File, 2004), 545.

Source: Interview with author in Georgetown, August 12, 1966.

Table 13.4. Dimensions of Foreign Policy: Positions of Various Public Affairs Organizations on Arms Expenditures in 1977

| | Multilateral | | Unilateral | |
	Coercive	Noncoercive	Noncoercive	Coercive
Proactive				Committee on the Present Danger; Amercan Security Council; American Conservative Union
Reactive		Center for Defense Information		

The CPD and American Conservative Union were MCA—unilateral because they emphasized national interests, coercive because they favored military expenditures, and proactive because they emphasized the benefits of possessing armaments.

The Center for Defense Information was MCA—multilateral because it favored a wider, international perspective on defense, noncoercive because it wanted to limit military expenditures, and reactive because it was concerned with the costs of unlimited military expenditures.

members of CPD had been prominent officials in former administrations and regularly served as advisors to the government, they talked Bush into allowing them to challenge the regular CIA estimates of Soviet strength on the basis of new information that was available to them. Accordingly, Bush appointed a number of them as an outside alternative Team B that could compete with the government's regular Team A that estimated Soviet military strength. Shortly before leaving office after the election of 1976, Bush, a Republican, accepted the higher Team B estimate of Soviet strength. This was significant because the CIA estimate was used throughout the government as the basis for planning American force needs.

In the meantime the Democratic president-elect Carter was forming his transition team to fill the positions in his new administration. As many as 53 out of approximately 100 members of CPD applied for one or more of these positions, largely in the defense or foreign policy field.[34] Carter selected none of them. Then in the first few months of his administration, Carter challenged the Soviet Union to join with him in reducing military forces. Soviet Premier Alexey Kosygin rejected the idea, but Carter continued to believe that this was the direction U.S. policy should take.

In the summer of 1977 a number of CPD members met with Carter to discuss military preparedness. The meeting went badly for the CPD. During the meeting Carter used public opinion polls to argue that the public favored efforts to keep arms expenditures down. The CPD became convinced that the only way for them to influence defense policy was to go to the public and change public perceptions of America's readiness to deal with the Soviet threat.[35]

The CPD used the higher Team B report figures to support their call for more arms expenditures. Since many CPD members were well-respected defense experts, they were able to gain access to public forums. For example, Paul Nitze had been one of the architects of America's containment policy and was thoroughly familiar with nuclear strategy. Nitze and others like him spoke at large public forums in major cities around the country, where their speeches were widely reported in the national media.

The CPD members who compiled the Team B report had argued that CIA estimates of Soviet military expenditures were too low for several reasons. For one thing, some line items that the United States included in its budget, like the heating of military barracks, had not previously been included in estimates of the Soviet military budget.[36] But the main difference between the Team A and Team B reports involved the estimation of military expenditures in the Soviet Union. Team B insisted that the CIA should estimate the cost of Soviet material and men on the basis of what it would cost the United States to provide the same men and material.[37] Since manpower was especially expensive in the volunteer military now in place in the United States, the much larger Soviet units appeared all that much more expensive in comparison.[38]

Of course, there were items that would be cheaper for the United States to produce than the Soviet Union, and those costs would be underestimated by this formula. Nevertheless, Team B estimated that the Soviet Union was spending almost twice as much as the United States on its military. This was the basis for the arguments that CPD was propounding across the country. It is interesting to note that the comparison was always made between the United States and the Soviet Union, because if the comparison was made between NATO and Warsaw Pact countries, the situation would not appear nearly so dire. Of course, the Soviet Union also had to focus some of its forces on China.[39]

As academic scholars and the CIA would later demonstrate, this comparison of Soviet–American strength was largely false. But it was not challenged either by the Carter administration or by the press. The failure of the press to expose this misrepresentation will be dealt with in the next chapter. But at least part of the explanation for Carter's failure to challenge the CPD presentation was Carter's preoccupation with other major issues, particularly the Panama Canal. The credibility of CPD members was sufficiently high that the administration would have had to launch a major effort to reverse the CPD position. Besides the military benefited from an overestimation of Soviet strength. Even if Team B estimates were inaccurate, they might lead to an increase in U.S. military expenditures.

By the time that Carter realized the extent to which CPD spokespersons were winning the public opinion battle, external events seem to confirm the idea that the Soviet Union was stronger because of their apparent successes abroad. The shah of Iran, who was one of the United States' closest supporters in the Middle East, was deposed. Then the Soviets decided to intervene in Afghanistan on behalf of a faltering Marxist regime, despite the United States' protestations. The CPD quickly linked these foreign policy situations to America's deteriorating situation in relation to the Soviet Union.

In the meantime, Ronald Reagan, the Republican candidate in the 1980 election, had become a member of the CPD, and one of his major campaign issues was the need for increased military expenditures. Although Reagan had a number of advantages in this election, the widespread belief that Carter had allowed the Soviets to gain an advantage in the cold war was clearly one of Carter's greatest vulnerabilities, and Reagan's commitment to increased military expenditures was a key element in uniting the West and the South behind him.

The CPD's success demonstrates how effective a small formal organization, even one with only several hundred members, can be in shaping public opinion on a foreign policy issue. Once Reagan was elected, he appointed Nitze, Jeane Kirkpatrick, and Eugene V. Rostow, all members of CPD, to key foreign policy positions in his administration. From these positions they were actually able to shape military policies of the U.S. government through much of the 1980s.

This section has emphasized formal organizations and political movements that promote various security and community values. The next section focuses attention on organizations that focus on prosperity values and represent the interests of various sectors of the economy.

Organizations Based on Prosperity Values

Prosperity was one of the most important motivations for settling the New World. This was true not only for the sponsors of the early settlements but also for the people who settled there. Indeed, most of the early colonists fled the class-bound societies of the Old World in search of greater freedom to pursue their own fortunes. Differences in class did emerge in America, and as one might expect, most of those who identified with the upper classes tended to favor more active participation in world affairs and those who identified with the lower classes to oppose such participation. But explaining foreign policy opinions in terms of these self-identities has never been very useful in America because most Americans identify themselves with the middle class. Of course, as inequalities grow in American society, class distinctions may become more useful in the future.

Since Americans generally accept income as a measure of achievement, income is usually a better predictor than class of foreign policy opinions.

Generally speaking, the higher the income, the more likely a person will favor a proactive policy; the lower the income, the more likely the person will favor a reactive policy. But as in the case of value organizations, these informal categories form parallel publics whose differences are interesting but do not in and of themselves explain foreign policies. In order to account for differences in foreign policy, one needs to look at the formal interest organizations that represent various sectoral interests in the economy. This section considers three kinds of economic organizations—business, labor and professional—as well as regional economic interests.

Business Organizations

There are hundreds of thousands of individual businesses in America as well as thousands of associations that represent various kinds of businesses. For example, Gale's Encyclopedia of Associations lists several thousand business and trade associations. Each of these associations struggles to define a niche for itself in the business world, and individual companies subscribe to these associations much in the same way that individuals subscribe to magazines. One of the most important functions of these associations is to represent the collective interests of their members before the government. Thus when a business wants help or relief from government, it can choose which of these associations is in the best position to represent its interests effectively.

Since Americans have had such a strong propensity to establish formal organizations to represent their various economic interests, these organizations are as diverse as the economy they represent. At first manufacturing, mining, agricultural, and labor organizations predominated. But as the economy became more service-oriented, the number of banks, insurance, real estate, communications, transportation, health, welfare, and other professional or service-type organizations increased. These organizations typically pursue an inside strategy because they control valuable resources that government policy makers may need to implement their own policies overseas. They also have large staffs and close relations with government officials, particularly those in the executive branch of the government.[40]

Of course, not all of these business organizations are equally interested in foreign affairs. On the basis of the Transnational Project it is estimated that about 20 percent of these business organizations have a primary or strong secondary interest in foreign affairs. The primary reason this figure is so low is that the large service sector is mainly a domestic market, whereas manufacturing, agriculture, and mining sectors are heavily engaged in the international market. But since Americans are now buying and especially selling more services overseas, this estimate is likely to be on the low side. Now that so many American businesses are involved in mergers, most large businesses will have a mix of products, some of which will be exposed to the international market. Thus the interests of a given business organization (association) will depend on the particular mix of products at a given time.[41]

In order to understand the kinds of pressures that businesses significantly affected by international markets are likely to bring to bear on government, one needs to make two distinctions among these organizations. First, American businesses that can take advantage of more than ample capitalization or land resources, such as some financial institutions and agribusinesses, are going to be primarily interested in the international market, whereas business organizations that depend extensively on labor will focus mainly on the domestic market, because businesses with high labor costs in America, such as textiles, will not be that competitive abroad. Thus **capital-intensive businesses** in the United States will be proactive, whereas **labor-intensive businesses** in the United States will be reactive.

Now that the reduction of trade barriers has made it possible for American businesses to produce goods and services overseas for the U.S. market, it is necessary to introduce a second distinction. American overseas businesses that are capital-intensive can prosper in any environment in which host governments give them access and accept the international rules of the market. But American businesses overseas that are more labor-intensive can only prosper if the host government protects their local acquisitions and helps them keep their local labor costs down. Thus some American businesses operating abroad are prepared to work with any host government that will play by liberal market rules, whereas others can operate only when the host government is conservative because it extends special privileges to them.

Thus those capital-intensive American businesses that are affected by international markets need U.S. government assistance either to facilitate the international movement of goods, money, services, and ideas or to restrict such movement. Those capital-intensive American businesses that have made direct investments overseas need U.S. government help in maintaining access to these economies and keeping them afloat. Those labor-intensive American businesses that have invested in land and labor abroad need to maintain their privileged position in those societies and easy access to the American market. Since the economic interests of many of these business enterprises are diametrically opposed, the pluralist model is useful in explaining the pressures that these organizations bring to bear on the U.S. government both at home and abroad. These pluralist influences can be illustrated by looking at business pressures on U.S. foreign policy toward Central America and the Caribbean.

Business Pressures on U.S. Foreign Policy in Central America and the Caribbean from the late 1940s to the early 1960s. In the late 1940s and early 1950s, capital-intensive businesses were especially important in formulating American foreign economic policies. These businesses were represented by organizations such as the Council on Foreign Relations, National Planning Association, and the National Foreign Trade Council and wanted government assistance in developing the kind of infrastructure abroad that would make foreign direct investment (FDI) by the largest corporations in the United States more attractive. These business interests were instrumental in establishing the Export-Import Bank, the World Bank, and the Point Four Program. The Commerce Department established a Business Advisory Council (BAC) to promote these institutions. The U.S. government funds to be dispensed by these institutions were not to compete with private capital but rather to open the way for private investment in these countries. Thus the Truman administration developed a "trade, not aid" policy.[42]

At first there was little business opposition to this foreign economic policy, but when Eisenhower became president, a number of more conservative business organizations such as the U.S. Chamber of Commerce, the National Association of Manufacturers, and the Committee of Industry, Agriculture and Labor on Import-Export Policy were formed to oppose tariff liberalization because many medium and small-sized businesses in the United States feared that the industries being established abroad by these investments would compete with them. This protectionist effort was led by several industry associations such as the National Coal and the National Chemists Associations and key manufacturing and agricultural interests such as textile and watch manufacturers, sugar refineries, and lead and zinc producers.[43] These nationalist business organizations were partially successful in working through Congress to limit reciprocal trade agreements with other countries.

The ability of nationalist businesses to limit reciprocal trade with other countries led capital-intensive businesses to push for an increase in official government assistance in order to stimulate investment opportunities abroad. For example, after the 1954 U.S.-backed coup in Guatemala, the Eisenhower administration agreed to increase economic assistance to that country.[44] By the late 1950s and early 1960s, business internationalists had convinced the government that American aid to less developed countries (LDCs) had to be increased in order to prevent the advance of communism. This new "trade and aid" policy became known as the "Alliance for Progress" in South and Central America.

There was a significant increase in official government assistance to these countries in the early 1960s, but when the Central American Common Market failed partly as a result of the soccer war between El Salvador and Honduras, business internationalists turned increasingly to agriculture.[45] Some of these businesses, such as lumber and ranching, were more labor-intensive, and they favored strong, local governments that were anti-communist and anti-labor. These businesses hoped to produce agricultural and other goods in these countries that they could then sell in the American market.[46] Of course, the nationalists were aware of these efforts and fought in Congress to ensure that expanded economic aid abroad would not harm firms producing similar goods in the United States. The foreign policies pursued by American business in the early cold war period are shown in Table 13.5.

Business Pressures on U.S. Foreign Policy in Central America and the Caribbean from the 1970s to the 1990s. American businesses continued to compete for influence over U.S. foreign policies in Central America throughout the 1970s and 1980s. By the end of the 1970s, American banks had become heavily exposed in countries such as Nicaragua. Thus in 1979, even as the communist rebels, the Sandinistas, were closing in on the local dictator, Anastasio Somoza, these banks were eager to refinance $600 million of Nicaragua's debt in order to protect their investments. The Rockefeller Foundation, the Committee for Economic Development, the Council on Foreign Relations, and the Business Group for Latin America all favored liberal trade policies because they had extensive investments in Central America. Other businesses that supported this policy included

Table 13.5. Dimensions of Foreign Policy: Positions of Various Business Organizations on U.S. Foreign Policy in Central America in the 1950s and 1960s

| | Multilateral | | Unilateral | |
	Coercive	Noncoercive	Noncoercive	Coercive
Proactive			"Trade, Not Aid" groups in 1940s and early 1950s; "Trade and Aid" groups in late 1950s and 1960s	
Reactive				Protectionist groups in 1950s, such as U.S. Chamber of Commerce and National Association of Manufacturers

"Trade, Not Aid" and "Trade and Aid" groups were MCA—unilateral because they emphasized their own business interests, noncoercive because they favored DFI and more liberal trade, and proactive because they were preoccupied with benefits.

Protectionist groups such as the U.S. Chamber of Commerce and the National Association of Manufacturers were MCA—unilateral because they were concerned with their own business interests, coercive because they wanted to employ government restraints, and reactive because they were concerned with the costs to U.S. domestic producers.

Exxon, Quaker Oats, Nabisco Brands, IBM, and NCR. The Carter administration also developed a $75 million loan for Nicaragua "to influence the direction" of the new Sandinista government.[47] Although the Carter administration felt that this new initiative in Nicaragua made sense in the security domain, given the broad criticisms leveled at American policy in Cuba throughout South and Central America, the Carter administration was also heavily influenced by the capital-intensive businesses with a stake in Nicaragua to take this position.

Of course, this policy came under direct attack in the presidential campaign of 1980, and the policy was reversed when Reagan came to power. Reagan's policy of ousting the Sandinista regime in Nicaragua not only had the support of conservative security organizations such as the Committee on the Present Danger but also the support of labor-intensive international businesses that had to leave Nicaragua when the Sandinistas gained power in 1979. Most of these businesses were part of an enclave along the Atlantic coast of Nicaragua, where they had been protected by the Somoza regime. They included Caribbean/Central American Action, Association of American Chambers of Commerce in Latin America, Rosario Resources, Robinson Lumber, Peterson Ranching, and Atlantic Chemical Corporation.[48] Since the Sandinistas wanted to increase the wages of local workers, give land to peasants, and otherwise eliminate the privileged position of American businesses as part of their reform policy, the policies of the new Nicaraguan regime were antithetical to these American businesses, and they sought to overthrow that government. The types of foreign policy pursued by the U.S. government along with various businesses in Central America that supported the different policies are shown in Table 13.6.

What is particularly instructive about this situation is that both Presidents Carter and Reagan received strong support from American business. The capital-intensive businesses in Nicaragua supported Carter's policy of "economic stabilization" because they could work with the Sandinistas to develop the country economically at the same time that they were protecting loans they had previously made to Somoza. The labor-intensive businesses in Nicaragua supported Reagan's efforts to oust the Sandinistas from power because that government would not tolerate the exploitation of Nicaraguan land and workers. These businesses actually preferred an authoritarian government that could maintain the privileged position of foreign companies on Nicaraguan soil.

Although U.S. labor-intensive business organizations operating abroad take advantage of low social and environmental standards in other countries, labor-intensive businesses in the United States seek protection from these foreign imports. And although American labor organizations have sometimes worked with their business counterparts to strengthen the position of U.S. businesses overseas, it has become increasingly clear that American labor competes directly with labor-intensive businesses over-

Table 13.6. Dimensions of Foreign Policy: Positions of U.S. Government and Various Businesses in Central America in the 1970s and 1980s

| | Multilateral | | Unilateral | |
	Coercive	Noncoercive	Noncoercive	Coercive
Proactive				Businesses favoring the Reagan administration's support for Contra forces, such as Association of American Chambers of Commerce in Latin America; Caribbean/Central American Action; Robinson Lumber; Peterson Ranching
Reactive			Businesses supporting Carter administration's refinancing of loans under the Sandinistas such as Exxon, Bank of America, IBM Quaker Oats and National Cash Register	

The businesses supporting the Reagan administration in Nicaragua were MCA—unilateral because they were looking out for their own interests, coercive because they wanted the U.S. government to use force to dislodge the Sandinistas, and proactive because they expected benefits from the Reagan foreign policy.

The businesses supporting the Carter administration in Nicaragua were MCA—unilateral because they were looking out for their own interests, noncoercive because they did not favor using force against the Sandinistas, and reactive because they were prepared to accommodate Sandinista restrictions in order to continue their operations.

seas. American labor unions also play an important role in foreign policy making.

Labor

The AFL-CIO, which is America's largest labor organization, has a sizeable international department in Washington, D.C., staffed by some 100 professionals and offices in nearly 40 other countries.[49] The AFL-CIO conducts most of its overseas policies through four regional organizations: (1) American Institute for Free Labor Development (AIFLD), (2) the African-American Labor Center (AALC), (3) the Asian-American Free Labor Institute (AAFLI), and (4) the Free Trade Union Institute (FTUI). These regional organizations are primarily engaged in promoting the free labor movement on the grounds that American labor can only compete successfully with foreign labor if the social and working conditions for laborers abroad are comparable to those in the United States.

However, the impact of American labor both at home and abroad has never been as strong as its numbers would suggest. Domestically, the labor movement has been weakened by the fact that it has always been divided by ethnicity, race, and gender.[50] Internationally, labor has been weakened by its refusal to join forces with some of the more radical labor movements abroad. Beth Sims explains the AFL-CIO's inability to unify all labor interests in terms of the AFL-CIO's commitment to **business unionism**.[51] In this form of unionism, workers fight for the wages and benefits that the market will bear, and organizing takes place at the level of the factory, industrial sector, or confederations among sectors.

Business unionism excludes the notion that workers form a class with widely shared characteristics. By emphasizing narrow, sectoral interests, business unionism tends to isolate groups of workers from one another. It likewise hampers the creation of coalitions with other sectors in society, such as environmental activists or the homeless and unemployed.[52] Thus business unionism may account for the domestic weakness of American unions as well as their international weakness.

As a consequence of business unionism, American labor initially assisted internationally minded businesses in expanding abroad on the grounds that it would expand markets overseas that would absorb excess capital in the United States. For many years this form of cooperation between labor and business benefited workers because it meant that new jobs were created with business expansion.[53] But the benefits of this cooperation disappeared once FDI resulted in the manufacturing of products abroad, which would compete with those produced in the United States. Under these circumstances American businesses benefited at the expense of American labor.

Of course, the AFL-CIO regional institutes were actively engaged in promoting the free labor movement abroad, but this policy got caught up in anti-communism in a way that distorted the impact of the labor movement abroad. The AFL-CIO supported radical unions such as Solidarity in Poland against communist governments, but it would not support radical unions in other parts of the world.[54] As a consequence, the AFL-CIO supported the unions in the so-called free countries that would accept only the more limited demands of workers. This meant that social and working conditions in these countries remained low in comparison with those in the United States, and American workers suffered as a result.

Professional Organizations

There are also a large number of professional organizations in American society, for example, the American Medical Association, the American Bar Association, and the American Political Science Association. These organizations are primarily concerned with the interests of their professional members, but they do have an important impact on American society as a whole. On the one hand, the persistent opposition of the American Medical Association to socialized medicine has significantly narrowed the choices that Americans face with respect to health care. The high cost of American health care compared to that of other developed countries has now become a significant factor in the ability of U.S. companies to compete with foreign companies in the international market. On the other hand, professional organizations provide a number of important international services. For example, they work with counterpart organizations in other countries and with INGOs to promote universal standards.

So far this section has looked at the way in which business organizations in various sectors of the economy have competed with each other over foreign economic policy. But it is also useful to consider this competition from a regional perspective. Peter Trubowitz calls attention to the fact that these sectors are distributed unevenly throughout the United States.[55] As a result, various regions of the country have very different economic interests. Trubowitz shows that these regional differences manifest themselves in the kinds of foreign policy choices America made at three critical junctures in its history.

Regional Differences

Regional economic differences have existed in the United States since colonial times. By the 1890s these regional differences were more pronounced than ever before. The Northeast region of the United States had become more industrial than either the South or the West.[56] But the manufacturing interests of the Northeast had not been that successful in gaining access to European markets, and so they sought to compete elsewhere around the world. They wanted to "pry open" these other markets by using tariffs as a bargaining instrument. The Northeast also wanted the United States to build up its navy so that the government could support business internationalism abroad. The largely agricultural interests in the South opposed both policies. They feared that a large American navy and aggressive tariff-bargaining with non-European states would threaten European interests elsewhere in the world and indirectly jeopardize the South's lucrative agricultural markets in Europe. The agrarians in the

West finally sided with the Northeast because they needed outside markets for their surplus goods, and they hoped that they could gain some advantage from the bargaining tariff. Thus the manufacturing interests in the Northeast won over the agrarian West at the expense of the agrarian South.[57] Table 13.7 shows the foreign policy dimensions of the policies favored by the different regions.

By the 1930s the economic interests of various regions had shifted again. In the intervening years business internationalists in the Northeast had developed important markets in Europe. But Hitler threatened those markets, and so Northeastern business internationalists wanted to intervene on behalf of their trading partners in Europe in order to maintain those markets. The agricultural interests in the South were equally dependent on European markets. Although the South opposed big government, it too saw the need for government intervention in Europe. In the meantime the agricultural interests in the West were preoccupied with their domestic markets. They wanted protection from the agricultural goods being imported from Argentina, Canada, and other states. Since they did not have as much economic stake in Europe, they hoped to remain neutral if and when war came to Europe. In this case the Northeast and South were eventually able to pursue their preferred policies of free trade and intervention in Europe at the expense of the West. Table 13.8 il-

Table 13.7. Dimensions of Foreign Policy: Foreign Policy Preferences by Region in the 1890s

| | Multilateral | | Unilateral | |
	Coercive	Noncoercive	Noncoercive	Coercive
Proactive			The South favored free trade	The Northeast and West favored a bargaining tariff and a navy buildup
Reactive			The South opposed a navy buildup	

The South favored free trade, an MCA foreign policy—unilateral because they were concerned with their own interests, noncoercive because the trade was free, and proactive because they expected the benefits of free trade. The South also opposed a navy buildup, an MCA foreign policy—unilateral because they were concerned with their own economic interests, noncoercive because they did not want a forceful American foreign policy, and reactive because they were primarily concerned with the costs of such a program.

The Northeast and West favored the bargaining tariff and a navy buildup, MCA foreign policies—unilateral because they were looking out for their own economic interests, coercive because they expected the government to pressure other governments, and proactive because they expected to benefit from these measures.

Table 13.8. Dimensions of Foreign Policy: Foreign Policy Preferences by Region in the 1930s

	Multilateral		Unilateral	
	Coercive	Noncoercive	Noncoercive	Coercive
Proactive			The Northeast and the South favor free trade	The Northeast and the South favor intervention
Reactive			The West favors neutrality	The West favors protection

Both the Northeast and the South favored intervention, an MCA foreign policy—unilateral because they were primarily concerned with their own economic interests, coercive because they feared that Hitler would block their trade unless they interfered, and proactive because they emphasized the benefits of trade.

The Northeast and the South also favored free trade, an MCA foreign policy—unilateral because they were primarily concerned with their own business interests, noncoercive because trade did not normally involve the use of force, and proactive because they sought the benefits of trade.

The West favored high tariffs (protectionism), an MCA foreign policy—unilateral because they were concerned with their own economic interests, coercive because they favored high tariffs, and reactive because they were concerned with the costs represented by free trade. On the other hand, the West favored neutrality with respect to a possible European war, an MCA foreign policy—unilateral because they were concerned with their own economic interests, noncoercive because they opposed the use of force, and reactive because they were concerned with the costs of intervention.

lustrates the foreign policy dimensions of the different regions' views on involvement in a European war during the 1930s.

By the late 1960s the differential effects of the international economy on various regions of the country were beginning to change their foreign policy preferences once again. For the first time the manufacturing interests in the Northeast were finding it difficult to compete in the global market. The Northeast wanted protection both from other developed countries, namely Europe and Japan, and developing countries. The West, on the other hand, had developed new manufacturing interests and important agricultural markets in East Asia that could be expanded. And the South had mixed feelings about trade. "High-wage industries such as electronics, automobiles, chemicals, rubber and plastics, and non-electrical machinery" wanted freer trade, whereas "low-wage industries like textiles, apparel, leather, and lumber" wanted protection.[58]

The key to a coalition between the West and the South was defense expenditures. For almost a century the Northeast had favored defense expenditures because the largest share of defense dollars was spent in that region. But as military expenditures switched from "traditional weapons industries—tanks, ordnance, shipbuilding"—to "capital-and technology-intensive weapons systems," the Sunbelt with its cheaper energy and other advantages quickly replaced the Rustbelt as the dominant benefi-ciary of defense spending.[59] So the South joined the West in favoring lib-eral trade and especially high military expenditures. Table 13.9 shows the dimensions of the foreign policies favored by the regions in the 1980s.

What is especially interesting is that Trubowitz's analysis shows that these regional economic differences that became evident in the 1970s cre-ated the opportunity for the Republican Party to forge a new party align-ment. Regional differences over racial issues in the 1960s also created this opportunity. Using congressional votes on cold war foreign policy issues, Trubowitz shows that party conflicts were most prevalent in the late 1940s and in the mid-1980s. In the 1940s liberal Democrats, especially in the Northeast, favored cold war internationalism and conservative Republi-cans, especially in the West, opposed it. But in the mid-1980s liberal Dem-ocrats, especially in the Northeast, opposed cold war internationalism and conservative Republicans, especially in the West and South, supported it. Although differences in party and ideology existed throughout the period,

Table 13.9. Dimensions of Foreign Policy: Foreign Policy Preferences by Region in the 1980s

| | Multilateral | | Unilateral | |
	Coercive	Noncoercive	Noncoercive	Coercive
Proactive			West favors free trade; South has mixed views	West and South favor armament expenditures
Reactive			Northeast favors disarmament	Northeast favors protection

The West favored free trade, an MCA foreign policy—unilateral because it was primarily con-cerned with its own economic interests, noncoercive because it opposed government protection, and proactive because it expected to reap the advantages of free trade. The South had mixed views with respect to free trade.

Both the West and the South favored armament, an MCA foreign policy—unilateral because they were looking out for their own economic interests, coercive because they wanted increased defense expenditures, and proactive because they expected to benefit economically from these expenditures.

The Northeast favored disarmament, an MCA foreign policy—unilateral because it was looking out for its own economic interests, noncoercive because it wanted to reduce expendi-tures for the military, and reactive because it was absorbed with the costs of armament.

The Northeast also favored protection, an MCA foreign policy—unilateral because it was looking out for its own economic interests, coercive because it wanted the government to impose tariffs, and reactive because it was concerned with the costs of free trade.

the reversal of party positions took place in the 1970s, and Trubowitz is able to demonstrate that the underlying cause of this change in party alignment was change in the economic interests of the regions in which these parties had their strength, not changes in ideology.[60]

Up to this point this chapter has emphasized the pressures exerted on government by organizations in their primary areas of interest. But pluralism suggests a much wider array of organized pressures. The final section of this chapter deals with an issue in which pressures are exerted by all sorts of groups.

Pluralism and Fast-Track Authority

In 1974 Congress established a **fast-track authority** so the executive branch could negotiate a reduction in non-tariff barriers with other countries under the careful eye of Congress. This authority allowed informal participation by Congress during what would normally be the "mark-up" period, although Congress was formally limited to an up-and-down vote without amendments once the legislation was formally submitted to Congress.

This fast-track authority had been very useful to successive administrations in dealing with complicated non-tariff barriers that necessarily involved domestic as well as international issues. The authority was renewed four times, the last three in conjunction with negotiations involving the Uruguay Round of trade agreements and the creation of free trade areas with Canada and Mexico, before it lapsed in 1994. There was only a half-hearted effort to renew it at that time.

By 1997, however, liberal business organizations with the support of the Clinton administration launched a serious effort to reestablish fast-track authority. But they quickly ran into a new cohort of actors representing "non-commercial, non-establishment causes like human rights, environmental protection, workers rights, humanitarian relief, consumer interests, animal rights, and preservation of national cultural values." [61] What made this new coalition so effective was its mastery of the revolution in information technology and telecommunications. For the first time in history, warnings, calls for action, and solicitations for allies could be quickly and cheaply transmitted to people around the world who otherwise would never hear of, or pay attention to, international economic policy proposals.[62] As a result, groups like Global Trade Watch, a branch of Ralph Nader's organization, Public Citizen, were able to mobilize pressure to defeat measures that might directly or indirectly assist various business organizations.

In this case the Senate Finance and House Ways and Means committees fashioned fast-track bills that "would have effectively required trade agreements . . . to contain only provisions reducing trade barriers and trade distortions." [63] These bills did not allow labor, environment, health, and safety standards to be employed as a disguised trade barrier. Since the new coalition of NGOs would not accept bills that did not provide such standards and since business groups would not accept bills that did, the congressional committees were not able to fashion legislation that could garner majority support in the House of Representatives.

Since Vice President Gore was depending on the support of many of the coalition groups in the 2000 campaign, the Clinton administration was not prepared to give a high priority to fighting for fast-track renewal. Similar coalitions were also successful in blocking market-based strategies for assisting Africa, delaying increased lending resources to the International Monetary Fund, and blocking efforts to pass the Multilateral Agreement on Investment.[64]

By the time that President George W. Bush was elected in 2000, however, the supporters of fast-track legislation were prepared to make some concessions to opponents in order to get fast-track legislation. Thus in August of 2002 new fast-track authority narrowly passed the Senate with the amendments to the Trade Adjustment Assistance Act demanded by labor to protect its members. The primary aim of the Bush administration was to extend NAFTA to the rest of Latin America by passing a Free Trade Area of the Americas in 2005, but that now seems unlikely.

Key Concepts

business unionism   476
capital-intensive businesses   471
fast-track authority   481
formal organizations   448
generational data   463
informal organizations   448
inside strategy   449
interest-promoting
  organizations   449

labor-intensive businesses   471
movement   450
outside strategy   449
parallel publics   448
pluralism   449
sectoral interests   449
value-promoting
  organizations   449

Suggested Readings

1. Ambrosio, Thomas, ed. *Ethnic Identity Goups and U.S. Foreign Policy.* Westport: Praeger, 2002.

2. Rosati, Jerel A. *Readings in the Politics of U.S. Foreign Policy.* New York: Harcourt Brace, 1998.

3. Smith, Christian. *Resisting Reagan: The U.S. Central American Peace Movement.* Chicago: University of Chicago Press, 1996.

4. Trubowitz, Peter. *Defining the National Interest: Conflict and Change in American Foreign Policy.* Chicago: University of Chicago Press, 1998.

CHAPTER 14

Elitism:
Policy Planning and the Media

The picture above shows Secretary of Defense Donald Rumsfeld meeting several business leaders in Chicago, Illinois, where he spoke to a joint meeting of the Chicago Council on Foreign Relations and the Commercial Club of Chicago on Friday, August 6, 2004. Such meetings give foreign policy elites throughout the country an opportunity to assess and influence top government officials. Some of these elites represent the social upper class in the United States and have significant input into policy planning for American foreign policy. Owners, editors, and publishers usually represent the press at these meetings.

IF ORGANIZED PRESSURE is as important as suggested in the last chapter, then the leaders of such organizations may wield extraordinary powers, especially if these leaders form the principal clique in a dominant organization. Most people have had experience—whether real or imaginary—with small cliques that take over and run things to suit themselves. This chapter deals with that possibility in American foreign policy. But conspiracies are hard to prove, and so the standards of proof will have to be lowered to illustrate this approach. Because the connections that need to be made between elite individuals are usually private and enigmatic, some readers will find the evidence of conspiracy compelling, whereas others will believe that there are better explanations for what really happened.

Elite Theory and Its Limitations

One of the problems in studying elites is that there is so little agreement on who belongs to this group. Most authors who deal with the idea of a "ruling elite" or a "power elite" begin by identifying the most important institutions in American society, and then determine which individuals exercise the most power within these institutions. Political scientist Thomas Dye concentrates on the individuals who control most of the nation's resources in twelve sectors of society: (1) industrial corporations, (2) utilities and communications, (3) banking, (4) insurance, (5) investments, (6) mass media, (7) law, (8) education, (9) foundations, (10) civic and cultural organizations, (11) government, and (12) the military.[1] Dye's list of elite individuals includes only about 7,300 names. The problem with Dye's ruling elite for the purposes of this chapter is that the list is not restricted to individuals primarily concerned with foreign affairs.

Moreover, Dye does not claim that the individuals he has identified constitute a **governing class**, that is, members of a single social group that control the government. Although he acknowledges that many of these individuals have common backgrounds, he concludes that "a majority of people at the top are specialists, that corporate and governmental elites are not closely interlocked, and that there appear to be multiple, differentiated structures of power in America."[2] If Dye's analysis is true, it is difficult to claim that there is a single, dominant elite in society that controls foreign policy.

The sociologist William Domhoff provides a counterargument with his contention that the leadership of the power elite is actually provided by the "social upper class" in American society.[3] Domhoff defines membership in this class by the **social register**, attendance at certain private (mostly Ivy League) colleges, and membership in select social clubs. In some cases membership may also be conferred upon a few select outsiders who are fully accepted by members of this class. Domhoff concludes that there are perhaps 65,000 families and single adults in the United States that belong to this upper class,[4] but only a small fraction of this social upper class actually is engaged in policymaking. Thus Domhoff argues that it is a tiny fraction within the power elite and the social upper class that actually serves as the "governing class." This select group "owns a disproportionate amount of a country's wealth, receives a disproportionate amount of the country's yearly income, and contributes a disproportionate number of its members to the controlling institutions and key decision-making groups in the country." [5] Figure 14.1 shows the intersection of the power elite in business and government with the social upper class.

Elite theory presupposes the existence of a tight-knit group of individuals whose special interests and values dominate society. In the American context these interests and values are rooted in capitalism. Elite theorists assume that capitalist ideology so pervades the political system that a relatively small group of capitalists can not only unobtrusively control the majority of the nation's economic resources, but also decisively influence the government. They further assume that if a given policy is adopted, then members of this elite supported this policy. The evidence

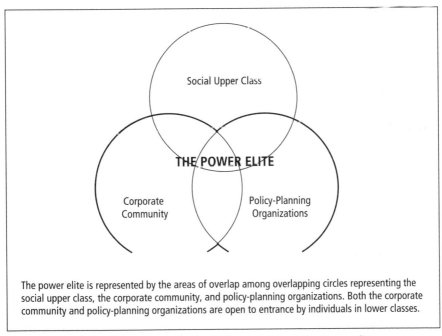

The power elite is represented by the areas of overlap among overlapping circles representing the social upper class, the corporate community, and policy-planning organizations. Both the corporate community and policy-planning organizations are open to entrance by individuals in lower classes.

Figure 14.1. Relationship between the Social Upper Class and the Power Elite
Source: Reprinted with permission from G. William Domhoff. *State Autonomy Or Class Dominance? Case Studies on Policy Making in America* (New York: Aldine de Gruyter, 1990). Copyright © 1996 Walter de Gruyter, Inc., New York.

for this theory requires the identification of links between specific individuals with both the resources and the political influence to convert their special interests into national interests. As Glenn Hastedt notes, elite theory differs from pluralist theory in that it emphasizes "the ties that bind policy makers together rather than the issues that separate them." [6]

Since elite theory stresses a number of exclusive ties between individuals, scholars and practitioners often have difficulty agreeing on who actually belongs to this core group. For example, were all of the half-dozen individuals who shaped American foreign policy during and immediately after the Second World War—Dean Acheson, Charles Bohlen, Averill Harriman, George Kennan, Robert Lovett, and John J. McCloy—members of the governing class?[7] Reasonable people can disagree. And since many of the individuals that people identify as part of the governing class are reluctant to claim membership in it, even among the purported elite, there is little agreement on who does or does not belong. Nevertheless, the concept of a governing class may be useful in understanding both the character and persistence of American foreign policy. In order to recognize the elitist character of American foreign policy it is important to identify the beliefs of the American social upper class.

Elite Beliefs

Identifying so-called elite beliefs is easier said then done. Given both the difficulty in reaching agreement on who belongs to the governing class and the reticence of many of these individuals to share their beliefs, it is not possible to measure the views of the governing class. But it may be instructive to compare the views of leaders with the general public. Using the CCFR data, Table 14.1 compares the views of elite leaders with the general public.

This figure shows that the largest and most consistent percentage differences between elites and the general public occur on the prosperity dimension. The elite is consistently less likely than the general public to consider the items on this dimension "very important." (Keep in mind that a low percentage score on this dimension is proactive and a high score is reactive.) The absolute percentage figures suggest that a concern for their prosperity after the September 11, 2001 attacks increased more among the general public than the elite.

The results are more mixed on the community dimension. A low score indicates a unilateral orientation, and a high score indicates a multilateral orientation. The elite was even more unilateral than the general public after the September 11, 2001 attacks with respect to both improving the global environment and strengthening the United Nations. But the positive scores in the community dimension indicate that the elite was more multilateral than the general public when it came to improving the standard of living of less developed countries. One might conclude that

Table 14.1. A Comparison of Elite and General Public Opinion on "Very Important" Foreign Policy Goals[a]

Chicago Council Foreign Policy Goal Questions	1974	1978	1982	1986	1990	1994	1998	2002
Community								
Combating world hunger	9	8	6	−2	n/a	**−15**	−6	−2
Helping to improve the standard of living of less developed nations	**23**	**29**	**20**	9	1	6	7	**12**
Improving the global environment	n/a	n/a	n/a	n/a	**14**	−9	−7	**−23**
Promoting and defending human rights in other countries	n/a	−4	−2		**−13**	−8	2	−1
Strengthening the United Nations	**−15**	**−21**	**−23**	**−24**	−5	**−18**	**−13**	**−29**
Strengthening international law and institutions	n/a	n/a	n/a	n/a	n/a	n/a	n/a	6
Security								
Maintaining superior military power worldwide	n/a	n/a	n/a	n/a	n/a	4	−1	**−16**
Helping to bring a democratic form of government to other nations	**−15**	**−11**	−6	−1	−2	−4	−2	−1
Preventing the spread of nuclear weapons	n/a	n/a	n/a	n/a	**35**	8	3	−2
Combating international terrorism	n/a	n/a	n/a	n/a	n/a	n/a	−5	−4
Protecting weaker nations against foreign aggression	−2	−4	9	−3	**−29**	−3	−3	**−14**
Prosperity								
Protecting the jobs of American workers	**−40**	**−44**	**−34**	**−34**	**−26**	**−33**	**−35**	**−14**
Securing adequate supplies of energy	2	8	2	3	1	5	−9	**−24**
Promoting market economies abroad	n/a	n/a	n/a	n/a	n/a	n/a	2	−9
Controlling and reducing illegal immigration	n/a	n/a	n/a	n/a	n/a	**−49**	**−34**	**−48**
Stopping the flow of illegal drugs into the United States.	n/a	n/a	n/a	n/a	n/a	**−28**	**−24**	**−36**
Protecting the interests of American business abroad	n/a	n/a	n/a	n/a	6	**−10**	**−16**	**−30**
Safeguarding against global financial instability	n/a	n/a	n/a	n/a	n/a	n/a	n/a	−5
Reducing our trade deficit with foreign countries	n/a	n/a	n/a	n/a	n/a	n/a	n/a	**−30**

a. Data appear in percentages and are placed in bold type if the difference is 10 percent or more. The elite percentages are subtracted from the general public percentages, so a positive number means that the elite was more positive than the general public. A negative number means that the elite was less positive than the general public.

Sources: Adapted from Chicago Council on Foreign Relations and German Marshall Fund of the United States, "U.S. Leaders Topline Report," *Worldviews 2002,* 33–41 and Chicago Council on Foreign Relations and German Marshall Fund of the United States, "U.S. General Population Topline Report," *Worldviews 2002,* 106–115.

poverty was more generally associated with the causes of the September 11, 2001 attacks among the elite than the general public, but after the attacks the elite was less inclined than the general public to associate either environmental improvements or the United Nations with solutions to global terrorism.

On the security dimension it appears that the elite was much quicker than the general public to realize the importance of preventing the spread of nuclear weapons and protecting weaker countries against foreign aggression at the point in time (1990) when the Soviet Union was dissolving. Later there was little difference between the elite and the general public in its recognition of the importance of preventing the spread of nuclear weapons or combating international terrorism. However, the elite placed less emphasis than the general public after the September 11, 2001 attacks both on maintaining superior military power worldwide and protecting weaker nations against foreign aggression, apparently because the elite discriminated more carefully than the general public among various security goals.

On the basis of the opinion data, one might surmise that the governing class is best represented by a unilateral, coercive, and proactive, or MCA, foreign policy in contrast to the general public's generally more multilateral, noncoercive, and reactive, or MCA, foreign policy preference, as Table 14.2 shows. (It is important to realize that these stances are defined on a relative rather than an absolute basis.)

In order to obtain a sharper picture of the beliefs of foreign policy elites, elite theorists look closely at those institutions that the power elite, and more specifically the governing class, consistently employ to further their

Table 14.2. Dimensions of Foreign Policy: General Foreign Policy Positions of American Elites and the General Public[a]

| | Multilateral | | Unilateral | |
	Coercive	Noncoercive	Noncoercive	Coercive
Proactive				Elites
Reactive		General Public		

Elites are more likely than the general public to favor MCA foreign policies—unilateral because they support nationalist policies, coercive because they favor the use of force, and proactive because they expect benefits. The general public is more likely than elites to favor MCA foreign policies—multilateral because they support global policies, noncoercive because they are less likely to support the use of force, and reactive because they are more concerned with costs.

a. The comparison is based on a difference of means test on individual factor scores on each of the three dimensions in the two data sets.

interests and values in the realm of foreign policy. No social institution is better suited to this purpose than the charitable foundations created by key families in the social upper class at the beginning of the twentieth century. The policies pursued by these foundations should provide important clues as to the preferred strategies of the governing class.

Elite Strategies

Although class distinctions existed in the colonial period, this chapter will focus on the social upper class in America at the beginning of the twentieth century. At that time the inequalities in American society were so manifest that they gave rise to a progressive social movement. The purpose of this movement was to "institutionalize certain reforms which would serve to preclude the call for more radical structural change." [8] This reform movement was particularly attractive to the social upper class because it held open the possibility of preserving elitism in a democratic society.

In order for these progressive reforms to work they had to create opportunities for common people to improve their economic and social status in society. If such people believed that those who rose to the top in society did so on the basis of merit and if the wealthy in society helped those with merit rise to the top, then there would be less pressure for revolutionary equality. By seeking "a more equitable political and economic path for the United States" the leaders of the progressive movement hoped to avoid revolution. "Rather than advocating the abolition of the system, progressive reforms represented attempts to harness the positive and eliminate the negative attributes of industrial capitalism." [9]

One of the primary instruments available to the social upper class for achieving more liberal reforms was the charitable foundation that emerged at the beginning of the twentieth century. Although there are now hundreds of such foundations, the strategies pursued by them have largely been set by the big three: the Carnegie, Ford, and Rockefeller foundations. These three foundations evolved slowly, giving *ad hoc* grants for a wide variety of purposes. But they eventually became effective instruments for promoting the interests of the social upper class as a whole.

In effect the governing class used the charitable foundations to convert their financial power into cultural and ideological power. The foundations placed most of their emphasis on education. The Carnegie Foundation is best known for building local public libraries throughout the country. The Rockefeller Foundation provided grants to elite schools for the purpose of improving medicine and reducing poverty, and the Ford Foundation also provided educational grants and scholarships. Thus "the dominant classes use[d] their privileged access to ideological institutions [among which can be included the mass media and the universities] to propagate values that reinforce its structural position." [10]

Perhaps "the most striking feature of the foundations' structures is the relative homogeneity of the trustees and staffs." They were either members of the social upper class or people clearly acceptable to them. Generally speaking, the foundations were very careful about the people who benefited the most from their largess. For example, political behavioralists and pluralists generally received strong support because they were interested in elite democracy. At the same time the "poor, dispossessed and minority groups in whose names many of their programs are launched infrequently participate in the decisions to initiate these projects." [11]

The gentlemen who sat on the boards of these foundations were very careful to preserve the principal funds on which their activities were based. For the most part, these foundations provided seed money for individual projects in the hopes that either the government would eventually take over the projects or that the projects themselves would become self-supporting. For example, in the 1950s the foundations sponsored foreign area studies programs at major universities, including Boston University, University of Chicago, Columbia, Cornell, Harvard, University of Michigan, Northwestern, Princeton, Stanford, University of Washington, and Yale. Foundation support for these international programs continued into the 1960s until the U.S. government finally provided institutional grants to support them.[12]

The foundations were also flexible; they were not hesitant to set up a variety of independent units to carry out their preferred projects. For example, the foundations sponsored organizations such as the Social Science Research Council, the Institute for International Education, the African-American Institute, and the Overseas Development Council, which operated quite independently from their sponsoring foundations. This had the advantage of at least partly disguising the huge role the foundations were playing in society as a whole because everything was not being done by one of the big three foundations but by a variety of independent organizations.

One of the most interesting things about both the social upper class and the foundations is that they were much more interested in the substance of policy than in politics itself. Although there are some notable exceptions such as the Roosevelts, the Kennedys, and the Bushes, the desire to give back to the community has seldom meant engaging in the rough and tumble of American politics. Rather it has meant involvement in education, the arts, and charities. Although it is widely believed that the wealthy exercise their influence on the political system by financing political campaigns, Domhoff shows that the upper class is less interested in politics than policy. He reports that the upper class as a whole does not contribute heavily to political campaigns on behalf of either Democratic or Republican candidates.[13]

Indeed, the evidence suggests that the upper class and the "corporate lawyers, top-level executives, and academic experts" who represent them in the policy process "tend to stay aloof from party politics." After all, it is the apparent "non-profit and nonpartisan image" of this network "that gives it effectiveness within the government whichever party happens to be in power." [14]

This brief foray into the beliefs and methods of the governing class suggests that there are two sets of institutions that are especially important in sustaining elite influence in society: policy-planning groups and the media of communication. Although the CCFR elite data for 1998 set out in Table 13.1 show that the leaders of think tanks favor MCA foreign policies, the editors and reporters associated with the media favor MCA foreign policies. But this chapter will show that media positions are explained as much in terms of the owners, advertisers, and authorities that control the media as with reference to the reporters and editors that assemble news stories.

Policy-Planning Functions

The elite studies of both Domhoff and Dye place particular emphasis on policy planning. One reason is that government officials are so tied up fighting so-called fires in the in-basket,[15] or immediate crises, that they have little time to plan for the future. With the attention of both the American Congress and president focused on the two-year and four-year election cycle, respectively, government preference for current policy is often the path of least resistance. Thus the foundations have found a niche that allows them to define the goals of foreign policy while government officials and bureaucrats are engaged in the day-to-day implementation of that policy. As Dye notes, "proximate [government] policy-makers tend to center about the means rather than ends of public policy." [16] This concentration of function leaves foundations and think tanks freer to center around the ends of public policy.

The policy-planning function has another advantage for elite organizations; it enables these organizations to train many of those who will become policy makers. For example, the Rockefeller Foundation alone has seen three of its top officials become secretaries of state: John Foster Dulles, Dean Rusk, and Cyrus Vance. Likewise a number of individuals well connected with the Ford Foundation have become key government officials, such as Paul Hoffman, John McCloy, McGeorge Bundy, and Robert McNamara.[17] All of these individuals played a prominent role in policy planning before they became government officials.

The Policy-Planning Network

Both Domhoff and Dye stress the importance of policy planning to elites. Domhoff describes four distinct kinds of elite institutions—foundations, think tanks, university institutes, and public discussion groups—as forming the **policy-planning network** in this country. And he argues

that of these four, public discussion groups are the most important because they "provide a setting wherein leaders in the upper class and corporate community can meet with each other and government officials to
exchange opinions and iron out possible differences on policy issues." [18]
Dye argues that discussion groups, which he calls *policy-planning groups,*
are the central coordinating points in the policy-making process" and
places them at the center of his "oligarchical model of national policy-
making." [19] These four kinds of institutions will be discussed briefly below.

Foundations.   Foundations are the parent organizations that fund most of
the other institutions in the network. Since all of the other institutions
need foundation funds to survive, foundations have the last word on what
kinds of initiatives will be sustained. By shifting funds from one organization or purpose to another, foundations largely determine the priorities for
policy planning. Foundations are also unique in that only they have sufficient resources to go beyond policy planning to implement policies on their
own. For example, foundations initially established the agricultural research centers around the world that brought the "green revolution."

Think Tanks.   Given the interest of the ruling elite in policy planning, it
is not surprising that foundations have helped to create a number of independent think tanks devoted to specific kinds of policy planning. As early
as 1916, for example, the Carnegie Foundation funded an Institute for
Government Research that merged with an Institute for Economics and
the Robert Brookings Graduate School in 1927 to form the Brookings Institution.[20] Brookings is one of the best-known liberal think tanks in the
country; but in the 1970s, a number of more conservative institutes
emerged, such as the American Enterprise Institute and the Heritage
Foundation. The Hudson Institute, the Rand Corporation, the Center for
Defense Information, and the American Security Council are just a few of
the one hundred or more think tanks that have surfaced across the
country. Each has carved out a particular area of foreign policy in which
to engage in policy-planning activities. For example, the Center for Defense Information is particularly interested in military expenditures.

Since most of these think tanks are focused on specific issues, they are
thought to be an ideal place to bring academia and government together;
thus bridging the gap "between the world of ideas and the world of action." [21] Of course, the relationship between academia and government is
sometimes strained because those who occupy positions in think tanks are
often critical of official policy. Indeed, many of them hope to replace these
officials. Thus in the year or two before presidential elections these policy
planners visit their foreign regions of expertise both to update information
and to renew personal ties with foreign leaders. They also try to publish
innovative ideas about U.S. foreign policy toward particular areas of the

world or on selected global issues in order to attract a following among those who would advise the president-elect on appointments to top-level positions.

Think tanks now cover the whole range of foreign policy ideas captured by our framework for analysis, as Table 14.3 shows. The Center for Defense Information believes that the United States can significantly cut back on defense expenditures. The Carter Center stresses negotiations and seeks improvements in the health of Third World populations. The Heritage Foundation favors a strong national defense.

University Institutes.   As early as the 1920s, the three major foundations were investing in research centers at private and public universities around the country. This effort was extended in the 1930s as the upper

Table 14.3. Dimensions of Foreign Policy: Foreign Policy Orientations of Various Think Tanks[a]

	Multilateral		Unilateral	
	Coercive	Noncoercive	Noncoercive	Coercive
Proactive	World Federalist Association	Carter Center		Heritage Foundation
Reactive		Center for Defense Information	Cato Institute	

The World Federalist Association generally favors an MCA foreign policy—multilateral because it perceives the world as one society, coercive because it wants to give the world federation sufficient authority to enforce law, and proactive because it wants to solve problems at the level at which they occur.

The Carter Center favors MCA foreign policies—multilateral because it believes in universal human rights, noncoercive because it favors preventing and resolving armed conflicts, and proactive because it believes people can improve their lives when they are provided with the necessary skills, knowledge, and access to resources.

The Heritage Foundation generally favors MCA foreign policies—unilateral because it emphasizes traditional American values, coercive because it favors a strong national defense, and proactive because it even wants to increase the capacity of the private sector to perform traditional military missions.

The Center for Defense Information generally favors MCA foreign policies—multilateral because it assumes a multilateral perspective on security, noncoercive because it prefers cooperative solutions, and reactive because it emphasizes prudent oversight of spending on defense programs.

The Cato Institute generally favors MCA foreign policies—unilateral because it favors strategic independence, noncoercive because it resists military intervention unless American vital interests are at stake, and reactive because it feels that an extended defense perimeter is outmoded.

a. This comparison is based on an inspection of websites on the Internet.

class policy planners became alarmed with public unwillingness to grapple with events in Europe. Then in the 1950s and 1960s the foundations not only created a series of foreign area studies programs across the country, but also a number of more general international centers such as Harvard's Center for International Affairs, MIT's Center for International Studies, Georgetown's Center for Strategic Studies, Berkeley's Institute for International Studies, the Stanford University Institute for Communications Research, and the Center for International Studies at Princeton University.

In the 1980s and 1990s academic entrepreneurs continued to build international centers on specific topics so that they could compete for foundation grants. In recent years there have been a number of new programs built around the reputation of former presidents, senators, or other notables such as the LBJ School of Public Affairs at the University of Texas, the Sam Nunn School of International Affairs at Georgia Tech, and the James A. Baker III Institute for Public Policy of Rice University. In addition to providing a link between government and academia, these centers and institutes are particularly useful in selecting and training future policy officials.

The policy-planning centers at universities have the advantage of bringing new talent into the policy-making process. Because of the education and outreach programs of these universities, these centers are an ideal way to involve the wider opinion-policy community in the policy-making process.

Public Discussion Groups.   Finally, there are the public discussion groups such as the Council on Foreign Relations, the Committee for Economic Development, and the Conference Board, as well as the Foreign Policy Association and various World Affairs Councils scattered across the country. Many of these organizations were founded between the First and Second World Wars when the liberal elite feared that the American public would not support proactive foreign policies. For example, the Council on Foreign Relations formed Committees on Foreign Relations in eight other cities in the 1930s, with the help of the Rockefeller Foundation. The Carnegie Foundation created a similar organization at the regional level in the South that eventually became what is now the International Studies Association.[22]

These policy discussion groups provide an opportunity for various sectors of the power elite to meet and to discuss important foreign policy issues; but, more important, Domhoff suggests that they also "provide a setting in which informal selection of members of the upper class and corporate community capable of serving in government can take place." These groups also "provide a setting wherein members of the upper class and corporate leaders can assess the skills, perspectives, and personalities of the experts who provide advice to them through speeches, discussions, written reports, and committee meetings." [23]

Now it is important to show how the policy-planning network enables ideas that are important to the governing elite became part of U.S. foreign policy. The fact that the elite takes the initiative in policy planning, however, does not mean that other people are not involved in developing these same policies.

Foreign Policy Contributions

There have been at least two critical junctures in the twentieth century at which the ruling elite felt compelled to redefine its objectives. One critical point occurred during the 1930s when the United States had to address the challenge of German and Japanese aggression. The second took place in the early 1970s when the United States faced both military defeat in Vietnam and the possible collapse of its economic hegemony. A third shift may now be required to deal with the turbulence caused by the end of the cold war and America's diminished standing in the world.

War and Peace Studies: 1939–1945.   The Council on Foreign Relations played a key role in planning for the cold war even before America's entrance into the Second World War. The Council's role originated at the end of the First World War, when Col. Edward House, President Wilson's principal advisor, formed a group of young experts to advise Wilson on matters to be discussed at the Versailles peace conference. Walter Lippmann, a journalist and a graduate of Harvard, managed the group that became known as the Inquiry. Although Wilson did not make much use of this group in France, members of the Inquiry did establish close ties with their counterparts from other countries, particularly Great Britain.

At the end of the Versailles conference the young British and Americans advisors decided that much remained to be done because the principals at Versailles had been "severely limited by the state of public opinion in their countries." [24] They determined to establish an Anglo-American Institute of International Affairs after the war with branches in London and New York.[25] But when the Americans returned to New York, they had second thoughts about the bilateral structure of the proposed organization. Lacking funds and power themselves, in 1921 they eventually decided to join an existing policy-planning group of New York financiers and international lawyers that had been organized under the leadership of Elihu Root, Theodore Roosevelt's former secretary of state.

The initial membership of the new Council on Foreign Relations was composed of two groups: the financiers and lawyers from Wall Street and the young intellectuals from the Inquiry. In order to extend their impact they decided to add "a number of carefully chosen individuals." [26] There was no requirement that members be listed in the social register, but many belonged to the same small group of social clubs in New York and

Washington, and the social upper class and Ivy League schools were well represented in the council's growing membership.

Over the first twenty years of its existence the council worked to develop a "reputation for confidentiality and nonpartisanship." [27] Although council members were an elite, they struggled to represent a wide range of views and dealt with the difficult topics of isolationism, the international causes of the Great Depression, American policy toward Japan, and the emerging situation in Germany.

However, the defining moment in the development of the council took place in September 1939, when Germany invaded Poland. At that point several council leaders, including Hamilton Fish Armstrong, the editor of the journal *Foreign Affairs,* visited the State Department and proposed that the council resurrect its role as the Inquiry by engaging in policy planning in concert with the government. Secretary of State Cordell Hull agreed, and with the financial help of the Rockefeller Foundation the council established its War and Peace Studies program. Over the next five years, four research committees, dealing with economic and financial issues, security and armaments issues, territorial issues, and political issues, met more than 250 times and produced some 682 memoranda that they shared with the government.[28]

A banker named Norman Davis, the president of the council and a close personal friend of President Roosevelt and Secretary of State Hull, best exemplifies the linkage between the council and the government at this time. The key figures on the council's Economic and Financial Group, Jacob Viner, a professor of economics at the University of Chicago, and Alvin Hansen, a professor of economics at Harvard University, exemplified the council's academic connections. In reports prepared as early as June 1940, this group concluded that "the Far East and Western Hemisphere probably bore the same relationship to the United States as America had to Europe in the past—a source of raw materials and a market for manufacturers." Moreover, the reports concluded that the economies of Great Britain and Japan could not function harmoniously with the American economy "without a large part of the world as markets and suppliers of raw materials." [29] This is an early indication of the council's formulation of American hegemony, even before the United States entered the Second World War.

Once the United States was actively at war, some of those engaged in the council's War and Peace Studies were brought into the government; others remained with the council. It is never easy to trace the influence of ideas within such a network, but the evidence suggests that the council had a profound effect on the government's own planning activities. Although only a few of the government's actions during and following the war could be attributed solely to the work of the council's committees, State Department officials acknowledged that the council's contribution had been "extremely important" and "very essential." [30]

The council illustrates not only the extent to which both private and public officials became engaged in the planning process but also the extent to which key individuals moved back and forth between policy planning and policy making. For example, William Stephenson, who was an aide to Colonel House during the First World War, became one of the early primary organizers of the Council on Foreign Relations and then held prominent positions in foundations. Leo Pasvolsky, who worked for the Brookings Institution before the war, became Roosevelt's chief advisor on United Nations affairs during the Second World War and then headed the foreign affairs studies program for the Brookings Institution. This interchange of key personnel continued throughout the cold war.

Trilateralism. By 1973 elite policy planners were confronting a whole new set of challenges. In January, President Nixon devalued the U.S. dollar by an additional ten percent to stop the run on U.S. reserves caused by growing competitiveness with Western Europe and Japan. Later that spring the last American troops pulled out of Vietnam. Then in September the developing countries meeting in Algiers demanded a New International Economic Order, which was followed in October by OPEC's oil embargo. In the face of these events America's ability to maintain its dominant position in the world was in doubt. It was an appropriate time to re-think America's goals and strategies for the rest of the millennium.

It was at this point that David Rockefeller, president of Chase Manhattan Bank, began to take some key policy-planning initiatives. As chairman of the board of the Council on Foreign Relations, Rockefeller launched the 1980s Project, which was "the largest, single research and studies effort the Council on Foreign Relations has undertaken" up to that point, comparable to the council's War and Peace Studies.[31] The project was funded by grants from the Ford, Lilly, Mellon, and Rockefeller foundations and the German Marshall Fund.

Despite its size, the 1980s Project was overshadowed by another Rockefeller initiative, the Trilateral Commission. The Trilateral Commission was particularly important both because it reveals the emergence of a transnational elite and because one of its former members, Jimmy Carter, became president in 1977. (Carter's appointment to the Trilateral Commission shows how key outsiders are incorporated into the elite.) And Zbigniew Brzezinski, the director of the Trilateral Commission, became Carter's special assistant for national security affairs. (Brzezinski also became important later in shaping foreign policy during the Clinton administration.) Other Trilateral Commission members such as Richard B. Cheney and Donald Rumsfeld became important in the George H. W. Bush and George W. Bush administrations.

Trilateralism can best be understood as an effort to create a broad coalition among the trilateral regions of the United States, Europe, and

Japan for the purpose of ensuring a healthy, not debilitating, competition among developed countries so that they might manage the dependence of developing countries. Among other things this would require them to thwart radical nationalist movements in some of these same developing countries.[32] Trilateralists believed that many of these radical nationalist movements were sponsored by the Soviet Union.

Some trilateralists were more concerned than others with the contradiction between liberal capitalism and liberal democracy. Liberal capitalism offers countries unprecedented growth, but it puts pressure on and creates inequalities within society. Thus in democratic societies, a counter pressure naturally rises to curtail liberal capitalism in order to realize greater equality. This contradiction is particularly evident in developing countries where transnational capital is putting great pressure on debt-ridden societies such as Nigeria. Since popular forces were challenging the authoritarian regimes that the United States had been backing in these countries, transnational corporations and international banks were looking for alternative forms of governance in these societies, which would neither be too radical nor too conservative.

In this context it is important to recognize that the Trilateral Commission included a broad spectrum of foreign policy elites. Some trilateralists, such as Carter, were shocked by the contention of Samuel Huntington and others that trilateralists should advocate a more moderate form of democracy in developing countries because participant democracy would make it more difficult to ensure the dominance of capitalist influence in these countries.[33] These contradictions were never resolved in the 1970s, and as we shall see, various elites belonging to this broader group later steered American foreign policy in very different directions. By 1980 many trilateralists had become disenchanted with Carter, and they looked first to George H. W. Bush, then a candidate for the Republican nomination, and eventually to Ronald Reagan for support.[34] One thing these trilateralists wanted was to replace the covert political activities of the CIA, which had largely fallen from grace under Nixon and Kissinger, with more open methods of promoting democracy abroad.[35]

Although much of the initial planning occurred earlier, President Reagan actually launched Project Democracy in a speech before the British Parliament in 1983. Project Democracy was designed to assist developing countries in their efforts to establish democratic governments. Because many of these countries already had radical national movements, Project Democracy was supposed to supplant these movements with more moderate democratic institutions. This initiative was implemented later in 1983, when Reagan signed National Security Decision Directive 77. The directive identified three functions for the new program: "public diplomacy"; an expansion of covert operations under the CIA; and creation of a "quasi-governmental institute," which became the National Endowment for Democracy (NED).[36]

The National Endowment for Democracy.   The NED appeared to be a private organization, but the State Department approved all the plans and programs funded by NED. Coordination between the State Department and private organizations was provided by a series of interlocking boards for the private organizations that received most of the NED funds. Among these boards were the National Democratic and Republican Institutes for International Affairs (NDI and NRI), the Center for International Private Enterprise (CIPE, a branch of the U.S. Chamber of Commerce), the Free Trade Union Institute (FTUI, a branch of the AFL-CIO), Freedom House, the Council on the Americas, the Center for Democracy, and a number of other American institutions, including the YMCA. Project Democracy first came under heavy attack in the mid-1980s. As a result of the Iran-Contra scandal in the fall of 1986, the General Accounting Office (GAO) ruled that the Office of Public Diplomacy (the first element of the project) was "an illegal domestic propaganda operation." [37] Congress eventually disbanded the second element: Col. Oliver North's covert activities. But the project's third element, the NED, has continued to function.

Many liberals criticize the NED because they believe that the NED, with its complicated and deceptive structure, is promoting **polyarchy** rather than democracy. Polyarchy is the "contentious but less mature brother" of democracy.[38] It was developed by political scientist Robert Dahl to deal with the fact that many societies do not have the conditions (popular sovereignty and political equality) "necessary to maximize those values in operating political systems." [39] Therefore, Dahl attempted to place countries on a democratic scale based on the political competition among leaders, who are in turn responsive to non-leaders.

Critics charge that polyarchy is a "system in which a small group actually rules and mass participation in decision-making is confined to leadership choice in elections carefully managed by competing elites." [40] They believe that polyarchy is a way of making democracy more practical in modern society by redefining it in terms of the institutions employed to select officials rather in terms of the rule by the most populous segment of the population. In their view polyarchy emphasizes free elections, a free press, and other institutions that would give the semblance of choice to the general population, without undermining the institutions required for transnational capital to operate in society. They would argue that all the governments that receive assistance through the NED, such as Chile and Nicaragua, are at best examples of polyarchy, not democracy.

Although NED funds were funneled through mainline American NGOs, these funds were sometimes disguised at the point where they were dispensed to foreigners. For example, NED funds handled by American private organizations were sometimes dispersed through local or regional organizations abroad such as the Center for Democratic Consultation (CAD), the Center for Electoral Assistance and Promotion (CAPEL), and the Delphi International Group.[41] The NED used these intermediaries both to make these interventions more acceptable to locals and to bypass congressional prohibitions on the use of covert funds for the Nicaraguan Contras.[42]

The strategy for promoting polyarchy through the NED was first implemented in the 1980s in the Philippines, Haiti, Chile, and Nicaragua. The first step in this strategy was to create a polarized referendum in which a democratic opposition, led by moderate, pro-U.S. elites, opposed the dictator. Although all opposition parties were initially encouraged to participate in the seminars and training sessions organized by the NDI and NRI, there was a heavy emphasis on uniting these parties around a single person in order to ensure the defeat of the dictator. Since more radical democratic forces opposed to these dictators were already in the forefront, however, it was essential "to transfer leadership of the democratization process from the mass movement to the political parties; and then to strengthen the center by isolating the parties on the left which were supporting the popular movement and weaning the parties on the right away from the dictator." [43] So the NED created labor organizations that would compete with the more radical and Marxist labor unions in these countries and formed groups that would attract businessmen tied to the dictator. The NED also worked with unorganized groups such as women and youth to build support for its candidates. (If the U.S. government engaged in similar activities in the United States, it would be considered undemocratic.) The NED continues to play a key role in countries such as Venezuela and Iraq today.

Elites and Policy Planning in the Post–Cold War World

When the Soviet bloc and even the Soviet Union itself collapsed in the early 1990s, trilateral elites began to adapt other measures. Although each of these adaptations were pushed by different elites, they could all be traced to ideas contending for trilateral support: economic assistance to Russia, NATO expansion, and the Project for the New American Century.

Economic Assistance to Russia.   When Poland, Hungary, and Czechoslovakia broke with the Soviet Union in 1989, the United States and its European allies had already established limited contacts with reform leaders in these countries. Since these leaders expressed an interest in establishing new market democracies, trilateralists were eager to develop what some called a "new Marshall Plan" for Eastern and East Central Europe. Such efforts were first made in East Central Europe, but early in 1992 a similar plan was hastily devised for Russia. What is especially interesting about the Russian aid program from the standpoint of elitism is that it quickly became an elite-to-elite aid program, which served the interests of these elites rather than either the United States or the Russian people.[44] Members of this Russian elite had developed contacts in the United States during Gorbachev's rule, and then became prominent in the new Russia.

The prominence of the individuals on both sides is important in explaining their operations. For example, whereas USAID usually develops a program of competitive grants for this kind of effort, the U.S. government was induced into turning much of its aid program to Russia over to a small group representing the Harvard Institute for International Development (HIID). The principal figures in the HIID group were Jeffrey Sachs, a Harvard professor of economics; Andrei Schleifer, a Russian-born émigré and Harvard economics professor; Jonathan Hay, a graduate of the Harvard Law School and former World Bank consultant; and Lawrence Summers, a Harvard professor who was the chief economist of the World Bank before he became a key U.S. Treasury official under President Clinton.

The HIID group funneled U.S. economic assistance to "a single group of self-styled Russian reformers called the Chubais clan." The Chubais clan was led by Anatoly Chubais, a young Leningrad economist, and included such persons as Yegor Gaidar, the first economic reform czar in Russia. They held key positions in the new Russian government and largely dictated the flow of U.S. and Western funds to Russia for an economic reform package that "encompassed privatization, legal reform, capital markets, and the development of a Russian security and exchange commission." [45] Harvard University itself profited by trading in the high-yield domestic bond market in Russia, which relied heavily on IMF lending.[46] The Chubais clan in Russia benefited by using the money provided by the United States to leverage even larger amounts from other Western sources. When the GAO finally began to investigate this arrangement in 1996, it discovered that the whole scheme was a fraud, and some of the funds made available to HIID in the spring of 1997 were recovered.

This entire episode had a very negative impact on U.S.-Russian relations because the purportedly people-oriented privatization program designed by the Chubais clan was actually a scheme calculated to enrich the Russian managers of the program at the expense of the Russian people.[47] Of course, this made ordinary Russians much less trustful of the United States and its capitalist system.

> Part of the [Russian] public came to associate the terms "market economy," "economic reform," and "the West" with dubious activities that benefited only a few people while others experienced a devastating decline in their standard of living—a far cry from their secure, albeit stark, lives under socialism.[48]

Although elitism usually involves a substitution of elite interests for the national interest, the Chubais fraud is a particularly flagrant example.

The second case of elite involvement in post–cold war foreign policy is more enigmatic, but it is no less consequential for American foreign policy.

Air War in Kosovo.   In the spring of 1999, NATO conducted a 78-day air war against the Yugoslav Federation in order to protect the large Albanian population living in the Serbian province of Kosovo. The alleged reason for taking this action was humanitarian, but most of the hundreds of thousands of Albanians who fled Kosovo did so after the NATO bombing had already begun.[49] This has led critics of U.S. foreign policy to suspect that the real purpose of the bombing was not humanitarian at all but rather to demonstrate NATO's ability to use force outside its territory.[50]

In order to place these allegations in context one needs to consider briefly the evolution of U.S. foreign policy toward Eastern Europe in the 1990s. In the years immediately following the break-up of the Soviet Union, East European countries actively sought NATO membership. At first the Clinton administration was divided on the issue.[51] Most experts in the Bureau for European Affairs in the Department of State and many in the Department of Defense wanted to stick with the existing Partnership for Peace (PFP) policy in which the United States provided assistance to countries, depending on their individual circumstances; but Anthony Lake, Clinton's first national security advisor, and Madeleine Albright, who was then U.S. representative to the United Nations, favored rapid NATO expansion. The choice of the latter strategy can largely be explained in terms of elitism.

In fall 1993 Zbigniew Brzezinski, who had been the director of the Tri-lateral Commission and Carter's national security advisor, convinced Lake, a student of Brzezinski, and Brzezinski-protégé Madeleine Albright that NATO should expand eastward.[52] Although the rest of the foreign policy bureaucracy was divided, Lake was able to get President Clinton to commit to NATO expansion in early 1994.[53] At the beginning of Clinton's second term, Sandy Berger replaced Lake as national security advisor, Albright replaced Warren Christopher as secretary of state, and, most important, William Cohen replaced William Perry as secretary of defense. These shifts allowed the administration to move ahead with NATO enlargement.[54]

The key to rapid NATO expansion was to turn the original emphasis on collective defense of NATO territory itself into effective action by a "coalition of the willing" outside NATO territory.[55] Although Brzezinski himself was primarily interested in broad political objectives, his protégés needed to demonstrate to the world that NATO could be an effective instrument for U.S. foreign policy in Europe as a whole. Slobodan Milosevic's aggression in Kosovo provided the perfect opportunity for this demonstration.

The first step in creating a broader role for NATO was Albright's efforts to replace Boutros Boutros-Ghali, who opposed U.S. efforts to use NATO forces in Bosnia, as secretary general of the United Nations. The second step was to force Milosevic to accept NATO forces on Serbian territory, which was the main thrust of NATO's negotiations at Rambouillet, France, in the winter of 1999. When Milosevic refused to go along, the United States was prepared to use force to compel him to accept NATO forces. The opportunity to do so came in March 1999 when the Kosovo Liberation Army (KLA) and Serbia clashed in southwestern Kosovo.[56]

The air war in Kosovo was a mere foretaste of what **neoconservative** critics of Clinton's foreign policy planned during his second term. Key members of this group, such as Donald Rumsfeld and Paul Wolfowitz, had been members of both the Committee on the Present Danger and the Trilateral Commission as well as prominent officials under previous Republican administrations. They set out to transform America's foreign policy by promoting an increased defense budget, citizen involvement ("expanded forms of reserve service"), and moral clarity ("democracy, free markets, and respect for liberty") into a foreign policy of "benevolent global hegemony."[57] The neoconservative instrument for planning this new foreign policy was the Project for the New American Century (PNAC).

Project for the New American Century. The project, which was housed in the conservative think tank American Enterprise Institute, was established in 1997. The project is important because of the forty individuals who originally participated, ten became high-level officials in the George W. Bush administration in 2001, including Vice President Cheney, Secretary of Defense Donald Rumsfeld, and his former deputy Paul Wolfowitz. Although the ties between these neoconservatives and the upper-class elite in this country is largely confined to the Bush family (Jeb Bush was one of the original participants in the project), the PNAC grew out of the web of elite institutions that has dominated American foreign policy since World War II.

It is evident that the neoconservatives associated with PNAC planned to remove Saddam Hussein from power long before George W. Bush was elected president.[58] Their plans were given a tremendous boost by the terrorist attacks on New York and Washington on September 11, 2001 because the attacks created an atmosphere in which any military action associated with the perpetrators of these attacks would have broad public support. Although the George W. Bush administration initially justified the 2003 invasion of Iraq in terms of WMD and purported ties between Saddam Hussein and al Qaeda, these claims were later proven to be false. The third argument of the administration and its defenders—that it was in America's interest to plant a democratic regime in the center of the Persian Gulf region—was the final pretext offered for the invasion, although democracy may not be an achievable goal.

Having discussed the role of the elite policy-planning network in foreign policy making, it is time to turn to another institution that is vital to maintaining elite interests and values in American society: the mass communications media. Even in an elite democracy, communications with the general public is essential.

The Mass Communications Media

The mass media involve over 25,000 different entities. They include "some 1,500 daily newspapers, 11,000 magazines, 9,000 radio and 1,500 TV stations, 2,400 book publishers and seven movie studios in the United States."[59] This does not include the millions of personal computers and handheld devices connecting to the Internet. However, the number of media that actually produce news at the national and international level is much smaller. The **mainstream media** include: television networks ABC, CBS, NBC, and Fox News; leading newspaper empires such as *New York Times, Washington Post, Los Angeles Times, Wall Street Journal,* and the holdings of Knight-Ridder, Gannett, Hearst, and Scripps-Howard; major news and general interest magazines such as *Time, Newsweek, Reader's Digest,* and *U.S. News & World Report*; major book publishers such as McGraw-Hill, and cable-TV systems such as Murdoch, Turner (CNN), and Cox.[60] Although most people rely on local outlets for national and international news stories, the mainstream media produce most of this news. But the key question is not who produces the news, but rather for whom do they produce it?

Elite or Mass?

Democratic theory would argue that the answer to this question is the general public. After all, the public must be informed in order to participate in the democratic process, particularly at election time. Thomas Jefferson once said, "Were it left to me to decide whether we should have a government without newspapers, or newspapers without a government, I should not hesitate for a moment to prefer the latter."[61] The First Amendment underscores Jefferson's point by protecting "freedom of the press." The Supreme Court has interpreted this concept of a free press very liberally, and generations of reporters have incorporated these ideas in their definition of what it means to be a professional journalist: they represent the "peoples' right to know."

But when it comes to describing the audience for news about public and international affairs a different picture emerges. Nearly three-quarters of the American people follow the news sometime during the day. But the reading, watching, and listening habits of people have changed remarkably over the last ten years. The regular evening television news programs of the major networks now reach only about 30 million people, just a fraction of the general public. People are watching and listening to news throughout the day. They rely on a variety of other news sources, including radio, cable TV, newspapers, and increasingly the Internet. Moreover, many get the news from these sources inadvertently while doing other things, such as listening to a radio broadcast with streaming audio while playing a computer game.[62] This is especially true of the younger generation that also relies heavily on Internet blogs and Comedy Central's *The Daily Show* for information.

This greater accessibility of news has largely discredited the old notion that there was a "two-step flow" of information to the public, with information first reaching elites (a more attentive public) and then only later extending to the general public. But even though the general public is getting the news at about the same time as the elite and the attentive public, this does not mean that it is not important to differentiate among various audiences. One of the most striking developments in recent years is the politicization of the news. Certain media are increasingly identified with particular parties and ideologies. For example, Fox News and talk radio is identified with Republicans and conservatives, whereas the PBS *News Hour* and National Public Radio resonate with Democrats and liberals.[63]

This politicization of the news should largely discredit the old myth that there was a "liberal" bias in the media. As media critic Eric Alterman indicates, conservatives have been "working the refs" for decades.[64] Academic studies show that reporters themselves are centrists. If there is a bias among them, it is a conservative one. More important, media are a business and "[b]usinesses are not in the habit of producing products that contradict their fundamental economic interests. . . . [T]he major commercial media in this country—not surprisingly—tend to favor style and substance which is consonant with their corporate interests; as do their corporate advertisers." [65]

Of course, the media claim to represent public opinion, especially in terms of letters-to-the-editor, call-in programs, and other mechanisms for tapping the responses of their audience. But although these public inputs may be interesting, they cannot seriously be compared either to elections or polling results as evidence of public opinion. For the truth is that neither the owners, the editors, the reporters, or in most cases the audiences of news programs in the mainstream media accurately represent the general population.

To assess who the media represent, one needs not only to examine who they are but also how they function, that is, what the mainstream media have to say. This chapter looks at the mainstream media in general, and then looks more closely at how the press functions in the area of foreign policy.

Ownership. The mainstream media are a big business—one of the most profitable industries in the United States, averaging profits of 20–30 percent per year. Moreover, the ownership of the mainstream media is concentrated in just a few prominent families who are associated with the upper class in this country. "With each passing [year] . . . the number of controlling firms . . . has shrunk: from fifty corporations in 1984 to . . . twenty-three in

1990. . . to close to ten media corporations by 1996." [66] By 2001 five media conglomerates owned the main media markets in the United States, including film, TV, magazines, music, books, cable, and newspapers.[67]

Of course, some may object that even though the mainstream media are controlled by just a handful of elite families, there is enough competition among them to ensure that they represent the best interest of the general public. But this pluralist argument has become less and less plausible with the passage of the Telecommunications Act of 1996 that established local rules that "made it possible, for the first time, for a single company to own more than one radio station in the same market. A single owner was now permitted to own both TV stations and cable systems in the same market. License periods for broadcasters were expanded." [68] Then, in 2003, the Federal Communications Commission (FCC) proposed that a company could own television broadcast stations that could reach up to 45 percent of the national television audience, although Congress set the limit at 39 percent in January 2004.[69] Liberals now fear that the 1975 rule against "cross-ownership," preventing a company that owns a television or radio station from owning a daily newspaper in the same market, will eventually fall.[70]

Despite this concentration of private ownership, frequent assertions of the importance of a free press lead most Americans to draw a sharp distinction between our media and the media in more authoritarian societies. Yet the American upper class has historically used its position of power to deal with journalists who insist on presenting the wrong news. For example, the Sinclair Broadcasting Group Inc., a conservative corporation that "owns or controls 62 television stations in 39 markets, reaching about a quarter of the nation's population," fired its chief political correspondent, Jon Leiberman, when he objected to running an anti-Kerry film as part of the news broadcast on all Sinclair Broadcasting stations just before the 2004 presidential election.[71]

The effect of this corporate pattern of ownership is evident in the business content of media throughout the country. For example, "almost every metropolitan paper in the country has a whole section devoted to 'Business.' " But perhaps the most obvious evidence of the glorification of private business in the media is "in the public impression that public-sector activities are essentially flawed and should be limited while private enterprises are essentially sound and have no need for change," despite a series of corporate scandals such as Enron and WorldCom.[72]

But the control exercised by owners is not the only problem faced by those journalists that take their professional standards seriously; reporters must also contend with the problem of advertising. Everyone knows that advertising plays an important role in American media. The question is, does this advertising affect news coverage in the media?

Advertising. Historically there has been a strong tie between the media and local communities throughout the United States. However, these ties began to change after the Second World War when the media's "pursuit of advertising" reduced "its responsiveness to reader desires." Now newspapers sell for about a third less than the cost of the paper on which they are printed,[73] and some newspapers, like *USA Today*, give away as many as 18 percent of their papers in order keep up their circulation numbers. Most of their income comes from advertising. Other media are even more dependent upon advertising. "TV and radio get nearly 100 percent of their income from advertisers, newspapers 75 percent and magazines about 50 percent.[74] And the clout of advertisers may be even stronger now that advertisers are turning more to cable TV and the Internet.

As newspapers and other media became more and more dependent upon advertising for their high profit margins, the competition among them for advertising dollars initially increased. But in the case of newspapers, for example, once one of the papers won this battle, it severely reduced the competition as its competitors gradually went out of business and were bought up, with the result that fewer and fewer communities now have their own newspaper. This change illustrates the growing separation between the media and their audience.

Now "[p]rofessional journalists, including their top editors, are largely powerless in determining the areas of strategic news coverage. That task has been taken over by market analysts and business consultants. The focus of journalistic effort has shifted from what the community needs to what the advertiser wants." Most advertisers prefer "fluff" and entertainment to news because this puts people more in the mood to buy. As a consequence, the amount of news has declined; and "puzzles and horoscopes, comics, nonlocal human interest and lifestyle articles, business and finance, and crime" has increased.[75]

Moreover, the corporations who advertise in the media are not just interested in the number of subscribers, viewers, or listeners; they want to reach people with disposable income. That means that advertisers have introduced important class differences in the media. "The magazines tend, actually, to universalize upper-middle-class practices as if they were shared by all Americans." [76] Television advertising also emphasizes elite buying.

So far this chapter has emphasized the extent to which the mass media are more responsive to the upper class and upper-middle class than to the lower-middle class or working class. But the discussion has been limited to the media in general. Now it is necessary to concentrate more on the news that deals specifically with U.S. foreign policy and international relations.

Foreign Policy News

The *New York Times* proudly proclaims in the upper-left hand corner of its first page that it contains "All the News That's Fit to Print." If one stops to think about it, this claim can hardly be true even if one is referring to local or domestic news, much less foreign or international news. Although the

United States only represents about five percent of the world's population, it dominates the news reported in this country. Even when one considers the fact that in normal times perhaps only a third of the news stories on network evening television shows deal with foreign affairs, it is important to remember that many of those international stories are either about U.S. citizens abroad or U.S. foreign policy.[77]

It is not just that there is less foreign than domestic news in the media; it is also that the coverage of foreign news is much less balanced than domestic news. Most foreign news is concerned either with security issues or with the global economy. Less attention is given to history, culture, or other aspects of societies abroad. Since most Americans have been conditioned to believe that proximate events are more important than distant ones, it is not too surprising that whereas one death may justify a local story, many hundreds or even thousands of deaths may be required in order to justify a foreign story. Stephen Hess estimates that "half of foreign television news stories involve violence."[78]

Moreover, news coverage is much more likely in some areas of the world than others. Despite the fact that perhaps 80 percent of the world's population is located in developing countries, most foreign news reported in the United States originates in developed countries. For example, there is very little news coverage of Africa. Hess concludes that "[t]he narrow span of TV foreign news, largely government related and driven by events, differed markedly from the broader and more balanced array of subjects in domestic news. International environmental problems, education, science, and the arts were rarely mentioned. Half the world's 180 or so countries were never noted. Coverage by continent distorted the map of the world."[79]

As Hess notes, there are several reasons for the paucity of foreign news. One is the cost of maintaining foreign correspondents abroad. Despite soaring profits, American newspapers have cut the number of regular foreign correspondents. Hess estimates that there are still about 1,500 foreign correspondents, but most of them are now freelancers, that is, they are not salaried but sell individual stories to various media. The Associated Press alone has over one-fourth of these; UPI has many fewer. The elite newspapers still carry a substantial number of foreign correspondents, but "CNN has more than ABC, CBS, and NBC combined."[80] For example, CBS only has eight foreign correspondents, and half of those are located in London.[81]

And if foreign news is more likely to deal with some people and places than others, it may be that this bias partly reflects the backgrounds of the correspondents who produce these stories. Hess notes that foreign correspondents are more likely than domestic reporters to have attended Ivy League colleges and have graduate degrees. He compares their backgrounds and educations to those of members of New York law firms. And he discovered that among those hired since 1990, "78% of their fathers were managerial or professional," or in other words, upper-middle class.

But in order to understand foreign news coverage by journalists working for the American media, we need to know more about the news organizations for whom they work and the bureaucracies with whom they must deal. In this context it is important to remember that elites largely determine the tasks that these reporters have and the resources available to them to perform these tasks.

This analysis will focus on what one writer refers to as the **routines of journalists**, that is, four phases that describe the work of reporters; they are: (1) *detecting occurrences,* (2) *interpreting occurrences as meaningful events,* (3) *investigating their factual character,* and (4) *assembling them into stories.*[82] The first two phases emphasize the extent to which these journalistic routines enable government, and possibly elite, sources to "manage the news" and the last two phases show how both officials and reporters, who may themselves be elites, "manufacture news."

Managing the News.   Since most mainstream media have only a few diplomatic reporters and foreign correspondents to cover U.S. foreign policy and the world, they assign them to **beats** where they are assured of getting news even on "bad news" days. A beat defines where reporters go, and whom they talk to.[83] All kinds of interesting events may be taking place in the world, but unless someone on a reporter's beat draws these occurrences to the reporter's attention, the reporter is unlikely to turn these events into news stories.

These "territorial or topical" beats are assigned to individual reporters by their immediate supervisors. These supervisors, or those who control them, exercise considerable power over individual reporters, not only by assigning specific beats and stories to them, but also by reviewing their stories prior to publication in the print media or broadcast on TV or radio and by deciding where, when, and how much of the story will appear in the media. Ironically, it is usually these supervisors, not reporters or the public, who decide what is newsworthy and what isn't. Moreover, these influences are particularly important in the early stages in the development of a story, or series of stories, because today's news is usually conditioned by yesterday's news.

In Washington, D.C., most foreign affairs reporters are assigned beats in the Golden Triangle: the White House, the State Department, and the Pentagon. Each of these beats is quite different. White House reporters "tend to see presidential actions as motivated more toward *political strategy* of maintaining leadership and power rather than toward policy." State Department reporters are "oriented more toward policy formulation." And reporters who cover the Pentagon tend to emphasize substantive issues such as "guns and ammo." [84]

Most diplomatic correspondents in Washington, D.C., organize their beats around the State Department's regular noon briefing. This briefing is scheduled so that reporters working for both evening and morning papers can make maximum use of the information provided by the State Department. Reporters working for afternoon papers use this information for fast-breaking news stories, while reporters working for morning newspapers use the extra time to develop news stories in more depth. The noon briefing also meets the needs of radio, television, and magazine reporters. In addition to the noon briefing, diplomatic reporters spend much of their time with information and policy officers throughout the State Department as well as contacts on Capitol Hill and in foreign embassies, and these reporters depend on their colleagues on other beats to cover other parts of the Golden Triangle.

The beats of correspondents abroad are remarkably similar to those of diplomatic reporters in Washington, D.C. Foreign correspondents may be more dependent on the wire services for hard news than their counterparts in Washington, but they too base their beats mainly on official government sources such as the foreign ministry and the U.S. embassy. Of course, these beats include a wider range of sources when correspondents are stationed in one place than when correspondents are on temporary assignment to other locations.

Most U.S. foreign correspondents operating abroad are located in a few large capitals. The country in which they are stationed largely defines their beats. Thus one study found that only 21 out of a total of 191 countries "accounted for 79 percent of the foreign dateline stories on network television from 1988 to 1992." [85] There was fairly "constant" coverage for only 6 countries: Great Britain, France, Germany, Russia, Japan, and Israel; "crisis" coverage only in another 15 countries: Iraq, Saudi Arabia, South Africa, China, Panama, Poland, Czechoslovakia, Jordan, Somalia, Kuwait, Iran, Colombia, Yugoslavia, Canada, and Syria; and a few preassigned stories in another 70 countries. Except for crises situations, the news coverage from abroad is often stereotypic: "If the story was about Colombia, the subject must be drugs; in Italy, the Mafia; in Germany, neo-Nazis." [86]

Thus reporters' beats affect the news in two ways. First, they determine which officials influence the news. Because the reporter is focusing on U.S. foreign policy rather than a situation abroad, the action occurs in a capital city rather than in the field. Thus in the coverage of the succession of wars in Yugoslavia from 1991 to 1995, the action occurred mainly in Belgrade and Washington in 1991:

"By 1993, it was in Sarajevo . . . . By late 1995, the action had moved to Dayton, the site of the peace conference." When news stories came out of Washington or Dayton, the character of the war in Bosnia largely disappeared. Moreover the locales from which the reports originated affected not only the perspectives that reporters brought to the conflict but also the kinds of experts they interviewed. Even when reporters were covering the war from locations in Yugoslavia, "press conferences got more coverage than (other) events" because they were the most important part of the reporter's beat.[87]

Second, reporters' beats encourage journalists to emphasize procedural rather than substantive issues.[88] Because officials are the main source of news on a beat, their agenda and their actions become the focus of media attention, rather than the basic causes of the international events or the implications of these events for various actors throughout the world. Unfortunately, these procedural matters—"when will the president or the Secretary of State make a statement"—not only receive more attention than they deserve but also divert attention away from more substantive issues. They frequently allow officials to substitute rhetoric for policy. No wonder many people get much of their international news inadvertently!

But the dependence of the media on government sources for news is not restricted to the identification of occurrences; it is also facilitated by standards developed by the media for guiding reporters in interpreting events. These standards were developed in the mid-nineteenth century when a large audience for standardized news first emerged, and later rationalized to provide a professional code of ethics.[89] Although the six **standards for professional journalism** listed below are intended to ensure objective coverage of the news, they often work against it as we will show throughout the remainder of this chapter.

1. The professional journalist assumes *the role of a politically neutral adversary*.

2. The journalist resists [sensationalism] by *observing prevailing social standards of decency and good taste*.

3. The truthfulness and factuality of news is guaranteed by *the use of documentary reporting practices*.

4. News objectivity is reinforced further by *the use of a common or standard format for packaging the news: the story*.

5. *The practice [is to] train . . . reporters as generalists* (as opposed to specialists).

6. The above practices are regulated and enforced by the important practice of *editorial review*.[90]

In considering how the news is interpreted, it is also useful to distinguish between the three phases in the development of a critical news story: the initial phase, the reflective phase, and the action phase.[91]

In the initial phase the six professional standards mentioned above largely ensure that reporters will faithfully report what government spokespersons say even when reporters have strong personal doubts, supported by countervailing details obtained from other sources. As long as all government sources adhere to the same policy line, reporters seldom question the information provided. Such uniformity leads to passivity on the part of the media audience, and government information officers work hard to ensure such uniformity.

For example, within the first week after Iraq's invasion of Kuwait on August 2, 1990, the mainstream media was promoting the administration line that the Iraqi leader, Saddam Hussein, was a madman and intent on invading Saudi Arabia. In October the same media reported on atrocities in Kuwait. One particularly sensational story involved a teenage girl testifying that Iraqi soldiers had taken 15 babies out of incubators and "left them to die on the floor of the hospital." Then shortly after the midterm elections in November 1990, George H. W. Bush justified doubling U.S. troops in Saudi Arabia on the grounds that the Iraqi military was massing along the Saudi border. But "if commercial satellite photos are accurate, it could be that Iraq increased their forces in the Gulf as a response to the U.S. troop buildup," and not as a precursor.[92] All of these stories were crucial in developing support for the war effort. (And the reporters who wrote these stories were all following "documentary reporting standards.") Yet we now know that the incubator story was a complete fabrication, and the other two stories are questionable.

If reporters "defined their roles more self-consciously as stimulator of public participation and debate" in the initial phase (which might be perceived by officials as violating social standards of decency and good taste), they could give "opposition voices equal play with administration leaders." [93] Such an airing of the issues at stake would affirm some of the questions ordinary citizens already have about proposed policies. But reporters usually wait until the main story line has been set. By the time reporters begin to pick up opposing views in the second, reflective phase, media coverage of the event begins to decrease.[94]

Congressional leaders also contributed to this failure to air opposing viewpoints in the Persian Gulf War by postponing the debate in Congress until just days before the beginning of the action phase, on January 15, 1991. This timing largely ensured the outcome of the vote to declare war. (Would Tocqueville have been proud of this example of democracy in action?) By that time "patriotic journalism" had taken over, and the media, particularly the local media, assumed the perspective of the soldier and rallied around the troops. This essentially "denies to the public the information and detached perspective people need to make sound decisions." [95]

Once the war had begun, the U.S. government made a concerted effort to showcase the accuracy of its new weapons. Western sources inside Iraq reported that the bombing campaign was resulting in significant civilian casualties. The Bush administration denied it. When an air-raid shelter in the Amiriya section of Baghdad was hit, and Western reporters in Baghdad said that hundreds of Iraqi civilians appeared to have been killed, the media downplayed the story because Bush labeled it as propaganda. At first the administration refused to even investigate the incident. Later they argued that the structure was a legitimate military target. But it is now estimated that around 1,600 Iraqi civilians lost their lives in that one incident.[96]

In all these instances the American media accepted the authoritative statements of the U.S. government and conveyed them to the American public. The media also downplayed discrepant and contradictory information that came to its attention. From the standpoint of media reporters, they were simply providing the most authoritative information available—that coming from government sources. Unfortunately, all of these government interpretations have subsequently been challenged. But the harm had already been done because the initial reports have the most impact. In this sense the government was successful in managing the news.

Because reporters were embedded with U.S. troops in the Iraq War, the "story" was largely controlled by the government and uniformly uncritical partly because these reporters were "generalists" and lacked the military background necessary to assess the action. During the postwar period in Iraq the insurgency seriously limited the ability of reporters to cover a variety of issues because it was dangerous for them to go outside of Baghdad.

But if the routines and standards developed by the media for covering the news often enable the government and elites to manage the news, then it is also true that the way reporters fill in the gaps and assemble news stories allows the government and sometimes reporters themselves to manufacture news. The next section explores the role of officials and reporters in interpreting the news and assembling stories.

Manufacturing the News.   When governments control news sources as they did in the Gulf War, there is little opportunity for the media to investigate events for themselves. But when reporters for whatever reason have unique access to breaking news as CNN did during the early bombing phase of the Persian Gulf War, they become the primary news source, forcing the government to respond. This so-called CNN effect is purported to have led George H. W. Bush to send troops to Somalia in 1992 and George W. Bush to increase U.S. disaster relief ten-fold to countries affected by the tsunami in the Indian Ocean in late 2004.

In normal times, however, reporters supplement the facts given to them by government spokesmen by talking to a range of other officials. Reporters cultivate a wide range of sources, but these sources are often reluctant to provide information that might call into question administrative policy. They usually find it safer to follow the president's lead on foreign policy issues, and reporters are reluctant to disclose information that would reflect badly on the institutions that they depend on for information. The unwillingness of reporters (and military officers) to question

Secretary of Defense Rumsfeld's policies during the post–war debacle in Iraq in 2003–2004 was particularly embarrassing. It took a lowly National Guard specialist to get Rumsfeld to acknowledge publicly that American forces were still going into combat in Iraq in late 2004 without adequate armor. This may be another case in which "standards of decency" or decorum prevent important stories from getting out.

Editors and producers sometimes assign investigative reporters to stories during the reflective phase, but they do not always give them the latitude they need to cover such stories. Moreover, when investigative reporters are given enough latitude, they sometimes allow themselves to be manipulated by their high-level sources. For example, Judith Miller, a former *New York Times* correspondent, wrote a series of exclusive articles on WMD in Iraq in which she propounded the myth that Saddam Hussein had such weapons.[97] Later the *New York Times* acknowledged that its editorial staff failed to question her stories sufficiently even though her sources never provided any solid evidence to support their claims.[98] As it turns out, she was misled by her high-level sources and was unwilling to challenge them because this would put her own exclusive access to them in jeopardy.

The Miller illustration is part of the larger Plame case that concerns the alleged efforts by top officials in the Bush administration to misrepresent the evidence for WMD in Iraq before the Iraq War. A number of reporters, including Miller, were called before a grand jury to testify about their relations with officials in the Bush administration in this case. Top officials in the administration had evidently leaked the name and identity of Valerie Plame Wilson, a CIA operative, to the news media, because her husband, Joseph C. Wilson IV, had criticized the administration's handling of a story involving the alleged sale of uranium by the African country of Niger to Iraq. This alleged sale was one of the few concrete stories the Bush team had used to justify going to war with Iraq. Although only one official, Lewis I. Libby Jr., Vice President Cheney's former chief of staff, has so far been charged by a grand jury for lying about the incident, the case shows how difficult it is for reporters to be "politically neutral adversaries" and for editors to provide meaningful editorial "review." The public editor for the *New York Times* suggests that in the future the use of anonymous sources should be an exception rather than a routine, and when confidential sources such as White House officials are used, editors should require reporters to explain why anonymity was granted to an official in the story itself.[99]

Even when reporters know information is false, they may not be prepared to challenge it. In the late 1970s defense reporters were confronted with discrepant information on Soviet defense expenditures. In this case the information was not leaked by officials, but rather presented by former officials who were members of the Committee on the Present Danger

(CPD). This case is particularly interesting because the information they used was actually official government information, which some of them working as an alternative analysis team, Team B, had produced under the Ford administration. In this case the mainstream media used the CPD version of the facts, which showed higher numbers for the Russians, even though many of the reporters involved, as well as officials in the Carter administration, must have realized these numbers were exaggerated.

Of course, professional formulas provide some guidelines for dealing with discrepant information. When reporters discover gaps in the information provided to them, they are expected to fill in these gaps on the basis of the knowledge they obtain while covering their beats. One way of filling in the gaps is by taking into account SOPs within the government in keeping with an organizational behavior model. In short, reporters are supposed to piece together a coherent story, assuming that the discrepancies are based on the differing positions or perspectives of their sources. (Of course, this doesn't work if officials are distorting the truth.) When things don't make sense, reporters, in consultation with their editors, publishers, or producers, are expected to rely on their own good judgment.

In many ways the press sidesteps these difficult questions by turning the debate function over to newspaper columnists, television and radio commentators, and politically oriented magazines. But the views of these more biased news sources "are more often asserted and announced than joined or judged." Despite the abundance of "opinion-mongering" though, the range of perspectives in the mass media is quite limited, compared to what is available in some other countries. "Few reactionaries and even fewer radicals have prominent platforms in the American media." [100]

The standard method for presenting adversarial information on television is to have experts advocating different views. Unfortunately, these adversarial exercises are often so bland or one-sided that it makes a mockery of debate. In too many cases the moderator refuses to ask the follow-up questions that would make the debate interesting. As the public editor of the *New York Times* noted in 2004, reporters often prefer to stand behind the appearance of objectivity rather than stand up for the truth. [101]

The other way that reporters manufacture news is by **framing** stories, that is, by interpreting them in ways that lead to evaluation. [102] Because people generally discount new ideas and embrace old, more familiar ones, officials and possibly the elite have a decisive advantage over their adversaries in framing international stories. The importance of framing is illustrated by the difference in the way the American media covered two air tragedies in the 1980s. The downing of a Korean passenger plane in 1983 over Soviet airspace was framed as a "murder." The downing of an Iranian passenger plane in the Persian Gulf in 1988 was framed as an "accident." [103] Although government information officers are adept at selling reporters a preferred story line, reporters may develop their own frame or script, especially if they have new or different information.

There are generally two kinds of framing: episodic and thematic. Episodic coverage usually involves concrete events such as a natural disaster or a terrorist attack. Thematic coverage refers "to policy debate, historical background, or possible political consequences." [104] Of course, reporters do not always have much choice as to what kind of story they write, but it is striking how infrequently they do choose to deal with thematic stories. For example, the media often prefer concrete events such as the destruction of the Old Bridge of Mostar to more abstract ones such as "the internal structure of the Bosnian political process or . . . Croatian policy." [105]

After all, by covering the destruction of the Old Bridge, the reporter can tell a story that all American audiences can relate to, whereas an effort to get at the real causes of the Balkan war could easily implicate some of the institutions, such as the IMF, that the United States is still relying on to control events in Eastern Europe.[106] In short, American reporters "amplified differences between Croats and Muslims, assumed conspiracies between Tudjman and Milosevic, and focused on rape and ethnic cleansing." All of these were dramatic stories, but there were other important stories that were equally crucial for the public to hear or read if it was going to understand the underlying causes of the war in Yugoslavia.[107]

Moreover, there is a tendency for the media to put a positive spin on what the United States is doing in conflict situations. This leads the media to focus on efforts to end the conflict rather than to cover the sources of conflict. It leads the audience to accept any arrangement offered in negotiations, regardless of whether it deals with the most important issues.

> Like fictional TV, the news represents dominant individuals and groups [the United States, NATO, and the EU] as performing positive actions. Subordinates [Muslims and Croats] are deviant and negative; conflict is the norm [rather than something whose causes need to be explored] and has specific functions [negotiations] to help the story along. News stories mediate the real using conventions, and reporters fill in local details for preconceived news stories.[108]

Most of this discussion has focused on reporters as intermediaries between the government and the public. But the relations between reporters and nongovernment leaders are also important in this regard. Since reporters are naturally suspicious of NGOs, it is particularly difficult for NGOs to deal with the routines of reporters.[109] NGOs are usually not on the reporter's beat. They are not normally considered objective sources. And so they often have to force gaps and contradictions on reporters as well as frame stories for them.

From this perspective it is instructive to look at the efforts of various NGOs in the 1980s to get their views on the conflicts in Central America covered by reporters. One group, Witness for Peace, which was profiled in

Chapter 13, sent Americans to Nicaragua to witness the fighting there. In order to capture media attention, this group had to schedule dramatic events such as "religious commissioning services to send off its first delegation" to Nicaragua and to create catchy phrases such as "human shields" to capture media attention. Then it had to contend with reporters' notions of objectivity and convince them to accept these witnesses as authoritative sources for what was actually taking place in Nicaragua. Only then would reporters for the mainstream media assemble stories in which they juxtaposed government statements with what these witnesses were saying about events in Nicaragua. "When the administration claimed human rights progress by the Salvadoran regime, the movement publicized its continuing, documented military and death-squad atrocities." [110]

Another group that struggled to get media attention in the 1980s was Pledge for Resistance, also profiled in Chapter 13. In 1986 alone, the leaders of the group "sustained seven months of protest that involved one thousand separate demonstrations and vigils in which some two thousand Pledge protesters were arrested." [111] Such large-scale actions are usually the only way that private citizens, such as the members of these two groups, can get the mainstream media's attention. But even though these individuals may be educated, intelligent, and thoughtful, they are not qualified in the minds of reporters to make authoritative statements about the war in Nicaragua. The media preferred to talk to them about their arrest rather than why they opposed the conflict.

Once such groups do get past the initial hurdles (newsworthiness and objectivity), they still have to come up with attractive ways of framing the issue so that journalists would have something to counter Reagan administration stories. These groups used at least four different frames to make events in Nicaragua understandable from their perspective: (1) El Salvador was another Vietnam, (2) the Reagan administration was botching diplomacy in the area, (3) America was doing things contrary to its culture, and (4) the United States was involved in imperialism. [112]

Because officials and the press are engaged in an interactive process, it is not easy for them to change their methods and procedures. This makes it incumbent on the consumers of international news to develop their own guidelines for reading, watching, or listening to the news. Generally speaking, consumers of international news must "recognize and discount the use of stereotypes, loaded descriptions, and standard plot formulas in the news." They also need to pay attention to stray facts. They need to recognize the signs of news control in action. And they need to be critical of factual claims that support only partisan positions. [113]

Conclusion

This chapter has shown how institutional elites and possibly the governing elite can influence foreign policy both by the role they play in policy planning and by their control over the media of communications. Policy planning provides the elite with a unique access and influence because it is a function that government generally performs badly. The media also provide a singular resource for the elite because they serve as the main intermediary between the government and the public.

Having now considered the role of both government and non-government institutions in the American foreign policy making process, it is time to reassess the question raised at the beginning of the text. What does all this portend for the relationship between democracy and foreign policy in America?

Key Concepts

beats   509
elite theory   485
framing   515
governing class   484
mainstream media   504
neoconservative   503
policy-planning network   491

polyarchy   499
routines of journalists   509
social register   484
standards for professional
  journalism   511
trilateralism   497

Suggested Readings

1. Ali, Tariq, editor. *Masters of the Universe? NATO's Balkan Crusade.* New York: Verso, 2000.

2. Entman, Robert M. *Projections of Power: Framing News, Public Opinion, and U.S. Foreign Policy.* Chicago: Chicago University Press, 2004.

3. Cavell, Colin S. *Exporting 'Made-In-America' Democracy: The National Endowment for Decmocracy and U.S. Foreign Policy.* Lanham, MD.: University Press of America, 2002.

4. Hess, Stephen. *International News and Foreign Correspondents.* Washington, D.C.: Brookings Institution, 1996.

5. Parmar, Inderjeet. *Think Tanks and Power in Foreign Policy: A Comparative Study of the Council on Foreign Relations and the Royal Institute of International Affairs, 1939–1945.* New York: Palgrave MacMillan, 2004.

6. Robinson, William. *Promoting Polyarchy: Globalization, US Intervention, and Hegemony.* New York: Cambridge University Press, 1996.

7. Wedel, Janine R. *Collision and Collusion: The Strange Case of Western Aid to Eastern Europe 1989–1998.* New York: St. Martin's Press, 1998.

CHAPTER 15

Democracy and Foreign Policy

A French observer of American democracy in the nineteenth century, Alexis de Tocqueville doubted that democracy was compatible with the exigencies of foreign policy. But America has largely been effective in foreign affairs in part *because* it is a democracy. In a rapidly changing world, American foreign policy has required cooperation with other countries, as well as the ability to hold its own in conflict. From this perspective the methods that have proven so useful in settling conflicts within the United States might be applied with equal vigor to its dealings with other countries. By turning democracy inside out, that is, using some of the methods employed inside the country to deal with some of the problems on the outside, Americans may find that democracy is more compatible with foreign policy than Tocqueville ever dreamed. In the picture above the finance ministers and central bank leaders of each of the G-7 countries and Russia, as well as the principals of leading world banks, meet in Washington, D.C. in 2005 to plan joint economic action at the global level.

NEARLY 175 YEARS AGO Alexis de Tocqueville, a visitor from France and early observer of the new republic, warned Americans that the requirements of democracy and foreign policy were quite different, and that their government might experience some difficulties in international affairs.[1] Although Tocqueville withheld final judgment, he felt at the time that the virtues of democracy had little to offer to those who must deal with the exigencies of foreign policy. This chapter assesses this judgment on the basis of the foregoing discussion of the history, substance, and processes of American foreign policy.

Tocqueville recognized that democracies might have many fine qualities. He was encouraged by the extent to which democratic governments might foster a more healthy economy, a more favorable public spirit, and a more stable system of laws, but Tocqueville knew that in his day governments regularly deceived one another through skillful and urbane diplomats and had to have the unity and patience to sustain unpopular policies. He feared that democracies might topple because they lacked such qualities. Thus the very things that he found so attractive about democracy in America might not be enough to sustain democratic governments in the end simply because they would have to deal with non-democratic countries in order to survive.

Now all these years later, the American democracy has not only survived, but it has become the world's only superpower. Did democratic methods of government have the kinds of consequences expected by Tocqueville? Did the international system place the kind of demands on the U.S. government that Tocqueville predicted? If so, did the American democracy learn to overcome or compensate for its democratic tendencies? Or did the international system itself change partly because of the influence of democratic regimes? These are some of the questions about democracy and foreign policy that were raised in the introduction to Part I and that will be answered in this concluding chapter.

Since foreign policy involves both domestic and international affairs, this issue will be explored at both levels. At the domestic level the questions are how some of the domestic factors the founders most feared—majoritarianism, factionalism, and elitism—have affected foreign policy in America and how the institutions they created to alleviate these dangers have worked out. At the international level the question is, how the attributes of a democratic foreign policy, namely the opportunity for dissent, responsiveness to public opinion, and openness have measured up to the requirements of foreign policy.

Different assumptions come into play at each level. At the domestic level there is rarely a clear separation between domestic and foreign policy. After all, there are few external threats that affect all domestic sectors of society in the same way. As a consequence, domestic political parties usually take different positions on foreign policy just as they do on domestic affairs. In this sense foreign policy, like domestic policy, involves compromises among different sectors of society. Under the pressures to compromise, issues are not likely to remain entirely separate. Decisions on one issue will depend at least in part on how other issues have been handled or will be handled.

Moreover, foreign policy at the domestic level is seldom entirely rational. At this level foreign policy must take into account a variety of domestic factors that have nothing to do with the international situation. For example, President Truman campaigned in 1948 on the basis of both cold war and domestic economic issues. Although the foreign policy of containment had been prescribed by that time, Truman had planned to keep defense expenditures down so that he could also pursue his Fair Deal domestic social programs. When he finally became convinced that defense expenditures needed to increase, however, he was not in a position to implement increases because both his budget advisor and his secretary of defense opposed increased defense expenditures.[2] Even after he had replaced these individuals, he was forced to abandon his domestic social programs and pass an Internal Security Act, which he despised, in order to get support for the military buildup.

Although the requirements of foreign policy provide a rationalization for efforts such as Truman's, each action requires a separate explanation. In each case these actions have to take into account the interests and ideas of a different set of groups and individuals. One cannot explain how each of these decisions was made without considering the domestic settings within which these groups and individuals function. That is why one needs so many different approaches to explain foreign policy from the standpoint of the domestic politics of foreign policy making.

Entirely different assumptions come into play at the international level. The international level involves the relationship between an entity, usually the government of a state, and other international actors. The state is assumed to be a coherent actor with a single set of preferences. The crucial question is not how the entity arrived at these preferences; rather, it is how to account for the outcomes of actions taken on behalf of these preferences. In short, one assumes that decisions are made on a rational basis.

As a result, the approach taken reflects the objective environment. If the international system is one in which the relevant others are enemies, as posited by the political philosopher Thomas Hobbes, then it is likely that one will rely on a realist approach. If it is a Lockean system in which relevant others are basically rivals, as described by the political philosopher John Locke, then one should probably employ a liberal approach. And if it is a system in which relevant others are essentially friends, as assumed by the political philosopher Immanuel Kant, one should rely more fully on a constructivist approach. Realists are preoccupied with power; liberals, with achievement; and idealists (constructivists), with social affiliation.

Because each of these approaches assumes a given preference ordering, the foreign policy actor would presumably employ means that are most likely to maximize its preferences or possibly minimize its costs (prospect theory). Since foreign policy outcomes depend on the interactions and relationships among two or more entities, great emphasis has to be placed on the perceptions of the preferences of relevant others. These perceptions are based both on a characterization of these others and on an appreciation of what kinds of actions will bring about what sorts of consequences in this setting. Although each approach assumes an objective environment, each recognizes the possibility that other entities may perceive that environment differently, and the differences in perception lead to a great deal of uncertainty.

The framework used in this book is uniquely suited for this kind of multilevel, multivariate analysis because its three dimensions can be employed both as the dependent variables in efforts to trace the effects of various domestic factors on foreign policy and as independent variables in efforts to trace the international consequences of a democratic foreign policy. At the domestic level, the three dimensions take into account both individual motives and the incentives built into the institutions of a society. At the level of individual motivations, the framework takes into account three basic needs or desires: power, achievement, and affiliation. At the organizational level, these motivations are incorporated into the design of institutions that serve the organizational functions of control, specialization, and coordination, respectively. Although power and control are most relevant on the security dimension, achievement and specialization on the prosperity dimension, and affiliation and coordination on the community dimension, all three dimensions need to be taken into account in every foreign policy.

Democratic and Undemocratic Sources of Foreign Policy

Part III examined the role of a range of actors in making foreign policy, including political leaders, foreign policy experts, small groups of top-level decision makers, the public, organized groups, and domestic elites. It also introduced the approaches used to explain the foreign policies associated with each of these actors: institutionalism, the organizational process model, the bureaucratic politics model, majoritarianism, pluralism, and elitism, respectively. To what extent do these various actors and approaches affect foreign policy in the United States?

Democratic Sources

This text distinguishes between three kinds of majorities: simple, pluralist, and deliberative. All three kinds of majorities are relevant as sources of foreign policy in a democracy.

Simple Majorities. As children of the Enlightenment, the founders wanted a government based on the participation of many individuals; but they were frankly suspicious of the general populace. So they limited participation to male citizens who owned property. Some modern commentators on democracy and foreign policy share the founders' fears of the general public. These individuals are referred to as traditionalists, and they include such notables as Walter Lippmann, the journalist, and George Kennan, the diplomat. Traditionalists raise two concerns about the general public's competency to participate in foreign affairs. First, they argue that the general public is so ignorant of foreign affairs that they should not be given a major say. Second, they contend that public views are so unstructured that they are unstable. Thus they argue that a simple majority of the population should determine the foreign policy of a country in only the most abstract way.

The most frequently cited example of public irrationality with respect to U.S. foreign policy occurred in the mid-1930s when President Franklin Roosevelt refused to take concrete steps to meet the rising danger in Europe because he felt constrained by an apparently isolationist public in the United States. Although it is true that Roosevelt bided his time in order to continue his domestic programs, during this period a majority of the American people actually supported involvement in foreign affairs, even though the isolationists were more vocal. By waiting to pursue a more proactive foreign policy, Roosevelt not only sustained support for his domestic programs but also discredited isolationism for at least the rest of the twentieth century, as the crisis in Europe intensified.

In fact, Roosevelt was not so much constrained by a simple majority as he was constrained by the pluralist majorities that the framers devised to prevent a tyranny of the majority. By dividing the government into distinct branches and then by requiring concurrent majorities from each of these parts, the framers tried to ensure that government policies were supported by a broad consensus of the public. But the closer the framers came to insisting on something approaching unanimity, the more they strengthened the position of minorities in the political system, because it became easier for minorities to prevent one or more of these concurrent majorities. This leads one to consider the composition of majorities.

Pluralist Majorities. So far the public has been treated as an undifferentiated mass of individuals. However, societies are organized into a myriad of informal and formal organizations. These organizations become increasingly important when one attempts to build extraordinary majorities because one must increasingly appeal to the special interests as well as the general interests of these organizations.

The danger lies in the nature of the organizations involved in the process. Informal organizations based on gender, class, and income seldom dictate specific foreign policies because these parallel publics are usually subject to cross-cutting influences. It is only when key leaders are able to use events to shape large-scale political movements that informal groups begin to have a significant effect on foreign policy. In contrast, formal organizations can exert an inordinate amount of influence on foreign policy decisions because at least some of the members of these organizations are prepared to act primarily in accord with their special interests. In short, the members of formal organizations are not as subject to cross-cutting influences as members of informal organizations.

Because formal organizations often represent narrow, fixed interests, they can develop exclusive influence in particular parts of the government. Such influences are most evident in those local constituencies where the members of formal organizations are most concentrated. But such influences are also possible in very large constituencies if formal organizations can convince elected or appointed officials that they control the balance of power in these constituencies.

If these organizations use their influence only to ensure that their particular interests are taken into account, then they can contribute to the search for a broader consensus. But these groups can sometimes achieve complete control over specific issues by gaining exclusive access to the congressional committees and administrative departments and agencies responsible for specific foreign policy issues. This results in "rule by minorities" or factionalism.

Unfortunately, some formal organizations appear to have undue influence on specific foreign policies in the United States. AIPAC's power in relation to Israel and some Middle East issues and CANF's power in relation to U.S. foreign policy toward Cuba are clear examples of group pressures. Although the inside strategies of these formal organizations are well-known, the outside strategies of other ideological groups such as the Committee on the Present Danger, Human Rights Watch, and the Sierra Club are also examples of group pressures. In addition, there are specific economic groups such as the Seven Sister oil companies, key banks, and even broad regional economic blocs that can exercise major influence on U.S. foreign policy.

What keeps these factions under control is the idea that there is a national interest that has precedence over these more parochial interests and ideas, and this national interest is defined in a consensus-building process that tries to take all these individual interests into account. When one party dominates the rest, this consensus-building process fails. Thus the leaders of society must continue to search for ways in which more general public interests can prevail.

Deliberative Majorities.   In recent years, some political scientists have come to the conclusion that it is possible to achieve concurrent majorities on foreign policy issues if political leaders will only respect the positions taken by a deliberative majority of the American people. These revisionists acknowledge that the public is often unable to name the persons or locate the places that are involved in foreign affairs, but this does not necessarily mean that they are incompetent to make foreign policy choices. For example, the public may be in a better position than those who got us involved in the Iraq war to decide when it is time to get out. As Miroslav Nincic argues, information is not the only factor that enters into making foreign policy decisions, and the explanatory contexts in which individuals put this information, their sentiments, and their aspirations are equally crucial.[3] The context includes the judgments individuals make about cause and effect relationships that are relevant to foreign policy and encompasses implicit theories about how the world works. Since everyone experiences life, everyone develops some understanding of this context.

Revisionists do not challenge the fact that the public often lacks information so much as they question the idea that the public's opinions on foreign policy are unreliable. Careful analyses of the CCFR data discussed throughout this text show that public opinion on foreign policy is not only stable but also is structured in much the same way as elite opinions are structured on those same foreign policies.[4] That means that the general public and foreign policy elites both put foreign policy issues in similar contexts. Of course, that does not mean that they necessarily reach the same conclusions.

Opinions on foreign policy also reflect the sentiments and aspirations of the specific individuals involved. The CCFR data also show that there are consistent differences in the stances that the general public and foreign policy elites take on specific foreign policies. For example, the general public is more likely than elites to believe that the purpose of foreign policy should be to strengthen the U.S. domestic economy. The public is also more likely than elites to believe that the United Nations should play an important role in American foreign policy. However, both the public and the elite are divided on these matters, and it would be difficult to prove that one position is better than another.

But public opinion in the form of a simple majority cannot be relied upon to guide the actual decisions of foreign policy makers as long as it differs markedly from political culture. Public opinion is what people themselves think about events; political culture is what people think others are thinking about those same events. The problem is that political culture usually trumps public opinion. So it is not enough to have majority opinion on one side because the opposite site may be able to invoke political culture in a way that undermines the majority opinion. That is why political leadership is so important in democratic foreign policy. Political leaders must be willing to interpret political culture in ways that will buttress, rather than cripple, public opinion.

Public interest or deliberative polling is particularly intriguing because it infers that the public might come to accept its opinions as consistent with political culture if given appropriate background information. The general lack of interest in public interest polling as opposed to traditional public opinion polling suggests that key elites are not that interested in working with the public to reinterpret its political culture. Until elites do so, minorities and elites will continue to undermine majority opinion.

Undemocratic Influences

Democratic sources of foreign policy are important because if they fail, there are always uniquely qualified individuals or groups waiting in the wings to take control of the country's foreign policy. The founders were most fearful that the republic would resort to the alternatives most common in other governments at the time, that is, rule by a monarchy or an aristocracy. They were determined to prevent either of these contingencies. But there were other possibilities, some foreseen and others not foreseen.

Military Takeovers.   The founders were particularly concerned about the possibility of a military takeover. They realized that the new government would face military threats to its security. Although they were quite conscious of such external threats, they felt that a large standing army was inimical to democracy. Consequently, they felt that the first line of defense should lie with the people themselves, providing for the "right of the people to keep and bear arms" in the Second Amendment to the Constitution. They also insisted that a militia be organized at the sub-state level. These constitutional safeguards have generally worked out quite well in laying the foundation for a civilian-based defense.

But eventually it became clear that a large peacetime military force would be necessary. The National Security Act of 1947 provided that this force should be under civilian control. However, the civilian secretaries of the service departments—army, air force, and navy—have never been as strong as the service chiefs. And the individual services continue to resist the efforts of secretaries of defense and the chairmen of the Joint Chiefs of Staff to exercise effective control over them.

Despite the constitutional and statutory constraints, the military is a potentially dominant factor in American society. President Eisenhower was one of the first to recognize the threat posed by the military-industrial complex in American society. U.S. military forces now absorb about 60 percent of the federal discretionary budget. Although threats to American security are more diffuse than they were before the end of the cold war, willingness to make sacrifices in order to deal with individual threats does not seem to have diminished that much. For example, there is support for a national missile defense system, even in the absence of major enemies and the requisite technologies.

Religious Elites. The framers were also cognizant of the potential danger posed by a religious elite. Those who fear that the religious right may be gaining too much influence in government have raised this danger in the wake of the 2004 election. President Bush, an avowed evangelical Christian, has facilitated the efforts of religious organizations to receive and dispense government assistance. However, the fact that the United States is a diverse religious society, plus the constitutionally mandated separation of church and state in America, has largely prevented any one religious group from gaining power. The same cannot be said for economic groups.

Capitalist Elites. The founders appeared less conscious of the dangers posed by economic elites. The fact that both economic and political liberalism emphasized individualism may have led them to see capitalism and democracy as largely complementary. The freedom of individuals to invest and consume were considered almost as important to the American way of life as the right to assemble and to vote. No special barriers were erected to protect American society from those who owned a dominant share of the economic resources of society.

In the latter part of the nineteenth century the inequalities of wealth under capitalism became so manifest that it became the overriding theme of one of the political parties—the Progressives. Some of the ideas of the Progressives were later used to mediate the relations between the rich and the poor in this country. Wealth not only became the primary measure of one's individual success in life but also provided the means necessary to influence an increasingly mass culture. Is there a danger that the social upper class could seek to govern America?

A growing number of capitalists are seeking major elective offices in the United States, and they have found other, more indirect ways of influencing foreign policy in America. The charitable foundations created by leading capitalists provided an ideal vehicle for promoting their views. By investing in think tanks, university institutes, and policy discussion groups they have found ways to identify individuals and ideas that would further their interests in the country's foreign policy. They also control the media of mass communications that play such a crucial role in a democracy. A number of wealthy families—the Roosevelts, Kennedys, and Bushes—have succeeded in gaining the highest office in the land; however, they must cater to a variety of congressional, regional, and sectoral interests in order to exercise that power.

Foreign Affairs Experts. Another group that was largely ignored by the founders were members of the foreign affairs bureaucracy. Initially this group was so small that it posed no particular threat to democratic government. Even now that the number of such experts is in the thousands, they both represent society as a whole and take an oath to support the U.S. Constitution.

But in trying to separate some of the unsavory aspects of politics from administration, bureaucracies have developed the capacity to act more or less autonomously. Considering that bureaucrats may actually make 99 percent of foreign policies, there is at least a hypothetical danger that these experts could make foreign policy choices that the majority of the public would reject. The primary danger is that these experts will follow their own SOPs and biases in making foreign policies rather than under-taking the new initiatives preferred by the party in power. For example, they may prefer to exercise unilateral diplomacy over multilateral diplomacy, support Europe over Asia, etc.

In order to deal with this kind of inflexibility the political leader have employed several measures. First, they have inserted an increasing number of political appointees between these foreign affairs experts and top decision makers. This layering at the upper levels of government may have become so prevalent that it substitutes political considerations for substantive expertise. The second method is to politicize the appointment of senior career officers in the foreign affairs bureaucracy so that these of-ficers can be depended upon to serve the interests of their political supe-riors. Of course, the primacy of politics in bureaucratic functioning gives rise to another danger.

Foreign Policy Advisors.   When conflicts of interest and discrepant ideas make it difficult for foreign affairs experts to make decisions at lower levels, these issues naturally rise to the top of the government. Such deci-sions are either worked out in interdepartmental committees under the watchful eyes of the White House or they go to the president and possibly Congress for decision. In many ways this is as it should be in a democracy because the people have elected the president and Congress.

However, the foreign policy decisions attributed to the president and Congress may actually be made by political appointees whose actions may be personally or ideologically motivated, rather than actions preferred by responsible, elected officials. One of the dangers at this level is that some of these individuals will take extreme measures to ensure the success of foreign policies that they assume to be favored by the president. For ex-ample, Henry Kissinger is widely known to have taken a number of ini-tiatives in arms control negotiations with the Soviets in 1971, which neither the president nor the State Department was fully aware of.[5] Kis-singer ultimately justified these independent actions on the grounds that he achieved the best possible results.

Although the threat of this elite arises from the potential that it will substitute its interests or ideas for those of the public on a more or less per-manent basis, anyone at the top could act in such ways. Moreover, such rogue actors would frequently blame democracy for their decisions. The ultimate remedy for these rogue actors is a free and independent press, although the press cannot do its job unless it is truly independent and unless members of the opposition party and the bureaucracy are prepared to speak out. This check on government also requires an alert and active citizenry.

So far, a wide range of domestic factors can influence foreign policy in a democracy. Problems can arise in conjunction with some of these democratic sources as well as undemocratic sources. Now it is time to consider the effects of democratic decision making on foreign policy outcomes at the international level.

Democratic Foreign Policy and International Outcomes

Democratic foreign policies are actions taken abroad that can be attributed to domestic factors associated with democratic rule rather than international factors. For example, the United States refused to annex Texas in 1836 because President Jackson realized that annexation would divide the Democratic Party in half. Southern Democrats supported annexation because Texas would join the Union as a slave state, but northern Democrats opposed bringing another slave state into the Union. Of course, Texans favored immediate annexation because they feared that Mexico would attempt to reestablish the status quo antebellum. So how do the domestic factors associated with democracy affect foreign policy outcomes?

This section assumes that a democratic foreign policy will have different outcomes depending on whether one lives in a Hobbesian, Lockean, or Kantian world. A Hobbesian world presumes outcomes will largely be determined by the security dilemma. A Lockean world assumes that outcomes will be determined by the free exchange of capital, goods, people, services, and technology. And a Kantian world assumes that outcomes will be determined by the acceptance of ideas.

Outcomes Implied By a Hobbesian World

Since Tocqueville assumed a Hobbesian world of rough and tumble politics where foreign policy actors must have unity of action, perseverance, and the ability to deceive others when necessary, the effect of the inverse features attributed to democracy—divisiveness, impulsiveness, and openness—will be discussed in this section. Does evidence show that these attributes of a democratic foreign policy are as detrimental to the country's interests as Tocqueville assumes?

Democratic Discord versus the Need for Unity in Foreign Policy.   Democratic government preserves the right of minorities to dissent. Although the founders may have underestimated the likelihood that differences over foreign policy would create havoc in the new government, differences among the leadership over how to deal with the French Revolution quickly emerged during Washington's administration. Such differences have plagued U.S. leaders throughout American history. For example, President Woodrow Wilson initially feared that if America entered the First World War, it would divide the country.[6]

However, the need for unity of action is not equally imperative on all occasions. The distinction between three kinds of foreign policy issues is key to determining when unity is imperative: crisis policies, strategic policies, and regular policies. The historical record suggests that the unity of democratic foreign policies varies, depending on the kind of issue.

Crisis foreign policies allow no time to develop new resources in order to meet a discrete international threat. Historical examples show that the opposition party and Congress have been reluctant to oppose presidential initiatives in a crisis. If the opposition party cannot give bipartisan support in a crisis, it usually accepts a co-partisan decision in which it reluctantly supports the president at the last minute. This is precisely what the Republican opposition chose to do in Bosnia in 1995 and in Kosovo in 1999, and what the Democratic opposition chose to do in Iraq in 2003. Thus in crisis situations U.S. foreign policy is generally unified.

The case is somewhat different with strategic foreign policies because there is time to develop new resources to deal with discrete international threats to American interests. In these cases the parties usually remain divided until they work out a solution. Although it may take several years to resolve strategic issues, once settled, the United States can usually count on pursuing a united policy. Although such divisions occurred at the beginning of the First and Second World Wars, the parties arrived at a common bipartisan or cross-partisan position in both situations. Of course, the parties could not reach similar agreements during the reassessment of the containment policy in the 1970s. In the cases of Vietnam and Nicaragua, Congress and the public ultimately forced a reluctant president to sue for peace. But before concluding that the failure to reach agreement was a fault of democracy, consider that these particular foreign policies were arguably dubious, and involvement should have been subject to debate regardless of the form of government. Indeed, public division on such issues may help democracies identify questionable foreign policies before it is too late to correct them. (Perhaps the real issue with Iraq in 2003 was that the Bush administration treated Iraq as a crisis situation rather than a strategic situation.)

Finally, regular foreign policies are those that involve no immediate threat. Such policies would include trade, foreign aid, defense expenditures, immigration, and regular diplomatic expenditures. Since regular policies are not usually developed in relation to a specific threat, they are often decided on the bases of tentative compromises only to be raised again at the next real opportunity. The failure of democracies to address these recurrent issues may be a serious weakness of democracy. For example, the failure of the United States to support state-building by the United Nations in non-crisis periods or to appropriate sufficient funds to run its own diplomatic missions may have serious long-term consequences for American diplomacy.

But domestic differences over foreign policies are not the only problem that Tocqueville attributes to democracy. Since democracies give minorities a chance to overtake majorities, the prospect for turnover in democratic leadership is fairly high. This raises the question of whether democracies have the ability to persevere in the pursuit of long-term foreign policy goals.

Changes in Democratic Leadership versus the Need for Perseverance in Foreign Policy. Many of the most important goals of foreign policy involve long-term objectives.[7] If a democratic country cannot persevere in difficult undertakings, then it may have little success in reaching those important goals. For example, the United States needs to maintain good relations with key countries on the Eurasian continent. The failure to do so may deprive this country of key resources when they are most needed. Yet it is tempting for democracies to overlook these long-term requirements of foreign policy when specific countries such as Iran violate the public's sense of comity.

With elections for Congress every two years and the president every four years, there are frequent opportunities for candidates to raise foreign policy issues. Indeed, partisan differences on foreign policy have been a feature of every presidential election since World War II.[8] Of course, these differences can also manifest themselves between elections. For example, on June 5, 2001, Senator James M. Jeffords of Vermont decided to quit the Republican Party. That gave the Democrats control of the Senate, including the chairmanship of all the relevant foreign affairs committees.

But even when elections and other factors do not affect party control, they can influence foreign policy. For one thing, electoral contests usually have a negative effect on foreign policy discourse. They make foreign policy seem more combative than it would otherwise be. The propensity of both incumbents and challengers to seek voter support by emphasizing international dangers is well known. During the cold war it was customary for candidates to seek votes using communist scare tactics. For example, it is no accident that most disarmament agreements were reached in the third rather than the first year of presidential terms.[9]

Moreover, when a change in political leadership does occur, it gives winning candidates the incentive to introduce innovations rather than to sustain existing foreign policies. Since the next election is only two to four years away, winning candidates are tempted to think in terms of the short run. For example, there is less to be gained by sticking with a modestly successful aid project started by one's predecessor than there is in initiating a project of one's own. As a consequence, foreign policy initiatives are both more common and more prized than foreign policy completions. In order to appreciate the effects of the election factor in a democratic foreign policy, one needs to look at the results from the standpoint of other states. Since diplomacy often involves pursuing long-term objectives across many different administrations, the propensity of democratic governments to emphasize differences between states and to take new initiatives rather than follow through on tested policies is disquieting. For example, North Korea is a very isolated country. If it is going to normalize its relations with the United States and Japan to say nothing of South Korea, then it needs to feel that any steps it takes in that direction are meaningful. In fact, one might expect the North Koreans to test that proposition periodically. If the United States itself publicly reexamines its foreign policy toward North Korea largely for domestic partisan reasons, then U.S. foreign policy actors lose opportunities to assure that government and its people that they can trust the United States.

This suggests that a democratic diplomacy is handicapped at least in relation to enemy states because each new administration needs to be convinced that it is pursuing the proper course. Such a handicap might be minimized if democratic diplomacy could reexamine its foreign policies in private. However, that is often not possible, especially if the new party is making this reassessment largely for domestic political reasons.

On the other hand, the United States has shown itself capable of undertaking difficult foreign policies over long periods of time. Perhaps the best of example of this is the containment policy itself. But in order to get public support for the containment policy the Truman administration probably oversold it to the American public. As a result, it is still an open question whether the United States has made the necessary adjustments now that the cold war is over.

Openness versus the Need for Deception and Covert Action in Foreign Policy. There is little doubt that access to information is important in a democracy. Freedom of speech, press, and assembly are vital to any system that requires the public to play a deliberative role in government. The minority could hardly replace the majority if it could not disclose the shortcomings of majority foreign policies. But this begs the question if deception, misrepresentation, and covert activities are necessary for the conduct of foreign policy.

When a country is engaged in armed conflict, many believe that even a democratic government should be allowed either to withhold information from the public altogether or to disguise it in such a way that that information will not endanger American lives. For example, in 1991 the Bush administration controlled much of the military and political information available to the public on the Persian Gulf War. The problem with government censorship, though, is that the real purpose for controlling this information is often to thwart dissent rather than to protect American lives. The issue of censorship becomes even more difficult when American lives are not immediately at stake.

Generally the public and Congress give the administration some latitude in determining information policies, but they must ultimately hold the administration responsible for any deception or misrepresentation that cannot later be justified. One of the persistent questions during the 2004 campaign was whether or not the Bush administration purposively misled the public and the press about the situation in Iraq both before and after the war. But secrecy is not the only kind of action considered unacceptable in a democracy. There are a number of other foreign policy actions that are thought to be inconsistent with democratic governance, such as covert intelligence operations.

At various times throughout American history the government has engaged in illicit activities abroad. Such acts undermine the sense of fair play that is so important in a democracy. Ironically, some covert actions may be more damaging in a democracy than they would be in other forms of government because they violate democratic rules. For example, the efforts of the National Endowment for Democracy to promote democracy by undemocratic means, that is, by making large amounts of money available to favored candidates, damaging out-of-favor candidates, or otherwise fixing foreign elections fall in this category.

If such actions are really necessary to an effective foreign policy, then democratic government might be at a disadvantage. But there is no good evidence that such measures are essential or successful. Although the U.S. intelligence agencies have claimed successful operations in Iran in 1953 and Guatemala in 1954, these actions have clearly backfired in the long run.

Given some of the constraints that simple majorities and pluralist majorities place on foreign policy in a democracy, it is easy to see why Tocqueville was concerned. But these problems are least severe in the crisis situations envisaged in a Hobbesian world where the United States has demonstrated a capacity for unity, perseverance, and secrecy and most problematic with respect to regular policies in a Lockean or Kantian world, which emphasize more openness.

Outcomes Implied By a Lockean World

Democracy is obviously more at home in a Lockean world in which prosperity is as important as security. Tocqueville recognized that democratic government had the ability to promote economic growth because liberal democracy embraces capitalism. After declaring its independence, the first act of the Continental Congress was to establish a model treaty for the purpose of establishing free trade with other states. In over two and a quarter centuries since that time, the United States has not only become the world's strongest economy but also a leading advocate of free trade in the world.

Democracy versus Globalization.   As the world's strongest state, it is not surprising that the United States favors an open world market. Early in the cold war, the U.S. economy provided the engine for development for former industrialized areas, with programs such as the Marshall Plan. Even though U.S. trade and investment in developing countries was limited, the American example served as a beacon of hope to non-industrialized areas of the world as well.

The desire on the part of people throughout the world to share the fruits of an American-dominated global market has been the paramount strength of American diplomacy since World War II. The power of the American economy both in a physical and symbolic sense could not be clearer than in the desire of former communist states to emulate both its economic and political system. The peoples of the communist and non-industrial areas of the world have literally voted with their feet to show their preference for a western-style economy.

If globalization is defined as the free exchange of people, goods, services, and money across international borders, then globalization has created unprecedented opportunities for American musicians, artists, writers, athletes, and entrepreneurs. Whether the growth and standardization that accompany globalization will be the tide that lifts all boats will largely depend on the ability of democratic forms of governance to ensure growth with equity.

Democracy versus Global Inequality.   The danger of globalization is that everyone may not share its benefits. If globalization begets the exploitation of workers, of the environment, and of social and cultural values, then it will lead to the kind of global inequality that will invite violence in the form of war and revolution.

In order to prevent such outcomes the international community must find ways to ensure equitable growth. But this requires political leaders around the world to find ways to regulate the world market. Many argue that new forms of governance must emerge at the global level in order to ensure global equitability. Yet the only democratic forms we know are at the state level, and the governments of states have been reluctant to surrender their democratic sovereignty to institutions at a higher level.

In the face of this deadlock at the inter-governmental level, international nongovernmental organizations (INGOs) provide one way of releasing the tension. Some believe that INGOs are already beginning to fill the void of governance at the global level. But if these INGOs are going to deal effectively with issues of equitable growth, they must reform themselves. After all, these organizations cannot help to make the global system more equitable until they themselves have become democratized. Thus the challenge of the future in foreign policy is to make international relations more democratic.

Outcomes Implied By a Kantian World

Immanuel Kant best captures the vision of peace with justice. Kant built his conception of "perpetual peace" on three definitive precepts. The first precept envisaged a number of liberal republics governed by civil constitutions. The second precept provided that these republics would establish a liberal peace among themselves by extending the methods used internally to their mutual relationships. And the third precept foresaw these liberal republics embracing the cosmopolitan law of "universal hospitality" in their relations with all other states.[10] Each of these precepts defined a step in the progression toward a democratic peace.

Democracy versus the Democratic Peace.   The idea of a democratic peace is one of the contemporary visions for the community of democratic states in today's world. But for Kant this was not a mere hope, it was inevitable.[11] In effect Kant argued that the moral commitments and material incentives embraced by these three precepts would produce "perpetual peace." Although Kant thought that political leaders would persuade themselves to embrace the democratic peace, he did not base his expectations on the assumption that men were "angels" rather than "devils." Kant believed that each conflict—even the most violent of conflicts—would teach people that their only salvation would come from reaching mutually acceptable, joint actions with others.

According to Kant, the worst the conflict, the more graphic the lesson. That lesson is that democracy must be turned inside out. That is, the rules, norms, and laws that democracies employ in their internal affairs must be utilized in their relations with others; in other words, multilateralism. Of course, this requires a renunciation of the state as an exclusive body of citizens. It requires a cosmopolitan acceptance of others as persons with equal rights.

But simply breaking down the old walls of sovereignty will not automatically ensure peace and justice. The world does not necessarily become a more peaceful place simply because we consent to deal with everyone else on the basis of equality. The fact is that the dilemmas faced by the founders in creating a union of states is simply returning to today's world in a new form.

Democracy versus Injustice.   Equal participation in global governance cannot by itself ensure that all parties will feel that they are being justly treated. Simple majoritarianism at whatever level does not ensure either justice or peace. In effect it simply converts foreign policy into domestic politics. In order to pursue peace and justice, people must put human rights—a human interest—and the common good—a global interest—ahead of whatever partisan or partial interests often masquerade as the national interest. Peace and justice will depend on our ability to reconstruct many of the ideas and institutions that now define what some people call reality.

Many questions still remain about how those human interests can best be served. What measures can be taken to ensure equity as well as growth? How can one offer incentives without permitting exploitation? What role does the environment play in this equation? What role does science or religion play?

Chapter 1 defines foreign policy as the intersection of domestic and international politics. That recipe was based on the supposition that there was something different about these two spheres of politics. Now we have come to understand that difference is only manifest in the Hobbesian world. In many ways, the Lockean world is a halfway house between this Hobbesian world and the Kantian world, because both conflict and cooperation are possible. In the Kantian world, domestic and foreign policies are the same. Kant gives us some hope because there is only one politics, but governance in that unitary system is still subject to the vagaries of human motivation.

Suggested Readings:

1. Barrus, Roger M., John H. Eastby, Joseph H. Lane Jr., David E. Marion, and James D. Pantus. *The Deconstitutionalization of America: The Forgotten Frailties of Democratic Rule.* Lanham, MD: Lexington Books, 2004.

2. Curtis, Alan, ed. *Patriotism, Democracy, and Common Sense: Restoring America's Promise at Home and Abroad.* New York: Rowman and Littlefield, 2004.

3. Moore, John Norton: *Solving the War Puzzle: Beyond the Democratic Peace.* Durham: Carolina Academic Press, 2004.

4. Nincic, Miroslav. *Democracy and Foreign Policy: The Fallacy of Political Realism.* New York: Columbia University Press, 1992.

Notes

Chapter 1

1. Duelfer Report, www.cia.gov/cia/reports/iraq_wmd_2004/September 30, 2004.
2. Alexander Wendt, *Social Theory of International Politics* (Cambridge: Cambridge University Press, 1999), 219.
3. Ibid., 23.
4. Alexander Wendt's description of these three approaches is used here because it is easier to incorporate the idealist approach if all three approaches are described in terms of ideas. Wendt, *Social Theory,* 260, 279, 298.
5. Ibid., 260.
6. Hans J. Morgenthau, *Politics among Nations: The Struggle for Power and Peace,* rev. Kenneth W. Thompson (New York: Knopf, 1993).
7. Kenneth N. Waltz, *Theory of International Politics* (New York: Random House, 1979); John J. Mearsheimer, *The Tragedy of Great Power Politics* (New York: Norton, 2001).
8. Robert O. Keohane and Joseph S. Nye, *Power and Interdependence,* 3d ed. (New York: Longman, 2001).
9. Peter J. Katzenstein, *The Culture of National Security: Norms and Identity in World Politics* (New York: Columbia University Press, 1996), 19.
10. Wendt, *Social Theory,* 298–299.
11. Martha Finnemore, *National Interests in International Society* (Ithaca: Cornell University Press, 1996), 22.
12. Ronald L. Jepperson et al., "Norms, Identity, and Culture in National Security," in *The Culture of National Security: Norms and Identity in World Politics,* ed. Peter J. Katzenstein (New York: Columbia University Press, 1996), 59.
13. This is the term employed by Jonathan Mercer to describe neo-classical economic, behaviorist, and rational choice theories of rationality. See Jonathan Mercer, "Rationality and Psychology in International Politics," *International Organization* 59, no.1 (Winter 2005): 77–106.
14. Two of the leading classics in this genre of research are: Kenneth Boulding, *Conflict and Defense: A General Theory* (New York: Harper and Row, 1963) and Thomas Schelling, *Strategy of Conflict* (Cambridge: Harvard University Press, 1960). Some rational choice scholars are beginning to pay more attention to preferences and perceptions. For example, Bruce Bueno de Mesquita features preferences and perceptions as well as power in his *Principles of International Politics: People's Power, Preferences, and Perceptions,* 3d ed. (Washington, D.C.: CQ Press, 2005).
15. Harold Sprout and Margaret Sprout, *An Ecological Paradigm for the Study of International Politics,* Research Monograph No. 30 (Princeton: Princeton University Center of International Studies, 1968), 33–34.
16. Graham Allison and Philip Zelikow, *Essence of Decision: Explaining the Cuban Missile Crisis,* 2d ed. (New York: Longman, 1999), 109–120.
17. Sprout and Sprout, *An Ecological Paradigm.*

18. Susan T. Fiske and Shelley E. Taylor, *Social Cognition*, 2d ed. (New York: McGraw-Hill, 1991), 5.

19. David G. Winter, "Authoritarianism and Perceiving the Invasion of Iraq as a 'Just War' " (paper delivered at the annual conference of the International Society of Political Psychology, Lund, Sweden, 2004).

20. See Henry A. Murray, *Explorations in Personality* (New York: Oxford University Press, 1983); and David C. McClelland, *Human Motivation* (Cambridge: Cambridge University Press, 1987). Also see Richard W. Cottam, *Foreign Policy Motivation: A General Theory and a Case Study* (Pittsburgh: University of Pittsburgh Press, 1977); David G. Winter, "Leader Appeal, Leader Performance, and the Motive Profiles of Leaders and Followers: A Study of American Presidents and Elections," *Journal of Personality and Social Psychology* 52 (1987): 196–202; Margaret G. Hermann and Thomas Preston, "Presidents, Advisers, and Foreign Policy: The Effect of Leadership Style on Executive Arrangements," *Political Psychology* 15, no. 1 (1994); and Jonathan W. Keller, "Leadership Style, Regime Type, and Foreign Policy Crisis Behavior: A Contingent Monadic Peace?" *International Studies Quarterly* 49, no. 2 (June 2005).

21. Russell G. Geen, *Human Motivation: A Social Psychological Approach* (Pacific Grove, Calif.: Brooks-Cole, 1995), 71.

22. Kenneth Waltz, *Theory of International Politics*. Also see Joseph M. Grieco, "Absolute and Relative Gains in International Relations Theory," *International Organization* 42, no. 3 (1988): 485–507; and Jonathan Mercer, "Anarchy and Identity," *International Organization* 49, no. 2 (1995): 229–252.

23. Barbara Koremenos, Charles Lipson, and Duncan Snidal, "The Rational Design of International Institutions," *International Organization*, 5, no. 4 (Autumn 2001): 761–799.

24. See Craig Parsons, "Showing Ideas as Causes: The Origins of the European Union," *International Organization* 56, no. 1 (Winter 2002): 47–84; and Amitav Acharya, "How Ideas Spread: Whose Norms Matter? Norm Localization and Institutional Change in Asian Regionalism," *International Organization* 58 (Spring 2004): 239–275.

25. John E. Reilly, *American Public Opinion and U.S. Foreign Policy* (Chicago: Chicago Council on Foreign Relations, 1975, 1979, 1983, 1987, 1991, 1995, 1999, 2003). The responses to the questions asked in 1998 from 1974 through 1998 are shown in Chapters 12 and 13.

26. The 2004 data are based on a computer survey. See *Global Views 2004* (Chicago: Chicago Council on Foreign Relations, 2004).

27. Factor analysis is a form of analysis that allows social scientists to group questions by showing which questions were answered by individuals in the same way in the aggregate. The 1974–1986 factor analyses are found in William O. Chittick, Keith R. Billingsley and Rick Travis, "A Three-Dimensional Model of American Foreign Beliefs," *International Studies Quarterly* 39 (1995): 313–331; the 1994 factor analyses are included in William O. Chittick and Annette Freyberg-Inan, "The Impact of Basic Motivation on Foreign Policy Opinions Concerning the Use of Force," in *Public Opinion and the International Use of Force*, eds. Philip Everts and Pierangelo Isernia (London: Routledge, 2001) 31–56; and the 1998 factor analysis is included in William O. Chittick and Keith R. Billingsley, "Alpha and Gamma Changes in American Foreign Policy Beliefs" (paper delivered at the 1999 annual meeting of the American Political Science Association in Atlanta). [The factor analysis of the 2004 data is included in the CD-Rom.]

28. Tara E. Santmire, "The Characteristics of Multilateralism as a Link between States" (paper presented at the annual meeting of the International Studies Association, San Diego, 1996).

29. The United States specifically formed the Contact Group to provide a forum in which Russia could contribute to the discussion of issues relating to the former Yugoslavia. Its members are Britain, France, Germany, Italy, Russia, and the United States.

30. The question dealing with democratic government seems to be more in line with this ideological interpretation of the security domain.
31. Jan Willem Honig and Norbert Both, *Srebrenica: Record of a War Crime* (New York: Penguin Books, 1997), 86.
32. Richard Holbrooke, *To End a War* (New York: Random House, 1998), 219–222.
33. See Chittick and Billingsley, "Alpha and Gamma Changes." An analysis of the 2004 data is included in the CD-Rom.
34. This process is briefly described in the CD-Rom.

Part I

1. James G. March and Johan P. Olsen, *Rediscovering Institutions: The Organizational Basis of Politics* (New York: Free Press, 1989), 143–158.
2. Alexis de Tocqueville, *Democracy in America,* ed. J. P. Mayer (New York: Harper and Row, 1966), 226–230.
3. Tocqueville, *Democracy in America,* 229.

Chapter 2

1. Mark V. Kauppi and Paul R. Viotti, *The Global Philosophers: World Politics in Western Thought* (New York: Maxwell, Macmillan Books, 1992), 126–127.
2. This chapter is primarily based on the following accounts of American history: Thomas A. Bailey, *A Diplomatic History of the American People* (New York: Appleton-Century-Crofts, 1974); John Catanzariti, ed., *The Papers of Thomas Jefferson,* vol. 25, *1 January to 10 May 1973* (Princeton: Princeton University Press, 1992); Alexander DeConde, *A History of American Foreign Policy,* vol. I (New York: Scribner's, 1978); Robert B. Ekelund Jr. and Robert D. Tollison, *Politicized Economies: Monarchy, Monopoly, and Mercantilism* (College Station: Texas A&M University Press, 1997); Thomas Fleming, *The Man Who Dared the Lightening: A New Look at Benjamin Franklin* (New York: Morrow, 1971); Felix Gilbert, *The Farewell Address: Ideas of Early American Foreign Policy* (Princeton: Princeton University Press, 1961); Michael F. Holt, *Political Parties and American Political Development: From the Age of Jackson to the Age of Lincoln* (Baton Rouge: Louisiana State University, 1992); Michael F. Holt, *The Fate of Their Country: Politicians, Slavery Extension, and the Coming of the Civil War* (New York: Hill and Wang, 2004); Lawrence S. Kaplan, *Colonies into Nation: American Diplomacy, 1763–1801* (New York: Macmillan, 1972); Walter LaFeber, *The American Age: United States Foreign Policy at Home and Abroad,* 2d ed. (New York: Norton, 1994); Robert Roswell Palmer and Joel Colton, *A History of the Modern World,* 7th ed. (New York: Knopf, 1995), 69; Harold T. Parker and Marvin L. Brown Jr., *Major Themes in Modern European History: An Invitation to Inquiry and Reflection,* vol. I, *The Institution of the State,* vol. II, *The Institution of Liberty* (Durham: Moore Publishing, 1974); Merrill D. Peterson, ed., *The Portable Thomas Jefferson* (New York: Penguin, 1975); Harold C. Syrett, ed., *The Papers of Alexander Hamilton,* vol. 14, *February 1793–June 1793,* vol. 16, *February 1794–July 1794* (New York: Columbia University Press, 1972); Buchanan P. Thomson, *Spain: Forgotten Ally of the American Revolution* (North Quincy, Mass.: Christopher Publishing House, 1976); Robert W. Tucker, "The Jefferson Legacy in American Foreign Policy," in *Economy, Diplomacy and Statecraft,* Colorado College Studies No. 27, ed. Timothy Fuller (Colorado Springs: Colorado College, 1988); Robert W. Tucker and David C. Hendrickson, *The Fall of the First British Empire* (Baltimore: Johns Hopkins University Press, 1982); Stephan Viljoen, *Economic Systems in World History* (New York: Longman, 1974); Gary M. Walton, "The Colonial Economy," Diane Lindstrom, "Domestic Trade and Regional Specialization," Gerald Gunderson, "Slavery," James F. Shepard, "Economy from the Revolution to 1815," Wayne D. Rassmussen, "Agriculture," Morton Rothstein, "Foreign

Trade," Richard A. Easterlin, "Population," and Harold D. Woodman," Economy from 1815–1865," in *Encyclopedia of American Economic History*, vol. I, ed. Glenn Porter (New York: Scribner's, 1980); and Carl Ubbelohde, *The American Colonies and the British Empire, 1607–1763*, 2d ed. (Arlington Heights: Harlan Davidson, 1979).

3. Parker and Brown, *Major Themes,*1: 39.
4. Gilbert, *Farewell Address*, 96.
5. The use of the gender-specific terminology in this section is intentional. Extension of these rights to women was not even discussed, let alone granted, until more than a century later.
6. Parker and Brown, *Major Themes*, 2: 301.
7. The names of these French philosophers—Gabriel Bonnot de Mably, Victor de Riquetti Mirabeau, and Guillaume Thomas François Raynal—are not well known today.
8. Gilbert, *Farewell Address*, 64–65.
9. Parker and Brown, *Major Themes*, 1: 154–155.
10. The government organization established to conduct relations with the American colonies was the Board of Trade.
11. Gilbert, *Farewell Address*, 226.
12. Parker and Brown, *Major Themes*, 1: 222–225.
13. Ibid., 330.
14. Ubbelohde, *American Colonies*, 93.
15. Ibid.
16. All three countries provided money and supplies. France sent George Washington troops, and the French navy provided essential help in bottling up the British at Yorktown. Spain provided assistance to George Rogers Clark in the west and helped to take Pensacola.
17. France recognized the new government in 1778, the Dutch in 1782, and Morocco in 1787.
18. Spain did not formally recognize the American government at this time, because it was trying to retrieve Gibraltar from the British.
19. Walton, "Colonial Economy," 42.
20. After the revolution, the republican government in France quickly fell into disarray and came under siege by royalist forces. In 1793 Napoleon Bonaparte, an officer in the French army, led French forces to a decisive victory over the British and was acclaimed as a hero. Returning to Paris in 1799, he overthrew the struggling republican government and established himself as an emperor with dictatorial powers. He managed to unify France and bring it some domestic peace, but wars with Britain and other European countries persisted until his empire collapsed in 1814.
21. Syrett, *Papers of Alexander Hamilton*, vol. 16, *February 1794–July 1794*, 270.
22. Syrett, *Papers of Alexander Hamilton*, vol. 14, *February 1793–June 1793*, 386.
23. Catanzariti, *Papers of Thomas Jefferson*, 25: 615 (italics in original).
24. It is important to remember that the original Republican Party, espousing the Jeffersonian philosophy, was almost the exact ideological opposite of the modern Republican Party. Today's Democrats are the more natural philosophical descendants of Jefferson and Madison, and today's Republicans are the heirs of Hamilton.
25. Bailey, *Diplomatic History*, 94–95.
26. Woodman, "Economy from 1815–1865," 68.
27. Lindstrom, "Domestic Trade," 269.
28. James E. Lewis Jr., *John Quincy Adams: Policymaker for the Union* (Wilmington, Del.: Scholarly Resources Inc., 2001), 91.
29. Cited in LaFeber, *American Age*, 94–95.
30. Americans did not necessarily view the Pacific Ocean as a stopping point but "thought of Asia as the Far West, a natural extension of their movement across the continent." LaFeber, *American Age*, 101. The victories against Mexico also inspired the "All Mexico

Movement," which envisioned taking over the entire country as a "'civilizing mission' to rescue [Mexico] from anarchy." Bailey, *Diplomatic History*, 264.

31. LaFeber, *American Age*, 95.

32. Many historians now suspect that Polk deliberately provoked the war. Although there is no hard evidence of deliberate provocation, historians point to the obviously risky act of posting troops so close to the Rio Grande and the perfectly timed announcement of casualties, not to mention the extremely fortuitous presence of troops in San Diego, ready to fight on the California front. See LaFeber, *American Age*, 110–112.

33. Although coercion is usually associated with domination, Adams sought domination through diplomacy because he feared both the internal and external repercussions of rapid expansion.

34. See *Dred Scott v. Sanford* 60 U.S. (19 How.) 393 (1857). The court ruled that blacks could never become citizens of the United States and held that the Missouri Compromise (and by implication other congressional acts involving the extension of slavery) was unconstitutional.

35. See LaFeber, *American Age* 134–135.

36. Bailey, *Diplomatic History* 317.

37. Also, Napoleon III coveted North American land and viewed a divided United States as one more easily conquered in his bid for territory in North America.

38. Quoted in Holt, *Political Parties*, 331.

Chapter 3

1. This chapter is primarily based on the following accounts of American history: Robert Beisner, *From the Old Diplomacy to the New, 1865–1900*, 2d ed. (Arlington Heights, Ill.: Harlan Davidson, 1986); Wayne S. Cole, *Determinism and American Foreign Relations during the Franklin D. Roosevelt Era* (Lanham, Md.: University Press of America, 1995); Wayne S. Cole, *America First: The Battle Against Intervention, 1940–1941* (Madison: University of Wisconsin Press, 1953); Wayne S. Cole, *An Interpretive History of American Foreign Relations* (Homewood, Ill.: Dorsey Press, 1968); Wayne S. Cole, *Roosevelt and the Isolationists: 1932–1945* (Lincoln: University of Nebraska Press, 1983); Brian P. Damiani, *Advocates of Empire: William McKinley, the Senate and American Expansion, 1898–1899* (New York: Garland Publishing, 1985); Alexander DeConde, *A History of American Foreign Policy,* vol. 1, 3d ed. (New York: Scribner's, 1978); John Dobson, *Reticent Expansionism: The Foreign Policy of William McKinley* (Pittsburgh: Duquesne University Press, 1988); Aaron L. Friedberg, *The Weary Titan: Britain and the Experience of Relative Decline, 1895–1905* (Princeton: Princeton University Press, 1988); Manfred Jonas, *Isolationism in America, 1935–1941* (Ithaca: Cornell University Press, 1966); Thomas J. Knock, *To End All Wars: Woodrow Wilson and the Quest for a New World Order* (New York: Oxford University Press, 1992); Alan M. Kraut, *The Huddled Masses: The Immigrant in American Society, 1880–1921* (Arlington Heights, Ill.: Harlan Davidson, 1982); Walter LaFeber, *A History of American Foreign Policy,* vol. 1, 3d ed. (New York: Scribner's, 1978); Harold T. Parker and Marvin L. Brown Jr., *Major Themes in Modern European History: An Invitation to Inquiry and Reflection,* vol. 2 (Durham, N.C.: Moore Publishing, 1974); John Wesley Powell, *Report on the Lands of the Arid Region of the United States,* ed. Wallace Stegner (Cambridge: Harvard University Press, 1962); Harold and Margaret Sprout, *The Rise of American Naval Power, 1776–1918,* (Princeton: Princeton University Press, 1939); Randall L. Schweller, *Deadly Imbalances: Tripolarity and Hitler's Strategy of World Conquest* (New York: Columbia University Press, 1998); Betty Miller Unterberger, "The United States and National Self-Determination: A Wilsonian Perspective," *Presidential Studies Quarterly* 26 (1996); Philip Weeks, *Farewell My Nation: The American Indian and the United States, 1820–1890* (Arlington Heights, Ill.: Harlan Davidson, 1990); David M. Wrobel, *The End of American Exceptionalism: Frontier Anx-*

iety from the Old West to the New Deal (Lawrence, Kan.: University of Kan. Press, 1993); Fareed Zakaria, *From Wealth to Power: The Unusual Origins of America's World Role* (Princeton: Princeton University Press, 1998); Byrd L. Jones, "Government Management of the Economy," Arthur M. Johnson, "Economy Since 1914," Diane Lindstrom, "Domestic Trade and Regional Specialization," Albro Martin, "Economy from Reconstruction to 1914," Wayne D. Rasmussen, "Agriculture," and Paul Uselding, "Manufacturing," in *The Encyclopedia of American Economic History*, vol. 2., ed. Glenn Porter (New York: Scribner's, 1980).

2. Liberalism here refers to political beliefs such as individual rights and limited government.

3. The Tsar's action occurred one year before President Abraham Lincoln issued the Emancipation Proclamation in 1862.

4. Schweller, *Deadly Imbalances*, 17.

5. Ibid., 24–25.

6. Wayne D. Rasmussen, "Agriculture," in *The Encyclopedia of American Economic History*, vol. I, ed. Glenn Porter (New York: Scribner's, 1980) 352–355.

7. Paul Uselding, "Manufacturing," in *The Encyclopedia of American Economic History*, vol. I, ed. Glenn Porter (New York: Scribner's, 1980), 4, 409–410.

8. Rasmussen, "Agriculture," 352.

9. Kraut, *The Huddled Masses*, 2.

10. Albro Martin, "Economy from Reconstruction to 1914," in *The Encyclopedia of American Economic History*, vol. I, ed. Glenn Porter (New York: Scribner's, 1980), 97.

11. Quoted in Wrobel, *American Exceptionalism*, 56, 62, 64–65.

12. Ibid.

13. Damiani, *Advocates of Empire*.

14. Theodore Roosevelt's "big stick" approach to foreign policy was the forerunner of the Roosevelt Corollary. The term grew out of his expression "speak softly and carry a big stick," which appeared in his request for a large naval appropriation.

15. Knock, *To End All Wars*, 35.

16. Ibid., 39–40, 70–71.

17. Ibid., 30, 59, 97.

18. In 1917 German foreign minister Alfred Zimmerman sent a telegram to Heinrich von Eckardt, the German ambassador in Mexico, suggesting that, in the event of a U.S.–German conflict, Mexico should declare war on the United States. If Mexico cooperated, Germany indicated, it could recover its lost territories of Arizona, New Mexico, and Texas.

19. U.S. Department of State, *The Foreign Relations of the United States*, 1918, Russia, vol. 1 (Washington, D.C.: Government Printing Office, 1931), 253.

20. Wilson recognized different forms of national self-determination. For countries such as Poland national self-determination meant the creation or re-creation of historical states, particularly when these nations had been treated as colonies. For countries such as Hungary it meant autonomy within existing states. And for still other countries such as Yugoslavia it meant equal treatment of ethnic groups in multinational states.

21. Knock, *To End All Wars*, 263–264.

22. Cole, *Determinism and American Foreign Relations*.

23. Cole, *Roosevelt and the Isolationists*, 381.

Chapter 4

1. William R. Keylor, *The Twentieth-Century World: An International History* (New York: Oxford University Press, 1996), 178–179.

2. Ibid., 187.

3. Roosevelt did not attend the 1943 Moscow meeting. Truman, his successor, attended the Potsdam conference.

4. During most of World War II, France was governed by a regime headed by Marshall Petain that collaborated with the Germans. It was referred to as Vichy France, since the head of government was located in the town of Vichy. Charles de Gaulle headed an alternative government in exile, the French Committee of National Liberation in London, and as leader of the Free French forces fought with the Allies in North Africa and Europe.

5. Townsend Hoopes and Douglas Brinkley, *FDR and the Creation of the U.N.* (New Haven: Yale University Press, 1997), 174–175.

6. Melvyn P. Leffler, *A Preponderance of Power: National Security, the Truman Administration, and the Cold War,* (Stanford: Stanford University Press, 1992), 105.

7. Ibid., 112.

8. John Lewis Gaddis, *Strategies of Containment: A Critical Appraisal of American National Security Policy during the Cold War,* rev. and exp. ed. (New York: Oxford University Press, 2005), 29.

9. Undersecretary of State Dean Acheson chaired the committee and David Lilienthal, head of the Tennessee Valley Authority, chaired the committee's Board of Consultants.

10. Thomas Wallace Graham, "The Politics of Failure" (PhD. diss., Massachusetts Institute of Technology, June 1989).

11. Churchill said:

> From Stettin in the Baltic to Trieste in the Adriatic, an iron curtain has descended across the continent. Behind that line lie all the capitals of the ancient states of Central and Eastern Europe, Warsaw, Berlin, Prague, Vienna, Budapest, Belgrade, Bucharest, and Sofia, all the famous cities and populations around them lie in the Soviet sphere and all are subject in one form or another, not only to Soviet influence but to a very high and increasing measure of control from Moscow.

12. Martin J. Hillenbrand, *Fragments of Our Time: Memoirs of a Diplomat* (Athens: University of Georgia Press, 1998), 87.

13. For political leaders and many scholars of this period the term "third world" helped to differentiate between the largely poor developing countries from the northern capitalist countries—the "first world"—and communist countries—the "second world." See excerpts from Nehru's speeches, Internet Modern History Sourcebook, http://www.fordham.edu/halsall/india/indiasbook.html, accessed 10/14/05.

14. Thomas Risse-Kappen, "Collective Identity in a Democratic Community: The Case of NATO," in *Ideas and Foreign Policy,* ed. Judith Goldstein and Robert O. Keohane (Ithaca: Cornell University Press, 1993), 383–384.

15. Hillenbrand, *Fragments of Our Time,* 121.

16. Because the secretary-general of the United Nations could not, in Moscow's opinion, be neutral, the Soviet Union demanded a triumvirate of secretary generals (which it called a *troika* after the Russian three-horse-driven vehicle), one each representing the democratic West, the communist East, and nonaligned third world. Dag Hammarskjöld, the secretary general, reportedly pointed out that even a troika only has one driver, and Khruschev's proposal was defeated when the neutral, nonaligned powers refused to go along with it.

17. See www.creativequotations.com/one/742htm, accessed 10/17/05.

18. See Graham Allison and Philip Zelikow, *Essence of Decision: Explaining the Cuban Missile Crisis,* 2d ed. (New York: Longman, 1999).

19. In August 1964 two American ships in the neutral waters of the Gulf of Tonkin were fired upon under mysterious circumstances. The United States claimed that two North Vietnamese PT boats had attacked the ships. A short time later, President Johnson asked Congress to grant him the powers to order a retaliatory attack on North Vietnam. Both houses passed the Gulf of Tonkin Resolution nearly unanimously, which cleared the

way for escalated U.S. involvement in the Vietnam conflict. Later studies have suggested that the attack may have been a hoax constructed to provide an excuse for openly using military force in North Vietnam.

20. Theodore H. White, *The Making of the President 1968* (New York: Atheneum Publishers, 1969), 398.
21. In terms of the retreat from a global engagement to a concentration on key points, this policy appears to be a return to the strongpoint defense first employed during the Truman administration.
22. The United States had added MIRVs to many of their weapons earlier.
23. In this scandal of 1985–1986, high-ranking members of the Reagan administration arranged secretly, in direct violation of U.S. law, to sell arms to Iran in order to encourage the release of American hostages held since the Iranian revolution. Profits from the sale, totalling millions of dollars, were funneled to Nicaragua to help arm the right-wing Contra guerrillas, who were fighting the leftist Sandinista government.
24. William C. Wohlforth, ed., *Witnesses to the End of the Cold War* (Baltimore: Johns Hopkins University Press, 1996), 107.
25. George W. Bush, *National Security Strategy of the United States of America,* released September 17, 2002. See White House website: www.whitehouse.gov.

Chapter 5

1. Thomas Sowell has developed the notion of visions in politics. See *A Conflict of Visions: Ideological Origins of Political Struggles* (New York: Morrow, 1987).
2. Chris Brown, *International Relations Theory* (New York: Columbia University Press, 1992), 55.
3. Peter R. Baehr, *The Role of Human Rights in Foreign Policy* (New York: St. Martin's Press, 1994), 14.
4. Andrew Linklater, *The Transformation of Political Community: Ethical Foundations of the Post-Westphalian Era* (Columbia: University of South Carolina Press, 1998), 5.
5. James H. Billington, "Lecture at Rice University on March 26, 1998," *Baker Institute Report* no. 10 (June 1998), 7.
6. Gail V. Karlsson, "Environment and Sustainable Development," in *A Global Agenda: Issues before the 49th General Assembly of the United Nations,* ed. John Tessitore and Susan Woolfson (New York: University Press of America, 1994), 154.
7. Jonathon Porritt, "Introduction," in *The Way Forward: Beyond Agenda 21,* ed. Felix Dodds (London: Earthscan Publications, 1997), xvii.
8. United Nations Development Programme, *Human Development Report 1996* (Oxford: Oxford University Press, 1996), 13. For a different view see David Dollar and Aart Kraay, "Spending the Wealth," *Foreign Affairs* 81 (January/February 2002): 123–124.
9. Anthony Lake, "From Containment to Enlargement," speech at Johns Hopkins University, September 21, 1993, in *Department of State Dispatch,* July 12, 1993, 664.
10. William J. Clinton, *First Inaugural Address,* January 21, 1993.
11. William J. Clinton, *National Security Strategy of the United States, 1994–1995: Engagement and Enlargement* (Washington, D.C.: Brassey's, 1995), 6.
12. William J. Clinton, *Between Hope and History: Meeting America's Challenges for the 21st Century* (New York: Random House, 1996), 163.
13. Lake, "From Containment to Enlargement," 663.
14. Vienna Declaration and Programme of Action of the World Conference of Human Rights, June 25, 1993.
15. George W. Bush, *The National Security Strategy of the United States* (Washington, D.C.: U.S. Government Printing Office, September 20, 2002).
16. The term "axis of evil" was first applied to these three states on January 29, 2002. See George W. Bush, *State of the Union Address.*

17. Tara E. Santmire, "The Characteristics of Multilateralism as a Link between States" (paper presented at the annual meeting of the International Studies Association, San Diego, 1996), 3.

18. Tom Farer, "How the International System Copes with Involuntary Migration: Norms, Institutions, and State Practice," in *Threatened Peoples, Threatened Borders*, ed. Michael S. Teitelbaum and Myron Weiner (New York: Norton, 1995), 260.

19. Christopher Mitchell, *Western Hemisphere Immigration and United States Foreign Policy* (University Park: Penn State University Press, 1992), 14.

20. U.S. Committee for Refugees, *World Refugees During 2004*, Table 1, www.refugeesorg/wrs04/statistics.html.

21. It is estimated that more than 1 million illegal immigrants were apprehended in the southwestern states in 2005 alone. See Darryl Fears and Michael A. Fletcher, "Temporary Worker Program Explained As Administration Presents Plan, Bush Voices Tough Action Against Illegal Immigration," *Washington Post*, October 19, 2005.

22. Teitelbaum and Weiner, *Threatened Peoples*, 21.

23. News Broadcast (Channel 8, Georgia Public Broadcasting Network, June 25, 2004).

24. Kathryn C. Lawler, "Refugees," in Tessitore and Woolfson, *A Global Agenda*.

25. Kathryn Sikkink, "The Power of Principled Ideas: Human Rights Policies in the United States and Western Europe," in *The Culture of National Security*, ed. Peter J. Katzenstein (New York: Columbia University Press, 1996).

26. Ibid.

27. Stephen P. Marks, "Social and Humanitarian Issues: Human Rights," in Tessitore and Woolfson, *A Global Agenda*, 177.

28. Felice D. Gaer, "Protecting Human Rights," in *U.S. Foreign Policy and the United Nations System*, ed., Charles William Maynes and Richard S. Williamson (New York: W. W. Norton, 1996), 165.

29. Human Rights Watch, *World Report 2000*, www.hrw.org/wr2k/.

30. Gaer, "Protecting Human Rights," 156.

31. Peter R. Baehr, *The Role of Human Rights in Foreign Policy* (New York: St. Martin's Press, 1994), 53.

32. Lori Fisler Damrosch, *Enforcing Restraint: Collective Intervention in Internal Conflicts* (New York: Council on Foreign Relations Press, 1993), 1.

33. Robert W. Tucker, *The Just War: A Study in Contemporary American Doctrine* (Baltimore: Johns Hopkins University Press, 1960), 84.

34. Mihaly Simai, "Forward," in *The North, the South, and the Environment: Ecological Constraints and the Global Environment*, ed. V. Bhaskar and Andrew Glyn (New York: St. Martin's Press, 1995), xii.

35. The Kyoto Protocol did not come into effect until it was ratified by developed countries representing 44 percent of carbon dioxide emissions. Because the United States alone had 36 percent of these emissions, the pact could only come into existence when Russia, with 17 percent of emissions, ratified the pact.

36. See Steven Kull, "Survey on Global Warming" (University of Maryland: Program on International Policy Attitudes, November 27, 2000).

37. John Buell and Tom DeLuca, *Sustainable Democracy: Individuality and the Politics of the Environment* (Thousand Oaks, Calif.: Sage Publications, 1996), 31.

38. In January 2005 the EU launched a scheme allowing industrial companies to buy or sell rights to pollute to meet the bloc's commitment under the Kyoto Protocol. "Fledgling Carbon Market Starts to Fly: World Bank," *Agence France-Presse* May 11, 2005.

39. Robert O. Vos, "Introduction: Competing Approaches to Sustainability: Dimensions of Controversy," in *Flashpoints in Environmental Policymaking: Controversies in Achieving Sustainability*, ed. Sheldon Kamieniecki, George A. Gonzalez, and Robert O. Vos (New York: State University of New York Press, 1997), 14, 16–18.

40. Notice that the options outlined here basically involve the same type. This serves as a reminder that these are general types in that there may be greater differences between two multilateral, coercive, proactive, or MCA, policies than between that type and any other type.

Chapter 6

1. This debate can be found in opinion journals focusing on American foreign policy that highlighted this debate beginning in 1989, especially *Foreign Affairs, Foreign Policy, National Interest,* and *World Policy Journal.*
2. James DeNardo employs this terminology in *The Amateur Strategist: Intuitive Deterrence Theories and the Politics of the Nuclear Arms Race* (Cambridge: Cambridge University Press, 1995).
3. John Mueller, *Quiet Cataclysm: Reflections on the Recent Transformation of World Politics* (New York: HarperCollins, 1995).
4. Belgium, Bulgaria, Canada, the Czech Republic, Denmark, Estonia, France, Germany, Greece, Hungary, Iceland, Italy, Latvia, Lithuania, Luxembourg, the Netherlands, Norway, Poland, Portugal, Romania, Slovakia, Slovenia, Spain, Turkey, the United Kingdom, and the United States are members of NATO, with Bulgaria, Estonia, Latvia, Lithuania, Romania, Slovakia, and Slovenia joining in 2004.
5. Russia has been invited to participate in NATO deliberations except those involving the accession of new members and decisions regarding joint action.
6. In the mid-1990s the United States and Russia also signed the START II agreement, which banned all land-based, multiple-warhead ballistic missiles; but the 2002 Moscow Treaty superseded this agreement before it became operational.
7. Cuba, Iraq, Iran, Libya, North Korea, Sudan, and Syria are usually regarded as rogue states. The status of some of these states has changed. For example, the United States has resumed normal relations with Libya, and North Korea has once again shown some signs of being willing to discuss its nuclear weapons program.
8. The collapse of the security dimensions is described in William O. Chittick and Keith R. Billingsley, "Alpha and Gamma Changes in American Foreign Policy Beliefs," paper, American Political Science Association, Atlanta, 1999. See also CD-Rom.
9. George W. Bush, *State of the Union Address* (January 29, 2002).
10. The twenty-five member countries of the European Union at the end of 2005 are: Austria, Belgium, Cyprus, Czech Republic, Denmark, Estonia, Finland, France, Germany, Greece, Hungary, Ireland, Italy, Latvia, Lithuania, Luxembourg, Malta, Poland, Portugal, Slovakia, Slovenia, Spain, Sweden, the Netherlands, and the United Kingdom. Bulgaria and Romania are scheduled to become members in 2007. Turkey will begin negotiations in late 2005, but must complete social and economic reforms before membership will be granted and Croatia's application is on hold pending resolution of a number of issues before the UN War Crimes Tribunal in the Hague.
11. Paul Kennedy, *The Rise and Fall of Great Powers: Economic Change and Military Conflict from 1500 to 2000* (New York: Random House, 1987).
12. Richard Betts, "The New Threat of Mass Destruction," *Foreign Affairs* 77, no. 1 (1997): 40.
13. In 2003 there were 27 countries with PFP programs with NATO. See James M. Goldgeier, *Not Whether but When: The U.S. Decision to Enlarge NATO,* (Washington, D.C.: Brookings Institution Press, 1999), 152–155.
14. Zbigniew Brzezinski, *The Grand Chessboard: American Primacy and Its Geostrategic Imperatives* (New York: Basic Books, 1997).
15. By this time East and West Germany had already reunified into a single Germany.
16. DeNardo, *Amateur Strategist.*
17. Thomas P. M. Barnett, *The Pentagon's New Map: War and Peace in the Twenty-First Century* (New York: G. P. Putman's Sons, 2004).

18. Ibid.
19. See Eric A. Nordlinger, *Isolationism Reconfigured: American Foreign Policy for a New Century* (Princeton: Princeton University Press, 1995).
20. As of early 2005, these tests had failed.
21. In keeping with Reagan's rationale for sharing SDI with Gorbachev, President Putin of Russia has asked the United States to share its NMD system.
22. UN Security Council Resolution 1546 (2004).
23. UN Security Council Resolution 1267 (1999) had called upon the Taliban government to turn over bin Laden as a result of the terrorist attacks in Africa.
24. The NATO negotiators at Rambouillet, France, had earlier tried to get the Serbs to accept NATO forces in Serbia itself.
25. The other members of this team were Senator Sam Nunn and General Colin L. Powell.
26. Harold A. Feiverson, ed., *The Nuclear Turning Point: A Blueprint for Deep Cuts and De-alerting of Nuclear Weapons* (Washington, D.C.: Brookings Institution Press, 1999), 202.
27. Ibid., 24.
28. Launch-on-warning is the decision to retaliate with one's own missiles when the first credible warning of an enemy attack has been received. Ideally one would hope that one would not launch until the warning had been verified, or depending on the size of the attack, until the attack had actually been consummated on friendly territory. De-alerting refers to measures that might be taken to slow down one's reaction time so that one would be less likely to respond to false alerts. Deactivation involves removing warheads from missiles, so that one would not have the capability of responding to warnings by actually initiating a missile attack.
29. Feiverson, *The Nuclear Turning Point*, 15, 32, and 200.
30. Ibid., 18.
31. Charles V. Pena, "Missile Defense: Defending America or Building Empire?" *Foreign Policy Briefing* No. 77 (Washington, D.C.: CATO Institute, May 28, 2003), 8–9.
32. Zbigniew Brzezinski, *The Grand Chessboard: American Primacy and Its Geostrategic Imperatives* (New York: Basic Books, 1997).
33. This strategy should not be confused with the various proposals put forward by the Project for the New American Century or the specific policies implemented by neoconservatives in the George W. Bush administration, but they do belong to the same genre.

Chapter 7

1. E. Paul Torrance, *Manifesto for Children* (Athens, Ga.: Torrance Center for Creative Studies, 1983).
2. Jack Kemp and Felix Rohatyn, "The Mandate for Higher Growth," in *The Rising Tide: The Leading Minds of Business and Economics Chart a Course Toward Higher Growth and Prosperity*, ed. Jerry Jasinowski (New York: Wiley, 1996).
3. Joseph E. Stiglitz and Lyn Squire, "International Development: Is it Possible?" *Foreign Policy* (Spring 1998): 139.
4. Cited in Gregg Easterbrook, "The Capitalist Manifesto," *New York Times Book Review*, November 27, 2005, 16.
5. Roy D. Morey, "Using the United Nations to Advance Sustainable Growth with Equity," in *Delusions of Grandeur: The United Nations and Global Intervention*, ed. Ted Galen Carpenter (Washington, D.C.: CATO Institute, 1997), 204.
6. Paul Krugman, "The Joyless Economy," *New York Times*, December 5, 2005, A25.
7. Robert J. Barro, "Government Can Boost Growth," in Jasinowski, *The Rising Tide*, 192.
8. Ralph E. Gomory and William J. Baumol, *Global Trade and Conflicting National Interests* (Cambridge, Mass.: MIT Press, 2000).
9. Sylvia Ostry, *The Post–Cold War Trading System: Who's on First?* (Chicago: University of Chicago Press, 1997), 43–48.

10. Anne Y. Kester and Panel on International Capital Transactions, *Following the Money: U.S. Finance in the World Economy* (Washington, D.C.: National Academy Press, 1994), 19.

11. Because of the strength of the U.S. dollar in Europe, a virtual dollar market emerged in Europe, which was not backed by the U.S. government.

12. Joan Edelman Spero, *The Politics of International Economic Relations,* 3d ed. (New York: St. Martin's Press, 1985), 44, 51.

13. Ibid., 52–53.

14. Kester and Panel on International Capital Transactions, *Following the Money,* 20.

15. Spero, *Politics of International Economic Relations,* 204.

16. Ibid., 212.

17. Ibid., 73.

18. Ibid., 112–113.

19. Richard B. Freeman, "Doubling the Global Work Force: The Challenge of Integrating China, India, and the Former Soviet Bloc into the World Economy," Nov. 8, 2004, http://www.iie.com/publications/papers/freeman1104.pdf.

20. Thomas L. Friedman, *The World Is Flat: A Brief History of the Twenty-First Century* (New York: Farrar, Straus and Giroux, 2005).

21. Ray Marshall, "The Global Jobs Crisis," *Foreign Policy* (Fall 1995): 68.

22. Peter F. Drucker, "The Global Economy and the Nation-State," *Foreign Affairs* (September/October 1997): 162.

23. Clyde Prestowitz, *Three Billion New Capitalists* (New York: Basic Books, 2005), 37.

24. Organization for Economic Cooperation and Development, "Regionalism and the Multilateral Trading System: The Role of Regional Trade Agreements," *Policy Brief.* Paris (August 2003): 7.

25. Other RTAs in the world include: ASEAN, Central European Free Trade Agreement (CEFTA), MERCOSUR (a free trade agreement between Argentina, Brazil, Paraguay, and Uruguay), and the ANDEAN free trade agreement between Columbia, Ecuador, Peru, Bolivia, and the United States.

26. See Laurence Harris, "Will the Real IMF Please Stand Up: What Does the Fund Do and What Should It Do?" in *Global Instability: The Political Economy of World Economic Governance,* ed. Jonathan Michie and John Grieve Smith (London: Routledge, 1999), 201–202.

27. Gomory and Baumol, *Global Trade,* 4.

28. Jagdish Bhagwati, *Free Trade, "Fairness" and the New Protectionism* (London: Institute of Economic Affairs, 1995), 14.

29. Ibid., 10, 20.

30. Organization for Economic Cooperation and Development, "Economic Survey of the United States, 2004," *Policy Brief,* Paris (April 2004): 7.

31. Friedman, *The World Is Flat,* 257.

32. Freeman, "Doubling the Global Workforce."

33. Prestowitz, *Three Billion New Capitalists.* Also see Friedman, *The World Is Flat.*

34. William J. Clinton, "State of the Union Address 1993," *Vital Speeches* 59, no. 11 (March 15, 1993): 322.

35. Ibid., 323.

36. Gomory and Baumol, *Global Trade,* 8.

37. William J. Clinton, *Between Hope and History: Meeting America's Challenges for the 21st Century* (New York: Random House, 1996), 22.

38. Clinton, "State of the Union Address 1993," 290.

39. Clinton, *Between Hope and History,* 118.

40. Felix Rohatyn, "Ways to Achieve Higher Growth," in Jasinowski *The Rising Tide,* 21.

41. Stiglitz and Squire, "International Development," 141.

42. George W. Bush, speech to Economic Club of Chicago, January 7, 2003, www.whitehouse.gov/news/releases/2003/01/20030107-5.html.

43. Paul Krugman, *Pop Internationalism* (Cambridge, Mass.: MIT Press, 1996), 53.
44. See Nouriel Roubini and Brad Setser, "The U.S. as a Net Debtor: The Sustainability of the U.S. External Imbalances," November 2004, www.stern.nyu.edu/~nroubini/papers/Roubini-Setser-US-External-Imbalances.pdf, 18.
45. These investments are often referred to as industrial policies. For a discussion of such policies, see Laura D'Andrea Tyson, *Who's Bashing Whom? Trade Conflict in High Technology Industries* (Washington, D.C.: Institute for International Economics, 1992).
46. Mickey Kantor, U.S. Trade Representative, in "Statement before the Senate Finance Committee on March 9, 1993," *Dispatch* (U.S. Department of State), March 15, 1993, 144.
47. Steve Lohr, "How Is the Game Played Now? Many Young Workers Accept Fewer Guarantees," *New York Times*, C1, C8.
48. Gordon Myers, *Banana Wars—The Price of Free Trade: A Caribbean Perspective* (London: Zed Books, 2004).
49. Soren Ambrose, "Multilateral Debt: The Unbearable Burden," *Foreign Policy In Focus* 6:37 (Nov. 2001) www.fpif.org/ 11/4/2005.
50. Myers, *Banana Wars*, 164.
51. Friedman, *The World Is Flat*, 299.
52. Program on International Policy Attitudes, "Americans on Foreign Aid and World Hunger: A Study of U.S. Public Attitudes 2001," University of Maryland.
53. Curt Tarnoff and Larry Nowels, "Foreign Aid: An Introductory Overview of U.S. Programs and Policy," Congressional Research Service, Library of Congress, updated April 15, 2004.
54. Anup Shah, "Sustainable Development: The U.S. and Foreign Aid Assistance," www.globalissues.org/TradeRelated/Debt/USAid.asp.
55. Greg Palast, "Bill Gates: Killing Africans for Profit and PR," July 14, 2003, www.gregpalast.com/detail.crm?artid=232&row=0.
56. Anup Shah, Hunger, updated www.globalissues.org/TradeRelated/Poverty/Hunger/Causes.asp.
57. China is now receiving a large share of private investment and enjoying rapid development. If that situation changes, China would have to be included.
58. Michael O'Hanlon and Carol Graham, *A Half-Penny on the Federal Dollar: The Future of Development Aid* (Washington, D.C.: Brookings, 1997), 53.
59. Tarnoff and Nowels, "Foreign Aid," 2.
60. David F. Gordon, "The Politics of International Sanctions: A Case Study of South Africa," in *Dilemmas of Economic Coercion: Sanctions in World Politics*, ed. Miroslav Nincic and Peter Wallensteen (New York: Praeger, 1983), 184.
61. Richard N. Haass, "Sanctioning Madness," *Foreign Affairs* (November/December 1997): 74.
62. Edward Said, "The Treason of the Intellectuals," in *Masters of the Universe? NATO's Balkan Crusade*, ed. Tariq Ali (New York: Verso, 2000), 343.
63. Stuart E. Eizenstat, "Do Economic Sanctions Work? Lessons from ILSA and Other U.S. Sanctions Regimes," Atlantic Council of the United States, February 2004.
64. Duelfer Report, www.cia.gov/cia/reports/iraq_wmd_w004/Comp_Report_Key_Findings.pdf
65. United Nations Children's Fund, *Children and Women in Iraq: A Situation Analysis* (Baghdad: UNICEF, 1993), 27.
66. Eric Hoskins, "The Humanitarian Impacts of Economic Sanctions and War in Iraq," in *Political Gain and Civilian Pain: Humanitarian Impacts of Economic Sanctions*, ed. Thomas G. Weiss, David Cortright, George A. Lopez, and Larry Minear (Oxford: Rowman and Littlefield, 1997), 114.
67. Eizenstat, "Do Economic Sanctions Work?" 11.
68. Robert L. Paarlberg, "Using Food Power: Opportunities, Appearances, and Damage Control," in Nincic and Wallensteen, *Dilemmas of Economic Coercion*, 139.

69. Les de Villiers, *In Sight of Surrender: The U.S. Sanctions Campaign against South Africa, 1946–1993* (Westport, Conn.: Praeger, 1995), 167.

70. George E. Shambaugh, *States, Firms, and Power: Successful Sanctions in United States Foreign Policy* (Albany: SUNY Press, 1999), 171.

Chapter 8

1. Union of International Associations, *Yearbook of International Organizations* (Munich: K. G. Saur Verlag, 2005/2006), vol. 5.

2. Alan Hedblad, ed., *Encyclopedia of Associations: National Associations of the U.S.* (Detroit: Gale Publishing, 2003).

3. Union of International Associations, *Yearbook of International Organizations*, vol. 5, 148–153.

4. Ibid., vol. 5.

5. Hedblad, *Encyclopedia of Associations*, 12–13.

6. The Transnational Project is a series of mail surveys administered to government officials and NGO leaders by William O. Chittick in the summer of 1984. This research was supported by a grant from the Georgia Research Foundation, Inc. Although the data obtained from these surveys are dated, more current data do not exist.

7. A representative sample was drawn from a list of officials in Washington, D.C., who held international positions in the 1984 *Federal Yellow Pages*. The sample was generally representative of this population, but the population either did not represent or underrepresented some policy makers. For example, CIA officials are not listed in the *Federal Yellow Pages*, and representation from the Department of Defense was limited to the Office of the Secretary of Defense and the Joint Chiefs of Staff. In addition, none of the U.S. officials stationed outside of Washington, D.C., were included in the sample.

8. The population of church-related agencies includes ninety Protestant groups with mission budgets of over $1 million or with at least one hundred American missionaries stationed overseas; the twenty-two largest Catholic mission-sending agencies in the United States; and eleven Jewish organizations that provide overseas relief and assistance abroad. The leaders of 64 out of 123 of these agencies participated in the study. See S. Wilson, ed., *Mission Handbook: North American Protestant Ministries Overseas* (Monrovia, Calif.: MARC Publications, 1979); *U.S. Catholic Mission Association, 1983*; and *American Jewish Year Book, 1981*, respectively. Also the leaders of 95 out of 165 of the AID list of PVOs participated in this study.

9. A TNC was included in the sample only if it had affiliates in at least six foreign countries. Sixty-five of these 175 TNC executives responded. See *Fortune Magazine, 1984*.

10. Sixty-four out of 125 bank executives responded. See "Bank Scoreboard" of *Business Week* for April 1984.

11. Bruce Russett and Harvey Starr, *World Politics: The Menu for Choice* (New York: W. H. Freeman, 1985). The order of these three general criteria has been transposed.

12. John P. Lovell, *Foreign Policy in Perspective: Strategy, Adaptation, Decision Making* (New York: Holt, Rinehart and Winston, 1970), 208–211.

13. Margaret E. Keck and Kathryn Sikkink, *Activists beyond Borders: Advocacy Networks in International Politics* (Ithaca: Cornell University Press, 1998), 105.

14. Ibid., 166.

15. Ibid., 27–28.

16. Ibid., 24.

17. Please note that Spearman's rank-order correlation is 0.29 out of a perfect correlation of 1.0.

18. Peter Willetts, "Consultative Status for NGOs at the United Nations," in *"The Conscience of the World": The Influence of Non-Governmental Organizations in the UN System*, ed. Peter Willetts (London: Hurst and Co., 1996).

19. Richard Hoggard, "UNESCO and NGOs: A Memoir," in Willett, *Conscience of the World*, 99.

20. Jane Connors, "NGOs and the Human Rights of Women at the United Nations," in Willett, *Conscience of the World*, 166.

21. Angela Penrose and John Seaman, "The Save the Children Fund and Nutrition for Refugees," in Willett, *Conscience of the World*, 253–254.

22. Keck and Sikkink, *Activists beyond Borders*, 96.

23. Helena Cook, "Amnesty International at the United Nations," in Willett, *Conscience of the World*, 193–195.

24. Seamus Cleary, "The World Bank and NGOs," in Willett, *Conscience of the World*, 72, 92.

25. Michael Longford, "NGOs and the Rights of the Child," in Willett, *Conscience of the World*, 223, 227.

26. Penrose and Seaman, "Save the Children Fund," 255, 263.

27. Keck and Sikkink, *Activists beyond Borders*, 152–153.

Chapter 9

1. See Nicholas Onuf, "Constructivism: A User's Manual," in *International Relations in a Constructed World*, ed. Vendulka Kubalkova, Nicholas Onuf, and Paul Kowert (Armonk, N.Y.: M. E. Sharpe, 1998), 59. Also see N. G. Onuf, *World of Our Making: Rules and Rule in Social Theory and International Relations* (Columbia, S.C.: University of South Carolina Press, 1989); and N. G. Onuf, "Everyday Ethics in International Relations," *Millennium: Journal of International Studies* 27, no. 3 (1998).

2. Friedrich V. Kratochwil, *Rules, Norms, and Decisions: On the Conditions of Practical and Legal Reasoning in International Relations and Domestic Affairs* (Cambridge: Cambridge University Press, 1989), 21.

3. Ibid., 23.

4. For a broad historical account of these roots, read William R. Polk's *Neighbors and Strangers: The Fundamentals of Foreign Affairs* (Chicago: University of Chicago Press, 1997).

5. Walter W. Powell and Paul J. DiMaggio, "Introduction," in *The New Institutionalism in Organizational Analysis*, ed. Powell and DiMaggio (Chicago: University of Chicago Press, 1991), 12.

6. Ibid.

7. This typology is based on Samuel Huntington's distinction between crisis, strategic, and structural policy as well as Marie Henehan's distinction between the crisis, critical, and regular issues of foreign policy. Here strategic is preferred over critical because crisis and critical may be mistaken for one another; and regular is preferred over structural because structural may be mistaken for institutional. See Samuel P. Huntington, *The Common Defense: Strategic Programs in National Politics* (New York: Columbia University Press, 1961), 3; Randall B. Ripley and James M. Lindsay, eds., *Congress Resurgent: Foreign and Defense Policy on Capitol Hill* (Ann Arbor: University of Michigan Press, 1993), 8; and Marie T. Henehan, *Foreign Policy and Congress: An International Relations Perspective* (Ann Arbor: University of Michigan Press, 2000).

8. See Huntington, *Common Defense*.

9. See ibid. and Henehan, *Foreign Policy and Congress*.

10. Ripley and Lindsay, *Congress Resurgent*, 19. Henehan argues that Congress generally handles tariff, immigration, defense expenditures, foreign aid, and other foreign policies in the same way as domestic policies.

11. Later the Duelfer Report confirmed that the Iraqi regime had no WMD and no written strategy or plan to revive such weapons after sanctions. See http://www.cia.gov/cia/reports/iraq_wmd_2004/Comp_Report/,10/10/2004.

12. 9/11 Commission, *Final Report of the National Commission on Terrorist Attacks Upon the United States*, authorized edition (New York: W.W. Norton, 2004).

13. Michael Foley and John E. Owens, *Congress and the Presidency: Institutional Politics in a Separated System* (Manchester, England: Manchester University Press, 1996), 336.

14. *The Federalist Papers* no. 51.

15. Originally senators were selected by state legislatures. The Seventeenth Amendment, passed in 1913, provided for the direct election of senators.

16. A fuller account of this elite sample appears in Chapter 13.

17. These political executives and members of Congress were compared with business, education, interest groups, and labor, media, religious, and think tank leaders (see Chapter 13).

18. Foley and Owens, *Congress and the Presidency.* 335.

19. Arend Lijphart, *Parliamentary versus Presidential Government* (Oxford: Oxford University Press, 1992), 11.

20. Ibid. The argument that the presidential system is more "democratic" is partly confounded by the fact that compromises are often discouraged in a single-member district system of voting that emphasizes a winner-take-all result rather than a system in which multiple candidates are elected in a single district on the basis of proportional representation.

21. Edward S. Corwin, *The President: Office and Powers, 1787–1957* (New York: New York University Press, 1957).

22. Gordon Silverstein, *Imbalance of Powers: Constitutional Interpretation and the Making of American Foreign Policy* (Oxford: Oxford University Press, 1997), 8.

23. Ibid., 50–62.

24. 252 U.S. 416.

25. 299 U.S. 305.

26. Silverstein, *Imbalance of Powers*, 39.

27. *United States v. Belmont,* 301 U.S. 324 (1939); *United States v. Pink*, 315 U.S. 203 (1942).

28. Loch K. Johnson, *America as a World Power: Foreign Policy in a Constitutional Framework*, 2d ed. (New York: McGraw-Hill, 1995), 380–387.

29. At a small group session of ISA/South members with former secretaries of state, three out of four secretaries took the position that the president had this authority. See William O. Chittick, "The Secretaries on Continuity and Bipartisanship in American Foreign Policy," *International Studies Notes* 11:1 (Fall 1984), 1–9.

30. Silverstein, *Imbalance of Powers,* 77.

31. 343 U.S. 579.

32. The *Pentagon Papers* were an internal collection of historical papers on how the United States became involved in the Vietnam War. The documents were leaked to the *New York Times* by Daniel Ellsberg, a Department of Defense employee, in 1971. See 403 U.S. 713.

33. Aaron Wildavsky, "The Two Presidencies," *Trans-Action* 4 (December 1966) 7–14. Wildavsky himself later acknowledged that the two-presidency thesis was tied to a particular era. See D. Oldfield and Aaron Wildavsky, "Reconsidering the Two Presidencies," in *The Two Presidencies: A Quarter-Century Assessment*, ed. S. A. Shull (Chicago: Nelson-Hall, 1991).

34. Barbara Hinckley, *Less than Meets the Eye: The Myth of the Assertive Congress* (Chicago: University of Chicago Press, 2000).

35. Most analysts agree that the U.S. action in the Persian Gulf War was essentially unilateral. See Angela Celeste Denton, "Foreign Policy Beliefs and the House Decision to Use Force in the Persian Gulf" (M.A. thesis, University of Georgia, 1991).

36. James M. McCormick, *American Foreign Policy and Process*, 3d ed. (Itasco, Ill.: F. E. Peacock, 1998), 339.

37. The rest of this section is based on Silverstein, *Imbalance of Powers*, 142, 150, 158–159, 161–162.

38. George W. Bush, *The National Security Strategy of the United States of America* Sept. 17, 2002. www.nti.org/e_research/official_docs/pres/pres090002.pdf.

39. See Henehan, *Foreign Policy and Congress*, 5–6.

40. Ibid., 67–70.

41. Henehan used Senate roll-call votes to measure involvement between 1896 and 1985.
42. Richard Neustadt, *Presidential Persuasion: The Politics of Leadership* (New York: John Wiley, 1960), 33.
43. John H. Aldrich, *Why Parties? The Origin and Transformation of Political Parties in America* (Chicago: University of Chicago Press, 1995), 81.
44. Ibid., 45.
45. Ibid., 100, 110–111.
46. Wilfred E. Binkley, *American Political Parties: Their Natural History*, 4th ed., (New York: Alfred A. Knopf, 1965), 114.
47. Aldrich, *Why Parties?* 132.
48. This discussion of the two major parties is based on John Gerring, *Party Ideologies in America, 1828–1996* (Cambridge: Cambridge University Press, 1998), 15.
49. Ibid.
50. These differences, including those who identify themselves as independents, are all significant at the 0.01 levels. Independents (not shown) are close to the mean on all three dimensions. A comparison of Tables 9.1 and 9.2 shows that both positions in government and party identification have an influence on attitudes toward the three dimensions.
51. Miroslav Nincic, *Democracy and Foreign Policy: the Fallacy of Political Realism* (New York: Columbia University Press, 1992), 112–113.
52. Charles O. Jones, *The Presidency in a Separated System* (Washington, D.C.: Brookings, 1994), 19–23.
53. C. David Tompkins, *Senator Arthur H. Vandenberg: The Evolution of a Modern Republican, 1884–1945* (Ann Arbor: Michigan State University Press, 1970), 240.
54. See Chapter 4.
55. Benjamin O. Fordham, *Building the Cold War Consensus: The Political Economy of U.S. National Security Policy, 1949–51* (Ann Arbor: University of Michigan Press, 1998).
56. For an appropriate strategy for U.S. policy makers under these circumstances, see Robert A. Pastor, *Condemned to Repetition: The United States and Nicaragua* (Princeton: Princeton University Press, 1987), 297–314.
57. Henehan, *Foreign Policy and Congress*, 128–139.
58. This formulation and much that follows is based on Forrest Maltzman, *Competing Principals: Committees, Parties, and the Organization of Congress* (Ann Arbor: University of Michigan Press, 1997), 9, 133–134, 138–139.
59. Maltzman, *Competing Principals*, 132.
60. Barbara Sinclair, *Legislators, Leaders, and Lawmaking: The U.S. House of Representatives in the Post–reform Era* (Baltimore: Johns Hopkins University Press, 1995), 23.
61. It is not clear that the State Department actually objected to this reorganization.
62. Warren E. Miller, "Party Identification and the Electorate of the 1990s," in *The Parties Respond: Changes in American Parties and Campaigns*, 3d ed., ed. L. Sandy Maisel (Boulder: Westview Press, 1998), 109–127.
63. Ibid.
64. Morris Fiorina, *Divided Government*, 2d ed. (Boston: Allyn and Bacon, 1996), 153.
65. Rebecca K. C. Hersman, *Friends and Foes: How Congress and the President Really Make Foreign Policy* (Washington, D.C.: Brookings, 2000), 33.
66. John T. Tierney, "Interest Group Involvement in Congressional Foreign and Defense Policy," in *Congress Resurgent: Foreign and Defense Policy on Capitol Hill*, ed. Randall B. Ripley and James M. Lindsay (Ann Arbor: University of Michigan Press, 1993), 109.

Chapter 10

1. Graham Allison and Philip Zelikow, *Essence of Decision: Explaining the Cuban Missile Crisis*, 2d ed. (New York: Addison-Wesley Longman, 1999), 166, 169, 175.
2. Ibid., 153.

3. James Q. Wilson, *Bureaucracy: What Government Agencies Do and Why They Do It* (New York: Basic Books, 1989), 68.

4. 9/11 Commission, *Final Report of the National Commission on Terrorist Attacks Upon the United States* (New York: W. W. Norton & Co., 2004), 263, 268.

5. James G. March and Herbert A. Simon, eds. "Introduction to the Second Edition," in *Organizations,* 2d ed. (Cambridge: Blackwell Publishers, 1993), 8.

6. Allison and Zelikow, *Essence of Decision,* 165.

7. Michael R. Gordon and General Bernard E. Trainer, *The Generals' War: The Inside Story of the Conflict in the Gulf* (Boston: Little, Brown, 1995), 228, 230.

8. Israel was not engaged in the Persian Gulf War, and the United States wanted to keep Israel out of the hostilities to maintain the support of its Arab allies. Because Schwarzkopf's area of responsibility did not include Israel, he was not as apt as Cheney to consider this aspect of the war. Gordon and Trainer, *The Generals' War,* 234.

9. Ibid., 244–247.

10. Christopher M. Jones, "Trading with Saddam: Bureaucratic Roles and Competing Conceptions of National Security," in *The Domestic Sources of American Foreign Policy: Insights and Evidence,* 3d ed., ed. Eugene R. Wittkopf and James M. McCormick (New York: Rowman and Littlefield, 1999), 267, 272, and 274. The procedures set forth in the Export Adminstration Act have become so controversial that Congress has not been able to renew it since 1993.

11. Sherrod McCall, "Case: Reporting from Brezhnev's Moscow," in *Inside an Embassy: The Political Role of Diplomats Abroad,* ed. Robert H. Miller (Washington, D.C.: CQ Press, 1992), 25.

12. Robert H. Miller, "Case: Political Dynamics in Côte d'Ivoire," in *Inside an Embassy: The Political Role of Diplomats Abroad,* ed. Robert H. Miller (Washington, D.C.: CQ Press, 1992), 33.

13. Stephen Bosworth, "Case: Political Transition in the Philippines," in *Inside an Embassy: The Political Role of Diplomats Abroad,* ed. Robert H. Miller (Washington, D.C.: CQ Press, 1992), 72.

14. Robert H. Miller, "Negotiating," in *Inside an Embassy: The Political Role of Diplomats Abroad,* ed. Robert H. Miller (Washington, D.C.: CQ Press, 1992), 74.

15. Barry Rubin, *Secrets of State: The State Department and the Struggle over U.S. Foreign Policy* (New York: Oxford University Press, 1985), 258.

16. Wilson, *Bureaucracy,* 276.

17. The bureau of International Organization Affairs has not traditionally been grouped with the other regional bureaus, and the bilateral relationships emphasized by these bureaus historically receive more attention than multilateral relationships. However, this regional bias may eventually erode as a result of key global issues such as terrorism.

18. The swivel attaches the carrying sling to the rifle.

19. Anthony Lake, *Somoza Falling* (Boston: Houghton Mifflin, 1989), 71–72.

20. Ibid., 146–167.

21. Samuel P. Huntington, *The Common Defense: Strategic Programs in National Politics* (New York: Columbia Univesity Press, 1961), 413.

22. Arthur T. Hadley, *The Straw Giant, Triumph and Failures: America's Armed Forces* (New York: Random House, 1986).

23. Gordon and Trainer, *Generals' War,* 218.

24. Khafji is a city on the Gulf Coast in Saudi Arabia just south of Kuwait. It was the focal point of a major offensive by the Iraqis, which the marines and Arab forces repulsed with little effort. CENTCOM did not pay much attention to this episode because the army was emphasizing the strength of the Iraqi force in order to magnify the effectiveness of the maneuver they were planning in the eastern desert. See Gordon and Trainer, *Generals' War,* 289.

25. Ibid, 35–43.

26. Richard A. Lacquement Jr., *Shaping American Military Capabilities After the Cold War* (Westport, Conn.: Praeger, 2003), 2.

27. Ibid, 39–43.

28. Harlan K. Ullman, *In Irons: U.S. Military in the New Century* (Washington, D.C.: National Defense University Press, 1995).

29. Edward F. Bruner, "Military Forces: What is the Appropriate Size for the U.S.? Summary and Introduction," *Congressional Research Service Report for Congress*, September 3, 2003, www.fas.org/sgp/crs/natsec/RS21754.pdf, accessed 11/19/05.

30. Paul R. Viotti, "Civil-military Relations after the Cold War: Integrating the Armed Forces and American Society," in *Clinton and Post–Cold War Defense*, ed. Stephen J. Cimbala (Westport, Conn.: Praeger, 1996), 140.

31. Tom Ensign, *America's Military Today: The Challenge of Militarism* (New York: New Press, 2004), xi–xii.

32. Ibid., 171.

33. Duncan L. Clarke, *American Defense and Foreign Policy Institutions: Toward a Sound Foundation* (New York: Harper and Row, 1989), 107–108, 110.

34. Eric Schmitt, "Rapid Pullout from Iraq Urged by Key Democrat," *New York Times*, November 18, 2005, 1.

35. Stephen D. Cohen, *The Making of United States International Economic Policy: Principles, Problems and Proposals for Reform*, 5th ed. (Westport, Conn.: Praeger, 2000), 165.

36. Ibid., 88–89.

37. There is a difference between the Council of Economic Advisers (CEA) and the NEC. The CEA is the main source of economic advice available to the president; the NEC coordinates differences among executive departments and agencies.

38. I. M. Destler, *The National Economic Council: A Work in Progress* (Washington, D.C.: Institute for International Economics, 1996), 20–22.

39. I. M. Destler, *American Trade Politics*, 3d ed. (New York: Twentieth Century Fund, 1995), 71.

40. Ibid., 4.

41. Cohen, *Making of the United States International Economic Policy*, 250.

42. Destler, *American Trade Politics*, 318–319.

43. Ibid., 291.

44. Amy B. Zegart, *Flawed Design: The Evolution of the CIA, JCS, and NSC* (Palo Alto: Stanford University Press, 1999), 171–172, 187–189.

45. "Report of the Task Force," in *In From the Cold* (New York: Twentieth Century Fund Press, 1996), 6.

46. White House, *A National Security Strategy of Engagement and Enlargement* (Washington, D.C.: Government Printing Office, 1994), 1.

47. Gregory F. Treverton, "Intelligence since Cold War's End," in *In From the Cold* (New York: Twentieth Century Fund Press, 1996), 107.

48. 9/11 Commission, *Final Report*, 411–414.

49. Treverton, "Intelligence," 122. This is less true in some departments, such as the State Department, than in others.

50. See Iraq Survey Group, *Comprehensive Report of the Special Advisor to the Director of Central Intelligence on Iraq's Weapons of Mass Destruction*, http://www.cia.gov/cia/reports/iraq_2004/Comp_Report, 10/10/2004.

51. 9/11 Commission, *Final Report*, 403–404.

52. Anthony Lake, *Six Nightmares: Real Threats in a Dangerous World and How America Can Meet Them* (Boston: Little, Brown, 2000), 53.

53. 9/11 Commission, *Final Report*, 415–416.

Chapter 11

1. Graham Allison and Philip Zelikow, *Essence of Decision: Explaining the Cuban Missile Crisis*, 2d ed. (New York: Addison-Wesley Longman, 1999), 255.

2. Ibid.
3. Strobe Talbott, "Globalization and Diplomacy: The View from Foggy Bottom," in *The Domestic Sources of American Foreign Policy: Insights and Evidence,* 3d ed., ed. Eugene R. Wittkopf and James M. McCormick (Lanham, Md.: Rowman and Littlefield, 1999), 191.
4. Graham T. Allison and Morton H. Halperin, "Bureaucratic Politics: A Paradigm and Some Policy Implications," *World Politics* 24 (Spring 1972): 48.
5. Ibid., 43.
6. Jerel A. Rosati, "Developing a Systematic Decision-making Framework: Bureaucratic Politics in Perspective," *World Politics* 33, no. 2 (January 1980): 236–237.
7. Morton H. Halperin, *Bureaucratic Politics and Foreign Policy,* (Washington, D.C.: Brookings Institution, 1974), 21.
8. Rosati, "Developing a Systematic Decision-Making Framework," 248–251.
9. Arthur T. Hadley, *The Straw Giant, Triumph and Failures: America's Armed Forces* (New York: Random House, 1986), 10.
10. Ibid., 16–17.
11. Navy volunteers were initially asked to fly the helicopters, but when they found out what the plan was, two of the volunteers refused to fly, saying they felt the mission was beyond their abilities. In the meantime the Marines had insisted that their pilots could do the job. See Hadley, *The Straw Giant,* 10–11.
12. Ibid., 6.
13. Ibid., 16.
14. Ibid., 17.
15. Stephen D. Krasner, "Are Bureaucracies Important? (Or Allison Wonderland)," *Foreign Policy* (Summer 1971): 7.
16. Robert J. Strong, *Bureaucracy and Statesmanship: Henry Kissinger and the Making of American Foreign Policy* (New York: University Press of America, 1986), 48.
17. Allison and Halperin, "Bureaucratic Politics," 46–47.
18. Stephen Hess, *Organizing the Presidency* (Washington, D.C.: Brookings Institution, 1988), xi.
19. Ibid.
20. The persistent efforts of presidents are documented by Amy B. Zegart in *Flawed by Design: The Evolution of the CIA, JCS, and NSC* (Palo Alto, CA: Stanford University Press, 1999).
21. Since Rusk was not a member of Kennedy's inner circle, he may also have shied away from making statements in formal meetings because he feared that his comments would be leaked to people outside the White House.
22. See Martin J. Hillenbrand, *Fragments of Our Time: The Memoirs of a Diplomat* (Athens: University of Georgia Press, 1999).
23. See Paul D. Hoyt and Jean A. Garrison, "Political Manipulation Within the Small Group: Foreign Policy Advisers in the Carter Administration," in *Beyond Groupthink: Political Group Dynamics and Foreign Policy-Making,* ed. Paul 't Hart, Eric K. Stern, and Bengt Sundelius, (Ann Arbor: University of Michigan Press, 1997), 255, 257–258.
24. Deborah Welch Larson, "The Role of Belief Systems and Schemas in Foreign Policy Decision-Making," *Political Psychology,* 15, no. 1 (1994) 20.
25. Ibid.
26. Yuen Foong Khong, *Analogies at War: Korea, Munich, Dien Bien Phu, and the Vietnam Decisions of 1965* (Princeton, N.J.: Princeton University Press, 1992), 11.
27. Dean Rusk, *As I Saw It,* ed. Daniel S. Papp, (New York: Norton, 1990), 161.
28. Alex Roberto Hybel, "A Fortuitous Victory: An Information Processing Approach to the Gulf War," in Wittkopf and McCormick, *Domestic Sources,* 337.
29. Iraq Survey Group, *Regime Strategic Intent,* www.cia.gov/cia/reports/iraq_wmd_2004/comp_report.
30. Michael Lyons, "Presidential Character Revisited," *Political Psychology* 18, no. 4 (1997), 793.

31. Ibid., 796.
32. Ibid.
33. Miriam Steiner, "The Search for Order in a Disorderly World: World Views and Prescriptive Decision Paradigms," *International Organization*, 37, no. 3 (1983): 373–413.
34. Ibid., 389–392.
35. Alexander George and Juliette George, *Presidential Personality and Performance* (Boulder: Westview Press, 1998), 224.
36. Margaret G. Hermann and Thomas Preston, "Presidents, Advisors, and Foreign Policy: the Effect of Leadership Style on Executive Arrangements," *Political Psychology*, 15, no. 1 (1994): 75.
37. Thomas W. Milburn, "The Management of Crisis," in *International Crises: Insights from Behavioral Research*, ed. Charles F. Hermann (New York: Free Press, 1972), 264.
38. Margaret G. Hermann and Thomas Preston, "Presidents, Leadership Style, and the Advisory Process," in Wittkopf and McCormick, *Domestic Sources*, 363.
39. Ibid., 352–354.
40. Hermann and Preston, "Presidents, Advisors, and Foreign Policy," 86, 93.
41. Ibid.
42. Thomas Preston, "Following the Leader: The Impact of U.S. Presidential Style upon Advisory Group Dynamics, Structure, and Decision," in 't Hart, Stern, and Sundelius, *Beyond Groupthink*, 237.
43. Ibid.
44. Ibid., 237–238.
45. John P. Burke and Fred Greenstein, *How Presidents Test Reality: Decisions on Vietnam, 1954 and 1965* (New York: Russell Sage, 1989), 38.
46. Ibid.
47. Ronald H. Hinckley, *People, Polls, and Policy-Makers: American Public Opinion and National Security* (New York: Lexington Books, 1992), 80.
48. Three models are customarily associated with presidential decision making: a formal model, a consensus model, and a competitive model. See Richard Tanner Johnson, *Managing the White House: An Intimate Study of the Presidency* (New York: Harper and Row, 1974.)
49. Bob Woodward, *Bush at War* (New York: Simon and Schuster, 2002), 38.
50. Preston and Hermann, "Presidential Leadership Style," 375–376.
51. Hoyt and Garrison, "Political Manipulation within the Small Group, 252–257.
52. Burke and Greenstein, *How Presidents Test Reality.*
53. Ibid., 63.
54. Ibid., 131.
55. Steve Smith, "Policy Preferences and Bureaucratic Position: The Case of the American Hostage Rescue Mission," in Wittkopf and McCormick, *Domestic Sources*, 294.
56. James M. Goldgeier, "NATO Expansion: the Anatomy of a Decision," in Wittkopf and McCormick, *Domestic Sources*, 320.
57. Ibid., 325.
58. James C. Thomson Jr., "How Could Vietnam Happen? An Autopsy," in Wittkopf and McCormick, *Domestic Sources*, 244.
59. Ibid.
60. Margaret Hermann, "Presidential Leadership Style, Advisory Systems, and Policymaking: Bill Clinton's Administration After Seven Months," *Political Psychology* 15, no. 2 (1994): 365; Hermann and Preston, "Presidents, Advisers, and Foreign Policy," 81; and Hermann and Preston, "Presidents, Leadership Style," in *Domestic Sources*, 88.
61. Eric K. Stern, "Probing the Plausibility of Newgroup Syndrome: Kennedy and the Bay of Pigs," in *Beyond Groupthink*, 153–189.
62. Irving L. Janis, *Groupthink: Psychological Studies of Policy Decisions and Fiascoes*, 2d ed. (Boston: Houghton Mifflin, 1982).

63. Ibid.

64. Jaacov Y. I. Vertzberger, "Collective Risk Taking: the Decision-making Group," in *Beyond Groupthink*, 275–307.

65. Zegart, *Flawed by Design.*

66. Hess, *Organizing the Presidency*, 52.

67. Preston, "Following the Leader," 229.

68. Phillip G. Henderson, *Managing the Presidency* (Boulder: Westview Press, 1988), 136.

69. Hoyt and Garrison, "Political Manipulation within the Small Group," in *Beyond Groupthink*, 249–274.

70. Bob Woodward, *The Commanders*, (New York: Simon & Schuster, 1991), 320–321.

71. Hermann and Preston, "Presidents, Leadership Style," in *Domestic Sources*, 362.

72. Ibid., 369.

73. Woodward, *Commanders.*

74. See Lloyd S. Etheredge, *Can Governments Learn? American Foreign Policy and Central American Revolutions* (New York: Pergamon Press, 1987), 1

75. Ibid., 50–51.

76. Allison and Zelikow, *Essence of Decision.*

77. Burke and Greenstein, *How Presidents Test Reality*, 183.

Chapter 12

1. For a discussion of the differences between political culture and public opinion, see Alexander Wendt, *Social Theory of International Politics* (Cambridge: Cambridge University Press, 1999), 141–143, 161–164.

2. Jonathan Riley, "American Democracy and Majority Rule," in *Majorities and Minorities*, ed. John W. Chapman and Alan Wertheimer (New York: New York University Press, 1990), 272, 275.

3. Louis Wirth, "Preface" to Karl Mannheim's *Ideology and Utopia: An Introduction to the Sociology of Knowledge* (New York: Harcourt, Brace and Co., 1936), xxii–xxiii.

4. See Herbert McClosky and John Zaller, *The American Ethos: Public Attitudes toward Capitalism and Democracy* (Cambridge: Harvard University Press, 1984), 18–19.

5. Ibid., 106, 111.

6. See Louis Hartz, *The Liberal Tradition in America* (New York: Harcourt, Brace & World, 1955), 36.

7. Alexis de Tocqueville, *Democracy in America*, vols. I and II (New York: Vintage Books, 1961.)

8. This is a reference to the "democratic peace" literature. See Michael W. Doyle, "Liberalism and World Politics," *American Political Science Review* 80, no.4 (1986): 1151–1170.

9. See Robert Jewett and John Shelton Lawrence, *Captain America and the Crusade Against Evil: The Dilemma of Zealous Nationalism*, (Grand Rapids, Michigan: William B. Eerdmans Co., 2003); and Hans J. Morgenthau, *Politics Among Nations: The Struggle for Power and Peace*, 2d ed., rev. and enl. (New York: Alfred A Knopf, 1955).

10. Edward Everett, *Orations and Speeches* (Boston, 1836), 297.

11. Thomas L. Friedman, "Two Nations Under God," *New York Times*, November 4, 2004, A31.

12. McClosky and Zaller, 168–169.

13. Frank L. Klingberg, *Cyclical Trends in American Foreign Policy Moods: The Unfolding of America's World Role* (New York: University Press of America, 1983), 8–11.

14. See Philip J. Powlick, "The Sources of Public Opinion for American Foreign Policy Officials," *International Studies Quarterly* 39 (1995) 427–451.

15. Chicago Council on Foreign Relations, *Global Views 2004: American Public Opinion and Foreign Policy*, www.ccfr.org/globalviews2004.

16. See William O. Chittick, Keith R. Billingsley, and Rick Travis, "Persistence and Change in Elite and Mass Attitudes Toward U.S. Foreign Policy," *Political Psychology* 11 (1990): 385–401.

17. Bruce Russett, *Controlling the Sword: The Democratic Governance of National Security* (Cambridge: Harvard University Press, 1990), 87–88.
18. Benjamin I. Page and Robert Y. Shapiro, "Effects of Public Opinion on Policy," *American Political Science Review,* vol. 77 (1983), 175–190.
19. Alan D. Monroe, "Public Opinion and Public Policy, 1980–1993," *Public Opinion Quarterly* 62, no. 1 (Spring 1998): 6.
20. Thomas Wallace Graham, "The Politics of Failure," PhD. diss., Massachusetts Institute of Technology, June 1989.
21. Ronald H. Hinckley, *People, Polls, and Policy-Makers* (New York: Lexington Books, 1992), 83, 85.
22. Graham, "The Politics of Failure."
23. Program on International Policy Attitudes, "Americans on Iraq and the U.N. Inspections II" (University of Maryland, a joint program of the Center on Policy Attitudes and the Center for International and Security Studies, Feb. 21, 2003)
24. See Chicago Council on Foreign Relations, *Global Views 2004.*
25. See the PIPA/Knowledge Networks Poll, "The Separate Realities of Bush and Kerry Supporters," October 21, 2004.
26. See Philip E. Converse, "The Nature of Belief Systems in Mass Publics," in *Ideology and Discontent,* ed. David E. Apter (New York: Free Press, 1974).
27. Gabriel Almond uses such data to show that the public is subject to wide mood changes in *The American People and Foreign Policy* (New York: Praeger, 1950).
28. Hinckley, *People, Polls, and Policy-Makers,* 59.
29. Russett, *Controlling the Sword,* 116–117.
30. Benjamin I. Page and Robert Y. Shapiro, *The Rational Public* (Chicago: University of Chicago Press, 1992), 45.
31. James S. Fishkin, *Democracy and Deliberation: New Directions for Democratic Reform* (New Haven: Yale University Press, 1991), 81.
32. Alan F. Kay, *Americans Talk Issues,* Survey No.16, (Storrs, Conn.: Center for Public Opinion Research, 1991), i.
33. Alan F. Kay, *Locating Consensus for Democracy: A Ten-Year U.S. Experiment* (St. Augustine, Fla.: Americans Talk Issues, 1998).
34. Alan F. Kay, "Deliberative Survey Research to Uncover Citizen Competence and Judgment," unpublished paper dated 1/29/95, 24.
35. Chicago Council on Foreign Relations, *Global Views 2004,* 25, Fig. 2-2.
36. Alan F. Kay, Stanley B. Greenberg, Frederick T. Steeper, and Hazel Henderson, "Survey No. 21: Global Uncertainties" (St. Augustine: Americans Talk Issues Foundation, May 18, 1993), 12.
37. Alan F. Kay, "Deliberative Survey Research," 14.
38. Chicago Council on Foreign Relations, *Global Views 2004,* 24–25.
39. Ibid., 18–19.
40. Ibid., 20.
41. Alan F. Kay, Hazel Henderson, Frederick T. Steeper, Stanley B. Greenberg, and Christopher Blunt, "Survey No. 28," *Who will Reconnect with the People: Republicans, Democrats, or …None of the Above?* (St. Augustine: Americans Talk Issues, August 1995), 16.
42. Chicago Council on Foreign Relations, *Global Views 2004,* 15.
43. Alan F. Kay and Hazel Henderson, *Americans Talk Issues: Perceptions of Globalization, World Structures and Security,* Survey No. 17, 1991, 2–4.
44. Chicago Council on Foreign Relations, *Global Views 2004,* 43.
45. Ibid., 39–47.
46. See Chicago Council on Foreign Relations and Program on International Policy Attitudes (PIPA), "The Hall of Mirrors: Perceptions and Misperceptions in Congressional Foreign Policy Process," October 1, 2004, 5–19.
47. Ibid.

48. Jesse Helms, "Address by U.S. Senator Jesse Helms, R, N.C., Chairman, Senate Foreign Relations Committee before the United Nations Security Council," www.newsmax.com/articles/?a=2000/1/28/211810, accessed 11/21/2005.

49. Graham, "The Politics of Failure," 147–49.

50. See Ole R. Holsti and James N. Rosenau, *American Leadership in World Affairs: Vietnam and the Breakdown of Consensus,* (Boston: Allen & Unwin, 1984).

51. Richard A. Melanson, *Reconstructing Consensus* (New York: St. Martin's Press, 1991), 67. The other citations in the sections on Nixon and Carter are also from Melanson, 88, 121, 116, 149, 141, and 159.

52. Ibid., 88.

53. Ibid., 121.

54. Ibid., 141

55. Nathaniel Beck, Book Review, *Public Opinion Quarterly* 58, no. 3, 381.

Chapter 13

1. Benjamin I. Page and Robert Y. Shapiro, *The Rational Public: Fifty Years of Trends in Americans' Policy Preferences* (Chicago: University of Chicago Press, 1992), 178–179.

2. Douglas Van Bell, "Domestic Imperatives and Rational Models of Foreign Policy Decision Making," in *The Limits of State Autonomy: Societal Groups and Foreign Policy Formulation,* ed. David Skidmore and Valerie M. Hudson (Boulder: Westview Press, 1993), 155.

3. Thomas Risse-Kappen, *Bringing Transnational Relations Back In: Non-State Actors, Domestic Structures, and International Institutions* (Cambridge: Cambridge University Press, 1995).

4. See Doug McAdam, John McCarthy, and Mayer Zald, "Social Movements," in *Handbook of Sociology,* ed. Neil Smelser (Newbury Park: Sage, 1988).

5. Daniel J. B. Hofrenning, *In Washington But Not Of It: The Prophetic Politics of Religious Lobbyists* (Philadelphia: Temple University Press, 1995), 13.

6. Gallup briefly describes this sample in "Attitudes of Opinion Leaders Related to Foreign Policy 1998," vol. 2 (Princeton: Gallup Organization, 1998), Technical Appendix 1.

7. David Howard Goldberg, *Foreign Policy And Ethnic Interest Groups: American and Canadian Jews Lobby for Israel* (New York: Greenwood Press, 1990), 17–18.

8. William Chittick interview with NGO leader, Washington, D.C., July 28, 1966 (name withheld by request).

9. Patrick J. Haney and Walt Vanderbush, "The Role of Ethnic Interest Groups in U.S. Foreign Policy: The Case of the Cuban American National Foundation," *International Studies Quarterly* 43 (1999): 348–354.

10. Walt Vanderbush and Patrick J. Haney, "Policy Toward Cuba in the Clinton Administration," *Political Science Quarterly* 114, no. 3 (1999): 400, 405.

11. Martin Weil, "Can Blacks Do For Africa What Jews Did For Israel?" *Foreign Policy* 15 (1974): 109.

12. Samuel P. Huntington, *The Clash of Civilizations and the Remaking of World Order* (New York: Simon and Schuster, 1996).

13. Elizabeth S. Rogers, "The Conflicting Roles of American Ethnic and Business Interests in the U.S. Economic Sanctions Policy: The Case of South Africa," in *The Limits of State Autonomy: Societal Groups and Foreign Policy Formulation,* ed. David Skidmore and Valerie M. Hudson (Boulder: Westview Press, 1993), 191–192.

14. Rogers, "Conflicting Roles," 193.

15. E. Gangway and R. Payne, "The Influence of Black Americans on U.S. Policy Towards Southern Africa," *African Affairs* 79 (1980): 598.

16. Sterling Johnson, *Black Globalism: The International Politics of a Non-state Nation* (Aldershot: Ashgate, 1998), 173.

17. Hofrenning, *In Washington But Not of It,* 15–17.

18. Ibid., 5–6.

19. Ibid., 9, 11.
20. Christian Smith, *Resisting Reagan: The U.S. Central America Peace Movement* (Chicago: University of Chicago Press, 1996), 194.
21. Ibid., 141.
22. Ibid., 158.
23. Ibid., 78–79, 82, 86.
24. J. Bruce Nichols, *The Uneasy Alliance: Religion, Refugee Work, and U.S. Foreign Policy* (New York: Oxford University Press, 1988), 118–121.
25. Ibid., 128–131.
26. Ibid., 131.
27. The Canadian government did accept many of these Nicaraguans.
28. Smith, *Resisting Reagan*, 70.
29. Ibid., 70, 185.
30. Lee Ann Pingel, "Persephone's Daughters: Women's Contributions to a Post-Statist Morality"(master's thesis, University of Georgia, Athens, 1996).
31. Ole R. Holsti, *Public Opinion and American Foreign Policy*, rev. ed. (Ann Arbor: University of Michigan Press, 2004), 190.
32. Ibid., 196.
33. See Bruce Russett, *The Prisoners of Insecurity* (San Francisco: W. H. Freeman and Company, 1983) and Steve Chan, "Grasping the Peace Dividend: Some Propositions on the Conversion of Swords into Plowshares," *Mershon International Studies Review* 39 (April 1995): 53–95. This does not include the kind of regional argument made by Trubowitz later in this chapter.
34. Jerry W. Sanders, "Empire at Bay: Containment Strategies and American Politic at the Crossroads," in *World Policy Paper* no. 25 (New York: World Policy Institute, 1983), 7.
35. Ibid., 10–11.
36. William T. Lee, "Understanding the Soviet Military Threat: How CIA Estimates Went Astray" (New York: National Strategy Information Center, 1977), 13–15.
37. Arthur Macy Cox, "The CIA's Tragic Error," in *How the World Works: Critical Introduction to International Relations*, ed. Gary L. Olson (Glenview, Ill.: Scott Foresman, 1984), 255.
38. Ibid.
39. Ibid., 256–257.
40. Ronald W. Cox, *Power and Profits: U.S. Policy in Central America* (Lexington: University of Kentucky Press, 1994), 5–6.
41. Ibid., 136.
42. Ibid., 27.
43. Ibid., 46.
44. Ibid., 55.
45. In 1969 El Salvador invaded Honduras after Honduran landowners deported several thousand El Salvadorans. It is called the "soccer war" because it broke out during a soccer game between the two countries.
46. Ibid., 15.
47. Ibid., 112–115, 136.
48. Ibid., 117.
49. Beth Sims, *Workers of the World Undermined: American Labor's Role in U.S. Foreign Policy* (Boston: South End Press, 1992), 3.
50. R. W. Cox, *Power and Profits*, 441.
51. Sims, *Workers of the World*, 3.
52. Ibid., 4–5.
53. Ibid., 6.
54. Ibid., 3.
55. Peter Trubowitz, *Defining the National Interest: Conflict and Change in American Foreign Policy* (Chicago: University of Chicago Press, 1998).

56. Ibid., 54. The Northeast contains the New England, Middle Atlantic, and Great Lakes states. The South contains both states in the Southeast and Southwest. And the West includes states in the Great Plains, in the Mountain West, and on the Pacific Coast.
57. Trubowitz, *Defining the National Interest*, 88.
58. Ibid., 214–215.
59. Ibid., 227.
60. Ibid., 183–190.
61. Stephen D. Cohen, *The Making of United States International Economic Policy: Principles, Problems, and Proposals for Reform*, 5th ed. (Westport, Conn.: Praeger, 2000), 245.
62. Ibid., 246.
63. Ibid., 251.
64. Ibid., 251–257.

Chapter 14

1. Thomas R. Dye, *Who's Running America? The Clinton Years*, 6th ed. (Englewood Cliffs, N.J.: Prentice Hall, 1995.)
2. Ibid., 160.
3. G. William Domhoff, *Who Rules America Now? A View for the '80s*, (Englewood Cliffs, N.J.: Prentice Hall, 1983.)
4. Ibid., 20.
5. G. William Domhoff, "Where Do Government Experts Come From? The CEA and the Policy-Planning Network," in *Power Elites and Organization*, ed. G. William Domhoff and Thomas R. Dye (Beverly Hills: Sage Publications, 1987), 190.
6. Glenn P. Hastedt, *American Foreign Policy: Past, Present, Future*, 3d ed. (Upper Saddle River, N.J.: Prentice Hall, 1997), 245.
7. Waster Isaacson and Evan Thomas, *The Wise Men: Six Friends and the World They Made* (New York: Simon and Schuster, 1986).
8. Edward H. Berman, *The Influence of the Carnegie, Ford, and Rockefeller Foundations on American Foreign Policy: The Ideology of Philanthropy* (Albany: State University of New York, 1983), 15.
9. Ibid., 16.
10. Ibid., 30.
11. Ibid. 32, 108–109.
12. Ibid., 99.
13. G. William Domhoff, *The Power Elite and the State: How Policy is Made in America* (New York: Aldine de Gruyter, 1990), 229.
14. Ibid., 321.
15. John P. Leacacos, *Fires in the In-Basket: The ABCs of the State Department* (Cleveland: World Publishing, 1968).
16. Dye, *Who's Running*, 238.
17. Berman, *Influence on American Foreign Policy*, 62–63.
18. Domhoff, "Government Experts," 193.
19. Dye, *Who's Running*, 220–222.
20. James Allen Smith, *Brookings at Seventy-Five* (Washington, D.C.: Brookings Institution Press, 1991).
21. Ibid., 58.
22. See Fletcher M. Green, "The South Looks Abroad," *The South and World Affairs* (September 1943).
23. Domhoff, "Government Experts," 193–194.
24. Robert D. Schulzinger, *The Wise Men of Foreign Affairs: The History of the Council on Foreign Relations* (New York: Columbia University Press, 1984), 3.
25. The comparable British institution is the Royal Institute for International Affairs.

26. Peter Grose, *Continuing the Inquiry: the Council on Foreign Relations from 1921 to 1996* (New York: Council on Foreign Relations, 1996), 8.

27. Schulzinger, *Wise Men*, 61.

28. Grose, *Continuing the Inquiry*, 23.

29. Domhoff, *The Power Elite*, 115, 121–122.

30. Michael Wala, *The Council on Foreign Relations and American Foreign Policy in the Early Cold War* (Providence: Berghahn Books, 1994), 36.

31. Albert Fishlow, Carlos F. Díaz Alejandro, Richard R. Fagen, and Roger D. Hansen, *Rich and Poor Nations in the World Economy* (New York: McGraw-Hill, 1978), xi.

32. Holly Sklar, "Trilateralism: Managing Dependence and Democracy—An Overview," in *Trilateralism: The Trilateral Commission and Elite Planning for World Management*, ed. Holly Sklar, (Boston: South End Press, 1980), 8.

33. Michel Crozier, Samuel P. Huntington, and Joji Watanuki, *The Crisis of Democracy: Report on the Governability of Democracies to the Trilateral Commission* (New York: New York University Press, 1975). Also see Sklar, "Trilateralism," 38, and Laurence H. Shoup, "Jimmy Carter and the Trilateralists: Presidential Roots," also in Sklar, *Trilateralism*, 199–211.

34. Holly Sklar, "Trilateralism and the Management of Contradictions: Concluding Perspectives," in Sklar, *Trilateralism*, 573–574.

35. William I. Robinson, *A Faustian Bargain: U.S. Intervention in the Nicaraguan Elections and American Foreign Policy in the Post–Cold War Era* (Boulder: Westview Press, 1992), 10.

36. Ibid., 15–17.

37. Ibid., 16.

38. Donald J. Lee, *Polyarchy: The Political Theory of Robert A. Dahl* (New York: Garland Publishing, 1991), 14.

39. Ibid., 13–14.

40. William I. Robinson, *Promoting Polyarchy: Globalization, U.S. Intervention and Hegemony* (Cambridge, England: Cambridge University Press, 1996), 49.

41. Robinson, *Faustian Bargain*, 51, 93.

42. Ibid., 114.

43. Robinson, *Promoting Polyarchy*, 171.

44. Janine R. Wedel, *Collision and Collusion: The Strange Case of Western Aid to Eastern Europe 1989–1998* (New York: St. Martin's Press, 1998), 191.

45. Ibid., 122.

46. Ibid., 153.

47. Ibid., 132.

48. Ibid., 132–133.

49. Robin Blackburn, "Kosovo: the War of NATO Expansion," in *Masters of the Universe? NATO's Balkan Crusade*, ed. Tariq Ali, (New York: Verso, 2000), 363–364.

50. Ibid. 365.

51. James M. Goldgeier, "NATO Expansion: The Anatomy of a Decision," *Washington Quarterly*, 21, no.1 (1998).

52. Goldgeier, "NATO Expansion"; Michael Dobbs, *Madeleine Albright: A Twentieth Century Odyssey* (New York: Henry Holt, 1999).

53. Goldgeier, "NATO Expansion."

54. Berger, Albright, and most of the others involved had Ivy League backgrounds; they were all supportive of NATO expansion. Christopher had been neutral; and Lee Aspin, the first secretary of defense under Clinton, and William Perry were opposed. See Goldgeier, "NATO Expansion"; Ashton B. Carter and William O. Perry, *Preventive Defense: A New Security Strategy for America* (Washington, D.C.: Brookings Institution Press, 1999).

55. Gilbert Achcar, "Rasputin Plays at Chess: How the West Blundered into a New Cold War," in Ali, *Masters of the Universe?* 57–98.

56. Achcar, "Rasputin."

57. William Kristol and Robert Kagan, "Toward a Neo-Reaganite Foreign Policy," *Foreign Affairs* vol. 75, no. 4 (1996): 18–32.

58. William Kristol, interview by Ted Koppel, "The Plan," *ABC Nightline,* ABC, March 5, 2003.

59. Edward S. Herman and Noam Chomsky, *Manufacturing Consent: The Political Economy of the Mass Media* (New York: Pantheon Books, 1988), 4.

60. Ibid., 5.

61. Judith Raine Baroody, *Media Access and the Military: The Case of the Gulf War* (Lanham: University Press of America, 1998), 7.

62. Pew Research Center for the People and the Press, "Media Consumption and Believability Study," http://www.people-press.org, June 8, 2004.

63. Ibid.

64. Eric Alterman, "What Liberal Media?" *Nation,* www.thenation.com/doc.mhtml?I= 20030224=alterman2.

65. David Croteau, "Examining the 'Liberal Media' Claim," A FAIR (Fairness & Accuracy in Reporting) Report, June 1998, http://www.fair.org/reports/journalist-survey.html.

66. Ben H. Bagdikian, *The Media Monopoly,* 5th ed. (Boston: Beacon Press, 1997), xii–xiii, xxii.

67. Granville Williams, "Media Ownership 2001," http://www.medicachannel.org/owner ship/chart.shtml

68. Bagdikian, *Media Monopoly,* xiv.

69. Center for Public Integrity, http//www.openairwaves.org/telecom/default.aspx? act'rules, accessed 12/29/04.

70. Robert W. McChesney, "Making Media Democratic," *Boston Review* 23, nos. 3–4 (Summer 1998) 4–10, 20.

71. PBS *NewsHour,* Online, October 19, 2004, www.pbs.org/newshour/updates/sinclair_ 10-19-04.html.

72. Bagdikian, *Media Monopoly,* xix, 216.

73. Ibid., 134, 176.

74. Martin A. Lee and Norman Solomon, *Unreliable Sources: A Guide to Detecting Bias in News Media* (New York: Carol Publishing Group, 1990), 59.

75. Bagdikian, *Media Monopoly,* 137, 221.

76. Herbert J. Gans, *Deciding What's News: A Study of* CBS Evening News, NBC Nightly News, Newsweek, *and* Time (New York: Pantheon Books, 1979), 27.

77. Stephen Hess, *International News and Foreign Correspondents* (Washington, D.C.: Brookings Institution, 1996), 8.

78. Ibid., 34.

79. Ibid., 4.

80. Ibid., 3.

81. Michael Massing, "The Press: The Enemy Within," *New York Review of Books* 52, no. 20 (December 15, 2005), accessed at http://www.nybooks.com/articles/18555.

82. Mark Fishman, *Manufacturing the News* (Austin: University of Texas Press, 1980), 16.

83. Ibid., 28.

84. Timothy E. Cook, "Domesticating a Crisis," in *Taken By Storm: The Media, Public Opinion and U.S. Foreign Policy in the Gulf War,* ed. W. Lance Bennett and David L. Paletz (Chicago: University of Chicago Press, 1994), 109–110.

85. Hess, *International News,* 31.

86. Ibid., 32.

87. James J. Sadkovich, *The U.S. Media and Yugoslavia, 1991–1995* (Westport, Conn.: Praeger, 1998), 36, 114–116.

88. Robert M. Entman, *Projections of Power: Framing News, Public Opinion, and U.S. Foreign Policy* (Chicago: University of Chicago Press, 2004), 78.

89. W. Lance Bennett, *News: the Politics of Illusion*, 4th ed. (New York: Addison-Wesley Longman, 2001), 187–191.

90. Ibid, 186–187.

91. William A. Dorman and Steven Livingston, "News and Historical Content," in Bennett and Paletz, *Taken by Storm*, 63–81.

92. Douglas Kellner, *The Persian Gulf TV War* (Boulder: Westview Press, 1992), 20–23, 67, 368. It later became known that this woman was the daughter of Kuwait's ambassador to the United States.

93. Robert M. Entman and Benjamin I. Page, "The News Before the Storm," in Bennett and Paletz, *Taken by Storm*, 97.

94. Richard A. Brody, "Crisis, War, and Public Opinion," in Bennett and Paletz, *Taken by Storm*, 218.

95. Marvin Kalb, "A View from the Press," in Bennett and Paletz, *Taken by Storm*, 6.

96. Kellner, *TV War*, 297–310.

97. See Franklin Foer, "The Source of the Trouble," *New York Metro*, December 31, 2004, www.newyorkmetro.com/nymetro/news/media/features/9226.

98. "The Times and Iraq," *New York Times*, May 26, 2004.

99. Byron Calame, "Anonymity: Who Deserves it?" *New York Times*, November 20, 2005, 12.

100. David L. Paletz, "Just Deserts," in Bennett and Paletz, *Taken by Storm*, 281.

101. Daniel Okrent, "It's Good to Be Objective. It's Even Better to Be Right," *New York Times*, November 14, 2004, 4.

102. Entman, *Projections of Power*, 26.

103. Ibid., 29–30.

104. Shanto Iyengar and Adam Simon, "News Coverage of the Gulf Crisis and Public Opinion," in Bennett and Paletz, *Taken by Storm*, 167–185.

105. Sadkovich, *Media and Yugoslavia*, 34.

106. Susan L. Woodward, *Balkan Tragedy: Chaos and Dissolution After the Cold War* (Washington, D.C.: Brookings Institution Press, 1995), 47–81.

107. Sadkovich, *Media and Yugoslavia*, 34–35.

108. Ibid., 64.

109. William O. Chittick, *State Department, Press, and Pressure Groups: A Role Analysis* (New York: John Wiley and Sons, 1970), 261–264.

110. Christian Smith, *Resisting Reagan: The U.S. Central America Peace Movement* (Chicago: University of Chicago Press, 1996), 257–258, 262.

111. Ibid., 83.

112. Ibid., 242–249.

113. Bennett, *Politics of Illusion*, 201–205.

Chapter 15

1. Alexis de Tocqueville, *Democracy in America*, ed. J. P. Mayer (New York: Harper and Row, 1966), 226–230.

2. Benjamin O. Fordham, *Building the Cold War Consensus: The Political Economy of U.S. National Security Policy, 1949–1951* (Ann Arbor: University of Michigan Press, 1998), 30–40.

3. Miroslav Nincic, *Democracy and Foreign Policy: The Fallacy of Political Realism* (New York: Columbia University Press, 1992), 47.

4. The best evidence for stability is to be found in Benjamin I. Page and Robert Y. Shapiro's *The Rational Public: Fifty Years of Trends in America's Policy Preferences* (Chicago: University of Chicago Press, 1992); the best evidence for a stable structure is to be found in William O. Chittick, Keith R. Billingsley, and Rick Travis, "Persistence and Change in Elite and Mass Attitudes Toward U.S. Foreign Policy," *Political Psychology* 11, no. 2 (1990): 385–401.

5. Jean A. Garrison, *Games Advisors Play: Foreign Policy in the Nixon and Carter Administration* (College Station: Texas A & M University Press, 1999).

6. Melvin Small, *Democracy and Diplomacy: The Impact of Domestic Politics on U.S. Foreign Policy, 1789–1994* (Baltimore: Johns Hopkins University Press, 1996), 43.

7. Robert Strausz-Hupé, *Democracy and American Foreign Policy: Reflections on the Legacy of Alexis de Tocqueville* (New Brunswick, N.J.: Transaction Publishers, 1995), 177.

8. See Nincic, *Democracy and Foreign Policy,* 112–113.

9. Ibid., 109.

10. Immanuel Kant, *Perpetual Peace,* ed. Lewis White Beck (New York: Liberal Arts Press, 1957).

11. Ibid.

Index